God's
perfect
child

God's perfect child

LIVING AND DYING IN THE
CHRISTIAN SCIENCE CHURCH

CAROLINE FRASER

Metropolitan Books

Henry Holt and Company   New York

Metropolitan Books
Henry Holt and Company, LLC
Publishers since 1866
115 West 18th Street
New York, New York 10011

Metropolitan Books is a registered trademark
of Henry Holt and Company, LLC

Parts of this book originally appeared, in somewhat different
form, in *The New York Review of Books* and *The Atlantic Monthly*.

Library of Congress Cataloging-in-Publication Data
Fraser, Caroline.
God's perfect child : living and dying in the Christian Science
Church / Caroline Fraser. — 1st ed.
        p.   cm.
Includes index.
ISBN 0-8050-4430-2 (hb : alk. paper)
1. Christian Science—History.   2. Christian Science—
Controversial literature.   I. Title.
BX6931.F73   1999   99-17535
289.5'09—dc21   CIP

Henry Holt books are available for special promotions and
premiums. For details contact: Director, Special Markets.

First Edition 1999

Designed by Michelle McMillian

Printed in the United States of America
All first editions are printed on acid-free paper. ∞

1   3   5   7   9   10   8   6   4   2

For my brother and sister

And ye shall know the truth, and
the truth shall make you free.

—Jesus of Nazareth,

John 8:32

Contents

Son • The Mother Church • M.A.M. at Pleasant View • "A Power Not One's Own" • The C.O.P. and "The Corrective Work" • Mark Twain and "That Shameless Old Swindler, Mother Eddy" • Radical Reliance and Mrs. Eddy's Teeth • The "Excelsior Extension" and the "Next Friends" • Willa Cather's Secret • "Call It the Christian Science Monitor" • The Stetson Problem • "A Combination of Sinners That Was Fast" • Science and Health, 1910 Edition • Postscript: "Mrs. Eddy's Place"

Acknowledgments

For reasons that I hope will become obvious, I did not seek, nor was I given, access to the archives of the Christian Science Church. I did request an interview with Virginia Harris, chairman of the Church's Board of Directors, as well as photocopies of some documents pertaining to the biography of Mary Baker Eddy by Willa Cather, all of which I was granted and for which I am suitably thankful.

Although they will disagree with what I have written, several Scientists, most notably Stephen Gottschalk, Thomas Johnsen, Lee Johnson, and Judge Thomas Griesa, gave interviews when I was working on the *Atlantic Monthly* article out of which this book grew and were generous with time and information. Giulia Plum, Pamela Martin, and Karen Sutton James addressed my queries about becoming and being Christian Science practitioners. Andrew W. Hartsook answered questions on several occasions, as did Ann Beals of the Bookmark and Jerry Lupo of the Rare Book Company, who also helped me acquire important research materials.

Since this is a book critical of Christian Science, I am particularly beholden to those who, having left the Church, have chosen to speak fully about their experiences. Since 1993, Rita and Douglas Swan, of Children's Healthcare Is a Legal Duty, Inc., have been extraordinarily generous, answering questions and granting me interviews year after year, inviting me to attend CHILD meetings, and allowing me to examine the archives of their organization. Many members of CHILD, Inc., have likewise revisited their often difficult Christian Science pasts with me, including, but not limited to, Beth Young, C. J. Hyatt, Dale Lewis, Mark Woodall, Bonnie Deckerhoff, Suzanne

Shepard, Laura Franklin, Josy Fox Goodman, Pam Mundell, Sue Fraser, and Marion and Bill Cooley. I am deeply grateful as well to Gayle Quigley, Jack Schram, and Douglass Lundman, who spoke with me about the circumstances surrounding the deaths of their children.

A number of other former Scientists were kind enough to grant me interviews or to volunteer information. I would like to thank Spalding Gray, Rockwell Gray, Thomas Simmons, Christine Madsen, Ruth Cook, Caroline Kent, Joanna White, and Joan Surguine, as well as the many others who wrote to me after the *Atlantic* article appeared.

Several journalists, scholars, and writers supplied me with copies of hard-to-locate materials, including Andrew Skolnick of the *Journal of the American Medical Association*, William Jarvis of the National Council Against Health Fraud, Seth Asser, Alfie Kohn, Rodney Stark, William Franklin Simpson, and James Franklin, to whose invaluable coverage in the *Boston Globe* of the Church and its media disaster during the 1990s I am indebted.

William Whitworth and Mike Curtis at the *Atlantic Monthly* and Barbara Epstein at the *New York Review of Books*, in editing and publishing my articles about the Church and Mary Baker Eddy (which appear in somewhat different form here), encouraged me to pursue the subject and sharpened my approach to it. Pat Crow, formerly of the *New Yorker*, offered valuable advice. I'm grateful to them all.

I and my book owe a real debt to the brilliant editing and incisive judgment of Sara Bershtel at Metropolitan Books. It has truly been a pleasure to work with her. Also at Metropolitan, Carly Berwick, Riva Hocherman, Kenn Russell, Jolanta Benal, and Linda Elliot have been wonderfully helpful. John Ware, my agent, believed in this project from the beginning and has been a steady source of reassurance.

In 1996, during the early stages of writing this book, my husband and I had the good fortune to be selected for the Margery Davis Boyden Wilderness Writing Residency and to live for seven months at the Dutch Henry Ranch near the Rogue River in Oregon. Thanks to the big hearts and hard work of Frank and Bradley Boyden, their mother Margery, and John Daniel, who takes time away from his own writing to administer this PEN Northwest program, Dutch Henry has provided me and many others a retreat into a world with its own unique distractions, away from phones and fax machines, where thinking can be done.

My brother and sister, Christopher Fraser and Katie Wheatley, to whom this book is dedicated, lived the Christian Science life with me. They live, as well, with its legacy, and their support and encouragement have meant much to me. I would also like to thank my sister-in-law, Linda Warner, for assistance with several research matters; my mother-in-law, Elsie Espen; my good friend Harbour Fraser Hodder; and, for exceptional help, Colleen Konheim.

This book would never have been written had it not been for my husband, Hal Espen. He has supported me in every possible way—financially, emotionally, morally—urging me to devote myself to this undertaking and to see it through. I am enormously grateful for his unwavering, loving commitment.

God's
perfect
child

Preface:
God's Perfect Child

You can't pray a lie—I found that out.

—Mark Twain,
Adventures of Huckleberry Finn

1. At the First Church of Christ, Scientist, Mercer Island

I was God's Perfect Child. We all were, every last one of us, from the tiniest baby to the oldest old lady in the First Church of Christ, Scientist, Mercer Island, Washington. God was perfect, and so were we.

In Sunday school, we learned that There Is No Spot Where God Is Not. God was Everywhere and Everything, Omnipotent Supreme, Father-Mother, All-in-All, and we were His image and likeness. God was All. Matter was nothing. At the age of four or five, I gazed at the top of the Sunday school table, at my knees going under it, at the plastic chairs, at the scratchy sisal carpet. The table and the chairs and the carpet and the knees *looked* real, but they weren't. They weren't even there. They were matter, and matter was Error, and Error did not exist.

I believed all this for many years, the years when I attended the Christian Science Sunday school. I learned the books of the Bible, the Ten Commandments, the Beatitudes, and Mary Baker Eddy's Scientific Statement of Being. I learned how to *know the truth* by thinking over and over again that I was spiritual and perfect, not material and imperfect. For a time I believed that our Sunday school superintendent, an elderly lady with a halo of white hair, who led us in singing our hymns and saying the Lord's Prayer, was Mary Baker Eddy, our Beloved Founder and Leader, the author of *Science and Health with Key to the Scriptures*, our Textbook.

We were always talking about Mrs. Eddy and her book. We said her name slowly and lovingly. We stroked the books, tracing with our fingers The Cross and The Crown embossed on the soft old cloth covers. We talked about her every Sunday. Even after I realized that our superintendent was really old Mrs. Bolton, who had a big house down by the water, I continued to believe that Mrs. Eddy was still alive somewhere, with white hair like my grandparents', because we talked about her as if she were.

The Sunday school was a big room, sunny, with two walls of glass. There were hardly any decorations. There were no toys. We were not there to have fun. We were there to fight off Mortal Mind, where Error came from. Mortal Mind had gotten inside our heads, under our hair. Divine Mind was All Powerful but kept getting away from us. We couldn't keep our Mortal Minds on the Divine Mind. We were full of Error. Mary Baker Eddy was there to remind us.

It was hard to keep the whole thing straight, so we had to pray a lot and study, study, study. Mortal Mind was thinking we were hurt when we fell down. Mortal Mind was accidents. Mortal Mind was forgetting to go to the bathroom before Sunday school and wetting our pants. Mortal Mind was being jealous or hateful or nasty. Mortal Mind was having a tantrum. Mortal Mind was crying.

The hardest thing to understand about Mortal Mind was the fact that it didn't exist. We tried hard to *know* that Divine Mind was All and that there wasn't any room left for bad, old Mortal Mind. If we could *know* that we were Divine Mind, everything would get better. We'd stop crying. We wouldn't even want to cry. We'd never do anything wrong or feel bad, even if somebody pinched us or pulled our hair. Even if somebody did those things, we could squeeze our eyes shut and *know* that we were God's Perfect Child.

Often, on the drive to Nana and Granko's house after Sunday school, I would have trouble *knowing* that I wasn't carsick. Car sickness was Mortal Mind. Throwing up was Mortal Mind. I ran through my list of silent prayers that were supposed to make me feel better: "There Is No Spot Where God Is Not," "I Am God's Perfect Child," "Man Is Not Matter," snatches of the Scientific Statement of Being. But concentrating on the words made my hot head spin. I waited for God to fill up the world like the air in a balloon, but the air in the car just got worse and worse. Then I threw up, a horrible explosion of Error, the vomit snaking down my Sunday dress and the seat of the car. Now I was Error. Error was in me. *Error was me.*

My father thought so too. He was a real Christian Scientist, a Member of the Church. So were Nana and Granko. We had to pull over by the side of the road and clean the vomit out of the car, with hankies, so they wouldn't see it. When Error came calling, we weren't supposed to tell.

But it came so often. The ladies in Sunday school told us that Error was like a little man, a wicked little elf sitting on our shoulders, whispering words in our ears. Whispering Sin, Sickness, and Death. We read the Ten Commandments. Thou Shalt Not Kill. If we listened to the little man, we could kill with our own words, our own thoughts. If we thought bad things, or said them, they would happen. So we had to think good thoughts all the time.

But all the time was too much. I was always throwing up, or wetting the bed, or sneezing, or saying the wrong thing at the dinner table. One day at East Seattle Elementary, during the first grade's rehearsal for assembly, marching in line into our assigned spaces on the bleachers, my head spinning, I suddenly threw up in the middle of the gym, on the gleaming, waxed floor where the boys played basketball.

"Why didn't you *tell* me you were sick?" Mrs. Bruhn cried. Mrs. Bruhn was not a Christian Scientist, and she didn't realize that I couldn't have told anyone that I was sick. You couldn't *say* "sick." Saying it made it real. I was sent home, in more Mortal disgrace than the exasperated Mrs. Bruhn could ever have known. Because my parents were still at work, I had to go stay with the old lady who lived next door. She was not a Christian Scientist, but she was nice anyway. She made me lie down on her nubbly couch and covered me with one of her crocheted afghans. I lay there through the afternoon, thinking and thinking. What was the matter with me? Why wasn't I God's Perfect Child? Why couldn't I Know the Truth? If There Was No Spot Where God Was Not, where was I?[1]

When I was ten, we built a boat. It was a sailboat, a thirty-foot sloop, with a poured fiberglass hull and a teak cabin and toe rails. It slept four uncomfortably and six with great discomfort, if two people slept on the galley table. My father often boasted that the design of our boat guaranteed that it would roll: if its mast ever went below the water, it would roll back up. It was christened the *Sancocho*, Spanish for a kind of stew, but we always just called it the boat. It had a pump toilet and one pump faucet for cold water. As we sailed around Puget Sound, the boat began to make me wonder about Christian Science.

Alarming things were always happening on the boat. Innocent of seagoing skills, my mother, father, older sister, and I, we were often lost, marooned on mud bars, caught in gales or fog, or bashed by "deadheads," floating logs the size of our mast. Sails or lines inopportunely fell in the water. We had a depth sounder, life vests, and a compass, but the compass was brought out only during navigational emergencies, as a kind of offering to the gods of rationality, my mother performing frenzied calculations while my father shouted directions. We didn't have a radio because we knew we would never have an accident requiring the use of one. We also had no lifeline, the rope or guard line strung on stanchions around the toe rail, to clip ourselves to in bad weather. We had no lifeboat, except for an inflatable rubber dinghy that took a long time to blow up. We didn't need radios or lifeboats or lifelines. Christian Science was our Coast Guard.

Sometimes, when things looked bad and I was afraid we were all going to die, my father made us sing. Once, caught in a storm on the Strait of Juan de Fuca, the wide passage that opens to the Pacific between the coast of Washington and Vancouver Island, we sat in the cockpit while the boat flailed through whitecaps in the pelting rain and flying spray, and sang "Onward Christian Soldiers" and some of Mrs. Eddy's hymns, "Christ My Refuge," "Feed My Sheep," and "Satisfied": "It matters not what be thy lot, / So Love doth guide; / For storm or shine, pure peace is thine, / Whate'er betide."

We sailed between Trial Island and the coast of Vancouver Island, not a recommended route. Jagged rocks loomed nearby out of clouds of spray. Cormorants, shiny and black as the rocks, yards away, impassively watched us lurch by. They looked right at home. Through the rain, I could see tiny people and cars on the shore, going about their business. I knew then that no one was going to save us, not the cormorants, not the people safe on dry land, and not Mary Baker Eddy, wherever she was.

I was beginning to realize that other people had their doubts about Christian Science. My mother, for one. My parents had what was called in Christian Science a mixed marriage: the union of a believer and a doubter. Where my father was serious-minded, she was lighthearted and frivolous. She loved to go to movies—long, romantic movies like Lawrence of Arabia and Dr. Zhivago—and buy high-heeled shoes and make decadent desserts—"Grasshopper Pie" and "Chocolate Log"—out of recipes in the women's magazines. She let us take as many baths as we wanted, even though my father (like Mrs. Eddy) disapproved of paying too much attention to hygiene, especially children's. She taught kindergarten and first grade, and she never told the children that there were little men sitting on their shoulders, whispering about Error.

In her own way, she was impressed by Christian Science, by its intellectual airs and its aura of middle-class prosperity. She was always telling a story about buying our upright piano and how hard it was for the men from church to move it down the outside back stairs and into the basement. "We prayed it down the stairs!" she would say.

But she was a classic fair-weather Christian Scientist. During my childhood, she was not a member of the Church, perhaps because she took birth control pills. Christian Scientists don't believe in pills. When I was sick and my father wasn't watching, she would slip a couple of St. Joseph's orange-flavored children's aspirin out of a bottle she kept hidden in the pocket of her raincoat in the closet and palm them to me, telling me not to say anything. I liked them, because they tasted good, but once when we were out on the boat, I found a tin of aspirin in her purse and piously threw it overboard, watching it vanish into the green dark, leaving a little rope of bubbles.

My father had no doubts. He taught us to jump up and turn down the volume every time an aspirin or Geritol commercial came on TV. He railed against "materialism" and wielded a kind of compulsive penury against it. He was offended by seat belts—we never wore them—because they implied that accidents could happen. Between the two of them, we scarcely knew what to believe. But we knew what we were *supposed* to believe. We prayed and knew the truth like crazy, and when nothing happened, we thought it was our fault. Christian Science was supposed to make all our fears go away; that's what Mrs. Eddy said. But instead, we were afraid all the time, of things that nobody else was afraid of—of coughing, of sneezing, of living.

2. Raising the Dead

Michael Schram was a kid who went to my Sunday school. His sister, Sue, and I, who were several years older, were in the same Sunday school class, and I remember leaning on my elbow, staring across the open room, bored and restless, for months of Sundays, looking at Michael sitting quietly at his own table in his tidy seersucker jacket and bow tie. Michael had the look of a boy suffering silently his mother's sartorial pretensions. In the end, that wasn't all he suffered.

Betty Schram always accompanied her children to the door of the Sunday school to drop them off and reappeared to collect them an hour later. In my memory, she is perpetually dressed as if for Easter, in pastel dresses with matching shoes and bags. A pretty woman, she was always busily renouncing the material world that so became her; her ex-husband, Jack, later told me that she had been a high school majorette and Miss Daytona Beach in Florida, where they met.

In the late summer of 1979, when Michael was twelve, Betty and Jack Schram were in the final stages of divorce. They were separated; he was living in an apartment off Mercer Island, on the east side of Lake Washington. Their marriage seems to have been a direct casualty of Christian Science. He had attended church with her for many years, "to support her," he said, but had gradually grown estranged from his wife as her commitment to Christian Science became, in his view, deeper and more disturbing. He said that his wife objected to his taking their children fishing and hunting: "It was God's perfect fish and God's perfect duck, you see." He remembered her spending long hours seated on the beds of their children before they went to sleep, rehearsing Christian Science theology with them. On one occasion, he arrived home late for dinner after being caught in traffic caused by a violent two-car accident. Shaken by what he'd seen, he described the thirty-foot flames from the burning cars to his family, seated at the dinner table. The description infuriated his wife, who said sharply, "You're listening to error. You didn't see any car on fire."

On September 9, 1979, a Sunday, Michael began having stomach pains. Betty Schram contacted Juanita Caldwell, her Christian Science practitioner, or faith healer. Caldwell was not on the Church's official list of practitioners, but she had developed close relationships with several women in the Mercer Island church for whom she served as a healer and spiritual adviser. Michael was too sick to go to school on Monday, Tuesday, and Wednesday of that week, although he was brought to the regular Wednesday evening meeting at church by his mother. No one noticed anything amiss. If they did, they were Christian Scientists and knew the truth about it. According to one account that came out later, on Thursday, September 13, Michael vomited violently and repeatedly. On Thursday night, he got up, washed his face, brushed his teeth, and got back in bed. He told his mother, "It's all better, Mommy." Then he died.[2]

His mother did not call the funeral home until Sunday morning, September 16, two and a half days after his death. When employees of Green's Funeral Home arrived, the house was filled with the odor of decomposition. Betty Schram and Juanita Caldwell had been praying over Michael's body, hoping to resurrect him, to raise him from the dead.

That Sunday night, Jack Schram received a call from his wife, saying that she had something important to tell him and was coming over to his apartment. The last time he had spoken with her had been the previous Monday; he had asked to speak to his children and had been told that Mike was "not available." He assumed that Betty wanted to discuss their pending divorce. When he went down to the lobby to meet her, she was sitting, waiting. She looked up at him and said, "Mike got sick. We prayed for him, but he passed on."[3]

The scene was still fresh in his mind seventeen years later. "I started screaming," he told me. "I said, 'What are you talking about? What are you talking about? Why didn't you call 911?' I just about punched her. She said it so matter-of-factly."

Betty Schram told him that their daughter was out in the car and wanted to talk to him. They went out to the car. Jack Schram said, "I opened the door, and I said, 'What's going on? I can't believe it.' Sue said, 'Dad, I have a poem I want to read you,' just as cold as a lamb chop. And then she read me the most god-danged, stupidest poem." Betty Schram then opened the trunk of the car and removed five rockets that her husband had recently given Michael, who belonged to his school's pyrotechnics club. She gave him the rockets, patted him on the shoulder, told him that everything would be all right, and drove off.

The King County medical examiner's office conducted an autopsy, which revealed that Michael had died of a ruptured appendix. Jack Schram told the *Seattle Times*, "In a place like Mercer Island, where there's a doctor every six blocks, there's no excuse for this, no excuse at all," alluding to the fact that Mercer Island is, indeed, a notably wealthy suburb, home to many doctors.

There was a local uproar over the death. The Mercer Island church I'd gone to all my life was forced to cancel its Sunday service for the first time in its history, because of a bomb threat that turned out to be a hoax. Somebody broke in to Betty Schram's house, and the police cordoned off her street. The case received national press attention, and the Church's local public relations representative blamed Michael's death on the fact that the practitioner, Juanita Caldwell, was unlisted. He did not tell the papers that listed practitioners undergo two weeks of religious training only and have no way of recognizing the symptoms of a ruptured appendix or any other illness even if they believed such illnesses existed, which they don't. He told the papers that he was conducting an inquiry into the matter, on instructions from the Mother Church. If he ever did, its details and conclusions were not released to the public.

The prosecutor's office considered filing charges against Betty Schram and Juanita Caldwell but, in the end, declined to do so, saying that recent changes in the language of the Washington state law regarding criminal negligence made it impossible. Under the law, Schram and Caldwell seemed to have committed ordinary or simple negligence; there was not enough evidence to show that they had realized the seriousness of Michael's illness, an element of criminal negligence. There was, the prosecutor said, "a lack of proof that they were aware the kid was going to die." And that was the end of it.

Michael Schram died the month I left home to go to college. My mother sent me the newspaper clippings about his death. She whispered the whole story to me, dragging the phone into the laundry room where my father couldn't hear her. I have those clippings still, yellowed and creased.

During my last few months at home I had refused to go to church with my parents, a stand that outraged my father and worried my mother. I missed seeing my friends at church, and I missed playing the hymns on the old Sunday school piano. But I did not miss expressing gratitude to Mrs. Eddy and reciting the Scientific Statement of Being and the seven synonyms for God for the millionth time. I was tired of saying things I didn't understand and didn't believe. Even in the months before Michael Schram's death, I knew somehow, without even thinking about it, that I had never seen the healings that Christian Science promised. I had heard people *talk* about their healings, but I had never seen anyone healed at all, not anyone in our entire church. I had almost left Christian Science by the time Michael Schram died, but his death—and the manner of it—were the end of Christian Science for me. Michael Schram was not God's Perfect Child. He was a human being. Over time, his death taught me that it is better to turn your back on a religion than on a human being. It taught me why you can't pray a lie.

I did not write this book so that, as the cliché goes, children like Michael Schram will not have died in vain. Michael Schram *did* die in vain. So have dozens, or hundreds, or even thousands of other Christian Science children; no one will ever know how many. They died for nothing. They died for an idea.

3. The Cross and The Crown

The Cross and The Crown is the trademarked seal of the Christian Science Church. It is printed or embossed on official literature of the Church, including *Science and Health,* and is ringed by a circle of words taken from the Gospel: HEAL THE SICK, RAISE THE DEAD, CLEANSE THE LEPERS, CAST OUT DEMONS. Christian Scientists, with the encouragement of their church, interpret this as a literal exhortation.

Americans have always revered the power of the individual. This preoccupation has taken many forms—political, social, and religious—but one form has survived virtually intact, changing only the superficial spots of its rhetoric: the notion that everyone has the power to heal himself of whatever physical, fiscal, or spiritual ills ail him. Mary Baker Eddy's doctrine that man is a perfect manifestation of a perfect God is an extreme amalgam of Calvinist perfectionism (Jonathan Edwards's "seeing the perfect idea of a thing"), Ben Franklin's do-it-yourself pragmatism, the Transcendentalists' rejection of "the illusions of sense," and Emersonian self-reliance.[4] As F. O. Matthiessen writes in *American Renaissance:* "From the weaker aspects of Emerson's thought, the rocking chair of Mary Baker Eddy . . . is only just around the corner."[5]

Emerson saw around that corner, saw that the intellectual and spiritual self-reliance he had anatomized in the American character was vulnerable to coarsening, exaggeration, and simplification. Ruefully, in old age and declining health, the Sage of Concord admitted as much in an address before the Concord Lyceum in 1880, a few miles from the birthplace of Christian Science and five years after the publication of *Science and Health.* America, he said, was in the midst of a cataclysmic shift, "a war between intellect and affection; a crack in Nature," which, in schism after schism, was splitting the Christian world into fragments. The mind, he said, had become aware of itself. There was a new consciousness: "The individual is the world." Emerson identified the power and danger of this new radical reliance on the self: "This perception is a sword such as was never drawn before. It divides and detaches bone and marrow, soul and body, yea, almost the man from himself. It is the age of severance, of dissociation, of freedom, of analysis, of detachment. Every man for himself . . . driven to find all his resources, hopes, rewards, society and deity within himself."[6] He could have been talking specifically about Christian Science, which is self-reliance taken to its furthest extreme. Mary Baker Eddy was driven to find her deity within herself, and she became the ultimate American mystic, denying not just the reality of evil but the reality of matter itself.

Her brew of Christianity, self-denial, and self-empowerment has been profoundly influential. To judge by the number of offshoots of Christian Science—including the New Thought movement, which is still alive today—and by the fact that it has had an impact on American culture out of all proportion to its size as a sect, Eddy touched a fundamental American chord by asserting that the individual, through an understanding of the nature of God, wields ultimate physical control over the malleable and ultimately nonexistent body. Christian Science—the marriage of Christianity and science—was once in a class by itself: a religion that also claimed to be a science. Now, however, it is a half-forgotten old character at a crowded party, elbowed aside by dozens of other attractive, if wacky, nondenominational alternative-health-care faddists, herbalists, power-of-prayer healers, and peddlers of natural nostrums.

From the New Thought movement of the late 1800s to the self-help and New Age movements of our own day, the idea that healing lies within the self has become a vessel capable of containing all manner of modern anxieties and needs. The self-healers of the twentieth century have touted their connection to the great god Science, a connection which, as Eddy perceived, would be the ultimate twentieth-century imprimatur. Even as they borrow from the prestige of science, they have also rejected the powerful authoritarian figure of the Doctor/Scientist jealously protecting the inner sanctum of a fearsomely complex, secret knowledge. Anyone can have that knowledge, they say. Anyone.

The healers and self-helpers have been enormously successful, churning out best-seller after best-seller and movement after movement in each successive generation: Napoleon Hill and his *Think and Grow Rich*, which promises wealth to those who can tap in to "Infinite Intelligence"; Norman Vincent Peale's *The Power of Positive Thinking*; Werner Erhard's est; Dr. Joyce Brothers and her *How to Get Whatever You Want Out of Life*; Deepak Chopra's ayurveda and his dizzying proliferation of books on how to become "ageless" and "timeless"; Bernie Siegal and his *Love, Medicine, and Miracles*; Marianne Williamson and her popularization of *A Course in Miracles*, a textbook fundamentally inspired by Christian Science; Louise Hay (a former Scientist) and her *You Can Heal Your Life*; Andrew Weil with his wise family-physician face, his guru's white beard, and his *Spontaneous Healing*. They all came out from under Mary Baker Eddy's overcoat.

. . .

Mary Baker Eddy's early life contained little hint of what was to come. Having been born on a New Hampshire farm in 1821, and having lived in genteel poverty after two unfortunate marriages, Eddy wrote and published her book *Science and Health* at the age of fifty-four, after years spent wandering from boardinghouse to boardinghouse in Massachusetts. Her first followers were factory workers in Lynn, Massachusetts, humble men who made shoes and boxes, humble women hungry for a purpose in life. Eddy gave them that purpose, bestowing upon them the ultimate power over themselves and others: the power to heal. An early proponent of self-help, she preached the gospel that health, wealth, and prosperity were within the grasp of every man, woman, and child who would know the truth of his or her perfection as God's creation. Her followers called her Mother.

Moving to Boston, founding her church in 1879, Eddy became ever more visible, and her popularity soared as a result of her intense personal charisma. She opened a college to teach metaphysical healing; she lectured; she wrote; she ruled her growing religious empire with an iron hand, micromanaging its complex affairs. The vast edifice of her Mother Church in Boston, completed in 1906, became a mecca for Scientific pilgrims. Women, especially, flocked to her movement, eager to fill the positions of ecclesiastical authority that were closed to them in other churches: they became Eddy's "practitioners," healers who fanned out across the country and, eventually, the world, offering their services to those who had despaired of hopeless medical diagnoses or quack "miracle" cures. Although Eddy availed herself, on occasion, of medical treatment, she urged her followers to practice "radical reliance" on Christian Science and to refuse drugs and doctors. Many of her followers believed that she would demonstrate eternal life and defeat death herself, but she died in 1910 of pneumonia, at the age of eighty-nine. Once homeless and destitute, she left this world a millionaire, the only woman in history to found, single-handedly, a major religious movement.

Despite its humble beginnings, there was nothing modest about the early growth of Christian Science. It exploded across the country, the most successful new sect of the new century. Between 1906 and 1926, the number of Christian Science churches in the United States increased from 635 to 1,913, and the membership of the Church more than tripled, from 65,717 to 202,098, a growth rate exceeding that of any other American denomination.[7] By 1926, there were Christian Science churches in every state of the Union, an achievement few new sects could claim. According to one study that examined the value of church buildings and expenditures per member, Christian Science was among the wealthiest of all denominations.[8] The church founded by factory workers had become a church of middle-class aspiration and high society. And its followers, who believed that their religion could engender success in business as well as self-improvement in every other area of life, considered it only their due. Christian Science, Eddy had told them, would one day become the religion of the world; it would save the world.

The early popularity of Christian Science was tied directly to the promise engendered by its core beliefs: the promise of healing. The overwhelming majority of those attracted to the movement came to be healed, or came because a husband, wife, child, relative, or friend needed healing; the claims of Christian Science were so compelling that people often stayed in the movement whether they found healing or not, blaming themselves and not Eddy's teachings for any apparent failures. As the movement gained momentum through the 1920s, 1930s, and 1940s, it developed its own cachet. A host of institutions for Scientists sprang up and fanned out across the country, including a network of reading rooms selling Eddy's literature and located on the main streets of most cities and towns, private schools and a college near St. Louis called the Principia, and a number of Christian Science sanatoriums and nursing homes for Scientists where no medical treatment was allowed to interfere with prayer. Like the Christian Science branch churches and reading rooms, these homes were architecturally distinguished and luxuriously appointed: beacons of Christian Science success. This was the heyday of Christian Science, when my grandparents discovered it, along with the grandparents and great-aunts and godmothers of any number of my peers.

But in the decades to come, the vitality of Christian Science gradually faded, giving way to a new, darker phase, particularly following the life-saving medical discoveries made during World War II, which cast a shadow over the Church's healing. The Church had inherited from its founder and Mother not only money and property, but detailed, perversely autocratic, often eccentric, instructions on how the Church was to be run, as well as a certain haunted character. During the 1950s and 1960s, the Church increasingly retreated, holding itself aloof from modern life, venturing out into public realms only to seek what it called "accommodations" for its practices, which seemed, as medical innovation triumphed, ever more anachronistic.

Mary Baker Eddy was a deeply fearful person. She hid herself from her followers and from the world. Her child—her Church—has taken after her.

Christian Science church services are quiet, even spartan. There are no clergy, no ministers, no priests. Excerpts from *Science and Health with Key to the Scriptures* are read aloud in lieu of a sermon in every Christian Science church in the world every Sunday and Wednesday, along with passages from the Bible. During services, the two books are read by members of the congregation, elected for three-year terms. The Bible and *Science and Health* are, by Eddy's edict, the "dual and impersonal pastor" of this church, which has no vestments, no communion, no kneeling, no confession, no ceremonies, no Christmas Eve candlelight services, no baptisms, weddings, funerals, or rituals of any kind.[9] At every service, hymns are sung from the Christian Science Hymnal, usually including one of the seven hymns written by Eddy.[10] No food or drink is ever served in the churches. There are no bake sales, no raffles, no bingo games. There are no religious pictures of Christ, of the Crucifixion, or of the Stations of the Cross. There are no choirs, no candles, no frescoes, no marble angels. There are none of the community services offered by nine out of ten churches, mosques, and synagogues in the United States: no soup kitchens, food pantries, day care programs, summer camps, health screenings, marital counseling, or AA meetings.[11] The only decorations are quotations on the walls from the Bible and Mary Baker Eddy, and arrangements of fresh or dried flowers.

For a sect that can be secretive, Christian Science is remarkably open about its church services and sacred texts: "All Are Welcome" is the invitation issued from the lectern at every service. The tenor of the services is constrained assurance. One of the best introductions to Christian Science is to attend a Wednesday evening "meeting" at which Scientists, as they call themselves, rise to deliver impromptu testimonies of their healings. The testimonies speak of everything from finding lost car keys to recovering from cancer. There are no written rules about testimonies, but most follow a conventional form. Nearly every testifier closes his or her remarks with an expression of profound gratitude to "Mrs. Eddy," as she is called by the faithful, and to Christian Science.

Christian Science testimonies are also published in two Church periodicals, the monthly *Christian Science Journal* and the weekly *Sentinel*. The Church has parlayed these published testimonies into an extraordinary and unprecedented social achievement, using the sheer numbers of published letters to assure federal and state legislatures that Christian Science is at least as successful as traditional medicine at treating disease. These government bodies have passed numerous statutes protecting Scientists from prosecution for child neglect or manslaughter. Hundreds of private insurance companies cover the fees of Christian Science practitioners. Astonishingly, the federal government has also allowed Medicare coverage for services provided in Christian Science nursing homes, although those services are religious, not medical.

Christian Scientists are anything but diverse. They are overwhelmingly white and largely middle-class or wealthy: over 16 percent of Christian Science households earned more than $50,000 in 1990, a figure above the national average.[12] They are well educated: 42 percent of Christian Scientists have graduated from college.[13] Indeed, they must be educated enough so that they can read and understand the difficult nineteenth-century textbook that is the center of the religion. Most Christian Science practitioners are women. Internationally, Christian Science has always been strongest in English-speaking countries (Great Britain, Canada, Australia) and in societies with a prosperous professional class (Germany and Scandinavia).

Christian Scientists pride themselves on being "thoughtful," and the religion tends to attract those who enjoy or can tolerate a high degree of abstraction, because it demands constant study of Eddy's impersonal and abstruse text. (At home, most practicing Christian Scientists read assigned selections from *Science and Health* and the Bible every day, as part of the Church's Bible Lessons, published quarterly in booklet form.) It also, of course, still attracts those searching for healing, whether of an illness or of a more amorphous problem. The mien of the Christian Scientist is almost invariably friendly and cheerful, so much so that satirists have focused on the Scientist's constant smile as an indication of the "type." Students at Principia have a term for the smile on their own faces: "the Prin grin." A stranger attending a branch church service is liable to be approached with a friendly word or to find his hand squeezed by a pew mate. The placid atmosphere of the service is never troubled by allusions to any problems or conflicts that the congregation or the Church may be undergoing or, conversely, by ecstatic expressions of religious fervor; if the emotional range of the experience were plotted on a chart, it would be represented by a straight line.

In *The Great Chain of Being: A Study of the History of an Idea*, Arthur O.

Lovejoy discusses the prevalence throughout Western thought of two strains: "otherworldliness and this-worldliness."[14] "This-worldliness" is self-explanatory; it is a quality of people grounded in the tangible reality of this world. "Otherworldliness" is the mark of those who reject this world in favor of an ideal. Christian Scientists are otherworldly, in the sense of being intensely emotionally invested in an unseen world of perfection, and emotionally disassociated from the realities of this world. Scientists are smilers, happy-talkers, positive thinkers, and they simply refuse to allow the realities of the world, its tragedies and disasters, to penetrate. Christian Science periodicals often feature eerily surreal accounts of Scientists surviving natural disasters, earthquakes, storms, hurricanes, accidents, and acts of terrorism, which underline a central Scientific truth: nothing can touch the Scientist who clears his mind of fear. Thus, for Scientists, there is nothing to fear but fear itself.

The otherworldliness of Scientists is particularly pronounced in those who have been born and raised in the religion; often such Scientists have little experience with medical care, little knowledge of the human body and its diseases, little awareness of the realities of the flesh. This makes it all the easier for them to ignore their own illnesses and those of others, including their children. For those so steeped in the religion and its teachings, death is merely a "belief," which will inevitably be conquered by Life, Truth, and Love, and will itself pass away. To Christian Scientists, life on earth is an evanescent and illusory phase, and death a passing fancy. In the most extreme situations, this belief can lead Scientists into radical acts of denial.

4. I Tip My Hat

This book is a biography not of a person but of a church, the Christian Science Church. It is about the cost of living and dying according to its beliefs, about a religious idea that grabbed hold of America and did not let go. Everyone who has ever written at length about the Church and its teachings either believes or does not believe that Christian Science can heal. The Church itself recently acknowledged the intense reactions that Eddy and her religion have inspired. "Given the nature of the subject matter of Christian Science," wrote one Church editor, "it is probably unrealistic to anticipate any biography in which the author does not at least 'tip his hat.' "[15] Here, I tip mine.

I have been a Christian Scientist. I have believed its teachings, prayed its prayers, read its textbook, honored its beloved Founder and Leader, sung its hymns, and tried to follow its way. I failed—or, rather, Christian Science failed me. I no longer believe in Christian Science. I do, however, believe that it is a profoundly complex experience to be or to have been a Scientist, an experience worth understanding in its own right. It is also worth understanding because the practice of Christian Science is representative of the risks being taken, right now, by millions of people, in their search for alternative or spiritual healing. For those experimenting with everything from magnets to meditation, Christian Scientists are the test case. They have bet their lives on the potency of their beliefs, and not all of them have lived to tell the tale.

The aim of this book is not to malign the followers of this religion. Christian Scientists are productive members of society. There are Christian Science judges, lawyers, teachers, politicians, physicists, housewives, and newspaper reporters. They are your neighbors and mine. My own parents are Christian Scientists. The religion at its best encourages an adherence to the Golden Rule, best exemplified in the public realm by the Church's newspaper, the *Christian Science Monitor,* which has earned a well-deserved reputation for fairness and balance. It is no accident that perhaps the most common word used to describe Scientists is "nice." Most Scientists are nice, courteous, and thoughtful; as profoundly religious and Christian people, they are also sincerely concerned for the common good. They do not deserve to be mocked any more than Christians do for believing that Jesus rose from the dead, or than Catholics do for believing that the wafer and the wine literally become the body and blood of their Savior.

But there are beliefs that allow an honest recognition of the human condition, and beliefs that distort the human condition; there are beliefs that respect the basic human rights of men, women, and children, and beliefs that do not. Religion in all its innumerable forms is dedicated to helping humanity cope with death and the afterlife. It shouldn't hurry us on our way there. Christian Scientists deserve religious freedom as much as any other group. They deserve that much, and no more.

Because of the literary vigilantism of the Church's powerful propaganda machine, the history of scholarship pertaining to Christian Science has been a strange one. Rarely has writing about any subject been so polarized. Had biographers and scholars been allowed to write about Eddy and her church unharried, there might today be a variety of nuanced histories and biographies illuminating the subject. As it is, the subject has been the site of a pitched intellectual battle from the beginning; the few critical works that have been published, particularly those focusing on Eddy's life, have been subjected to incessant attack by the Church, which brands all criticism of Eddy and her religion "obnoxious" and forbids its members to frequent bookstores that sell such materials. It has organized campaigns to discredit such books and prevent their sale, and then blandly denied such actions. Scientists' response to what has been written about them reveals a deep intolerance of skeptical attention of any kind, an intolerance that typically characterizes fearful and reactionary movements.

The Church, for its part, has published an enormous apologist literature about Christian Science. In addition to multiple flattering biographies of Eddy, the Church publishes its daily newspaper, the weekly *Sentinel* and other religious periodicals, and books and pamphlets that rationalize the medical neglect of children in favor of Christian Science prayer treatment; these are distributed to public libraries, hospitals, airports, and bus stations, as well as Christian Science reading rooms. *Science and Health* is now widely available in retail bookstores. The Church has every right to publish and distribute such material, of course. But the information that the Church has left out of its literature should also be made available. An accurate historical record of a movement that has done much to skew society's perceptions of it, conjuring an elaborate fantasy of its healing prowess, is essential. Not only is it beyond the present ability of Christian Scientists to raise the dead to life, as the *Sentinel* recently acknowledged, it is beyond their ability to treat organic disease at all.[16] The Empress of Christian Science has no clothes. Christian Science has killed and maimed and materially damaged people. Their story has not been fully told. I have tried to tell it here.

In its zeal to ensure that protective legislation shields its members from the consequences of their most destructive practices, the Christian Science Church has long evaded responsibility for its actions. Making promises and assertions that have no basis in fact, it has led the U.S. Congress down a garden path for the past century. A Christian Scientist commented recently, regarding Church scandals, "It is the facts that are the problem."[17] This book is dedicated to presenting those facts: facts that have been suppressed, or dismissed, or obscured by the Church; facts that demonstrate that the Church has, throughout its history, been dedicated to an idea that can kill people; facts that demonstrate that the Church has had an unfortunate influence on the legislative and statutory level, seriously eroding the rights of children to equal protection under the law.

Christian Scientists, like everyone in a free society, have the right to *believe* whatever they want. They do not, however, have the right to *do* whatever they want. This book is about what Christian Scientists believe, but, above all, it is about what they have done. For too long, Christian Science, the purloined letter of American religion, has been hidden in plain sight. It has been content to live a veiled existence, relegated to passing mention in texts on American religious history, hiding behind a reputation for middle-class respectability. But "there is an hour to come," Nathaniel Hawthorne wrote in his classic story "The Minister's Black Veil," "when all of us shall cast aside our veils."[18] For Christian Science, it is about time.

Part I

Mary Baker Eddy:
"Mere Historic Incidents"

"Wickedness or not," said the traveller with
the twisted staff, "I have a very general
acquaintance here in New England."

> —Nathaniel Hawthorne,
> "Young Goodman Brown"

1. "A Very General Acquaintance"

The "traveller with the twisted staff" in Nathaniel Hawthorne's tale "Young Goodman Brown" is Satan. Goodman Brown, a newly married Puritan, encounters the Devil on an evening walk through the wild gloom of a New England forest. Tempted, he follows the Devil to a meeting in the heart of the woods where he watches as all of his pious, God-fearing, do-gooding neighbors and friends—even, to his despair, his young bride—perform a Black Mass and worship evil. After he returns to his village, not knowing if the fantastical night and its terrifying visions were real or a dream, Goodman Brown lives out the rest of his life in a state of deep and ominous suspicion, despising the hypocrisy of everyone he sees. "A stern, a sad, a darkly meditative, a distrustful, if not a desperate man did he become from the night of that fearful dream," Hawthorne writes.[1]

"Young Goodman Brown" is a parable not about the power of Satan but about the power of the *belief* in Satan. "Wickedness or not," the story seems to say, an overwhelming conviction of the evil of others can ruin human life. It is a parable about the perils of self-righteousness, something Hawthorne here, as in *The Scarlet Letter*, takes as a given of human nature and religious zealotry.

Mary Baker Eddy dreamt the same fearful waking dream as Goodman

Brown. For her, the world was peopled by beings governed by dark compulsions, wielding a terrible power that she later identified as "malicious animal magnetism." Nothing and no one was safe. Her creation of Christian Science was an attempt to protect herself from the terror around her and within her. But, although she became successful beyond her imagining in all the worldly ways, acquiring wealth and power, she never found refuge from those demons; she distrusted her own followers and even her own Church. So she stamped her people and the generations born after them with her peculiar paranoia, bequeathing her fears to an entire religious movement: fear of weakness, of powerlessness, of the needs and frailties of the human body, of sexuality, of death.

"Young Goodman Brown" is set in the New England of the 1600s, but Hawthorne wrote it in 1835. He knew who his neighbors were. He knew that beneath the placid surface of New England life beat a Puritan heart that yearned for perfection and punished its absence. He wrote it when another New England native, the girl Mary Baker, was fourteen years old.

2. "Mere Historic Incidents"

Mary Morse Baker was born in Bow, a rural township five miles from Concord, New Hampshire, the state capital of the first colony to declare its independence from Great Britain. She was delivered into this world on July 16, 1821, the sixth and last child of Mark and Abigail Baker. Those are among the few undisputed facts in the life of the woman who came to be known as Mary Baker Eddy. Just as she would be a compulsive revisionist of her own writings—issuing 432 editions of her textbook, *Science and Health,* and revising it until the month before she died—she was also an unapologetic revisionist of her own history.[2] She asserted her right to do as she pleased with the facts of her life in her highly idiosyncratic and much revised autobiography, *Retrospection and Introspection:* "Mere historic incidents and personal events are frivolous and of no moment. . . . The human history needs to be revised, and the material record expunged."[3]

Since her death, the Christian Science Church has followed her lead, revising and expunging, reshaping and elaborating the mythology she wove around herself, preferring that the world see Eddy as a religious genius and leader, divinely inspired. But the trajectory of her life as she progressed from humble farm girl to one of the wealthiest, most powerful women of her day tells a different story.

. . .

Mary Baker Eddy grew up on a farm. The Baker family had been in New England for seven generations, since the first Baker had emigrated from England, and the land Mary Baker grew up on had been cleared by her father's father. The Bakers were strict Congregationalists. The family home, two and a half stories with a sloping roof, on a hill above the Merrimack River, housed nine people: Mark and Abigail Baker; their six children—Samuel, George, Albert, Abigail, Martha, and Mary—and Mark's mother, Maryann Baker. It was a modest farm. Outside the house were two barns, a garden, and an orchard surrounded by a stone wall three feet thick. The house faced east and overlooked the Londonderry Turnpike, the road to Boston. At the time, Bow consisted of several farms, schools, and a meetinghouse.

Mark Baker, a tall, thin man, was apparently an adequate farmer; he kept oxen, cows, horses, pigs, sheep, and chickens and raised hay, wheat, corn, and other crops. To supplement his income, he also took on legal work for neighbors, drawing up wills and other documents, and he was the county coroner for Bow. He was notably pious, an active, even obstreperous member of the Congregational church in Bow. Shortly after his daughter Mary was born, he became clerk of the church, and his complaints about the "backsliding" of fellow members are still to be found in the church records.[4] The family prayed together morning and evening, seated on benches before him, while he read from the Bible and extemporized on the Scriptures, sometimes at great length. As a young child, Mary found her father's sermonizing tedious and once claimed to have stuck him in the behind with a pin during a particularly protracted session.[5]

Baker's neighbors remembered him as an inconsistent disciplinarian, thundering with righteous indignation one minute, relenting the next. He could hold a grudge and was estranged for years from one of his brothers, who lived on a neighboring farm. Baker's apparent rigidity may have derived at least in part from his religion; he was known for his orthodoxy, his "view that the vast majority of mankind must and would be damned for the glory of God."[6]

According to neighborhood legend, Mark Baker once lost track of the day and worked on the Sabbath, upbraiding his neighbors for their godlessness on his walk to church the next day. He was horrified when he learned that he had profaned the Lord's Day and prayed for forgiveness with his pastor. But on his way home, his outraged feelings got the better of him:

> A tame crow, a pet of the children of the neighbourhood, hopped on a bush in front of him, cawing loudly. In his perturbed condition, the sight of the bird made Mark angrier than ever, and raising his stick, he struck the crow dead. "Take that," he said in a passion, "for hoppin' about on the Sabbath," and he stormed on up the hill. At home he kept the day strictly as Sunday to atone for his worldliness of the previous day.[7]

Robert Peel, a Christian Scientist and the author of a three-volume biography of Eddy, noted that Mark Baker's farmhands and relatives considered him "kind-hearted," and other recent biographers have suggested that his portrayal as an unyielding parent and rigid religionist has been exaggerated.[8] The source of that image, however, was his youngest daughter. There is little doubt that Mark and Mary Baker had a fraught relationship. The only description he earns in Eddy's autobiography is a terse one: "My father possessed a strong intellect and an iron will."[9] This is one of several hints in Eddy's writings and other sources that she remembered her father with a certain coldness, even contempt; she once said of him, "Father kept the family in the tightest harness I have ever known."[10] There is only one extant photograph of him, a tintype revealing a lean, stern face with a penetrating gaze strikingly similar to his daughter's.[11]

As a child, Mary sporadically attended a one-room schoolhouse with her older sisters, Abby and Martha, when illness did not keep her at home; Eddy later attributed her frequent absences to her father who, she said, "was taught to believe that my brain was too large for my body and so kept me much out of school."[12] Late in life, she reported to her students a recollection of her first day at school, when she was asked what she wanted to be when she grew up. Most girls would probably have replied, "A mother" or something similar, assuming the question would have been asked at all. But Eddy described her four-year-old self as replying, "I want to write a book!"[13]

Apocryphal or not, the anecdote contains at least a grain of truth: the young Mary Baker developed a deep respect for the written word and began writing and publishing at a young age. Mainly verse, her compositions are collages of flowery Victorian language and imagery. In "Alphabet and Bayonet," an example of her "girlhood productions" that she chose to reproduce in her autobiography, there is a hint of preoccupations to come:

Forth from this fount the streamlets flow,
That widen in their course.
Hero and sage arise to show
Science the mighty source.[14]

Eddy's mother may well have been the inspiration behind her early love of reading and moral instruction. Remembered by her daughter with great tenderness and affection, Abigail Baker, of whom no photograph or other likeness exists, was said to have read to her youngest often from the Bible, and family letters and reminiscences show that Mary and her mother were particularly close.[15] Shortly after her daughter left home, Abigail Baker wrote to her, "Dear Child your memory is dearer to *me* than gold every thing reminds me of you. . . . sometimes I fear I worship mary instead of the great jehovah."[16]

Many of Eddy's other recollections of her childhood and her relationship to her mother significantly focus not on the work of daily life—milking, cooking, cleaning, weaving, sewing—but on extreme moral scrupulosity and higher pursuits. One anecdote that she was fond of telling was of a time when she brought home a pitch-pine knot she'd found on a neighbor's property; it was a popular children's pastime to throw these highly flammable knots of wood on the fire to see them flare. Discovering that the pine knot did not come from their own property, her mother reprimanded her for stealing it, a violation of the Ten Commandments, and made her return it.[17]

Another story Eddy told about herself and her mother—told years after her mother's death, to students whose own feelings about Eddy were worshipful—emphasizes the mother's idealization of her daughter. In that story, Eddy claimed that her mother experienced a divine visitation when she was pregnant with her youngest child. Eddy's student Clara Shannon recorded her teacher's account in her unpublished memoir, "Golden Memories":

One day, about four and a half months before [Mary's] birth, her mother, Mrs. Baker, went into the attic to get some wool in order to spin yarn for knitting. . . . Collecting her wool together, suddenly she was overwhelmed by the thought that she was filled with the Holy Ghost and had dominion over the whole earth. At that moment she felt the quickening of the babe.[18]

Eddy went on to say that her mother felt intense guilt for thinking such a thing. Adam Dickey, Eddy's secretary at the end of her life, relates a similar story:

> [Mrs. Baker] could not keep her thought away from the strong conviction that this child was holy and consecrated and set apart for wonderful achievements, even before her birth. She said, "I know these are sinful thoughts for me to entertain, but I cannot shake them off."[19]

According to Eddy, this was just one of the signs that she was destined for a sacred, scriptural mission. In her autobiography, she included a chapter entitled "Voices Not Our Own," which tells of one of "many peculiar circumstances and events connected with my childhood."[20] When she was eight years old, Eddy wrote, she repeatedly heard a voice calling her name three times in a row. When she went to her mother to ask what she wanted, her mother told her that she had not called. Alarmed, she read to her daughter the biblical story of the prophet Samuel, who was called three times by the Lord. Her mother told her to reply to the mysterious voice as Samuel did, by saying, " 'Speak, Lord; for Thy servant heareth.' "[21] Finally, Mary replied to the voice in this manner, and it ceased to trouble her. Many years later, Eddy told a more dramatic version of the tale to Dickey, who wrote in his memoir:

> [Eddy] then related in a voice filled with awe, that when she made the reply, a most unusual phenomenon took place. Her body was lifted entirely from the bed, on which she lay, to a height, it seemed to her, of about one foot. Then it was laid gently back on the bed. This was repeated three times. As a child she was afraid to tell the circumstance to anybody, but she pondered it deeply in her heart and thought of it many years afterward, when she was demonstrating the nothingness of matter and that the claim of the human body was a myth.[22]

The question of whether Eddy believed that these events actually happened or consciously invented them seems less important, finally, than what the stories themselves suggest about Eddy's image of herself, the image she wanted her followers to hold dear. The stories prophesy her mission. Acceptance of these signs as literal truth separates many believers in Christian Science from nonbelievers, just as an acceptance that Joseph Smith received golden tablets from the angel Moroni separates believers in

Mormonism from nonbelievers. In the first, simpler version of Eddy's story, God spoke to the child, Mary. The elaborated version introducing the element of levitation enlarges Mary's role and makes its point more literal. God picked her up. He picked her.

Although these annunciations were embraced by many true believers in Eddy's day, some modern-day Scientists have attempted to distance themselves from the supernatural elements of Eddy's self-mythologizing. Robert Peel does not recount these tales. Robert David Thomas, a scholar and non-Scientist who had access to the Church's archives while writing his psychological biography of her, reports: "The Baker family correspondence in fact fails to offer any corroborating evidence that both her mother and God had marked her as a chosen one."[23]

Eddy also mythologized another incident in her autobiography in a way that seems designed to offer a parallel between herself and Jesus. In the chapter "Theological Reminiscence," Eddy claims that "at the age of twelve I was admitted to the Congregational (Trinitarian) Church."[24] She goes on to describe the dramatic occasion. Unable to accept "my father's relentless theology" and the doctrine of predestination, Mary came down with a fever. Her mother joined her in prayer; her fever lifted; and "the 'horrible decree' of predestination . . . forever lost its power over me."[25] Queried about her belief in this harsh doctrine during a church meeting devoted to the interrogation of prospective members, Mary refused to accept it, wept, and cited a psalm; the church members wept with her. Even the hard-hearted pastor who put the cruel question to her was moved, and welcomed her into the church.

Records at the Bakers' church, however, show that Mary joined that church at age seventeen, not twelve.[26] Jesus, of course, was twelve when he entered the temple in Jerusalem and dazzled the rabbis with his wisdom, proclaiming "I must be about my Father's business."[27] Eddy's story about her precocity at age twelve, questioning the doctrine of predestination, seems designed to parallel the New Testament story, and, indeed, that is how many Scientists have interpreted it.[28] Eddy later acknowledged that "a mistake may have occurred" in her recollection of the event.[29] But, although a note was inserted in the autobiography referring readers to Eddy's acknowledgment, she never, in subsequent editions, took the opportunity to correct her original statement.

3. "An *Agreeable* Variety of Pain"

In 1834, at the age of twelve, Eddy attended a revival in Concord, New Hampshire—a "protracted meeting," as they were called—that lasted seven days. Waves of revivals were then sweeping through the state, and after one of Mary's early revival experiences, she enthused about leaving the Congregationalist for the Methodist church, but was discouraged by her father.[30]

Mary was born at a moment of intense revivalist and schismatic activity in American Christianity. Her birthplace, Bow, was less than a hundred miles from Sharon, Vermont, where Joseph Smith, the Mormon founder, was born in 1805. Smith would spend some part of his childhood in Lebanon, New Hampshire, even closer to Bow. The period of religious revivalism known as the Second Great Awakening ran from 1820, the year before Eddy's birth, to 1860, when she was thirty-nine, just a few years before she would experience her own great awakening.

The Second Great Awakening made it possible for practically anyone to found a new religion. Men and women who had never had a day of formal religious instruction, and members of social classes who previously would never have dreamed of partaking of a religious revolution, were awakened to the possibilities by evangelists. One such preacher, Charles Grandison Finney, told his audience of merchants and craftsmen in 1830 that "if Christians united and dedicated their lives to the task, they could convert the world and bring on the millennium in three months."[31] The news of this "shopkeeper's millennium" was galvanizing: "Scores of people rose from their seats, many of them weeping, and pledged their lives to Jesus. With that act they left the imperfect and confining world that God had made for corrupt man, and entered a world where men worked ceaselessly to make themselves and others perfect."[32]

Mary may also have sensed the excitement over the Millerite movement, born when William Miller, a farmer from New York and one of the founders of what became Seventh-Day Adventism, predicted that Christ would return and the world end between March 21, 1843, and March 21, 1844. When the world placidly prevailed on March 22, 1844, Miller was forced to recalculate his date for the millennium, suggesting that it would come the following October. Faced with considerable evidence to the contrary, his adherents ultimately felt their so-called Great Disappointment.

Seventh-Day Adventism was subsequently reorganized under the leadership of Ellen Gould White, and the Adventists swore off predicting the exact date of the end of the world.

And Mary could hardly have been unaware of the growing notoriety of Joseph Smith and his sect. The *Book of Mormon* was published in 1830, and by 1839 the entire country was following the news of how the Mormons had been driven out of Missouri and were building a new sanctuary in Nauvoo, Illinois, where their movement would grow to thirty thousand strong.[33] A new Mormon newspaper published eyewitness accounts of their persecution.[34] Eddy may have heard of the "spectacular healings" Smith was said to have brought about during an epidemic of typhoid or malaria among his people, and of Smith's murder and martyrdom at the hands of a mob in 1844.[35]

Revivals brought enormous excitement and spectacle to the dull and difficult lives of New England farmers, such as Smith's and Eddy's parents, and were often accompanied by news of mainline Protestant movements dividing into faction upon faction. One historian writes, "The Methodists split four ways between 1814 and 1830. The Baptists split into Reformed Baptists, Hard-Shell Baptists, Free-Will Baptists, Seventh-Day Baptists, Footwashers, and other sects. Unfettered religious liberty began spawning a host of new religions. . . . Faith healers and circuit-rider evangelists . . . stirred their audiences to paroxysms of religious frenzy.[36] One day, Mary would make her own split.

Even as these stirring spiritual events were occurring, life for the Baker family continued on a more worldly plane. Albert, Mary's favorite brother, graduated from Dartmouth College, the first Baker to achieve such an advanced education. Judging by the letters between Mary and her brother, she developed a taste for social recognition and intellectual sophistication through Albert's example. His future seemed bright. He studied law and began to be active in New Hampshire state politics. After being admitted to the bar, he was elected to the state legislature, and until his sister gained her notoriety as the founder of a new religion, his accomplishments would represent the pinnacle of the family's social success. Later, Mary would claim that Albert taught her "the ancient tongues, Hebrew, Greek, and Latin," but that "after my discovery of Christian Science, most of the knowledge I had gleaned from schoolbooks vanished like a dream."[37] There is no evidence, however, that Eddy ever knew these languages. Over her lifetime, she would display a talent for religious leadership, but languages and literature, for all her aspirations to be a writer, were not among her gifts. Neither formally educated nor a true autodidact, she would never develop any skill for narrative or clarity in writing.

Mary's health preoccupied the Baker family for many years. She suffered from a variety of ill-defined ailments, the nature of which has excited much speculation among her biographers. The first critical biography of Eddy described her frequent childhood "attacks" as a form of tantrum, citing the family doctor's diagnosis as "hysteria mingled with bad temper":

> At times the attack resembled convulsions. Mary fell headlong to the floor, writhing and screaming in apparent agony. Again she dropped as if lifeless, and lay limp and motionless, until restored. At other times she became rigid like a cataleptic, and continued for a time in a state of suspended animation. At home the family worked over her, and the doctor was sent for, and Mary invariably recovered rapidly after a few hours; but year after year her relatives fully expected that she would die in one of these spasms. Nothing had the power of exciting Mark Baker like one of Mary's "fits," as they were called. His neighbors in Tilton remember him as he went to fetch Dr. Ladd, how he lashed his horses down the hill, standing upright in his wagon and shouting in his tremendous voice, "Mary is dying!"[38]

The complaints that frequently kept Mary home from school and waited on by her parents and older siblings are now recognized as classic nineteenth-century manifestations of psychosomatic illnesses. In *From Paralysis to Fatigue: A History of Psychosomatic Illness in the Modern Era*, the historian Edward Shorter argues that "the symptom pool"—a group of complaints associated with a specific historical period—changed as advances were made in medical knowledge and as fads and fashions in medicine, influenced both by the wider culture and by physicians themselves, came and went.[39] In the eighteenth century, hysterical paralysis and catatonia were common, and in the nineteenth, neurasthenia, or nervous exhaustion, became a catch-all diagnosis. The young Mary Baker was diagnosed on various occasions as suffering from spinal irritation, neuralgia, dyspepsia, stomach cankers, and ulcers, all symptoms that were eventually to come under the umbrella of neurasthenia. The diagnosis became ever more popular, sparing families the far more painful, distressing labels associated with mental illness.

Most biographers, historians, and critics who are not affiliated with the Christian Science Church have recognized Eddy's illnesses as psychosomatic. In Harold Bloom's memorable description, she was "a monumental hysteric of classic dimensions, indeed a kind of anthology of nineteenth-century nervous ailments."[40] Even Robert Peel, an apologist for Eddy's more eccentric characteristics, hints at the likelihood that at least some of her childhood pain was psychogenic:

> There is no reliable evidence of the exact form Mary Baker's ill health took during the first fourteen years of her life. Whether it included the acute "spells" that occurred in the later years of her girlhood we do not know. What is certain is that it kept her out of school a good deal of the time.[41]

Peel attempts to explain the psychosomatic nature of Eddy's illnesses by suggesting that her symptoms physically manifested her "existential concerns,"[42] but he also acknowledges that "it is necessary . . . to distinguish between the genuine suffering that darkened her life in those years and the romantic melancholy she shared as a literary fashion with the age."[43] He grants that she was "the chief sufferer" in the family and that she was particularly attracted to fad diets and cures, experimenting as an adolescent with a diet of bread and water developed by Sylvester Graham, the Presbyterian minister and nutritional evangelist who invented graham flour.[44]

It is impossible to determine exactly what inspired Mary's various symptoms, but her own and other family members' letters suggest that her suffering may have been a combination of hypochondria, conscious histrionics and malingering, and unconscious rebellion against her father. Early in her life, Mary established a pattern of claiming to be gravely ill and then dramatically recovering; she seems to have discovered that such behavior unfailingly attracted the attention, sympathy, and concern of her family and friends.

Mary herself seemed relatively unconcerned by the grim prospect of suffering and death that she dangled before her loved ones. As a teenager, she wrote to a friend that she was suffering "an *agreeable* variety of pain," and her physical ills rarely seem to have kept her from the activities she enjoyed: writing poetry and letters, reading, and visiting friends.[45] It seems implausible that the illnesses of her youth were ever organic or potentially serious. Indeed, Eddy's complaints of ill health evaporated in middle age, immediately following her discovery of Christian Science.[46] Eddy survived to the age of eighty-nine, outliving all the other members of her immediate family. Christian Scientists, of course, interpret her long life and relatively good health after her discovery of Christian Science as the inevitable result of her healing method.

In 1836, when Mary was fourteen, the Baker family moved from Bow to a farm near Sanbornton Bridge, New Hampshire, a town twenty-odd miles away.[47] The move was agreeable to the three Baker girls; their proximity to the village gave them greater social opportunities, and soon, Mary's eldest sister was engaged to be married. In 1837, her brother Albert took over the law practice of his mentor Franklin Pierce, who had been elected to the U.S. Senate. (Thirteen years later, Pierce would become president of the United States.) And in 1839, Albert himself entered political life, elected to the New Hampshire statehouse.

But Albert's promising career soon came to an abrupt end. In 1841, he died of a kidney infection, and his sister Mary, twenty years old, suffering the first tragic loss of her young life, wrote a great deal of verse exploring the metaphysical ramifications of death.[48] After hearing that her brother had been impugned by his political rivals, she also wrote a verse defense of his honor, entitled "Lines on reading an attack upon the political career of the late Albert Baker Esqr."[49] During her later life, Eddy was preoccupied with defending herself from "attack"; this may be an early indication of that proclivity.

In 1843, two years after Albert's death, Mary married George Washington Glover, her thirty-three-year-old brother-in-law. She was twenty-two. George Glover's sister had married Mary's eldest brother, Samuel, in 1831, and legend has it that when George Glover met the young Mary at his sister's wedding, he took her on his lap and told her he'd come back to marry her when she grew up. Glover was from Concord, New Hampshire, but was making a career for himself as a builder in Charleston, South Carolina. He took his bride south with him, first to Charleston, then to Wilmington, North Carolina, and was preparing to take her with him to Haiti, where he had contracted to build a cathedral, when, in a disastrous financial setback, his building supplies were destroyed by fire or stolen. In June 1844, George Glover contracted a virulent illness, possibly yellow fever, and died within a matter of days, on June 27. The couple had been married less than seven months. Mary Glover was forced to return to her parents' home in Sanbornton Bridge, penniless and pregnant.[50]

This was a brief, sad chapter in Eddy's life, but—characteristically—she would later embellish it. One of the most specious elements of the Eddy mythology has been the recurrent claim kept alive by her church that she was a vocal opponent of slavery who wrote articles criticizing the institution. No such articles have ever been found. She claimed to have freed her husband's slaves, but it is doubtful that he had any; she also told several colorful and patently false stories about a slave named Bill, whom she claimed to have freed and who, in gratitude, was supposed to have rescued her from bandits.[51] In a 1902 message that Eddy delivered to her church, nearly sixty years after her first marriage, she informed her congregation that "my husband, Colonel Glover, of Charleston, South Carolina, was considered wealthy, but much of his property was in slaves, and I declined to sell them at his decease in 1844, for I could never believe that a human being was my property."[52]

Glover was apparently *not* wealthy; in fact, Peel found an entry in the records of the Masonic lodge to which Glover belonged which described him at the time of his death as "in indigent circumstances."[53] All in all, Eddy's gratuitous embroidering on the reality of her first marriage casts her narration of her life into lasting question.

4. Mother Mary

Eddy's only biological child, George Washington Glover II, was born on September 12, 1844. On his birth, Mrs. Glover lapsed into the state of chronic invalidism she had exhibited throughout her youth, and proved incapable of caring for her son. The baby was nursed by a local woman who had recently lost one of her twins, while his mother was cared for by a household servant, Mahala Sanborn. In one of his more implausible attempts at rationalizing Eddy's behavior, Peel blames the baby for his own abandonment, suggesting that he was far more demanding than most infants: "He wailed in protest long beyond the time that is held proper for babies to cry."[54] The suggestion originated with Eddy herself.[55]

Two years later, Mary had recovered enough to conduct a short-lived "infant school," a kind of kindergarten attended by local children, which, despite its failure, indicates her desire for some kind of station or occupation in life.[56] But she continued to suffer, as one of her sisters described it, from "dispepsia, liver-complaint and nervous disease."[57] During this period, she became known throughout the neighborhood for her predilection for the family's porch swing, which was said to ease her discomfort.

Eventually the family outfitted a sofa with rockers and employed small boys to rock her in it, a pastime that became known locally as "swinging Mrs. Glover."[58]

There are references in the family's letters to the rambunctiousness of young George Glover II and to the inability of his mother to mind him, but his uncle George, Mary's brother, provided something of a father figure until 1849, when he married and left home. That same year, Mary's mother died. By 1850, Mark Baker was planning to remarry and made it clear to his youngest daughter that her son would not be welcome to live with him and his future wife. She wrote an angry, defiant letter to her brother George, revealing the tension she felt between herself and her father:

> Last year . . . I went into that cold damp house with Father, helped cleanse and set it in order and lived alone with a little girl and him all winter; in the spring he told me if George was not sent away he would send him to the *Poor House* (after abusing him as he did through the winter). *Now* he comes to me to help arrange the things of his bride; but I will see them in the bottomless pit before doing it.[59]

Mary herself was not turned out of her father's house but was unwilling to continue there without her son; her sister Martha, however, recently widowed, continued to live there with her two daughters after her father's marriage. Mary sent young George on a series of visits to relatives and moved in with her other sister, Abigail Tilton, who had a son of her own to care for and who was also, according to Peel, not hospitable to George.[60]

The fate of Mary's son has been a source of never-ending controversy, a troublesome blot on Eddy's character that she and sympathetic biographers have struggled to erase. In 1851, his round of visits at an end, six-year-old George was sent to North Groton, New Hampshire, forty miles away from his mother, to live with the former servant, Mahala, who had married a farmer, Russell Cheney. Again, Peel blames the boy, who, he suggests, may have deserved his fate, being insufficiently sensitive for his mother's delicate nature: "In temperament he might almost have been the child of Mahala, who was good-hearted and coarse-grained, not particular about niceties of behavior and totally without 'nerves.' "[61] Eddy herself was only too eager to acquit herself of responsibility for the act of giving up the child, and never ceased blaming her family for his removal from her life.

In 1853, Mary married her dentist of seven months, Daniel Patterson, the groom carrying the bride down the stairs of her father's house for the ceremony and then carrying her back up to bed again.[62] Mary's father had warned Patterson about his prospective bride's invalidism, but the groom was undaunted. Although the couple lived near the Cheneys in North Groton in 1855, George Glover's adopted family took the boy with them when they moved to Minnesota in 1856. George Glover did not see his mother again for twenty-three years.

In the final edition of her autobiography, Eddy hints darkly that all these events were beyond her control:

> My dominant thought in marrying again was to get back my child, but after our marriage his stepfather was not willing he should have a home with me. A plot was consummated for keeping us apart. The family to whose care he was committed very soon removed to what was then regarded as the Far West.
>
> After his removal a letter was read to my little son, informing him that his mother was dead and buried. Without my knowledge a guardian was appointed him, and I was then informed that my son was lost. Every means within my power was employed to find him, but without success.[63]

In the earlier 1891 edition of this same work, Eddy complained that her son's removal "depriv[ed] me of the opportunity of having my son classically educated," revealing a preoccupation with her son's illiteracy that would surface again when they became reacquainted, years later.[64] But to date no evidence has been found to support the sympathetic assumption that Mary Glover yearned to regain custody of her son.[65]

In 1983, Jewel Spangler Smaus, a Christian Scientist and the author of a children's biography of Eddy's early life that was published by the Church, tried to offer such evidence, writing a series of articles about Eddy's son for the quarterly newsletter of the Longyear Museum and Historical Society, published by the Longyear Foundation, a private group of Christian Scientists that maintains many of the historical sites in New England dedicated to preserving Eddy's memory. Smaus's discoveries, which were also touted by the Church in the *Christian Science Journal* as "An Important Historical Discovery," were thought to document, finally, Eddy's claim that her child was taken from her by means of a "plot."[66] Smaus claimed to have discovered documents signed by Eddy, her father, and Daniel Patterson, which set in motion the process by which Patterson would have become George Glover's legal guardian, a procedure which,

Smaus wrote, Patterson never legally completed, thus voiding the documents. Other documents, however, she acknowledged, suggested that Patterson was indeed the boy's legal guardian. Yet another paper, signed by the boy's eventual guardian, Russell Cheney, claims that Mary Glover had given him her son when the boy was five.

Taken together, the various sets of documents raise far more questions than they answer. If Patterson was plotting to remove young George from his bride's life, why did he sign the guardianship papers, and why did the newlyweds move to North Groton, where the boy was living? If Patterson was never George's legal guardian, why did Mary's father—noted for his parsimony—pay a bond in 1860 for the then enormous sum of $200 that Cheney, the boy's guardian, claimed Patterson owed him as the former guardian? And, of course, how did these machinations go on without Mary's knowledge? Smaus conjures up a plot whereby Mark Baker and Daniel Patterson schemed to remove George from his mother's life; she does, however, admit in the *Journal* article that the confusion surrounding the documents "leaves the issue somewhat clouded." All the evidence suggests that Mary's long-suffering family lavished time, effort, and money attending to her needs; their letters show that they often believed her to be at death's door. The simplest explanation for the fate of her son remains that she was not well enough or not willing enough to care for him. There is no documentary evidence that Mary's family had any malicious intent toward her; there is no evidence of a plot; and there is no evidence that George was told that his mother was dead.[67] Nor has any evidence come to light confirming Eddy's claim that she employed "every means" to locate her son.

There is no doubt, however, that Mary expressed affection for her son and distress over his absence. In a letter written to George's aunt and uncle when he was staying with them, she wrote of sending him to live with the Cheneys:

> Oh! how I *miss him* already! There seems nothing left me now to enjoy. . . .
> I want very much to know how you have succeeded with him and if he has
> been a good boy (some naughty things of course). There is no child whom
> we expect mature in every respect, but take Georgy with the aggregate, is he
> not a pretty good and very dear boy?[68]

Her concern for her son, however, is often surmounted by her concern for herself ("There seems nothing left me now to enjoy") and by her concern for appearances. Her emotions were also expressed in melodramatic form in "Written on the 9th day of May on parting with my babe":

> Go little voyager, o'er life's rough sea—
> Born in a tempest! choose thy pilot God.[69]

Later in life, her encouragement of those followers who called her "Mother" and her repetitive, even obsessive, use of the mother-and-child metaphor in her writings suggest that her feelings of loss, guilt, or failure concerning her son remained alive and unresolved. For some time, she even stipulated that no one else in the Christian Science movement could bear the title "Mother." One of the seven hymns by Eddy is entitled "Mother's Evening Prayer." The room set aside for her sole use in the Mother Church in Boston was named Mother's Room. And in *Retrospection and Introspection*, she wrote, without apparent recognition of the irony, "The true mother never willingly neglects her children in their early and sacred hours, consigning them to the care of nurse or stranger. Who can feel and comprehend the needs of her babe like the ardent mother?"[70]

5. "Gems of Truth" and "Dewdrops of Wisdom"

The Patterson marriage was not a successful one. By all accounts, Patterson traveled frequently to find work, and his wife was chronically ill. North Groton was an isolated town in the White Mountains of New Hampshire, an area of rocky peaks, narrow gorges, and high winds. With her husband and child gone, Mary Patterson was at loose ends in a lonely place. She amused herself by spending time with neighborhood children, employed a blind girl as her servant, and dabbled in phrenology and homeopathy as a way to engage her neighbors.

She read constantly in the Bible, but, as Peel notes, she had no exposure to the great literature of her own or of any other day, except in collections of aphorisms and quotations in the newspapers. She collected these "Gems of Truth" and "Dewdrops of Wisdom" and pasted them in a scrapbook alongside poems, recipes, health tips, and home cures.[71] She became an eccentric and controversial figure in the community. She spent her days bedridden, prescribing homeopathic cures to her neighbors while lying on a peculiar wooden contraption with a headboard that she raised and lowered with a string. On one occasion she sent frantic word of her imminent death to her husband only to effect a remarkable recovery on his return.[72]

Patterson was not a consistent provider, and an item in the local newspaper reported how he came to blows with a man to whom he owed money for a load of wood. Mary's sister Martha had loaned the Pattersons money to purchase their house, but in 1859, when Martha faced straitened circumstances, she was forced to foreclose on their mortgage. The Pattersons were eventually evicted and their possessions auctioned off, whereupon they moved into a boardinghouse in Rumney, New Hampshire, probably with the financial help of Mary's sister Abigail.[73]

These traumatic events coincided with the onset of the Civil War. The war, which seemed of little interest to Mary Patterson, indirectly presaged the greatest upheaval and revelation in her life; it freed her temporarily from the constraint of her husband's presence. In 1862, while on a mission from the governor of New Hampshire to deliver money for the war effort to Washington, D.C., the hapless Daniel Patterson stopped in Virginia, thirty miles from the capital, to see the battlefield of Bull Run, site of the first major battle of the war. He was captured by the Confederates, transported to Richmond, and jailed.

With the shock of this news, and already suffering from her usual host of vaguely defined spinal troubles and weakness, Mary checked into the Vail Hydropathic Institute in Hill, New Hampshire, for a course of baths, one of several popular cures she had not yet sampled. Soon dissatisfied, she made arrangements to try yet another method. Developed by a doctor in Portland, Maine, it involved the laying on of hands, and Mary's exposure to it would alter the course of American religious history. The doctor's name was Phineas Parkhurst Quimby.

6. Dr. P. P. Quimby and His Disciple

In contrast with the famous tintype of Eddy's father, with long, stern, implacable visage and intense eyes, portraits of Quimby reveal him to have had a soft, round, bearded face. Quimby, in fact, resembles the kindly Geppetto of Disney's *Pinocchio* or the jolly Dr. Andrew Weil, whose white beard and New Age wisdom on medical matters have launched a million (or so) books. Eddy met Quimby when she was forty-one, and he became her surrogate father, her mentor, and her muse.

Phineas Parkhurst Quimby, known to his friends as Park, was born in Lebanon, New Hampshire, in 1802, not far from Bow, which would produce his most famous patient. Like Eddy's family, Quimby's was of extremely modest means; his father was a village blacksmith who eventually moved his family to Belfast, Maine. Quimby had little education, and, like Eddy, he never learned to write with confidence. During his youth he was apprenticed to a watch- and clockmaker and tinkered with various mechanical inventions.

Quimby was intrigued by the pseudoscience and spiritualism of his age. During his lifetime, phrenologists were measuring human heads and inspecting bumps and nodes on the skull to pronounce on the character traits and intelligence of their subjects. There was a fascination with the powers of electricity and magnets, the forces of which were thought to have healing powers. In 1848, the infamous Rochester Rapping Spiritualists—three sisters who lived in a reputedly haunted house near Rochester, New York—began communicating with a rapping spirit whom they dubbed Mr. Splitfoot, a man who had supposedly been murdered in the house. Seven years later, the sisters confessed to having produced the rapping noises with their double-jointed toes, but in the meantime spiritualism had become enormously popular, and parlor séances were all the rage.

Mesmerism was also experiencing a resurgence. In 1838, Quimby attended a lecture delivered by Charles Poyen, a Frenchman who performed acts of mesmerism, or what we would now call hypnotism, in front of crowds, and the lecture transformed Quimby into an enthusiast. He followed Poyen from town to town to observe this mysterious power that one person could exercise over another, puzzling over the process. Not long after his systematic observations of Poyen, Quimby would discover that he, too, was a natural mesmerist, and he went out on the lecture circuit himself.

Mesmerism had been debunked over fifty years before Quimby first discovered it. Franz Anton Mesmer, a German physician (1734–1815), achieved his notoriety in eighteenth-century Vienna and later Paris, where mesmerism, "the greatest vogue of the 1780s," transformed healing into a parlor game.[74] Mesmerism drew on the ancient theory of the humors, to which Mesmer had added the chic modern element of magnets. Stephen Jay Gould, in his essay on Mesmer, "The Chain of Reason versus the Chain of Thumbs," describes mesmerism as a belief that "a single (and subtle) fluid pervaded the universe uniting and connecting all bodies. . . . The same fluid flows through organisms and may be called animal magnetism. A blockage of this flow causes disease, and cure requires a reestablishment of the flux and a restoration of equilibrium."[75] Mesmer treated these "block-ages" by passing his hands or a magnet over the body of his patient, iden-tifying the "poles" of magnetic flow; then, sitting opposite the patient, he would touch knees and fingers with the sufferer and gaze intently into his or her (usually her) face.[76] The effects were galvanic. Patients screamed and shook involuntarily, moaned and wept, fainted and seemed insensible. It was all very exciting. Mesmer, who had married into high society and wealth, became the darling of the Austrian and French upper classes and was the friend of Mozart, Haydn, the Austrian empress Maria Theresa, and Marie Antoinette.

The theory behind Mesmer's practices had a long pedigree. The history of "magnetising" can be traced back to Paracelsus—Philippus Aureolus Theophrastus Bombast von Hohenheim (1493?–1541)—a Swiss alchemist and physician who was the first to attribute fantastical powers to the mag-net. (The first scientific treatise on magnetism, *De Magnete*, by William Gilbert, the English scientist and physician, was not written until 1600.) Charles Mackay, in his 1841 study of human suggestibility and gullibility, *Extraordinary Popular Delusions and the Madness of Crowds*, writes that Paracelsus "boasted of being able to *transplant* diseases from the human frame into the earth, by means of the magnet," and devised a theory of animal magnetism by which wounds inflicted by a metallic weapon, such as a sword, could be magnetically treated.[77] A "weapon salve," wrote Paracelsus, was to be applied to the sword itself, not the wounds:

> Take of moss growing on the head of a thief who has been hanged and left in the air; of real mummy; of human blood, still warm—of each, one ounce; of human suet, two ounces; of linseed oil, turpentine, and Armenian bole— of each, two drachms. Mix all well in a mortar, and keep the salve in an oblong, narrow urn.[78]

Other practitioners of magnetism believed that such unguents could be dried into a "powder of sympathy" that was far more efficacious; even-tually, the sympathy—or imagination alone—was seen as the active agent. William Maxwell, a disciple of Paracelsus, observed: "If you wish to work prodigies, abstract from the materiality of beings—increase the sum of spirituality in bodies—rouse the spirit from its slumbers."[79] Mackay's nineteenth-century interpretation of this was blunt: "Here, in fact, lies the whole secret of magnetism, and all delusions of a similar kind: increase the spirituality—rouse the spirit from its slumbers, or, in other words, work upon the imagination—induce belief and blind confidence, and you may do any thing."[80]

Though Mesmer did not exactly invent mesmerism, he did bring it to new heights of popularity. Indeed, he was rousing so many spirits with such regularity that his technique was given a featured role in Mozart's comic opera *Così Fan Tutte*. The two heroes, pretending to poison themselves out of unrequited love, are "healed" by a maid pretending to be a doctor, who produces a large magnet and rubs them with it.[81] The demand for Mesmer's services grew to be so great that he invented a bizarre method for treating large groups of people at once, involving a pot of "magnetized" water or what was, in effect, weak battery acid. A circle of patients would grasp metal rods dipped into the pot and move them to the "mesmeric poles" of their bodies, grasping each other's thumbs to allow the healing magnetism to flow through the circle.[82] Mesmer himself would move among his patients, dressed in lavender silk, touching them with a magnetized metal wand, entrancing them.[83]

But Mesmer's popularity was his undoing. On the advice of his competitors—doctors and scientists scandalized by his methods and success—Louis XVI formed a Royal Commission in 1784 to examine the strange claims. Benjamin Franklin, then living in Paris as ambassador from the United States, and Antoine Lavoisier, the founder of modern chemistry, were appointed to the commission, as were other French scientists and physicians, including the inventor of the guillotine. The resulting "Report of the Commissioners Charged by the King to Examine Animal Magnetism" is, Gould writes, "a key document in the history of human reason."[84]

The commission submitted Mesmer's methods to rigorous but fair examination. The scientists attempted to magnetize themselves and several other groups of people, devising a test that deceived its subjects into believing they were being magnetized when they were not. Their excited reactions revealed the psychosomatic power of the magnetizing procedure. Mesmer refused to take part in the testing, instead assigning to it one of his assistants who failed test after test posed by the commission. In their report, the scientists "unanimously" concluded "that nothing proves the existence of Animal-magnetism fluid; that this fluid with no existence is therefore without utility; that the violent effects observed at the group treatment belong to touching, to the imagination set in action."[85] The fad evaporated for the moment, at least in France.

Quimby may never have heard of the report, which was not translated into English until 1996, but he might not have cared even if he had. Mesmerism seemed to have the power to transform itself into a method to suit the needs of its practitioners and patients; Quimby would alter it to his own purposes. He would have no vats of magnetized water or groups of patients holding each other by the thumbs. His form of mesmerism leaned toward mind reading and the power of mental suggestion.

Quimby began conventionally enough, traveling and lecturing during the 1840s with a young man particularly susceptible to the mesmeric influence, Lucius Burkmar. Quimby lectured; Burkmar fell into mesmeric trances, whereupon he could be controlled by Quimby or members of the audience. Some of the pair's exploits resemble the deliberate hoaxes of contemporary psychics and faith healers who work with advance information. Burkmar claimed to be able to travel in his mind to distant places. Audience members were invited to take Burkmar mentally into their homes; he would respond by describing the furniture and other personal items, to the amazement of the crowd. Eventually, Burkmar advanced to the point where he could describe the inner organs of patients, and for a time, Quimby and Burkmar practiced mesmeric healing, diagnosing a patient's problem and prescribing a treatment through Burkmar's clairvoyance.

Although it is unclear how much of a showman Burkmar was and to what degree he believed in his own act, Quimby was a sincere believer in the powers of mesmerism. But he increasingly found himself less interested in Burkmar's proclivities than in the questions they raised in his mind about people's perceptions of their illnesses or symptoms and what role those perceptions might play in their suffering. He apparently suspected that Burkmar's talents lay not in the realm of the supernatural but in an ability to discern the needs or desires of the person under examination, much as psychics and palm readers are known to be adept at intuiting a subject's psychology from physical and behavioral cues. Quimby was particularly intrigued when Burkmar diagnosed and treated *him* for back pains he had been suffering:

On one occasion, when I had my subject [Lucius] asleep, he described the pains I felt in my back (I had never dared to ask him to examine me, for I felt sure that my kidneys were nearly gone) and he placed his hand on the spot where I felt the pain. He then told me that my kidneys were in a very bad state,—that one was half-consumed, and a piece three inches long had separated from it, and was only connected by a slender thread. This was what I believed to be true, for it agreed with what the doctors told me, and with what I had suffered; for I had not been free from pain for years. My common sense told me that no medicine would ever cure this trouble, and therefore I must suffer till death relieved me. But I asked him if there was any remedy. He replied, "Yes, I can put the piece on so it will grow, and you will get well." At this I was completely astonished, and knew not what to think. He immediately placed his hands upon me, and said he united the pieces so they would grow. The next day he said they had grown together, and from that day I never have experienced the least pain from them.[86]

This bizarre cure was Quimby's moment of epiphany. He surmised that, had Burkmar told him that his condition was incurable, he would probably have died, and that the real sickness had been not in his back or in his kidneys but in his mind. "I discovered that I had been deceived into a belief that made me sick," he wrote. "The absurdity of his remedies made me doubt the fact that my kidneys were diseased, for he said in two days they were as well as ever."[87] Quimby's newfound interpretation of the power of suggestion led to his profound distrust of the medical profession, whose members, he felt, were spreading "beliefs" in illness and disease to all their patients. Observing Burkmar's visit to credulous patients who drank up his diagnoses and agreed with them, no matter how absurd, Quimby grew increasingly troubled by the physician's power over his subjects: "Instead of gaining confidence in the doctors, I was forced to the conclusion that their science is false. Man is made up of truth and belief; and, if he is deceived into a belief that he has, or is liable to have, a disease, the belief is catching, and the effect follows it."[88]

Although Quimby's distrust of doctors may seem extreme today, it was not an unreasonable or unwise response to medicine of the mid-nineteenth century. In the report on mesmerism, Benjamin Franklin had suggested that the cures reported by Mesmer's patients resulted from their having avoided a doctor's care, and the prestige of physicians had not made much progress in the intervening years. There had been several extraordinary discoveries early in the century—the smallpox vaccine and the use of quinine to treat malaria, for example—but in most respects, medicine remained in its Dark Ages. Quacks peddled worthless or noxious patent medicines. No form of anesthesia for use during surgery was discovered until 1842, and one anatomist opined that "the only difference between a young and an old physician was that 'the former will kill you, the latter will let you die.' "[89] There was no understanding of the role of sanitation or the importance of a clean water supply, and medical treatment, besides being often worthless, if not hazardous, could be "ruinously expensive."[90] The germ theory of disease, antibiotics, and modern diagnostic tools all lay in the future. It was an age before the organization and standardization of medical licensure and medical studies; the title of "Doctor" was meaningless. Anyone could declare himself a doctor. In such a world, if medical science was false, a new science had to be created to fill its place, and Doctor Phineas Parkhurst Quimby was up to the job.

In 1859, Quimby opened an office in Portland, Maine, after several years spent treating the sick at his home in Belfast and during his travels. He treated his patients with a combination of panaceas, giving them glasses of magnetized water, rubbing their heads, and performing a laying on of hands, but he began to believe that these physical performances, accompanied by his reassurances, were almost wholly psychosomatic in their effectiveness. His practice of mesmerism had been transformed from a crude magic act to a simple application of psychological reassurance, a kind of medicine that was, by all accounts, including Eddy's, intensely satisfying to his patients. He believed—and often demonstrated—that he could argue his patients out of their conviction that dyspepsia or back pain or some other minor symptom was destroying their lives. Because his form of healing was largely mental, basically involving a dialogue with the patient, he could heal from a distance, and frequently engaged in a therapeutic correspondence with his patients.

It was the basis of what would become Christian Science. Indeed, in 1863, Quimby wrote an article (that went unpublished) in which he used the phrase "Christian Science."[91] And in 1859, three years before Eddy arrived at his door, Quimby had written essays on such topics as "Mind Is Spiritual Matter" and on the true nature of disease:

Disease is what follows the disturbance of the mind or spiritual matter. . . .
By the destruction of error comes the introduction of Truth or Science, or health; and as error is matter or mind, it is the instrument of its own destruction. The matter is not annihilated, but the opinion is. . . . This form which follows the disturbance of the mind the doctors call disease. Here is where all the error lies; they take the effect for the cause. . . . Disease is what fol-

lows an opinion, it is made up of mind directed by error, and Truth is the destruction of this opinion.[92]

Even before they met, Mary Patterson's relationship with Quimby had taken on a feverishly needy tone. She wrote to him that she would die unless he helped her, adding, almost hopefully, "I can sit up but a few minutes at a time. Do you think I can reach you without sinking from the effects of the journey?"[93] On her first visit to him, in October 1862, she was half-carried up the stairs to his office, but she left it under her own power, her spinal trouble healed. Entranced by Quimby's manner and philosophy—and having long been captivated by intriguing alternatives to medical science, such as homeopathy—she declared herself virtually cured of her catalogue of ailments in less than a week. In November 1862, she wrote a letter to the *Portland Evening Courier* to announce the news of her spiritual breakthrough and to analyze Dr. Quimby's "power":

> When by a falling apple, an immutable law was discovered, we gave it the crown of science, which is incontrovertible and capable of demonstration; hence that was wisdom and truth. When from the evidence of the senses, my reason takes cognizance of truth, although it may appear in quite a miraculous view, I must acknowledge that as science which is truth uninvestigated. Hence the following demonstration:—
>
> Three weeks since I quitted my nurse and sick room *en route* for Portland. The belief of my recovery had died out of the hearts of those who were most anxious for it. With this mental and physical depression I first visited P. P. Quimby; and in less than one week from that time I ascended by a stairway of one hundred and eighty-two steps to the dome of the City Hall, and am improving *ad infinitum*. . . .
>
> But now I can see dimly at first, and only as trees walking, the great principle which underlies Dr. Quimby's faith and works; and just in proportion to my right perception of truth is my recovery. . . . That this is a science capable of demonstration, becomes clear to the minds of those patients who reason upon the process of their cure. The truth which he establishes in the patient cures him (although he may be wholly unconscious thereof); and the body, which is full of light, is no longer in disease.[94]

In this same letter, Mary denied that Quimby healed through "spiritualism" or "animal magnetism."

A rival paper, the *Portland Advertiser*, mocked Mary's most extravagant claim: "P. P. Quimby compared to Jesus Christ? What next?"[95] Mary responded, again in the *Courier*:

> P. P. Quimby stands upon the plane of wisdom with his truth. Christ healed the sick, but not by jugglery or with drugs. As the former speaks as never man before spake, and heals as never man healed since Christ, is he not identified with truth? And is not this the Christ which is in him? We know that in wisdom is life, "and the life was the light of man." P. P. Quimby rolls away the stone from the sepulchre of error, and health is the resurrection. But we also know that "light shineth in darkness and the darkness comprehendeth it not."[96]

These letters are the most important early documents in the history of the evolution of Christian Science. They contain the essential language and concepts of the religion, already formed and presumably imbibed from Quimby himself. Mary couches her description of her healing—firmly attributed to Quimby—in the vocabulary she will later claim as her own: "an immutable law," "science . . . capable of demonstration," "truth," "principle," "error."[97] She equates it with the healing of Christ. But the fact that Eddy was indebted to Quimby for the basic concepts and language of mind healing is clear to scholars outside the Christian Science tradition although not to those in it.[98]

Much of the later defensiveness about the role that Quimby played in Eddy's "discovery" of Christian Science arose from her critics' exaggeration of it: their accusations that Eddy had plagiarized Quimby.[99] Quimby, with less formal education than Eddy herself, was a clumsy and untutored writer who never published anything during his lifetime; his scribbled notes, essays, letters, manuscripts, and transcripts of his remarks, hand copied by adoring patients and students, including Eddy herself, eventually became a source of controversy after his death, when Eddy's supporters claimed that others had edited or altered them to make them appear to predate her arrival on the scene. But just as there is no evidence proving that Eddy plagiarized from Quimby, so there is no evidence that the Quimby manuscripts contain ideas or language that came from anybody but Quimby.[100]

Indeed, despite all the denials and manuscript controversies, Eddy's own testimony in the *Portland Evening Courier* confirms that all of Quimby's concepts—the distrust of doctors and materia medica; the belief that disease is an illusion, an error of thought; the notion that matter is infinitely malleable through the power of mind; the idea that disease is a product of the mind—along with a number of his characteristic words and phrases ("error," "false belief," and "infinite Mind") were the inspiration for her own subsequent teachings and writings.

Eddy's letters to the *Courier* also suggest that Quimby's practice had a definite Christian component.[101] Earlier magnetizers had attributed Jesus' healings to the magnetic technique, and so did Quimby, developing a philosophical concept of the healing Christ (referring to the healing ideals Christ stood for, not to Jesus Christ, the physical man) which he equated with the highest ideals of Science. He wrote, "I say, repent all, and be baptized in the Science that will wash away your sins."[102] Eddy would also echo Quimby's scathing attacks on "priestcraft," his belief that the fearful or punitive aspects of Christianity had a negative impact on health:

> Disease was conceived in priestcraft and brought forth in the iniquity of the medical faculty. The priest prophesied falsely and the doctors flourished by their lies, and the people love to have it so. Then the question arises, what can you do to prevent it? . . . Come out from the world of opinion, and when a doctor says you have so and so, make him prove it.[103]

Quimby's association of his healing method with that of Jesus and his equation of "Christ" with "Science" were all adopted, for her own purposes, by Eddy.

Many philosophers had, of course, already made pronouncements that asserted the primacy of mind over matter. Eddy would imbibe them through Quimby. There were the theories of the Irish bishop George Berkeley (1685–1753) that there was no substance but spirit, and the German philosopher Friedrich Schelling (1775–1854), who held that "nature is spirit visible, and spirit is invisible nature." Emanuel Swedenborg (1688–1772) and other idealist philosophers proclaimed that "mind is the only *substance*."[104] Swedenborg interpreted heaven and hell as personal, almost psychological, states of mind, a concept paralleling Eddy's later view: "The sinner makes his own hell by doing evil, and the saint his own heaven by doing right."[105] Quimby was likely also influenced by the teachings of Andrew Jackson Davis, the "seer of Poughkeepsie," a spiritualist who spread Swedenborgianism during Quimby's day.[106] Quimby imbibed the patois of Davis and Swedenborg. And Eddy imbibed Quimby.

Over the next several years, Mary wrote regularly for newspapers in Maine and Massachusetts and lectured on several occasions, explaining and defending Quimby's teachings. Her husband, who had escaped from jail in 1862, began spending longer and longer periods of time away from his wife, and biographers allege that he was a known philanderer.

Throughout this period, which is one of the least well documented of her life, Mary grew increasingly dependent on Quimby, writing him letters beseeching his absent treatment when she was away, observing his practice and making handwritten copies of his manuscripts when she was in Portland. Invariably she was cured in his presence, but in his absence her symptoms returned. She needed his attention, his soothing hands, his teaching. She was his disciple. But later in her life she reversed her perception of their original roles, as if she could not bear to acknowledge her dependence on him. She claimed that Quimby had once said to her, "I see that I am John, and that you are Jesus."[107] In fact, she was closer to Peter. She would inevitably deny her Master.

7. The Fall in Lynn

Within months of each other, two of the most important men in Mary's life died, leaving her nearly alone in the world. In October 1865, Mark Baker, her father, died; he left the bulk of his estate to his widow and a dollar to each of his daughters. Dr. Quimby's death followed a few months later, on January 16, 1866. On February 1, 1866, two weeks after Quimby died, Mary Patterson fell on the ice while walking to a temperance meeting in Lynn, Massachusetts.

Now known to Christian Scientists as the "Fall in Lynn," this episode was resurrected by Eddy years after it happened as the moment of her discovery of Christian Science. There are widely divergent accounts of the seriousness of her injuries. The local newspaper, the *Lynn Reporter*, wrote that she was "severely injured" and "taken up in an insensible condition."[108] It was also reported that a Dr. Alvin Cushing, a homeopathic doctor called to the scene, determined her injuries to be "of a very serious nature, inducing spasms and intense suffering."[109] Three days after the accident, according to Eddy's account, she read one of the biblical accounts of the healings of Jesus—she never revealed which one—and arose from her bed and walked, startling her friends.

My immediate recovery from the effects of an injury caused by an accident, an injury that neither medicine nor surgery could reach, was the falling apple that led me to the discovery how to be well myself, and how to make others so.

Even to the homoeopathic physician who attended me, and rejoiced in my recovery, I could not then explain the *modus* of my relief. I could only assure him that the divine Spirit had wrought the miracle—a miracle which later I found to be in perfect scientific accord with divine law.

I then withdrew from society about three years,—to ponder my mission, to search the Scriptures, to find the Science of Mind that should take the things of God and show them to the creature, and reveal the great curative Principle,—Deity.[110]

Dr. Cushing, interviewed years later, had a different recollection. He recalled that Mary insisted that she be moved against his recommendation and that he administered morphine to lessen her pain. "I did not at any time declare, or believe, that there was no hope for Mrs. Patterson's recovery," he wrote in an affidavit.[111]

Whatever the exact circumstances of the fall, given Mary's predilection for "spells" and collapses, it is difficult to accept at face value her assertion that her accident was life-threatening. Julius Silberger, Jr., who wrote a psychoanalytic biography of Eddy, interprets the famous fall and its role in her life as neither the revelatory nor the insignificant event that her supporters and detractors held it to be, seeing it instead as a profound reaction to all her losses: "She now had no one on whom to rely. She was hurt, in the most literal sense."[112] And to salve that hurt, she looked to the Christianity of her mother and to Quimby's "science"—the "falling apple" of Newton cited here and in her first writing about Quimby—that she defines as "law."

Eddy claimed that her healing was "immediate" and implies that it was complete, but, in fact, it was temporary. Less than two weeks later, on February 15, 1866, Mary wrote to another of Quimby's patients and followers, Julius Dresser, asking him to take Quimby's place and help her:

> Two weeks ago I fell on the sidewalk, and struck my back on the ice, and was taken up for dead, came to consciousness amid a storm of vapors from cologne, chloroform, ether, camphor, etc., but to find myself the helpless cripple I was before I saw Dr. Quimby.[113]

She told him that she had recovered but that fear was overtaking her again. "I am slowly failing," she wrote. Dresser declined to help her, saying that he was no doctor and could not even help to heal his own wife of her ailments.

Mary's accident (serious or not) and recovery (epiphanic or not) did presage one of the most difficult periods in her life. The Pattersons continued to live together for the next few months, but later in the summer, Daniel Patterson deserted her, effectively putting an end to the marriage. (Eddy sued for divorce seven years later.) She received a little money from him intermittently, but, at forty-five, she was essentially destitute and homeless, moving from rooming house to rooming house, relying on the kindness of hosts and friends. Around the time that Patterson left her, she began writing a vast manuscript—not devotional but emulative and explanatory—an analysis of the book of Genesis.

8. Healing and Head-Rubbing

Mary Patterson moved at least eight times during that crucial year of 1866, from town to town in and around Boston, from the North Shore to south of the city, from Lynn to Swampscott, Stoughton, Amesbury, and back to Lynn. During that summer, she is said to have healed the clubfeet of a seven-year-old boy named George. According to the story, which is accepted unquestioningly by Robert Peel, the boy, who had never walked, was left for a few minutes on the beach at Lynn by his mother; when she returned, he was strolling with a strange woman. "The woman was of course Mrs. Patterson," Peel writes.[114]

Biographical accounts of this period in Eddy's life vary so enormously that they seem to be describing different women. Those written by Christian Scientists maintain that she was, at this juncture, just beginning to formulate her healing method and to discover its wondrous powers, passing them along to eager acolytes. Those written by outsiders concentrate on the accounts of the landlords and hosts who put her up. And these suggest that she was indeed a memorable houseguest, but not necessarily because she could heal: "She alienated her hosts by refusing to pay for her room and board or by justifying herself with the claim that she had cured some member of the household of this or that illness. Most of these beneficiaries denied that she had either practiced on them or healed them."[115]

Eventually, she met Hiram Crafts, a shoemaker in Lynn, in one of the houses where she boarded. He became her first student. In 1867, she urged him to enter the healing practice, and he placed an ad in the local newspaper:

TO THE SICK
DR. H. S. CRAFTS

Would say unhesitatingly, *I can cure you*, and have never failed to cure Consumption, Catarrh, Scrofula, Dyspepsia and Rheumatism, with many other forms of disease and weakness, in which I am especially successful. If you will give me a fair trial and are not helped, I will refund your money.[116]

Their relationship, however, was brief, because of a falling out over money or, according to some accounts, Mary's advice to Craft that he divorce his wife.[117]

From 1867 to 1868, Mrs. Glover, as she had once again begun to call herself, was taken in by the wife of a sea captain in Amesbury, an enthusiastic conductress of séances. When this woman's son-in-law, with his three orphaned children, returned to the home, he evicted Mary Glover and several other unwanted tenants, including a young man named Richard Kennedy, with whom Mary would continue to correspond. This eviction was perhaps the most grievous yet of her itinerant life; she was put out on the street with her baggage at night, in the rain.

Mary went to stay with yet another spiritualist in Amesbury and placed an advertisement in *Banner of Light*, a spiritualist paper:

ANY PERSON desiring to learn how to heal the sick can receive of the undersigned instruction that will enable them to commence healing on a **principle of science** with a success far beyond any of the present modes. No medicine, electricity, physiology or hygiene required for unparalleled success in the most difficult cases. No pay is required unless this skill is obtained. Address, MRS. MARY B. GLOVER, Amesbury, Mass., Box 61.[118]

She was soon offered what must have seemed the princely sum of $300 and room and board to instruct a Mrs. Sally Wentworth, a nurse, in how to heal. She stayed at the Wentworth home until the beginning of 1870, when she had an angry dispute with Mr. Wentworth, apparently over his refusal to give her the money to publish her manuscript, now a quite lengthy exegesis on Genesis. She left abruptly, without informing the family; Horace Wentworth, the Wentworths' son, would later claim in an affidavit that she had retaliated against them by destroying her bedroom, ripping up the carpets and the featherbed and leaving a shovelful of smoldering coals in the closet.[119]

Her next student was Richard Kennedy, her former rooming-house mate, with whom she forged a contract most favorable to herself. In February 1870, they agreed to go into a partnership in which Kennedy would pay her $1,000 for instruction in healing over the next two years; in the future, she was to receive half of all the money he made from practicing what was essentially the Quimby method of head-rubbing and healing talk. Together, in June, they moved into the upper half of a private school building in Lynn, Kennedy using part for an office and Mary using one room for her writing. She again advertised as a teacher of healing and by that fall had a dozen or so students. She required the students to pay, at first, a tuition of $100 (eventually it was raised to $300). Those wishing to go into the practice of healing were also required to pay either 10 percent of what they subsequently earned, or a lump sum of $1,000. Three hundred dollars, as Peel notes, was "almost one-third of the average annual income of a Lynn shoe worker."[120] These excessive demands would result in some of her students demanding the refund of their tuition money; a few actually took her to court to obtain it.

Mary was fearful of "practicing" herself, lest she take on the symptoms of the very illnesses she was trying to heal. (Quimby, too, had claimed that he felt his patients' symptoms.) Therefore, she generally split the physical side of her endeavor off from the mental side, delegating the healing duties to students, such as Kennedy and a succession of others, and reserving to herself the right to teach. Each of her three-week classes, meeting in the evenings because many students worked in the shoe factories by day, consisted of an initial head-rubbing by Kennedy, followed by her instruction. Each student received a handwritten copy of her latest manuscript, "The Science of Man, By Which the Sick Are Healed, Embracing Questions and Answers in Moral Science," a format she had picked up from Quimby, who had himself circulated a manuscript entitled "Questions and Answers." "The Science of Man," which was revised many times, contained the very essence of what was to become Christian Science: definitions of God, principle, life and intelligence, man, and matter, as well as a crude early explanation of how to heal the sick. One question in her 1870 version of the manuscript asked: "Is all sickness but a belief?" The answer was: "It is; there is no truth in inharmony, for truth would at once restore harmony."[121] Man is redefined as an "idea," not a physical being, and matter itself is said to be without true substance in God's creation. Like her Genesis manuscript, "The Science of Man" would become another crucial chapter in the book she did not yet know she was writing.[122]

Teaching and speaking publicly, Eddy was apparently a deeply charismatic figure. Most of her students seem to have been entranced by their teacher and by her extraordinarily single-minded devotion to the material. In a memoir of these early days, *Mrs. Eddy As I Knew Her in 1870*, Samuel Putnam Bancroft, a shoe worker and one of her students, described her, focusing particularly on her eyes:

> Was she attractive? Was she beautiful? Attractive: yes, very. Beautiful: not in an ordinary sense. . . . Her features were regular, and finely molded. The most noticeable were the eyes, large and deep-set, dark blue and piercing, sad, very sad, at times, yet kind and tender. Her figure was a trifle above the average height, and she carried herself very erect. While this gave the appearance of slimness, she was well-rounded. Although her resources were meager, she was always neatly and carefully dressed. Her hair was very dark, and was tastefully arranged, after the fashion of the times. Her manner was always ladylike and self-possessed, even on the most trying occasions. When in conversation, the animation she displayed added much to her attractiveness. It was the animation of conviction, not of excitement or agitation.[123]

Eddy's eyes seem to have taken on a myriad of colors to those who loved her and are alternately described as gray, brown, and blue. John C. Lathrop, whose mother, Laura Lathrop, was healed of a chronic illness in 1884, wrote that "Mrs. Eddy had remarkable eyes, deep and soulful. They seemed to look right through one into the distance, and similarly, when one looked into her keen, deep-set gray eyes, one seemed to look beyond the physical."[124]

But the eyes were not her only notable feature; to her followers, Eddy was the most vigorous, most methodical, most erudite, most dignified woman in the world, with the finest sense of humor. In old age, she would be described by them as having the youngest demeanor and the smoothest skin of any elderly person they had ever seen.

The partnership with Kennedy did not last. Mary, in her first move to put some distance between her own teachings and those of Quimby, had decided that the laying on of hands, by virtue of its very physicality, was contrary to her teachings that there was no life in matter. Silberger suggests that she may have been agitated by the intimacy of the act: "We have no way of knowing how much *conscious* conflict Mrs. Glover experienced when Kennedy laid his hands upon her. She was, Bancroft tells us, so often in need of healing care herself, at that time."[125] Kennedy—who had become immensely popular and successful in his practice—refused to give up his therapeutic touching, and in the spring of 1872, the two came to a parting of the ways and split their earnings. Mary Glover received nearly $6,000.

Mary's break with Kennedy was the beginning of a powerful obsession on her part; she could neither forgive nor forget her former partner. After the break, her income fell off sharply, and for a time she resumed her restless travels from town to town, house to house. On this round of visits, she told all of her hosts that she was hard at work on a new version of "The Science of Man," and that she needed quiet to concentrate. She gave up teaching between 1872 and 1875, possibly in order to finish her manuscript, possibly because there was less demand for her services.

One of her students, Wallace W. Wright, the son of a Universalist minister from Amesbury, decided, after taking one of her early classes, that her teachings amounted to little more than mesmerism and announced his disillusionment in the pages of the *Lynn Transcript* in early 1872. His comments were prophetic, the first to raise fundamental objections to Christian Science:

> To live as this so-called science teaches would sever the affection between parents, and children, brothers and sisters, and forbid all mingling with society or friends. Why? Because it tells us that man is a delusion; that man, the noblest work of God, the result of His creative genius, the flowers in the fields, the mighty forests, the hidden wonders of the world, are all delusions, and the work of imagination.[126]

Mary's published reply in that paper restates a thesis that would reappear in all her work, in many different formulations. But it reads less like a reply to Wright's objections than an Emersonian rhapsody:

> The idea that expresses moral science is physical, and we see this idea traced out in one continuous page of nature's bright and glorious character. Every

blade of grass, tree and flower, declare, "How manifold are thy works, O Lord! in wisdom hast thou made them all."

The entire creation of God symbolizes nothing else but wisdom, love and truth. All that He hath made is harmonious, joy-giving and eternal. He also hath made man in His "image and likeness," and this must be a perfect man.[127]

During this period, Mary's relationships with men, always troubled, took on a particularly disturbing cast. She demanded adulation and obedience; the men she encountered who refused to comply became, in her mind, demonic. Perhaps brooding on her abandonment by Patterson, she began to imagine that Wright and Kennedy were somehow plotting against her, and she accused them of practicing mesmerism, turning Wright's hurtful words back at him. Meanwhile, she relished the attentions of another young man, another George, George Barry, a foreman in a shoe shop.[128] Robert Peel acknowledges that Barry seemed to fulfill Mary's need for a son:

> So far as he could, young George Barry of Lynn took the other George's place. He felt that through the Science he had learned from Mrs. Glover he had been literally reborn. No task was too arduous to show his love for her: he ran errands, performed chores, hunted rooms, attended to her finances, and above all copied and recopied her growing manuscript. He was the first of her students to ask if he could call her "Mother," the term which Civil War soldiers had used for their nurses and which had come to be associated with woman's ministry of healing.[129]

In 1873, she submitted her new manuscript to a publisher. It was rejected, and, after much revision, rejected again in 1874. George Barry and another student each gave $1,500 to their teacher so that she could publish the manuscript herself. She contributed no money, however, to the publishing of her book, keeping her savings from her time with Kennedy to buy a house in Lynn, at 8 Broad Street. She first thought to title her volume *The Science of Life*, but learning that a book by that title was already in print, she renamed it. She called it *Science and Health*.

9. *Science and Health,* First Edition

In its first edition of 1875, *Science and Health* is an odd and unformed book. Even Robert Peel, who thought Eddy a genius, acknowledged its difficulties: "Sentences are chaotic, punctuation erratic, quotations inexact, meanings obscure."[130] Grammar and organization are so crude that a single paragraph can go on for over half a dozen pages, and run-on sentences, dangling participles, and overwrought language abound. Later in life, without acknowledging that she and an editor hired for the purpose had revised subsequent editions extensively in order to lend greater coherence to her theories, she claimed that her writings had been "dictated" by a "divine power":

> What I wrote had a strange coincidence or relationship with the light of revelation and solar light. I could not write these notes after sunset. All thoughts in the line of Scriptural interpretation would leave me until the rising of the sun. . . . It was not myself, but the divine power of Truth and Love, infinitely above me, which dictated "Science and Health with Key to the Scriptures." . . . I should blush to write of "Science and Health with Key to the Scriptures" as I have, were it of human origin, and were I, apart from God, its author.[131]

But if God was the author of the first edition, he was an uncertain and irritable one.

The radical teachings that would make up Christian Science are, however, present in the first edition. God, Mind, Love, Life, Truth, Soul, and Spirit, used as synonyms for each other, make up the whole of creation, and man is described as their perfect reflection. The material world, physical illness, and disease are an illusion, and a complete understanding of these revelations about man's true spiritual nature is said to heal illness, as well as sorrow, moral flaws, and all forms of suffering. But these basic concepts of Christian Science appear in a garbled, stream-of-consciousness style: "To admit physical effects is to conclude matter cause and effect, whence it follows there are two causes, viz., mind and matter, else that mind produces matter, or matter produces mind, which contradicts the science of Life in its demonstration, and is like saying dust originated man, and a serpent a dove."[132] The term "Christian Science" is present but, partially in lower case, it has not yet become the name of the religion: "Indifference to Christian science surprises one when we know it is the eternal right in which God holds the scales, and adjusts all harmonious balances."[133] Nonsensical and confusing statements occur with some regularity: "Life is the same yesterday, to-day and forever; anachronism and organization have nothing to do with it" and "a farm, a merchandise, a husband, wife, etc., may hide this science from individual perception."[134]

Mary took advantage of an interruption in the book's typesetting to write an addition, one that settled some scores. Here she is clearly referring to her old nemesis, Richard Kennedy:

> The modus operandi of the mal-practice is as follows: The doctor rubs the heads of his patients, communing with them mentally as he does this, but instead of speaking to them only Truth, and that which promotes harmony, he takes this opportunity to introduce into their minds side-issues, such as suit his sinister purpose, imparting his own likes and dislikes to the patients, either from vengeance or ambition. . . . Filled with revenge and evil passions, the mal-practitioner can only depend on manipulation, and rubs the heads of patients years together, fairly incorporating their minds through this process, which claims less respect the more we understand it. . . . None can track his foul course; the evil is felt but not understood. . . . Try it, whoever will, manipulate the head of an individual until you have established a mesmeric connection between you both; then direct her action, or influence her to some conclusion, arguing the case mentally, as you would audibly, and make the result. You will find, the more honest and confiding the individual, the more she is governed by the mind of the operator.[135]

As she often would in her writings, Mary revealed more than she knew. The fear and loathing of Kennedy here evident, the attraction and revulsion inspired by the "mesmeric connection" that she felt between them were overpowering to her. *She* is the "honest" and "confiding" individual "governed by the mind of the operator," the vulnerable, manipulated party, unable to govern her own mind. The paranoid scapegoating of "enemies" that breaks through the sugary rhetoric about light, Truth, and Love—characteristic of all editions of *Science and Health*, its hostility and aggression cloaked with maternal benevolence—appears fully formed in the first edition.

Reviews of the first edition of *Science and Health* were mixed; sales were dismal. Mary's following at this point consisted primarily of the eight people who had signed an agreement to pay small weekly sums to support her in exchange for her Sunday preaching, but this small band industriously sent copies to important personages and universities in the United States and abroad, including Queen Victoria, Thomas Carlyle, and the Archbishop of Canterbury.[136] There was little response. One reviewer wrote, "Its style is the oracular. The author does not give opinions nor elaborate theories, but announces laws and principles."[137] Notwithstanding these shortcomings, *Science and Health* would soon find readers eager to learn what it had to teach.

10. "A Touch of Fanaticism"

One reader who was not put off by the book's airs was Bronson Alcott. The Transcendentalist reformer and utopian thinker whose disdain for the practicalities of life inspired his daughter Louisa's tales of genteel poverty and family hardship in *Little Women*, Alcott was in his seventies when *Science and Health* was first published. Mary Glover herself seems to have sent a copy to him at his home in Concord, and he replied with a letter she found deeply gratifying, thanking her for her "remarkable volume," which he read with "profound interest."[138]

Early in 1876, he called on her and her small circle in Lynn, subsequently writing in his journal: "I find her a devoted student of the New Testament, a Christian in the truest sense, an idealist in apprehending the supremacy of mind over matter, and a faith in Spirit transcending any contemporary whom I have been fortunate to meet."[139] He vowed to "cultivate further acquaintance with a person of such attractions mentally and spiritually," but he eventually came to qualify his initially positive impression after meeting with Mrs. Eddy and her students in June 1878:

> The party consists of fifteen or more young gentlemen and ladies preparing to become healers of disease by Mrs. Eddy's theory. They call themselves "Christian Scientists," and their method the "Mental Method."
>
> I have but an imperfect acquaintance with this theory of healing, and infer that she may have still to remove, perhaps cure, some of the nervous maladies incident to improper modes of diet and regimen, both of body and mind. There is perhaps a touch of fanaticism, though of a genial quality, interposed into her faith, which a deeper insight into the mysteries of life may ultimately remove. I judge her present gifts are rather derived from her

nervous temperament, combined with the faith with which she ventures into hitherto unexplored crypts of psychology, than from any established philosophy concerning such recondite matters.[140]

It would be their last meeting.

Alcott happened to mention in one of his notes to Mrs. Eddy that a neighbor had also shown interest in her work: "Mrs. Emerson once expressed her wish to meet you."[141] But the tantalizing question of whether Mary Baker Eddy ever met Ralph Waldo Emerson himself remains unresolved.

Quimby inspired Eddy's vocabulary—not just individual words and phrases, "divine Mind," "malicious animal magnetism," "Christian Science"—but an entire language of ideas that would frame her inchoate desires, frustrations, and fears. But where Quimby gave her a vocabulary, Ralph Waldo Emerson framed the world in which she found herself, and the strange, distorted echoes of Emerson resound in everything she ever wrote.

She probably did not read the works of Emerson, arguably the most influential American philosopher of his century, except in fragments published in newspapers and in *Philosophic Nuggets*, her treasured collection of aphorisms from Ruskin, Carlyle, and other figures. But *Science and Health* and her other writings are shot through with Transcendentalist notions and language; in many ways, her work is an unconscious misreading of Emerson.

The theological logic of Christian Science, in particular, derives from Emerson and the Transcendentalists, who rejected Enlightenment methods of reason—observation and induction—and adopted new Romantic or idealistic methods, reliant on intuition and an anti-intellectual perception of truth, indifferent to the external evidence. Aping the Enlightenment men of science—Ben Franklin or Thomas Jefferson—Eddy called her experiments in healing scientific. But she followed the example that the Transcendentalists set in ventures such as Brook Farm, the failed experiment in communal living, by paying little heed to the physical results of her work, substituting fantasy for inconvenient fact.

The Transcendental Club had begun meeting in 1836, to explore the new work being done in theology, philosophy, and literature; its members included Emerson, Alcott, Henry David Thoreau, and Margaret Fuller. Emerson proposed, in his radical Divinity School Address of 1838, that there were spiritual laws running beneath the surface of life. Positing that there was "one mind" governing all of creation, he attacked the sentimentalization of Christian miracles and the "noxious exaggeration about the *person* of Jesus." He claimed that "God incarnates himself in man" and devalued doctrine:

> The world is not the product of manifold power, but of one will, of one mind; and that one mind is everywhere active, in each ray of the star, in each wavelet of the pool; and whatever opposes that will is everywhere balked and baffled, because things are made so, and not otherwise.[142]

Virtually every one of these points is made in some fashion in Eddy's writings. She too posited "one mind" and suggested that healing was simply part of the natural law of God, not a miraculous event. She too tried to demystify Jesus, the man, suggesting that the principles he stood for should be the Christian Scientist's primary focus. But Eddy's re-vision of Jesus—which was supposed to empower every Scientist with a practical knowledge of God's healing laws—ultimately minimized Jesus and inflated her own importance; *she* was the new revelator. Emerson, on the other hand, sought to knock down the walls of the "dead church" and restore self-reliance to the individual by celebrating nonconformity, intuition, and boldness.[143] While Eddy was busily writing new universal laws, Emerson was urging every man to be a law unto himself: "No law can be sacred to me but that of my nature."[144]

Eddy later claimed, in an undated letter to a friend, that she had met Emerson (who died in 1882) in his dotage:

> Waldo Emerson was a man fitting a nich in history well, and we all in Mass. love him. But he was as far from accepting Christian Science as a man can be who is a strict moralist. Bronson Alcott is far in advance of him. I saw Emerson some months before his demise; went for the purpose of *healing* him. Let no one but my husband, Dr. Eddy, who went with me, know it. As soon as I got into the deep recesses of his thoughts I saw his case was hopeless. I can work only by God's graces and by His rules. So when I said, in reply to his remark, "I am old and my brains are wearing out from hard labor,"—and then chattered like a babe,—"But you believe in the powers of God above all other causation, do you not?" He answered, "Yes," and this followed in substance: but it would be profane for me to believe a man does not wear out. I don't believe God can or wants to prevent this result of old age.[145]

The tale of this epochal meeting—documented nowhere else—hints at the scope of Eddy's ambition. Whether or not it took place, there is something truly Emersonian in the elderly Sage's remarks as she reported them. Ever the "transparent eyeball," he was willing to accept as divine every season in Nature's cycle whereas Eddy, although she often invoked the Transcendental correspondences between mind and nature in her painfully florid poetry, was not, dismissing the entirety of the natural world with a wave of her hand.[146] She inevitably dismissed as well her own sources, just as here she infantilizes Emerson in her zeal to outshine him. As with Quimby, so with Emerson: Eddy aspired to transcend all of those to whom she was indebted, even the fathers of Transcendentalism.

11. "I Shall Never Again Trust a *Man*"

Around the time of her book's publication, Mary Glover hung a sign at Number 8 Broad Street announcing her arrival on the healing scene: MARY B. GLOVER'S CHRISTIAN SCIENTISTS' HOME. The Broad Street house was furnished with heavy Victorian decorum, but the emotional machinations that took place within it, as Mary's followers competed for her attention, were anything but decorous. George Barry was soon supplanted in his teacher's affections by another student, Daniel Spofford, who had undertaken to send out review copies of *Science and Health* with a note indicating that only favorable notices were welcome. Spofford had been practicing some other brand of mental healing when he was introduced to Mrs. Glover's teachings by his wife. When Mary began to rely more and more heavily on him, Spofford attempted, unsuccessfully, to divorce his wife, apparently hoping to marry his teacher. This, however, was not to be, for, in late 1875, Mary Glover met Asa Gilbert Eddy.

The circumstances leading up to Mrs. Glover's marriage to Eddy are extraordinarily melodramatic and foreshadow the chaotic atmosphere that would become the norm in her movement in the coming years. At the time that he met Mrs. Glover, Eddy was a Singer Sewing Machine salesman. Compared to Spofford, who is described as an assertive man, Gilbert Eddy has always been painted as something of a Milquetoast. "People who knew Eddy well in Lynn," wrote one early biographer, "describe him as a quiet, dull little man, docile and yielding up to a certain point, but capable of a dogged sort of obstinacy. He was short of stature, slow in his movements, and always taciturn."[147] His own mother had been a profoundly eccentric character who left her family to shift for themselves and went for long daily drives wearing a shawl cut to include a large pane of glass to protect her face from the weather.[148] Gilbert Eddy's mother was also a regular client of a clairvoyant healer known as Sleeping Lucy, who diagnosed her patients while in a trance; she also introduced her son to spiritualism and séances.[149] He was instantly converted to Mary's cause. Soon they were calling each other by their first names, although Mary was always "Mrs. Glover" to her other students, and Eddy was called "Dr. Eddy."

Ever since the publication of her book, Mary had become increasingly convinced that her students' mental reliance on her—which she referred to as their "calling" on her—weakened her physically and emotionally. In February 1876, she wrote to a cousin, "I feel the weight of sick folks terribly since my book is at work."[150] In October of that year she wrote to Spofford, "I feel like a tired and wounded soldier of the cross, taken to the rear."[151] She often warned her students not to make a "Dagon" of her, referring to one of the blasphemous gods of Babylon found in the Bible.[152] In November, Spofford lost his suit for divorce; a month later, on December 30, Mary sent him a letter apparently in reaction to his jealousy over her favorable treatment of Gilbert Eddy. Mary's letter, with its overtones of a lovers' quarrel, is so wildly accusatory as to suggest a person on the brink of an emotional breakdown:

> Dr. Spofford won't you exercise *reason* and let me live or will you *kill me?* Your mind is just what has brought on my relapse and I shall never *recover* if you do not govern yourself and TURN YOUR THOUGHTS wholly away from me. Do for God's sake and the work I have before me let me get out of this suffering I never was worse than last night and you say you wish to do me good and I do not doubt it. Then won't you *quit thinking* of me. I shall write no more to a male student and never more trust one to live with. It is a *hidden* foe that is at work read Science and Health page 193, 1st paragraph.
>
> No STUDENT nor mortal has tried to have you leave me that I know of. Dr. Eddy has tried to have you stay you are in a *mistake*, it is God and not man that has separated us and for the reason I *begin* to learn. Do not think of returning to me again I shall never again trust a *man* They know not what manner of temptations assail God produces the separation and I submit to it so must you. There is no cloud between us but the way you set me up for a

Dagon is wrong and now I implore you to turn forever from this error of personality and go alone *to* God as I have taught you.

It is mesmerism that I feel and is killing me it is *mortal* mind that only can make me suffer. Now stop thinking of me or you will cut me off *soon* from the face of the earth.[153]

The paragraph of *Science and Health* to which she was referring is a bitter denunciation of sexual desire:

> Sin is thought before it is deed, and you must master it in the first, or it conquers you in the second instance. Jesus said, to look with foul desire on forbidden objects, breaks a moral precept; hence, the stress he laid on the character of a man that is hidden from our perception. Evil thoughts reach farther, and do more harm than individual crimes, for they impregnate other minds and fashion your body. The atmosphere of impure desires, like the atmosphere of earth, is restless, ever in motion, and calling on some object; this atmosphere is laden with mental poison, and contaminates all it touches. When malicious purposes, evil thoughts, or lusts, go forth from one mind, they seek others, and will lodge in them unless repelled by virtue and a higher motive for being. All mental emanations take root and bear fruit after their own kind. Consider, then, the guilt of nurturing evil and impure thoughts, that send broadcast discord and moral death. Sooner suffer a doctor infected with small-pox to be about you, than come under the treatment of one that manipulates his patients' heads, and is a traitor to science.[154]

The following night, Gilbert Eddy gave Spofford a note from Mrs. Glover, telling him that she planned to marry Eddy. In a victorious display of passive-aggressive power, she also instructed Spofford, the jilted lover, to pass this news on to the clergyman who was to perform the marriage. The next day, January 1, 1877, Mary Glover and Gilbert Eddy were married. On the marriage certificate, both of them declared that they were forty years old; in fact, Gilbert Eddy was forty-six, and his bride a decade older.

12. "Take Up Spofford"

The revulsion and anxiety that Mary felt about sex may have been an element in the breakup of her second marriage; they would not trouble her third. It is clear from her letters and comments about Gilbert Eddy that theirs was to be a chaste union. The night before they married, Mary had a dream "in which she wanted to cross a wheat-field but was prevented by 'dark swinish forms' moving about in it, until Gilbert appeared on the other side calling, 'Come on, Mary, I will help you.' "[155] Help her he did, by becoming her most obedient student, asking nothing for himself. He became the first Christian Science practitioner, hanging out a shingle at their home in Lynn. Two days after their wedding, Mary wrote again to Spofford, "I . . . feel sure I can teach my husband up to a higher usefulness, to purity, and the higher development of all his *latent noble* qualities of head and heart."[156]

Mary's handful of students, who had formed the Christian Scientist Association on the Fourth of July, 1876, were not, however, as sanguine about her marriage as she. There was much dissatisfied murmuring. The new Mrs. Eddy, after all, had advised some of her students against marriage, implying that it was a base state that hindered spiritual development.

Not all of them could forgive her. George Barry, who together with another student had certainly lost money on the publication of *Science and Health*, lost as well all reverence toward his "Mother" and sued her, shortly after her marriage, for $2,700, for services rendered over the previous five years. Spofford, who had handled the finances involved, testified on Barry's behalf (Barry was eventually awarded $350) and was promptly expelled from the Association, in what was perhaps the first Christian Science excommunication.

There would be many more. This was only the first of a series of lawsuits engendered by Mrs. Eddy and her followers, lawsuits so outrageous that they attracted more public attention than the publication of Mrs. Eddy's book. To the amusement of Lynn and eventually Boston, accusations flew back and forth in the local newspapers. Indeed, it was her scandals, not her metaphysics, that put Mary Baker Eddy on the American map.

The scandals originated in Eddy's fixation on the dangers presented by those personalities that were in opposition to her, particularly those of Kennedy and Spofford. She felt their conflicts with her in her body and identified this ache or that pain as proceeding from their minds. She counseled students to "take up Spofford," to pray to know that "he cannot affect his Teacher or her students to make them sick or turn them away from Truth and their Teacher."[157] She also interpreted her lack of money as a distressing symptom of their working against her. George Barry had filed an attachment on the house at 8 Broad Street, and neither Mrs. Eddy nor her husband was earning much by teaching. Mrs. Eddy empowered one of her more zealous followers, an attorney named Edward J. Arens, to sue former students for violating their contractual obligations to her. He began by filing suit, in 1878, against Richard Kennedy.

The Kennedy suit went well for Mrs. Eddy; she was awarded $250. Arens quickly filed two more, one against Spofford and another, for unpaid tuition, against two students. After the case against Spofford was dismissed, Arens immediately engineered another, the case that came to be known as the Salem Witchcraft Trial of 1878. Two centuries after nineteen "witches" were hanged in Salem, the scourge had returned.

On May 14 of that year, Arens and Mrs. Eddy appeared in the Supreme Judicial Court in Salem on behalf of a Miss Lucretia Brown, an elderly spinster, and presented a bill of complaint accusing Daniel Spofford of having practiced mesmerism against her. Miss Brown had originally been healed of a spinal injury by Spofford, according to the complaint, but had subsequently suffered an inexplicable relapse, the result of dark doings on Spofford's part:

> The plaintiff humbly complains that the said Daniel H. Spofford of Newburyport, is a mesmerist, and practices the art of mesmerism, and that by his power and influence he is capable of injuring the persons and property and social relations of others, and does by said means so injure them. That the said Daniel H. Spofford, has at divers times and places since the year 1875, wrongfully, maliciously, and with intent to injure the plaintiff, caused the plaintiff, by means of his said power and art, great suffering of body, severe spinal pains and neuralgia, and temporary suspension of the mind; and still continues to cause the plaintiff the same. . . . And the plaintiff says that said injuries are great and of an irreparable nature, and that she is wholly unable to escape from the control and influence he so exercises upon her, and from the aforesaid effects of said control and influence.[158]

It is the only instance in the history of U.S. jurisprudence in which the plaintiff accused the defendant of practicing witchcraft.

Not surprisingly, the court declined to hear the case, pointing out that it was not within its power to control the mind of Spofford. The local newspapers were happy to take up where the court left off. The *Newburyport Herald* wrote,

In the Supreme Judicial Court, at Salem, on Tuesday, a bill in equity was brought more befitting the new institution at Danvers [the State Hospital for the Insane] than the highest tribunal of the Commonwealth. . . . we suspect the real complainant is Mrs. Mary B. G. Eddy, of Lynn, who has a power of attorney to appear for the plaintiff in the case. Mrs. Eddy professes to cure disease miraculously, and to be able to impart her power, and Spofford was one of her pupils, with whom she has since quarreled. She tried some time since, to induce us to publish an attack upon Spofford which we declined to do, and we understand that similar requests were made to other newspapers of the country. At last the matter has come into court, and the bill in equity is a curiosity such as might have been looked for in the court records of two hundred years ago. The witchcraft delusion is not yet dead, even officially.[159]

Even with the court's dismissal, the matter did not end. In October 1878, Gilbert Eddy and Edward Arens were arrested on a charge of having conspired to murder Daniel Spofford. Some days prior to the arrest, Boston newspapers had reported Spofford's "Mysterious Absence"; in fact, tipped off by the police about the danger to his person, he had been hiding out in Cambridgeport.[160] A barkeeper, James Sargent, claimed that Arens, using an alias, had offered him $500 to kill Spofford; Sargent later identified Gilbert Eddy as Arens's accomplice. Alerting the police, Sargent had participated in a sting operation, encouraging Arens and Eddy to pay him for murder.

The Boston newspapers, the *Herald* and the *Globe*, went wild over the story, comparing Gilbert Eddy and Arens to the Borgias. Gilbert Eddy was locked up in the Charles Street jail awaiting a preliminary hearing and wrote to his wife, "I have enjoyed myself during this experience so far, having as I have the assurance of being accounted worthy to suffer persecution for the Masters sake."[161]

Meanwhile, Richard Kennedy appealed the decision against him, and, while the newspapers were having a field day with the Eddys, that decision was reversed. The plot thickened when it seemed as if Sargent, and possibly others involved in the case, had committed perjury. By January 1879, prosecutors had dropped all the charges, but Eddy and Arens were required to pay the court costs. Her husband was free, but now everyone in Boston knew about the infamous Mrs. Eddy.

It was in this atmosphere that Eddy and the students in the Christian Scientist Association voted to form a church, to be known as the Church of Christ (Scientist). In August 1879, a charter was granted. The Eddys moved to Boston—the home of the new church—for the winter of 1879, so that Mrs. Eddy could fulfill her obligations as its president and pastor. The new church had twenty-six members.[162]

13. "A Demonic Strain"

Out of court, Mary Baker Eddy's life continued to be every bit as dramatic. Mrs. Eddy—and, decades later, her biographer and champion, Robert Peel—believed that, somehow, Kennedy was the mastermind behind the entire attempted murder plot, if plot it was. Peel suggests that Eddy's fear of Kennedy (who later in life became a vestryman in the Episcopal church) was merited because Kennedy was, perhaps, a species of devil: "Scientific caution would suggest some attention to the possibility that among the hidden factors in the situation was a psychopathic or, to use the term which has again become fashionable, a demonic strain in Kennedy."[163] Peel cites the suspicions of both Eddys, but is finally forced to acknowledge that "Facts are hard to come by here."[164] Stephen Gottschalk, another Scientist and apologist for the religion, concurs with Peel's dark conclusion: "There may or may not be some significance in the fact that both [Arens and Kennedy] died in mental institutions."[165] Eddy herself, of course, needed no facts that pointed to Kennedy's involvement; she knew that he yearned to control her life mentally. By this point, Eddy's paranoia had become a part of her religion, from which it would never be divorced.

Her behavior grew more extreme after these trials. She stood to lose the house in Lynn to her lawyers, who had not been paid, and she and her husband went back to the familiar boardinghouse circuit. She planned to move to Cincinnati for a time to escape the demonic mental machinations of Kennedy and Spofford. She wrote to her son, George Glover, who had last seen her twenty-three years earlier, when he was eleven, to meet her there, but when he arrived, she was nowhere to be found. He was forced to contact the Lynn police to learn her whereabouts, and found out that she had decided to stay in Boston. Once reunited with his mother, George, who had been living and mining for gold in the wild west of Deadwood, South Dakota, was so alarmed by her terror of Kennedy (who, she felt, was preventing the Eddys from finding appropriate lodging) that he went to Kennedy's office, pulled out a gun, and ordered him to stop his satanic practices or, said George, "I will search you out and shoot you like a mad dog." Kennedy later denied that this ever happened.[166]

In October 1881, the first of many group defections and rebellions by Mrs. Eddy's students—who were later to be labeled disloyal—took place. During a meeting of the Christian Scientist Association at Eddy's home in Lynn, a declaration was read, signed by eight students (about a third of the entire movement), including several longtime and formerly devoted ones:

> We, the undersigned, while we acknowledge and appreciate the understanding of Truth imparted to us by our Teacher, Mrs. Mary B. G. Eddy, led by Divine Intelligence to perceive with sorrow that departure from the straight and narrow road (which alone leads to growth of Christ-like virtues) made manifest by frequent ebullitions of temper, love of money, and the appearance of hypocrisy, *cannot* longer submit to such Leadership.[167]

The signers went on to withdraw their names from the Association and from the Church of Christ (Scientist).

Mrs. Eddy listened and without responding left the room. She returned after the meeting to find her husband with two lone followers, one of whom was Calvin Frye, who would go on to serve as her devoted secretary until her death, some thirty years later. The four stayed up all night, and at dawn, Mrs. Eddy began to speak in an oracular biblical patois while her audience scrambled to take notes during this sacred visitation. According to their notes, she said:

> Is this humiliation, the humility the oppressor would heap upon me! O, the exaltation of Spirit! . . .
>
> Oh, blessed daughter of Zion, I am with thee. And none shall take my words out of thy lips. Thou art my chosen, to bear my Truth to the nations, and I will not suffer another messenger to go before thee.
>
> And this Absalom shall perish and this backsliding Israel shall eat the bread of bitterness.
>
> And I will lift thee up Oh daughter of Zion. And I will make of thee a new nation for thy praise.
>
> Get thee up! Depart, depart. This people are a stiff necked people.[168]

After delivering herself of this speech, Eddy arose and proclaimed, "Why, I haven't any body."[169] Another loyal student, Julia Bartlett, arrived and heard her ask those assembled to stay with her "three days." Bartlett later wrote,

> Those three days were wonderful. It was as if God was talking to her and she would come to us and tell us the wonderful revelations that came. We were on the Mount. We felt that we must take the shoes from off our feet, that we were standing on holy ground. What came to me at that time will never leave me.[170]

Mrs. Eddy had transformed the humiliating rejection by her students into a sacred event. Her talent for continuous self-creation would save her, time and time again, preserving the awe and respect of her followers, as it did here. Her students would learn that every pronouncement, every contradiction, every whim of their leader was divinely inspired. And those who did not learn that lesson would be summarily cast out.

14. *Science and Health,* Second and Third Editions

During this turmoil, Mrs. Eddy had prepared and, in 1878, brought out a second edition of *Science and Health.* The so-called Ark edition, featuring an illustration of Noah's Ark on the cover, is now the rarest of all the many editions of this book. It was to have been published in two volumes, but the first had so many typographical errors that Mrs. Eddy had it destroyed; only five hundred copies of the second volume were printed. On the flyleaf was this astonishingly solipsistic verse by Mrs. Eddy:

> I, I, I, I, *itself, I*
> *The inside and outside, the what and the why,*
> *The when and the where, the low and the high,*
> *All I, I, I, I, itself, I.*[171]

The second volume contained several new chapters, including one entitled "Mesmerism"; it was to this malicious force that its author attributed the many misprints.

Three years later, in 1881, the Eddys paid to have a third edition printed. It was a seminal revision. For the first time, the profoundly important statement of Christian Science, the "scientific statement of being," that all Christian Scientists memorize, appeared in the text, asserting that "there is no Life, substance, or intelligence in matter; all is Mind."[172]

Also making its first appearance, stamped in gold on the cover, was The Cross and The Crown, the seal that would become the trademark of Christian Science. Chapter titles and the organization of the content correspond more closely to their final form; Eddy had also added the epigraph from *Hamlet* that still opens the book: "There is nothing either good or bad, but thinking makes it so."

But the third edition was, if anything, even more defensive than the first; indeed, Eddy took the opportunity to go on the attack against her enemies. Two statements, both addressed "To The Public," the first signed by Dr. Asa G. Eddy and the second by thirty-one of Eddy's students, preceded the preface and took an unnamed "ignorant hypocrite" to task at some length for plagiarizing Eddy's works.[173] Both statements were actually addressed not so much to the public as to the hateful plagiarist himself, the Eddys' old partner in crime, Edward J. Arens, who, after breaking off relations with his coreligionists, had indeed borrowed liberally from *Science and Health* in a pamphlet he had had published anonymously in 1880. As she had when other followers defied or disappointed her, Eddy found demonic significance in Arens's betrayal.

In the same vein as the prefatory statements, Eddy also added a new forty-six-page chapter, "Demonology," to her book. It consisted of ringing denunciations of the likes of "Dr.——" (Richard Kennedy) and "D. S——" (Daniel Spofford), as well as a "brief sketch"—actually a lengthy account—of the farcical Eddy-Arens-Spofford murder conspiracy, here described as "one of the most diabolical conspiracies that ever disgraced the annals of history."[174] Eddy was immersing herself and her followers in obsessive fears of the dark side of Christian Science. She saw her enemies "reversing the arguments of Truth," much as satanists recite the Lord's Prayer backward or defile the sacraments by practicing them in perverted ways:

> Having instanced a few cases of the evil workings of the hidden agency in our midst, our readers may feel an interest to learn somewhat of the indications of this mental malpractice or demonology. It has no outward signs, such as ordinarily indicate mesmerism, and its effects are far more subtle because of this. Its tendency is to sour the disposition, to occasion great fear of disease, dread, and discouragement, to cause a relapse of former diseases, to produce new ones, to create dislikes or indifference to friends, to produce

sufferings in the head, in fine, every evil that demonology includes and that metaphysics destroys. If it be students of ours whom he attacks, the malpractitioner and aforesaid mesmerist tries to produce in their minds a hatred towards us, even as the assassin puts out the light before committing his deed.[175]

These attacks and paranoid ruminations, however, seemed to excite interest in the book among a certain segment of the society it reached. The third edition of *Science and Health* was the first to sell out.[176]

15. "Mesmeric Poison"

After the treachery of the students in Lynn had been revealed, the Eddys left that city for good and, in January 1882, repaired to Washington, D.C., and Philadelphia for two months. Mrs. Eddy did a great deal of lecturing, and the loyal students who had accompanied her took on patients, while, back in Boston, another student, Clara Choate, was attracting scores of new students, mostly women, to readings of *Science and Health* and lectures.

In one of the few passages in her writings in which she acknowledges political developments in the world outside of her small coterie, Mrs. Eddy, in a letter from Philadelphia to Clara Choate, alludes to the efforts of women on other fronts:

It is glorious to see what the women *alone* are doing here for temperance. More than ever man has done. This is the period of *women, they* are to move and carry all the great moral and Christian reforms. I know it. Now darling, let us work as the industrious Suffragists are at work who are getting a hearing all over the land. Let us work as they do in love "preferring one another." Let us work shoulder to shoulder each bearing their own part of the burdens and helping one another and then the puny kicks of mesmerism will give up the ghost before such *union.*[177]

This is the strongest feminist statement Eddy ever made; she was in no way an activist for women. *Science and Health* denounces "civil law" for establishing "very unfair differences between the rights of the two sexes," and supports women's property rights and their right to vote.[178] But Eddy also encouraged gender stereotypes, writing in her textbook: "Man should not be required to participate in all the annoyances and cares of domestic economy, nor should women be expected to understand political economy."[179] Christian Science is one of the few major religious movements to have been founded by a woman, but, although it encouraged women to become healers, its organization would be authoritarian and largely male.[180] (In her movement, Eddy elevated only men to the highest administrative posts, and on her death, left in charge a Board of Directors consisting of five men.) Although the majority of her followers were women, Eddy regularly engaged in power struggles with women Scientists who developed their own followings and denied to other women the authority she herself had gained.

When the Eddys returned to Boston in April 1882, Mrs. Choate hosted a lavish formal reception, to which curious Boston society flocked. Much interest had been aroused just prior to their arrival in the city by a flattering full-page article in the *Boston Sunday Globe* of March 26, 1882, about extraordinary Christian Science healings, announced with almost a full column of sensational headlines:

> MIRACLES? — Phenomena of a Startling Nature. — All Manner of Diseases Cured — Without Medicine or Ceremony. — What is "Religious Science?" — The Lame Walk and the Blind See. — Infirmities of Every Description Dissipated. — "Disease a Belief, Not a Reality." — Remarkable Facts For Metaphysicians. — The Science of Medicine Contradicted. — Startling Theory of God and the Bible. — The Divine Mind the Power Which Dispels Sickness.[181]

The article was as sensational as it purported to be. The reporter had attended the weekly lecture, held at the Choates' home in the Eddys' absence:

> The parlors were so greatly crowded that there was barely room for the lecturer to stand in the midst of the assembly. It was an audience composed of well-dressed, intelligent ladies and gentlemen. Mrs. Choate, a lady about 30 years of age, a picture of health, with a stout physique and frank and pleasant countenance, spoke for nearly an hour. In the course of her remarks she stated some of the leading features of the doctrine of the "Christian science." . . . Said the lecturer: "I would no more have a disease described

before my child than I would allow sin to be pictured before him. Either would sink into his mind and might bear evil fruit in after years."[182]

After the lecture, the reporter was introduced to one of Clara Choate's success stories, a Boston mother whose nine-month-old infant had been suffering with a terrible case of eczema which "five of the best doctors in Boston" had failed to heal. When Mrs. Choate was called in to the case,

> the child was emaciated and covered with eruptions, and its little arms were pinioned to the pillow on which it lay to prevent it from tearing its flesh. They were using five pounds of vasaline per day and did not attempt to dress the child. They had not dared to wash it for five weeks. After Mrs. Choate had looked at it the child immediately began to mend, was perfectly well in three months, and is still in the best of health. The writer asked Mrs. Choate what her method was in this case, and was informed that the cure was entirely carried on in the mind of the mother. From certain signs the "scientist" inferred that the trouble with the child could be traced to pre-natal causes. On questioning the mother the fact was developed that before the child was born a servant had come home intoxicated and threatened to kill her, thus giving her a fright. Mrs. Choate said that she could not explain the cure any further than that she destroyed the error in the mother's thought, and in so doing healed the child. No medicine, of course, was used.[183]

The article incited the wrath and disgust of Boston physicians and was succeeded a week later by a follow-up as critical as the original article was unquestioning, also announced with loud headlines: "WHAT THEY THINK OF IT. — Opinions of Prominent Clergymen and Physicians — In Regard to the 'Christian Scientists' and Their Work. — Interviews with Rev. M. J. Savage, Dr. Harris and Others."[184] Clergymen and medical men denounced the new healing method as "sublime rubbish" and "thundering humbug."[185] One doctor, asked about the "force or principle" behind Christian Science, replied, "Credulity, sir."[186] At the bottom of the page under this article was a brief, if ironic, advertisement: "A FULL feeling after meals, dyspepsia, heartburn and general ill health relieved by Brown's Iron Bitters."[187]

The Eddys moved into a house in Boston's South End, on Columbus Avenue, installing a plate near the door announcing that Mary B. G. Eddy was now a Professor of Metaphysics and Christian Science. And in

May, Mrs. Eddy opened her Massachusetts Metaphysical College, a school of metaphysics which she had been contemplating for the past several years. In addition to her teaching at the school, Mrs. Eddy held regular Thursday evening meetings, at which she lectured, and preached on Sunday afternoons.[188]

But two months after Mrs. Eddy's triumphant arrival in Boston, just as the Christian Science movement was being established on a solid footing, disaster struck. On June 3, 1882, Gilbert Eddy, who had seemed tired and weak for some time, died in his sleep. A medical doctor who had been living with the couple had earlier diagnosed heart disease and suggested that Gilbert's condition was grave, but Mrs. Eddy was convinced that the problem was her enemies at work again. The day after his death, Mary Baker Eddy announced to the world, via the *Boston Globe*, that her husband had been mentally murdered. She named no names to the *Globe*, but she confided in others that the murderer was none other than Edward Arens.

The doctor who had diagnosed Eddy's illness performed an autopsy, and the bereaved widow demanded to see her husband's diseased heart. He showed it to her, "pointing out the diseased portions," but, according to one account, "the only effect of this evidence was to confirm her disbelief in autopsies and physicians."[189] The doctor could find no poison in Gilbert Eddy's body, but Mrs. Eddy called a press conference to announce her own findings:

> My husband's death was caused by malicious mesmerism. . . . I know it was poison that killed him, not material poison, but mesmeric poison. My husband was in uniform health, and but seldom complained of any kind of ailment. During his brief illness, just preceding his death, his continual cry was "Only relieve me of this continual suggestion, through the mind, of poison, and I will recover." It is well known that by constantly dwelling upon any subject in thought finally comes the poison of the belief through the whole system. I have seen mesmerists, merely by a glance or a motion, make an arm or a leg of a subject stiff, and then relax it again or give pain and relieve it again. . . .
>
> Circumstances debarred me from taking hold of my husband's case. He declared himself perfectly capable of carrying himself through, and I was so entirely absorbed in business that I permitted him to try, and when I awakened to the danger it was too late. I have cured worse cases before, but took hold of them in time. . . . One of my students, a malpractitioner, has been heard to say that he would follow us to the grave. He has already reached my

husband. While my husband and I were in Washington and Philadelphia last winter, we were obliged to guard against poison, the same symptoms apparent at my husband's death constantly attending us. And yet the one who was planning the evil against us was in Boston the whole time.[190]

As in all the other disappointments and tragedies of her life, Mary Baker Eddy seemed to have been incapable of responding to loss in a direct way. Her immediate reaction to her husband's death was not to grieve at losing her helpmate, admirer, and supporter or to regret having misconstrued the seriousness of his condition. Her reaction—angry accusations and defensive concern over how her husband's death might be perceived as a black mark on her healing record—was to insist that Gilbert Eddy's death was not her fault.

Of course, it was not. But in the worldview of Christian Science, the worldview Eddy herself had created, death is not a natural event. Death is the failure to assimilate and demonstrate the "truths" of Christian Science. The deaths of Christian Scientists since Gilbert Eddy have also been accompanied by those same reactions: anger, defensiveness, and disassociation from the human emotions of grief and sorrow. The death of her husband was one of Mrs. Eddy's most confounding experiences, and the Christian Science response to death is in consequence one of her most painful legacies.

Part II

"You Will Have to Learn to Love Me More": Mrs. Eddy Builds Her Empire

A will! A wicked will;
A woman's will; a cank'red grandam's will!

—Shakespeare,
King John

1. Footman Frye

After Gilbert Eddy's death, Mary Baker Eddy's first inclination was to find a follower as obedient and tireless in her support as he had been. Her search for such a helpmate and healer fit a pattern in her life.[1] When Daniel Patterson, her second husband, was failing her, she wrote a pleading letter to Quimby; when Quimby quit the scene, she wrote in virtually the same manner and with the same request for attention to another of the doctor's former patients, Julius Dresser. She now sent a peremptory letter to her son, George, demanding that he come to her side. When he refused, she wrote to another student, who also balked.

Finally, Eddy, who, as one scholar has observed, had exhibited a "pattern of marrying men who were not her intellectual equals," settled on Calvin Frye.[2] Like Gilbert Eddy before him, Frye was a slow, stolid character with a troubled family background. His mother had become psychotic shortly after he was born and, except for brief periods, continued in that state for the rest of her life. Frye had been married briefly and widowed; when Mrs. Eddy called him into her service, in the fall of 1882, he was thirty-seven years old. For the rest of his Leader's life—the next twenty-eight years— Calvin Frye never left Eddy for so much as a day.[3]

Frye and his exacting mistress never married, but their relationship was, in many ways, the closest and most emotionally dependent of Eddy's life.

The long-suffering Frye drove Eddy on her daily carriage ride, handled her correspondence, buffered her from the importunings of followers, nursed her during illnesses, worked ceaselessly to protect her from the dangers of malicious animal magnetism, and submissively suffered her rebukes and demands. More than any other individual in her household, he was privy to her pains, her secrets, her daily struggle. And he kept a diary. That diary—as well as notebooks in which Frye apparently took dictation from Eddy about her religious visions, or dreams, and other theological matters—are among the most mysterious and coveted documents held by the Church. No outside scholars have ever been allowed to see the originals, but some of the material has made its way out into the world.[4] In 1917, just before his death, Frye apparently excised portions of the diary that seemed most incriminating or damaging to Eddy's memory. Immediately after his death, these portions were entrusted to John Dittemore, then a Director and the Clerk of the Church (who, two years later, broke with his fellow Board members and was exiled by them). He had them transcribed and photostated, keeping copies for himself. The originals of these portions were then burned. Excerpts from the photostats were published in both Dittemore's own critical biography of Eddy and in the controversial *Mrs. Eddy* by Edwin Franden Dakin; transcripts of them have been circulated throughout the Christian Science underground by samizdat. Thus, ironically, the so-called noxious portions of the Frye diary have been those that have seen widespread circulation. Frye's diary, much of it written in desk calendars in shorthand, captured in detail the volatile behavior of the woman he worshipped, providing a crucial portrait of her later years. Calvin Frye, Eddy's most obedient servant, would unwittingly open an unauthorized window into her unusual private life.

2. The Boston Craze

With her strange pronouncements following the death of her husband, Mary Baker Eddy became a household word in Boston. The fin de siècle in the city known as the Athens of America—dominated by hothouse movements like Christian Science, temperance, and women's suffrage—was daringly resurrected in Henry James's *The Bostonians*. Its characters offer tantalizing glimpses of Eddy and her followers: the coldly zealous and asexual Olive Chancellor; the spooky mesmeric healer Selah Tarrant and his daughter Verena, whose lectures hypnotize willing audiences; and the

harried reformist Miss Birdseye, who was apparently inspired by the educational reformer and abolitionist Elizabeth Peabody. The fevered, melodramatic intrigues of the early women's movement that are the focus of
that novel bear an unmistakable resemblance to the intrigues of Eddy's set.
In Verena Tarrant, James had Eddy to the life:

> She had been nursed in darkened rooms, and suckled in the midst of mani-
> festations; she had begun to "attend lectures," as she said, when she was
> quite an infant, because her mother had no one to leave her with at home.
> She had sat on the knees of somnambulists, and had been passed from hand
> to hand by trance-speakers; she was familiar with every kind of "cure," and
> had grown up among lady-editors of newspapers advocating new religions,
> and people who disapproved of the marriage tie. . . .
>
> The sort of thing she was able to do, to say, was an article for which there
> was more and more demand—fluent, pretty, third-rate palaver, conscious or
> unconscious, perfected humbug; the stupid, gregarious, gullible public, the
> enlightened democracy of his native land, could swallow unlimited draughts
> of it.[5]

If the public could swallow unlimited draughts, Eddy would serve them. In
1883, the sixth edition of *Science and Health* appeared, now with a new
"Glossary" of biblical terms heralded by a grand new subtitle: *With a Key to
the Scriptures*.[6] That year Eddy also established the first Christian Science
periodical, the *Christian Science Journal*, which appeared at first bimonthly
and eventually monthly. It would be enormously influential in reaching
Scientists across the country and eventually the world, instructing them in
the appropriate behavior and practices of Scientists and printing testimonials of the faith. In 1884, Eddy taught in Chicago, attracting scores of followers there.

Throughout this time, as she would for the rest of her life, Eddy was
revising *Science and Health*. In 1885, she hired a former Unitarian clergyman, James Henry Wiggin, to help her edit the "textbook," as it was now
called. Wiggin, who was alternately condescending to Eddy and impressed
by her energy, polished and reorganized her prose, lending the book a
crisper, more authoritative tone.

In March 1885, facing a largely hostile audience of two thousand in
Boston's Tremont Temple, she answered her Protestant critics—Reverend
Joseph Cook and Reverend A. J. Gordon—in one of the most prominent
public addresses of her career. Granted only ten minutes to respond to the

charges of pantheism, spiritualism, and blasphemy leveled against her during Cook's popular lecture series, Eddy tersely asserted her Christian credentials: a belief in one God and a belief in the atonement of Christ, although she did not explain that her view of atonement entailed achieving a mystical sense of "at-one-ment" with the divine Mind, whereas most Christians believed it was the reconciliation of God and man through Jesus Christ's sacrifice on the cross. She also offered a brief description of the Christian Science healing method. "It is not one mind acting upon another mind," she said. "It is not the transference of human images of thought to other minds; it is not supported by the evidence before the personal senses,—Science contradicts this evidence; it is not of the flesh, but of the Spirit. It is Christ come to destroy the power of the flesh; it is Truth over error."[7] She denied that Christian Science was faith healing and asserted that the new religion "combines faith with understanding," a distinction that Scientists would insist upon as crucial in the decades to come.[8]

She convinced neither Cook nor Gordon, and the reception afforded her was chilly. But her determination in the face of disdain seems to have impressed other, more liberal clergy, and it was around this time that she and the movement began to attract the vocal support of sympathizers. Critics denounced Christian Science as the "Boston Craze"; the *Times* of London reported that clergy believed it to be "the most dangerous innovation that has threatened the Christian Church . . . for many years."[9] But others went so far as to respectfully attend her classes; one Congregational minister wrote: "If they can heal, as they claim they do, they will carry the day, and they ought."[10] Negative and positive, it was all attention, and attention begat growth.

Also in 1885, the Scientists moved their services from Hawthorne Hall, with only 250 seats, to Chickering Hall, which could hold five hundred; services there were soon packed. The *Christian Science Journal* began to run notices from around the country, "News from Abroad," attesting to the growth of Christian Science in far-flung cities. In 1889, Brooklyn, New York, reported that the movement begun there in 1886 with "a few earnest seekers" had, over the course of the next few years, given instruction in Christian Science to "over one hundred students . . . about half of whom have become members of the [Christian Scientist] Association."[11] That same year, Buffalo, New York, reported that a group that began with a series of "Parlor Talks" for half a dozen people had grown into a full-fledged church with an attendance of "160 or more."[12] Duluth, Minnesota,

Oshkosh, Wisconsin, and Oakland, California, also reported great progress.[13] The 1890 U.S. Census of Religious Bodies counted 8,724 members of the Christian Science Church in 32 states.[14]

This was the period of Eddy's greatest social success. Frances Hodgson Burnett, who would publish the sensationally successful *Little Lord Fauntleroy* in 1886, came to call at one of Eddy's Thursday evening meetings. In 1885, when Louisa May Alcott complained in the *Woman's Journal* of the unpleasant "mesmeric sensations" she suffered after consulting a practitioner of mind cure, Calvin Frye set her straight in the *Journal*, asserting that her practitioner was not one of Eddy's own and suggesting that Miss Alcott was the victim of "demonology."[15]

In September 1888, the *Christian Science Journal* announced the opening of the first Christian Science reading room. It was conceived of as "a publication-room for our JOURNAL, and a salesroom for other Christian Science publications," as well as "a reading-room and social place for our friends,—a sort of clubroom."[16] Great pride was expressed in its location, "one of the most eligible locations in all Boston . . . in the Hotel Boylston, over the Steinert piano warerooms . . . where some of the best concerts are held."[17]

Boylston Street was also the location, in 1889, of the first of the short-lived Christian Science "dispensaries," where Eddy's practitioners offered indigent patients the mental treatments she had taught them. The dispensaries would be the only foray Christian Science ever made into traditional Christian mission-style work—indeed, this first dispensary was called "a Christian Science Mission and Free Dispensary"—and would be opened in a number of cities over the next few years. But, according to one historian, they were not a complete success; the volunteers who ventured into the "slums of the city to serve the sick . . . encountered a great deal of disbelief, and . . . a great deal of resistance."[18] After a few years the dispensaries were shut down, considered to be superfluous because of the proliferation of practitioners.

3. "Mind-Quacks"

The growing number of practitioners of Christian Science spelled not only success for Eddy's movement but also competition. A number of Eddy's followers, including former editors of the *Journal* and others who had held positions of trust within her movement, split off to form their own

Christian Science groups; by the late 1880s, there were over thirty self-proclaimed colleges and schools and almost a dozen periodicals claiming to teach Christian Science, including the *International Magazine of Christian Science* and the *Mental Healing Monthly*.[19] The dizzying array of books, magazines, groups, and leaders all proclaiming to offer some form of Christian Science or mental healing proved confusing to the public and the press; Mrs. Mary H. Plunkett, a prominent defector from Eddy's camp, became known in the New York City papers during the 1880s as "the high priestess of Christian Science."[20]

What's more, Mary Patterson had not been Dr. Quimby's only disciple. With the publicity her movement began to attract, particularly after the move to Boston, other Quimby enthusiasts began to see the wisdom of promoting their own version of their master's teachings. What would come to be called the "mind cure," "mind science," or "New Thought" groups sprang from the same humble examining room where Quimby first met Mary Patterson and healed her. But, in large part, they were spurred on by Eddy's success.

Julius Dresser was one of Quimby's patients who had known Mary before she became Mrs. Eddy; she had turned to him for aid after Quimby's death.[21] Dresser's own health had failed while he was studying for the ministry in Maine. He came to Quimby for healing in 1860 and subsequently married another of Quimby's patients. Dresser, like Mary Patterson, became an enthusiastic convert to Quimbyism and began teaching it to others. After some years in the newspaper business, he and his wife began practicing and teaching mental healing in Boston in 1882, the year after Eddy chartered her college.

The Dressers were troubled by what they saw as Eddy's wholesale misappropriation of the Quimby method, and, through circulars and statements to the press, challenged her corner on the healing market. Some years after she launched the *Christian Science Journal* in 1883, they began to publish *New Thought*, in 1890, which gave yet another name to the rather nebulous movement. It was Horatio Dresser, Julius's son, who later edited *The Quimby Manuscripts*, a book that became one of the few sources on Quimby's biography and his writings.

New Thought gave rise to a number of organizations. The Unity School of Christianity was founded in 1889 by Myrtle Fillmore, a convert to Christian Science who believed she had been healed of tuberculosis through Science. She ultimately left Christian Science and was influenced by Emma Curtis Hopkins, another Scientist who had had a falling-out with

Eddy. Unity, which produces millions of copies of inspirational pamphlets and other publications from its headquarters, Unity Village, near Kansas City, is still renowned for its experimentation with twenty-four-hour-a-day prayer vigils. Although less well known to the general public than Christian Science, it has arguably had a far wider reach; in recent years, it has reported receiving over two million letters annually.

Divine Science was also founded in 1889, and Hopkins also contributed to its development. A former editor of the *Christian Science Journal* and member of Eddy's inner circle, Hopkins set up shop in Chicago after their break, founding the rivalrous Christian Science Theological Seminary, which taught many New Thought leaders and writers. The Institute of Religious Science and Philosophy was founded in Los Angeles in 1927 by yet another of Hopkins's students, Ernest Holmes. It has been one of the more successful of the mind-science organizations, attracting such celebrity followers as Norman Cousins (of the *Saturday Review*), and the actors Robert Stack and Robert Young. It established over a hundred churches in the United States by the mid-1970s and has its own cadre of practitioners. Both Unity and Religious Science groups hold worship services on Sundays at New York's Lincoln Center and other prominent venues.

All of the mind sciences share with Christian Science an emphasis on positive thinking, on the banishment of evil through an understanding of the power of good, and on spiritual treatment for a variety of physical and other ills. Christian Science stands alone, however, in its insistence on a complete repudiation of medical care. Indeed, Eddy's reluctance to reconsider her most adamant rejections of medicine—even after she had broken her own rules in her later years—may have arisen out of a desire to distinguish Christian Science from all its offshoots and rivals. "Adulterating Christian Science," she wrote in *Science and Health*, "makes it void."[22]

There is no doubt that Eddy was threatened by her competitors. In 1886, in the *Journal*, she asserted that false teachers, "in their witless ventilation of false statements and claims," were misleading and defrauding the public.[23] Such practices represented "the froth of error passing off"; Eddy's faithful followers were assured that "Christian Science will some time appear all the clearer for this filth that has been poured into it."[24] She used the phrase "Mind-Quack" to describe her rivals, accusing Emma Hopkins of "fraud" and suggesting that those teaching any form of mind science were plagiarizing from her. In 1887, she published this extraordinary statement about her rivals in a pamphlet: "They are spreading abroad patchwork books, false compendiums of my system, crediting some ignoramus or infidel with teachings they have stolen from me. The unweaned suckling whines while spitting out the breast-milk which sustained him, 'I was a man before I saw my mother.' "[25]

Eddy, who was often accused of plagiarism herself, did not take imitation as a form of flattery; indeed, the proliferation of rivals and counterfeiters seemed to cause her no end of grief.[26] With growing numbers of Scientists out in the Field, teaching and distributing their own versions of Science, versions that did not always conform to Eddy's own, she no longer wielded total control over the creation, and questions began to be raised about the methodology behind Christian Science treatment. What was a treatment? What were practitioners supposed to do? What were they forbidden to do? What exactly was Mary Baker Eddy teaching at her Massachusetts Metaphysical College?

4. At the Massachusetts Metaphysical College

The theology and practice of Christian Science were forged in the fiery furnace of the Massachusetts Metaphysical College. Historically and legally, the college was a unique institution, state chartered under a broadly construed 1874 act (soon repealed) that encouraged the formation of educational corporations in the Commonwealth without establishing any standards by which they might be investigated or regulated.[27] Just as *Science and Health*, which Eddy revised virtually from its first publication until her death, had a thirty-five-year gestation, the teaching and practice of Christian Science, including the work of practitioners and teachers, were works in progress that Eddy amended and improved at her whim.

Refinements to the curriculum of the college and a defense of its uniqueness were constant preoccupations in the early numbers of the *Journal*. In November 1886, Eddy addressed the question "Can Christian Science Mind-healing be taught to people who are absent?" She advised her readers that the science of Mind could not be taught "silently," and moreover, that those who tried it were practicing animal magnetism.[28] For true teaching, students had to come to the college. In June 1887, those wishing to attend were instructed that only those students who were "perfectly well" could be admitted: "A sick person is not in the proper condition for learning Christian Science."[29] Students who were ailing could not be treated by Mrs. Eddy, since she did not have the time to take up their cases; their illnesses might also encourage the forces of "chemicalization," a bubbling up or throwing off of distracting physical or emotional symptoms—almost a purging of negativity—that was an occasional byproduct of Christian Science treatment. "Those who would follow Christ," reads the *Journal* note on "Invalidism in the College Classes," "should be presented to him without spot or wrinkle."[30]

Most of Eddy's teaching was organized in two main courses. The "Primary class" was a two-week, twelve-lesson course consisting of instruction in how to heal the sick and be a practitioner. It initially cost $300, equivalent to some $4,600 in today's money and at a time, notes one scholar, when Harvard Medical College charged $200 for an entire year's tuition.[31] It has survived to this day under the same name, although it is also called "Primary class-instruction," "class-instruction," or simply "class." Scientists who have completed Primary class-instruction are referred to as having been "class taught." The second and more advanced class was called the Normal class; this six-lesson course was designed to teach students who had completed class-instruction how to become teachers of Christian Science. (Primary class was supposed to be taken before Normal class, although early on in the history of the college some students took the Normal class first.) Some of Eddy's students took her classes several times, since each presentation seemed unique. Primary classes were taught by Eddy or by her assistants, but only Eddy, the president of the college, taught the Normal course.

Over the coming years—after she closed the college and relinquished the teaching to others—Eddy would place many restrictions on the teaching of Christian Science. She gradually cut back on the number of students allowed in each Primary class, on the number of classes that could be taught by each teacher in any given year, and on the number of meetings teachers could hold with former students. Teachers of Primary class were eventually allowed to instruct no more than thirty students per year, and the tuition was standardized at $100. Normal class was to be taught only once in the world every three years; class size was also limited to thirty; and tuition was also set at $100. Eddy felt that these restrictions would keep teachers from gaining their own followings. In 1895, she established a rule that no students who had been taught by her could subsequently take instruction from other Christian Science teachers.

Although note-taking in Eddy's classes was not allowed, many of her students apparently disobeyed, keeping notes and writing memoirs of their class experiences; class notes taken from teachers who had been taught by Eddy have also been preserved. Thus, Eddy's teachings, which seem to have involved both free-form lectures and asking and answering questions of her students, have survived in a number of written accounts, many of which describe the experience of her teaching as life-transforming. C. Lulu Blackman, a young woman from Nebraska, described herself as facing a life of "inevitable invalidism."[32] After correspondence with Mrs. Eddy, she was "called to" the class of 1885, which began with an arresting vision of the teacher:

> When she entered the classroom, I saw her for the first time. Intuitively, the members of the class rose at her entrance, and remained standing until she was seated. She made her way to a slightly raised platform, turned, and faced us. She wore an imported black satin dress heavily beaded with tiny black jet beads, black satin slippers beaded, and had on her rarely beautiful diamonds. These she spoke of in one of the later sessions. She stood before us, slight, graceful of carriage, and exquisitely beautiful. Then, still standing, she faced her class as one who knew herself to be a teacher by divine right. She was every inch the teacher. She turned to the student at the end of the first row and taking direct mental cognizance of this one, plainly knocked at the door of his thought. It was as if a question had been asked and answered, and a benediction given. Then her eyes rested on the next in order and the same recognition was made. This continued until each member of the class was included. No audible word voiced the purely mental contact.[33]

Eddy's presence, for Blackman and others, was overwhelming: "In my own experience, she seemed to have obliterated everything I had deemed substantial and actual. The word 'God'—'God'—'God' was repeated over and over in my consciousness to the exclusion of all else."[34] At the close of the third lesson, the students were instructed to go out and find their first patient and heal them.[35] After the final lesson, Mrs. Eddy shook hands and spoke a few individual words to each student. Blackman writes, "As she held my hand she looked directly into my eyes and said, 'Thou art mine, saith the Lord, and none shall pluck you from out my hand.' "[36] And so C. Lulu Blackman came to be Mrs. Eddy's. She went back to Fremont, Nebraska, and became a practitioner.

The current teaching of Christian Science is just as Eddy left it, with only minor exceptions. All Scientists may now take Primary class-instruction only once in their lives (unless their teacher is demoted by the Church, in which case they must repeat class with an approved teacher), but those who wish to go into the "practice" or "healing ministry" of

Christian Science in order to become "*Journal*-listed" practitioners and nurses must take it. (Listing of practitioners' names and addresses in the monthly *Christian Science Journal* is the only official Church recognition or licensing of practitioners.) Students of class-instruction are admonished to keep even the fact of their attending class secret, lest malicious animal magnetism prey upon them. Class-instruction is offered by Christian Science "teachers" who have completed the single additional instructional level that exists within the Church, the Normal course, given once every three years at the Church Center in Boston by a teacher appointed by Church authorities. Teachers meet annually with all of their Primary class students once a year in a gathering known as Class Association. Associations continue to meet annually even after a teacher's death, so long as there are students to attend.

Although class-instruction is based, according to Eddy's rule, on the twenty-four questions and answers in "Recapitulation"—the chapter in *Science and Health* in which Eddy defines God, man, error, and other crucial concepts—students are nonetheless taught intriguing lessons that seem to fall outside the literal language of that chapter. These lessons derive directly from Eddy's own teachings. Students are urged to begin each day of their lives with a study of the Bible lesson for the week and of the "scientific statement of being" in order to protect themselves and their families against the threat of misfortune, illness, accident, or "aggressive mental suggestion," images of materiality presented by the outside world. In addition, they are taught a form of preventative, protective prayer in which they "deny" the reality of evil in its most dangerous, specific forms: mesmerism, hypnotism, numerology, and other dangerous black arts. They are taught to "deny" that any other religions can harm them, specifically religions that were feared by Eddy herself, such as Roman Catholicism.[37] These teachings are preserved in the "Notes from Primary Class as taught by Laura Sargent." Sargent herself had taken two of Mrs. Eddy's own Primary classes, as well as the Normal class and other instruction; she served in Eddy's household intermittently from 1890 until Eddy's death. Sargent described Roman Catholicism as "a belief of mortal mind, parading in a religious guise . . . a belief in personality, punishment and damnation."[38] "Romanism," she taught, had three principal beliefs: "1. That man needs a human priest. 2. That God has a mother named Mary—a personalization of the Motherhood of God. 3. That we need saints in order to get favors."[39] (Judaism was described as "the belief that the spiritual has to be materialized and personalized, before it can be of any value. It is an attempt to crucify the Christ. It is a misconception.")[40] Beginning in 1904, Eddy made it impermissible to teach Roman Catholics Christian Science, "except it be with the written consent of the authority of their Church," and candidates for Normal class are asked about any Roman Catholic connections in their background.[41]

The essential elements of how to give a Christian Science treatment are as they were when Eddy taught them. Thus, present-day adherents of Christian Science are in the strange position of following teachings about bodily health and functions that were formulated in the mid- to late nineteenth-century. Their systematic denials and abstract assertions of spiritual truths rely fundamentally on rejection of a whole host of disciplines: all advances in medical science, surgery, medical technology, and emergency medical care; psychiatry and psychology; dietary and nutritional knowledge; and stress- and pain-management. Their solution to the mind-body problem is essentially premodern, and a glimpse into their healing methodology is a glimpse back in time.

Scientists often attempt to heal themselves through what they call consecrated prayer: an intense study of and concentration on Eddy's writings and biblical texts that excludes all other thoughts. But at times they may choose to go to a Christian Science practitioner, or professional healer, for treatment, often when their own efforts have fallen short, when they feel they need additional help handling a problem on their own, or simply when they seek a deeper spiritual understanding of an issue. While an individual's prayers may be based on virtually any text chosen from the Bible and Eddy's writings, the prayers of a practitioner follow a more standardized form.

Anyone—Scientists, non-Scientists, or those who belong to other faiths—may avail themselves of a practitioner's services as long as they are not taking any drugs or receiving medical care and express a serious commitment to the process of Christian Science healing. According to accounts by those who have taken class-instruction and those who have worked as practitioners, a Christian Science treatment is broken down into the following steps:

First, the practitioner knows the truth about God, declaring the allness of God using Eddy's seven synonyms—Life, Truth, Love, Spirit, Soul, Principle, and Mind. Then she declares the truth about man. She relates the synonyms of God and truths about man to each other, arguing, for example, that Spirit, Substance, is the only Mind, and man is its image and likeness; that Mind is intelligence; that Spirit is Substance; that Love is wholeness; that Life, Truth, and Love are the only reality. The practitioner meditates on the many permutations and relationships between God and man's true nature as a manifestation of God.

Next she "dips into error but doesn't wallow in it." She knows that "there are no isms, no -ologies, no animal magnetism, no mesmerism, no demonology, no numerology, no astrology, no hexes." She denies other religions, Romanism, the devil, and evil, knowing that there is no other power apart from God. She denies whatever is specific to that case: the various symptoms of the illness or trouble at hand. In Christian Science, there is a peculiar, Swedenborgian correspondence between troublesome emotions or feelings (anxiety, fear, anger, jealousy, disappointment) and physical symptoms. Fear corresponds to fever and fever to fear; tumors can be affiliated with the burden of anger; rashes or skin problems can be interpreted as outbreaks of nagging frustration. Such symptoms are treated by asserting the nothingness of both the root emotional cause and the symptom. For example, in a recent Christian Science periodical, a man recounted how his recurrent back pain was healed when he realized that he had been persistently resentful of a family attorney; after a cordial conversation with the lawyer, his resentment and the pain dissolved.[42] Practitioners will often "diagnose" these connections between uncomfortable emotions and uncomfortable bodily sensations or pains. If the individual for whom a practitioner is praying "seems" to have a fever, she knows that fever is the physical manifestation of fear and that eliminating the cause will eliminate the symptom. "Destroy fear, and you end fever," Eddy wrote.[43] In children, fever is thought to be caused by the fear of the parents.

The practitioner brings the treatment to a conclusion by reaffirming the truth that man is the image and likeness of Love, of divine Mind, of intelligence, of Truth. She knows that disease is a lie and that the five material senses are liars. She may invoke Eddy's reformulation of Jesus' denunciation of the devil ("he is a liar, and the father of it") by asserting that "Mortal mind is a liar and the father of it."[44] Finally, she declares that her statements and affirmations are the very word of God and that the word goes out with the power to heal. She concludes that "this cannot return unto me void."

The rhetorical argument of Christian Science treatment thus can be broken down into statement, assertion, contradiction of what is thought to be the false logic of mortal existence, and summation. "Mentally contradict every complaint from the body," Eddy writes.[45] The expression of gratitude for Christian Science, for man's perfection, and all blessings is also an important part of both the treatment and the resulting testimonials about the healing.

Generally, the practitioner does not perform these prayers out loud. Christian Science treatments, whether administered by oneself or by a practitioner, are usually delivered silently; practitioners, moreover, generally conduct their practice at home or in their offices, away from their patient. This is called absent treatment.

But, while a patient may not hear these silent, absent prayers, important transactions do take place between practitioner and patient, either on the phone or in person. Practitioners suggest certain courses of study, certain passages from the Bible or Eddy's writings, certain hymns, or certain statements that seem helpful for the situation, often focusing on passages that mention the affected part of the body or the particular condition or problem. The Christian Science periodicals are full of testimonial examples of patients working and praying, with the help of practitioners, on specific textual passages. Recently a woman in London wrote to the *Sentinel* to testify that she had been healed of the fear of driving a car through praying with the help of a practitioner, concentrating on a line from Isaiah: "And an highway shall be there, and a way, and it shall be called The way of holiness."[46] A woman in Portugal described in a recent *Journal* the healing of a sore on her leg after studying, with a practitioner, a passage from *Science and Health* that instructed her, "Have no fear that matter can ache, swell, and be inflamed as the result of a law of any kind, when it is self-evident that matter can have no pain nor inflammation."[47]

Any problem, no matter how unremarkable or trivial, can be addressed through Christian Science: a wart on a toe, cancer, joblessness, poverty, feelings of anger or resentment toward others, and, especially, fear. Fear, indeed, is seen as great cause for alarm, and many testimonies allude to "overcoming" it; sorrow or grief, likewise, is something that must be healed in order to restore harmony to the mind and body.

Testimonies often mention feelings of warmth, comfort, and support arising from the practitioner-patient relationship; it often seems to carry overtones of the relationship between doctor and patient or therapist and patient. But while medical doctors may alarm patients with graphic diagnoses and prognoses, and therapists may push patients to explore painful feelings and experiences, practitioners seek to calm and allay all fears by denying the disease or problem any reality. Practitioners often delve into what they interpret as the underlying causes behind an illness or an upset, seeking the emotional source of disease or pain in a patient's frustration, anger, or impatience with family members, bosses, or coworkers. Once upset feelings are healed, the logic goes, the body will fall into line.

Although testifiers in both branch church meetings and in the periodicals express complete confidence that their healings have come through the practice of Christian Science, those outside the religion may interpret them differently. Often it seems that the process of "healing" is really a narrative process, rather than a physical one, in which the sufferer revises his experience, using the rhetoric and logic of Christian Science. In the place of a person who is ill or has some other physical problems such as an injury or deformity, or is experiencing turmoil, depression, or some misfortune, the Scientist eventually comes to see a well person, a happy person, a whole person. Quite often the "healings" of conditions described in testimonies take as much time as any unassisted recovery; sprained ankles, bruises, minor cuts, scrapes, and burns are "healed" over the course of days or weeks. One recent testimony in the *Journal* described a woman's "healing" of a propensity to faint that took fourteen years.[48] "Instantaneous healings," of which Scientists are very proud, are often of conditions that seem scarcely to warrant the attention given them; the real "healing" seems to have been a process of calming or rejecting fear and distress.

The placebo effect of Christian Science seems to have been particularly powerful and compelling during Eddy's day, when medicine was more hazardous than salutary; historians have noted that the new faith was particularly successful in facilitating childbirth by calming the nerves and soothing the justifiable fears with which women then faced labor.[49] There are many testimonies in the *Journal* attesting to painless, or at least easier, births, including this one from a woman with six children:

I have always suffered very severely at childbirth, except with my last babe. (The others were born before we turned to Christian Science.) My last one caused so little suffering that it seemed like a miracle. I was awakened about three o'clock in the morning, but not by pain, and knew that the time for the birth had come. I called my husband, and told him to get Science and Health and read some, and help me the best he knew. I then began to treat myself, and in a short time (I do not know exactly how long, but before day) my little one had arrived, and everything was all right. About three in the afternoon I arose and sat up a little while. The next week I commenced to run the sewing machine; before my babe was a month old we moved a distance of over three miles; I went in a cart, helped to fix my things, in fact, I was well, and stronger than I ever was before in three months.[50]

Not all births attended by Christian Science, however, were as uncomplicated as this, and it was an obstetrical disaster that plunged Eddy into her most severe crisis since the death of her husband.

5. Metaphysical Obstetrics

Eighteen eighty-eight was a year of turmoil. In the spring, Mrs. Abby Corner, a Christian Science practitioner in West Medford, Massachusetts, administered Christian Science treatment to her daughter as she was giving birth; her daughter hemorrhaged and died, along with the infant. Mrs. Corner was indicted for manslaughter.

Mrs. Eddy had offered two one-week classes in "Metaphysical Obstetrics" at the college only the previous year. She taught these first obstetrics classes by herself, and they focused on mentally protecting the mother and infant during childbirth. The course contained no practical instruction on human physiology or on midwifery techniques; instead, it taught practitioners how to deny the "false claim"—the false material picture—presented by the human body and its functions. There was also much instruction in overcoming mesmerism or malicious animal magnetism, the sinister mental force sent out by Mrs. Eddy's disloyal students and enemies that could kill or wound the unwary. As one critic wrote, "Mrs. Eddy's obstetrical course . . . consisted of instructions to 'deny' everything except the child itself."[51]

The "Notes on Metaphysical Obstetrics," which were prepared by a Dr. Alfred E. Baker, a medical physician who subsequently became a Christian Scientist and who led a later obstetric class under the auspices of Eddy's Board of Education (formed after her college was closed), are quite astonishing, consisting of brief declarations of truth to be made by the practitioner. The notes are organized under a variety of headings. Under "Seed Egg," for instance, it says: "Error has no seed. . . . Menstrual function does *not* accompany egg formation, simply a superstition. Belief of necessity for that can be overcome. A false claim against women."[52] "Organs of Generation" are redefined metaphysically: "Uterus: Place where anything is generated or produced. If it could choose Christ it would. So you must choose for it. Matter is never a producer. . . . The pelvis enclosure is not the place where anything is generated or produced. Could God get into a bottle and produce anything there?"[53] Under "Dry Birth," the metaphysical obstetrician is instructed: "No such thing as a dry birth. No such thing as a Sahara desert. . . . No material bag of water. Mind lubricates."[54] And "Intercourse" ("no sexual desire or genital sense . . . no tomb, no gloom, no doom") is defined as "*Ecstatic* sense, as in courtship, a belief of mesmerism to be handled."[55]

Mrs. Eddy's response to the Corner indictment, published in a letter to the *Boston Herald* in April 1888, wreaked havoc in her movement. She went on the attack, expressing no sorrow or sense of responsibility for the death of Mrs. Corner's daughter or of her baby. She lashed out at Mrs. Corner herself and at the "medical scoffers" who saw fit to criticize Christian Science.

> The lamentable case reported from West Medford of the death of a mother and her infant at childbirth should forever put a stop to quackery. . . . Mrs. Abby H. Corner never entered the obstetrics class at the Massachusetts Metaphysical College. She was not fitted at this institute for an accoucheur, had attended but one term, and four terms, including three years of successful practice by the student, are required to complete the college course. No student graduates under four years. Mrs. Eddy, the president of this college, requires her students to use the utmost precaution in practice, and to be thoroughly qualified for their work. Hence the rapid growth of this system of mind-healing, its safety and success. The West Medford case, so far as is known, is the first instance of death at childbirth in the practice of Christian science. This fact is of vital importance, when compared with the daily statistics of death on such occasions caused by the use of drugs and instruments. Does medical malpractice, and the mortality that ensues, go unnoticed because of their frequency? Christian scientists are called daily to heal chronic cases of disease caused by the malpractice of physicians of the regular school, and they heal these cases in a majority of instances. . . . Are the medical scoffers who sit in judgment on mind-healing willing to lift the veil on the charnel house for others to read the records of their blunders and count the number of their victims.[56]

Although Mrs. Eddy herself wrote this notice, it was signed by the "Committee on Publication, Christian Scientists' Association," in one of the first uses of the name. It established for all time the methodology of the Committee on Publication, the institution that continues to deflect questions and concerns about the safety of Christian Science practices, particularly those involving children, by attacking the flaws and failures of medical science. (The C.O.P. now, as then, never addresses the specific circumstances involved in any Christian Science death). Of course, the college standards that Mrs. Eddy makes much of in the notice did not really exist; the college offered only the three courses, Primary, Normal, and Obstetrical Metaphysics, totaling some twenty-four lectures; "terms" at the college lasted a mere few weeks; the "four-year" program consisted primarily of the student's own healing work.

When Mrs. Corner was acquitted after evidence suggested that her daughter's hemorrhage probably could not have been successfully treated medically, Mrs. Eddy claimed to have always known that she would be. But the damage had been done. Christian Scientists were outraged that Eddy had attacked, rather than defended, one of their own. In any event, in September 1888, Eddy announced in the *Journal* that Dr. Ebenezer J. Foster, a medical doctor, would take over the teaching of "the anatomy and surgery of obstetrics," while she herself would address its metaphysics.[57] In 1902 she declared, "Obstetrics is not Science, and will not be taught"; thus, this controversial material disappeared from the Christian Science curriculum, and the teachings are only available in the notes of Baker and Eddy's own students.[58]

6. Another Son

On June 12, 1888, at an uproarious meeting of the Christian Scientist Association in Boston, thirty-six members, about a fifth of the group, resigned. The next day, in Chicago, Mrs. Eddy appeared to have trumped this defection by appearing before an adoring audience of four thousand at the annual convention of the National Christian Scientist Association, an event that captivated the Chicago press and public. There were claims of instantaneous healings of the lame and diseased. Certainly, according to the *Chicago Times*, there was rapture:

> When the speaker [Mrs. Eddy] concluded the audience arose en masse and made a rush for the platform. There were no steps provided for getting

on the rostrum, but that did not deter those who wanted to shake hands with the idolized expounder of their creed. They mounted the reporters' table and vaulted to the rostrum like acrobats. They crowded about the little woman and hugged and kissed her until she was exhausted and a man had to come to her rescue and lead her away.[59]

The adulation was not shared by all. Back in Boston there was rancor among Eddy's followers and growing resentment of her peremptory ways.

Those feelings were exacerbated when, in November 1888, at the age of sixty-eight, Mrs. Eddy adopted a son. Dr. Ebenezer J. Foster, who, after his legal adoption, changed his name to Dr. Ebenezer J. Foster Eddy, was then forty-one years old, a medical and homeopathic physician with a degree from the Hahnemann Medical College in Philadelphia who had begun to study at the Metaphysical College the year before. Eddy appointed him to be a teacher of obstetrics at the college just after the Abby Corner affair and the defection of the Association members. His adoption followed a six-month visit by George Glover and his family which, in Peel's opinion, consisted of a "plaintive" wife and three "wailing" children.[60] Mrs. Eddy seems to have become ever more offended and disappointed by George, apparently feeling that his unrefined manners and illiteracy reflected badly on her. It is clear, however, that George yearned to be accepted by his mother, asking if his wife could take her class. Mrs. Eddy had tried to forestall his visit, writing to tell him,

> You are not what I had hoped to find you, and I am wholly changed. . . .
> When I retire from business and into private life then I can receive you if
> you are *reformed*, but not otherwise. I say this to *you* not to *any one else*. I
> would not injure *you* any more than myself.[61]

George might well have had cause to doubt the sincerity of such protestations when, in March 1888, his mother castigated him again:

> I want your children *educated*. No greater disgrace rests on my family
> name than the ignorance of the parents of these darling children.
> You could read in the Bible very well when you left your Mother long ago.
> It should be a shame to any one at any age not to be able to read. . . .
> If [your wife] will read to me a page of Science and Health *wherever I open
> to it*, I will then talk with you about her joining my next class.[62]

The Glovers visited anyway, but they were not allowed to stay in Mrs. Eddy's home, which was filled with her students and staff.[63]

It may have seemed to her that she could replace the flawed and troublesome George with a finer model of a son. Foster Eddy was apparently more suggestible than George, and he had no wife: "He never offered Mrs. Eddy advice, never interfered with her wishes, never questioned her wisdom or demurred to her projects—as even Mr. Frye was sometimes known to do," wrote one biographer.[64] Interviewed years after his adoption, Foster Eddy could not recall "ever having crossed his adopted mother in anything."[65] He played the piano for her and affected the grand style of his new mother, wearing a fur-lined coat and a diamond solitaire pinky ring she had given him. But as one of her critics noted, Mrs. Eddy tired of people easily; it was a pattern throughout her life:

> Each of her favourites gave her, as it were, a new lease of life; with each one her interest in everything quickened. . . . She must altogether absorb the new candidate; he must have nothing left in him which was not from her. If she came upon one insoluble atom hidden away anywhere in the marrow of his bones, she experienced a revulsion and flung him contemptuously aside.[66]

She would eventually tire of Foster Eddy—"Bennie," as she called him—but not before her preference for him had brought additional strife to her household and her movement.

By 1889, all of Mrs. Eddy's endeavors were thriving. There were far more applications than could be accepted at the Massachusetts Metaphysical College; *Science and Health* was selling briskly as students were encouraged to purchase each new edition as it became available in improved form; her own classes were overflowing; the church in Boston had had to find bigger and bigger halls to accommodate its services. It was at this point that Mrs. Eddy chose to shut everything down.

In September, she "recommended" that the Christian Scientist Association be dissolved. It was. In October, she closed the college. In December, the Church of Christ (Scientist) in Boston was dissolved as well, also on her recommendation. The National Association was put on hiatus for three years. She gave up her editorship of the *Christian Science Journal*, leaving it to others to pay the bills of that not-yet-profitable periodical. God had commanded her to do these things, she said. She announced in the *Journal*, in the oracular third person, that she was "taking a vacation, her first in twenty-five years," and that "her desire is that God may permit her to continue to live apart from the world, free from the toil and turmoil in which her days have been passed for more than a quarter century."[67] Those among her stunned followers who pressed her about her decision were told that she was "*tired, tired,* of teaching and being the slave of so many minds."[68] She declared herself disgusted by the "poor teaching" that was going on in the Field.[69]

She could easily have delegated her teaching responsibilities and other duties to her many loyal followers; indeed, she was already doing so. But she clearly felt no responsibility to maintain the institutions she had created. The extraordinarily abrupt way in which she brought her whole movement to a halt was an exercise of power reminiscent of her announcements to loved ones earlier in her life that she was on the verge of death, reminiscent of her abandonment of her son. It was also, more specifically, an angry reaction to the 1888 rebellion against her and an attempt to gather institutional power into her own hands, an attempt that would prove completely successful.

At this point, Mrs. Eddy began, once again, restlessly moving from place to place, but she could now afford a more lavish style than the boarding-houses of her itinerant period. First she went to Barre, Vermont, then to Concord, New Hampshire, then to a suburb of Boston. But she encountered disappointments wherever she went. In Barre, a loud brass band playing in the town square refused to accommodate her need for quiet. In the Boston suburbs, she thought that the neighbors were mesmerized. Malicious animal magnetism, or M.A.M. as she had taken to calling it, now threatened her everywhere, and she sent her adopted son to scout out locations for a safe house. According to one biography, "She stipulated that to be safe it must be a certain distance from mailboxes, post-offices, telegraph and express offices, and stations; all such terminals she regarded as the favorite lurking spots for M.A.M. sent out by her enemies."[70]

Finally, in 1891, she settled in Concord, taking a house in town while a grander, more isolated place was erected for her on the outskirts. It was to be called Pleasant View.

7. The Mother Church

Mrs. Eddy's peremptory actions were not inspired entirely by whim. As certain writers have pointed out, the Massachusetts attorney general was, at the time Eddy closed down her college, investigating institutions that were granting spurious medical degrees. One of Eddy's more obstreperous "disloyal" students, Mrs. Josephine Woodbury, eventually suggested that the possible legal consequences of running the Massachusetts Metaphysical College inspired Mrs. Eddy's desire to move out of state.[71]

Mrs. Eddy's role in the closure of the Boston church also merits a closer look, especially as she was simultaneously encouraging other branch churches across the country to continue organizing. But while she allowed the Boston church to keep on meeting informally, she was insistent it formally dissolve its organization.

The Church had been structured democratically; its members had the right to choose its pastors and participate in its administration. In the remonstrative letter she sent to the Boston congregation on November 28, 1889, she demanded that they "drop all material rules" and relinquish those rights:

> Dear Brethren:
>
> The Church of Christ (Scientist) in Boston was my patient seven years. When I would think she was well nigh healed a relapse came and a large portion of her flock would forsake the better portion, and betake themselves to the world's various hospitals for the cure of mortal maladies. These straying sheep would either set up claims of improvements on Christian Science and oppose the mother Church, or sink out of sight in religious history. . . .
>
> So I admonish this Church after ten years of sad experience in material bonds to cast them off and cast her net on the spiritual side of Christianity. To drop all material rules whereby to regulate Christ, christianity, and adopt alone the golden rule. . . .
>
> When this is done I have already caused to be deeded to those who shall build a Church edifice, the lot of land designed for the site of such an edifice, and which is now valued at $15,000.
>
> This offer is made on condition that the question of disorganization shall be settled by affirmative vote at the annual meeting of this Church held December 2nd, 1889.[72]

In 1886, after years of meeting in rented halls, the Boston church members had decided to buy land and put up their own church building. With a down payment of $2,000 and a mortgage of $8,763.50, they purchased a vacant lot in the Back Bay, at the corner of Falmouth and Caledonia Streets. After two years, they had paid off nearly $4,000 but could not raise the final mortgage payment. The mortgage was foreclosed in the summer of 1889, and it appeared that the Boston Scientists had lost their land.

What they did not know was that in December 1888 Mrs. Eddy had secretly bought up the mortgage, and it was she who foreclosed on them, after which, through what one biographer describes as "a series of complex and dubious financial transactions conducted by a lawyer who was later disbarred," she sold the land at public auction, with her lawyer's son acting as agent, for $5,000, roughly half its estimated worth.[73] But she essentially sold it to herself, or rather to a handpicked representative, her loyal follower Ira O. Knapp. (As one wag eventually put it, "She took it out of one pocket and put it in the other.")[74] She then sent the Boston members the letter quoted above, assuring them that the land was theirs if they agreed to relinquish their previous form of church organization. They did, but not without murmuring and complaint from some members who suspected that her methods were underhanded and possibly illegal.

In 1892, she had a deed of trust drawn up that transferred the property to four of her closest, most obedient followers: the aforementioned Knapp, William B. Johnson, Joseph S. Eastaman, and Stephen A. Chase. These trustees would constitute the Church's first Board of Directors (later a body of five members) which would take over the institutional powers previously held by the members of the Boston church, including the power to appoint pastors and Readers and to make any other regulations governing the church. According to the deed of trust, if they failed to erect a church costing at least $50,000 within five years, the property and the church would revert to Mrs. Eddy.

Thus Mrs. Eddy succeeded in "disenfranchising," as one writer put it, not only the Boston congregation but the entire church membership.[75] This was the beginning of the Mother Church as the Vatican of Christian Science and of Eddy's handpicked and ultimately self-perpetuating Board of Directors, who together constitute a power that, throughout the movement it governs, is papal in its reach and scope. In the *Journal*, Eddy defended her byzantine legal maneuverings by revealing that a higher power was at work. "I had this desirable site transferred in a circuitous, novel way," she wrote, adding "but this was God's business, not mine."[76]

No less a power justified her actions.

8. M.A.M. at Pleasant View

In June 1892, the renovations at Pleasant View were finished, and Mrs. Eddy moved in. Living with her at this time were Calvin Frye; Martha Morgan, the first of several cooks; Laura Sargent and Clara Shannon, aides and housekeepers; and Foster Eddy; later, various maids, an overseer, a coachman, and a groundsman were added to the staff.[77]

Pleasant View, about a mile and a half west of the town of Concord, New Hampshire, was set in a partially cultivated, partially wooded valley in farming country. Originally an old farmhouse, the three-story structure had been renovated to include a covered front porch, three wide verandas at the back running the full length of the house, bay windows, a fountain with goldfish, and a corner tower with a balcony, where Eddy kept her study, which had views down the valley in the direction of Bow. In years to come, from the tower balcony, Eddy would address the throngs of Christian Scientists who gathered once a year to pay her homage. It was in 1892 that Eddy, already called Mother by most of her followers, decided on her official title: "Discoverer and Founder of Christian Science."

She gradually bought more land to add to the estate and made a number of improvements; it was a working farm while she lived there, with fruit trees, vegetable and flower gardens, hay fields, and a windmill. Soon after she moved in, a group of her students donated the money to construct a pond overhung by willows on the rear lawn; in 1893, the Toronto Scientists donated a boat for it.

Eddy became famous for her daily afternoon drive, during which she sat alone in the carriage, with Calvin Frye in the box up front. She was often seen pacing on the rear verandas, a vision that impressed itself on the mind of one devoted follower, an artist making his first visit:

> I was sketching some details of the house from the rear, at the lower end of the grounds, some sixty rods away from it, when a *dark* figure came out upon the upper veranda . . . and began to walk the length of the veranda and back. I was there sketching some fifteen minutes or more and the black figure walked vigorously back and forth the length of the piazza and return [sic] constantly. . . . I noticed the fashion of the garb, that it was very peculiar, particularly the bonnet or hat, which was large in size in proportion to the

figure, which looked very short and small. The hat was so large and bent so around the head that no face was visible to me, although no veil was worn, and the depth of the black to my sense seemed beyond description and left an impression upon my mind of sackcloth and ashes as the Bible hints, or has it. . . . Perhaps my imagination magnifies, but it seemed to me the Founder of Christian Science was thus typifying in outward appearance the inner throes of anguish, perhaps habitually borne.[78]

Mrs. Eddy wrote frequent panegyrics on the peacefulness and beauty of her new home, but, in many ways, Pleasant View was anything but pleasant for its inhabitants. (Or, as Peel would write, "One had to have moral and spiritual stamina to live in such an atmosphere.")[79] Many of the bizarre practices that Mrs. Eddy had intermittently and experimentally employed to thwart malicious animal magnetism during her time in Boston hardened over the sixteen years she spent at Pleasant View into rigid ritualistic behavior.

M.A.M. was not only in the mail, it was widespread throughout the physical world, a colorless, odorless, insidious influence affecting Mrs. Eddy's health, her food and clothing, the air she breathed, and the weather outside her home; it also preyed on her students and aides. It made lost objects impossible to find and ruined the printing of her books. It required constant vigilance. In *Mary Baker Eddy: Her Spiritual Footsteps*, Gilbert C. Carpenter, who spent a year in Mrs. Eddy's employ, described with great reverence "a representative day at Pleasant View."[80] Most of Carpenter's recollections coincide with those of other "household workers," as they came to be called, including Laura Sargent, Clara Shannon, Adam Dickey, and Calvin Frye.

Mrs. Eddy insisted on round-the-clock "Watches," in which household employees were assigned to stay awake and alert, praying to resist M.A.M. The frequent failures of the workers to adequately "watch" resulted in Mrs. Eddy's intense anxiety and caused her to experience difficulty in breathing, sinus congestion, and insomnia. The term itself came from Jesus' rebuke of his disciples when they fell asleep in the Garden of Gethsemane: "Could ye not watch with me one hour?"[81] Carpenter describes the average daily watch:

Each student returned to his or her room to do the mental work to destroy fear, and to recognize the presence and power of God as supreme in the home as well as in the whole universe. . . . Watching instructions were written out either by Mrs. Eddy or by Mr. Frye under her supervision, and were passed around to us. One of these papers that is representative of her specific instructions to what line of thought to take up, reads as follows: "No fear; no poison, arsenic, etc; no suffering caused here by the readers of S. & H. [*Science and Health*]; no evil minds; no feeling the beliefs of patients; no relapse, no reversal of truth. There is but *one* Mind, God, good. Evil *is not* mind, it has *no power*. . . . We are not self-mesmerized. God, good, alone *controls us*. We feel no mind but *His*.[82]

The consequences of failing to alleviate the mental or physical suffering of Mrs. Eddy during a watch were severe. Calvin Frye described several such punishments in his diary; with him, they seem to have escalated at times to physical abuse. On one occasion, Eddy pulled Frye's hair. On others, she rebuked and reviled him. One of Frye's 1895 entries reads, "Mrs. E. was disturbed with my driving yesterday called me an idiot insane etc. Last eve she asked me if I knew I was insane. She says WATCH."[83] It was so difficult to stay awake for the night watches that Calvin Frye would sometimes knock on Clara Shannon's door and say, "Sister Clara, are you at your watch?" She would call back, "Yes, you can come and see; I am standing up!"[84]

Mrs. Eddy hated storms, heavy rains, thunder and lightning, and heavy snow. One of her weather watches reads: "Make a law that there shall be no more snow this season."[85] A household worker recollected in his memoir, "I have heard our Leader describe in a number of instances how she has dissipated a thunder cloud by simply looking upon it."[86] Clara Shannon claimed to have seen Mrs. Eddy produce rain out of a cloudless sky during a drought.[87]

A series of long-suffering cooks tried and failed to prepare Mrs. Eddy's food to her satisfaction, but their efforts were frequently spoiled by M.A.M. Extreme measures were warranted, as Carpenter explained: "The cook . . . often prepared two complete dinners for Mrs. Eddy, calling one the *incase*, meaning thereby that in case Mrs. Eddy sent back the first meal served, because she did not like it, there would be a second to offer." But Carpenter, who venerated Eddy, insisted that his Leader was not "overparticular about her food" and often "hardly knew what she ate." Nevertheless, "she did require that it be flavored with scientific right thinking, cooked with spiritual understanding, and served with a loving consciousness of man's oneness with God."[88]

. . .

In obedience to Mrs. Eddy's deed, the Board of Directors had begun building her Mother Church in 1893, but the construction of that building was, in the eyes of Eddy and her Scientists, bedeviled by a veritable plague of M.A.M. Outsiders might nonetheless conclude that Eddy herself had had a hand in the delays through her tendency to interfere in fund-raising and construction details. She drastically shortened her previous timetable for building the church, demanding that it be completed no later than the end of 1894, during a severe financial depression and despite problems posed by the building site and difficult building regulations.[89] In September 1893, she had written to the Board of Directors of the Church, saying, "Why in the name of *common sense* do you not lay the foundation of our Church as GOD BIDS YOU, AT ONCE?"[90] Days later, she importuned them again, "Do not delay one other day to lay the foundation of our Church"; when the work had not begun by October, she wrote, "Nothing but M.A.M. is preventing the foundation of our church being laid in *this month* as God has *bidden* it to be done!"[91] According to Peel, Eddy was insistent that all delays in the construction of the Church "*must* be handled as animal magnetism."[92] Joseph Armstrong, one of the Church Directors, who later wrote the official Church account, *Building of The Mother Church*, described the many difficulties in completing the building as proceeding not from Eddy but from the forces opposed to her: "Error was, or seemed to be, in possession and would yield only as Truth and Love were manifested. Every law of matter seemed opposed."[93] Laboring around the clock, workers completed the building at midnight on Saturday, December 29, 1894, and church services were held the next day, with a dedication scheduled for January 6, 1895.

The Mother Church is an extraordinary building, an intimate, eccentric, triangular Romanesque structure of granite, graced by stained-glass windows illustrating biblical scenes, including "Woman God-Crowned," "Mary First at the Resurrection," "Mary the Mother of Jesus," and "Mary Anointing the Head of Jesus," all subjects chosen by Eddy. There are also two illustrative rose windows, one depicting Jesus raising Jairus' daughter from the dead (long rumored to be the New Testament passage that healed Eddy after her famous fall in 1866) and another—known as the "Window of the Open Book"—displaying an open copy of *Science and Health* at its center. An inscription in pink granite wraps around the exterior of the church's bell tower, reading:

THE FIRST CHURCH OF CHRIST, SCIENTIST
ERECTED ANNO DOMINI, 1894.

A TESTIMONIAL TO OUR BELOVED TEACHER, THE REVEREND MARY BAKER EDDY; DISCOVERER AND FOUNDER OF CHRISTIAN SCIENCE; AUTHOR OF ITS TEXT-BOOK, SCIENCE AND HEALTH WITH KEY TO THE SCRIPTURES; PRESIDENT OF THE MASSACHUSETTS METAPHYSICAL COLLEGE, AND THE FIRST PASTOR OF THIS DENOMINATION

Eddy refused to attend the first service or the dedication, a decision Scientists and later Christian Science historians interpreted as a step in the direction of abolishing "personality" from her church.[94] But the memoir of one of her household workers, Clara Shannon, suggests otherwise. Shannon's memoir is a poignant evocation of how religious adoration of an omnipotent leader can entail humbling disappointments.

Clara Shannon was an unmarried British woman in her late thirties who was so devoted to Mrs. Eddy's service that for an entire year she left the house at Pleasant View only once, to walk down the drive. She wished for nothing more than to give Mrs. Eddy a dress to wear to the dedication of the church. M.A.M. was routinely held responsible for problems with Mrs. Eddy's clothes; she often found, to her distress, that her dresses were suspiciously ill-fitting, too short, or wrinkled. In an attempt to defeat M.A.M. on this important occasion, Shannon withdrew all the money in her bank account, over a hundred dollars, bought gray satin, velvet, and pearl trimming, and took it all to a dressmaker. "In the meantime," she wrote, "I watched and prayed for a harmonious result and to break the so-called law of malicious malpractice, which argued that Mrs. Eddy could not get anything to wear."[95] On Christmas Day, 1894, Shannon presented the gown to Mrs. Eddy, telling her it was "from Divine Love."[96] Mrs. Eddy was so pleased with it that she ordered a matching bonnet, clearly planning to attend the dedication: "Mother felt that Love had provided her with a dress in which to go to the dedication service of The Mother church on January sixth, 1895; so a few days after, she sent me to Boston to Wethern's store, to ask them to make her a bonnet of the same gray velvet with pearl trimming and two small gray feathers."[97]

But withholding herself from those who yearned for her most seems to have been a compulsion for Mrs. Eddy. She did not attend the dedication of the Mother Church, and the occasion for Clara Shannon's gift went unmarked. "It is not necessary to explain the reasons," Shannon wrote sadly. "I did all that I could to make it possible for her to go, but she suffered so much that she thought it wisest to remain home."[98] Mrs. Eddy was not the only one who suffered.

9. "A Power Not One's Own"

Over the next twenty years, Mary Baker Eddy became more haughty in manner and autocratic in mien, issuing a veritable whirlwind of orders, counterorders, accusations, and recriminations. She began to suggest that her role on earth was unique—even, perhaps, divine. Her forecasts of the future of her movement became more global and grandiose; Christian Science would be the savior of the race, of humanity, of the world.

She upbraided her followers at every opportunity. On one occasion, she told her Chicago students, who came to her in fear that they had lost their healing powers, "You will have to learn to love me more."[99] To a group of her followers who had gathered at Pleasant View, she delivered this abrasive speech:

> My dear Students, Guard your tongues. When you see sin in others, know that you have it in yourselves, and become repentant. If you think you are not mortal, you are mistaken. I find my students either in an apathy, or in a frenzy. I am astounded at your ignorance of the methods of animal magnetism. Your enemies are working incessantly while you are not working as you should. They do not knock, they come with a rush. They do not take me unawares. I know before they come. Would that my head were a fountain of waters, and my eyes rivers of tears that I might weep, because of the apathy of the students and the little that they have accomplished. You have never seen me in my real home, but you may sometime. Come with me into it.[100]

During this same period, Christian Scientists by the thousands began making regular annual appearances at Pleasant View, usually on or just after Communion Sunday (when the names of new applicants to the Mother Church were read during the service and Scientists engaged in one of the few sacraments left to them, kneeling in silent prayer), to pay her homage. On these occasions, she would appear briefly on her balcony, like a queen, wearing elaborate costumes and wraps trimmed with fur. Photographs of Mrs. Eddy on these appearances continue to be treasured possessions of Christian Scientists and can still be bought at Christian Science reading rooms.

Eddy had grown more acquisitive and flamboyant over the years, wearing glamorous gowns, bonnets, and jewelry—including a cross made of diamonds that appears in some portraits—often given to her by her followers. She began the practice of listing her Christmas gifts in the *Journal*; in 1889 she received a hand-painted silk patchwork "bed-scarf" of seventy-two squares, each embroidered by a different Scientist. She was also given, among other things:

> Eider-down pillow, white satin with gold embroidery. Eiderdown pillow, blue silk, hand-painted, and fringed with lace. Pastel painting of Minnehaha Falls, with silvered easel. Silver nutpick set. Painted Sevres China teaset. . . . Stand for lemonade-set. . . . Chinese jar. . . . Large variety of books and poems. Face of the Madonna, framed in oak and ivory. . . . Blue silk-embroidered shawl. . . . Silver holder for stereoscopic views. Two fat Kentucky turkeys. Hosts of bouquets and Christmas cards.[101]

Within a decade, she would be approving the design and motto to be placed on the Mary Baker Eddy Souvenir Spoon, produced by the Christian Science Souvenir Company of Concord, New Hampshire, described rapturously in the *Journal*: "About the handle appears gracefully wreathed the Mother's favorite flower, the rose, and surmounting the whole is the emblem of the Cross and Crown."[102] Eddy refused to divulge the words of the motto and warned Scientists not to ask: "Mother requests that Christian Scientists shall not ask to be informed what this motto is, but each Scientist shall purchase at least one spoon, and those who can afford it, one dozen spoons, that their families may read this motto at every meal, and their guests be made partakers of its simple truth."[103] (The motto was "Not Matter but Mind Satisfieth."[104]) Scientists could also purchase pictures of Mrs. Eddy, as well as "cuff-buttons, rings, brooches, watches, and pendants," also adorned with her favorite flower.[105]

Her imperious ways seemed to encourage her followers and to entice newcomers to the religion eager to partake of the wonders that enraptured others. Eddy had early on developed the practice of sending certain hand-picked followers to far-flung cities or regions of the United States—Chicago, New York, St. Louis, and California—in order to shepherd the growth of the movement. Now she widened her field, dispatching Julia Field-King, a homeopathic physician who had converted to Christian Science, to London in 1896, to establish the religion there, where it was received with enormous enthusiasm, attracting a number of socially prominent people, including a smattering of lords and ladies. The First Church of Christ, Scientist, London was dedicated the following year. During the 1890s Frances Thurber Seal, a practitioner in Dresden, and others in Stuttgart and Hannover spread the movement with phenomenal success, so that Germany eventually became the largest stronghold of Christian Science outside the English-speaking world.

Christian Science was also showcased at the 1893 World's Parliament of Religions, an adjunct to the Chicago World's Fair. Four thousand Scientists attended a denominational meeting of their own, one of the largest held at the Parliament. The Scientists were also invited to give a presentation to the entire Parliament, including contingents representing branches of Christianity, Judaism, Islam, and Buddhism, as well as the Parliament's most exotic guest, Swami Vivekananda, whose appearance famously introduced Hinduism to a wide American audience. Eddy, who disdained the proceedings by referring to them as "Vanity Fair," dispatched one of the movement's most venerable public speakers, Judge Septimus J. Hanna, a former Iowa county court judge and convert to Science, to read a speech she had written for the occasion.[106] Hanna's delivery of the speech was such a sensation that the newspapers clamored for copies, which he supplied, only to learn that he had excited his Leader's wrath. Eddy suggested that his conduct in releasing the speech to the press could wreak incalculable spiritual harm and that the speech, which had been slated to be published in a volume about the Parliament, would now have to be withdrawn: "Since the newspapers devoured it contrary to my solemn charge God has shown me by *signs* and *wonders* that it must not be published at this date. The dose is *too great*, the chemicalization will do incalculable harm," she admonished, using her term for spiritual purging.[107] The "harm" she had in mind was the kind of malicious evil she had once attributed to Kennedy and Spofford; now she felt that larger forces, including the Catholic Church, were working against her. "This published dose has unified parties against us in prayer," she wrote, later adding, "It would seem since the World's Fair that [the Catholics] are afraid of the power of Christian Scientists and would exterminate the Leader."[108] Eddy eventually relented, allowing parts of the speech to be printed, but she forced Hanna and the other Scientists involved to acknowledge the grievous error of their ways.

The vehemence of her response was matched by her frequent dramatic assertions and suggestions about her place in religious history, surprising to her public and often even to her followers. Early in 1893, she wrote a poem she called "Christ and Christmas," about the spiritual meaning of that holy day. Later that year, she began to discuss the possibility of publishing the poem in an illustrated volume. For the illustrator, she had in mind an unlikely self-taught artist named James F. Gilman, the artist who had been struck by his first sight of her, pacing on the veranda. He had been drawn to Concord to be near her by his reverence for Christian Science, which only deepened as he got to know its creator. His illustrations would imply a relationship of Eddy to Jesus Christ that went far beyond the import of the poem itself.

Gilman, a handsome man with a salt-and-pepper beard, may have struck a chord with Mrs. Eddy. He, too, was something of a wanderer and an itinerant and lived his life propelled by emotional forces he did not understand. He was also frank and direct, speaking bluntly to her about the disappointments he had experienced during his class instruction with Foster Eddy. Now nearly seventy-two and surrounded by acolytes and their flattery, Mrs. Eddy seems to have been smitten with Gilman's honesty, flirting and behaving girlishly in his company. He noted in his diary that she often seemed "childlike."[109] She spent a great deal of time showing him photographs and paintings of herself, instructing him on how the illustrations were to look. Like the members of Mrs. Eddy's household staff, Gilman came in for his share of sharp words and rebukes—on one occasion, she told him his angels looked like tadpoles—but he always returned to her good graces.[110] For what was to be the final illustration in the book, she had special instructions. He wrote in his diary,

> In the last illustration which she wants I should make very impressive, showing Truth at the door of mortal mind, she wants to have one bare foot show, and she said she could remove the hose from one foot and let me sketch the foot from the life if I desired. She said her students would think much of the picture if they knew it was her foot represented from nature.[111]

In two of the illustrations, an idealized young woman dressed in flowing white robes appears as the figures of "Christian Science" and "Truth." Peeping from beneath her toga is one bare foot. Eddy was so proud of the illustrations that she took partial credit for them; the last page of the book reads: MARY BAKER EDDY AND JAMES F. GILMAN, ARTISTS.[112]

When *Christ and Christmas* was published, in December 1893, the response was delight from Christian Scientists and outrage from Protestant and Catholic clergy.[113] Readers of the volume thought that they recognized the likeness of Mrs. Eddy in several illustrations, including one of a woman adorned with a halo and bearing a scroll marked CHRISTIAN SCIENCE, holding hands with Jesus Christ.[114] The haloes encircling the heads of Christ and the woman were of equal size, critics noted, surmising that Eddy meant to suggest that she was equal to Christ. Eddy hastened to reassure the clergy, writing in the *Journal*, "The clergymen may not understand that the illustrations in 'Christ and Christmas' refer not to my personality, but rather foretell the typical appearing of the womanhood, as well as the manhood of God, our divine Father and Mother."[115] The clergy's misperception was not surprising, considering that Eddy had encouraged Gilman to use her image as a model, but she professed to be appalled, writing to Foster Eddy, "I have stopped my book Christ & Xmas being printed! The students made a golden calf of it and therefore I pull down this dagon."[116] As she habitually did when faced with adulation or reproach—in this case both—she retreated, stopping the presses and withdrawing the book just weeks after it had gone on sale. *Christ and Christmas* was reissued several years later, with its illustrations somewhat altered.[117]

Eddy's irrepressible students might well have been forgiven their tendency to glorify the accomplishments of their Leader, given that she was routinely elevating herself and her book to an exalted level. At the same time as the flap over *Christ and Christmas*, Eddy was pressuring her longtime publishers at the University Press in Cambridge, Massachusetts, to print *Science and Health* on thin "Bible paper," which was both difficult to obtain outside England (where the Oxford University Press used it to print Bibles) and problematic to print on.[118] Eddy's justification for her desire to have *Science and Health* printed on this special paper was elaborate: "It has always been my desire and expectation," she told William Dana Orcutt, an employee at the University Press, "that my book should encourage more and more people to read the Bible. Through sharing the revelation of the spiritual meaning of the Bible which has come to me, Christian Scientists recognize the messages more clearly, and understand better what these messages mean to them. Many have suggested the desirability of having the Bible and Science and Health more similar in physical appearance as an aid to using them together."[119] The press bowed to her wishes, experimenting with a variety of papers and printing processes throughout the 1890s, and *Science and Health* has been available on Bible paper ever since.

One of the most important projects of Eddy's later years was her constant revision of the *Manual of The Mother Church*, first published in 1895. The eighty-ninth edition of the *Manual*, published just weeks after her death in 1910, would determine the future course of her Church.

In the *Manual of The Mother Church*, Mary Baker Eddy laid down the law. Eddy claimed that the *Manual*, like *Science and Health*, originated from a sacred source. The rules, she wrote, "were not arbitrary opinions nor dic-tatorial demands, such as one person might impose on another." They were, in fact, "impelled by a power not one's own."[120] As sacred writ, these by-laws could not be opposed, contradicted, or disobeyed. But evidently, the "power" that impelled these laws had as changeable a mind as the power that wrote *Science and Health*. They were constantly revised and rewritten, added to and subtracted from the *Manual* by Eddy herself virtu-ally until the day she died.

One of the central bylaws was written not long after Eddy made the first of her two visits to her Mother Church. She had missed its dedication in January 1895, but three months later, in April, she came without notifying the congregation. She spent a Saturday night in "Mother's Room," an apartment elaborately furnished and decorated for her sole use, located in the tower of the church. Paid for in part by the collections of the "Busy Bees," children of local Christian Scientists, the room had gold-plated plumbing and African red marble in the bath, three stained-glass windows, a mantel over the fireplace made of onyx blocks from Mexico that had been exhibited at the 1893 World's Fair in Chicago, an Eskimo rug made out of one hundred eider duck skins, and a number of lamps, embroideries, vases, and other knickknacks donated by Eddy's adoring subjects. Eddy herself contributed a large oil painting of the haircloth rocking chair in which she wrote *Science and Health*. As Joseph Armstrong, one of the Directors who supervised its construction, wrote in *Building of The Mother Church*, "everything was provided for the beloved mother's actual occu-pancy, as witness such tokens as a handkerchief, a tiny pincushion, dress-ing gown, slippers, and every needful toilet article."[121] But the beloved mother spent only that night and one other in her room.[122] In 1908, after the room had come to the attention of critics, she had the furnishings removed and the room closed.

The Sunday morning after her night in "Mother's Room," she appeared at the service, causing a sensation. She recited the Ninety-first Psalm and the hymn "Guide me, O thou great Jehovah."[123] The bylaw that she com-posed soon after this appearance stipulated that, henceforth, preaching was abolished in her church.[124] In its stead, she ordained "the BIBLE, and SCI-ENCE AND HEALTH WITH KEY TO THE SCRIPTURES, Pastor over The Mother Church . . . and they will continue to preach for this Church and the world."[125] She claimed that this rule of the "impersonal pastor," like so many of her other rules, was designed to abolish the importance of "personality" in her church; it had and continues to have the effect of elevating her personality above all others, making it impossible for any individual pastor or preacher to establish a following, to elucidate her teachings, or to serve as a figure of authority.[126] To this day, branch churches and the reading rooms they maintain have only limited autonomy and can make only minor changes to their own services.

The most democratic element of the *Manual* was its inclusion of application forms for membership in the Mother Church; indeed, just as the services and sacred texts of Christian Science were open to outsiders, so membership in the Mother Church was remarkably easy to come by. The forms (there were different versions for those who already had a Christian Science teacher and those who did not) required the applicant to sign a statement verifying that he or she did not belong to any other church (except a Christian Science branch church), made a practice of reading the Bible and *Science and Health* "understandingly," and accepted Church teachings. The only other information the applicant was required to divulge, aside from his name and address, was the name of his Christian Science teacher, if he had one; the form had to be countersigned by one Mother Church member. Children could not be born members of the Church, through the affiliation of their parents, but they were allowed to join at the age of twelve. Joining a Christian Science branch church (which was not required in order to join the Mother Church) was only slightly more complicated, involving an interview at which one might be asked if one was "free" of reliance on alcohol, tobacco, or medicinal drugs. The simplicity of the process of joining the Mother Church and its branches—requiring no lengthy examinations, memorization of texts or prayers, abstruse knowledge, or proofs that one could heal or had been healed—significantly contributed to the growth of Eddy's church. Many people who believe Eddy's teachings, however, join neither Mother Church nor branch and still consider themselves Christian Scientists.

The preface to Eddy's *Science and Health* includes this bold statement: "The time for thinkers has come."[127] But in her *Manual*, Eddy included several bylaws that would discourage Scientists from thinking too much and would limit and control what members of her church could read and write. One bylaw instructed every member who could afford it to subscribe to the Church periodicals. Another concerned "obnoxious books": "A member of this Church shall not patronize a publishing house that has for sale obnoxious books."[128] The bylaw concerning "Uncharitable Publications" prohibits Church members from publishing "an article that is uncharitable or impertinent towards religion, medicine, the courts, or the laws of our land."[129] Yet another, "No Incorrect Literature," forbids the buying, selling, or circulating of any Christian Science literature that is not "correct in its statement of the divine Principle and rules and the demonstration of Christian Science."[130] The "Obnoxious Books" bylaw does not define "obnoxious," but its phrasing does not merely forbid the *reading* of such books; it aims to punish those who sell them, by mandating Christian Science boycotts of any store selling books critical of or "obnoxious" to the Church.

Such rules are not particularly unusual in organized religions. Those who join churches are usually aware of the restrictions that may be placed upon them; Scientists certainly are. The Catholic Church has its famous Index of Forbidden Books. Mormons are discouraged from reading anything but "faith-promoting" materials and have been excommunicated for publishing books or articles critical of their church and its policies.[131]

But Eddy was not satisfied with censoring the reading of her own members. Deliberately, she attempted to censor the reading of those who are *not* Christian Scientists. And, through the Committee on Publication, a Church office created especially for the purpose, she has posthumously succeeded.

10. The C.O.P. and "The Corrective Work"

Josephine Curtis Woodbury—one of the most outrageous figures in a movement peopled by colorful characters—was the inspiration for Eddy's Committee on Publication. Woodbury began as one of Eddy's disciples in the 1870s and assumed the role of Christian Science teacher in 1886. Her penchant for melodrama reportedly rivaled Eddy's own; although she had never met Richard Kennedy, her teacher's great enemy, she assumed Eddy's animus toward him and appeared to be deeply fascinated with the powers and hazards of M.A.M.

Indeed, Woodbury's florid mimicry of Eddy's darkest fears and her popularity as a teacher most likely aroused her "Mother" 's suspicions regarding those who rose too high in the movement and threatened her exclusive leadership. In the 1880s, Woodbury opened her own Christian Science school in competition with the Massachusetts Metaphysical College. Eddy tolerated her until 1890, when Woodbury, married and already the mother of two children, gave birth to a baby boy. The joyous event was tainted by the fact that Woodbury had made it clear to her students that she had given up all sexual congress with her spouse in pursuit of her higher spiritual calling (a not uncommon pretension among early Scientists). Those in her inner circle surmised, accurately enough, that the infant derived from a liaison at Niagara Falls with a student and was not the offspring of her neglected husband.

Woodbury rose to the occasion. She announced that the child had been spiritually conceived through a preternatural understanding of Eddy's teachings on the superfluity of sex; Woodbury's was actually a radically exaggerated interpretation of Eddy's strange and confusing teachings on obstetrics. Gathering a group of her students around her, she baptized the little "Prince of Peace," as he was christened, in an extraordinary ceremony held in a tidal pool at Ocean Point, Maine, reading aloud from *Science and Health* one of Eddy's unlikeliest anecdotes: "It is related that a father plunged his infant babe, only a few hours old, into the water for several minutes, and repeated this operation daily, until the child could remain under water twenty minutes, moving and playing without harm, like a fish."[132] Woodbury attempted to follow suit with her own infant and, according to eyewitnesses, nearly drowned him.[133] When word of these proceedings reached Eddy, she was appalled but continued for several years to try to negotiate her fallen pupil back into her good graces. But after a series of second chances and rapprochements, in 1896 Woodbury found herself excommunicated from the Christian Science movement.

She was soon joined in disfavor by Eddy's adopted son, Foster Eddy, who had been tolerated by his "mother" for only a decade, roughly the same amount of time that Eddy's biological son had. Eddy broke with him permanently after several years of castigating him for his misdeeds: he was rumored to have had an affair with a married woman and, like Woodbury, seemed to crave power and attention. She often warned others against him, including her board of directors, on one occasion writing to Joseph Armstrong, "He will *ruin you* unless you defend yourself mentally against his influence. . . . What shall I do to defend the cause against him?"[134] In 1897, she exiled him from the movement.

Woodbury, for her part, did not go quietly. After her banishment, Eddy's apostate student began publishing subversive criticisms of her former teacher. When Mr. Woodbury, who had apparently accepted his wife's explanation of the miraculous addition to his family, died not long after her banishment, his widow attributed her loss to a species of M.A.M. practiced by Eddy. In June 1899, shortly after this latest effrontery, Eddy shot back in her Communion message to the Mother Church, making graphic reference to "this woman, 'drunken with the blood of the saints' . . . 'drunk with the wine of her fornication' . . . retaining the heart of the harlot and the purpose of the destroying angel." In case anyone had missed her point, Eddy added a ringing announcement of her triumph over this enemy: "The Babylonish woman is fallen, and who should mourn over the widowhood of lust, of her that 'is become the habitation of devils, and the hold of every foul spirit, and a cage of every unclean . . . bird'?"[135]

Woodbury sued for libel, claiming that Eddy's cutting remarks regarding "the Babylonish woman" were directed at her. She retained a lawyer named Frederick W. Peabody, who would become a relentless critic of Eddy's and a foe of her movement, instigating a great deal of negative press coverage, further lawsuits, and his own denunciatory books and articles. Although they eventually lost the nuisance suit, in 1901, Woodbury and Peabody, thorns in Eddy's side, subjected her to two agonizing years of litigation. Calvin Frye wrote in his diary on April 7, 1900:

> Mrs. Eddy had a severe experience all day yesterday being tormented with a sense of evil all day long. She found Clara told dressmakers wrong and thereby had her dress skirt made 1 ½ in. too short in back & spoiled. Laura & I both caused her trouble thro stupidity & sin so that she declared I was the cause of influencing others to abuse her. . . . An atmosphere & hate & revenge from testimony being taken in Montreal on W suit &c &c. . . .[136]

The emotional toll of the ordeal spurred Eddy, in 1900, to create the Committee on Publication, whose "duty" was, she wrote in the *Manual*:

> To correct in a Christian manner impositions on the public in regard to Christian Science, injustices done Mrs. Eddy or members of this Church by the daily press, by periodicals or circulated literature of any sort. This Committee on Publication shall be responsible for correcting or having corrected a false newspaper article which has not been replied to by other Scientists. . . . Furthermore, the Committee on Publication shall read the *last proof sheet* of such a [corrective] article and see that it is published according to copy.[137]

Eddy's dismay over her treatment by the press was sometimes warranted; the yellow journalists of Joseph Pulitzer's New York *World* and other tabloid papers followed and harassed her, publishing sensational and often inaccurate stories about her health, her net worth, and the goings-on in her household. There were stories about how she'd gone insane, and, on one occasion, premature speculation that she was dying or dead. The press's excitement over Eddy's doings, however, was often inspired by her own behavior: her feuds with former followers, such as Woodbury, the lawsuits and countersuits filed by those apostates and by herself, the dramatic and contradictory announcements she continually made in her own publications and in the major papers, including the *Boston Globe*. During her long reign as the head of the Church she founded, Mary Baker Eddy was news.

The Committee on Publication was—and is—the Church's watchdog, its strongman. It is a committee of one person, whose office is at the Mother Church, in Boston, but that one person functions as manager of Committees in every state in the country (one per state, two in California) and is supported by a large staff. Each Committee is a committee of one individual who answers to the manager. There are also, in accord with Eddy's directive, a plethora of one-man Committees in Canada, Great Britain, and Ireland and a few dozen more in countries that have enough of a Christian Science presence to warrant them. The Committee on Publication does not publish much besides its "corrective" articles and pamphlets and letters to the editor "correcting" what it takes to be errors. (The "Publishing Society" is the Church's publishing arm; Eddy seems to have been using "Publication" to refer to publications emanating from outside the Church.)

Interestingly enough, Eddy stipulated: "The Committees on Publication shall consist of men generally," and so they have, except when a "suitable man" was not to hand.[138] But the manager has always been a man. Many committeemen are lawyers who make it their business to keep a close eye not only on the press but on state legislatures, ever vigilant to guard against the passage of laws "restricting" the practice of Christian Science.

In her definition of the duties of the Committee on Publication, Eddy did not explain what she meant by such terms as "impositions" or "injustices," but the first man she chose for the job of manager, Alfred Farlow, a Christian Scientist from Kansas City, knew exactly what she meant. The word "imposition," in fact, means both burden and deception, and Farlow, with Eddy's blessing, began to treat all forms of critical comment on

Christian Science—indeed, anything that did not agree with the Christian Science view—as "lies" that placed an intolerable burden on the movement.[139] Describing the ideal man for the job, Farlow wrote: "He should understand the tricks of the evil one and know how to meet them and how to defend himself against evil mental influence."[140]

Following Farlow's lead, subsequent managers of the Committees have made it a policy to cultivate newspaper editors and reporters and to flatter legislators. Of editors, Farlow was patronizing: "I sit and chat with them, even listen to their yarns and laugh and joke with them. I accommodate them by reporting certain matters . . . I make them see that I am their friend and this serves as a barrier against the publication of things which they know are offensive to me."[141]

Libraries, too, have always received the special attentions of the Committees, who have taken their cue from Eddy's remarks in 1891: "The advantage of having *Science and Health* in the public libraries is very great. I would advise that the students see to it that a copy of the new revised *Science and Health* be put into the public libraries in the towns and cities where they reside."[142] Committees eventually went so far as to ask libraries for permission to paste labels identifying Church-approved books in all works pertaining to Eddy or Christian Science: "Where it is permitted, this list is pasted in both the approved and the unapproved books. In some libraries the approved books are segregated in the card indexes and so marked."[143]

The Committees on Publication may also have been responsible for urging Merriam-Webster to include dozens of Christian Science definitions in its dictionaries. For much of the past century, Merriam-Webster's definitions of such words as "truth" (*"cap, Christian Science* : GOD") and "principle" (*"cap, Christian Science* : a divine principle : GOD") have included Mary Baker Eddy's interpretations. Why and under what circumstances those definitions were added seems to have escaped the institutional memory of the Merriam-Webster Company. A spokesman for the firm believes that, long ago, "someone in Christian Science vetted" the definitions; the company is now considering dropping them from future editions.

But at the turn of the century, much of the Committees' work in the libraries, dictionaries, and legislatures of this land lay in the future. One of the Committees' first pieces of business was its attempt to correct the impositions of Eddy's most irritating, intemperate, and famous foe: Mark Twain.

11. Mark Twain and "That Shameless Old Swindler, Mother Eddy"

In July 1902, in a letter to the *Concord Monitor*, Mary Baker Eddy claimed that Christian Science would one day replace all other religions, prophesying that "Christian Science is destined to become the one and the only religion and therapeutics on this planet."[144] In the last decade of his life (it was the last decade of Eddy's life as well), Mark Twain grew to fear and hate Christian Science, becoming something of a crank on the topic. He grimly conceded the accuracy of Eddy's forecast, declaring Christian Science the "Standard Oil" of religion and predicting "that the new religion will conquer the half of Christendom in a hundred years."[145] Eddy and Twain were both wrong, but their predictions were understandable given the excitement surrounding the explosive growth of Christian Science at the turn of the century.

The religion could scarcely have failed to come to Twain's attention. The U.S. census of 1890 showed Church membership at 8,724; by the 1906 census, it had increased to 65,717.[146] In the first years of the century, Christian Science was being debated by Roman Catholic and Protestant clergy, some of whom termed the new sect demonic. Medical doctors attempted to legislate it out of existence, and editorialists vigorously debated the fate that awaited these bizarre religionists. Christian Science was so frequently the subject of rumor and sensational report in newspapers, magazines, books, and lecture halls that most Americans had an opinion about it and could discuss it in detail.

Twain's *Christian Science*, which appeared in 1907, was the first "obnoxious book," a compilation and expansion of articles he had published in *Cosmopolitan* in 1899 and the *North American Review* in 1902 and 1903. It seems to have been the first book that the Church attempted to suppress; initially, the attempt was successful. Harper & Brothers, Twain's publisher, advertised and took orders for the book in 1903 and then withdrew it for several years. Twain's explanation invoked the power of the Church:

> The Harpers considered the publication inexpedient, as it might injure the house with the Christian Scientists. . . . The situation is not barren of humor: I had been doing my very best to show in print that the Xn Scientist

cult was become a power in the land—well, here was proof: it had scared the biggest publisher in the Union![147]

Twain may have exaggerated the Church's influence, as he did else-where, but one Twain editor and scholar, Paul Baender, speculates that Harper & Brothers chose to wait and issue the book at a time when "Christian Science and Mary Baker Eddy were once again under strong attack in newspapers and periodicals, as they had not been in 1903."[148] The Harpers had earlier excluded the Christian Science material from one of Twain's collections but included it in British and German editions; this suggests that the publisher was concerned about the reaction of Scientists in America, where they were most numerous. (In 1901, for instance, there were 485 Christian Science churches in the United States, sixteen in Canada, and only two in Great Britain.)[149]

Certainly, the Committee on Publication attempted to intervene with Twain himself. William McCrackan, the C.O.P. for New York State, met with Twain several times and exchanged a series of letters with him. McCrackan, a writer himself, wrote a response to Twain's articles on Christian Science in the *North American Review* that Twain seems to have considered including in his own book; although this did not come to pass, Twain did include a number of footnotes correcting mis-takes that McCrackan had pointed out. The two became friendly for a time, Twain apologizing for abusive letters he had sent early on in their correspondence. But Twain was also meeting and corresponding with Frederick Peabody and Josephine Woodbury and seems to have been unable to reconcile McCrackan's genial nature with what he saw as the bizarre nature of Eddy's cult of personality. Twain ruefully wrote to McCrackan that he was occasionally impelled to rise in the middle of the night and write shrill, denunciatory letters to Eddy—whom he called "that shameless old swindler, Mother Eddy"—letters that he subsequently tore up.[150] Twain would never learn that McCrackan interpreted these letters as the result of Josephine Woodbury's mesmerism of him.[151] In fact, Twain's disdain for Eddy's character was prompted not by mesmerism but by despair.

In 1896, Samuel Clemens, desperate over the illness of his favorite daugh-ter, Susy, instructed his wife, Olivia Langdon Clemens, to consult a Christian Science practitioner. (Peel claims that Clemens had sought treatment himself from a practitioner in New York City during the 1890s and "benefited from the treatments.")[152] Susy died later that year, at the age of twenty-four, of spinal meningitis. Although Clemens blamed medical doctors for her death (he had quickly given up on the practitioner), the hope and frustration Christian Science had aroused continued to prey on his mind. When he began his first essay on Mrs. Eddy and her religion two years after Susy's death, in 1898, it was apparent that he was personally affronted by Eddy, who, with her imperious manner and whimsical pronouncements, may have reminded him uncomfortably of the dynamics of his own household. Scholars of Twain have noted an anxious, overinsistent quality in Twain's attacks on Christian Science and linked it to his distress over the illnesses of his wife and surviving daughters, illnesses which he clearly felt were psychosomatic and that possibly derived from his own, often tense dealings with them.[153]

After Susy's death, Twain's relationship to his wife and her maladies grew increasingly troubled. An invalid throughout her life, plagued by "nervous prostration" and paralyzed for two years in her youth, only to be raised to her feet again by a mind-healer named Dr. Newton, Olivia Clemens, who was more interested in medical and spiritual fads than in Christian Science, frequently sequestered herself from her husband for weeks at a time, believing that his bombastic, excitable behavior exacerbated her symptoms. It probably did; after years of psychosomatic illnesses, she suffered from heart problems during her final years. After Olivia's death in 1904, Twain's daughter Clara repeated the pattern of withdrawal, suffering a nervous breakdown and refusing to see her father or communicate with him for a year. His youngest daughter, Jean, an epileptic in an age when epilepsy was thought to be a form of mental illness, drowned in the bath during a seizure in 1909.

Olivia Clemens's chronic invalidism may well have been at the root of Twain's sarcastic endorsement of Christian Science as the perfect panacea for hypochondriacs:

How much of the pain and disease in the world is created by the imaginations of the sufferers, and then kept alive by those same imaginations? Fourfifths? Not anything short of that, I should think. Can Christian Science banish that four-fifths? I think so.[154]

Twain echoed this same sardonic admiration when his biographer Albert Bigelow Paine admitted to him that Christian Science had cured a nervous condition. According to Paine, Twain said to him,

Of course you have been benefited. Christian Science is humanity's boon. Mother Eddy deserves a place in the Trinity as much as any member of it. She has organized and made available a healing principle that for two thousand years has never been employed, except as the merest kind of guesswork. She is the benefactor of the age.[155]

Twain's sarcasm was lost not only on the Christian Scientists who have cited this passage as evidence that Twain recanted his harsh appraisal of Eddy, but also on his daughter Clara. The only one of Twain's children to outlive him, Clara defied her famous father by eventually converting to Christian Science. After his death, Clara Clemens, with Paine's help, censored the anti-Scientist statements in her father's autobiographical writings and published her own book, *Awake to a Perfect Day: My Experience with Christian Science*. It opens with the claim that her father's words to Paine were an expression of his "wholehearted reverence" for Christian Science.

Although not Twain's finest work, *Christian Science* is an impassioned, wickedly caustic book, hilarious, mocking, and occasionally mean-spirited. The structure suffers from a lack of coherence as Twain eviscerates one outrageous Eddy quotation after another, but he conveys the force of his subject's ego better than anyone else before or since. His analysis of her character and the quality of her writing is ruthlessly accurate. "None but a seasoned Christian Scientist can examine a literary animal of Mrs. Eddy's creation and tell which end of it the tail is on," he wrote. "She is easily the most baffling and bewildering writer in the literary trade."[156]

In an earlier essay, Twain had mocked Eddy for calling herself "Mother" and her Church "the Mother Church." In her "Reply to Mark Twain," published as a letter in the *New York Herald*, Eddy instructed her followers to drop "Mother" as her honorific, a title she had, in an earlier *Manual* bylaw, reserved for herself.[157] Not content to leave well enough alone, however, she also suggested, in typically ambiguous fashion, that she might "prove" to be something analogous to "Mother":

I have not the inspiration nor the aspiration to be a first or second Virgin-mother—her duplicate, antecedent, or subsequent. What I am remains to be proved by the good I do. We need much humility, wisdom, and love to perform the functions of foreshadowing and foretasting heaven within us. This glory is molten in the furnace of affliction.[158]

Twain knew false modesty and bad faith when he saw them. In his book he wrote, "Mrs. Eddy has herself created all these personal grandeurs and autocracies . . . . although she may regard 'self-deification as blasphemous,' she is as fond of it as I am of pie."[159]

In his assault on Eddy, Twain left no stylistic stone unturned, citing her for "affectations of scholarly learning, lust after eloquent and flowery expression, [and] repetition of pet poetic picturesqueness," and he apes her worst offenses.[160] He saw her pretensions to education, poetry, and breeding in practically every passage she wrote:

> She usually throws off an easy remark all sodden with Greek or Hebrew or Latin learning; she usually has a person watching for a star—she can seldom get away from that poetic idea. . . . she often throws out a Forefelt, or a Foresplendor, or a Foreslander where it will have a fine nautical foreto' gallant sound and make the sentence sing; after which she is nearly sure to throw discretion away and take to her deadly passion, Intoxicated Metaphor. At such a time the Mrs. Eddy that does not hesitate is lost.[161]

Twain's sharpest criticisms found their mark. Her denials and protestations to the contrary, Eddy was so stung by Twain's contempt that she not only dropped her controversial honorific title but also closed down the lavishly furnished "Mother's Room" in the Mother Church. Twain also savagely criticized her and her Church for a lack of organized charity, a charge that was, in part, unfair.[162] Eddy privately gave both small and large sums to a wide array of causes, including a local hospital near Concord, earthquake and flood victims, children's aid charities and orphanages, the Y.M.C.A. and the Masons, and to other religious communities or churches in need, even to a Shaker colony in New Hampshire after a fire.[163] But Twain was accurate enough in pointing out that the Church itself had as yet done little to organize or participate in charity work, believing, as Eddy taught, that the practice of Christian Science itself, with its healing effects on the world, was the finest form of charity.[164]

Whatever its flaws, Twain's critique of Christian Science and its Leader established a precedent that has never been overturned. Withering under the scorn of one of America's most beloved writers, the Church became perpetually defensive, a position it remains frozen in today.

12. Radical Reliance and Mrs. Eddy's Teeth

Among the ways in which Eddy was particularly "baffling and bewildering" as a writer were her ambiguity and her contradictions. Mark Twain had pointed this out for posterity, but those most affected by Eddy's inconsistent teachings—which are, for practical purposes, impossible to render coherent—were her own followers. Eddy neatly dismissed the problems created by the contradictions in *Science and Health* by declaring that "in this volume of mine there are no contradictory statements,—at least none which are apparent to those who understand its propositions well enough to pass judgment upon them."[165] For her followers, however, it has not been so easy.

Eddy had established a strict rule in *Science and Health*, known to Scientists forever after as the rule of "radical reliance." She wrote, "The scientific government of the body must be attained through the divine Mind. It is impossible to gain control over the body in any other way. On this fundamental point, timid conservatism is absolutely inadmissible. Only through radical reliance on Truth can scientific healing power be realized."[166] "Radical reliance" is just a single phrase in *Science and Health*, but it has come to govern many Scientists' lives. The passage in which it occurs seems to brook no alternative to absolute rejection of medical science and absolute reliance on Eddy's teachings.

But as quickly as Eddy made her rules, she broke them. And when her conduct—her breaking of the rules—became public, she was forced to devise exceptions to them that are every bit as bewildering as the rules themselves. One of the most extraordinary exceptions was contrived after it was revealed in a Boston newspaper in 1900 that Mrs. Eddy had been to the dentist and had had some of her teeth pulled.

Scientists had had no specific instructions from their Leader with regard to dental hygiene until Eddy's own dental problems came to light. The *Boston Herald* of December 2, 1900, reported that, at a meeting of the Episcopal Congress in Boston, a lecturer criticized Eddy for claiming to be able to cure diseases of the bone while she herself was known to have visited a dentist and to have had teeth extracted. Her reply was also published in the *Herald*:

> If I employ a dental surgeon, and he believes that the extraction of a
> tooth is made easier by some application or means which he employs, and I

object to the employment of this means, he thinks I must suffer because his method is interfered with. Therefore his mental force weighs against a painless operation, whereas it should be put in the same scale as mine, thus producing a painless operation as a logical result.[167]

While this explanation did not, perhaps, clarify matters, it was followed by notices placed by Eddy in the *Christian Science Sentinel* and *Journal* suggesting to Scientists that they might, if they wished, go to dentists.[168] And so they have, ever since, even though many of them are not able to explain where this loophole originated. (There is nothing in the *Manual* concerning teeth, although Eddy, in *Science and Health*, assures her readers that she knew a woman who, at ninety years of age, had somehow spontaneously generated "new teeth, incisors, cuspids, bicuspids, and one molar."[169]) Scientists often draw the line, however, at accepting painkillers, such as novocaine, and may postpone dental surgery while trying to heal themselves mentally.

The Scientific compromise with regard to dentists has come to haunt subsequent generations, particularly when juries sitting in judgment on Christian Science parents after a child has died without medical treatment have learned that the parents availed themselves of dental surgery.[170] The policy seems utterly irrational to outsiders, although it is oddly consistent with Eddy's concessions to physical reality. When some early followers questioned whether they needed to eat, she dashed their absolutist hopes: "To stop eating, drinking, or being clothed materially before the spiritual facts of existence are gained step by step, is not legitimate. When we wait patiently on God and seek Truth righteously, He directs our path."[171] When Scientists questioned whether it was really necessary to engage in sexual intercourse in order to bear children, she averred that "marriage is the legal and moral provision for generation among human kind."[172]

The Church, following Eddy's lead after the Abby Corner case, has also encouraged its members to employ the services of licensed doctors or midwives in childbirth. In an exception to what is known as the "no mixing" rule, practitioners are allowed to pray for expectant mothers who are under the care of obstetricians. The Church has justified this position by assuring members in this country that there are state laws requiring licensed doctors to be present at childbirth. In fact, there are no such laws, and some Scientists do bear their children at home, eschewing medical care. Many refuse drugs or procedures that are recommended by their obstetricians.

They reassure themselves that the Scientific method is superior; there are many testimonies suggesting that Christian Science has saved mother and child during difficult births when doctors found themselves at a loss.[173]

There are other loopholes as well, some of them big enough to drive an ambulance through. As with the exception allowing dental care, these exemptions from the law of radical reliance originated in Eddy's failure to heal herself mentally of her own illnesses and the encroaching effects of old age. She allowed that "it is better for Christian Scientists to leave surgery and the adjustment of broken bones and dislocations to the fingers of a surgeon," at least until there was a wider acceptance of the religion (although she followed this by asserting that "Christian Science is always the most skilful surgeon").[174] She urged Scientists who failed to receive aid from "their brethren" to consider "the right use of temporary and eternal means."[175] And any Scientist "seized with pain so violent that he could not treat himself mentally" might "call a surgeon, who would give him a hypodermic injection." The hypodermic, of course, was just one of those "temporary . . . means": "then, when the belief of pain was lulled, he could handle his own case mentally."[176] Tragically, however, she did not— perhaps could not—clarify her instructions.

Eddy inserted the latter passage regarding "hypodermic injection" in *Science and Health* in 1905. It was her way of acknowledging and rationalizing what had happened in 1903: at nearly eighty-two years of age, she had suffered several bouts of pain caused by renal calculi, or kidney stones, pain so severe and debilitating that she had called in a physician who diagnosed the illness and administered morphine.[177] She did not, however, edit her writings to remove either the "radical reliance" statement or other passages dissuading Scientists from accepting medical aid.

While a non-Scientist might read these loopholes and interpret them to sanction surgery and drugs for those not helped by Christian Science, Scientists have developed their own unique interpretations. The "hypodermic" passage is strictly interpreted as allowing only painkilling medication in extreme instances where an individual has lost the ability to pray for himself, but it is worth noting that Scientists routinely refuse painkillers for themselves and their children, even in the most extreme cases of pain caused by cancer and other life-threatening diseases and accidents. The surgery passage—even though, as written, it allows "surgery *and* the adjustment of broken bones"—is generally taken to refer only to the setting of broken bones.[178] It is thus far more common for Scientists to allow themselves a cast on a broken bone than to allow themselves surgery. Surgery itself is generally considered to be completely at odds with Christian Science practice, and practitioners are instructed never to "mix" Christian Science with medical care and to refuse to treat any Scientist who is undergoing a surgical procedure or receiving drugs. "'Temporary means,'" according to Robert Peel, "have been taken to include crutches, eyeglasses, hearing aids, nursing care without medication, the setting of a broken bone by a surgeon, and other expedients obviously not intended to heal the impairment or diseased condition but to help a person carry on in some fashion until a genuine healing could take place."[179] Scientists often refer to such things as walkers or canes as "mechanical" aids. These physical aids that exist outside the body, while occasionally frowned upon, are clearly more tolerable to Scientists than anything intrusive that must penetrate, be taken into, or be placed inside the body: drugs, surgery, implants, etc. It is also common for Scientists to refuse to hear diagnoses of their own or others' medical conditions, following Eddy's instructions to "avoid speaking aloud the name of the disease," believing that "talking disease" allows it greater power over the mind.[180]

Scientists are never excommunicated from the Mother Church for availing themselves of medical care, but if they acknowledge having relied upon drugs or surgery, they may be stripped of positions they hold within their branch church until they can prove that they have once again freed themselves of such means. Christian Science practitioners, nurses, and nursing homes will not treat those who have recently strayed from the path of radical reliance. The Mother Church has routinely removed practitioners and teachers from their official positions after finding that the officials had either accepted medical treatment for themselves or turned a blind eye to it in patients or students.[181]

For legal reasons, the official Church emphasizes repeatedly that all decisions about whether to rely on Christian Science or to turn to medical care are the province of the individual. In practice, however, this issue is far more gray than black-and-white. The Church's disclaimers, insisting that every decision concerning health care is left up to the individual Christian Scientist, fail to take into account the ineffable but nonetheless powerful peer pressure that urges Scientists to follow the official teachings. Christian Science is a way of life as much as it is a religion, and sociologists have noted that Scientists often socialize largely with other Scientists.

No Christian Scientist wants his fellow church members to know that he is flouting accepted practice. The disclaimers also echo the ambiguity of Eddy's own statements about medicine, surgery, and drugs in which she seems to permit Scientists access to such methods with one breath and then belittles them with the next.

13. The "Excelsior Extension" and the "Next Friends"

The last years of Eddy's life were chaotic. Increasingly frail, she was racked by recurrent bouts of pain caused by kidney stones, fears of malicious animal magnetism, the attacks of critics, and disappointment in her hand-picked leaders. Biographical accounts of Eddy's final decade vary sharply. Peel contends that Eddy was robust and lucid to the end; Edwin Franden Dakin describes her as physically and mentally feeble. Julius Silberger may be right in suggesting that Eddy had good days and bad, appearing at times hearty, at times frail, depending on whether she was suffering physical pain. It was one of her attacks of renal calculi that seems to have precipitated the most famous lawsuit of Eddy's later years, the so-called Next Friends suit of 1907 in which it was argued that she was senile, incompetent to conduct her own affairs, financial and otherwise, and in thrall to her household workers, most notably Calvin Frye.

The suit was prompted, in part, by Eddy's increasing reclusiveness, which gave rise to exaggerated rumors; she compounded the suspicions of the press by her eccentric behavior. In June 1904, Eddy had not made an expected personal appearance at a service in the new Christian Science branch church in Concord, New Hampshire, near Pleasant View, to which she had donated most of the construction funds. Instead, she drove by in a closed carriage, only stopping for a moment and refusing to emerge. Secretaries handled more and more of her correspondence and refused all requests for interviews.[182]

Even more remarkably, she failed to attend the dedication of the new "Excelsior Extension" of the Mother Church in June 1906, an occasion so grand that her absence could not help but attract attention. The planning of a new church, less than a decade after the Mother Church was completed, was inspired, in part, by the rapid growth of the movement, which the original building could no longer accommodate. It was also, apparently, inspired by jealousy. In 1903, Augusta Stetson, one of Eddy's most fervent and energetic practitioners, had founded and built the First Church of Christ, Scientist, in New York City, a grand Gothic pile of a building on the corner of Central Park West and Ninety-sixth Street. When it was finished, it was the largest Christian Science church in the world; it apparently inspired the Board of Directors in Boston to begin plans immediately for the Extension to the Mother Church, so that the Boston church would not long be eclipsed.

As had been the case with the original Mother Church, the building of the Extension was fraught with complications and delays incited by M.A.M.; Eddy instructed her Board of Directors to form a special committee to protect the architects mentally.[183] She ordained through a new *Manual* bylaw that the original church could never be demolished or removed, thus complicating considerably the plans for the new church, which was to be built on adjacent property and would seat four or five thousand.[184] The enormous Extension had to be grafted onto the original structure; it shares a wall with the Mother Church and is connected to it by a passageway. John Valentine Dittemore, the disgruntled former Director of the Church said, not inaccurately, that on the "broad cheek" of the Extension, "the little Mother Church stuck out like a wart."[185]

The new building was as grandiose as the old one was modest; Peel acknowledges that it has "a touch of both St. Peter's and Santa Sophia about it."[186] It transformed the Mother Church by projecting an enormous new structure out from its back wall: an extraordinary wedding-cake Renaissance basilica with rows of arched windows, balustrades, and columns. Inside, seven balconies look down on an auditorium of twenty-five thousand square feet, unobstructed by columns, furnished with a Reader's platform of imported marble. It was furnished with a mile and a half of mahogany pews and one of the largest pipe organs in the world. Throughout the building dozens of inscriptions line the walls, matched quotations from Paul and Mrs. Eddy, Luke and Mrs. Eddy, John and Mrs. Eddy, Christ Jesus and Mrs. Eddy. It was and is still the largest church in the city of Boston, its vast dome an instant landmark, its spire topping even the Bunker Hill Monument.[187] Mary Baker Eddy never set foot in it.[188]

The ostensible reason, hints Peel, who glosses over her absence, was Eddy's stern disapproval of materialism, her refusal to partake of "the American worship of the great bitch-goddess Success."[189] In fact, Eddy, who had approved the floor plan and other details of the building, was too ill to attend; she had suffered from pain throughout the winter of 1905–1906.[190] She did, however, send a message. "The modest edifice of The Mother Church of Christ, Scientist, began with the cross," it concluded. "Its excelsior extension is the crown. . . . Methinks this church is the one edifice on earth which most prefigures self-abnegation, hope, faith; love catching a glimpse of glory."[191]

She missed an extraordinary occasion. On June 10, 1906, Christian Scientists took over Boston: crowds brought by special trains gathered at dawn for the first of six services; the church's chimes played Eddy's hymns throughout the day; congregations five thousand strong recited the Lord's Prayer in unison. This unprecedented event in American religious history was covered by newspapers from all over the world, which noted with awe that some $2 million had been raised to pay for the vast project in full and that the Church treasurer had requested that no more donations be given.[192] At the first testimonial meeting in the new church the following Wednesday, crowds packed the Extension, the original church, and seven additional large halls in the neighborhood, spilling out into the streets as hundreds of Scientists arose to testify to the healing power of their faith, calling out the names of their hometowns: " 'Chicago!' 'London!' 'Kalamazoo!' 'Habana!' 'San Francisco!' 'Wichita!' 'Dresden!' 'Peoria!' 'Indianapolis!' 'Duluth!' "[193]

While Scientists basked in the sympathetic attention of the world, however, Eddy herself would not benefit from it. Later that year, the *New York World*, aware as ever that Eddy and her church made for some of the best copy of the day and eager to compete with *McClure's Magazine*, which was rumored to be preparing an exposé of Eddy's life, began intensively investigating the situation at Pleasant View, hoping to discover what had kept Eddy from attending the dedication of the Extension. In October 1906, the *World* ran an outrageously speculative and wildly inaccurate article—MRS. MARY BAKER G. EDDY DYING / FOOTMAN AND "DUMMY" CONTROL HER— alleging that Eddy was dying of cancer while Frye, the "Supreme Power" and evil henchman of her household, held her purse strings firmly in his hands.[194] Of course, the truth was much the reverse: Eddy controlled Frye more than Frye controlled Eddy. But the mysteriousness that surrounded life at Pleasant View—Eddy's increasing reclusiveness and her household's inability to deal with the press in an open and straightforward way— worked against Eddy's stated desire for privacy, attracting attention rather than repelling it.

Meanwhile, George Glover had begun to have his own suspicions. In 1903, he had visited his mother and found her in a paranoid state, talking incessantly of M.A.M. and the plots against her, including attacks on her life. She had always behaved in contradictory fashion toward him, treating him contemptuously in some letters, affectionately in others; refusing to see him, then relenting. In 1899, she had made him a gift of an elaborate mansion in Lead, South Dakota. An itinerant gold panner and millworker, he had never made the kind of money required to live in the style that the house seemed to warrant. But when he asked her for money for its upkeep and to start his own business, she refused, saying that Calvin Frye wouldn't let her spend any more on him. This, in fact, was not true—she had full control over her own money—but her attempt to put Glover off seems to have excited his anxieties and resentments.

In 1907, Joseph Pulitzer, the owner and publisher of the *World* and himself something of a recluse, decided to smoke Eddy out by engineering a lawsuit alleging that she was not in control of her own affairs. Pulitzer was apparently hoping not only to sell papers but to steal some thunder from his rivals at *McClure's*, whose multipart series on Eddy was announced in its December 1906 issue. Feminist biographers have noted, with some justification, that Pulitzer's machinations were not only greedy but sexist, trading on the public perception of old women as feebleminded and hysterical; Eddy's own comment, made to one of her household, that "if I were a man, they would not treat me so" undoubtedly has a great deal of truth in it.[195] What is also true is that Eddy's paranoia to some extent played into Pulitzer's hands; it both spurred the lawsuit to come and was spurred by it.

A reporter from the *World* was sent to persuade George Glover, who theoretically stood to lose the most if his mother was indeed being exploited by her minions and who had always resented Frye's interference in his relationship with his mother, to file the suit. Glover initially resisted the idea but was moved to take action after he met again with his mother and detected confusion in her responses to his questions. She had gotten wind of the possibility of a lawsuit being filed and begged him to return letters she had written him, letters that documented her fears and rages. While he was in Washington, D.C., conferring with a lawyer Pulitzer had hired to prepare the filing, she sent him a telegram offering him money to encourage him to return home:

> DONT LOSE ANY TIME HURRY HOME AND GET THE
> MONEY THAT I HAVE SENT TO LEAD CITY ENJOY IT[196]

In March 1907, George Glover; his daughter, Mary Baker Glover; and one of Eddy's nephews, George W. Baker, legally declared themselves the "next friends," or closest relatives, of Eddy and filed suit in her name against Calvin Frye and a number of other members of her household, alleging that she was incompetent to handle her affairs. Several days later, Eddy's estranged adopted son, Ebenezer Foster Eddy, and another Eddy nephew, Fred W. Baker, signed on as additional "next friends." They all petitioned the Superior Court in Concord, New Hampshire, to appoint a receiver to handle Eddy's property, thereby attempting to withdraw it from the control of Frye and the others. Not surprisingly, one of the lawyers representing the "next friends" was Eddy's old nemesis, Frederick Peabody.

Eddy retaliated by placing her property in a trust administered by three men: Archibald McLellan, a member of the Church's Board of Directors; Henry Baker, one of Eddy's cousins; and Josiah Fernald, a president of Eddy's bank. The trustees asked the court to make them the petitioners in the suit, thereby eliminating the "next friends" entirely; the court demurred, but declared that if Eddy was found competent to have formed the trust, then the original petitioners—and the suit—would be dismissed. This led to the examination of Mrs. Eddy by a panel of three appointed masters of the court, consisting of an alienist, or forensic psychologist of the day; a judge; and an attorney. By all accounts, she acquitted herself well, being in good health at the time of the interview. As a critical biographer of Eddy later wrote, "No one who heard Mrs. Eddy talk to the distinguished Masters could have believed her any less competent to manage her business affairs than any other old lady of her years."[197]

Before the masters could render their verdict on Mrs. Eddy's sanity, the petition was dropped. But the whole affair left her shaken, and 1907 continued to be a year of assaults on her equilibrium.

A month after the "next friends" suit was filed, Mary Tomlinson, sister of Irving Tomlinson, both of whom had been Readers at the Concord Church for many years and together formed Eddy's "Committee on Business," which was to provide her with "metaphysical" support, jumped from a window of Boston's Parker House Hotel one floor below where the "next friends" and their lawyers were gathered to discuss their strategy. According to one account, Mary Tomlinson

> had become deranged because of her horror at being asked to "treat" Mrs.
> Eddy's son George and his lawyer by putting metaphysical arsenical poison

into their veins, or by killing them by any other means at her imagination. Christian Science was denying officially that it used absent treatment to harm anyone, and Miss Tomlinson was . . . so disillusioned by the recrudescence of the old practices that she repudiated Mrs. Eddy, became depressed, and killed herself.[198]

Irving Tomlinson later wrote a sycophantic memoir, *Twelve Years with Mary Baker Eddy: Recollections and Experiences,* in which his sister's suicide is never mentioned.[199]

In December 1907, Joseph Armstrong, one of Eddy's Board members, died suddenly. Mrs. Eddy became convinced that the entire state of New Hampshire was suffering from malicious animal magnetism, and in January 1908, under conditions of great secrecy, she moved from Pleasant View to a thirty-four-room mansion in the neighborhood of Chestnut Hill, in Boston. By special arrangement with the railroad authorities, Mrs. Eddy and her entourage were transported in a private train, preceded by an extra engine. Like the food tasters in the house of the Borgias, it was sent on ahead as an indicator of danger. The Chestnut Hill house had been renovated at great expense "to reproduce exactly the arrangement of the rooms with which she was familiar at Pleasant View," but Mrs. Eddy immediately ordered another round of renovation, finding the rooms too large.[200] She is said to have exclaimed on seeing her new home, "O splendid misery!"[201]

14. Willa Cather's Secret

The publication of and reaction to the *McClure's Magazine* series about Eddy, eventually collected into a book, was—and continues to be—a multifaceted drama encompassing the rich eccentricity of Eddy's character, her intolerance of criticism, and the institutional engine of censorship and suppression she set in motion. The long-running series and the subsequent book, *The Life of Mary Baker G. Eddy and the History of Christian Science,* were published under the name of Georgine Milmine, a Canadian who ultimately married of a newspaperman in Rochester, New York. Milmine, about whom little is known, had studiously compiled—apparently with some help from those industrious Eddy enemies Frederick Peabody and Josephine Woodbury—an impressive collection of documentary sources concerning Eddy.

But Milmine was not, in fact, the true author. It was ultimately revealed, some eighty-five years after the articles first appeared, that Willa Cather wrote most of the articles that became the book. At the time the articles appeared, Cather was a young editor at *McClure's*. She suppressed her role in writing *The Life*, apparently because of a distaste for the notoriety that ensued and a desire that her reputation as a writer of fiction not be sullied by this controversial nonfiction work.[202]

The connection, however, was long suspected by her biographers. In 1922, Cather wrote to Edwin Anderson, the director of the New York Public Library, who had questioned her about her work on the series, and admitted that she had written all of the articles, except for the first install-ment, based on materials collected by Milmine and purchased by McClure. She said that McClure had chosen her for the job because he felt she was unprejudiced and had no ax to grind with regard to Christian Science. She had enjoyed the work, which involved traveling around New England and completing the research Milmine had started, but had no interest in own-ing up to her role in writing the pieces or defending them. There was some irony, she noted, in the fact that Milmine did not write a word of the book that bore her name.[203]

The *McClure's* series was anything but flattering to its subject. It exposed Eddy's vanity, her fabrications and exaggerations about her past, and the intrigues of her bizarre household. The articles *were* sensational exposés, as the Church has emphasized over and over again. What the Church leaves out of its denunciation of them as yellow journalism, how-ever, is the fact that the articles were also documented and fact-checked.[204] Both Cather and Milmine had interviewed many of those still living who had known Eddy during the years before she "discovered" Christian Science, and they collected numerous sworn affidavits testifying to Eddy's eccentricities, which included her desire, long into adulthood, to be rocked in special couches or cradles constructed for the purpose.

Eddy's representatives tried to quash the series before it started. A biog-raphy of McClure, *Success Story: The Life and Times of S. S. McClure*, by Peter Lyon, relates the story of how three Christian Science officials con-fronted Witter Bynner, the poet and playwright who was managing editor of *McClure's* when the series on Eddy appeared, in the editorial offices of the magazine before the articles' publication. They demanded to see McClure himself:

> The Christian Scientists came in. Before they sat down, they stood on chairs and closed the transoms over the two doors to the room. Then they

made their demand: the series must not be published. S.S. scowled at them and said nothing. To fill the silence, Bynner began rather nervously to assure the Scientists that the articles were not sensational, not offensive; that there was no cause for apprehension; that all the facts had been most carefully verified. . . .

One of the Scientists cut in to suggest that perhaps there would be no objection to publication of the material if the Scientists were permitted to edit it as they might please.[205]

McClure refused to entertain any such proposition; before the Scientists left his office, they let him know that "he would soon notice a distinct loss of advertising in his magazine."[206] Lyon notes that "advertising lineage in McClure's did decrease, during and after publication of the series on Christian Science," but he insists there was "no cause-and-effect relationship."[207]

Legend has it that Christian Scientists bought and destroyed many copies of the Milmine book and continually borrowed or stole them from libraries in order to prevent their circulation.[208] There were reports that the copyright was purchased by a Scientist and that the plates from which the book was printed were destroyed. The Mother Church acquired the original manuscript. Few reviews of the book appeared, apparently because editors feared the consequences of offending Christian Science advertisers and readers.

In any event, The Life disappeared from circulation almost immediately; the Christian Scientists essentially succeeded in suppressing it for the entire time in which it was under copyright. The book would not be reprinted until 1971, after it entered the public domain, when the Baker Book House, a Christian publishing firm, reissued it "in the interest of fairness and objectivity."[209] Until then it was virtually unobtainable except in a few libraries, and, as one observer remarked, any reader was "likely to have to borrow the only copy from the chief librarian's safe, and be watched by a detective while reading it."[210] This is no exaggeration. Even today, in the card catalogue volumes in the New York Public Library, the cards for controversial books concerning Eddy and Christian Science carry cautionary notes restricting the use of these books to "the Cage," a room under the watchful supervision of a librarian.

In the introduction to the University of Nebraska Press edition of 1993, the scholar David Stouck noted that the book had originally carried for Christian Scientists "the same heretical status as Salman Rushdie's Satanic

Verses does to many Muslims today."[211] The press would soon discover that it still did. When Victor Westberg, then manager of the Committees on Publication, learned of Nebraska's plans, he called the press, expressing "great fear" that the reprint would scar the reputation of the Church and Mrs. Eddy. It eventually became clear to the press, which was primarily interested in disclosing Cather's authorship of the book and its importance in her development as a writer, that Westberg "felt it was his responsibility to try to bully us into stopping publication or into saying that the book was worthless." Finally, fearing for the jobs of those in the Church archives who had helped his researcher uncover the Cather-"Milmine" manuscripts, Stouck agreed to issue a statement, printed separately from the book. It read like the Church press release that it essentially was:

> Since the [University of Nebraska] re-issue of *The Life of Mary Baker G. Eddy and the History of Christian Science* went to press new materials have come to light which suggest that Ms. Eddy's enemies may have played a significant role in organizing the materials for the "Milmine" biography. New information about Georgine Milmine, moreover, suggests that she would have welcomed biased opinion for its sensational and commercial value. The exact nature of Willa Cather's part in the compiling and writing of the biography remains, accordingly, a matter for further scholarly investigation.[212]

In fact, there is no "new information." The Church unearthed items in its files—letters of Alfred Farlow and other early Church figures—attesting to the fact that Milmine, and later Cather, used sources suggested by Peabody and Woodbury, which hardly invalidates the book. The question, with any sources, including biased ones, is: Do the facts stand up? In the case of the *McClure's* articles, they largely did.[213] The only specific mistake the Church has uncovered is that a photo thought to be of Eddy and used to illustrate the editorial announcement of the *McClure's* series turned out to be a photo of the mother of one of her followers. On all other details of the work, however, the Church is silent.

At the Church's 1993 annual meeting—the annual meetings are open to the membership—Victor Westberg gave a report in which he boasted of his success in correcting this particular imposition:

> A major corrective opportunity this year involved the rerelease of one of the earliest malicious biographies of Mrs. Eddy, *The Life of Mary Baker G.*

Eddy and the History of Christian Science by Georgine Milmine. Dating from the yellow journalism period, this book was published in an attempt to discredit her. The current publisher, after much correspondence with our office, instead issued a statement accurately characterizing its bias. The book has received almost no attention in the public, proving if Truth isn't spoken, nothing is said.[214]

The anxiety inspired in the Church by even the most innocent scholarly interest in Eddy originates, of course, with Eddy herself. Eddy initially objected to the publication of the first official biography sympathetic to her, *The Life of Mary Baker Eddy,* by Sibyl Wilbur O'Brien, which was financed by her followers. O'Brien was a journalist who had earlier interviewed Eddy for a magazine called *Human Life;* although not a Scientist, she experienced a conversion to Eddy's cult of personality the moment she met her. She was so enamored of her subject that she bowed to the Christian Scientists' prejudice by acceding to their request that she drop her married name from the book, because it was "considered to smack of Irish Catholic antecedents."[215] In 1908, learning that the Wilbur biography had appeared in bookstores without her knowledge, Eddy instructed Alfred Farlow: "Put it into the public notice to-night that I forbid the publication of my history or autobiography [*sic*] by Sibyl Wilbur or any other person without my written endorsement or consent."[216] Eddy was eventually persuaded to grant her approval of this lavishly sympathetic biography when it was pointed out to her that the only existing alternative was the fearsome "Georgine Milmine" "attack."[217]

Around the same time, Eddy paid a handsome sum, "amounting to many thousands of dollars," to another journalist, Michael Meehan, the Catholic editor of the Concord, New Hampshire, *Patriot,* also sympathetic to her cause, to withdraw the book he had written at her request about the Pulitzer lawsuit, *Mrs. Eddy and the Late Suit in Equity.* After five thousand copies had been printed, Eddy decided that the book, which exonerated her, would "keep alive a memory of bitterness and discord," and she wrote to Meehan:

> You will render me a statement of all expenses to which you have been put. Make liberal allowance for those who have aided you in the work. Put a value upon your own time and service while engaged on it, and when you have done this, double the value you have placed on your own work, and double it again, and then send me the bill.[218]

There is some irony in the fact that the Church has also attempted to suppress some of the early works of Mary Baker Eddy herself. Preserved in the papers of the New York Public Library's Edwin Anderson is a letter to Willa Cather describing Scientists' attempted suppression of the first edition of Eddy's *Science and Health*, a volume so controversial within the movement that its very presence in the Church archives has reportedly inspired fear in those who work there.[219] The first edition of Eddy's textbook remains troublesome to the Church because its stream-of-consciousness style, its uncertain grammar, and the variations in theological points between it and later editions call into question Eddy's claim that *Science and Health* was divinely inspired.

Eddy herself, however, had no problem with her inconsistencies and recommended that her followers keep *all* editions of her books, for comparative study. She instructed them, on the publication of the fiftieth edition (which was far from the last): "*Do not attempt to dispose of the earlier editions. . . .* Fortunate is he who has all former revisions, together with the original edition of 1875! . . . Keep them all; they will prove a '*treasure trove.*' Again: Let the new volume be studied *in connection with earlier editions.* The very contrasts help to see how the thoughts have risen only as we have been able to receive them."[220] Mark Twain surmised that Eddy's injunction to buy and keep all the editions as they appeared must have been motivated by simple greed, but Eddy's hunger for approval, attention, and love—her need to see everything connected with herself as a "treasure trove"—far exceeded any lust for mere money.

15. "Call It the Christian Science Monitor"

Despite the dispiriting events of these years, Eddy was gaining the approval she craved. In 1908, Clara Barton, founder of the American Red Cross, said of Eddy in a newspaper interview, "Love permeates all the teachings of this great woman,—so great, I believe, that at this perspective we can scarcely realize how great,—and looking into her life history we see nothing but self-sacrifice and selflessness. Never has Mrs. Eddy tried to bring her personality before the public."[221]

The confidence inspired by such endorsements, as well as her residual anger over the attacks of Pulitzer's *World*, may have contributed to Eddy's decision, in 1908, to strike out in a new direction and provide her followers with an energizing project to rally them: she founded a newspaper, the

Christian Science Monitor. She had been pondering the idea for some years. In 1896, she wrote,

> An organ from the Christian Scientists has become a necessity. After looking over the newspapers of the day, very naturally comes the reflection that it is dangerous to live, so loaded seems the very air with disease. These descriptions carry fears to many minds, to be depicted in some future time upon the body.[222]

Increasingly, as the millennium approached, Eddy had turned her gaze to politics and human affairs. A national furor over yellow journalism had exploded in 1898, when sensational reporting in newspapers owned by William Randolph Hearst and Joseph Pulitzer had inflamed popular opinion about the outbreak of the Spanish-American War. In 1899, she announced to Church members gathered at the Mother Church for her annual Communion address: "I reluctantly foresee great danger threatening our nation,—imperialism, monopoly, and a lax system of religion. But the spirit of humanity, ethics, and Christianity sown broadcast—all concomitants of Christian Science—is taking strong hold of the public thought throughout our beloved country and in foreign lands, and is tending to counteract the trend of mad ambition."[223]

Eddy had always seen Christian Science as the means to save the world. In *Science and Health,* she interpreted Jesus' parable of the woman, hiding three measures of leaven, or yeast, in a lump of meal, as a parable of Christian Science, hidden in plain sight until the whole world was leavened by it: "Did not this parable point a moral with a prophecy, foretelling the second appearing in the flesh of the Christ, Truth, hidden in sacred secrecy from the visible world? Ages pass, but this leaven of Truth is ever at work. It must destroy the entire mass of error."[224] The *Monitor* would be yet another form of leaven, transforming "the entire mass of error" that was Eddy's view of the world outside her doors.

In March 1908, John L. Wright, a Christian Scientist and a newspaperman, wrote to Eddy encouraging her to establish a newspaper. In August of that year, she sent this command to the Trustees of the Christian Science Publishing Society:

> It is my request that you start a daily newspaper at once, and call it the Christian Science Monitor. Let there be no delay. The Cause demands that it be issued now.[225]

Wright and others advised her to leave the words "Christian Science" out of the title of the paper, but she refused.

The establishment of the *Monitor* was undoubtedly the most brilliant of all Eddy's organizational maneuvers; for decades, the *Monitor* would be the ambassador of the religion, the public face that the Church turned to the world, friendly, fair, intelligent, and impartial, dedicated not to sensationalism but to measured analysis. But the *Monitor* was not merely good public relations; it was nothing less than the savior of mankind. It was the Trojan horse of Christian Science; dressed as newspapermen, Scientists would glide past the defenses of a secular and scornful world and deliver the moral essence of Christian Science to those who didn't even know they needed it. Editor after editor of the *Monitor* has employed Eddy's reading of the parable of the leaven to define the paper's mission, "dedicated," in the words of one, "to the task of leavening human thinking."[226] Whatever missionary spirit Scientists had was invested in the *Monitor*.

The *Monitor* was never intended to be merely a Boston paper. Long before the *New York Times* developed into a national newspaper and before the appearance of other modern national papers, such as *USA Today*, the *Monitor* fashioned itself not only as a national organ, but as an international one, specifically because of the missionary role assigned it by its creator. Just weeks before the appearance of the paper, Archibald McLellan, its first editor, announced in an editorial published in the *Christian Science Sentinel:*

> It will be the mission of the Monitor to publish the real news of the world in a clean, wholesome manner, devoid of the sensational methods employed by so many newspapers. There will be no exploitation or illustration of vice and crime, but the aim of the editors will be to issue a paper which will be welcomed in every home where purity and refinement are cherished ideals. . . . From the "news" standpoint the Monitor will be of far wider scope than a merely local daily would cover and will be read with interest from Maine to California and from Canada to Mexico. Even our friends across the sea will find the Monitor interesting from this standpoint.[227]

The first issue of the paper was published on November 25, 1908. It was twelve pages, packed with advertising drummed up by enthusiastic Christian Science salesmen, featuring a front-page story on the building of the Charles River Dam, as well as the first in a prophetic series on the crisis in the Balkans, an early instance of the kind of international reporting that would make the *Monitor*'s reputation.[228] In an unusual move for that time, the entire back page was devoted to editorials, of which Mrs. Eddy wrote the first. In it, she proclaimed that the aim of the *Monitor* was "to spread undivided the Science that operates unspent." Its object was "to injure no man, but to bless all mankind."[229]

From the beginning, the *Monitor* was truly unique. According to postal regulations and tax law, it was a religious newspaper; but in the eyes of the world that read it, it seemed a regular newspaper, not a denominational paper or house organ for Christian Science.[230] With few exceptions, the only overt religious content appeared in its single daily religious article, labeled as such.[231] And yet every article in the *Monitor*—and every photograph, every headline, every decision behind every feature—would be informed by religious principles. As one of its editors wrote, "Christian Science thinking does indeed underlie all the conclusions presented in *The Christian Science Monitor*."[232] Instead of emphasizing negative developments in dramatic and sensational ways, it would report the facts constructively, emphasizing possible solutions to conflict, or progress toward resolution. It would refuse to engage in sensationalism of any kind, generally eschewing coverage of crimes or disasters unless they had a significant bearing on social issues of the day.

The *Monitor* would develop its own idiosyncratic house style based on the principles that inspired it. Scientists did not believe in using alcohol, tobacco, stimulants, or drugs, so the paper would not advertise them; it would also refuse to publish photographs depicting drinking or smoking, even retouching images to remove offending cigarettes or glasses of whiskey or wine.[233] For a time in the 1920s, it refused to countenance references to "jazz bands" and "ballroom dancing," which were thought to be racy.[234] Its coverage of medical news was, as might be expected, extremely limited. It developed a whole new genre of obituary writing, preferring, on the occasion of the deaths of prominent public figures, to publish analyses of careers or appreciations of the accomplishments of newsworthy souls who had "passed on."[235] It was traditionally so decorous in its language and approach that one apocryphal anecdote circulated to the effect that the caption under a photograph of a World War I battlefield littered with the corpses of pack animals alluded to "passed-on mules."[236]

Its editor in chief met weekly not with a secular publisher or owner but with the Board of Directors of the Christian Science Church, which directed its coverage of world events.[237] It was a newspaper that set out to reform journalism but its "clean, wholesome manner" and muted presentation of Christian Science principles was also intended to reform something much larger: the ways of a materialistic world.

16. The Stetson Problem

Before she died, Mary Baker Eddy made sure that there would be no leader after her. There is considerable evidence that, like many leaders of religious movements, she could not bear to establish a successor, an heir to her position in Christian Science. The adoption of Foster Eddy had been her one step in this direction, but she had stepped back soon enough. In concluding the "next friends" suit, she had mollified Foster Eddy and her own son with financial settlements that were guaranteed them if they did not challenge her will. Now, in the last two years of her life, she set out to vanquish the only woman who had ever shown enough authority and charisma to replace her, Mrs. Augusta Stetson.

Born in 1842, Augusta Stetson discovered Christian Science during its early years. Living in Somerville, a suburb of Boston, she was struggling to support herself and her husband, who was afflicted with heart damage caused by rheumatic fever contracted while a prisoner of the Confederates during the Civil War. Stetson wrote in a memoir: "During the spring of 1884, I heard of several cases of Christian Science healing in Boston and was invited to attend a lecture which was to be given by Mrs. Eddy. . . . I went to the lecture weighted with care and nearly prostrated from the effects of watching for one year in the room of an invalid husband. During this lecture I lost all sense of grief, physical weakness, and prostration."[238] That winter, Eddy encouraged Stetson to attend her Primary class in Christian Science, waiving the tuition; by the following year, Stetson, who had been pursuing a career as an elocutionist and public speaker before discovering Science, was fully involved in healing work as a practitioner, which, along with lecturing, fund-raising, and other work as a regional Christian Science leader, would become her livelihood. Eddy was both captivated by her new protégée's charisma and suspicious of it, "testing" her on one notable occasion by deliberately not showing up to deliver a lecture to which Stetson had invited a number of clergymen. In Eddy's absence, Stetson was forced to improvise a lecture of her own. In her memoir, she recalled asking Eddy the following day for an explanation. "[Eddy] answered, 'I was there.' I did not know at the time what she meant and thought her *personal* presence was necessary. She smiled at my innocence and ignorance of her methods of testing her students. She said, 'But you stood, Augusta. You stood, you did not run.' She referred to this nearly every time I saw her after that event. "[239]

Augusta Stetson never ran. Although she did not succeed in healing her husband—who died in 1901 because, Stetson claimed, "he was not in a receptive condition to be treated by our faith"—she became an ardent Scientist, devoting her life to the Cause, as Eddy and her followers called it. In New York, where she was sent by Eddy in the late 1880s, she flourished, helping to found the First Church of Christ, Scientist, New York City in 1887 and becoming its regular preacher. She was a brilliant fundraiser, inspiring wealthy Scientists in New York to donate over a million dollars for the construction of the church. If anything, she was too successful, inspiring rivalry in some fellow Scientists; soon there were a number of branch churches in the city, many of them trying to compete with her lavish church.

She had a tumultuous relationship with Eddy; the letters they exchanged feature, by turns, Eddy's protestations of affection and gratitude for Stetson's innumerable gifts and her reprimands for Stetson's mistakes. In a letter to Stetson in 1889, Eddy wrote, "Yes, darling, you are learning . . . and growing like a sweet, fat, promising baby, like a beautiful sapling, like the reeds by the river, like the child Jesus."[240] In 1901, Eddy took her to task for what was to be a common confusion among her students:

> But darling, you injure the cause and disobey me in thinking that I am Christ or saying such a thing. And m.a.m. is causing you to do this. Read my books on this subject and you will find I always explain Christ as the *invisible* and never corporeal. . . . I am corporeal to the senses even as Paul was. But God has anointed me to do His work, to reveal His Word, to lead His people. . . . I am only a Godlike woman, God-anointed, and I have done a work that none others could do.[241]

Stetson was extraordinarily solicitous of her Leader, sending her books of poetry, fruit, flowers, diamond jewelry, gowns, tea jackets, bonnets, cloaks, muffs, a feather boa, a live bird (which Eddy returned), and furs.

She had portraits made of Eddy, making sure that every detail of hairstyle and expression met the subject's specifications. Eddy grew dependent on her, ordering specific items of clothing as needed, and, as always with those on whom she relied, growing irritable and petulant when Stetson inevitably disappointed her: "I am working for you and all students *continually*," she wrote to Stetson in 1906, "and so have no time to care for my wardrobe"; in 1907, she wrote to her, "I cannot believe that you are forgetting your duty to your teacher and leader, so I write to you myself to learn of *you why* my three recent requests that you would send to me a Spring bonnet—have not been even *noticed*? . . . Do *not allow* the *evil one* in your midst to turn you away from me in this hour of crucifixion, or history will repeat itself, and Christian Science will once more be lost as aforetime."[242]

Stetson tried to counter Eddy's anxieties, letting no opportunity lapse to let her know that she herself was merely a humble cog in the mighty wheel of Christian Science. But Eddy clearly detected signs of ambition in Stetson and tried to thwart it, writing bylaw after bylaw in an attempt to rein her in. She restricted the term of Readers in branch churches to three years (Stetson had long been the Reader at her New York City church) and forbade practitioners to keep offices in branch churches (there were offices for some twenty-five practitioners in Stetson's church). When Eddy read in a New York newspaper in November 1908 that Stetson was planning to build a new branch—a branch of her branch—on Riverside Drive that would rival any Christian Science church, including the Mother Church, in size and grandeur, she summoned her errant student to Boston, where Stetson agreed to abandon her plans. It would be their last meeting. According to Peel's account, Eddy embraced her rival, holding her face in her hands as Stetson knelt before her, and said to her, "God bless you forever and forever and forever."[243]

Augusta Stetson was not the loopy Josephine Woodbury with her illegitimate offspring and her melodramatic christenings, and Mrs. Eddy apparently feared confronting her directly. In 1909, acting on reports that Stetson was encouraging her cadre of practitioners to pray for the destruction of rival branches in New York City, Eddy ordered the Board of Directors to deal with her once and for all. It took over a year. Stetson was accused of a number of grievous errors: practicing M.A.M. on her enemies, including the Board of Directors, and encouraging idolatrous behavior among her followers. She was hauled before the Board, interrogated, stripped of her titles of teacher and practitioner, and excommunicated. Stetson continued to believe that Mrs. Eddy loved her and had been misled by her household henchmen. But she lost much of her authority and was forced to resign from the New York church she had built.

17. "A Combination of Sinners That Was Fast"

By 1910, the last year of her life, Mrs. Eddy had grown increasingly frail and querulous, demanding that every item in her house be returned to the exact same spot after cleaning, delivering sharp rebukes when things were misplaced. Adam Dickey, a new secretary who had been brought in to supplement the efforts of Calvin Frye, much to Frye's dismay, solved the problem by placing tacks beneath every item in the house so that all the knickknacks, trinkets, and pieces of furniture could be correctly replaced.

In 1908, Eddy had called Dickey to her side as she lay ill on a couch. Holding his hand, she made him promise her that, if she were to die, he would "write a history" and explain to the world that she had been "mentally murdered."[244] She then made him raise his right hand and swear to do so. After their meeting, she sent him a note reiterating her request. She had previously enacted the same scene with Frye.

In the memoir that he finally, obediently wrote, long after Eddy's death, Dickey revealed a number of fascinating details about life with the Discoverer, Founder, and Leader of Christian Science. Dickey recounted his experiences trying to give her Christian Science treatment for her ailments:

> On one occasion when she was in need of encouragement I said to her, "Mother, you cannot have a return of an old belief." Up came the warning hand: "Don't put it that way," she said. "At one time I had a belief of excellent health, and your declaration, if carried out, would prevent me from expressing that belief of health, and that is what I am striving for." So I promised her I would never again be so careless.[245]

On another occasion, he saw that she was "having trouble with her throat":

> At once I saw that the belief was that there was a gathering of phlegm in her throat, and I began to declare that mortal mind could not create and

that there was no such thing as phlegm in her throat. She stopped me at once and said, "Do not say that; there is a natural and normal secretion of phlegm in the throat, and if we declare against that, we are likely to interfere with the natural function of the glands of the throat." Then I changed my statement and said, "There is and there can be no such thing as an abnormal secretion of phlegm in your throat." This she approved.[246]

Dickey's most gripping revelation—one that would become renowned throughout the Christian Science Field—was the story of how Mrs. Eddy raised Calvin Frye from the dead. One evening, Dickey writes, shortly after Eddy had retired for the night, Laura Sargent came to his door "in great trepidation" to tell him that she had found Frye unconscious on a lounge chair in his room and had been unable to rouse him. They rushed back to him, and Dickey found him slumped in the chair, "breathless and with no pulse or indication of life whatever."[247] After shaking and calling to him for some time, they finally went to inform Eddy. On her instructions, they placed him in a rocking chair and dragged him into her room, where Eddy sat in bed, a shawl around her shoulders. As Dickey notes, "It was an interesting moment." Eddy placed her hand on the unconscious man's shoulder and commenced to address him "in a loud voice":

> "Calvin, Calvin, wake up. It is Mother who is calling you. Wake up, Calvin, this Cause needs you, Mother needs you, and you must not leave. Calvin, Calvin, wake up. Disappoint your enemies. You shall not go. I need you here. Disappoint your enemies, Calvin, and awake."

This continued for a half hour. At one point, Dickey tried to prop up Frye's head, but Eddy instructed him not to touch the man:

> The time seemed to pass without any appreciable response to her work. This did not discourage her. She redoubled her efforts and fairly shouted to Mr. Frye her commands that he awake. In a moment he raised his head and drew a long, deep breath. After this his respiration became regular and he was restored to consciousness. The first words he uttered were, "I don't want to stay. I want to go." Mrs. Eddy paused in her efforts and turning her gaze to the workers around the room, said, "Just listen to that." She again turned to Mr. Frye and in her commanding tones insisted that he awake and remain here.[248]

The next day, Frye resumed his duties. Dickey concluded: "The fact remains that Calvin Frye had passed through what mortal mind calls 'death,' and the grave had been cheated of its victim by our Leader's quick and effective work."[249]

In the last weeks of her life, Eddy elevated Adam Dickey to the highest status, appointing him to the Board of Directors. He died in 1926; the following year, his widow published his *Memoirs of Mary Baker Eddy* and distributed the book to members of her husband's Christian Science Association. When the Board of Directors learned of the book, they professed themselves horrified by it and rebuked Dickey's widow, who had acted in obedience to her husband's sacred trust. The Board wrote to every member of Dickey's Association, requesting them to return the copies and sending them a letter justifying the censorship. The Board did not appear to doubt the accuracy of Dickey's claims. Rather, they explained, these unwarranted revelations about Eddy's private life would fall into the hands of the enemies of Christian Science; clearly, the Board members realized that the details of Eddy's unhealed illnesses and supernatural doings (raising the dead, levitating) would appear outlandish to those outside the faith. They suggested that Eddy had only asked Dickey to *write* a history saying that she had been mentally murdered, not publish it. They concluded that the book violated the *Manual* bylaw against "publications unjust."[250] The Church suppressed the book so successfully that it became one of the rarest and most sought-after of all Christian Science texts. Scientists who traveled to the Library of Congress and the New York Public Library to read the few copies available to the public found on several occasions that the book was mysteriously missing; one of the two Library of Congress copies had been lent to a Christian Scientist Congressman who claimed to have "mislaid" it.[251]

During her final days, weakened and racked with pain caused by kidney stones, Eddy was beset by the fears she had entertained all her life. In September 1910, Calvin Frye captured the despairing scene around Eddy's bed:

> Mrs. Eddy called [the household workers] and demanded of us to heal her, for she was tired of going on in this way confined to her bunk &c &c; she added that she would give any one of us $1000. to heal her.
>
> A.H.D. [Adam Dickey] said he would give $1000. to be able to heal her &c. so said the others in substance. I did not reply for some time for I felt quite confused & discouraged, but finally said "Well all we can do is to keep

up our courage and work on up to our highest understanding. She replied "Has it come to this! She afterward said If you all feel like that turn your (mi)nds away from me & know that I am well.[252]

Five days before her death, on November 28, 1910, she dictated to Laura Sargent this statement: "It took a combination of sinners that was fast to harm me."[253] Her last written words were "God is my life."[254] That last week of November, she caught cold, and the cold developed into pneumonia. Mary Baker Eddy died on the evening of December 3, 1910.

The next day was a Sunday, and at the end of the service at the Mother Church, a special announcement was read by the First Reader, Judge Clifford Smith:

> My Beloved Students:—You may be looking to see me in my accustomed place with you, but this you must no longer expect. When I retired from the field of labor, it was a departure, socially, publicly, and finally, from the routine of such material modes as society and our societies demand. Rumors are rumors,—nothing more. I am still with you on the field of battle, taking forward marches, broader and higher views, and with the hope that you will follow. . . . All our thoughts should be given to the absolute demonstration of Christian Science. You can well afford to give me up, since you have in my last revised edition of *Science and Health* your teacher and guide.[255]

That announcement had been written in 1891, two years after Mrs. Eddy closed her college. Judge Smith then read this: "It has now become my duty to announce that Mrs. Eddy passed from our sight last night at 10:45 o'clock, at her home in Chestnut Hill."[256] She was dead, but she was not gone.

It had been a remarkable life. Mary Baker Glover Patterson Eddy had survived the rigors of a New Hampshire farm child's life, survived dyspepsia, widowhood, homelessness, divorce, injury, and insult to become the first American woman—the only American woman—to single-handedly found an international religious movement. She left an estate estimated at over $2 million.[257] She left a newspaper that would become world-famous and world-respected.

Mary Baker Eddy also left a book. And the book *is* Mary Baker Eddy. Peremptory and imperious, ambiguous and contradictory, cunning and accommodating, fearful of life and dismissive of death, *Science and Health with Key to the Scriptures* is the perfect reflection of its author. Eddy believed herself to be called by God and to speak in his voice, commanding the people to rise above their puny and fallible bodies, but the theology and practice of Christian Science were forged in the frailties, eccentricities, and pride of Eddy's character.

Slavishly attended by her followers throughout her life as Leader of her Church, Eddy now leads only through her book, which has sold millions of copies and been translated into sixteen languages; it is now her words that are worshipped. Through the book, she still stands at the pulpit of her Mother Church and Christian Science branch churches throughout the world during every Christian Science service. She walks with every Scientist on her or his journey through life. She stands by Scientists as they pray, suffer, raise their children, grow old, fall ill, and die. In the most literal way, her *Science and Health* is considered a lifeline by its people; it is their medicine cabinet, their nurse, their doctor, their hospital. In a religion without clergy, it is also their adviser, pastor, therapist, and friend. The great irony of Eddy's textbook lies in the fact that—despite her virulent attacks on human individuality and her energetic attempt to resolve the entire human race into one oceanic Mind—her personality powerfully lives on in *Science and Health*.

18. *Science and Health*, 1910 Edition

More than any other Christian sect, Christian Science is a religion of the book, a book other than the Bible. Other indigenous American religious movements are also based on original texts: *The Book of Mormon* and other Mormon writings; *The Great Controversy*, by Ellen Gould White, the originator of Seventh-Day Adventism; *Dianetics*, by L. Ron Hubbard. But Scientists are unsurpassedly devoted to theirs.

All Scientists worthy of the name devote a significant amount of time weekly, if not daily, to its study. They study the Bible, too, but the Bible, in some ways, plays a secondary role. Scientists share the Bible with other Christians, but *Science and Health* is their identity. Every Christian Science service features readings from *Science and Health*, and it is the so-called First Reader who reads it. The Second Reader reads the Bible.

Science and Health is a long and difficult text. By anyone's estimate, it is not an easy read. Its detractors have had a great deal of fun with it: Mark Twain suggested that it be translated into English; Harold Bloom identified its prose style as "one of the great ordeals of the American Religion."[258] At seven hundred pages, written in the nineteenth-century manner and diction unique to its author, with line numbers and extensive marginal notes, it is a daunting text to tackle from cover to cover. Although at times they may read the entire text, most Scientists work with the book in ways that render it more digestible: studying short passages organized around the theme in the Church's official weekly lesson sermon, printed in *Christian Science Quarterly Bible Lessons;* searching out words or phrases of particular interest with the help of printed or electronic concordances; or simply opening the book at random to see what inspiration they are, in the spiritual sense, led to find.

Science and Health is repetitive, as are many religious texts, including the Bible, but Scientists seem to find the reformulations and reiterations of the book's major points consistently useful. Where one passage may seem opaque, another will leap out in clarity, leading the Scientist to grasp some essential spiritual truth. To a critic, the book's chapter headings seem less like definitions of content than starting points; any chapter may range over the whole of the book's concerns. (Indeed, Eddy shuffled, rearranged, and retitled the chapters of her book through dozens of editions; one Eddy biography offers a daunting chart illustrating "the amazing extent to which she carried this rearranging."[259]) Likewise, the end of one paragraph often jumps to the beginning of another without discernible transition. But such stylistic concerns do not trouble the faithful. *Science and Health* is considered a divinely inspired and sacred text among Scientists. For them, there is no questioning it, from its bold opening declarations—"To those leaning on the sustaining infinite, to-day is big with blessings" and "The time for thinkers has come"—to its concluding testimonies of healing.[260] Christian Scientists interpret *Science and Health* as literally as Christian fundamentalists interpret the Bible.

The main section of *Science and Health* contains a preface and fourteen chapters, with titles such as "Prayer," "Marriage," "Christian Science versus Spiritualism," "Animal Magnetism Unmasked," "Physiology," "Some Objections Answered," and "Christian Science Practice." The "Key to the Scriptures" at the end of the volume consists of three chapters: "Genesis," "The Apocalypse," and "Glossary," a compendium of Eddy's definitions or readings of important words, biblical names, and phrases. The last chapter,

"Fruitage," is a collection of letters attesting to healing from early Christian Scientists. All the testimonies date from Eddy's day, and many of them—"Depraved Appetites Overcome," "Liver Complaint Healed," "Through Great Tribulations"—reflect the same antique sensibility that suffuses the rest of *Science and Health*.[261]

"Prayer" is the first chapter in the book, and the Christian Science way of prayer is the Christian Science way of life. Scientists pray continually; "Desire is prayer," writes Eddy, "and no loss can occur from trusting God with our desires, that they may be moulded and exalted before they take form in words and in deeds."[262] Prayer for Scientists is the logical argument of their faith; it often involves mentally reviewing Eddy's characteristics of God and man, which are the cornerstones of the Scientists' description of reality. Prayer is the vehicle for "knowing the Truth."

Although their obsessive focus on certain phrases and passages from *Science and Health* can seem like a hypnotic practice to outsiders, Scientists see themselves as eschewing rote repetition. Indeed, Scientists take pride in the belief that their prayers are more felt and sincere than the repeated "Hail Mary" and "Our Father" of the Catholic rosary, in part because Scientists never petition or ask God for a particular result. Their prayers are conceived as revisions of their own thinking, bringing their thought in line with God's. The British critic and novelist V. S. Pritchett, who was raised as a Scientist, acknowledged the argumentative nature of Christian Science prayer: "The closely reasoned prayers of our faith . . . were more like conversations with Euclid than appeals to God."[263] The sociologist Bryan Wilson also observed the logical nature of Christian Science prayer: "Prayer is the means used to heal the sick, but prayer means something other than what is usually meant by Christians. It is neither praise nor supplication, but an attempt to bring subjective attitudes into accord with what Science proclaims to be objective reality. It is largely silent affirmation, the application of logic to certain given premises."[264] A good example of such a Scientific argument appeared recently in a testimony published in the *Christian Science Sentinel*, in which a woman described her prayers following a painful fall on a flight of brick stairs:

As I got up I was declaring out loud, "I'm all right. I *am* all right!" We slowly continued down the walk while I prayed. My metaphysical treatment went something like this: I am a spiritual idea, a representative of God. The brick walk represented an idea of God. Spirit is substance, so there was no material substance in the body, head, or brick step to collide. And I did not need to fear the results of two spiritual ideas touching. Thank you, God![265]

Several core beliefs characterize Christian Science: a reliance on the first chapter of Genesis as the true story of creation; a belief in a "Father-Mother" God synthesizing the highest qualities of both; a rejection of the physical or material world, typified by Scientists' "radical reliance" on prayer to heal and their refusal to engage medical doctors or to partake of drugs or alcoholic or caffeinated drinks; a preoccupation with the specter of "animal magnetism," a devilish or malicious force of evil also known as malicious animal magnetism or mesmerism; and an emphasis on "primitive Christianity" as represented by the sect's singular interpretation of Jesus' teachings and healings.[266] Eddy, who had been on her way to a temperance meeting when she had her famous fall on the ice in 1866, came to equate not only alcohol and tobacco but also caffeine with drugs; all were noxious foreign substances that could alter and control human behavior. She wrote in *Science and Health*, "The depraved appetite for alcoholic drinks, tobacco, tea, coffee, opium, is destroyed only by Mind's mastery of the body."[267]

The essential "truths" which are so often repeated throughout *Science and Health* are all contained in Eddy's famous "scientific statement of being," which she described as "my first plank in the platform of Christian Science."[268] They can also be found in her definition of man. Both statements are emphasized heavily in Christian Science Sunday schools and are memorized by Scientists as a kind of catechism:

> QUESTION.—What is the scientific statement of being?
> ANSWER.—There is no life, truth, intelligence, nor substance in matter. All is infinite Mind and its infinite manifestation, for God is All-in-all. Spirit is immortal Truth; matter is mortal error. Spirit is the real and eternal; matter is the unreal and temporal. Spirit is God, and man is His image and likeness. Therefore man is not material; he is spiritual.[269]

> QUESTION.—What is man?
> ANSWER.—Man is not matter; he is not made up of brain, blood, bones, and other material elements.[270]

As these passages show, one of Eddy's characteristic stylistic devices, which appears throughout *Science and Health*, is a reliance on synonyms. There are seven synonyms for God, memorized by the faithful: "Mind, Spirit, Soul, Principle, Life, Truth, Love."[271] Intelligence shares many of those synonyms: "Intelligence is omniscience, omnipresence, and omnipotence. It is the primal and eternal quality of infinite Mind, of the triune Principle,— Life, Truth, and Love,—named God."[272] The synonyms recur and recur: "Mind is God"; "God is Mind"; "Mind is the divine Principle, Love"; "God is the only Mind"; "God is Love."[273] The positive synonyms are accompanied by numerous negative ones: "Evil is not Mind"; "Nerves are not Mind"; "Error is neither Mind nor one of Mind's faculties."[274] These are common poetic devices, as in Shakespeare's lines "Love is not love / Which alters when it alteration finds," but unlike a poem, which develops an argument through a series of figures of speech or rhetorical devices, Eddy's synonymous parallels remain on a simple, abstract level. They can seem tautological to the unbeliever. Eddy rarely stoops to describe in vivid or concrete terms the objects of her reverence or dismissal. In *Science and Health*, God is All Good, but he is not the God of the Old Testament, an active character in the drama of human life.

The interpretation of the creation stories of Genesis is crucial. In the first chapter of Genesis, God creates man "in our image, after our likeness," and calls his creation "good."[275] In the second, more specific chapter, he fashions Eve out of Adam's rib and allows Eve to choose whether knowledge of good and evil, in the form of an apple offered by a serpent, may enter the world. Christian Scientists hold to the literal truth of the first chapter of Genesis. They interpret the second chapter, the story of Eve's temptation and the expulsion of mankind from paradise, as a false story, "the history of error in its externalized forms, called life and intelligence in matter."[276] The story of Adam and Eve, therefore, is read as a metaphor of man's mistaken belief in the material world; the "Lord God" of the second chapter who replaces the "God" of the first is held to be a false god. Scientists believe that man is created perfect by God and that he can never fall short of that perfection. For them, the second chapter of Genesis is an allegory of the illusion of matter in which we seem to live.

The Scientists' God is the embodiment of all positive characteristics of the feminine and the masculine, a Father-Mother God. The inclusive gesture of the name, common also to the Shakers and other sects of the nineteenth century, hints at the sects' origins in a time when women had no ecclesiastical power. In much of the third, or 1881, edition of *Science and Health*, Eddy used feminine pronouns exclusively in referring to God. Interestingly, this practice was not retained in later editions, and, while it is now common to hear Scientists speak of their "Father" or "Father-Mother God," it is unusual to hear them speak of God as "Mother."

In her most ambitious, audacious, and heretical act of religion-making, Eddy revised the most sacred of all Christian prayers, the prayer taught to man by Jesus Christ himself, the Lord's Prayer, in order to accommodate her gender-inclusive deity. Eddy's "spiritual interpretation" is read at every Christian Science Sunday service as the congregation recites the traditional version; it also appears in the chapter "Prayer" in *Science and Health:*

> Our Father which art in heaven,
> *Our Father-Mother God, all-harmonious,*
> Hallowed be Thy name.
> *Adorable One.*
> Thy kingdom come.
> *Thy kingdom is come; Thou art ever-present.*
> Thy will be done in earth, as it is in heaven.
> *Enable us to know,—as in heaven, so on earth,—God is omnipotent, supreme.*
> Give us this day our daily bread;
> *Give us grace for to-day; feed the famished affections;*
> And forgive us our debts, as we forgive our debtors.
> *And Love is reflected in love;*
> And lead us not into temptation, but deliver us from evil;
> *And God leadeth us not into temptation, but delivereth us from sin, disease, and death.*
> For Thine is the kingdom, and the power, and the glory, forever.
> *For God is infinite, all-power, all Life, Truth, Love, over all, and All.*[277]

Eddy's cosmic view of a realm where God and man are perfect, blameless, and eternal involves disposing of the material world, error, and evil. *Science and Health* teaches that a belief in the physical reality of the world and all its inherent flaws and failures—including death—is error, an illusion to which we are temporarily drawn, an illusion that seems impossible to vanquish completely in this life. In order to overcome the belief in the illusion of the material, Scientists must recognize or "know" that God is all, not filling all space and time but eradicating those ghostly specters. Man, a reflection of God, is only and entirely spiritual, and explicitly not carnal. As Harold Bloom interprets Christian Science belief, "Whatever it is that God loves in us, it is certainly not our bodies, since they are far too flawed for him to have made."[278] Since God did not make our bodies, they do not exist. Therefore, sin, sickness, and death—the trinity of ills that flesh is heir to—are essentially as unreal as our material manifestations. Unreal but inescapable: Eddy invokes the words "sin," "sickness," and "death" again and again throughout *Science and Health*. One scholar wrote: "It has been estimated that sickness, suffering, sin and death are denied at least three thousand times in the pages of *Science and Health*."[279]

Science and Health is full of odd, inaccurate, or obsolete statements about the physical body, the physical sciences, and human history—anachronistic assertions that may be particularly startling to a modern reader. Parents of newborns are instructed that "the daily ablutions of an infant are no more natural nor necessary than would be the process of taking a fish out of water every day and covering it with dirt in order to make it thrive more vigorously in its own element."[280] Mothers are informed that the pain of childbirth is illusory: "Mind controls the birth-throes in the lower realms of nature, where parturition is without suffering. Vegetables, minerals, and many animals suffer no pain in multiplying; but human propagation has its suffering because it is a false belief."[281] Eddy asserts that her Pilgrim forebears "had less time for selfishness, coddling, and sickly after-dinner talk. . . . Damp atmosphere and freezing snow empurpled the plump cheeks of our ancestors, but they never indulged in the refinement of inflamed bronchial tubes. They were as innocent as Adam, before he ate the fruit of false knowledge, of the existence of tubercles and troches, lungs and lozenges."[282] (Innocent they may have been, but they were also carried off in droves by malnutrition, smallpox, pneumonia, diphtheria, and other contagious diseases and respiratory illnesses.) But Scientists are capable of forgiving Eddy her nineteenth-century ignorance, believing, with her, that "the less we know or think about hygiene," or any other method of preserving or improving the material body, "the less we are predisposed to sickness."[283]

It is the aim and life's work of every Christian Scientist to overcome the "claims" of error, or mortal mind, arising from the pernicious belief in matter. While Christian Scientists have never overcome death, many strongly believe that they have "demonstrated" the truth of their spiritual existence by vanquishing various physical or emotional problems, including illnesses, broken bones, tumors, depression, accidents, joblessness, homelessness, divorce, anxiety, and so forth.

Yet the very nature of Scientists' "demonstrations" raises a question. Scientists spend immense time and effort on their Scientific obligation to overcome the false belief in matter, to realize that all forms of evil and sickness, no matter how trivial, are unreal. And yet their demonstrations of power over the unreality of matter—the healings to which they testify— are themselves physical and are regarded by them as real, indeed, as *essential* evidence of the truths of Christian Science. This raises a philosophical question: Why are all positive or beneficial physical results of Christian Science treatment—examples of regained health, wealth, or prosperity— spoken of as real? If the material world does not exist, why is prosperity more real than poverty? Why is health a more real, a more *desirable* state, than sickness? If all matter, sick or well, is unreal, why attempt to alter its seeming characteristics?

The answer lies in the fact that Scientists maintain their absolute beliefs while living in a relative reality. Wilson described Scientists' philosophical relationship to the physical world as a compromise between idealism and pragmatism:

> Christian Science holds that in the absolute sense man is spiritual and there-fore cannot be sick. In so far as the system claims to heal it does however recognize that, at the level of the world's understanding, man thinks of him-self as material and subject to decay and death. In fact this belief is an illu-sion, says Christian Science, although it is an illusion so powerful that it causes man to see, feel, suffer just the conditions which it specifies. In fact there is nothing to heal, except a false belief which a man entertains of him-self, or which others entertain about him, or both.[284]

Another central question raised by such beliefs is one of theological logic. If God created all, and all is perfect, where does the illusion of error come from? How can so potentially damaging and divisive a belief seem to exist, even as an illusion? It is, after all, a not insubstantial illusion, one so powerful that every human being subscribes to it in this life. In "Recapitulation," the chapter of *Science and Health* in which the "scientific statement of being" and the definition of man appear, this question is not directly asked or answered, nor is it specifically addressed anywhere else in *Science and Health*. Whatever answer is offered by the book seems to come in the form of circular logic: error never has existed and does not exist now; the illusion of it does not exist; therefore, the illusion has no source or origin. To Christian Scientists, this is apparently satisfying. But the problem of evil in Christian Science belief has long posed a puzzle or a stumbling block not only for observers but also for potential converts. Critics such as Mark Twain and sympathetic observers of the religion such as William James have identified Eddy's evasion of the origin of evil as the Achilles heel of Christian Science. The intellectual historian Arthur O. Lovejoy laid bare this very contradiction, exposing the pathos and the logical absurdity of the wholesale denial of reality:

> To call the characters of actual experience "illusion," blank nonentity, though it is a kind of poetry which has a very potent metaphysical pathos, is, philosophically considered, plainly the extremest kind of nonsense. "Unreal" those characters may conceivably be in the sense that they have no existence or no counterparts in an objective order outside the consciousness of those who experience them. But to speak of them as absolutely unreal, while experiencing their existence in oneself and assuming it in other men, and while expressly pointing to them as imperfections to be transcended and evils to be overcome, is obviously to deny and affirm the same proposition in the same breath. And a self-contradiction does not cease to be meaningless by seeming sublime. Thus any otherworldly philosophy which does not resort to this desperate subterfuge of illusionism seems to have this world, whatever its ontological deficiencies, on its hands as an unaccountable mystery, a thing unsatisfying, unintelligible, and evil, which seemingly ought not to be, yet somehow undeniably is.[285]

In a world in which every human being to some extent suffers and certainly dies, and in a century in which humanity has become intimately acquainted with total war, genocide, and the specter of nuclear annihilation, Christian Science has been extremely self-limiting, perhaps in part because it has never been able to account, except to its own satisfaction, for the world, the "unaccountable mystery" which it evidently still has on its hands.

The yawning gulf between Christian Scientists and other Christians is caused by Eddy's unusual view of Jesus Christ. Scientists use the name "Jesus" to refer to the man who lived on earth, "Christ" to refer to the "divine manifestation of God."[286] Throughout *Science and Health*, there are frequent references to the "Christ, Truth," which is the "truth" that matter is error (something Jesus never preached) and that man is the reflection of God. *Science and Health* teaches that Jesus was "the son of a virgin," but Scientists do not see him, as other Christians do, as God incarnate in the flesh.[287] They do not believe in the flesh. Eddy sharply diverged from the mainstream Christian view when she wrote that "Jesus of Nazareth was the most scientific man that ever trod the globe"—that he was, in essence, the very first Christian Scientist, who taught his followers how to heal and demonstrated supremacy over matter through rising from the dead and ascending to an immaterial plane.[288] "He was at work in divine Science," she wrote. "Jesus bore our sins in his body. He knew the mortal errors which constitute the material body, and could destroy those errors; but at the time when Jesus felt our infirmities, he had not conquered all the beliefs of the flesh or his sense of material life, nor had he risen to his final demonstration of spiritual power."[289] Eddy interpreted the words of St. John, "He shall give you another Comforter, that he may abide with you *forever*," as a prophecy of the coming of Christian Science: "This Comforter I understand to be Divine Science."[290] She believed that she had rediscovered the Science of Christ that Jesus had originally brought to the world. Thus, Jesus' healings are the cornerstone of Scientists' Bible study; the Church's lesson sermons frequently focus on one or more of them. This is what Scientists mean when they claim that Christian Science is the rediscovery of "primitive Christianity," Christ's power to heal made available to all.

Christian Scientists do not subscribe to the Apostles' Creed or the Nicene Creed, those distillations of orthodox Christian belief.* The Apostles' Creed establishes Christians' belief in the Trinity of God the

---

*Scientists have no creed, but they do have these Tenets of the Mother Church, which appear in *Science and Health* (p. 497) and are reprinted in every copy of the Church's Bible Lesson:

1. As adherents of Truth, we take the inspired Word of the Bible as our sufficient guide to eternal Life.

2. We acknowledge and adore one supreme and infinite God. We acknowledge His Son, one Christ; the Holy Ghost or divine Comforter; and man in God's image and likeness.

3. We acknowledge God's forgiveness of sin in the destruction of sin and the spiritual understanding that casts out evil as unreal. But the belief in sin is punished so long as the belief lasts.

4. We acknowledge Jesus' atonement as the evidence of divine, efficacious Love, unfolding man's unity with God through Christ Jesus the Way-shower; and we acknowledge that man

Father, Jesus his Son, and the Holy Spirit, and in the essential facts that Jesus Christ was conceived and born, suffered, died, was buried, and was raised up from the dead. In the most profound sense, Christian Scientists do not believe in the Trinity because they do not believe in the *literal* fact of Jesus' sacrifice: his physical presence was part and parcel of a material world that has no true existence. In class-instruction, Scientists are taught that Jesus did not rise from the dead, because he never died; he only appeared to die "to the personal sense of those watching."[291] This emphasis on Christ's evanescent existence rather than Jesus' physical life and death explains, in part, why Scientists do not practice the sacraments of baptism or communion.

Scientists also do not believe in a literal hell. There are few allusions to the next world and virtually no description of what awaits man after death. Nevertheless, there is a pervasive sense among Scientists that life on earth is but a mere, passing phase, and that death needn't be a source of grief or even great concern.[292]

For Scientists, salvation is not a matter of accepting Jesus as their savior but of "knowing" the Christ, Truth: recognizing that man is perfect, here, now, and always. There is thus no fallen state from which they must be saved. Scientists are more likely to refer to Jesus as "the Master," for his masterful demonstration of Christianly Scientific healing, than as the Savior.[293] For Scientists, Jesus has been transformed from savior to Scientific authority. One important implication of this view of Jesus is that redemption loses its traditional Christian meaning and import; since man is not inherently flawed or sinful, he does not need to be redeemed by Jesus' suffering. He needs only to realize his atonement, or, as Eddy defines it, "at-one-ment" with God.

Because of these deviations from the literal word of the Bible and from traditional Christian beliefs and practices, evangelical or fundamentalist Christians believe that Christian Science, along with many other

---

is saved through Christ, through Truth, Life, and Love as demonstrated by the Galilean Prophet in healing the sick and overcoming sin and death.

5. We acknowledge that the crucifixion of Jesus and his resurrection served to uplift faith to understand eternal Life, even the allness of Soul, Spirit, and the nothingness of matter.

6. And we solemnly promise to watch, and pray for that Mind to be in us which was also in Christ, Jesus; to do unto others as we would have them do unto us; and to be merciful, just, and pure.

distinct Christian sects such as those of the Mormons and Jehovah's Witnesses, are cults, satanic in origin. Christian Science was also rejected and attacked in its infancy by the mainstream Protestant clergy and by medical doctors on the grounds that it was neither Christian nor a science, but it has gradually, over the years, become accepted by many Protestant denominations in the ecumenical spirit that has characterized the last few decades of American religious life.

Science and Health has no clear narrative line, virtually no sense of pace or movement toward a revelation, and few illustrative stories, parables, or examples. The one startling exception to the unrelieved oracularity—an exception much loved by children in Christian Science Sunday schools for breaking up the tedium of reading vast tracts of their textbook—is a strange playlet in the chapter "Christian Science Practices," a drama with speaking parts enacting the struggle of a man with his liver. Mortal Man is the defendant, on trial for his life; Personal Sense is the plaintiff; Judge Medicine is set to render his predictable verdict: Death. The jury is composed of a fearsome collection of Mortal Minds: Materia Medica, Anatomy, Physiology, Hypnotism, Envy, Greed, and Ingratitude. A variety of unsavory witnesses are called to testify against the hapless victim of "liver-complaint": Sallow Skin, Coated Tongue, Nerve, Morbid Secretion, etc.[294] (In my Sunday school classes, we actually enacted this play, and there was intense jockeying for these coveted roles.)

The trial does not go well for the defendant, whose illness is perceived as his own fault: Coated Tongue gives graphic testimony regarding the "foul fur" with which it is covered due to the failing liver; Sallow Skin complains of being "dry, hot, and chilled by turns"; and Mortality and Death, albeit the trial seems to be a civil one, urge the court to execute the defendant. The jury, acting with undue haste, declares the proceedings at a end, and the Judge announces their guilty verdict.[295]

Enter Christian Science, attorney for the dying man (although where Christian Science has been until this point is somewhat unclear). Christian Science demands a hearing and delivers a lengthy speech, beginning: "The prisoner at the bar has been unjustly sentenced. His trial was a tragedy, and is morally illegal. Mortal Man has had no proper counsel in the case. All the testimony has been on the side of Personal Sense, and we shall unearth this foul conspiracy against the liberty and life of

Man. The only valid testimony in the case shows the alleged crime never to have been committed."[296] There is an abortive attempt by the opposing counsel, False Belief, to have Christian Science declared in contempt, but great effusions of further rhetoric from Christian Science, alleging skulduggery by the witnesses, save the day: "Morbid Secretion is not an importer or dealer in fur, but we have heard Materia Medica explain how this fur is manufactured, and we know Morbid Secretion to be on friendly terms with the firm of Personal Sense, Error, & Co.," etc., etc.[297] After putting everyone, including Judge and jury to shame, Christian Science succeeds in having his client declared not guilty, whereupon "Mortal Man, no longer sick and in prison, walked forth, his feet 'beautiful upon the mountains,' as of one 'that bringeth good tidings.' "[298]

It is an astonishing performance of some twelve pages. While it does suggest that Eddy could never have made her living as a dramatist, it reveals her preoccupation with bodily sensations and symptoms as insidious foreign invaders, attackers, and destroyers. It demonstrates, more graphically than any other passage of Eddy's writings, how Christian Scientists are taught to regard their bodies. As a fantasy, it suggests that Eddy was herself disassociated from her body; as a religious parable or teaching, it demands that Scientists divorce themselves from their physical existence—coated tongues and morbid secretions—and reestablish their experience on a higher plane. The repellent quality that the human body takes on for Scientists is captured most succinctly in one of Eddy's hymns, which calls for her followers to "Cleanse the foul senses within."[299]

Postscript: "Mrs. Eddy's Place"

In 1943, the Church published in the *Sentinel* a statement signed by the Board of Directors and entitled "Mrs. Eddy's Place." The result of intensive study by a special committee of editors of all of Eddy's pronouncements about herself and her role, it was subsequently published as a pamphlet and distributed through Christian Science reading rooms from 1943 to 1971.[300] This document, which became famous among Scientists and was commonly known as "The Six Points," reflected the ambiguity that Eddy often expressed about her role. It asserted that "Mrs. Eddy . . . understood herself to be the one chosen of God to bring the promised Comforter to the world, and, therefore, the revelator of Christ, Truth, in this age." Scientists considered this a crucial distinction: Eddy was not *herself* the Second Coming; she had merely brought it to the world. It further affirmed that "Mrs. Eddy regarded portions of Revelation (that is, Chapter 12) as pointing to her as the one who fulfilled prophecy by giving the full and final revelation of Truth; her work thus being complementary to that of Christ Jesus." Eddy "revealed God's motherhood; she represents in this age the spiritual idea of God typified by the woman in the Apocalypse."* Eddy, the pamphlet claimed, "considered herself to be the 'God-appointed' and 'God-anointed' messenger to this age . . . the revelator cannot be separated from the revelation." The Six Points, the Church's attempt to instruct Scientists on their Leader's role, only deepened the confusion about Eddy's divinity.[301]

Eddy had encouraged this exalted view. In her statements about herself, she went back and forth, slyly suggesting that her existence was prophesied in the Bible, then denying it. At times she tried to discourage her followers from worshipping her; at other times, she fanned the flames of their idolatry. When Eddy was asked about her role, her answers were coy and ambiguous. In response to a query from the press about whether she regarded herself as the second Christ, she answered:

> Even the question shocks me. What I am is for God to declare in His infinite mercy. As it is, I claim nothing more than what I am, the Discoverer and Founder of Christian Science, and the blessing it has been to mankind which eternity enfolds. . . . But to think or speak of me in any manner as a Christ, is sacrilegious. Such a statement would not only be false, but the absolute antipode of Christian Science, and would savor more of heathenism than of my doctrines.[302]

Eddy denied being a second Christ but told her followers that her teachings were the Comforter promised in the Bible, the Second Coming of Christ, which, of course, she had discovered. If she had discovered the Second Coming, was she not a part of it? Seeing Eddy as special, divinely inspired, and marked by God to receive His message, Scien-

---

* According to Revelation 12:1, that woman was "clothed with the sun, and the moon under her feet, and upon her head a crown of twelve stars."

tists have elevated her to a stature that others, particularly other Christians, find inexplicable, blasphemous, or offensive. Scientists' response to this has been to claim publicly that they do not worship her while, in the sanctuary and privacy of their churches and their lives, they do. They cannot let go of her. She is their Discoverer, their Leader, their Mother.

Part III

"Nothing Has Gone Right
Since 1910": Christian
Science After Death

For if a man know not how to rule his
own house, how shall he take care of the
church of God?

—1 Timothy

1. The Telephone in the Tomb

It is hard to miss the Mary Baker Eddy Memorial and Tomb in Mount Auburn Cemetery, in Cambridge, Massachusetts. Mount Auburn is the burial place of Boston's most celebrated families and most famous intellectuals: the Eliots and the Lowells, Josiah Quincy and Fannie Farmer, Henry Wadsworth Longfellow, B. F. Skinner, and Buckminster Fuller. One of the largest and most elaborate of the many grand memorials in this renowned garden cemetery, Eddy's memorial rises from a high bank on Halcyon Lake, a still, green pond surrounded by weeping willow and Japanese maple. On sunny days, the surface of the water reflects the white granite of the tomb. Stairs from the lake sweep up either side of the monument to a ring of eight fifteen-foot-tall columns supporting a crown, open to the sky, that bears these words: MARY BAKER EDDY DISCOVERER AND FOUNDER OF CHRISTIAN SCIENCE AUTHOR OF SCIENCE AND HEALTH WITH KEY TO THE SCRIPTURES. Inside the columns is a bed of flowers. Two stone tablets flanking the columns are carved with lengthy quotations, one from Eddy, the other from Christ Jesus. There are no dates of birth or death. It is impossible to tell where the body is buried.[1]

She was dressed in white silk and lace, like a bride, for the funeral service. It was held five days after her death on December 8, 1910, to allow George Glover to travel from South Dakota. After the service, the bronze casket was taken to Mount Auburn to await interment in the tomb under construction at the site of the present monument (which was not completed until 1917); it was guarded around the clock until, as one hostile biographer put it, "sufficient time had elapsed for complete decomposition."[2]

The irrepressible Augusta Stetson took this opportunity to suggest to the press that the guard had been posted by her personal enemies, the ambitious Board of Directors, in order to thwart the resurrection of Mrs. Eddy and force her back into the tomb so that they could take over the Christian Science movement; other Scientists believed that the guard was on duty to welcome their Leader back to the world.[3] Alfred Farlow was eventually forced to make the official statement that "while Christian Scientists believe the Scriptural teaching that the time will come when there will be no more death, they take the common-sense view that centuries may pass meanwhile before this exalted spiritual estate is reached."[4] Although he himself had earlier contributed to the notion that Eddy would demonstrate eternal life, Farlow flatly stated at this time that Christian Scientists "do not look for her return to this world."[5]

Since Eddy's death, the Committee on Publication has been indignantly correcting "the myth" that there is a telephone installed in the tomb for Mrs. Eddy's use should she rise from the dead. Robert Peel chided the "sober historians at Harvard who only need to stroll over to Mount Auburn or pick up their own telephone to find out the real facts" and who tell the famous telephone tale "as a droll dinner-table story of unimpeachable authority."[6] He explained that the telephone had been installed for the guard's "added security" as a "normal safety precaution" without, however, suggesting why such a precaution was felt to have been necessary.[7]

Peel and other Church-sanctioned historians have also kept alive the sense of absurdity inherent in the telephone-in-the-tomb story by dwelling with pride on the condition of Eddy's body. Perhaps unconsciously, Peel, in emphasizing her body's youthfulness and slowness to decay, recalls accounts of the bodies of Catholic saints, which are said to remain sweet and fresh long after death. He quotes both the medical examiner's comments on the "extraordinary beauty" of Eddy's "dead face" and the undertaker's assessment of the corpse: "In the process of embalming we found the body at sixty hours after death, in as good condition of preservation as we always find at twelve to twenty-four hours after death."[8] Peel claims that this statement is of "evidential value," but as evidence of what he does not say.[9]

. . .

Whatever the condition of Eddy's body, the condition of the Christian Science movement at the moment of her death was grave. On December 7, before she was even laid to rest, the Board of Directors held a "special meeting" that resulted in a press release claiming that "the authority given to the Board of Directors by the Church Manual remains intact, and is fully adequate for the government of the organization in all its affairs."[10] The Board was also moved to declare that "hundreds of telegrams and letters received from branch churches and societies throughout the world show that it has the unswerving loyalty and support of the entire denomination."[11] This preemptive defensiveness was a natural reaction to the uncertain situation Eddy had left. Indeed, within a decade of Eddy's death, the question of the Board's authority and the "unswerving loyalty" of the Christian Science Field would be thrown wide open. The question of who was to lead the Church would become, in fact, the most divisive issue facing it.

Mrs. Eddy had left some unfinished business. In the years before she died, against the repeated and ever more urgent advice of her lawyers, her Board of Directors, and other advisers, Eddy let stand in the *Manual*, the primary governing document of her Church, a number of so-called estoppel clauses, which require her approval before certain actions can be taken.

Nearly a hundred years after her death, Eddy still maintains the right to summon any Church member to come to her home and work for her for three years; she still instructs members of the Church not to "haunt" her drive or "stroll by her house"; she still objects to any member publishing "profuse quotations" from her works "without her permission."[12] The Mother Church cannot be moved or demolished without her consent. By virtue of the most mystifying and potentially crippling of the estoppel clauses, the election of officials to the Church's most important posts still awaits her approval: neither its Board of Directors, nor the Trustees of its Publishing Society, nor the manager of its Committees on Publication can be appointed without her. Having failed to demonstrate the eternal life she promised, Mary Baker Eddy left her followers in the legal straitjacket of her immortal *Manual*.

Moreover, Eddy had never made it exactly clear who or what was to run the Church as a whole after her departure from the scene. She had left a fairly simple structure: a Board of Directors to oversee the Mother Church, a Board of Trustees to run the Publishing Society, the Committee on

Publication to deal with the press, a Clerk to deal with the Field, a Board of Education to instruct Christian Science teachers, and a Board of Lectureship to give lectures around the world. All of these boards and committees were considered part of the Mother Church, which had gradually and uneasily been assuming its place as the official governing body of the movement in the final years of Eddy's life. The Board of Directors ran the Mother Church, but the question of how far the powers of that church extended over the entire movement was largely unresolved at Eddy's death. The *Manual* described the branch churches as self-governing and the Mother Church as "unique," occupying "a position that no other church can fill," but what exactly those words meant was yet to be determined.[13]

The five-member Board of Directors had been nominally in charge of many aspects of Church organization for some years, but the Board was required to seek Eddy's approval in virtually all important matters. Throughout her career, Eddy expressed ambivalence about her Church organization, not least when she closed down her college and the Boston church in 1889. She wrote in her autobiography, "Material organization has its value and peril, and . . . is requisite only in the earliest periods of Christian history. After this material form of cohesion and fellowship has accomplished its end, continued organization retards spiritual growth, and should be laid off,—even as the corporeal organization deemed requisite in the first stages of mortal existence is finally laid off, in order to gain spiritual freedom and supremacy."[14] In other words, a material church was as unnecessary, in her view, as a material body; but, bowing to the inevitable, she made provisions for it in this seemingly imperfect stage of life. She was also known to express irritation and distrust toward her Board of Directors, and she rebuked them as often as she did her household workers, referring to them once, according to one of those workers, as "trained monkeys."[15]

Eddy's Board members and lawyers had pleaded with her to remove the estoppel clauses from the *Manual*, but she had refused. Only a few months before her death, the Board approached her, begging her to make some provision so that the Church organization could continue. According to Adam Dickey, she later dictated to him this statement: "I have no right or desire to change what God has directed me to do and it remains for the Church to obey it. What has prospered this Church for thirty years will continue to keep it."[16]

Now the Church faced the first and perhaps the most important of the decisions that had to be made without its Leader's guidance: whether to honor her wishes or preserve itself. If the Church continued to obey the letter of Eddy's bylaws after her death, its official bureaucracy—headquartered in offices near the Mother Church and considered to be part of the Mother Church—would eventually grind to a halt. As Board members retired or died, there would be no mechanism by which to replace them. The *Manual* could not be obeyed for the Church to survive, and yet it *had* to be obeyed. To Christian Scientists, the *Manual* is sacred writ. "Eternity awaits our Church Manual," Eddy wrote, and she went on to emphasize that it would outlast the guiding documents of other, inferior religions: "[It] will maintain its rank as in the past, amid ministries aggressive and active, and will stand when those have passed to rest."[17] Eddy strictly forbade any revision, amendment, or annulment of any bylaw in the *Manual*: "This Manual shall not be revised without the written consent of its author."[18]

One of Eddy's last official acts, just days before she died, was to appoint Adam Dickey, her new favorite among her household staff, to the Board of Directors; he would serve for fourteen years, eventually becoming chairman. In 1910, neither he nor the other Directors was about to step aside because of confusion about Eddy's intentions. The Church was in the middle of its most explosive period of growth: in 1906, there had been some two hundred congregations; by 1910, there were over six hundred.[19] Between 1911 and 1923, the Church gained 753 new branches throughout the world.[20] The Directors, Dickey included, were bent on encouraging that growth and could not see how the Church could prosper without a guiding institution.

On December 17, two weeks after Eddy's death, the Board published a new edition of the *Manual*, the 89th edition, which remains in use today. They did not announce the publication in the *Sentinel*, as was the custom. The glaring discrepancy between the 88th and the 89th editions, soon noticed by observant Scientists, involved the removal of Eddy's name and title, Pastor Emeritus, from the head of the list of officers of the Church. This had the effect, at least in the minds of many shocked Scientists, of elevating the Board of Directors to Mrs. Eddy's singular status as Leader. Her name and title were restored in 1924, but by that time the Board's authority was assured. The Board also added to the *Manual*'s "Present Order of Services in The Mother Church"—the list detailing the proper order of hymns, readings, and prayers during the services—the words "and Branch Churches," thereby effectively locking the branches into the same rigidly fixed services as those observed at the Mother Church, preventing innovation or services tailored to specific congregations.[21]

To outsiders, these changes may seem necessary, even reasonable, intended to maintain the organization. Indeed, the Board was well within its legal rights in disregarding the estoppel clauses and continuing its operations without Eddy's approval; the *Manual*, after all, was merely the governing document of a Church, not state or federal law. But some of Mrs. Eddy's followers saw the Board's continued existence and the removal of Eddy's name as Pastor Emeritus as a devious act of betrayal, designed to demote Mrs. Eddy, and a violation of one of the key estoppel clauses, the *Manual* bylaw that states that the *Manual* itself can only be revised with Eddy's consent.

To this day, the Board of Directors continues to break many of the bylaws of the *Manual* in order to ensure its own existence, and a substantial group of dissident Christian Scientists continues to revile them for it. The Board dismisses as hidebound the arguments of those who believe in strict construction of the estoppel clauses, but their uneasy conscience regarding the issue can be detected in the lengths to which they have gone to obey those clauses that *can* still be obeyed. Many Scientists, reading the estoppel clauses, have interpreted them literally and believed that Eddy meant to dissolve the Mother Church organization, as she had done once before, leaving the branch churches to be truly self-governing, to fend for themselves. Eddy, having declared the *Manual* the work of God, knowingly left the Church on the horns of this dilemma, and no one has ever understood why.

The estoppel clauses in the *Manual* were not the only confusion that Eddy left to her church. Among the other governing documents of the Church are various deeds of trust bequeathing to the Church Eddy's interest and control in Church properties, buildings, and the business of the Christian Science Publishing Society; two of these deeds are actually printed in the *Manual* and have assumed *Manual* status as sacred documents. In 1892, the Board of Directors of the Church was assigned various properties, powers, and responsibilities under a trust deed. In 1898, the Christian Science Publishing Society was established under a *separate* deed of trust that granted to its three-member Board of Trustees the responsibility of publishing the *Christian Science Journal* and *Sentinel*, and *The Christian Science Monitor*.

But the two boards (the Board of Directors of the Mother Church is generally referred to as "the Board" or "the Directors" and the publishing board as "the Trustees") were assigned overlapping duties and responsibilities, and the directions Eddy left for how to replace the Trustees were unclear. In the *Manual*, she granted the Directors the power to *declare* vacancies on the Board of Trustees, but she reserved to herself the right to fill those vacancies; in her absence, if she did not "elect to exercise this right," the "remaining trustees" were allowed to fill the open seats.[22] Eddy may have intended the two boards to provide checks and balances on each other's power, but their powers were so ill-defined that it was inevitable that they would clash. It took less than a decade for the two to come to legal blows, and for the divisions Eddy had written into the *Manual* and the deeds of trust to tear the Church apart. "Dissensions are dangerous in an infant church," she once wrote.[23] About that, she was right.

2. The Great Litigation

What made the Great Litigation great? On the face of it, not much. There were no courtroom dramatics, no surprise witnesses, no smoking gun. The Great Litigation, which occupied the years from 1918 to 1921, was actually a fairly dry, technical lawsuit that ultimately determined who was to run the Church. The drama lay, not in the suit itself, but in the acrimony it inspired among Scientists.

The Church, by this time, was a going concern, having inherited most of Eddy's millions and some valuable property. The Publishing Society was doing a million dollars' worth of business a year; all profits were turned over to the Board of Directors. Scientists were donating handsomely to the Church, and it was beginning to inherit estates from members who had passed on. Much was at stake in the lawsuit: money, prestige, and momentum.

By its end, the Church periodicals—*Journal, Sentinel,* and *Monitor*—had lost most of their subscribers, and the Publishing Society had lost hundreds of thousands of dollars. A vast rift had opened up between those who supported the Trustees of the Publishing Society and those who supported the Board of Directors. The Great Litigation was the Civil War of the Christian Science Church, and the Church emerged with permanent scars, with the Board of Directors winning the war, but the Trustees inflicting heavy losses, still felt today. Indeed, in 1997, the Massachusetts Supreme Judicial Court was forced by disgruntled Scientists to revisit the core issues raised in the Great Litigation.

• • •

The catalyst who forced the fight into the open was a man named Herbert W. Eustace, a respected Christian Science practitioner and teacher from San Jose, California, who had served in most of the offices of his branch church. In 1912, he was asked by the Publishing Society to become one of its three Trustees. Eustace had already expressed his loyalty to the Board of Directors; in a speech to Christian Science teachers he had compared the Church to an army that demanded obedience from its soldiers.[24] But in 1916, when the Board demanded that the Trustees sign a "memorandum of understanding" in which they would "acknowledge the directors as the supreme governing power of the Christian Science movement," Eustace and the other Trustees balked.[25]

The Trustees had grown suspicious of the Board's increasing interference with editorial policy at the Publishing Society, a situation that seemed to Eustace to be the work of darker forces. He wrote later:

> I had not long been a member of the board of trustees before I began to feel an indefinable element at work with the directors of the Church, an apparent attempt to dictate to the trustees on matters wholly within the province of the trustees' duties as set forth in the Deed of Trust. I soon realized that it was the age-old demand of ecclesiasticism to rule, to allow nothing to interfere with its thirst for power and authority. I saw clearly, also, that while it might appear as persons trying to acquire power and prestige, it was not primarily person* at all, but evil appearing as ecclesiastical despotism in an effort to substitute itself for the demands of Principle.[26]

The Board began to raise frequent objections to minor expenses incurred by the Trustees for such items as stationery and transportation. Eventually, an argument blew up between the Board and the Trustees over what the Publishing Society would be allowed to publish.

Eustace had been class-taught by Edward Kimball, a figure close to Mrs. Eddy (she had, during one of her lawsuits, entrusted him with the copyrights to all her works). Considered a Christian Science pioneer by his

---

* Here, Eustace uses "person" in the Christian Science sense, to mean "personality." In Scientific parlance, this suggests the ambitious, grasping, and selfish human mind, which should be, by definition, dissolved into the one Mind of God.

Mark Baker, the father of Mary Baker Eddy, who subscribed, she wrote, to a "relentless theology"

George Washington Glover, Mary's first husband, who died six months after their marriage

Mary, when she lived in North Groton, New Hampshire, with her second husband, Daniel Patterson (Corbis)

Daniel Patterson, Mary's second
husband, an itinerant dentist
with a wandering eye

Mary Patterson in a photographer's
studio in Amesbury, around 1867,
dandling an unknown infant

Phineas Parkhurst Quimby,
Eddy's mentor and muse in
the art of mind-healing

Richard Kennedy in 1871, when he was Mary Glover's partner; after their break in the following year, she came to believe that he was mentally working to destroy her.

Daniel Spofford when he was a student and suitor of Mary's in Lynn, Massachusetts. Suspected by Mrs. Eddy of practicing malicious animal magnetism, he was the supposed target of a murder plot by Eddy loyalists.

Asa Gilbert Eddy, Eddy's third husband and the first Christian Science practitioner. His wife believed that he was murdered by "mesmeric poison."

Mary Baker Glover in 1876, the year after
Science and Health was published

Calvin Frye, around 1882. He served as
Eddy's secretary, servant, and footman for
twenty-eight years; Eddy was said to have
raised him from the dead.

A Christian Scientists' Picnic, July 16, 1885. Augusta Stetson is third from the left in the
third row; Josephine Woodbury is in the top row.

Josephine Woodbury, following the birth of her "Prince of Peace," whom she claimed to have spiritually conceived, and her excommunication from the Mother Church

Ebenezer J. Foster Eddy, adopted by Eddy in 1888. She broke with him in 1897.

"Christian Unity," one of the illustrations by James F. Gilman for Eddy's poem of 1893, "Christ and Christmas." The figure of "Christian Science," whose foot was drawn from Eddy's own, brought criticism from those who believed she was equating herself with Jesus Christ.

Mary Baker Eddy addressing an audience of 10,000 Christian Scientists from her balcony at Pleasant View, June 29, 1903

Eddy returning to Pleasant View
from her daily drive, Calvin Frye
holding the reins

Adam Dickey, at Eddy's last home, Chestnut Hill, Massachusetts, in 1910. He would later write an extraordinary memoir about his time with Eddy that was suppressed by the Church.

Augusta Stetson, Eddy's student and eventual rival, founder of the First Church of Christ, Scientist, New York City, excommunicated in 1909

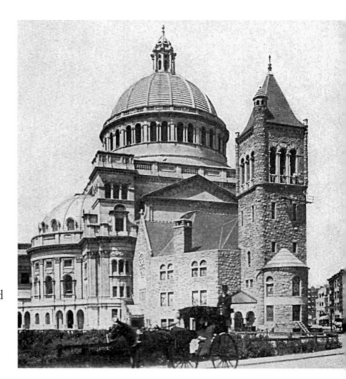

The Mother Church and its new Extension, after its completion in 1906

students, Kimball had suggested to them that Eddy's works were a kind of springboard for an evolving Christian Science. In the coming years, the Board would harshly suppress this view. When editorials promoting it ran in the periodicals under Eustace's watch, the Board of Directors issued an edict: nothing published by the Church could go beyond what Mrs. Eddy had written. There could be nothing exploratory, analytical, theoretical: nothing new. The irony of the Board's rigidity in suppressing new interpretations of Eddy's writings while simultaneously ignoring her estoppel clauses—an act that was itself a form of interpretation—was not lost on their subjects and would, in years to come, engender enormous resentment.

The Board members also forbade the Trustees to publish without their express permission "Purification," a collection of religious articles about various metaphysical points that had been culled from the *Monitor*. The articles had been written by Frederick Dixon, a well-known newspaperman who had been appointed editor of the *Monitor* by Eddy herself and eventually became editor in chief of all the periodicals; he, too, was becoming suspect in the eyes of the Board for refusing to proclaim his allegiance to them publicly.

After years of haggling over the Trustees' refusal to sign the agreement acknowledging their supremacy, the Directors, in January 1918, demanded the resignations of all three Trustees. Eustace considered the Directors' behavior to be a direct violation of Eddy's deed of trust and possibly illegal. The *Manual* gave the Directors this right, but the deeds, unlike the *Manual*, were legally enforceable documents. Eustace stubbornly began to assert the rights of the Trustees, consulting several lawyers, including the esteemed Charles Evans Hughes, who would later become the Chief Justice of the U.S. Supreme Court. The lawyers, having examined the relevant documents, confirmed what Eustace privately believed: the Trustees were legally bound to obey not the Directors but the separate deed of trust that had established their own positions as heads of the Publishing Society. All of the Trustees refused to resign.

Two months later, the Board moved to oust the chairman of the Trustees, Lamont Rowlands, the least known and least influential of the three. The Trustees immediately responded by petitioning the Supreme Judicial Court of Massachusetts for an injunction prohibiting the Board of Directors from interfering in their affairs, and the Great Litigation was launched.

The hearings, to determine whether the Board of Directors of the Church had final authority over the affairs of the Publishing Society or whether that Society could govern itself, were held before a master of chancery, a single member of the Court. They began in June 1919 and lasted the entire summer. The text of the proceedings was printed, verbatim and without comment, daily, in the *Christian Science Monitor*; when the litigation came to an end, the transcripts and other court documents would fill over a thousand pages of *Proceedings in Equity 1919–1921 Concerning Deed of Trust of January 25, 1898 Constituting the Christian Science Publishing Society*. This collection was published by the Publishing Society.

Charles Evans Hughes revealed more than he knew about the divided nature that the Christian Science movement had inherited from its founder when he talked about harmony, unity, and despotism in his final argument for the Trustees:

> A good deal has been said with respect to the importance of harmony. No one could dispute the desirability of harmony. But there are two conceptions of harmony. One is the harmony produced by despotic power; the other is the harmony that results from a unity of ideas and common views of religious truth. It seems to us most unjust to Mrs. Eddy, most contrary to her teachings, to assume for a moment that she relied upon the exercise of the despotic power which these Directors have arrogated to themselves. . . .
>
> The unity which these gentlemen [the board of directors] wish, the unity of despotic power, the control absolutely of this entire government of Christian Science in the church and in the publications and everywhere else—that is the unity which might very well destroy the very faith or the organization for the propagation of the faith to which they profess to be devoted.[27]

Anyone familiar with the history of Eddy's own exercise of power might well have been startled by this argument, but it won the day. On March 6, 1920, the master decided the case in favor of the Trustees, essentially upholding the position that they could not be fired by the Board and were responsible for governing the Publishing Society strictly according to the deed.

The Board of Directors immediately struck back. In public, they asked that the decision be reviewed by the full panel of the court. In private, the Board encouraged a whispering campaign, carried out in part by Christian Science lecturers and other Scientists loyal to the Board who urged other loyalists to cancel church advertisements in and subscriptions to the religious periodicals. The *Monitor* routinely carried advertisements placed by branch churches, whose members in turn solicited Monitor advertising from local businesses and encouraged friends, neighbors, and libraries to subscribe. The aim of this whispering campaign, an extended boycott of all the products of the Publishing Society, was to bankrupt it. So-called executive or emergency committees, such as the "Executive Committee of the Christian Science Delegates of New York State," began publishing news bulletins inciting Scientists to participate in the boycott on the grounds that the Trustees were disobeying the Manual. The Board could order no reprisals or boycotts on its own authority lest it be found in contempt of court. But the Board could attempt through underground channels, as one writer put it, "to starve out the Trustees."[28]

Of course, in so doing, they were destroying the business of the Publishing Society and, inevitably, their church. Over the next year, 80 percent of subscriptions to the Journal and the Monitor were canceled, and the Sentinel suffered a 70 percent loss in circulation. In January 1920, 6,581 practitioners—who relied on the Board for the privilege and prestige of becoming "Journal-listed"—had advertised in the Journal; by July 1921, all but about 2,000 had pulled their advertisements. The gross proceeds from the sales of Eddy's works fell from $775,544 in 1919 to $375, 241 in 1924.[29] While this was undoubtedly discouraging to the Trustees, it inevitably hurt the entire Christian Science movement. It would be years before the periodicals could regain their subscription base. In addition, the tactics of the Board caused bitter divisions within branch churches and between Christian Science teachers and their students who went separate ways.

Various individual Scientists attempted to enter the legal fray by filing their own petitions. The attorney general of Massachusetts, for example, was pressured to petition the court on behalf of the Board during their appeal—an unprecedented act—and was rebuked by the court for "dragging himself in here as the fifth wheel."[30] But in the end, on November 21, 1921, the full court reversed the earlier decision and found for the Board, granting it complete authority over the Publishing Society. Although the court upheld most of the findings of the master, it could not find a legal solution to the problems posed by the separate deeds that did not grant full power over the entire institution to the Board of Directors. One body—not two, with conflicting responsibilities and warring powers—had to run the Church, or the Church, as it was constituted by Eddy in the Manual and in the conflicting deeds of trust, would fall to pieces. The historian Charles Braden described the court's dilemma and its resolution: "From the practical standpoint it is difficult to see how the court could have decided otherwise. Had it done so, there is no doubt that there would have been an endless succession of charges and countercharges before the court. The *Manual*, on any literal interpretation, is plainly inoperable."[31]

Through its decision, the court washed its hands of any attempt to interpret the ecclesiastical scripture that was the *Manual*; it gave the Board of Directors carte blanche to interpret the *Manual* as it pleased and granted that the Board had the right to remove the Trustees as it saw fit. The Board's first move, in December 1921, was to take punitive action, accusing the Trustees of mismanaging the Publishing Society and causing the disastrous drop in periodical subscriptions, of financial malfeasance, and of the terrible act of bringing the Great Litigation down upon the Church in the first place.

Herbert Eustace refused to attend a Church hearing on these charges, writing to the Board, "Since you would be both accusers and judges, what profit could there be in my joining in this idle ceremony?"[32] He also wrote, "You know in your hearts, and every Christian Scientist knows, that the injury to the periodicals was caused by the insidious propaganda which you have wholly inspired and approved."[33] He pointed out that the chaotic state of the Publishing Society's accounting records about which the Board had complained was also the Board's doing: "Practically our entire accounting department suddenly and without a moment's notice left their appointed tasks, many of them going immediately into your employment. Our books were left in a condition positively disgraceful; pages were torn and mutilated. . . . This occurrence . . . had the approval of the Directors if it was not directly inspired by them."[34] In January 1922, all of the Trustees resigned. In October 1922, Herbert Eustace was dropped from the rolls of the Church, and the Committee on Publication announced to the press that "Mr. Eustace is excommunicated forever."[35]

Thus the Board of Directors became the reincarnation of its Leader, Mary Baker Eddy. Eddy *had* risen from the dead, but now there were five of her, who, while they might pass from the scene individually, would represent her on into eternity. In the aftermath of her death, the Board of Directors became a body every bit as autocratic, contradictory, and punitive as its creator. The question of how far the powers of the Board and the Mother Church extended over the Field was now answered: it extended as far the Board saw fit. Over the decades to come, the Board would wield its authority through announcements in the *Journal* and the *Sentinel*, instructing Scientists not to read the first edition of *Science and Health*, not to take drugs or medicine if they wished to be considered Scientists, not to circulate their own theological writings, not to declare themselves conscientious objectors during wartime on the basis of their religious beliefs. Scientists were told how branch church services were to be held and how they were to behave.[36]

Superficially, the Board's dictatorially enforced unity would lead to material prosperity and social respectability for the Church: all proceeds from the Church's publishing endeavors and fund-raising would flow to the Mother Church, and the Board would determine how they were spent. But in suppressing all dissent from the Field, the Board encouraged not only reformers, like Eustace, who merely favored a looser, less formal, more democratic form of leadership and theological as well as demographic growth and independent writing on Christian Science topics. By providing no outlet for grievances or frustrations and no mechanism by which change or reform might take place, the Board also encouraged every disgruntled member with an ax to grind to organize against it, some of whom would resort to methods far less decorous than those of Eustace and his fellow Trustees. The dissident element in Christian Science has always been dismissed by the Church leadership as a tiny minority, but it has had a lasting influence on Church affairs, forcing the Board into defensive positions and airing the movement's dirty linen in the public press. Since the Great Litigation, dissidents in one form or another have been a permanent fixture in the Church, and they have recently come into their own, claiming up to a third of existing Scientists.

The dissidents have themselves become publishers, putting out volumes of protest letters, pamphlets, analytical prose, and compilations of relevant documents arguing their case. They frequently cite a passage from a letter written by the beloved Christian Science teacher Bicknell Young in May 1937. Young, a nephew of the Mormon leader Brigham Young, had been sent by Eddy herself to teach Christian Science in England; he became known as the Dean of Christian Science Teachers. His lecture at the Albert Hall in London in 1909 attracted some ten thousand people, and the following year he became the first lecturer to conduct a world tour. Bicknell Young had been taught by Edward Kimball (as was Eustace), and he, too, believed that the estoppel clauses in the *Manual* should have been obeyed and the powers of the official Church, the Mother Church, gently diminished and eventually ended in keeping with Eddy's *Manual* requirements after her death. In this oft-quoted letter, he wrote:

What we have now to "run" the Christian Science organization, our Leader never established. She set up two coordinating boards with Deeds of Trust to serve as a balance. They worked together while she was here to control them, but as soon as she left, they each wanted the power, especially the Board of Directors. They appealed and resorted to the advice of human lawyers and the courts (Paul appealed to Caesar). Nothing has gone right since 1910 when she left; it has not been carried on according to Mrs Eddy's intentions.[37]

In one sense, nothing *has* gone right for Christian Science since Eddy died. Struggling to present a uniform face to the world while suffering the throes of what is essentially an endless schism, Scientists have lurched from crisis to crisis. The Church itself, built on the cracked foundation Eddy left, has been shaken by one dissenter after another, each pointing out what is obvious to anyone who can read the *Manual*.

But in another sense, in the worldly sense, much *seemed* to go right for the Church in its early decades, despite, even during, the turmoil of the Great Litigation. In 1916, acting on a proposal Eddy had made near the end of her life to establish "a Christian Science resort for the so-called sick," the Board announced to the Field plans for the building of the first sanatorium of the Christian Science Benevolent Association, to be located on twenty acres in Brookline, Massachusetts, donated by Mary Beecher Longyear, a friend of Eddy's who had long been promoting the idea.[38] Completed in 1919, Chestnut Hill, as it is still known, served several functions over the coming years. It was a rest home for elderly or poor Scientists; a nursing home for Scientists too ill to care for themselves and who didn't wish to go to a hospital; and a training institute where Christian Science nurses learned the basic concept of nonmedical Christian Science nursing. A beautiful brick structure in the Collegiate Gothic style, with peaked roofs and leaded-glass windows, featuring a parlor with carved-wood paneling, furnished with a grand piano, library tables, and overstuffed chairs, Chestnut Hill was designed to impress the Field and the world with the style and substance of Scientists. Christian Science, it declared, would take care of its own.

In 1927, on the site of Eddy's former New Hampshire house, Pleasant View, torn down several years after her death, the Board opened the Pleasant View Home for retired practitioners and elderly or indigent Scientists, an equally grand estate with several wings. The same year, a second sanatorium of the Benevolent Association was opened on the West Coast. Arden Wood was built on a spectacular wooded site in San Francisco between Twin Peaks and the ocean; like Chestnut Hill, it is an imposing structure with beautifully furnished parlors and manicured lawns. During the same period, a Committee on Christian Science Homes was formed in England, where several Christian Science nursing homes were being established. Over the next few decades, a number of other sanatoriums and nursing homes would be opened in the United States; Chestnut Hill and Arden Wood were run by the Church, and the rest were privately operated but accredited by a Church committee.

Principia, the first Christian Science school, also experienced its greatest growth during this period. Inspired by the Christian Science use of the word "principle," Principia began modestly in 1897 when Mary Kimball Morgan, a Christian Science practitioner in St. Louis, developed an educational curriculum for home-schooling her two sons after deciding that the public schools were too materialistic. Established with the blessing of Mary Baker Eddy but without any official relationship to the Mother Church, it celebrated its first high school graduation in 1906 and expanded to serve over six hundred students during the 1920s. Its first college graduation was held in 1934. Principia eventually established two large campuses. A boarding and day school for kindergarten through high school was built in St. Louis. The college campus, completed in 1935, designed by the noted California architect Bernard Maybeck (who also designed the landmark Christian Science branch church in Berkeley) was located on a stunning piece of property, comprising over two thousand acres and four miles of bluffs, high above the Mississippi River surrounding the town of Elsah, Illinois, about forty miles upriver from the city. Principia remains the only Christian Science college in the world, but other private schools for Scientists' children opened around the country, as did summer camps where children could sing Mrs. Eddy's hymns and suffer the usual insect bites and sprained ankles without fear of being subjected to unwanted medical attention.

Branch churches continued opening around the world, including several in Africa, South America, Australia, and Asia. The U.S. Census in 1926 counted 202,098 Christian Scientists, compared to 65,717 in 1906.[39] In 1930 there were 2,451 churches; by 1933, there were 2,639, along with forty-seven college or university organizations for students.[40] Worldwide, there were 10,747 practitioners and over 500 Christian Science nurses.[41]

One historian of Christian Science asserted that, in 1925, *Science and Health* "was second only to the Bible as the most widely read book in the English language."[42]

World War II provided an extraordinary opportunity for the spread of Christian Science; the Church opened hundreds of reading rooms for servicemen and -women in Africa, Asia, Europe, and the United States and intensified distribution of Christian Science literature and the *Monitor* throughout the world. Christian Science became fashionable over these years, the trendy movement of the moment for politicians and movie stars and high society. The 1930s and 1940s were the time of the Church's greatest worldly success. For one brief, shining moment, Christian Science was chic.

3. Lady Astor Leads the Way

In 1914, Lady Nancy Astor—one of the "five or six most famous women in the world" during her lifetime, according to one biographer—fell ill with a mysterious "abscess."[43] Confined to her bed, told by doctors that she needed surgery, she began reading the first chapter of *Science and Health*. She converted immediately. She said later that after her discovery of Christian Science, "My life really was made over . . . I was no longer frightened of anything."[44]

Born Nancy Langhorne in Virginia, in 1879, and raised an Anglican, she was, during the first phase of her life, a renowned beauty of the Gilded Age and a Southern belle, sister of Irene Langhorne, the "Gibson Girl." After a brief, unhappy first marriage and divorce, she married Waldorf Astor in 1906, a union that would lead to her groundbreaking career in politics.

Waldorf Astor, who would eventually be converted to Christian Science by his wife, was the great-great-grandson and heir to the fortune of John Jacob Astor, the wealthiest man in America on his death in 1848. John Jacob Astor had made his money in the fur trade, and he imprinted his family name on New York City, endowing the Astor Library, which became, in time, the New York Public Library. In 1919, Waldorf Astor succeeded his father (an American-British financier who had acquired several magazines and a newspaper in England and had lent financial support to Britain during World War I) as viscount and was himself a leader in Tory politics. Lord and Lady Astor entertained lavishly at Cliveden, one of their estates, and Lady Astor on occasion debated the merits of her religion with her friends the writers Hilaire Belloc and George Bernard Shaw. Shaw, in particular, was scathing on the subject, once writing to Lady Astor that his wife "is in bed with a swamping headful of sin and error, known to the mob as a bad cold."[45] Lady Astor, known for her own wit, apparently had enough of a sense of humor not to take offense.

She was the first woman to sit in Parliament, elected in her husband's place in the House of Commons after he acquired his title. Famous for her outspoken lobbying for the reform of laws affecting the rights and welfare of women and children, she served as a Conservative member from 1919 to 1945. Her religious beliefs may have influenced her intense opposition to alcohol and her support of temperance legislation, but her primary influence as a Scientist was as a powerful and prominent member of society. An eager proselytizer for her faith, Lady Astor spread not only the gospel according to Christian Science, but a sense of its respectability and presentability as well. Painted by John Singer Sargent, hostess to a generation of great literary and political figures—Henry James, Edith Wharton, Rudyard Kipling, T. E. Lawrence, Winston Churchill—at one of England's most famous estates, Lady Astor permanently raised the image of Christian Science from its working-class origins and transmuted it into a religion of high society.

Nor was Lady Astor the only well-placed and influential Christian Scientist of the time. In Germany, Count Helmuth von Moltke and his wife, Dorothy, were Scientists who contributed to the translation into German of *Science and Health*.[46] Helmuth von Moltke, who became a Christian Science practitioner and teacher, descended from a line of high-ranking German army officers and politicians; the Moltkes' son, Helmuth James von Moltke (who was not a Scientist), would eventually be executed during World War II for his role in conspiring to assassinate Hitler in the famous bomb plot of July 1944. Like the Astors in England, the Moltkes lent their own prestige to the religious movement.

Lady Astor's most famous convert to Christian Science was Philip Kerr, who inherited the title of Lord Lothian in 1930. Soon after reading the copy of *Science and Health* she had sent him in 1914, in her first excitement at discovering Christian Science while recovering from her illness, he became a devoted Scientist. He, too, would become an influential ambassador of the religion. Over the next few years, Kerr served as private secretary to Prime Minister David Lloyd George, participated in drawing up plans for the League of Nations, and was present at the Paris Peace Conference of 1919.

Kerr also edited *The Round Table*, a journal promoting the views of the secretive international Round Table groups inspired by the political teachings of Cecil J. Rhodes (many members had been Rhodes scholars). The groups were discussing ideas later influential in the formation of the United Nations. Christian Science became the religion of the Round Table groups and the so-called Cliveden Set.[47] Kerr, in particular, articulated the potential advantages of an international "one world" government, a notion that has recently served as a component of the overwrought conspiracy theories of radical right-wing and white-supremacist groups in this country. In 1937, in an address delivered at Oxford University, he suggested that a unified, international governing body was the only alternative to endless war. His language recalled Eddy at her darkest and most paranoid:

> Few people seem to realize the far-reaching and demonic effects which the almost universal acceptance of national sovereignty as the basis of our present-day world order has both in producing war and in making impossible fidelity to the moral law or to Christian principle. . . . There is, indeed, no ultimate remedy for the demonic evils which spring from national sovereignty save the creation of a common sovereignty representing all men and nations.[48]

The "demonic effects" and "demonic evils" were vintage Eddy, language she often employed in her preoccupation with malicious animal magnetism, but, what's more, Lothian's notions of a united world and a "common sovereignty" may well have been inspired by his Leader's tantalizingly grand, if vague, visions of a future world that might materialize before the entire affair dissolved altogether. On various occasions, Eddy had let slip her certainty that she saw signs foretelling the day when Christian Science was "destined to become the one and the only religion and therapeutics on this planet."[49] She found it a "cause for joy" that "the loosening cords of non-Christian religions in the Orient are apparent," and suggested that the world would eventually be unified under her flag: "Competition in commerce, deceit in councils, dishonor in nations, dishonesty in trusts, begin with 'Who shall be greatest?' I again repeat, Follow your Leader, only so far as she follows Christ."[50]

Of course, Eddy's oratory was just as likely to veer off into the patriotic as to stray into millennial prophecy. And her offbeat preserved wisdom was just as likely to be used by right-wing Scientists to condemn communism and socialism as it was to be used by Lothian (who achieved even greater prominence when he was appointed British ambassador to the United States in 1939), as the inspiration for his one-world government musings. Thus, following their Leader down the twisted paths she laid for them, Scientists would stray into different political camps, using Eddy's rhetoric to justify their positions. And Lady Astor and Lord Lothian, the two jewels in the crown of Christian Science, would form a nexus for Christian Science's own modest crop of conspiracy theories, which focused on fears of one-world government and a communist takeover of the *Christian Science Monitor*.

Having turned its attention to international politics and away from the often lurid local concerns of city papers, the *Monitor* gradually gained a reputation for thoughtful, analytical coverage of world affairs, particularly over the course of the world wars. By the 1950s, the paper had over thirty thousand advertisers, six editions, and enormous prestige and respect. All Scientists, even those who did not live in Boston or work for the Church, were encouraged to promote the success of their paper by urging local businesses to advertise in it, by distributing free copies in Church distribution boxes or train and bus stations, and, of course, by subscribing.

One man—Erwin D. Canham, born in Maine in 1904, editor of the *Monitor* from 1945 to 1964 and editor in chief from 1964 to 1974—was largely responsible for the paper's development into a world-class journalistic institution. He also left some enduring questions about the influence on the paper of his political beliefs. During the 1920s, while a Rhodes scholar and a cub reporter on leave from the *Monitor*, the young Canham was entertained at Cliveden by Philip Kerr and the Astors, who owned their own newspaper, *The Times* of London. At Oxford, he covered the birth of the League of Nations for the *Monitor*. He, too, was a member of one of the Round Table groups. Unusually for a newspaper editor, Canham frequently and eagerly accepted positions in government, thinking to promote his religion along with its newspaper; his government service, however, also raised questions of conflict of interest. In 1948, he was vice chairman of the U.S. delegation to the United Nations Conference on Freedom of Information. In 1959, he was president of the U.S. Chamber of Commerce. During the Eisenhower administration, he served as chairman of the National Manpower Council and on the Commission on Information, which determined U.S. policy on information and propaganda. During the 1970s, he was a member of President Nixon's Commission on Campus Unrest and of the board of the Public

Broadcasting Service. He served as a director of the John Hancock Insurance Company and chairman of the board of the Federal Reserve Bank of Boston. When he died, in 1982, he was editor emeritus of the *Monitor* and had recently completed a term as resident commissioner of the Northern Marianas Islands.

During Canham's reign as editor of the *Monitor*, editorials favoring the United Nations were a staple, and Lord Lothian occasionally contributed to the paper. Some conservative Scientists became convinced that Canham was harboring Communists at the *Monitor*, particularly after two of its foreign correspondents were labeled Soviet spies during the McCarthy era.[51] Liberal Scientists, on the other hand, have long suspected that a connection was formed during the Canham years between *Monitor* staffers and the CIA; they point to Canham's frequent government service and involvement with international affairs, even while serving as editor.

While no evidence has ever surfaced to prove either theory, Canham's long service as *Monitor* editor and in government positions, along with Lady Astor's and Lord Lothian's in politics, established Christian Scientists in public life, where they would become firmly entrenched for decades to come. But Lady Astor did more than just attract the high and mighty to Christian Science. She became a role model for the religion, a beacon and symbol for all who were drawn to Christian Science as a populist success theology.

4. Nothing Succeeds Like Supply

Lady Astor was the highest embodiment of the wealth and rank that drew so many to Christian Science, but the promise of social and material success was already built in to the theological underpinnings of the religion. Such a promise was not unusual for what was essentially a Protestant sect; Max Weber had famously connected Calvinism's doctrine of predestination with what came to be known as the Protestant work ethic. The intense anxieties instilled in the followers of Calvinism and Puritanism by the harsh belief that only a few could be saved as God's elect, Weber argued, inspired the belief that hard work—materially demonstrated by the accumulation of capital—was a possible sign of salvation. The success theology of Christian Science constitutes a fascinating subset of the relationship between the Protestant work ethic and what Weber called "the spirit of capitalism." Scientists believe that the accumulation of material wealth is what Eddy called a "demonstration" of Christian Science. Indeed, demonstration is the point of one of her beloved sayings—"Divine Love always has met and always will meet every human need"—which is now engraved on the walls of most Christian Science churches throughout the world.[52] The expectation of perfect wealth, along with perfect health, follows from Eddy's teachings about a perfect world. The Christian Science notion of the spiritual significance of worldly goods is concentrated in Scientists' idiosyncratic use of a single word: "supply."

"Supply" is discussed only glancingly in Science and Health and Eddy's other writings, but, inspired by her exhortations to practice "radical reliance" and demonstrate the practicality of the new "Science" as a methodology that could address any problems in life—from the physical to the fiscal—her followers picked up the notion and ran with it. The concept of "supply" comes up hundreds of times in the early issues of the Christian Science periodicals.

It has its origin in the New Testament story of Jesus feeding the multitudes. Eddy writes, in Science and Health: "In the scientific relation of God to man, we find that whatever blesses one blesses all, as Jesus showed with the loaves and the fishes,—Spirit, not matter, being the source of supply."[53] Elsewhere she establishes a "deific law that supply invariably meets demand."[54] Many of Eddy's references to supply emphasize God's infinite supply of love, good, and other spiritual qualities; some references, however, refer to more worldly commodities. In an undated dedicatory message to a branch church in New Hampshire, Eddy wrote, "Rest assured that He in whom dwelleth all life, health, and holiness, will supply all your needs according to His riches in glory."[55]

Scientists have subsequently used "supply" to invoke God's infinite material, as well as spiritual, largesse. As they struggled to put their Leader's teachings into practice, "supply" congealed into Scientific jargon, suggesting that Scientists had access to an infinite supply of whatever they might need, including money. Countless testimonies in the Church periodicals report that imminent destitution or want was staved off by a successful demonstration of supply. A report from the Cleveland Association of Scientists in the Christian Science Journal of August 1889 asserted, "Workers in Science know that the supply is always equal to the demand," and Alfred Farlow, Eddy's first manager of the Committees on Publication, wrote in the Journal in 1893: "The divine Mind can and does supply all things. . . . If we learn to avail ourselves of God's supply, there will be plenty for all, and no occasion for disappointment, contention or want."[56] The *Journal* specifically addressed "the Business man of to-day" in an article in July 1897, explaining that Christian Science could heal ailing businesses as well as bodies and could benefit the bottom line: "To establish and conduct a business successfully under present conditions, money as *part* capital is certainly necessary, but this does not underrate the fact that understanding, or wisdom, is the part which not only secures the balance, but retains and increases it."[57]

Augusta Stetson's interpretation of supply was representative of the most materialistic Scientists; she boasted of being able to "demonstrate money."[58] One of her students recalled that her dining room was invariably decorated with "gorgeous silver and china" and beautiful floral arrangements: "One night as I sat next to her at dinner she was talking of God as our infinite Source of Supply, and with a gesture toward the roses said that when she needed anything she just put out her hand as she would to take one of the roses, Love meeting the need of the moment, whatever it might be."[59] On another memorable occasion, she explained to her pupils the logic behind the law of supply that guaranteed Scientists not just adequate possessions but elegant ones:

> We need health and strength and peace, and for these we look to God. But let us not forget that we also need *things*, things which are but the type and shadow of the real objects of God's creating, but which we can use and enjoy until we wake to see the real. We surely need clothes. Then why not manifest a beautiful concept? Clothes should, indeed, be as nearly perfect as possible, in texture, line and color. . . . It is certain, too, that we need homes. Then why not have beautiful homes? Our homes should express the highest sense of harmony and happiness. . . . We have a right to everything that is convenient, most comfortable, most harmonious. God made all things, though we only see their shadows, and all things are for His children. Everything is *ours*. It does not belong to mortal mind.[60]

To demonstrate supply, as Stetson and so many Scientists did, was to demonstrate that no Christian Scientist need ever want for anything. It became a self-fulfilling prophecy: the wealth and material success of prominent Scientists proved that the law of supply was in force and enforceable.

Scientists' emphasis on supply did not mean that it was acceptable to pray to become rich; indeed, it was considered to be unacceptable Scientific practice "to outline," to pray for any particular outcome. Outlining was anathema to Scientists, as described in this 1910 *Journal* article on "Effectual Prayer": "The genuine Christian Scientist . . . does with his own desires as Abraham did with Isaac, and nothing short of such complete surrender can make his prayer prove true. He must renounce all that constitutes a material sense of existence, and lay down his personal outlining of plans, if he is wholly to trust his welfare to the law of God. He must, in short, mean 'thy will be done' when he prays it."[61] But if, having renounced all specific desires and surrendered his human will, the Scientist found that his prayers were answered by worldly success, then that success was considered a manifestation of his true identity as a reflection of perfection.

Stephen Gottschalk, alone among Scientists to write astutely about the religion's appeal to businessmen, notes that "an increasing concern with business affairs" could be seen in the Church's religious periodicals as early as the 1890s, particularly during the depression of 1893–1897.[62] Just as the Neoclassical architecture of financial institutions around the turn of the century drew on ancient models to evoke an image of stability and prosperity, so the architecture of Christian Science churches did as well; many of these early churches resemble banks. "Though [Scientists] did not speak of wealth as an end in itself," Gottschalk writes, "they often justified the acquirement of material riches as an expression of spiritual riches."[63] Eventually, financial and hence social success came to seem a given for Scientists, a "demonstration" of the truth of their religion. Scientists still interpret financial windfalls and business triumphs in this way. In an interview in the *Christian Science Journal*, Bette Graham, the Scientist and secretary who invented Liquid Paper and turned it into a successful business, said, "I've been grateful for profit because it has represented to me the outcome of radical reliance on God."[64]

In 1961, the British sociologist Bryan Wilson published the first lengthy study of Christian Science. Examining the social class structure of Christian Scientists in the United States and Britain, Wilson concluded that Scientists are largely middle-class in makeup and refuted the Church's attempt to characterize Christian Science as appealing to all classes.[65] The lower classes, Wilson wrote, are "unaccommodated by its formality, sophistication, reserve and complex terminology—this last itself a frequent evidence of psychological need for assertion of superiority."[66] Identifying it as a "basically hedonistic faith" in its emphasis on success and prosperity,

Wilson found Christian Science to be "the religious expression of the well-to-do and comfortable, or those who would be so; it confirms them in the righteousness of their possessions, or of their striving."[67] Wilson's precise analysis, supported by over a dozen tables examining the demographics of the religion, explained why the faith held little appeal for the lower class in this country, including blacks, and for the populations of Third World countries where other American religions, including Mormonism, have successfully recruited.

Christian Science as a road to wealth and social status appears in enough early-twentieth-century novels to constitute a miniature genre of its own. Many of the novels were by women—*The Awakening*, by Mary Hornibrook Cummins (1905); *Glad Tidings*, by Lillian De Waters (1909); and *The Seamless Robe*, by Ada Carter (1909)—and their odd combination of a taste for the material good life with a distaste for sensuality became a hallmark of the movement.[68] The portentously named protagonist of *The Seamless Robe*, Robert Saul, a preacher who belittles Christian Science in his sermons, falls in love with Cecil Gwynne, a lovely Scientist who (like Astor) is a member of the aristocracy. After many pages in which our hero struggles to suppress his contempt for the new religion, Saul, like his forebear on the road to Damascus, sees the light of Truth, and he writes to Lady Gwynne to renounce his impure desires for her:

> I am only slowly climbing toward that plane of thought which you have reached before me, but at last, my sister, I see; still, "through a glass darkly," but less darkly every day. The fiery trial has been mine, but the baptism of tears has washed away the dross of selfish desire, revealing something of that selfless love which holds the brotherhood of man with bonds which never can be severed. . . . You know better than I what it means to watch the pure child thought unfold in Mind, revealing the whiteness of Soul.[69]

These spiritual potboilers suggest that, just as death was eroticized in literature about tuberculosis, for Scientists, the renunciation of sexual desire (as well as sexual relations in marriage) characteristic of the superior, refined Christian Science lifestyle was likewise a source of excitement and promise. In *The Diary of Jean Everts*, by Charles Francis Stocking (1912), the intriguing Christian Science "stranger" who arrives at the side of the heroine, wasting away from what seems to be TB, heals her with the Truth and then delivers what amounts to a uniquely Scientific proposal of marriage: "I know that marriage is a serious problem, even though it is seldom taken up as such. And I fully agree with Mrs. Eddy, that unless it is a step in the line of progress it should not be entered into. . . . Will you join me in laying all human desires upon the altar of Love, and ask that we may be led to see the way clearly?"[70]

One of those who was led to the magnificent renunciations and potential remunerations of the new religion was the father of one of the great literary men of the twentieth century, V. S. Pritchett. Pritchett's life, which nearly spanned the century (1900–1997), *did* span the formative years of Christian Science, and he captured the spirit of those years as no one else could, particularly the hope for prosperity that Christian Science brought to the lives of lower middle-class ne'er-do-wells like his father, Walter Pritchett.

Invariably described as "Micawber-like" in biographical essays about his son, the ebullient, petulant Walter Pritchett seems to have discovered Christian Science around 1910, when it was the height of religious fashion in London. He eagerly grasped at it, much as Americans would later grasp at Norman Vincent Peale's populist pull-yourself-up-by-your-bootstraps psychology; he clearly believed that the religion would lead him to the wealth and status he coveted. V. S. Pritchett, in the first volume of his memoirs, A Cab at the Door (a reference to the Pritchett family's many abrupt flights from creditors), remarks on Science's enduring appeal to those, like his father, who worshipped the elusive gods of prosperity:

> The heirs of the Transcendentalists were businessmen; they blandly denied the reality of matter in order to justify themselves in raking in more and more of it. . . . [Christian Scientists] gave up drink, tobacco, tea, coffee— dangerous drugs—they gave up sex, and wrecked their marriages on this account, and it was notoriously a menopause religion; they gave up politics; they gave up art but, oddly, they did not give up business.[71]

Pritchett captured the middle-class aspirations of Scientists drawn to the faith by its pretensions to learning, its clubbiness, its rarefied airs:

> Many of the good people—though mostly the bossy ones—in the church that met at the Town Hall were knowing the Truth about each other right and left. And even more, they were enjoined to "voice" it when it was opportune; it was constantly opportune and rarely complimentary. Father "voiced" very often to a Mrs. E., who "voiced" back. Not to "know the

Truth" was a certain way of "letting Error into consciousness"—I have since discovered that this, like the word "problem," is a common Americanism: perhaps, after all, Christian Science is a normal product of the middle-class American ethos.[72]

He observed the irony of Scientists' obsession with a material world that their faith rejected:

> Once or twice [Father] was asked to take the collection at the church and then he was in a state only to be compared with that of an actor on a first night. His lotions and perfumes made the air heady, as he changed from shirt to shirt and went through his collars minutely examining them. . . . At last, on these occasions, he appeared downstairs, in a tail-coat, a waistcoat discreetly outlined by a white, piqué under-waistcoat, and a pair of trousers of astounding and tigerish stripes. He wore a winged collar, a silk stock, a pearl tie-pin, and a button-hole. On his feet were spats. . . . If anyone of that crowd appeared to be the image and likeness of the Divine Mind, we felt, that man was our father.[73]

V. S. Pritchett had a scattered and frequently interrupted education that came to an abrupt end when he was apprenticed in the leather trade at the age of fifteen. He had followed his father's religion during adolescence but quickly left it behind during his struggle to become a writer, recognizing that there was no way to reconcile Christian Science—with its absolute unwillingness to countenance the physical life of the body, not to mention death—with art and literature. At twenty, he escaped to Paris, impecunious and with his parents' disapproval. The *Christian Science Monitor*, which had impressed him as an enormously sophisticated organ in his youth, hired him in the 1920s to report as a foreign correspondent from Ireland and then Spain, and his first books—short stories and a travelogue—were inspired by his travels. He eventually read himself into the role of a self-educated critic of considerable wit and acumen, writing and reviewing for the *New Statesman* for some forty years.

In much of his later fiction, Pritchett returned to his father and his father's absorption in Christian Science, dwelling on the manner in which religious rigidity warps human behavior. His 1951 comic novel, *Mr. Beluncle*, is based on his father; in it, the Christian Science Church is fictionalized as "the Church of the Last Purification" of Toronto, Canada;

and Mrs. Eddy is rechristened "Mrs. Parkinson." Mr. *Beluncle* follows its protagonist's blithe path through life, reigning as a spiritual guru over his beleaguered family, gaily building up a fantasy life of fine houses and fancy clothes bought on credit, only rhetorically wondering "if God wants it for me."[74]

All of Pritchett's fictions about the Church explore the self-absorption unwittingly fostered by religious teachings that try to discourage individuality and personality. He wrote in his memoirs that "the many tragic failures to heal are not the important aspect of this religion." He located the true evil of Christian Science, or of any similar sect, not in the actual deaths it caused but in the *living* deaths: "The real objection is to the impoverishment of mind, the fear of knowledge and living that Christian Science continuously insinuates; the futility of its total argument and its complacency."[75] His most masterful evocation of this theme and of the pomposity and joylessness of the faith, particularly as it was lived by the hopeful lower classes, can be found in his 1947 short story, "The Saint."

The first-person narrator of "The Saint," a seventeen-year-old boy whose family also belongs to the Church of the Last Purification, expresses doubts about the religion and is taken under the wing of a visiting Church lecturer. The lecturer, Hubert Timberlake, is a "wide upright man in a double-breasted navy-blue suit . . . [with] a pink square head with very small ears and one of those torpid, enamelled smiles which were said by our enemies to be too common in our sect."[76] Timberlake insists on going punting on the river with the boy, determined to have a quiet word with him and put him straight.

But Mr. Timberlake is not the punter he imagines himself to be. As he poles inexpertly under a low-hanging weeping willow, Mr. Timberlake finds himself dangling by a tree limb over the river, a situation grossly at odds with his metaphysical perfection. Witnessing the scene, the young man is struck by an embarrassing epiphany:

> I saw the shoes dip, the water rise above his ankles and up his socks. He tried to move his grip now to a yet higher branch—he did not succeed—and in making this effort his coat and waistcoat rose and parted from his trousers. One seam of shirt with its pant-loops and brace-tabs broke like a crack across the middle of Mr. Timberlake. It was like a fatal flaw in a statue, an earthquake crack that made the monumental mortal. The last Greeks must have felt as I felt then, when they saw a crack across the middle of some statue of

Apollo. It was at this moment I realized that the final revelation about man and society on earth had come to nobody and that Mr. Timberlake knew nothing at all about the origin of evil.[77]

Abruptly confronted with his inability to walk on water, Mr. Timberlake, rescued by his shocked host, lies down with the young man in a field of buttercups to dry off; when he arises in his sodden navy-blue suit, he is "transfigured," covered in buttercup pollen, "as saintly as any of those gold-leaf figures in the churches of Sicily."[78] But, steeped in his religion, Mr. Timberlake cannot speak of what has happened: "By no word did he acknowledge the disasters or the beauties of the world. If they were printed upon him, they were printed upon a husk."[79]

Pritchett's Timberlake is the distillation of the aspirations and pretensions of the emotionally straitjacketed Christian Scientist, and, as a portrait of the mental confinement imposed by the religion, it is dead on. But "The Saint," which seems to take place in Canada shortly after the turn of the century, does not take into account the one worldly event that truly captured the imagination of the Scientists, a disaster of such overwhelming enormity and undeniability that even they were forced to acknowledge it, albeit in their own inimitable way. It was World War II.

5. "Three Cheers for the Christian Scientists"

Mary Baker Eddy disapproved of war. Asked her opinion in 1898 of the Spanish-American War, she told the Boston Herald: "Killing men is not consonant with the higher law whereby wrong and injustice are righted and exterminated."[80] In 1904, responding to a query about the Russo-Japanese War, she wrote in the Boston Globe: "Nothing is gained by fighting, but much is lost. . . . War is in itself an evil, barbarous, devilish. Victory in error is defeat in Truth."[81] She claimed that "for many years I have prayed daily that there be no more war, no more barbarous slaughtering of our fellow-beings; prayed that all the peoples on earth and the islands of the sea have one God, one Mind," although she allowed that "at this hour the armament of navies is necessary, for the purpose of preventing war and preserving peace among nations."[82] On occasion, she requested that her followers pray for the resolution of hostilities taking place around the world.[83] But Eddy did not live to see the global warfare of the twentieth century, and her church, while following her law to the letter in most other instances, has taken little heed of her pacifist sentiments since her death.

During World War I, any question of Christian Science conscientious objection was drowned out by the *Monitor's* editorial position; it announced that "the demand of Principle has required the entrance of the United States into the war."[84] The Church was far too distracted, in any event, by the looming specter of the war within its own ranks, the Great Litigation, to take up any philosophical issues. The Scientists collected money for a War Relief Fund for the aid of their displaced brethren in Europe; they opened "rest centers" for servicemen, resembling Christian Science reading rooms; and they distributed their literature. For the first time, they were allowed to appoint chaplains; eleven served.

But in World War II, the question of pacifism was raised by several dissident groups of Scientists, such as the Peace Association of Christian Scientists and the Pacifist Principle Fellowship, who believed that Eddy's remarks on war meant that Scientists should refuse to serve.[85] The Church took a hard line with conscientious objectors who wished to oppose the war on religious grounds, not only refusing to support their position but actively seeking to deprive them of the right to make such a claim. Months before Pearl Harbor and the official entry of the United States into World War II, the Church, in articles and editorials in its religious periodicals and in the *Monitor*, announced its acceptance of the war and asserted that Scientists could not conscientiously object on religious grounds without "misrepresenting Christian Science."[86] The reasoning was that the Church Tenets made no specific reference to "participation in war" and no specific provision for refusing to serve.[87]

The Church's position was undoubtedly influenced in part by Hitler's increasingly negative treatment of Scientists. The *Monitor* ran one of the first interviews with Hitler, on October 3, 1923, in which he opined that the Ruhr district, rather than being handed over to France in war reparations, should have been "burned down as Moscow was burned by the Russians. The French would never have found a single bridge or tree there."[88] He also made his political intentions plain, saying, "What has been possible in Italy also is possible in Germany, where the German people, given a Mussolini, would fall down on their knees before him and worship him more than Mussolini ever has been worshipped in Italy."[89] After this, the *Monitor* frequently criticized Hitler and National Socialism, much to the despair of many German Scientists who, according to Erwin Canham's account, "tried with earnestness, with desperation, sometimes with anguish to persuade the *Christian Science Monitor* to support and praise the Hitler movement."[90] To the Church's credit, the *Monitor* never wavered in this regard and never supported appeasement, only occasionally running letters to the editor from its "indignant" German readers.[91]*

In 1933, when Hitler assumed power, the movement in Germany was popular and growing: there were sixty-four Christian Science branch churches and societies, and over a hundred practitioners. Scientists, along with many other religious minorities, as well as leaders and members of mainstream Christian religions, suffered increasing persecution under Hitler, despite a personal interview that Lord Astor arranged with the Führer to plead their cause.[93] In 1936, the importation of Christian Science literature into Germany was banned; on June 9, 1941, less than two months before Hermann Göring ordered the "final solution of the Jewish question," all Christian Science churches, reading rooms, and practitioners' offices were closed and their property seized. The following month, "Christliche Wissenschaft"—Christian Science itself—was banned "for the entire Reich," by order of the German minister of the interior, who declared the religion, which was, of course, a foreign institution imported from the United States, "hostile to people and state."[94] Christian Scientists who could be identified as such were arrested and questioned. Practitioners were pressured to disclose the names of their patients, past and present. Scientists who refused to cooperate were jailed, as were those who attempted to keep copies of the Church's Bible Lessons and other religious literature. Albert Telschow, the Committee on Publication for Germany, was seized by the Gestapo and subjected to repeated interrogations; he died after a mock trial and several weeks of confinement under harsh conditions. His assistant, Friedrich Preller, was jailed for six weeks and was ordered to find other employment on his release. One Scientist who had sold advertising space in the *Monitor* to Jews was sent to the Ravensbruck concentration camp, but survived her imprisonment.[95]

But there may have been another motivation, aside from the German persecution, behind the Board's embrace of the war and its refusal to

---

* In what may have been, in part, a quid pro quo arrangement, Lord Lothian and Lady Astor were supporters of Neville Chamberlain's appeasement policy; in 1927, when Chamberlain was serving as minister of health, he had successfully argued for a religious exemption clause for Christian Science nursing homes, defending the faith by saying, "Christian Science is not carried on as medical treatment; it is not a species of quackery which pretends to be something it is not."[92]

consider conscientious objection to it. Christian Scientists and their Church have always been exquisitely sensitive to society's expectations and approval. Although willing to oppose society on what it sees as a central religious issue—requirements for medical care for their children—the Church has rarely taken controversial positions on other matters. During the war, it publically relaxed its standards in several ways. It allowed that Church members could, in good conscience, take first-aid courses during times of war; it urged those who were drafted into the armed services to comply with vaccination requirements; and it expressed no disapproval of Christian Science wounded who accepted medical treatment, going so far as to print testimonies that included reference to such treatment in *The Story of Christian Science Wartime Activities, 1939–1946*, a book about the heroic efforts of Scientists in relief work, on the battlefield, and in prison camps, published by the Christian Science Publishing Society.

One Christian Science airman, whose face was badly burned when a shell exploded in his cockpit, wrote, "I had six operations in which skin was grafted from other parts of my body to my eyelids. The doctors were amazed at my recuperative ability after each operation." This open acknowledgment of acceptance of medical aid—aid that is characterized as benign rather than worthless—is unprecedented in Christian Science literature. Dozens of testimonies coming out of the war—of fortuitous survival, of spirits uplifted, of fortitude in prison camps, of such miraculously swift recoveries as that of the unnamed airman—emphasized that Scientists could benefit from their religious principles while not insisting on them. For Scientists, the Second World War was an anomaly: a time of public compromise, concession, and accommodation that brought them into close contact with huge numbers of non-Scientists, many of whom were deeply impressed by the charity and practicality of a religion that could be practiced seemingly by anyone, whether they were members of the Church or not. For Scientists, World War II was a public relations coup.

But while the Church was publicly accommodating of the compromises forced on Scientists in wartime, it was quietly moving to enforce a stricter obedience to the rule of "radical reliance" upon its membership. In 1942 and in 1945, perhaps in response to situations in which Scientists wounded during World War II accepted medical care, the Christian Science periodicals printed this "Item of Interest Concerning Use of Drugs or Medicine," designed to prevent branch churches from adopting a more relaxed position toward medicine:

> Should Christian Science churches accept as members applicants who use medicine, drugs, or material means for healing? The teachings and works of the great Master, Christ Jesus, and our beloved Leader, Mrs. Eddy, clearly indicate that they should not. . . . Jesus did not use drugs and did not recommend them for human use. He knew that drugs could not possibly heal, because there is but one healing agency—even God, the divine, infinite Mind.[96]

In 1957, the Board of Directors placed this directive in the editorial section of the *Christian Science Journal*, referring specifically to Eddy's statement on radical reliance: "This unequivocal statement of the Christian Science method of healing is not modified by any other statement in the textbook or in our Leader's other writings." They went on to spell out the requirements that radical reliance placed on Church members: "In order to be completely free from materia medica, one must reject its theory and opinions as to the origin, name, nature, symptoms, and effects of disease and must recognize that disease is never a material condition, but is a false mental state which is healed only by the Christ, Truth."[97]

The problem, as the Board well knew, is that Eddy never made an unequivocal statement in her life, and the assertion that her statement on radical reliance was "not modified" by any of her other writings was simply not true. The well-known exceptions to the radical reliance rule allowing Scientists to rely on medical doctors for surgery or other forms of medical treatment, including drugs, were still there, in *Science and Health*, but the board simply chose to ignore them. This hard-line position on radical reliance would have grave consequences in the years to come.

During World War II, Scientists were allowed to serve as wartime ministers, and, by the end of the war, there were over 250 Christian Science ministers assigned to the various armed services, as well as several thousand paid or volunteer war workers assigned to staff the 225 "welfare centers" and "rest rooms," wartime reading rooms for servicemen offering free literature, stationery, aid in reaching family members, indeed, just about everything but coffee. Enormous quantities of free Christian Science literature were distributed: over fifty thousand pocket-sized copies of the Bible and *Science and Health*, a million dollars' worth of Christian Science periodicals and books, and over 22,000 daily copies of the *Monitor*. Scientists also collected and distributed overseas some $4.5 million worth of clothing—all bearing labels with the words "Christian Science" on them—as well as food and other goods and services, largely dispelling the criticism that Mark Twain had made so bitterly years before, that Scientists were not charitable.

The Story of Christian Science Wartime Activities tells of one occasion when several Air Force companies, amounting to around six hundred men, were outfitted on short notice by volunteer Scientists with sweaters, scarves, and socks. One of the volunteers recalled: "Many took Christian Science pamphlets from the bookcase shelf, though we did not mention Christian Science. . . . After one company was lined up outside ready to leave, we suddenly heard their sergeant shout, 'Three cheers for the Christian Scientists,' followed by rousing volleys of 'hip, hip, hooray' from the assembled company." There is no telling how many people the world over were exposed to similar acts of Christian Science benevolence, but *Christian Science Wartime Activities* confirms that a number of new Christian Science "societies" (small groups of Scientists who may eventually form branch churches) got their start during this era: "Growth of the Christian Science movement was further indicated in the reports of Wartime Ministers, which showed a total of more than thirteen thousand 'newly interested' students."[98]

World War II was also the catalyst for the Church's last release of its membership numbers in this country: 268,915, far lower than the "millions" blithely alluded to by Eddy and Church officials in the past.[99] In the flush of its successful wartime contributions, the Church seemingly paid little attention to the evidence suggesting that, while the movement's growth was continuing, it had noticeably slowed. Between 1931 and 1941, the number of Christian Science practitioners increased from 8,420 to 8,680, a growth rate of slightly more than 3 percent, and the growth in the number of new branch churches had fallen to 10 percent, compared with its high of 200 percent during the first two decades of the century.[100] But Scientists themselves seemed to feel no alarm over the state of their union at this point, particularly as ever more famous, glamorous, and important people continued to be drawn to Christian Science. Not the least of them were movie stars.

6. Healing in Hollywood

Hollywood sets trends in spirituality just as it does in everything from fashion to food to hairstyles. Marianne Williamson's miracles were the fashionable spiritual flavor of the 1980s, and Scientology is the fad of the 1990s. But in the Hollywood of the 1930s and 1940s, Christian Science reigned supreme, attracting Cecil B. DeMille, Ginger Rogers, Joan Crawford, Doris Day, and others, some for just a few years, others for life. Even William Randolph Hearst, though not a Christian Scientist, endorsed the faith; after his infant son was treated for a serious illness by a practitioner and recovered, Hearst ordered that there be no criticism of Christian Science in his newspapers. In 1941, Hearst told the *Los Angeles Examiner* that the "best doctors in the world" had failed his son before the practitioner was brought in as a last resort.[101]

Christian Science enjoyed the shallow respect that avant-garde practices involving health and spirituality traditionally attract in Hollywood, but the religious movement's most intense closeup came on June 7, 1937, the day "the Baby" died. "The Baby" was Jean Harlow, also known as "the Platinum Blonde" and "the Blonde Bombshell." Her death, of acute nephritis, or kidney failure, after a brief illness, was widely blamed by the Hollywood rumor mill and the press on her mother, who professed to be a Scientist. Jean Harlow, the story went, had been kept by her selfish Christian Scientist mother from doctors and hospitals until it was too late. Christian Science was denounced as "nothing but legalized murder" by none other than Louis B. Mayer, head of Metro-Goldwyn-Mayer, Harlow's studio, and one of the most powerful men in Hollywood, who was offended when Harlow's mother refused his offer of his own personal physician.[102] But most of the blame fell on Harlow's mother rather than on the religion itself. Myrna Loy captured the prevailing sentiment when she wrote, "I hold that woman responsible for Jean's death."[103]

Today it is hard to imagine the furor that greeted Harlow's death. At the time, she had surpassed in popularity and box-office draw such stars as Joan Crawford, Greta Garbo, and Norma Shearer. She had been dating William Powell, and her death interrupted the filming of *Saratoga* with Clark Gable. Her funeral, at Forest Lawn Memorial Park, was "the first big Hollywood funeral," a "spectacle" surpassing any premiere gala.[104] Attending were Lionel Barrymore, Carole Lombard, Spencer Tracy, Mickey Rooney, Norma Shearer, Myrna Loy, Wallace Beery, and the Marx Brothers, as well as Mayer, Gable, and Powell. There were some $15,000 worth of flowers, including "exotic roses" from Howard Hughes. Harlow was dressed in a pink negligee from her *Saratoga* wardrobe, and after the casket was closed, it was covered with fifteen hundred lilies of the valley and five hundred gardenias. A moment of silence was observed at all Hollywood studios as the service began. Jeanette McDonald sang "Indian Love Call," said to be one of Harlow's favorites, and was accompanied by the trilling of a caged bird.[105] The eulogy was delivered by Genevieve Smith, a Christian Science practitioner. Smith read the Twenty-ninth Psalm and, according to one account, Mary Baker Eddy's "scientific statement of being."[106] Nelson Eddy (no relation) closed the service with his rendition of "Ah, Sweet Mystery of Life."

Wild rumors about the cause of Harlow's death swept Hollywood. It was a miscarriage, polio, a "septic abortion," or syphilis.[107] Cary Grant claimed that the peroxide from Harlow's famous bleached-blond hair had "seeped into her brain and killed her."[108] In 1964, a sensationalistic "intimate biography" by Irving Shulman revived the story of how Christian Science killed Jean Harlow, portraying Harlow's mother as a deranged religious fanatic who kept her dying daughter locked away from doctors in the hope of healing her through Science. One of the films inspired by this book starred the Scientist Ginger Rogers in the role of Harlow's mother, "Mama" Jean.[109] But a more objective recent biographer, David Stenn, reveals that Christian Science played only a minor role in the melodrama of Harlow's death.

In fact, although her kidneys had apparently been failing for years, ever since complications following a bout of scarlet fever as a teenager, Harlow's suffering and death may have been exacerbated by a medical doctor's misdiagnosis. Neither Harlow nor her mother was a particularly serious or devout Christian Scientist. Neither of them joined the Mother Church, and Mama Jean, a stage mother apparently drawn to a religion that she interpreted as glorifying human willpower, called on both practitioners and doctors simultaneously.[110] During Harlow's last illness, her mother turned Harlow's Palm Drive house into a virtual home hospital, hiring a doctor and three private nurses (as well as a Christian Science practitioner) to attend her, hoping to control her daughter's treatment, as she could not in a hospital. Harlow's isolation may have resulted in the initial doctor's misdiagnosis of cholecystitis, an inflammation of the gallbladder; his dextrose injections, moreover, may have hastened his patient's death—which was, however, inevitable, as there was no cure for kidney failure in 1936.

Keeping her daughter at home, using Christian Science as her excuse, Harlow's mother also hoped to hide Harlow's alcoholism. Anxious studio executives and friends who tried to see Harlow were often turned away, and those who urged taking Harlow to the hospital were adamantly, if inaccurately, told, "We are Christian Scientists."[111] Harlow was not taken to the hospital until the evening before she died. Thus the tale that Christian Science killed "the Baby" was born. Stenn points out, however, that, at the age of twenty-six, Harlow had lived a hard life: "forty-two movies, three marriages, two abortions, scandal, alcoholism, gonorrhea, and heartbreak."[112] Her death, under such circumstances, hardly seems the result of religious zealotry. But thanks to the Shulman biography and to the elephantine Hollywood memory for gossip, Christian Science is still rumored to have been responsible for the star's early death.

Many of the stars attracted to Christian Science, however, especially women, were serious about the religion, which seemed to provide them with a sense of stability and self-respect in an environment characterized by fickle audiences and an obsession with appearances. Ginger Rogers was something of an exception among them, having been a Scientist since childhood. Her mother, Lela, had turned to Christian Science when her baby daughter, then Virginia McMath, born less than a year after Mary Baker Eddy died, was kidnapped during a custody battle with her estranged husband. Stumbling through Kansas City after a fruitless search for her child, Lela McMath found herself in front of the office of a Christian Science practitioner, who took her in and prayed with her to know that the child was safe. Several days later, Lela recovered her daughter in Texas. She always attributed their reunion to her newfound religion.[113]

Rogers was brought up attending Christian Science Sunday school, and in her autobiography, *Ginger: My Story*, describes her healing, in childhood, of warts on her hands, her stepfather's healing of flu, and a husband's healing of boils. Like many Scientists, she was proud of her record of never missing work because of illness, and she tells of recovering from pneumonia while onstage in the lead role of *Mame*:

The last six days of *Mame* were a memorable time because my record of not missing a performance was in jeopardy. I came to work on Monday with a heavy cold and was feeling very ill. My voice had vanished and I despaired. Each day the challenge was there: "Give up!" No, I thought. One on God's side is a majority. I called a practitioner in California, explaining and requesting metaphysical, prayerful help. I had all the symptoms of pneumonia: the fever, the perspiring, and so on. Still I reported to work on Tuesday, praying constantly.

Thank heavens I had a tiny microphone attached to my bra; otherwise I don't think I would have been heard past the first row. Between the dialogue, I uttered to myself parts of the Lord's Prayer and the 23rd Psalm, and kept my thoughts Godward. My strength slowly returned. My voice became stronger. My dancing became lighter.[114]

Rogers, who finished her run in Mame without breaking her perfect record, later learned that the cast had been placing bets on when she would collapse.

Rogers never took Christian Science lightly. She died in 1995, at the age of eighty-three. Her last act was to call her Christian Science practitioner and listen as passages from the Bible were read to her over the phone.

Many new religious sects or cults that have initially aroused suspicion in the American public have embraced celebrities in often successful bids to domesticate or normalize their image. The Transcendental Meditation movement became associated in the public mind with the Beatles, and Scientology has exploited the reputations of dozens of its celebrity members, most notably actors John Travolta and Tom Cruise, to promote its acceptance. The Christian Science Church, however, perhaps because of the guilt by association it suffered in the case of Jean Harlow, perhaps because of its abhorrence of any publicity it cannot control, has shied away from affiliating itself too closely with its own celebrities. No incident better illustrates the Church's gun-shy attitude toward its own glamour than the flap over which Hollywood starlet would play the part of Mary Baker Eddy.

There was to have been a movie about Eddy's life. In the late 1940s, Arthur Corey, a Scientist with Hollywood ties, was asked to write a screenplay about Eddy's life, in which Olivia de Havilland, of Gone With the Wind fame, and other stars had expressed interest; Jesse Lasky, one of the founders of the studio that became Paramount, was to produce and Dorothy Arzner, a pioneering woman director, was to direct. But the movie was scrapped in 1949, having foundered on the rocks of official Christian Science disapproval.

Before the project was abandoned, Mary Pickford, a self-professed Christian Scientist, had signed on to play Eddy. The gossip columnist Louella Parsons broadcast this tidbit, and a Christian Science letter-writing frenzy was set in motion by Church officials. Scientists' response to the sacrilegious notion that an actress—Scientist or not—would step into the shoes of the woman who had brought the Second Coming to the world was quick and sharp, Corey reported. "Audacious! A sacrilege! Unauthorized!"[115] Because of Scientists' opposition, Pickford bowed out, only to be replaced by Joan Crawford, another erstwhile Scientist who, herself a troubled mother given to grandiosity, might well have captured Eddy's queenly manner with her family and followers. But Crawford eventually wrote to Corey, in Christian Science code, to say, "I feel it extremely dangerous for anyone to try to put this on the screen. We have enough to work out of daily, and certainly enough to work with I know, but I see no reason to add to the malpractice."[116] And the Committee on Publication for California, James Vincent, also tried to discourage the project, announcing to the press in 1949: "While we agree that mankind would be benefited by an appreciative understanding of Mrs. Eddy's life, we realize that it would not be possible rightly to portray her character either in a picture or on the stage."[117]

Five years later, Warner Brothers tried to revive the Corey treatment, and Joan Fontaine and Greer Garson both expressed interest in the role. But, again, it was not to be. Jack Warner lost interest after learning what a fraught subject Eddy had become.[118] Not even the Mormon church could keep movies from being made about Brigham Young; the Saints settled for ensuring that film depictions of their movement were positive ones. But the Christian Science Church, through pressure tactics that it would resort to repeatedly over the years, succeeded in quashing any movie about Eddy's life.

Christian Science's appeal extended beyond Hollywood to artists and writers who saw it as a glamorous form of mysticism. Hart Crane, the poet, was raised by a Christian Science mother and retained a belief in its effectiveness; Mina Loy, the Surrealist poet, became an ardent Scientist, on occasion attending a branch church in Florence, Italy, with Gertrude Stein and her brother Leo (a surreal moment in Christian Science history); Henry Miller, that reprobate of American letters, found Eddy a "great soul."[119]

The visual artist most profoundly influenced by both Hollywood and Christian Science was Joseph Cornell (1903–1972). When Cornell was a child, his father died of leukemia, and his brother Robert was born with a paralyzing illness later identified as cerebral palsy. Burdened by a prematurely adult pressure to care for his family—he was the eldest son—the young Cornell discovered Christian Science in the early 1920s and seems to have found the religion enormously comforting as a means to organize and soothe his extreme moods, panic attacks, and recurring nightmares.

He also seems to have found it useful in his difficult relationship with his nagging, unappreciative mother, with whom he lived all his life because he was convinced that his crippled brother needed him. Obsessed with a series of unapproachable, unattainable women—ballerinas, movie stars, waitresses—he also dreamed of Mary Baker Eddy, his spiritual mother. He wrote in his journal in 1963: "strange dream of . . . Mrs. Eddy in 1910 costume . . . (one of phenomenal stages of preoccupation with maiden)."[120] His own mother was continually disapproving and critical; Christian Science gave Cornell the means by which to disapprove of her, writing to his sister, "I'm sick and tired of mother going to the end of her days doing everything in the world but looking into a healing truth."[121]

Cornell's journal is a unique published record of the emotional life of a Christian Scientist; unlike the Church's testimonies, which have a cookie-cutter sameness, Cornell captured the meditative quality of the religion in his own language. On August 17, 1945, shortly after the surrender of Japan, he identifies the day as "Christian Science Holiday—second V-J Day." He had "decided to go out back alone and do some mental work to know the unreality of the claim of pressure at back of head. A beautiful feeling of gratitude for atmosphere of garden and woods in the back of garage and of being *rid of a feeling* of always *wanting to be somewhere else*."[122] Cornell, a middle-class dreamer whose lonely existence was enlivened by the energy of art and popular culture, found in Christian Science a religion overlaid with sophistication that transported him away from the small, sordid, disappointing details of life.

Cornell fused his Science and his art, using his readings in *Science and Health* to spark spontaneous associations, much as he used the images and techniques of Surrealist art, literature, and film. He once wrote to his friend and fellow Scientist Mina Loy: "My Science and healthy thoughts about the unconscious in Surrealism (about which I know nothing) combined to give me extraordinary emotions."[123] He told Julien Levy, Loy's son-in-law, who owned the art gallery that first displayed his work, that he thought that Surrealism was marked by "deviltry." His art, he said, would be "white magic," as opposed to malicious animal magnetism, the black magic of Christian Science.[124]

Cornell's first tentative works of art were "pill boxes," small round paperboard boxes. The cover of one of these pill boxes reads SURE CURE FOR THAT TIRED FEELING.[125] Cornell removed the original contents of these boxes and filled them instead with "tiny shells, sequins, red ground glass, rhinestones, beads, black thread, scraps of blue paper," and other magical talismans.[126] The work of an already committed Scientist, his pill boxes are fascinating, childlike revisions of materia medica, the bête noire of every Scientist. Instead of the worthless pills that could not cure his beloved brother, the boxes have been filled with ephemera invested with special powers by the artist, a kind of physical manifestation of the magic Christian Science cure.

The work for which Cornell would be known—the shadow boxes and collages—teem with references to the world as seen through the scrim of Christian Science. Like his pill boxes, Cornell's many "pharmacy" boxes, corked or stoppered glass bottles ranged in compartmentalized rows, filled with unlikely *objets*, scraps of paper with occasionally visible words, a fragment of a butterfly's wing, a seashell, varicolored liquids or paints, and gold dust, hark back to the religion's roots: mesmerism and alchemy in which any humble natural object could be magnetized into a healing or transforming power, turning sickness into health or dross into gold.

The use in many Cornell boxes of mirrors, glass, and reverse images recalls the Christian Scientist's overweening concern with man as the reflection of perfection, and with corporeality and materiality as the physical manifestations of imperfection. Overwhelmed by the material world, Cornell tamed it by collecting, collating, boxing, labeling, and organizing it. A virgin all his life, overwhelmed by the pressing anxieties of sexuality and desire—anxieties so palpable in *Science and Health*—he caught those explosive feelings and framed them in the boxes paved with tiny, repetitive images of Lauren Bacall, a beautiful Medici prince and princess, balls, birds, and feathers. One of the boxes made for and inspired by Mina Loy featured her photograph "recessed . . . beneath a layer of glass shards."[127]

In Joseph Cornell, worlds collided. Friend of the artist Marcel Duchamp, the writer Susan Sontag, the ballerina Allegra Kent (also intrigued by Christian Science), the actor Tony Curtis; lover of Borges and Beethoven and Emily Dickinson—Cornell was as powerful an American original as Mrs. Eddy, the "maiden" who inhabited his dreams. His mind, both sophisticated and naive, met an American religion, and its words, phrases, and images seeped into his mysterious world. Science is still in there, in his boxes, preserved under their creator's imperfect control, fragile, impermanent, falling to pieces.

Other celebrity associations with Christian Science have composed a public image of the religion that seems almost schizophrenic: by turns doctrinaire and accommodating, unyielding and flexible. According to her biographer Fred Lawrence Guiles, Joan Crawford seems to have been attracted to the religion's tone of high-minded superiority, once chatting about its advantages with Marilyn Monroe.[128] But Crawford did not strictly follow its teachings. Toward the end of her life (she died in 1977 of cancer, at the age of seventy-two), she was visited regularly by her Christian Science practitioner, who read to her from the works of Mary Baker Eddy, apparently not deterred by Crawford's acceptance of medical care and medication for her condition.

Doris Day converted to Christian Science as an adult, and for many of her colleagues and fans, her famously cheerful disposition became associated with her religion, although her beliefs apparently also made her reclusive and anxious. In 1954, Louella Parsons wrote of Day in *Cosmopolitan*, "She lives in the belief that happiness has to be made—and can be made—by the individual. In her sunny exuberance, she seems to be a living proof of it."[129] Day's attraction to Christian Science may have come from personal unhappiness. As a young dancer, she was badly injured in an automobile accident and spent over a year in hospitals; after she became a star, she had a series of unhappy marriages. Like other actors who encountered Day's religious practices on the set, Rex Harrison, who starred with her in the 1960 murder mystery *Midnight Lace*, was bemused by her devotion: "We used to hold what amounted to Christian Science sessions on the set—or so it seemed to me—when all the lights would be put out and the director could be heard telling Doris, sotto voce, 'God is in the studio, God is in the flowers, God is on the set.' "[130] Retired from acting, Day lives in northern California; she is still a devout Scientist.[131]

Carol Burnett, in her memoir, *One More Time*, has recalled her unsettled childhood growing up with a Christian Science grandmother, an inventive hypochondriac who tied a rolled-up *Christian Science Monitor* to her stomach with string so that her " 'insides wouldn't fall out.' "[132]

According to Burnett, this grandmother was of the school of Scientists who believe in covering all bases, with a copy of *Science and Health* and a medicine cabinet full of pills and potions:

> She'd lie down and put a cold rag on her forehead and clutch the Bible and *Science and Health* to her breast, moaning, "There is no death, God is all in all. . . ." I'd start to panic when she'd jump up again, swallow some medicine, then give up and say, "Watch me . . . I'm going. Know the truth for me!" One time I banged my head against the wall and begged God to take me first.[133]

The celebrity most eager to associate herself in the public mind with Christian Science—and perhaps the person who has caused the most confusion about its beliefs—is also the one with the finest Christian Science pedigree: Carol Channing, star of the original—and endless revivals of—*Hello, Dolly!* In virtually every interview she has given in recent years, Channing has alluded to Christian Science. She grew up in its heyday, and many of her comments about it recall the awe in which it was once held by a middle-class America convinced that it conferred worldly success upon its adherents.

During a spate of interviews in 1995, when Channing was seventy-four and launching the thirtieth-anniversary *Dolly* tour, she told the *New York Times*, "I'm a Christian Scientist and we have no such thing as age."[134] At an opening-night party in New York City, she announced to the audience that she was never sick and would never be too old to work: "Age doesn't interest me. Besides, I'm a Christian Scientist and we don't believe in birthdays. Now, isn't that a nice religion to have?"[135] Like many Christian Scientists, she is deeply proud of a near-perfect attendance record; she has never missed a performance because of illness, only once ducking out to accept a Tony award for lifetime achievement. Her father would be proud.

George Channing, whom his daughter remembers with deep affection—she jokes that, dressed as Dolly, she looks like her father in drag—was a beloved Christian Science lecturer during the 1930s and 1940s who also served as manager of the Committees on Publication.[136] Transcripts of his public lectures and addresses to his Class Association are still distributed as "The George Channing Collection" by dissident Christian Science organizations that are not afraid to flout the Church's policy against circulation of "unauthorized literature." In an interview with the *Washington Post* in

1995, Carol Channing poignantly recalled the pitfalls and delayed gratifications of a Christian Science upbringing:

> I got Pygmalioned into that Christian Science mold. I don't know any differently. I mean, I was raised to believe that there is no such thing as age. I never had a birthday growing up. I had to get everybody else a present, but I never got one myself. Never! I thought it was terrible. My father sneaked me a pair of roller skates for one birthday. I'll never forget it. He said, "Just don't tell Mary Baker Eddy." Wasn't that sweet of him? But as I got older, I realized, yes, you don't tell people what age you are, because if you do, they make you that age.[137]

Channing's endurance, which verges on masochism, rivals that of Ginger Rogers. While in her mid-sixties, appearing in a tour of the stage show *Legends!*, Channing tripped and fell in one scene but jumped up and finished the show. At the curtain call, a fellow actor reached down to grab her hand, and she said, "Don't—my arm's broken."[138] After the show, she went to the hospital, had her arm set and put in a cast, and continued with the tour. She has also performed with a high fever, in a wheelchair, and in a neck brace, as well as while suffering from severe allergies caused by her hair dye.[139] At the time of the thirtieth-anniversary tour, her vision was so poor that she could barely see her way down the stairs during her famous final scene, and she was scheduled to have eye surgery.[140] She forced herself to finish the cast album with an infected trachea. Channing's interpretation of her behavior is classically that of the Christian Scientist, refusing to let reality impinge on perfection: "Nothing will stop us from lifting other people's lives. That's the goal, and as long as that is the goal, it fits in with the laws of the universe."[141]

Glorifying her role and belittling herself, Channing expresses a self-image typical among Christian Scientists, who routinely minimize the importance of their individuality. "If you dwell on yourself," she told a *Vanity Fair* interviewer, "it gets sickening."[142] Channing's view of the world, which, for her, is the audience, is also quintessentially a Christian Science view:

> Actors are totally dependent on their faces, voices and bodies to tell a story. But Christian Science says there's nothing so strong as the power of thought. So it doesn't matter if you don't have a voice, or if you're sitting in a wheelchair doing a show. It's the thought that counts, how you understand and

project the character mentally. You know, the smartest mind in the world is an audience. There's a truck driver here, and a housewife there and a whiz of a businesswoman next to her. All kinds of mentalities are sitting there. Together, they form the perfect mind. . . . Sometimes, I think it's like facing God Almighty.[143]

Channing's blithe acceptance of surgery and other forms of medical care that Scientists usually reject or indulge in only secretly, and her glorification of such trivial Christian Science traditions as not missing a day of work and not celebrating birthdays, presents a romanticized image of the Science lifestyle. That image is now firmly fixed in the public perception: Scientists don't "believe" in doctors, but they probably use them anyway. Clashing with the occasional breaking news story concerning Christian Science parents on trial for the deaths of their children, this image has created a split in the public response to Christian Science. The religion is seen as somehow respectable *and* scandalous, admirable *and* contemptible, familiar *and* troubling—an impression only reinforced by the sharply differing responses of other celebrities and public figures. For every Christian Science cheerleader like Carol Channing, there's a bitter accuser like James Hetfield, the lead singer and guitarist for the heavy-metal group Metallica. Raised as a Scientist, he has denounced the religion in songs such as "The God That Failed" and "Dyers Eve": "Dear mother / Dear father / What is this hell you've put me through / Believer / Deceiver / Day in day out live my life through you."[144] In an interview in 1991 he said, "Both my parents are Christian Scientists; I think that they got into it after they got married, but it's always been a difficult topic for me. My mom passed away because she didn't go to a doctor or a hospital when she had cancer. I guess I'm still kind of angry at myself for not forcing her."[145]

Even those who rarely, if ever, speak publicly about the religion embody its contradictions: Shannon Miller, the Olympic gymnast, was raised as a Scientist but quietly agreed to have surgery on a sports-related injury in 1992.[146] Tommy Vardell, the All-American Stanford fullback who went on to play for the Cleveland Browns, occasionally refused to take anti-inflammatory drugs but, in order not to bring his career to a complete halt, agreed to take medications recommended by NFL doctors and trainers.[147] At a talk he delivered at the Principia College campus in 1992, Vardell affectionately recalled singing Mrs. Eddy's hymn "Shepherd Show Me How to Go" while playing baseball as a child and "yelling at my brother for not knowing the Truth when I struck out."[148] He also acknowledged that NFL scouts consider Christian Science "a negative" in football.

The astonishing number and variety of Hollywood celebrities who are Scientists or who bear the early imprint of Science from their families suggest the extent to which Christian Science once permeated the culture and, in almost imperceptible ways, still does. Robert Duvall was raised as a Scientist and attended Principia Upper School, the Christian Science preparatory school in St. Louis, as well as Principia College. He almost flunked out of the college until he changed his major from government to drama, a specialty at Principia, which regularly stages elaborate theatrical productions. The playwright Horton Foote, also a Scientist, discovered Duvall in an early performance of one of his plays and subsequently offered him his first movie role, as Boo Radley in Foote's Academy Award winning screen adaptation of *To Kill a Mockingbird*.[149]

What is one to make of the fact that Elizabeth Taylor, perhaps the world's most famous actress, as well as a notable hypochondriac and serial invalid, was raised as a Scientist by her devout mother?[150] That actors as disparate as Mickey Rooney, star of dozens of MGM musicals, and George Hamilton, Hollywood's perpetually tan playboy, are Scientists?[151] That the comedian Robin Williams was raised by a Christian Science mother ("I call her a Christian Dior Scientist," he has said. "She is basically optimistic, which is frightening sometimes")?[152] That the Scientist Val Kilmer, who stars in Dreamworks' animated *Prince of Egypt*, has said in a recent interview in the *Christian Science Sentinel* that Eddy's "wonderful, revealing" comments on Moses inspired his portrayal?[153] That Monica Lewinsky, having consulted a Christian Science practitioner about her fear that Linda Tripp would betray her, whiled away her incarceration in the Ritz-Carlton by compulsively reading the Ninety-first Psalm on the practitioner's recommendation? That the Christian Science Church has been a client of Ken Starr's? Christian Science is a chameleon among religions, blending into the background, harmless to some, deadly to others. Its true nature has always been most evident, however, when its defenders are drawn out into the open and forced to go on the attack.

7. "The Blight That Failed"

No matter how many movie stars and millionaires and artists the chic new religion attracted, Christian Science continued to be subject to skeptical curiosity, disbelief, and ridicule. Mary Baker Eddy, in creating her Committees on Publication specifically to deal with "impositions" against her, had tried to inoculate her movement against criticism. But she did not live to see the most infamous imposition of all, Edwin Franden Dakin's *Mrs. Eddy: The Biography of a Virginal Mind.*

Dakin's book, published by Scribners in 1929, became one of the most famous battlegrounds of the Eddy biography wars. The Scientists' suppression of Cather's book had gone unnoticed and unprotested, but, unlike Cather, Dakin was not a shadow author who refused to acknowledge his own work. Dakin relished a good fight, and the Church's organized attempts to suppress his book blew up in its face.

One of the most extraordinary things about Dakin's book is the fact that it was written at all. Dakin was not a journalist or a professional writer, and *Mrs. Eddy* would remain his only original work.[154] Born in 1898 in Hannibal, Missouri, Dakin graduated from Washington University in 1921 and immediately found success in the business world, serving on the editorial staff of a weekly, *Commerce and Finance,* and eventually as a public relations adviser to various companies. As Dakin wrote years later in a new introduction to Scribners' 1970 paperback reissue of *Mrs. Eddy,* his interest in his subject sprang from a spiritual quest engendered by his experiences while serving with the Washington University Ambulance Corps from 1917–1919:

> As a youth just turned twenty-one, I awoke one morning with what I thought a startling idea: if one wanted to know the real truth about God— and what belief about Him, if any, might hold water—then why not explore the personal lives of folk who devoutly embraced one belief or another? What happened to these people? Did their own beliefs do them any good? Could one find any evidence, in the final life-outcomes for any of these true believers, that one assortment of beliefs was any more valid than another, or any more reliable a guide to useful truth?
>
> I was then just returned from over two years in France. There I'd had my hands in human blood and pus for days on end. That was the Medical Corps

for you. And I came out of that World War I experience intensely troubled by one of man's most ancient wonderings: if there be a God worthy of man's least veneration, how could He possibly permit such horrors—the flesh-rendings of countless decent youths—as I'd seen with my own eyes?[155]

With these questions in mind, Dakin embarked on an intellectual march through the history of Christianity, beginning with Paul and moving on through the lives of the saints; he then explored Eastern religions and the Koran. He eventually wound up his search with the colorful exploits of "modern figures as various as Mme. Blavatsky, Mrs. Besant, Brigham Young, and Mrs. Eddy."[156] He was intrigued by Eddy and disturbed to find so little biographical material about her, dismissing Sibyl Wilbur's " 'authorized biography' " as a "pious insignificance."[157] He eventually discovered a rare copy of "Milmine" 's biography in a used-book store on New York's Lower East Side, "and paid $25 for it—not a small sum in the mid-20's."[158] He learned that, though Eddy herself was dead, the passions she had inspired survived. He called on the formidable Augusta Stetson, "still living in her palace just off Central Park West."[159] He also found living in the city John Valentine Dittemore, once a member of the Church's Board of Directors, excommunicated after quarreling with his fellow members. Talking with these exiled insiders and reading Stetson's own voluminous writings, Dakin was captivated by the dark doings and strange spiritual exploits still unfolding: "It seemed to me great drama. I had never seen such a magic tale in print outside of fiction, and somewhere at this point I suddenly thought, *Why not do this tale myself?*"[160]

With the help of his mother, who enthusiastically conducted much of the research for the book at the New York Public Library, Dakin set out to fill the hole he had found in Eddy research, working at his job six days a week and writing at night. On November 28, 1928, he delivered the unsolicited manuscript to Charles Scribner's Sons, where it was "accepted at once."[161]

It was not long before the Christian Scientists showed up at Scribners' door. An announcement of Scribners' fall books was distributed May 1, 1929; a few days later, Orwell Bradley Towne, the Committee on Publication for New York State, visited the publisher's office to confirm the fact that a biography of Mrs. Eddy was set to appear. Towne immediately made an appointment to meet with executives of Scribners. According to a pamphlet about the ensuing publishing controversy, "The Blight That Failed," which was distributed with later editions of Dakin's book, "The interview began by Mr. Towne producing from his pocket, apparently without embarrassment, one of twenty copies of a confidential memorandum supplied to the members of the Scribner sales department. Mr. Towne was not asked how he procured this copy, and did not volunteer that information."[162]

During the meeting, Towne disagreed with the editors' assertion that Dakin's book was not a sensational exposé; he insisted that the sales department's description of the book—he had not read the book itself—showed that it was "false" and "unworthy." He questioned Dakin's character and qualifications as a writer "but desisted when he was obliged to admit that he knew nothing of Mr. Dakin personally."[163] Towne warned that Scribners would face serious consequences if they proceeded to publish the book, saying, "It is a very serious matter to offend several million people," a rather extraordinary claim given that the U.S. Census of Religious Bodies conducted in 1926 had found just over 200,000 Christian Science Church members in the United States, a figure given in Dakin's book.[164] Towne also asked to see the book prior to publication, saying, "I suggest you submit the manuscript to our committee on publications so that the reliability of its sources and the accuracy of its data be checked." Towne offered no reciprocal editorial aid; he did not "offer to open the church archives to Mr. Dakin so that he might make his own investigations into the official records of Mrs. Eddy's church."[165]

Scribner declined. In July, a month before the publication date of the book, Henry Saylor, editor of *Architecture* magazine, which was then published by Scribners, received a letter from an old college acquaintance, Albert Lombard, who also happened to be the Committee on Publication for Southern California. Lombard urged Saylor to wield any influence he might have at Scribners to halt publication of the book:

It appears that the proposed biography has been written without dependable data, for I understand that no information regarding Mrs. Eddy has been sought from the archives of the Church she established. . . . An inaccurate, inadequate, or unfair account of Mrs. Eddy's character and work would not only give offense to a large number of respected citizens, but it would also do an injustice to a religion which furnishes unquestionable proofs of the good it is doing for mankind. . . . Some years ago *McClure's Magazine* suffered serious loss of prestige as a result of publishing a series of articles which contained misleading statements concerning Mrs. Eddy. . . . I know that you are interested in seeing the high standard of Scribners maintained as I am interested in seeing justice done to Mrs. Eddy, and if you are in a position to discuss this subject with the proper person so that it will receive judicious consideration, the best interests of both of us may be served.[166]

The book was published on August 16, 1929, to overwhelmingly favorable reviews. H. L. Mencken wrote, in the *American Mercury*, "Mr. Dakin's book is well ordered and competently written. He has been at pains to unearth the precise facts and he sets them forth carefully and pleasantly. He has made a valuable contribution to American history."[167] Lewis Mumford praised the book in the *New Republic:* "The total effect of his work is sympathetic; it is the facts that alienate us, and [Mrs. Eddy's] own absurd pretensions that are deflated, by the mere act of exposure. In short, Mr. Dakin has committed an unforgivable offense against Mrs. Eddy: he has done her justice."[168]

He did her justice in an almost voyeuristic, page-turning style, placing us in Eddy's classroom, at her bedside, in her tiny attic room as she laboriously scrawled out the hundreds of pages of *Science and Health* by hand. He captured the process by which a human being transmuted herself into myth. In the chapter "Twilight of a God" he relates how Eddy, ensconced in Olympian splendor at Pleasant View, developed the habit of taking violent exception to new arrivals. When physical pains or problems in the movement coincided with the appearance on the scene of a new servant, she inevitably concluded that the newcomer had "brought along a fresh supply of M.A.M. in his trunk" and dispatched the unfortunate forthwith.[169]

Mrs. Eddy is not a modern biography. Published today, such a book would undoubtedly have more extensive footnoting, and the apparent re-creation of dialogue would raise eyebrows. But, as Mencken, Mumford, and other reviewers acknowledged, it brought its subject vividly to life, exploring the psyche of a woman devoted to the precept that matter is not real as only a man who had recently had his hands in "human blood and pus for days on end" could. Occasionally arch and patronizing, Dakin is also admiring of Eddy's "indomitable will," which to his mind entitled her to "comradeship among the great."[170]

Scholars still consider his book a valuable contribution to Eddy studies.[171] Dakin's *Mrs. Eddy* should have become the accepted source for Eddy researchers for some time; the fact that controversy and doubt have attached themselves to the reputation of the book, which is now unfortunately out of print, derived from what Scribners called "a threefold attempt to smother it."[172]

That "threefold attempt" consisted of visits by Christian Scientists to bookstores and libraries; letters of protest from Christian Scientists and Christian Science churches to Scribners; and letters from Committees on Publication to virtually every newspaper or magazine that reviewed the book. In a time when independent booksellers regarded the goodwill of their customers as essential to their business, the visits, some made directly by those representing the Committees on Publication of particular states, were initially the most damaging. Booksellers were asked by Scientists to stop selling the book; those who balked were asked to compromise by keeping it hidden under the counter or in a back room. Particularly stubborn booksellers were threatened with boycotts.[173]

"The Blight That Failed" quotes from seven representative letters that booksellers sent to Scribners describing complaints from customers and Committees on Publication regarding the book; three of the booksellers requested permission to return unsold copies:

An Atlanta bookseller on September 12:
We have on hand three copies of "Mrs. Eddy," by Dakin, and beg to advise that Atlanta has a number of followers of Mrs. Eddy who resent us having this book on sale. We do not feel that it would pay us to antagonize this class of people, and ask that you allow us the privilege of returning the three copies for credit. . . .

A Burlington, Vermont, book dealer on November 13:
Some very good friends of ours who are Christian Scientists feel that we should not discriminate against the Christian Science religion, and they are justified in asking us to refrain from selling the book. If agreeable to you, we will return for credit the two copies you recently sent us.

On November 23 one of Detroit's leading booksellers wrote:
Due to the violent protest of the Science Church in our city and boycott on our store by these good people, we have been forced to withdraw the sale of your book "Mrs. Eddy" from our store. We are not in business to offend classes, and this group of people are good book buyers and are very close

friends of our establishment. We are the third bookstore in our city to withdraw the sale of this book. The first company was the largest department
store in our city. It is quite evident from our experience that we made a great
mistake in displaying this book at all. As time goes on you will probably feel
that you have made an error in publishing this title.[174]

A bookseller in Cleveland wrote that the Committee on Publication for
Ohio had "been quite insistent that we discontinue the sale" of Dakin's
book. He refused to comply, noting that he had sold "about thirty copies
up to the present time," but agreed not to feature the book in promotional
materials.[175]

Some booksellers were outraged by the pressure brought to bear upon
them. In January 1930, a bookseller in southern California wrote to
Scribners:

> It may interest you to know that way out here in the West solemn meet-
> ings have been held to blacklist the stores carrying "Mrs. Eddy." The row has
> given us just the opportunity we wanted to cancel a very unprofitable adver-
> tisement which has been running in the *Christian Science Monitor* for several
> years. In the beginning a very good customer told us that, much as she liked
> to trade with us she would have to go elsewhere if we did not advertise in
> the Christian Science paper. The advertisement cost at least half of her
> annual purchase, but we ran it until we became thoroughly disgusted with
> Christian Science tactics. This year she did not enter the store—so much for
> freedom of action.[176]

Throughout October and November of 1929, sales of *Mrs. Eddy*
declined noticeably. In a publishers' note included in subsequent editions,
Scribners acknowledged the initial success of the boycott: "For many
weeks it seemed as if the sale of Mrs. Eddy might actually be so reduced
that the book could not be kept on the market. Many stores were forced by
threats to renounce its sale, and many to conceal it."[177] Scribners responded
by sending letters to booksellers and by running a series of ads in newspapers designed to expose the Church's campaign. One of the ads read:

> "We have been forced to take off our tables all copies of 'Mrs. Eddy,' by
> Edwin Franden Dakin."
> This is from a bookseller who writes that because of pressure from

individuals who are trying to smother this biography, he has been obliged to return his stock of copies and compelled to write a letter of apology to "two agencies" in his city. Personally this bookseller endorses the book.

This is a sample of many letters which have come to us from coast to coast.

The result is a situation almost incredible in a free country. You may find that your bookseller either will regret his inability to sell you this biography, universally endorsed by the press of the country, or he may produce a copy hidden away under a counter. Some booksellers actually have the courage to display the book. We hope your bookseller is one of these.

Throughout some eighty-five years of publishing, we have been able to say of our books, "on sale at all booksellers." We regret that in this one instance we must qualify this statement.[178]

As early as 1906, the Committees had begun to petition libraries to reclassify *Science and Health* as religious literature rather than one of the "mental philosophies."[179] With Dakin's book, they attempted to influence libraries' choice and display of books. The November 1929 issue of *Carnegie Magazine*, the journal of the Carnegie Institute of Technology, described an organized attempt to remove Dakin's book from the Carnegie Library in Pittsburgh, Pennsylvania:

When this book appeared a group of members of the Christian Science Church called at the Carnegie Library with the request that it be excluded from the collections. Director Munn gave very careful consideration to the matter, but after conference he decided that, while consenting to keep the book out of the "Monthly Notes" published by the library and off the shelves that are open to visitors, his duty to the people of Pittsburgh obliged him to carry it in his circulation department, and since that time it has been one of the most sought-for of all the present-day publications. It was not alone in Pittsburgh but throughout the country that the officials and publishing committees of the Christian Science Church have resorted to every form of pressure up to the threat of a boycott in their feverish efforts to suppress this masterful and illuminating book.[180]

There is evidence that the campaign to suppress Dakin's book was approved, if not planned, by the highest levels of Christian Science officialdom. The October 5, 1929, issue of the *Christian Science Sentinel* lauded the Committees on Publication for interfering with the circulation of critical books, probably Dakin's, in libraries:

At the insistence of a Christian Scientist, a misleading book concerning our religion was moved from the shelves near Mrs. Eddy's writings in a branch of the Los Angeles Public Library; and through the alertness of an Assistant Committee on Publication an incorrect biography of Mrs. Eddy was removed from the open shelves of the public library of the assistant's city and placed on the closed shelves.[181]

Branch churches around the country wrote to Scribners, protesting their publication of the book, an action that could not have been contemplated without the assumption that it would be approved by the Mother Church; likewise, Committees on Publication do not act on their own. The letters from individual Scientists, according to "The Blight That Failed," betrayed "similarities which varied according to geography, so that letters from Missouri, for example, were alike in their central idea and varied only in introductory and concluding phraseology," suggesting that state Committees had supplied their constituents with templates that were widely copied.[182]

After the Scribners ads denouncing the Christian Science boycott appeared toward the end of 1929, a backlash began. There were articles in the *New Republic*, the *Saturday Review of Literature*, the *Christian Advocate*, and the *Nation* condemning the campaign, and the Church soon tried to disassociate itself from the actions of its own members, publishing a long self-justifying statement in the *Sentinel* of December 23, 1929: "Many people are opposed to what they regard as censorship. For one reason, the word 'censorship' is often used loosely by people who think vaguely."[183] Having put their critics in their place, the *Sentinel* urged restraint upon Church members, even though "an author and a publisher may have shown a lack of feeling, or even positive injustice."[184] Responding to the *New Republic*'s disapproval, Orwell Bradley Towne, the Committee on Publication for New York who had visited Scribners in the beginning, went so far as to deny that his Church had engaged in any form of attempted censorship, even though *he himself*, in his official capacity as the Church's representative, had tried to persuade Scribners not to publish the book:

Protests of individual Christian Scientists may not be properly interpreted as a boycott or as suppression, and reiteration of assertions to the contrary cannot alter that situation. The protests made in this case have been by individuals.[185]

Unimpressed by the Church's penchant for revising history, the *New Republic* responded to Towne by calling a boycott a boycott:

> This statement is simply not true. For instance, one letter received by Scribners came from a Christian Science church in Kansas City, written over the names of the members of the executive board, and signed by the hand of the clerk. This letter quoted the Church Manual of the First Church, Scientist, of Boston, which "governs every branch throughout the world," to the effect that "a member of this church shall not patronize a publishing house or bookstore that has for sale obnoxious books." . . . If this is not an official threat of an official boycott, we wish Mr. Towne would tell us what it is.[186]

The Christian Science Church continues to deny that it attempted to suppress the Milmine and the Dakin books. The *New Republic* of March 10, 1997, printed a letter received from Victor Westberg, then manager of the Committees on Publication, responding to what he perceived as a slur on the Church's reputation, a reference to the fact that Scientists had bought and disposed of many copies of the Milmine book. "Since its founding in 1879," Westberg wrote, "there has been no time when the Church of Christ, Scientist has had in place, or exercised, a policy of buying up books critical of its founder, Mary Baker Eddy. Our church's policy remains the same as always, to balance views on Mrs. Eddy or the church we consider incorrect or misleading by offering information we see as accurate, as we are doing in this case."[187] Given the extensive history of censorship and suppression in which the Christian Science Church has engaged, Westberg's claim, like Towne's before it, was hardly forthright.

In the years since the Dakin boycott, the Church has continued to wage letter-writing campaigns against books or articles that pose an "imposition"; to attempt intimidation of authors or publishers planning on releasing material the Church fears; and to insert Church propaganda whenever and wherever it can.

Charles Braden, in his Church history *Christian Science Today*, reported many instances in which the C.O.P. and Church members pressured writers, as well as publishers and editors, including his own. As a professor of religion at Northwestern University in Chicago during the late 1930s, Braden, long before beginning his book on Christian Science, wrote to a local Christian Science group, inviting them to send someone to his class to answer questions about the religion. He writes:

> I received a reply saying it was not their custom to do such things, and that I must rather ask the Board of Directors in Boston. All the other local religious groups had freely sent their representatives without reference to any superior authority.
>
> Accordingly, I wrote to the Mother Church Directors. Their reply was that they would be glad to send one of their lecturers, for a fee of one hundred dollars; but no questions or discussion would be permitted. We did not, under the circumstances, have a Christian Scientist address the class![188]

Writing his book, Braden, an impartial scholar with no religious ax to grind, was, predictably enough, denied permission to use the archives at the Mother Church. (One Church official did suggest that, if Braden submitted his manuscript to the Church, it might be possible for someone in the Church to consult the archives and verify his facts. As Braden says, "Obviously this was no help at all."[189]) While completing another book about modern scriptural texts, including *Science and Health*, Braden asked for permission to quote from Eddy's writings, which were then still under copyright protection; the Church asked him to supply the context for each quote. He did and was told that permission could only be given once he had supplied page proofs of the book. Braden explained that, if permission were denied at such a late stage, the result would be unreasonably costly to his publisher. Only after asserting that he would include a note in his book to the effect that "for some reason known to themselves, the Christian Science authorities had refused to grant permission to make a direct quotation from their copyrighted material," did the Church relent.[190] But the Church was still not satisfied. Before long, "representatives of the church" appeared at Braden's publisher's office, asking to read the relevant portions of his manuscript, which the publisher allowed without asking the author's permission, much to his disgust. Braden was left to wonder, "can it be that such publishers are overestimating the power of this particular minority?"[191]

The Church still employs such tactics. Recently, Robert David Thomas, the author of a psychoanalytic biography of Eddy, *"With Bleeding Footsteps": Mary Baker Eddy's Path to Religious Leadership*, was granted partial access to the archives of the Mother Church. Every year in which he requested new materials, Thomas was asked to sign a waiver allowing the Church to check his completed manuscript for "footnoting accuracy."[192] After submitting the manuscript to the Church, he was told that permission to quote from the Church's copyrighted materials was denied, forcing him to spend months revising his text in order to comply with copyright law. Thomas attributed the Church's change of heart to political infighting then going on at the Church Center. While politics probably played a role, his experience was surely another chapter in the Church's history of manipulating the media and academics.

Inevitably, the attention generated by the Christian Science campaign to suppress Dakin's *Mrs. Eddy* boosted demand for the book, and in 1930, it was reprinted in a Blue Ribbon Books edition, one of a series of hardcover best-sellers priced at a dollar. Unlike some of the volumes about Eddy and her Church that have become more rare over the years, Dakin's book went through so many printings that it is still readily available, even though out of print. In the end, it was a draw: the Church succeeded in smearing Dakin's book, but Dakin succeeded in dramatizing Eddy's paranoid personality so that it lived on in the minds of his readers. People still remember it. In 1995, I received a postcard from an elderly gentleman in Paris, France, that read: "You should read Dakin's *fascinating* book on Mary Baker Eddy (1929, I think). It is invaluable for any student of the old fraud."

8. Paul Revere Rides Again

Hypervigilant in policing outside biographies of Eddy, the Church also pursued its own members who had the gall to publish their opinions about their religion. The success of Christian Science in some quarters had not quieted critics within the Church, where the old divisions continued to rage: Who shall lead the Church? Should the estoppel clauses be obeyed? Did all authority in the Church lie with the Board, or should individual Scientists have a voice?

In the years following their triumph in the Great Litigation, the Christian Science Board of Directors began to exercise its newly authorized power over the Field through announcements in the *Journal* regarding "right" conduct for individual Christian Scientists and for branch churches. It also began to respond to any challenge to its authority by disciplining the most powerful members of those churches, the practitioners and the teachers, whose influence over patients and students the Board has historically feared. Now the Board began to wield liberally the disciplinary tools at its disposal, withholding or withdrawing the all-important *Journal* listing for practitioners and teachers, conducting disciplinary hearings, and ultimately threatening probation or excommunication.

But one of the Board's victims bit back. In 1922, a Christian Scientist named Walter Wilson fell out of the Board's good graces almost as soon as he had been accepted into them. His name had first appeared in the *Journal* as a practitioner only that January; it was withdrawn later that year. The Board had discovered that Wilson had sided with the Trustees of the Publishing Society during the Great Litigation.

The manner by which Wilson's transgressions became known to the Board is not uncommon in the Christian Science movement; Scientists make charges to Church authorities against other Scientists, often anonymously, often motivated by jealousy, anger, or greed. (Teachers have accused each other of "stealing" students; since it was once possible to make a comfortable living teaching Christian Science, this was regarded as a grievous offense.) A number of practitioners in Rochester, New York, where Wilson practiced, signed a petition that was sent to the Board, attesting to the fact that Wilson had continued to subscribe to the periodicals during the litigation. Wilson vehemently defended himself in a correspondence with the Board that stretched on for the next twenty-one years. After his third application for reinstatement in the *Journal* had been rejected in 1943, he and a friend, Karl Smith, began writing an incendiary series of pamphlets, sent to Christian Scientists all over the world, under the pen name of Paul Revere.

The "Paul Revere" pamphlets, published first monthly and then semi-annually between 1943 and 1955, are an extraordinary indictment of the Mother Church bureaucracy and the behavior of the Board of Directors. As "Paul Revere," Wilson and Smith made much the same argument as others have before and since: under the estoppel clauses, which Eddy herself inserted into the *Manual*, the Church organization, including the Board of Directors, was meant to come to an end after her death.

But "Paul Revere" did not simply set out to tear down the existing Church. The pamphlets proposed a way by which Christian Scientists could faithfully follow the letter of the *Manual* and still maintain their individual branch churches and the movement as a whole. The plan was essentially Congregationalist in nature, reestablishing the Mother Church as simply another independent branch with no overarching authority. The

Board would continue to administer the affairs of that church but not those of the movement as a whole; branch churches and individual Christian Scientists would be self-governing. As would many other Christian Science writers at odds with the Board, "Paul Revere" accused that body of being authoritarian, going so far as to compare Boston to Rome, a stinging slur in light of Eddy's animus toward Catholicism. The writers made frequent references to the "Romish" nature of the Board and to the "medieval" actions of those Scientists who evinced such blind obedience to it that they literally burned the books that the Board had denounced. (Book burning among Scientists began when the *Christian Science Journal* urged its readers in 1890: "Burn every scrap of 'Christian Science literature,' so-called, except *Science and Health*, and the publications bearing the imprint of the Christian Science Publishing Society of Boston."[193]) "Paul Revere" 's plan promised to abolish the Christian Science "Vatican." The Publishing Society, operating under its own trust deed, would continue to govern itself, much as Herbert Eustace had wanted it to.

Although amateurish, repetitious, and occasionally bigoted, the pamphlets were apparently well received by at least a segment of the Christian Science Field. The writers never revealed any circulation figures but often alluded to the large volume of supportive mail they received, printing extracts from illustrative letters. They claimed that requests for the pamphlets came to them from around the world; soon they began selling collections of the pamphlets, which are still circulated today.

The publications certainly excited a great deal of attention from the Board itself, which had been describing "Paul Revere" as a "disgruntled practitioner," and had instructed at least one "loyal" Christian Science teacher to tell his flock that Christian Scientists should avoid reading his pamphlets at all costs.[194] The periodicals also began running thinly veiled responses to the charges made in the pamphlets, without mentioning "Paul Revere" by name.

For the first five years of publication, Wilson and Smith did not reveal their identities, sending and receiving mail at a post office box in Washington, D.C. But "Paul Revere" alleged that the Board of Directors had surreptitiously learned their identities from a postal employee long before they willingly disclosed their names in 1948. In 1945, a telegram was sent from "Paul Revere" to the Board, listing only the number of the post office box as a return address. "Almost immediately," Wilson wrote, "a long distance telephone call came from headquarters at Boston to Mr.

Walter H. Wilson in Washington D.C.," responding to the telegram.[195] Wilson contends that the Board could not act on its knowledge of the guilty parties' identities because it had come by its information illegally. In any event, when Wilson and Smith acknowledged in an open letter that they were "Paul Revere," they were promptly excommunicated.

"Paul Revere" had, in fact, exposed far more than disgruntlement with the Board. The pamphlets aired a number of cases in which practitioners and teachers were disciplined and excommunicated on the basis of anonymous accusations and rumors. Many so disciplined were among the most dedicated, enthusiastic, and ambitious members of the movement. Some had written their own books on Christian Science only to discover that the Board of Directors was pursuing a policy—nowhere supported in the writings of Eddy herself—that only books published by the Publishing Society were "authorized" Christian Science literature and that anything else was prohibited on the basis that it was spurious and detrimental to the movement. This policy actually seemed to contradict Eddy's statement in her autobiography: "Christian Science is not copyrighted. . . . A student can write voluminous works on Science without trespassing, if he writes honestly, and he cannot dishonestly compose *Christian Science*."[196]

"Paul Revere" defended many of those who were being disciplined, including Gilbert C. Carpenter and his son, Gilbert C. Carpenter, Jr. The Carpenters, both longtime practitioners in Providence, Rhode Island, are now renowned throughout the dissident Christian Science movement for their compilations of Eddy's writings and remarks recorded by the students who lived in her home. (From 1905 to 1906, the elder Carpenter lived with Eddy at Pleasant View, serving as a secretary.) Both father and son were avid collectors of Eddy's letters and articles, and of early editions of *Science and Health*, eventually amassing a remarkable private cache of primary source materials on Christian Science, including complete sets of the early years of the periodicals and most editions of the textbook. The Carpenter home, a sixteen-room Victorian mansion, was furnished with a number of items that had belonged to Eddy—a desk, a dining room table, and a variety of decorative objects—accompanied by duplicates where originals could not be obtained. But in the 1930s, when the elder Carpenter began giving daily talks in his home inspired by his recollections of life with Eddy, and, in 1934, published *Mary Baker Eddy: Her Spiritual Footsteps*, a glimpse of life at Pleasant View accompanied by truly extraordinary theological justifications for Eddy's strange habits and sharp temper, the Board withdrew the Carpenters' *Journal* listings and began a campaign to discredit them. Eventually, they were put on probationary status (an interim step before excommunication) and banned from their branch church.

Her Spiritual Footsteps contains revelations about Eddy that are nothing less than astonishing. The Carpenters so deified Eddy that they found spiritual significance even in her criticism of a servant's haircut (see the chapter in *Footsteps* entitled "Mr. Stevenson's Haircut as a Text for Spiritual Unfoldment") or in her occasional use of morphine. As a condition of copyright, the Carpenters deposited two copies of the book in the Library of Congress. Although shunned by their local church, the Carpenters at their home, and their books in the nation's capital, soon became popular way stations on the Christian Science pilgrimage. Even Scientists who did not identify themselves as dissidents believed that important material about Eddy and her teachings, particularly regarding malicious animal magnetism, existed that the Church refused to make available.

In 1945, the younger Carpenter established the Carpenter Foundation to preserve the collections. After his death in 1952, the foundation went bankrupt and the most valuable materials were eventually obtained by the Mother Church, which signed an agreement with the foundation asserting that "qualified Christian Scientists" could examine the collection, an agreement that has not been honored to the satisfaction of many in the movement. But before it disappeared into the official archives, much of the collection was copied, and is still available today through dissident mail-order supply houses.[197]

"Paul Revere" criticized the Church's treatment of the Carpenters, pointing out that the Carpenters' enthusiastic reverence for Eddy was not essentially different from the view of Eddy promoted by the official Church in its own pamphlet "Mrs. Eddy's Place." "Paul Revere" also protested the disciplining and excommunication of a series of popular lecturers who had attained positions of respect in the movement. John Doorly, an Englishman and member of a branch church in London who served as a lecturer from 1914 to 1929, was excommunicated in 1946 for exploring the metaphysical meanings of Eddy's synonyms for "God," and of the Lord's Prayer, and expanding on Eddy's writings about the days of creation. The Board decided that Doorly, by teaching his own opinions and holding discussion groups, was breaking *Manual* bylaws, and it sharply informed him, "You have so strayed as not to be fit for the work of a teacher of Christian Science."[198] Doorly responded by writing a description of the Church's pressure tactics leading up to his excommunication and sending copies to every practitioner listed in the *Journal*. Likewise, Max Kappeler, a follower of Doorly's, was excommunicated that same year, for publishing and teaching original views on Christian Science. (Kappeler is now the leader of a Christian Science movement of his own, the Kappeler Institute for the Science of Being, with offices in the United States, Germany, and Switzerland.) Bliss Knapp, son of Eddy's loyal follower, Ira O. Knapp, and a popular lecturer in his own right, was also severely chastised by the Board in 1948 for writing a book promoting views almost identical to those in "Mrs. Eddy's Place."

Like their namesake who warned his fellow dissidents of danger, "Paul Revere" awakened many Scientists to the problems within their church government. After their excommunications, however, Walter Winslow and Karl Smith seem finally to have lost heart, and their letter about their banishment was their last. But there were plenty of other dissidents waiting to take their places.

9. Behind the Scenes with the Metaphysicians

During the 1940s and 1950s, while most of the Field exhibited a certain complacency about the continued popularity of Christian Science, some concerned Scientists had discerned that interest in the religion was subsiding. In 1943, John Doorly openly challenged the Board, urging them to acknowledge that the Church "was adding between 90 and 95 branches yearly twelve years ago, but has since steadily declined so that for the past three years it has lost more branches than it has added."[199] Charles Braden cites a letter from one Chicago branch church to another, dated 1944, confirming that sales of *Science and Health* in Chicago reading rooms had fallen by as much as two-thirds and that membership in Chicago churches had also begun to decline.[200]

Arthur Corey was one Scientist who was troubled by the drop-off in the movement. Born in 1900, Corey had gone into the theater after college, appearing on Broadway during the 1920s. His entry in *Who's Who* portrays him as something of a Renaissance man or, at least, a jack-of-all-trades. He worked as a secretary to a high official of the New York Central Railroad; "directed pioneer research in fluorescent lighting for a leading laboratory chain"; and was a "national consultant" on parliamentary law for "the standard guidebook."[201] Living in Chicago during the 1930s and 1940s,

Corey was active in Chicago's Twelfth Church and took class-instruction with Bicknell Young before Young's death in 1938.

From all accounts, Corey was a tremendously charismatic man, with a dramatic voice and a gift for transmitting his enthusiasm about Christian Science to others. He served two terms as a First Reader in his church and eventually became a popular *Journal*-listed practitioner with a wide and successful practice. Sensing the stasis that had settled over the movement, Corey, who described himself as a "man of action," was determined to do something about it.

Corey felt that greater openness from the Church about its teachings— particularly its secret class-instruction—combined with modern public- ity methods, could help revive interest in Christian Science. He began discussing the problems facing the Church with other practitioners and with teachers, holding a series of luncheons, which were brought to a halt when Corey learned (as the Carpenters and John Doorly had earlier) that such open discussion was anathema in the movement. Refusing to be intimidated, he collected all the Christian Science literature he could find, everything from first editions of Eddy's works to notes taken in the classes of well-known Christian Science teachers, their Association addresses (delivered annually by teachers to their Class Associations), and other writings that had been suppressed by the Church. Working with these materials, he began writing a book detailing the forbidden fruit of Christian Science class-instruction.

Christian Science Class Instruction was published in September 1945. In the foreword, Corey made a prediction:

> Consternation will greet the publication of this book in many quarters, for Christian Science Class Instruction has come to be one of the most closely guarded secrets of this age. In fact, it has become so sacrosanct that whenever a pupil discloses even a part of what has been said in his Class, he is branded with the scarlet letter of "disloyalty" and the flames of religious intolerance are fanned against him.[202]

"Consternation" was something of an understatement. The book inspired everything from threats of legal action by Church authorities to boycotts to implied death threats, and the scandal over its publication lasted for years, even as the book itself went into multiple printings, becoming a best-seller.

G. P. Putnam's Sons had agreed in 1943 to publish the book as well as

to keep the manuscript out of the hands of Church officials before publication. But a Putnam president showed the manuscript to a Christian Scientist employee—without informing Corey—and the outraged
employee predicted disaster for the publishing house. Putnam backed out
of the deal, arguing that a large number of Christian Scientists would
undoubtedly follow the lead of the official church in shunning Corey's
book and possibly boycotting other Putnam books as well. Corey then
brought his book to the Farallon Press in San Francisco, founded in 1930
by Hugh Studdert-Kennedy, yet another Christian Science dissident
who had written a book challenging the Board's right to rule the Christian Science movement, *Christian Science and Organized Religion*.[203] Corey
agreed to pay for the publication of his book and to donate all proceeds to
Farallon's nonprofit foundation.

But before Corey's book was even published, a letter-writing campaign,
similar to that organized by the Church against Edwin Franden Dakin's
book, was begun. In his foreword, Corey had claimed that his book was
based on students' written notes—copies of which were in his possession—
taken during the class teachings of Mary Baker Eddy herself, as well as during the classes of a number of other Church luminaries, whom he also
named. Many of these Christian Science teachers—who, after all, held
their positions only at the Church's discretion—somehow learned of the
content of Corey's book before it was published and wrote to him forbidding the use of their writings "in any manner." One teacher claimed that
she would "repudiate" anything he attributed to her.[204]

The Christian Science Committees on Publication were also assigned
the task of interfering with the book's publication and sales. James Vincent, the Northern California C.O.P., visited and called the Farallon office
repeatedly during August 1945, the month before publication, asking to
see Corey; in October, a process server came to the office to deliver an
"injunction" that was later discovered to be simply an intimidating letter.
The server threatened a secretary at Farallon with legal retaliation when
she refused to divulge Corey's home address.

Other Committees on Publication around the country sent similar
letters to newspaper editors who had run—or were only considering
running—reviews of the book or advertisements for it; they also visited
booksellers, urging them not to sell the book on the basis that it was "unauthorized." Public librarians were handed statements to paste into the book.
Charles Braden describes a copy of *Christian Science Class Instruction* that
he found in the public library in Des Moines, Iowa. Handwritten on the

title page are the words "This book is not An Authorized Christian Science Publication." The statement "Explaining A Controversy About This Book," pasted on the back cover, reads, in part, "In a letter dated November 13, 1945, Mr. William D. Kilpatrick, manager of committees on Publication, the First Church of Christ Scientist in Boston, Massachusetts states that many of the authors' and publishers' claims are false."[205]

Kilpatrick was not satisfied with "protesting the deceptive and unauthorized" nature of Corey's book; he also held a meeting in Chicago for all local Church members at which he denounced it.[206] According to one exasperated Chicago bookseller who had received numerous anonymous letters from Scientists threatening to boycott his store if he sold the book, the day after Kilpatrick's meeting, all the bookshops in the city were deluged with requests for it. Gilbert Carpenter, Jr., wrote to Corey, "If you wanted to stir things, believe me, feller, you have! Committees on Publication all over the land are on a hot griddle over it."[207]

Farallon donated gift copies of Corey's book to public libraries all over the country, only to hear later that they had disappeared or become unavailable. The Boston Public Library placed its copy in its Rare Book Department and refused to release it to general circulation. The copy in the Los Angeles Public Library was defaced, and the pages listing the names of teachers whose class notes had been used as source material were ripped out. The library in Kansas City was sent more than one copy, but the book was not made available to the public despite demand. In 1955, Braden discovered that the copy at Northwestern University "had been surreptitiously removed, and that even the index card had been taken out of the file drawers, a feat which required the withdrawal of the locking rod through the cards."[208]

In the face of such concerted opposition, many booksellers refused to sell the book, others to display it. Some apparently kept it hidden under a counter, only handing it over after persistent inquiry. A man from Long Island City wrote to Farallon to order the book, saying that Macy's refused to. Meier & Frank, a department store in Portland, Oregon, removed it from its shelves after receiving complaints. Clerks there told subsequent interested buyers that the book was "unauthorized" and unavailable.[209]

Christian Scientists spread the rumor that Corey had written the book solely in order to make a fortune, comparing him to Judas betraying Christ for a handful of gold; in fact, as per his arrangement with Farallon, all the earnings were donated to its foundation. Corey received threatening letters suggesting that he might meet the same fate as Jesus' disloyal disciples: "a violent death."[210] *Journal*-listed practitioners reached for scatological language to revile the book, describing it as "garbage," "vomit," and Corey himself as "a stinkin' mess."[211] Rumors were circulated about his death.

But some practitioners were drawn to the book as the first accessible exegesis of the Christian Science healing method since Eddy's day; several even took class-instruction with Corey in 1946 and 1947 after reading it. Soon after, *their* names were turned in to the Church by an informer who was also in attendance. The Board demanded an explanation from them and forced their resignations.

In spite of all this opposition, Corey's defiance of the Board's strictures against publishing was the most successful yet; his book ultimately went through twenty-three reprintings and was sold all over the world. Photocopies of the book are still sold by dissident booksellers.

For all the hysteria it inspired, *Christian Science Class Instruction* is a simple, straightforward book, an excellent introduction to Christian Science. It openly addresses many of the difficulties presented by Eddy's book, offering philosophical explanations for her many contradictions in logic, providing answers to the most frequently asked questions about Christian Science, explaining the difference between Eddy's absolute and relative statements.

Part of Corey's enterprise was an attempt to modernize the teaching of Christian Science and to dispel some of its hoary mystification. He revealed that students taking class-instruction were traditionally immersed in the fear-mongering that had characterized Eddy's own instruction. "It has become the custom in church sponsored class instruction to discuss 'the cults,'" he wrote.[212] Class-instruction included denunciations and incantations, which students were instructed to recite every morning, to mentally combat the fearsome "Romanism" proceeding from the Catholic Church, as well as the pernicious mesmerism being practiced on Scientists by faceless Theosophists, Hypnotists, Spiritualists, Occultists, and other Necromancers. Corey gently suggested that these practices be laid to rest: "Do not fear the inroads of the denominations, the cults, the isms or the ologies. . . . As a human being, if you are sticking to your own knitting, you are finding the Christ and helping others to find the Christ."[213]

Most threatening to the Church, Corey's *Class Instruction* urged discretion and compassion on practitioners in cases when their patients clearly

needed medical attention, ignoring Eddy's stricture prohibiting practitioners from treating patients in hospitals or under a doctor's care:

> Be thankful for the comforts and conveniences made available through the
> kindly ministrations of doctors and nurses, for Love alone provides such
> things. . . . It goes without saying that the Christian Science practitioner is
> neither technically equipped nor legally permitted to diagnose physical ail-
> ments or recommend physical treatment of any kind. And it is well to
> remember that advising a patient to discontinue medication, to have an
> operation or to refrain from having an operation, may be construed as falling
> into these categories. Your business is, under the law, to keep your patient in
> your prayers, not to keep his physical activities under your direction. The
> requirements of the law on this score are plain. You can "render unto Caesar
> the things that are Caesar's" and still maintain your inner integrity as a
> metaphysician.[214]

Corey's next book, *Behind the Scenes with the Metaphysicians,* published in
1968, is a chatty introduction—at times unintentionally hilarious—to the
social aspirations and metaphysical airs of country club Christian Science
as well as an argument for Church reform. An unabashed name-dropper,
proud of his celebrity students—Mark Twain's daughter, Clara Clemens
Samossoud; choreographer Robert Alton; Lillian Fontaine, mother of Joan
Fontaine and Olivia de Havilland; television producers and corporation
presidents; moonlighting members of the Church—Corey took Scientists
to task for their metaphysical pretentions while parading some of his own:
he conducted his Los Angeles classes in a suite at the Bel-Air Hotel, plying his students with "daily high-teas" in order to keep them awake.[215]
(The frontispiece of the book is a photograph of Ruth St. Denis, a modern
dance pioneer and spiritualist in 1940s Hollywood, mooning about beside
the swimming pool chez Corey in a cape and floor-length gown.)

But Corey also had an unerring sense of where the Christian Science
movement had gone wrong. He identified the Church's gradual insistence
after Eddy's death on "radical reliance" as a bad political mistake, forcing
Scientists to take a hard line that made the religion unappealing to outsiders and critics. Corey is virtually the only Scientist ever to acknowledge
honestly and directly the dangers that the religion posed to children, publishing a description of children who had suffered and died as a result of

overzealous reliance on Christian Science. He was particularly scathing about those who pressed on with Christian Science treatment even when it became painfully absurd and absurdly painful:

> We have all known misguided martyrs of this persuasion who lost their jobs by refusing to wear needed spectacles. How often do we see church Readers stumbling embarrassingly through their delivery, in spite of the large-type Reader's text, because substituting for glasses the undemonstrated statement that "Mind sees"! And do you remember the woman who urged her blind daughter to walk alone through hazardous New York traffic and down the church balcony steps to the very brink, all in the belief that they must refuse literally to recognize blindness? With what pride this dunce told her hair-raising story in an open letter, and with what zeal like-minded faithsters circulated it throughout the church ranks! . . . What dangerous nonsense to say, as is often done by impractical absolutists, that resort to needed practical expedients militates against metaphysical healing![216]

Corey emphasized Mrs. Eddy's own reliance on medicine and eyeglasses and pointed out the illogic of accepting dental care while refusing medical care. He descried the "officially fostered *materia medica* tabu [that] operates increasingly to deprive us of medical testimony," testimony that might buttress the claims of Christian Science.[217] He pointed out that, although Christian Scientists fear and shun medicine, they seem not to realize that food and drink themselves often contain "extractable drugs" and chemical components.[218]

The irony of Arthur Corey's life and career as an outcast Scientist lies in the fact that he represented, on many levels, the best qualities of his religion. He embodied the kindness, compassion, and temperateness of the moderate Scientist, the Scientist who chooses not to force his beliefs on others or push his patients and students beyond what they can stand. He acknowledged, as no Christian Scientist publicly has before or since, the mental anguish that is caused by not knowing the potential severity of any given illness: "I have seen more than one patient relieved of unbearable terror by a medical diagnosis which revealed that a particular disorder was benign instead of malignant," he wrote. "It is nonsense to think the doctor produces disease."[219] His teaching stripped the religion of its darkest impulses toward paranoia and extremism. He stood for what Christian Science might have been at its best: a devotion to exploring the meaning of life, health, and true morality. Arthur Corey died in 1977, dismissed by the Church but, nonetheless, a popular and enthusiastic Christian Science teacher to the end.

A significant proportion of the Christian Science population read Corey's books and took them to heart, troubled both by the reaction of the Church and by the implications of what he had to say. One such Scientist was Robert Merritt, a lifelong Church member and graduate of Principia College who had taught for some years at the Daycroft School, a Christian Science prep school in Greenwich, Connecticut. Merritt had been an ardent Scientist until, in 1968, he read Corey's book along with Charles Braden's study of Christian Science, which painstakingly details the Church's attempted suppression of Corey's work.

At the time that he discovered these books, Merritt was the First Reader of the New London, Connecticut, branch church, and he attempted to discuss his questions about the Corey affair, as well as concerns about the declining attendance at the church, with two of his fellow members, the Second Reader and the reading room librarian. Soon after, Merritt was called in to a private meeting with the two women he had taken into his confidence and was advised to repent:

> The librarian said she had recently been attacked by an inexplicable temptation to stay away from church. When she said this, I thought to myself that many others in the community apparently had the same temptation to stay away, and this long before I ever joined the congregation or became elected Reader. . . . [She] said that one Sunday morning she had felt physically paralyzed and could not rise to sing a hymn with the rest of the congregation. Experiencing pain and discomfort—a touch of mental arsenic?—she remained through the service only with heroic effort. Later it dawned upon her what this lurking "malicious animal magnetism" was and why she felt so uneasy about Church recently. She recalled a statement I had made several months previously to the effect that *independent* Christian Scientist Arthur Corey had written some helpful material on our faith. She informed me that studying such officially-unapproved literature was in disobedience to the *Church Manual*, and, by clear implication, to Mary Baker Eddy and God.[220]

Disillusioned, Merritt ultimately resigned from the Church and became a correspondent of Corey's. Eventually, with Corey's help, he wrote his own book, entitled *Christian Science & Liberty*, published in 1970. He criticizes the Church for taking Christian Science away from the public and even its own adherents by means of its punitive ecclesiastical bureaucracy. Merritt, like scores of others who resigned or were banished from the Church, remains an independent Christian Scientist, practicing his faith in his own way, happy to do without the trappings of the official religion. Describing himself as "sick and tired of Boston's arbitrary control," he has in recent years grown interested in the Plainfield Christian Science Church of Plainfield, New Jersey. Plainfield is a renegade branch church that was dropped from the *Christian Science Journal* in 1977 after it refused to comply with the Board of Directors' demand that its trustees be replaced with members willing to swear an oath of loyalty to the Board. The Mother Church sued the Plainfield church in 1983 to prevent it from using the words "Christian Science" in its name but lost its case in 1987. The Plainfield church is currently thriving, with a membership of Scientists from around the country. Its church, which seats 250, is often full. It publishes its own lesson sermons and its own religious periodical, *Healing Thoughts*. Mary Baker Eddy's great-granddaughter is a member.

10. "The President's Son of a Bitch"

Even as the Church was struggling with criticism and rebellion in the field, Christian Science was reaching the pinnacle of its political power. At various points since the late 1960s, Scientists have served as heads of the FBI and the CIA; there have been powerful Scientists in Congress; and two Scientists have acted as close advisers to the president of the United States. In 1971, the astronaut Alan Shepard, whose mother and wife were Scientists, took a microfilm copy of the first issue of the *Christian Science Monitor* to the moon on *Apollo 14*.[221] For decades Scientists in positions of power had been dedicating themselves to achieving unprecedented legislative and bureaucratic gains for the Church and its members, winning the recognition of insurance companies and protection under the law—and those gains had engendered a sense of entitlement, even hubris. In ways profound and petty, large and small, Scientists now considered themselves, if not above the law, at least capable of revising it to their advantage.

William Webster, a former federal judge with an image as a squeaky-clean straight arrow, spent nine years (1978–1987) as director of the FBI, having been tapped by President Carter to reform that institution, marred by charges of widespread civil rights violations and illegal investigative practices.[222] He followed his fellow Scientist Admiral Stansfield Turner as director of the CIA; Webster and Turner were classmates and friends during their student days at Amherst College in the 1940s.[223] Christian Scientists, like Mormons, have proved to be appealing recruits for both agencies; their beliefs prohibit the use of alcohol and recreational drugs, making them good security risks, and their cultures encourage respect for authority.

Turner's and Webster's appointments may have been simple coincidences, but they are also testaments to the extraordinary degree of respectability and trust that accrued to Christian Science. It is impossible to imagine the appointment to those positions of individuals with allegiances to less well-established or trusted sects, such as those of the Reverend Moon or the Hare Krishnas. But, although Webster was a close friend of George and Barbara Bush (who offered him their Kennebunkport home as a retreat after his wife, also a Christian Scientist, died of breast cancer in 1984), both he and Admiral Turner kept relatively low profiles during their tenures.[224] This would not be true of two of the most famous Christian Scientists in American political life: H. R. Haldeman and John Ehrlichman.

"The President's son of a bitch," as Haldeman once called himself, was a devout Christian Scientist. It may seem difficult to reconcile the White House of Richard Nixon and its reputation for illegality, profanity, and deceit with the religion of Mary Baker Eddy, but Christian Science teaches its adherents to deny the reality of evil. Some Scientists have construed that denial to be absolute. Christian Scientists are demonstrated masters of situational ethics, and H. R. Haldeman and John Ehrlichman, his fellow Scientist in the White House, simply took that mastery to a new level.

Haldeman met John Ehrlichman while they were students at the University of California at Los Angeles. He introduced Ehrlichman to Nixon in 1960, and both men worked on a succession of Nixon campaigns. After Nixon was elected president in 1968, Haldeman was appointed White House chief of staff, and Ehrlichman became Nixon's domestic policy adviser. The two Scientists subsequently played starring roles in the long national melodrama of Watergate. Ehrlichman supervised the notorious "Plumbers" and approved the break-in at Daniel Ellsberg's psychiatrist's office. The eighteen and a half missing minutes on the White House tapes featured a conversation between Haldeman and Nixon; other tapes revealed that he and the president had plotted a cover-up together. Ehrlichman and Haldeman resigned in April 1973, and each subsequently served eighteen months in prison, convicted of conspiracy, obstruction of justice, and perjury.

Ehrlichman's name, as pundits never tired of pointing out during the Watergate years, means, in German, "honest man." But neither Ehrlichman nor Haldeman were particularly honest or forthcoming about (among other things) the role their religion played in their conduct. Ehrlichman barely mentions Christian Science in his pathologically self-serving memoir, *Witness to Power,* and only hints at the odd Christian Science nepotism of the Nixon White House.[225] Besides Haldeman and Ehrlichman, Egil "Bud" Krogh, a young protégé of Ehrlichman's who had worked in his Seattle law office before joining the White House staff, was also a Christian Scientist; Krogh would eventually serve four months in jail for his role as one of the Plumbers. John Andrews, one of Nixon's speechwriters, also had ties to Christian Science, as did Henry Paulson, one of Ehrlichman's aides, who is now the chief executive officer of Goldman Sachs. Walter Annenberg, the publishing tycoon and major contributor to Nixon's campaigns who was named ambassador to Great Britain by Nixon, was married to a member of the Christian Science Church.

Were Haldeman and Ehrlichman too busy obstructing justice to concern themselves with their religion? Haldeman, for his part, never discussed the faith in his Watergate memoir, *The Ends of Power,* and no mention of it is to be found in the thousands of pages of his journal, released as *The Haldeman Diaries: Inside the Nixon White House,* in 1994. But Haldeman and Ehrlichman took time out from their other activities in 1971 to see to it that President Nixon signed a private bill essentially drafted by the Christian Science Church and designed to prevent any other entity from publishing *Science and Health with Key to the Scriptures,* which was soon to enter the public domain. Mark Twain, obsessed with American copyright law and its bearing on his own publications, had predicted that such a day would come to pass. Mrs. Eddy, he wrote, "thinks of everything. She knows she has only to keep her copyright of 1902 alive through its first stage of twenty-eight years, and perpetuity is assured. A Christian Science Congress will reign in the Capitol then."[226] He was only off by forty-one years.

In order to see this bill through, Haldeman and Ehrlichman were forced to fraternize with a fellow Christian Scientist, Senator Charles Percy of Illinois, who had earned himself a spot on Nixon's "enemies" list by opposing the president's defense budgets and Supreme Court nominees, as well as the escalation of the war in Vietnam. Percy's life was an American classic of rags to riches. Born in 1919, he was ten when his family was impoverished by the stock market crash of 1929. Through his Christian Science Sunday school teacher, he got his first job at Bell & Howell; by the time he was twenty-nine, he was head of the company, the youngest chief executive of a major American corporation. In 1966, he was elected to the U.S. Senate where he remained until 1985, eventually serving as chairman of the powerful Committee on Foreign Relations.[227]

By 1971, copyrights on all editions of *Science and Health*—except for the 1906 edition—had expired. In May 1971, a bill designed to protect and restore the Church's copyrights on the book was introduced into the Senate, cosponsored by Percy and by North Dakota senator Quentin Burdick, whose wife was a Scientist; they arranged that it be numbered "S.1866," 1866 being the year that Eddy "discovered" Christian Science after her fall on the ice. The bill proposed a law establishing a seventy-five-year extension—until 2046—of the copyright of *Science and Health;* it covered, as well, all of Eddy's other published and unpublished works, including those that had previously entered the public domain. Hearings were held. The manager of the Committees on Publication, Dr. J. Buroughs Stokes, came down from Boston to argue that the purity of Eddy's "unique" work was in danger of being "adulterated" without special protection.[228] He also testified that "not a single member of our church has indicated any opposition to the passage of this bill."[229]

On the face of it, the bill was unconstitutional. Two senators, Jacob Javits of New York and Philip Hart of Michigan, along with the Bar Association of the City of New York and a number of lawyers who were experts in copyright and constitutional law raised the objection that the proposed legislation violated the First Amendment: "Congress shall make no law respecting an establishment of religion."[230] Javits moved to delay the bill and was promptly besieged, after the Committee on Publication for New York State mobilized New York Scientists, with some five hundred identical telegrams from constituents—including many Sunday school students—all reading: "Please release Bill S.1866 protecting copyright of *Science and Health,* our pastor."[231] Lacking the will to hold a pastor hostage, Javits capitulated; the bill was passed by both houses, albeit with a rider by Javits suggesting that it was constitutionally flawed.

The bill then made its way through the hands of Haldeman and Ehrlichman to the desk of Richard Nixon, who signed it on December 15,

1971. At the Church's annual meeting the following year, J. Buroughs Stokes announced to the assembled Christian Scientists that "from the beginning it was clear that S.1866, as it was numbered, was under God's protection."[232]

Contrary to the C.O.P.'s testimony before Congress, some Christian Scientists did object to the bill. Many of those who felt that the Board had arrogated an unseemly degree of power to itself—who, because of the *Manual's* estoppel clauses, questioned the Board's very right to exist— believed that Christian Scientists ought to have the right to distribute any and all versions of Eddy's texts, including those that the Church itself had sought to suppress, such as the first edition of *Science and Health* and earlier editions of the *Manual.* In 1980, a group calling itself United Christian Scientists, led by a Principia graduate, David Nolan, began legal proceedings challenging the extended copyright on Eddy's works. In 1987, they prevailed: the U.S. Court of Appeals for the District of Columbia declared that Bill S.1866 was an unconstitutional violation of the separation of church and state. *Science and Health,* along with Eddy's other works, entered the public domain. Since then, dissident Scientists have enthusiastically set about reproducing, purchasing, and studying all the variorum editions of Eddy's works that their Church abhors.

H. R. Haldeman died in the manner peculiar to his faith. In 1994, Peter Haldeman, his youngest son, published a memoir of a household dominated by the chaos of Watergate and the strange practices of Christian Science. Describing his father's sickness and suffering, he wrote of calling his father's practitioner as he neared death and urging her to discuss with his father the possibility of receiving medical care.[233] She refused. His mother, also a Scientist, suggested that Peter's questions were "ruining" his father's chances for recovery.[234] Ultimately, watching his father choose his painful end (untreated cancer), Peter Haldeman discontinued his protest with the weariness common to those dealing with Scientists' passivity: "I knew I was no longer ruining it for him, but I also knew I wasn't saving him."[235]

11. The Kerry Letters

Despite the movement's political success, by the 1960s it had become clear that Christian Science itself needed some saving. Even the most positive-minded Scientists perceived that their movement was in a serious slump. As early as the summer of 1965, the *National Observer* published an article, "Christian Science Assumes New Posture," in which Church officials, while not divulging actual figures, for the first time publicly acknowledged that the Church had suffered a decline in membership so precipitous that advertising and public relations specialists had been hired to advise the Church on how to appeal to the modern age.[236] In language that was startlingly down-to-earth, Ralph Wagers, head of the Church's Board of Lectureship, told the *Observer*, "We haven't been doing a very good job of explaining ourselves.... When 85% of the people out there are gray-haired or non-haired, you begin to ask yourself, 'What's going to happen to Christian Science?' "[237]

It was a question that more and more Scientists were asking themselves. What would become of a church already so small that many congregations were numbered in the dozens, not the hundreds, that were largely female and largely aging, to which young people were not attracted? Christian Science lectures, enormously popular in the 1920s and 1930s, were now sparsely attended, lackluster affairs, stiffly delivered by middle-aged stuffed shirts. Church officials faced with such facts usually pointed out that organized religion in the United States was experiencing declines across the board. (They make a similar claim today.) But even if such decline was a universal phenomenon, Christian Science was clearly declining faster than most faiths and could afford it less. The *Christian Science Monitor*, while still highly respected, reached its top circulation in 1971—271,000—but was beginning to run deficits. By 1983, circulation had fallen to 141,000. The number of practitioners had also entered a decline, falling from a high of 11,200 in 1941 to 7,100 in 1970.[238] The number of churches in the United States had fallen to 2,277 in 1976, down from 2,411 in 1966.[239] A recent study showed Christian Science with the "lowest rate of retention of any American denomination for which data are available"; only 33 percent of one sample of those raised in the Church remained as members.[240] Nor has the Church traditionally reached out to different constituencies. Christian Science has never been attractive to minorities. It offers little sense of community and historically little welcome to African-Americans. Although there have been a few black practitioners, until the 1960s their names were accompanied by a parenthetical "colored" in the *Christian Science Journal*, and they were advised to limit their practice to their "own people."[241] The numbers of Hispanic-Americans and Asian-Americans attracted to the religion has always been negligible.[242]

. . .

The Church's response to this malaise was to announce, in 1966—the hundredth anniversary of Eddy's fall in Lynn and subsequent discovery of Christian Science—its intention to build a new multimillion-dollar Church Center designed by the firm of I. M. Pei. The elaborate plans called for the transformation of the Mother Church in Boston into a fourteen-acre campus with an extensive complex of buildings: a new Sunday school building, the "Colonnade" office building, and a twenty-eight-story administration building. A grand new portico entrance was added to the Mother Church Extension. A huge plaza with a 670-foot-long reflecting pool now sweeps past the Mother Church, culminating in a spectacular fountain. It was as if the Board thought that by inflating their own center of power, they could somehow inflate the sense that Christian Science was a growing movement, a movement to which millions would flock, a movement where something, *anything,* was happening. As a political maneuver, the grandiloquent plans for the Church Center seemed inspired by the building prowess of the Mormons, known for their gargantuan temples in Salt Lake City and around the world—physical statements of the power and glory of the Latter-Day Saints—the only difference being, of course, that the Mormons had the bodies to fill their edifices.

That the Church Center project was eventually regarded as an embarrassing fiasco by many Christian Scientists who were troubled by the vast sums spent and not accounted for to the Field became apparent to the outside world only after the Center was completed, in 1975. That year, a man named Reginald Kerry sent copies of an open letter to every Christian Science practitioner and branch church executive board in the country—six thousand in all. The first of the "Kerry letters"—as they would come to be known—charging the Church with all manner of corruption, threw the official bureaucracy into a frenzy of retaliation and opened up the dissension within the Church to a curious public.

By the time he began sending out his infamous letters, Reginald Kerry had assembled an eclectic résumé. Born in 1914, he grew up in Santa Barbara, California. He told friends that he had discovered Christian Science at the age of eighteen, when he was cured of cancer—a healing that, he said, enabled him to grow from five feet four inches tall to six feet two.[243] Following this remarkable event, Kerry's entire family converted and experienced many healings, his father of alcoholism, his sister of nearsightedness, and his mother of arthritis. After several years spent as a trumpeter in various dance bands, Kerry went into the restaurant business in Santa Barbara. He eventually became police and fire commissioner of that city and served on the California State Parole Advisory Board for twelve years. He also worked as a labor negotiator and was active in several local political campaigns. He was a member of a branch church in Santa Barbara for over forty years, serving as First Reader, chairman of the church board, Sunday school teacher, and in a variety of other positions.

His first job at the Church Center came about unexpectedly at the Church's annual meeting in 1969, during what was surely one of the strangest—indeed, one of the only—interruptions ever to disturb that staid event. The Church's annual meetings, held in the Mother Church, are scripted, opening and closing with hymns and organ music, featuring formal addresses by Church officials: the president, the Clerk, the treasurer, the manager of the Committees on Publication, and the chairman of the Board of Directors. No questions are taken from the floor. But on June 2, 1969, a black man named Hayward Henry, representative of a militant group calling itself the Metropolitan Boston Committee of Black Churchmen, strode into the Mother Church with several other Churchmen, walked up to the podium, and took over the meeting. Henry read a three-page "statement of demands," one of which was for Boston religious organizations to donate $100 million to his organization as "reparations for 520 years of slavery." A newspaper photograph, taken from behind Henry and looking out over the congregation, shows a sea of puzzled elderly, white faces.

Apparently because of his experience with law enforcement, Reginald Kerry was recruited by frantic Board members to help escort Henry and his fellow protesters over to the Publishing Society, located next door to the Mother Church, to negotiate terms. After threatening to burn that building down, the protesters were eventually subdued, and Kerry was credited with helping to save the day.

The Churchmen's action had, in fact, been inspired in part by the building of the Church Center. In order to erect the Center on the scale proposed, the Church, which owned a number of rental properties surrounding it, had evicted tenants and razed the low-cost housing, much of which had been occupied by blacks.

As a consequence of his triumph in saving the 1969 annual meeting from disaster, Kerry was asked by the Board to do a number of disparate jobs. He was invited to address a number of Christian Science college groups. In 1973, the Board asked him to negotiate an agreement between the Carpenter Foundation and the Church, which had been locked in litigation over the fate of the foundation's archival materials for years. During construction of the Church Center, he was asked to help design a new security system. But familiarity with Boston and the Board had brought Kerry only intense disillusionment, not helped by the fact that his application to become a practitioner was turned down by the Church.

Like Jesus throwing the money changers out of the temple, Kerry became bent on overturning the corruption he saw around him. Nor was he alone in his mission. One of his disciples was a middle-aged woman named Ann Beals, the daughter of a Christian Science lecturer and a lifelong, class-taught Scientist, listed in the *Journal* as a practitioner since 1967. Shortly before meeting Kerry, Beals had moved from Decatur, Georgia, to Boston. Greatly concerned about the decline of Christian Science, she believed that there were no absolute prohibitions in Eddy's writings against Christian Scientists publishing their own works. New interpretations and explanations of Science, she felt, could only help attract others to the movement. She approached Board members, Publishing Society trustees, and the Committee on Publication, asking for clarification of their policy against Christian Scientists publishing their own work, but she was never satisfied with what she felt were their evasive answers: "I soon began to realize that I would not find anyone there who would even take the time to listen to me. They were not in the least interested in my books or my ideas. . . . Finally after four years of futile effort, I gave up."[244] In 1974, Beals put out a pamphlet of her own metaphysical writings, "Animal Magnetism," because she believed that the Church was not adequately addressing this all-important issue. She was eventually told, by Church authorities, that her writings were incorrect. She asked for a specific explanation of her errors, which was never forthcoming. She withdrew her *Journal* listing, putting an end to her work as a practitioner. It was during this personal rebellion that, shortly after Labor Day 1975, Reginald Kerry turned up on her doorstep, wearing a badge identifying him as a worker at the Mother Church.

Over several meetings in the fall of 1975, Kerry told Ann Beals about what he saw as "gross mismanagement, corruption and discord" at the Church Center.[245] He had heard rumors that the construction site was so poorly guarded that thousands of dollars' worth of building materials had been stolen, that branch churches which had approached the Mother Church for desperately needed loans were ignored or turned away, and that

Church funds and congregations had been declining at an alarming rate. He was outraged by what he saw as rampant immorality at the Center and suggested that many workers there had engaged in adultery, sexual harassment, or homosexuality; he spoke of the atmosphere at headquarters as being tainted by fear and suspicion. When, in October 1975, Kerry proposed to write a letter about his complaints to practitioners and branch churches, Beals immediately offered to help him.

But before he mailed the letter, Kerry, in obedience to what Christian Scientists call the Matthew Code—the biblical prescription for the resolution of conflict, which Eddy included in her *Manual* as a model for her followers—took his complaints to the Board.* He met with them in December, telling them his specific charges; the Board demanded evidence. According to Beals's account, the meeting turned ugly when Kerry was sharply instructed not to interrupt the chairman of the Board and he responded by slamming his fist on the table. Kerry also warned the Directors that he had informed the Massachusetts and New Hampshire attorneys general that a grand jury should be convened to investigate his untimely death should any harm come to him, and that all his hard evidence would be sent to the newspapers.

Several days after the meeting, Kerry gave a copy of his letter to the Board, apparently hoping that they would respond with a commitment to address the problems he had outlined. After receiving no reply, however, he instructed Ann Beals to proceed, and thousands of copies of the letter were sent out on December 11, 1975. Eight single-spaced, legal-sized pages, it addressed all of the same issues Kerry had discussed with the Board—the decline in membership, financial questions posed by the enormous sums spent on the construction of the Center, the problems faced by branch churches and practitioners, and "immoral conditions at the center"—and suggested that Church members send "prayerful protests" to the Board and demand an independent financial audit of the Church books and a new independent committee to look into his charges. He closed with a promise

---

*"Moreover if thy brother shall trespass against thee, go and tell him his fault between thee and him alone: if he shall hear thee, thou hast gained thy brother.

"But if he will not hear thee, then take with thee one or two more, that in the mouth of two or three witnesses every word may be established.

"And if he shall neglect to hear them, tell it unto the church: but if he neglect to hear the church, let him be unto thee as an heathen man and a publican" (Matt. 18: 15–17).

to send "quotations, names, dates and places" in a second letter to all *Sentinel* subscribers and to the media if "corrective action" were not taken.[246]

The Board retaliated with its own letter to practitioners and branch churches—sent first class and thus beating Kerry's bulk-rate mailing—instructing them to disregard the Kerry letter. The Board's letter dismissed Kerry himself and characterized his charges as an "attack," a response often used by the Committee on Publication. It counseled the wise Christian Scientist to "quietly turn to God in prayer rather than reacting with excited gossip or speculation." The Board also, however, tentatively acknowledged that the current situation in Boston was under review, promising to "take every appropriate action to correct whatever needs correcting."[247]

The Board's letter, of course, only served to heighten interest among all but the most hidebound Board sympathizers. "To some members," Beals wrote in her self-published memoir of the Kerry years, "the Board's letter was an advance notice to be on the lookout for Letter #1, and they couldn't wait to read it."[248] Others destroyed the Kerry letter; still others, she reports, "hid it and did not discuss it or share it with other members. Thus, this first letter reached only a percentage of the Field."[249] The percentage it did reach, however, was vocal. Letters and phone calls demanding a response to Kerry's charges began overwhelming the staff at the Church Center, and the Board asked Kerry if he would sign a "cease-fire," agreeing not to send any further letters until his next meeting with the Board on January 26, 1976. In addition, the Board created a committee of three Church Center employees to investigate Kerry's charges.

Then, on January 23, the Board sent a second, fifteen-page letter to the same practitioners and churches, explaining with some specificity the committee's results, acknowledging that a few of Kerry's concerns were verifiable—such as the fact that the movement had reached its peak in the 1950s and that some five hundred branch churches had no practitioners in their congregations (though the *Manual* required each church to include one)—but denying most of the serious charges of financial and moral improprieties.

The Board's second preemptive letter took Kerry by surprise. In an angry letter to them, he described it as a "breach of our cease fire agreement . . . full of God-damned lies (damned by God's allness)" and "a real double-cross."[250] The Board had asked him repeatedly to supply them with whatever evidence he had; he replied:

The "evidence" is already in your possession. You have the statistics concerning church membership, periodical subscriptions, and numbers of branch churches and practitioners. You have all of the financial records of the church. You are aware of the cutback in personnel and the sale of real estate. The conditions in the Treasurer's Office are within your jurisdiction and are documented by your own files.[251]

Desperate to head off a second Kerry letter to the Field, the Church retained an attorney to meet with him. The meeting, which took place in March, in New York City, is recounted in some detail in both Kerry's subsequent letter and in Ann Beals's book, and seems to have entailed threats and attempted bribery. The attorney first told Kerry that if he sent further letters he would be sued for libel in all fifty states; he then read him a list of state prison terms for libel. Kerry laughed this off, comparing himself to Joseph, Paul, and John, who had all suffered in prison for teaching spiritual truths to their people. The attorney threatened him with excommunication. Kerry responded by mocking excommunication as a "tool of the Catholic Church."[252] Finally, the attorney suggested that, if Kerry sent no more letters, he would be offered a "top spot in the movement," apparently referring to the Board in saying, "They have big plans for you."[253] To this inducement, Kerry was immune, and the two men concluded their meeting by going out to dinner and a Broadway show. The second Kerry letter went out later that month.

Kerry's second letter, addressed to practitioners, reading rooms, branch churches, and "experienced Christian Scientists everywhere," was practically a volume unto itself, over seventy pages long, with separate chapters and a series of exhibits that supplied some evidence for the charges Kerry had made.[254] It was even more vehement in tone than the first letter, accusing the Board of Directors and others of lying and of engaging in a "cover-up" of what Kerry termed the "Christian Science 'Watergate.' "[255] The first letter had been relatively subdued, a warning. Interpreting the Board's admonitions and rebukes as a rejection of that warning, Kerry took off the gloves, and his true style began to emerge.

Judging by his remarks about "Communists" and "homos," Kerry was an archconservative politically. He was intensely homophobic, and his letters also betray the same fear of Roman Catholicism that appears in other

Christian Science literature, including the Paul Revere pamphlets. There are slurs against Jews and Judaism. The style of the Kerry letters—they continued over the next fifteen years—became increasingly uninhibited, characterized by profanity, paranoia, and a disturbing violence of tone and of language; they have much in common with the tracts of conspiracy theorists. The second letter opens with Kerry's assertion "I am sure you know that if Letter No. 1 had not been true, I would either be in jail for criminal libel or dead."[256]

In the third letter, sent in October 1976, he named the names of those working in the Church Center, including Robert Peel, who had never married, as well as members of the Board of Directors and the Committee on Publication and other high-ranking officers, whom he considered to be homosexual. In the fifth letter, sent in November 1978, he invoked the traditional conspiracy theorists' bogeymen, accusing the Church treasurer, Marc Engeler, who was from Switzerland, of being an "advisor to the Rothschilds and Onassis," and vilifying the longtime editor of the *Monitor*, Erwin Canham, and other Church officials, for being affiliated with the Council on Foreign Relations. Although the letters provide no evidence for it, there is much talk throughout of wiretaps and "bugging" at the Church Center. Kerry's name-calling, often ugly and distasteful, has its own lunatic vigor: referring to David Sleeper and DeWitt John, both members of the Board, Kerry writes in one of the letters, "Double-talk Sleeper and hot-head DeWitt are now running the Board."[257]

The paranoia and anger expressed in the letters, as well as their failure to support accusations with verifiable evidence, call into question Kerry's emotional stability. Ann Beals reveals that "a few months before the mailing of Letter #1, he lost both his mother and his wife," and perhaps these losses contributed to the angry despair so evident in the letters.[258] But Kerry's fears are also a standard expression of the Christian Science belief in malicious animal magnetism, and many Christian Scientists did not see him as unbalanced. Christian Scientists believe—as Eddy taught—that M.A.M. can, literally, sicken and kill its victims; hence Kerry's assertions that only the righteous truth of his accusations saved him from death.

Likewise, Ann Beals was convinced that she was being followed, that her phone was tapped, and that her apartment had been searched. Particularly when she was in Boston, she also felt she was subject to the malevolent thoughts of those at the Church Center who disapproved of her connection with Kerry:

> In addition to [the] spying, I faced another challenge in Boston—one that was deeply hidden, extremely subtle. This was the secret hypnotic work I met after moving there. Being a serious student of Christian Science, I was very much aware of the power of evil mental forces. . . . I could detect when my thinking was being influenced by harmful mental suggestions. . . .
>
> Early in November [1976] a feeling of depression, acute loneliness, futility, and hopelessness began to build up in my mind. At times, a dull aggravating headache would appear, and my eyesight would begin to blur. . . . Such hypnotic work comes in the guise of one's own thinking and is very deceptive. Mental manipulation has many forms—depression, insomnia, extreme excitement, sleepiness, mental numbness, confusion, mental disturbance. It also produces physical effects such as headaches, heart problems, etc. . . . This evil work grew stronger as the winter wore on, and my mental condition worsened. Waves of futility would sweep over me and I wanted to give up the struggle. But this I knew I could not do. I did believe that I could out-last the attacks because I understood what was taking place, but the struggle was constant and severe.[259]

Both Beals and Kerry, who was also living in Boston when the early letters were sent, moved to California in 1977, after sending the fourth letter, in order to escape this "mental work."[260]

Their own work was having devastating consequences on the already shrinking Church membership. The third letter, mailed in 1976, in which Kerry accused Church officials of homosexuality, resulted, according to Beals, in thousands of morally offended Christian Scientists leaving the Church, and hundreds of practitioners withdrawing their names from the Journal.[261] The Board sent yet another conciliatory letter to members, this one explaining that the Church would not be suing Kerry, because he did not have assets that were "collectable." But scores of members apparently believed Kerry when he wrote that the Church did not sue him because everything he said was true.

At the Church Center, things were in turmoil. As Kerry delightedly reported in his letters, many of those he had accused of homosexuality or other moral infractions had resigned or been "phased out," including several Board members; the Church Clerk; the First Reader of the Mother Church; the heads of the Department of Branches and Practitioners, the

Speech and Editorial Department, the Committee on Publication, and the Benevolent Association. Kerry's claims are difficult to evaluate. Turnover at the Church Center is generally steady; salaries are not high, and people often serve the Church for a time, considering it a spiritual privilege, and eventually return to their lives outside. What is certain, though, is that resentment had been accumulating for years over how money was being spent and accounted for by the Church; over how Church members, practitioners, and teachers were treated by the bureaucracy; and over whether the Church was—or was not—dealing with the sharp decline of Christian Science. All of that resentment was reinforced by Kerry's letters. In letter after letter, he printed mail that had come to him, supporting his exposés. One typical writer asserted that turmoil stirred up by the Kerry letters was part of a preordained plan. "Our forever Leader [Eddy] . . . knew it was coming. . . . it is a time of 'Armageddon' and in it we'll find the Crown of rejoicing."[262] In his fifth epistle, Kerry included a letter that had been sent by a Principia graduate to the Board, castigating them for soliciting funds for the Christian Science Monitor Endowment plan. The writer had not been in touch with the Church for years and was offended that he had been tracked down for mercenary reasons: "All of this effort—not to inquire lovingly after a long-lost sheep—but to solicit money! Thank you for verifying my estimation of a cold, calculating and desperate business organization. I don't think this is what Mary Baker Eddy had in mind. I would appreciate it if you would please remove my name forever from The Mother Church membership list."[263] Many letter writers expressed intense gratitude to Kerry for criticizing Robert Peel's biography of Eddy, widely disliked throughout the movement for exposing, with scholarly documentation, Eddy's flaws: one former state Committee on Publication wrote to the Board, "What has happened in the last 24 years that permits an account as contemptible as this to appear in an authorized biography of our Leader? . . . How do you think people like me who owe so much to Mrs. Eddy feel about a governing body that permits such disrespect of its Founder?"[264]

Kerry also began to include court transcripts, copies of memos sent between Church departments, and excerpts from letters by other dissident Christian Science writers who, inspired by his example, were beginning to publicize their own grievances. In 1976, Mrs. Grace Ross, a *Journal*-listed practitioner and former secretary to the Gilbert Carpenters, sent a sixteen-page letter to the Field, accusing the Board of not abiding by their agreement to make the Carpenters' archival material available to the membership. In 1977, Mrs. Rosalind M. Pickett of Indianapolis wrote a forty-seven-page indictment of the Board entitled "The Boston Situation" and sent it to twenty-two Church officials. After receiving no reply, Mrs. Pickett then sent it out to thousands of Christian Scientists in the Field. It read, in part:

> Of all the Kerry charges none are more shocking to us in the Field than the morals issue. The resulting tongue-clucking on this topic has obscured consideration of other questions that need answering. . . .
>
> Surely nobody but a fool or a madman would (without substantiation) make up such bottom-of-the-barrel charges, sign his name to the document, and put it in the United States Mails.
>
> And surely the person so vilely accused would not, if innocent, stand passively by.[265]

As trouble spread, all the old unresolved issues came to the surface. The group calling themselves United Christian Scientists, with which Kerry himself had been involved, began sending newsletters to the Field, arguing that the eighty-ninth edition of the *Manual*, issued after Eddy's death, was illegitimate, and that the estoppel clauses should be obeyed, bringing an end to the Board's power. They also promoted the notion that independent Christian Science churches could take the place of officially sanctioned ones. In addition, the newsletters and conferences held by the United Christian Scientists publicized the Kerry letters and the issues addressed by them.

The worst publicity, from the point of view of the Church, came in the mainstream media. *Newsweek* wrote about Kerry's allegations of financial mismanagement and immorality in 1976. Though David Sleeper, then a Board member, denied the charges, saying that "financially, we're at the strongest point in our history," the damage was done.[266] On Sunday, March 12, 1978, the *Boston Globe* ran a lengthy story, "A Rift Among Christian Scientists," which painstakingly outlined all of Kerry's charges, as well as those of his supporters, such as Ann Beals and Grace Ross. The Church, in its response, called the accusations "wild and half-baked," and Allison Phinney, Jr., the assistant manager of the Committees on Publication, suggested that those making them "might as well not be" Christian Scientists.[267] Ann Beals, who had hoped that the Kerry letters would incite Church members to active protest, was discouraged by the effect they did have: "Instead of fighting for the church, members left it. I couldn't say I blamed them."[268]

. . .

The Church had long shied away from taking an official stance on homosexuality, only beginning to address the issue during the sexually permis-
sive 1960s and 1970s.[269] (Eddy, squeamish about all sexual matters, never
mentioned the issue in her writings, but she certainly implied that sexual
relations were acceptable only when sanctioned by marriage.) In a panic
over the effects of the Kerry letters, the Church, in its most heavy-handed
manner, repeatedly insisted, in editorials in the *Christian Science Monitor*
and in its religious periodicals, that homosexuality was immoral and could
be healed through Christian Science.[270] Soon after, the periodicals began
to run testimonies by those who claimed to have been "healed" of impure
desires.[271]

It seems that the Church authorities were sufficiently out of touch with
their members that they were taken by surprise to learn that a significant
proportion of them were not only fundamentally conservative when it
came to such issues but were capable of being outraged by allegations of
immoral behavior at the Church Center. Reliable sources suggest that it
was widely rumored throughout the movement that several high-ranking
Church officials at that time were, indeed, homosexual. Rather than publicly admit the facts, or simply dismiss the letters as scurrilous hate mail,
the Church responded to the charges with its own reactionary and intolerant rhetoric, running articles and editorials denouncing immorality;
as a sop to the Field, it also purged two minor employees suspected of
homosexuality.

The Kerry letters may have inspired the Church, in January 1982, to fire
Christine Madsen, a young reporter who had worked for the *Monitor* for
seven years, after an anonymous informant alleged that she was a lesbian
and had tried to "entice" a coworker's wife. Madsen was a lesbian and
admitted as much when questioned in the office of one of the trustees of
the Publishing Society. She was also a Christian Scientist who had studied
Eddy's writings closely enough to know that nowhere in Eddy's work did
any reference to homosexuality appear. She was told to read Leviticus, the
book of the Bible that, in certain translations, contains a harsh condemnation of homosexuality. "I couldn't see any way you couldn't be a
Christian Scientist and a lesbian or vice versa," Madsen told a Boston
weekly at the time of her firing. "When I joined I thought that the church
must be full of [liberal-thinking] people."[272]

Several months after Madsen was dismissed, James Ogan, a thirty-six-year-old business and cost analysis supervisor for the Buildings and Grounds division of the Church, who was also gay, was fired after nine years of employment. The Church admitted firing Madsen for being a lesbian but claimed Ogan was dismissed for having "told a lie."[273] The lie he was accused of telling was, however, related to his homosexuality. Ogan's supervisor, irate over his involvement with a gay theater group, instructed him to call his Christian Science teacher and discuss the matter with him; Ogan claimed that he had; the supervisor checked his story with the teacher and discovered that he had not.

The Christian Science Church and its newspaper are both considered religious organizations under the law and as such have the legal right to discriminate against whomever they choose. Madsen and Ogan sued anyway. Their cases were eventually settled out of court for undisclosed sums.

The most astonishing thing about the Kerry letters, finally, is the fact that they were taken so seriously by all concerned: by the Board and the Field and, consequently, by the press. As Beals herself acknowledged, "To this day, I am amazed at the power of these Letters . . . [which] were nothing more than poorly edited gossip sheets exposing the sins at the Center to anyone who would read them."[274]

A bizarre combination of the serious and the trivial, the silly and the libelous, accurate analysis and fantastical rumor, the Kerry letters and the other dissident writings they inspired filled a vacuum that the Board itself had created in forbidding Christian Scientists to write, debate, or discuss their own Church, its teachings, its prospects, and its future. Without any officially approved outlets through which to satisfy the human need to air grievances and to seek guidance and information, the Field blew off steam in its own ad hoc ways. Ever since the Great Litigation, for every modernizing reformer like Herbert Eustace or Arthur Corey there has also sprung up an aggrieved letter writer like Walter Wilson of "Paul Revere" and like Reginald Kerry. The result has been untold damage to the movement, the disillusion of scores of the faithful, and a climate of pervasive frustration and distrust.

There is no way of knowing just how many Scientists resigned their membership in the Church or turned against the official movement as a result of dissident activity. But judging by the sales of Arthur Corey's books and by the fact that Kerry's letters can still be bought today (from Ann Beals's mail-order firm, the Bookmark), the number could be considerable. Both Kerry and Beals asserted that the responses to his letters numbered in the thousands, and the Church's overwrought reaction would tend to support that claim.

In the decades since Mary Baker Eddy's death in 1910, the Church's progress has resembled an arc, rising higher through the 1920s and 1930s as the glamour of Hollywood rubbed off on Christian Science and membership continued to grow, then leveling off, stagnating, and falling through the 1950s, 1960s, and 1970s. Throughout this time, the Church was in fact losing a battle it could never have won, a battle it has barely acknowledged: the battle against medicine. As the extraordinary life-saving medical advances we now take for granted came into being—antibiotics, insulin, penicillin, vaccines—they incrementally and inevitably won over the segments of the population that might once have turned to Christian Science, eroding a mainstay of the Church's reason for being. But, while medicine began attacking from without, the Church's own intrinsic weaknesses and vulnerabilities—Eddy's estoppel clauses and the rebellion they inspired, the Board's lack of flexibility and spontaneity, its utter indifference to the issues outlined by members like Eustace and Corey and Kerry—were killing the institution from within. As the Church entered the 1980s, its leadership was distracted by the Kerry letters and by what truth they told. The movement was coming dangerously close to the edge of viability, losing membership, losing its tenuous grasp on what little unity it had ever enjoyed, losing faith in itself. It was in this climate of precarious survival that the Church would endure its greatest trials. It was in this climate that Christian Scientists would be arrested and tried for the neglect, abuse, and manslaughter of their own children.

Part IV

"God's Law": Christian Science Goes to Court

Wherefore by their fruits ye shall know them.

—Jesus of Nazareth,
Matthew 7:20

1. Breaking the Law

On January 7, 1911, only a little over a month after the death of Mary Baker Eddy, a Christian Science practitioner named Willis Vernon Cole was plying his trade in an office on the ninth floor of a building at Fifth Avenue and Twenty-sixth Street in New York City. He was praying with a woman, Mrs. Isabelle Goodwin, who, unbeknownst to him, was a police matron. Goodwin had told the practitioner she was sick and wanted treatment; she accepted his prayers and paid him two dollars.

A week later, after Goodwin filed an affidavit about her experience in the practitioner's office, Cole was arrested and charged with practicing medicine without a license. He was not the first Christian Science practitioner to be so charged. Indeed, by the time of his arrest, Christian Scientists had learned only too well that their true enemy was not M.A.M., or malicious animal magnetism, but A.M.A., the American Medical Association.[1]

The American Medical Association, founded in 1847, during Eddy's lifetime, brought together in one organization all of the local, state, and county medical societies that had already formed across the country. Beginning in the mid-nineteenth century, both together and individually, the national and local medical societies began aggressive campaigns to influence public health policy and legislation. Just as Christian Science was becoming established, medical doctors, researchers, and institutions were engaged in a struggle to establish their own professional respectability. Increasingly, that struggle involved public denunciation by medical professionals of those considered to be "quacks" as well as the promotion of legislation establishing allopathic medicine—based on drugs, surgery, and scientific criteria—as the gold standard of health care.

Frequently, the AMA and its member organizations engaged in vituperative legal, legislative, and public relations battles with the rivals of allopathic medicine: practitioners of homeopathy, hypnotism, hydropathy, so-called electric medicine, and the like, as well as purveyors of patent medicines and nostrums of all kinds. In California, in 1876, there was a bitter debate in the legislature over the future of homeopathic medicine; it was legalized that year despite the angry objections of medical doctors and their organizations. When Christian Science came to prominence during the last two decades of the century, it too set off alarms in medical societies across the country, and the AMA began to mobilize against it.

The campaign of the professional medical societies against Christian Science took several forms. Beginning in 1888, with the manslaughter indictment of Mrs. Abby Corner, and on into the 1890s, several Christian Science practitioners were tried for manslaughter or murder following the deaths of their patients; some of these charges were instigated by outraged medical doctors, whose testimony was a feature of the trials. The practitioners were acquitted or their cases dismissed, largely because of the prosecution's inability to prove conclusively that medical science could have saved the patients' lives or that the practitioners had committed any criminal act by performing what was essentially a religious, not a medical, service.

One of the most sensational of these cases involved Harold Frederic, a well-known American novelist and the European correspondent for the *New York Times*, who died in London, in 1898, at the age of forty-two after an illness described as "brain fever." Author of *The Damnation of Theron Ware*, a popular novel about a Methodist minister seduced away from his uncomplicated faith by the ambiguities of modern science and secular criticism, Frederic had consulted a Christian Science practitioner near the end of his life. The British press was quick to blame his death on Christian Science, which the *Times* of London denounced as "a dangerous importation" from America.[2] Both the woman who gave Frederic Christian Science treatment and the woman who sent for her were charged with his murder.

Like the American practitioners, they were acquitted: Frederic's case had apparently been pronounced hopeless by medical doctors before he sent for the Scientists, and there was no evidence that he had not freely chosen to consult with them.[3] But the *Journal of the American Medical Association* used the Frederic case to launch an extended denunciation that was apoplectic in tone and libelous in nature. Before the trial and without access to any of the facts of the case, in language equal to Eddy's at its most melodramatic, *JAMA* asserted that Frederic could have been saved by doctors:

> Nature, aided by science, would have soon repaired the injury, but at the moment when the clear eyes were darkened and the strong mind was help-less, a miserable creature appeared, stretching out rapacious hands for the sick man's gold. She got it, and Harold Frederic is dead. . . . The woman who killed Mr. Frederic has confessed her utter lack of legal qualifications to act as a doctor, and that she accepted fees for treatment.[4]

The facts of the Frederic case did not stop the editors of *JAMA* from repeatedly alluding to this practitioner and others as greedy charlatans, pur-veyors of spiritual snake oil. In issue after issue throughout 1899 and on into the new century, *JAMA* continued to castigate Christian Scientists as "dupes and victims" and "cranks"; the editors went so far as to associate Scientists, without explanation or evidence, with what they termed the "sensual prac-tices" and "the frequent sexual aberration displayed by many fanatic sects."[5] In November 1899, the editors of *JAMA* outlined their policy:

> Steps should be taken to restrain the rabid utterances and irrational prac-tices of such ignorant and irresponsible persons. Liberty is one thing, and license another, and the crime of even suggesting such obviously false doc-trines and immoral practices should be prevented by severe punishment. Those who speak thus should know better, or their ignorance is criminal.[6]

Undaunted by considerations of basic constitutional freedoms of religion or speech, the AMA was determined to make Christian Science illegal.

Attempts to legislate Christian Science out of existence began in the 1880s. Some of the proposed bills, such as the "Health Act" brought before the Illinois legislature in 1887, would have made it a crime for anyone who had not graduated from a medical school or passed an examination set by the medical board to practice healing of any kind. Others, such as the one introduced in the New York legislature in 1889 that would have made it a misdemeanor to practice Christian Science "Mind-healing," addressed themselves specifically to that one religion.[7] Few of these bills passed, and those that did were vetoed by state governors. The *Chicago Tribune*, noting that mental healers were as thick in Chicago as " 'fleas in Vallombrosa, or candidates for office,' " mocked the proposed Illinois legislation:

> Every old auntie who prescribes vermifuge for an ailing infant, or pepper-mint for a pain under the baby's apron, would be liable to be summoned . . . and be required to show a diploma from some reputable medical college, or else be fined or imprisoned for the unauthorized practice of medicine. . . . The mother who suspects constipation in the little one, and gives it a dose of castor oil, without first getting a prescription from a regular physician, would be sent to jail for thirty days.[8]

The laws that singled out Christian Science itself were clearly discrimi-natory; moreover, they classified Christian Science religious beliefs as medi-cal practices. Legislatures quickly learned that to hold hearings on these bills was to invite the considerable wrath and growing clout of Christian Scientists down upon their heads. Over a thousand defenders of the faith turned up in Albany, New York, in March 1898, when that state's Senate Committee on Public Health considered yet another bill banning practices such as Christian Science. No less a personage than one of the state's for-mer Supreme Court justices, a Judge Talman, addressed the packed cham-ber and its galleries in defense of Christian Science. Though not a believer himself, Talman said that his wife had been healed through Christian Science of typhoid fever and nervous prostration, and he scolded the leg-islators for entertaining such a narrow-minded, punitive bill:

> A majority of the Scientists have come into this faith through being healed and saved from death when given up by the doctors. They know it is true, and no legislative power on earth can compel them to call medicine to their aid. Look at this gathering. Do they look like cranks? Are they puny and sickly? Is there not health, cheerfulness, and kindliness there? . . . Fifty thou-sand in this state can bear testimony to the power of Science. Will you deny this? Can you disprove this assertion? Can the doctors deny it?[9]

In the face of such opposition, the senator who had introduced the bill meekly agreed to withdraw it or amend it to *exempt* Christian Scientists. The *Christian Science Journal* triumphantly reported that, on the eve of their victory, "senators and members of the Assembly called at the hotels of the Scientists who remained in the city overnight" to convey their congratulations, and "the subject of Christian Science was the general topic of conversation about the Capitol and throughout the city of Albany, so that, indirectly, great work has undoubtedly been done for our Cause where its opposite was intended."[10]

The AMA and local medical societies redoubled their efforts, and soon virtually every state in the Union considered legislation aimed at controlling or eliminating the professional practice of Christian Science. In 1899, medical doctors in Philadelphia announced in the *Albany Morning Express* that they would "commence a national war against the Christian Scientists" to influence Congress to take action against the movement; that same year, the Medical and Legal Relief Society, a gathering of hundreds of doctors and lawyers, convened in New York City, at the Waldorf-Astoria, to organize their opposition to the religion.[11]

These aggressive tactics eventually antagonized many fair-minded medical doctors, clergymen, and legislators who spoke up for the rights of Scientists. In March 1898, William James eloquently testified before the Massachusetts legislature against a bill proposing that only physicians and surgeons could be legally licensed to treat the sick:

> I come to protest against the bill simply as a citizen who cares for sound laws and for the advance of medical knowledge. Were medicine a finished science, with all practitioners in agreement about methods of treatment, a bill to make it penal to treat a patient without having passed an examination would be unobjectionable. But the present condition of medical knowledge is widely different from such a state. Both as to principle and as to practice our knowledge is deplorably imperfect. The whole face of medicine changes unexpectedly from one generation to another in consequence of widening experience, and as we look back with a mixture of amusement and horror at the practice of our grandfathers, so we cannot be sure how large a portion of our present practice will awaken similar feelings in our posterity.
>
> I am here having no axes to grind, except the axe of truth, that "Truth" for which Harvard University, of which I am an officer, professes to exist. I am a Doctor of Medicine, and count some of the advocates of this proposed law among my dearest friends, and well do I know how I shall stand in their

eyes hereafter for standing to-day in my present position. But I cannot look on passively, and I must urge my point. That point is this: that the Commonwealth of Massachusetts is not a medical body, has no right to a medical opinion, and should not dare to take sides in a medical controversy.[12]

Supporting the Scientists had its price, as James privately acknowledged, writing to a friend that he had never done anything "that required as much moral effort. . . . Bah! I'm sick of the whole business, and I well know how all my colleagues at the Medical School, who go only by the label, will view me and my efforts."[13] He himself had no great love for Christian Science, but he admitted to a sincere intellectual curiosity about what Scientists were experiencing when they felt themselves being healed. "Why this mania for more laws?" he wrote. "Why seek to stop the really extremely important experiences which these peculiar creatures are rolling up?"[14]

Other medical doctors acknowledged the powerful placebo effect that Christian Science could have on patients whose illnesses or discomforts were psychosomatic. In 1898, the *New York Times*, in a piece about the Frederic case, interviewed a Dr. S.B.W. McLeod, president of the Medico-Legal Society of New York, who was of the opinion that "there are thousands of people who are willing to go to bed, suffering from imaginary complaints. Every doctor has had experience with such. Frequently they are given up by their physicians to become victims to their own imaginations, but often complete cures could be effected if sufficient mental force could be exerted on them. With such patients, I don't doubt that Christian Science would be efficacious."[15] Even Mark Twain, hardly a friend of Christian Science, laconically noted in 1903 the irony posed by these proposed bills: "It is curious, but if the Second Advent should happen now, Jesus could not heal the sick in the State of New York. He could not do it lawfully: therefore He could not do it morally; therefore He could not do it at all."[16]

By 1910, the legislative crusade of the AMA against Christian Science had markedly failed, just as its former crusade against homeopathy had also failed. Not only did it fail, it inspired Christian Scientists to pressure legislators to pass statutes exempting Christian Scientists from medical licensing requirements, or to revise prohibitive legislation. So, when the medical societies fell back on their first line of defense—the prosecution of Christian Scientists for practicing medicine without a license—they found themselves stymied. The case of the hapless Willis Vernon Cole, arrested

in 1911 in New York City for his unsuspecting prayers over a police matron, would prove to be a watershed of sorts.

Only a few days after his arrest, Cole was back in his office, awaiting
trial, when a Mrs. Frances Benzecry came in and asked for treatment.
Evidently, Cole's immersion in the divine Mind had not sharpened his
ability to smell a rat, for Mrs. Benzecry was an investigator for the New
York County Medical Society, come as an undercover agent to gather yet
more evidence against him. Over the next five days, she put the practitioner through his paces. First she complained of "eye trouble."[17] The next
day, it was back pains; a few days later, gas from eating potatoes and bread.
Then she brought in her young daughter who also had eye trouble and, in
addition, needed to be cured of a head cold. The account of these visits, in
the Court of Appeals records of *People v. Cole*, assumes, at times, a farcical
air, particularly when the devious investigator, Mrs. Benzecry, on her second visit, dashes Cole's placid expectations of immediate healing:

> I went in and he said to me, "Why, you are looking very well." And I said,
> "I feel about the same." And after that, why, he spoke about God is good and
> we must have love and faith in God. And then he says, why, he will give me
> a treatment. So that Mr. Cole placed his chair facing mine again, closed his
> eyes and put his hands up to his face and we remained in perfect silence for
> about fifteen minutes.

She testified that she had tried to elicit a diagnosis from Cole before he
began his treatment, telling him:

> "Mr. Cole, I have a pain in my back." I then said that I had a porous plaster
> on my back at that time; and I said to him what did he think about the pain
> I had in my back. He said it was some kind of disease, but he could not tell
> me what kind it was; he said, "I can cure it." He said "you must now take off
> that porous plaster because Christian Science cannot cure with plasters on."
> He said that I must take off my glasses as well as remove the porous plaster
> from my back. . . . That I should have more faith and understanding; that I
> must have courage. . . . I said I must keep my glasses as I cannot go without
> them. . . . He said if I wanted to be cured by Christian Science I must remove
> the glasses.[18]

Cole's first jury could not determine a verdict; the second found him
guilty. The *New York Times* was quick to gloat, writing, "The decision will

be a stunning blow to the exploiters of the particular form of suggestion to which Mrs. Eddy gave vogue among the credulous and erratic." It went on to suggest "a persistent infliction of fines" as a suitable deterrent to other offenders.[19] But two years later, the New York State Court of Appeals overturned the verdict in a decision that would establish precedent.

The Public Health Law of the state of New York provided that "no person shall practice medicine, unless registered and legally authorized." The definition of the practice of medicine had an important exception that had not been pointed out in the instructions to the jury:

> A person practices medicine within the meaning of this article, except as hereinafter stated, who holds himself out as being able to diagnose, treat, operate or prescribe for any human disease, pain, injury, deformity or physical condition, and who shall either offer, or undertake, by any means or method, to diagnose, treat, operate or prescribe for any human disease, pain, injury, deformity or physical condition. . . .
>
> This article shall not be constructed to affect . . . the practice of the religious tenets of any church.[20]

Cole did "treat" Mrs. Benzecry, but he did not diagnose, query her about symptoms, take her temperature, lay on hands, massage, prescribe drugs, perform surgery, or anything that a medical doctor would do; his treatment—silent prayer—was within the practice of the religious tenets of his church.

One of the judges sitting on the Court of Appeals that reversed the judgment against him was Benjamin N. Cardozo, who would be appointed to the U.S. Supreme Court in 1932. In another Court of Appeals case, *People v. Vogelgesang* (1917), Cardozo returned to *People v. Cole* in affirming that a self-proclaimed member of the "New York State Association of Spiritualists" was guilty of practicing medicine without a license for having massaged a man suffering from fatal heart disease with "a liniment, compounded of angle worms, turpentine, sweet oil and benzine" while "indulg[ing] in silent prayer."[21] In his opinion, Cardozo revisited the numerous state statutes, including New York's, that exempted those practicing spiritual forms of healing from medical licensing requirements, and he reiterated his finding in *Cole*: "Through all this legislation there runs a common purpose. The law exacts no license for the ministration by prayer or by the power of religion. But one who heals by other agencies must have the training of the expert."[22] Cardozo was specific about the line to be drawn between faith healers and physicians:

> While the healer inculcates the faith of the church as a method of healing, he is immune. When he goes beyond that, puts his spiritual agencies aside and takes up the agencies of the flesh, his immunity ceases. He is then competing with physicians on their own ground, using the same instrumentalities, and arrogating to himself the right to pursue the same methods without the same training.[23]

Therefore, the spiritualist, with his worms mashed in turpentine, was guilty; the Christian Scientist was not.

Thus did the persistent harrying of Christian Scientists by the AMA result in exactly the opposite of what the medical community intended: not less but greater freedom and expanded rights and responsibilities for Christian Scientists. Few Christian Scientists could have predicted, however, where those greater responsibilities would lead.

2. Writing the Law

If there was one arena where Christian Scientists could not seem to prevail, it was in the court of public opinion with respect to their treatment of children. This became more marked as the century and the state of medical knowledge progressed.

It is clear from reading the early years of the *Christian Science Journal* and *Sentinel* that Mary Baker Eddy and her followers had no idea that the birth of their movement coincided with the greatest advances in medicine, sanitation, and preventative care yet seen in human history. In 1897, a vaccine to prevent typhoid was developed; in 1890, the first formulation of the diphtheria antitoxin was introduced, with improved forms to follow in 1913 and 1923; and insulin was discovered as a treatment for diabetes in 1921. Insulin was a particularly dramatic discovery, changing the fate of diabetics practically overnight from a death sentence to the prospect of a normal span of life. Appendectomies became the standard treatment for appendicitis before the end of the nineteenth century.

Through the 1890s and on into the new century, Christian Scientists claimed dozens of healings of diphtheria, appendicitis, and other serious illnesses and contagious diseases. But as deaths in the general population rapidly declined with new treatments and vaccines, Christian Scientists continued to die, and their deaths—particularly children's deaths of diphtheria, diabetes, measles, and appendicitis—stood out in sharper relief, attracting widespread attention in communities across the country, from neighbors, newspaper reporters, morgue attendants, coroners, and district attorneys.

Medical doctors grew increasingly contemptuous of Christian Science and impatient with the sometimes gruesome results of its treatment. In his *Autobiography*, William Carlos Williams remembered his grandmother: she converted to Christian Science and willfully ignored a cancerous growth on her face, which, he wrote, "I knew must, in the end, destroy her."[24] As both a poet and a physician, he was uniquely observant:

> I had been, in fact, called the Christian Scientist doctor of Rutherford. When they were ill, seriously ill, or dying they always wanted me: for "diagnosis only," it was made clear, or to sign the death certificate. I paid no attention to them, but always did what I could.
>
> I've seen some terrible cases: a woman with six children living over a tobacco shop who died following a criminal abortion; a case of placenta previa with every joint in her body infected (I drained them one after the other over a period of at least three months while she lay there) and she got well; an untreated case of diphtheria strangling on the floor because of an excess of religious fervor on the part of the parents; a woman shrieking in a room over a candy store from an inoperable cancer of the uterus while her bemused husband, overwhelmed by doctrinaire convictions, looked at her with stony eyes.[25]

Where death, particularly the death of children, was once viewed with a passive acceptance by society, Christian Science as a treatment came to seem more and more eccentric, and the deaths of Christian Science children more preventable and unnecessary, even shocking, horrifying, terrible.

As the numerous early arrests of Christian Science practitioners for practicing medicine without a license suggest, Christian Scientists, like Mormons and other advocates of new religions, were widely held in suspicion, and they were brought up on charges when their children died, while other bereaved parents were considered blameless. Indeed, the argument that children died under medical care as often as, if not more often than, children under Christian Science care became one of the most effective legal tools in Scientists' defense. In Los Angeles, in 1902, Merrill Reed and his wife, both Scientists, were tried for manslaughter after their young daughter died of diphtheria without medical care. Their lawyer argued, among other things, that the diphtheria antitoxin was still considered an experimental, controversial treatment among doctors; that a significant percentage of diphtheria sufferers still died even after receiving the antitoxin; and that the Reeds had believed that their daughter's condition was improving shortly before she died. In 1902, the Reeds were acquitted. Later in the century, using some of the same arguments in court, Christian Science parents would not fare so well.

One of the first signs of a hardening of public opinion against Christian Science was the notorious case of Audrey Kay Whitney. In 1937, Edward Whitney, a widowed insurance investigator who was not a Christian Scientist, arranged to leave his ten-year-old daughter in the care of her aunt, who lived in Chicago, while he went on a business trip. Audrey was a diabetic, and her aunt was a Christian Scientist. Without consulting Edward Whitney, Audrey's aunt put her under the care of a Christian Science practitioner, William F. Rubert, who advised that she be taken off insulin. She died, in a diabetic coma, on December 10, 1937.

Audrey Kay Whitney would have become just another Christian Science child who quietly perished, if not for her father's rage. Immediately after his daughter's death, Rubert, the girl's aunt, and the Christian Science nurse who had presided over her death were brought up on manslaughter charges, which were, however, subsequently dismissed. In 1941, Edward Whitney was arrested in La Salle, Illinois, for grabbing the governor of that state, Dwight Green, and demanding that he look into the case. In 1946, Whitney mailed a threatening letter to the practitioner which read, in part, "I will return to Chicago and . . . kill you"; he was eventually indicted and acquitted on charges arising from the mailed threat.[26]

On January 30, 1959, some twenty-one years after his daughter's death, Edward Whitney, having traveled from his home in Birmingham, Alabama, to Chicago, walked into William Rubert's office on the eighth floor of Orchestra Hall where the practitioner sat alone, pulled out a .32 automatic, and said, "I've waited a long time for this." He shot Rubert twice, and then, as Rubert ran down the hall and into a waiting elevator, shot him again through the elevator's glass door. Whitney was clearly seen firing the gun by Francis Houston, the elevator operator, and was immediately apprehended and arrested for attempted murder. A photograph of him that appeared the next day in the *Chicago Tribune*—"Practitioner Shot by Dad of Girl Who Died / Revenge Shooting"—shows him standing in a detective bureau in trench coat and fedora, calmly smoking a cigarette. Beneath that photograph is one of William Rubert, flat on his back on a hospital gurney, a doctor bending solicitously over him.

Rubert was seriously injured, shot in the right arm, right hand, and chest. He was taken to St. Luke's Hospital, where he underwent surgery; he eventually recovered. The *Tribune* quoted a Christian Science Church spokesman solemnly opining that emergency operations are not contrary to the teachings of the religion. This must have been news, indeed, to Rubert, who had counseled against emergency measures for Audrey Kay Whitney, and to the Christian Science Board of Directors, who have long been publicly proclaiming the opposite.

Perhaps the most astonishing element of the whole story was the fact that Edward Whitney, tried for attempted murder, was acquitted. Whitney premeditated his crime, threatened it, planned it, and carried it out, expressing no immediate remorse for it; he shot a man at close range twice and then ran him down and shot him again in front of an eyewitness. But sympathy was with the father, not the Christian Science practitioner.[27]

As medical science grew more accepted and sophisticated, particularly following advances made during and after World War II, the Christian Science Church grew more persistent in pressing for what it defined as its "rights," particularly in the United States, where the Church was headquartered and where it would develop powerful and effective lobbying techniques. In Great Britain and Canada, countries where the climate has not been so accommodating to Christian Science, members of the religion have always been required, along with everyone else, to provide their children with medical care. Here, however, the Church increasingly made it known that Scientists' constitutional right to freedom of religion was being violated by society's growing reliance on medicine. Vigorously pursuing a course that would protect and expand this right, the Church won—not only for itself but for members of all kinds of religious groups that oppose medical care, vaccinations and inoculations, and medical education for children—a vast array of legal privileges that have eroded the right of their children to equal protection under the law.[28]

People v. Cole had put to rest in New York State the question of whether Scientists were practicing medicine without a license. Although several states, including Texas, West Virginia, and Ohio, retained laws that prevented spiritual healers from charging fees for their services, many others were persuaded to grant great leeway to faith healers in general and Christian Scientists in particular. In Maryland, for example, "any Christian Science practitioner duly recognized in the *Christian Science Journal*" was allowed to treat people for disease or illness and to charge for the service.

But the Church was not satisfied with the grab bag of untested state statutes that lay between Christian Scientists and possible prosecution. Committees on Publication aggressively pursued changes in the law, encouraging members to wage letter-writing campaigns. As a result, the New York State legislature, for example, after intensive lobbying by Scientists, passed a law in 1950 exempting Christian Science children from studying certain subjects: "A pupil may be excused from such study of health and hygiene as conflicts with the religion of his parents or guardian."[29] In 1950 as well, Ohio, the last holdout in the nation in refusing to allow practitioners to charge for their services, dropped that restriction. Andrew Hartsook, a Christian Scientist, a historian of the Church, and a longtime resident of Ohio, has written that, while this triumph "was hailed as a great achievement, it was known to those close to the state C.O.P.'s office that favorable consideration for the change in the state statute was accompanied by a large donation to the Ohio Republican party from Christian Science sources."[30]

In 1955, the U.S. Senate announced that it would hold hearings on the freedom of religion; the Church replied with a lengthy document outlining all the infringements on Scientists' freedom. The Church requested exemption on religious grounds from compulsory vaccination and inoculation; compulsory X-ray chest exams; compulsory physical examinations of schoolchildren; compulsory periodical medical examination for federal, state, or city employees; compulsory study in public schools of medical disease theory, of detailed descriptions of diseases and their symptoms, of films, books, and other materials graphically portraying forms of disease or its effects, or of material which insists or implies that medical treatment is the only effective method of treating human ailments; requirements that people receive medical treatment in order to qualify for disability benefits, including workmen's compensation; fluoridation of the public water supply; and World Health Organization regulations.[31] The 1955 hearings were broken off before they were completed, but the Church would dedicate itself over the next several decades to the enactment of federal and state statutes and legislation guaranteeing Scientists this laundry list of exemptions, or what they prefer to call "accommodations."

The accommodations the Church requested and received were legion, many involving exemptions from criminal and civil child abuse and neglect laws. Arizona, for example, declared that "no child who in good faith is being furnished Christian Science treatment by a duly accredited practitioner" could be considered neglected or abused.[32] Other state statutes contained language that was sufficiently vague or broad so that it seemed to allow Scientists to treat their children as they wished and to practice their religion without interference. The Church also began issuing to its members special cards demanding exemptions from school medical examinations for their children; Scientists were encouraged to order their children's schools not to provide any medical care. The Church pursued an aggressive campaign against the fluoridation of the water supply, describing it as a kind of mass medication of the populace, akin to forcing Catholics to eat meat on Fridays. (Braden notes, however, that the Church, in one of its most baffling rationalizations, did not disapprove of the chlorination of water. According to Scientists, chlorination was treatment of the water itself and not of persons.[33])

But Scientists were successful in gaining much of what they were after. The Internal Revenue Service now allows the fees of Christian Science practitioners and nurses to be deducted as medical expenses.[34] The Workmen's Compensation Act makes a provision for Christian Science treatment, and the federal government covers such treatment in its group health and hospitalization plan.[35] In many states, Christian Science nurses are exempt from registration.[36] Forty-eight states allow religious exemptions from immunizations; some exempt Scientists or other objectors from routine procedures given to most newborns: the treatment of a baby's eyes with silver nitrate to prevent blindness, and tests for metabolic diseases or mental retardation.[37] Some of the allowances make no logical sense: practitioners—who cannot diagnose disease or illness—are allowed to sign certificates for sick leave and disability claims, although the Church has never explained how practitioners can verify conditions they don't believe in.[38] Practitioners, as health providers, are required by some states to report contagious illnesses or suspected cases of child abuse or neglect, but the religion teaches the contradictory practice of denying such conditions.

To explain these myriad statutes and laws, the Church published and distributed booklets to Scientists in every state. Entitled, for example, "Legal Rights and Obligations of Christian Scientists in Minnesota," these booklets describe in great detail how Scientists, and particularly Christian Science parents, can bypass all the onerous practices of society with regard to the physical body, no matter how petty. The Church has even gone so far as to request that Christian Science Camp Fire Girls, "who wish to qualify for any of the Torch Bearer programs" that require vigorous physical exercise, be relieved of the requirement of having a physical exam.[39]

The Church's success in gaining this extraordinary array of special rights and privileges was linked to one key development: during the 1950s, insurance companies began to cover the services of Christian Science practitioners. The Church has been loath to explain its role in convincing insurance companies to cover Scientists in health, accident, and hospitalization policies, preferring to suggest that such coverage was a "recognition" of Scientists' healing prowess. Robert Peel, representing the Church's position, argued that the acceptance of Christian Science healing by legislatures, courts, insurance companies, and public health agencies was not attributable to "skillful public relations" by the Church. "Mere skill could never have achieved such a result," he wrote, "unless it had been backed up by the known lives of its adherents."[40] In 1995, Victor Westberg, then the manager of the Committees on Publication, denied that the Church had anything to do with the insurance coup, saying merely that Scientists had, of their own free will, individually asked for this coverage from their insurers.[41] The Church doubtless played a role, however, probably by encouraging Scientists themselves to lobby insurance companies individually, much as they lobby their legislators, and by providing companies with their own unique form of statistics: the numbers of healings published in Christian Science periodicals. One writer even refers to "a study" that "showed no deaths occurred [among Scientists] from suicide, homicide, or automobile and home accidents."[42]

"Recognition" of Christian Science by insurers marked a new phase in the history of the Christian Science movement, a phase in which the Church would come ever closer to crossing the line that Justice Cardozo had drawn between faith healers and physicians. In much of its previous wrangling with legislatures, the Church had emphasized the fact that Christian Science deserved protection under the First Amendment because it was a *religion*; with insurance coverage, it was about to become much more: an alternative health care "system," proven "effective" by the

Church's own claims and statistics (which would be based, invariably, on the number of healings published in its own periodicals). Ironically, the benefit that individual Scientists derived from insurance coverage was minimal, and insurance companies offered it largely because they knew they were risking little by doing so. Christian Science treatment is undoubtedly one of the cheapest forms of treatment available and always has been; practitioners' charges, compared with the expenses of medical testing, specialists, hospitalization, and drug therapies, are minuscule, from $10 to $50 for a treatment. Since the majority of Scientists are middle-class, relatively few needed even to avail themselves of their insurance benefits; it would prove beneficial largely to those entering Christian Science nursing homes. Insurance companies—motivated, as always, by considerations of the bottom line—must have realized that Scientists neither smoke nor drink; are unlikely to defraud insurers by malingering or faking accidents; and, when they do contract serious illnesses, are likely to die swiftly, without recourse to expensive tests, treatments, or lengthy hospitalizations.

The real value of insurance coverage to the Church lay in the shell game it enabled. The Church parlayed the insurance coverage into a semblance of the scientific evidence—which it has never had—of the efficacy of its healing method. Church representatives brought lists of insurers covering Christian Science to state legislators and offered them as public "recognition" that Christian Science worked. Over and over again, the Committees on Publication told legislators that insurance companies would never cover Christian Scientists unless they were convinced that Christian Science treatment was a successful healing method. And over and over again, legislators believed them.

During the 1950s, certain signs of impatience with the special accommodations that Christian Scientists requested of local and state officials, and a concern over Scientists' apparent willingness to flout regulations concerning contagious disease, began to show up. In 1951, Cora Sutherland, a Christian Scientist in her fifties who taught shorthand at Van Nuys High School in Los Angeles, contracted tuberculosis. At that time, the approximately thirteen thousand public school teachers in that city were required to submit a chest X ray every three years in order to identify carriers of active TB; Cora Sutherland, along with one hundred other teachers, received a religious exemption from this regulation. Although she had developed a persistent cough and had lost an alarming amount of weight, she submitted, in lieu of an X ray, an affidavit affirming that she did not have any communicable disease.

It seems, however, that both Sutherland and her practitioner had made a pretty good guess about the nature of the disease she was suffering from. When she became so ill that she had to apply for a leave of absence, her practitioner certified that her symptoms included "lung congestion aggravated by activity."[43] By March 1954, Sutherland had become so desperately ill that her brother insisted that she go to a hospital. She died the day after she was admitted. The coroner's report confirmed that Sutherland had had active tuberculosis, probably for the past two years. She had exposed dozens of her students to the disease, and the Los Angeles health department was forced to comb the city for seventy-two graduates of Van Nuys High School in order to recommend that they have X rays taken. The health department was so irritated by the situation that it petitioned the board of education to eliminate the religious exemption and require X rays of all teachers, pointing out that those who remained exempt could be "exposing the school population of 463,719 to tuberculosis, a leading killer."[44]

As the decade wore on, there were signs that the relationship between Scientists and the law was gradually growing more volatile. In 1955, David Cornelius, the seven-year-old son of Edward and Anna Cornelius, of Swarthmore, Pennsylvania, members of the Mother Church, grew ill and was treated by a practitioner. After the treatment failed, his parents sought medical care. David was diagnosed as having diabetes, treated with insulin, and released from the hospital after his condition improved. His parents were told that he must have regular injections of insulin to survive, but they discontinued the treatment, placing the boy once again under the care of a Christian Science practitioner. After he again grew ill, he was moved to a Christian Science nursing home in Philadelphia; he died on February 14, 1956, in a diabetic coma. His parents were indicted for involuntary manslaughter and narrowly escaped being tried on that charge. The Church, represented by Dr. J. Buroughs Stokes, of the Committees on Publication, persuaded the district attorney to drop the case by insisting that the Corneliuses had sincerely believed that they could save their son through prayer.[45]

In 1957, a Chicago Superior Court judge ordered a Christian Scientist mother to allow a physician to administer the polio vaccine to her child.[46]

In 1958, a family in San Mateo, California, sued a Christian Science neighbor for breaking the California quarantine law after their son contracted the same strain of tuberculosis that the Christian Scientist had.[47] In 1959, the New Jersey Superior Court ruled that a local school board had the legal right to require a Scientist to have her children immunized before enrolling them in public school.[48]

But these isolated cases remained isolated; there was no public outcry, no investigation, no analysis by the press or public authorities that led to an understanding of the fact that Christian Science practices were increasingly coming into conflict with society. Therefore, it is not surprising to find that the Church encountered no resistance when it asked Congress to cover services provided in its sanatoriums and nursing homes under Medicare, a health-insurance system designed to provide medical care for the elderly. In 1965, Dr. J. Buroughs Stokes, who had been so helpful to the Church in resolving the matter of the death of David Cornelius (and who would go on to defend Senate Bill 1866), appeared before the U.S. Congress several times to ensure that all aspects of the Christian Science nursing services would be covered under Medicare to the same extent that services provided to inpatients in medical facilities and the services of registered nurses would be.

In this, as in all requests submitted by the C.O.P. to legislative bodies, the language employed was subtly misleading, designed to soothe and reassure anyone who might be troubled by the strangeness of Christian Science. Dr. Stokes, who was not a medical doctor but had a doctorate in education from Harvard, submitted to the Congress information about Christian Science and its nursing care that described the religion as "a healing system"; he asserted that the Church "accredits a list of Christian Science practitioners and nurses and certifies Christian Science sanatoriums"; and he explained that, while Scientists do not use medical methods, "they do not ignore or neglect human ailments, diseases or injuries."[49] He referred to "the countless thousands who rely upon Christian Science for health care" and reported that, at the Sanatorium at Chestnut Hill, in Massachusetts, there had been "healings during the past year of broken limbs, broken pelvis, all without surgery: cerebral thrombosis; stroke; paralysis; ulcers; cancer, to name but a few."[50] He also made a point of mentioning that "hundreds of insurance companies in the United States recognize and pay for Christian Science treatment and care in their group insurance agreements and their various casualty and accident lines."[51] He concluded: "The facts that Christian Science treatment and care are established on a definite basis, that thoroughly documented records of healings extend over many years, and that Christian Scientists are reasonable and law-abiding people, have had considerable influence on the recognition afforded us by insurance companies."[52]

Stokes's rhetoric, describing a "healing system" complete with processes of accreditation and certification, with its own established sanatoriums and nursing homes in which "patients" were cared for by nurses "equipped to give skilled nursing care," was certainly familiar to the congressmen; they asked few questions. A Senator Anderson did ask whether "Christian Scientist nursing homes would involve any religious counseling," but Stokes assured him that the only thing of that nature "might be the reading of religious matter to a patient unable to read by himself, much as a medical nurse might read to a blind patient in a medical nursing home."[53] The Church was not asking that Medicare cover the fees of the practitioners that patients are required to retain during any sanatorium stay (indeed, private insurance would cover that); they were asking for coverage of the nursing care and the cost of the stay. Nevertheless, Stokes's assurance that the Medicare coverage would simply be paying for services available in any hospital—"changing bandages and teaching patients how to walk again, etc."—was a distortion of the truth: Christian Science nurses have no medical training in how to change bandages or provide physical therapy and are not "skilled" in any meaningful sense.[54] Their main purpose, aside from bathing, turning, and moving patients, was then, as it is now, to provide a religious atmosphere and defend themselves and their patients against materia medica and malicious animal magnetism. What Stokes did not tell the Congress was that Christian Science nurses would not notify a medical doctor of a potentially dangerous change in a patient's condition, would not provide oxygen to a patient who was smothering, would not even call for emergency help. Essentially—and this is something that the Congress surely did not understand—Medicare would be paying them *not* to be nurses.

The modern era of Christian Science religious exemptions and the toll they have taken in the deaths of children begins in the spring of 1967, when Lisa Sheridan, five and a half years old, of Harwich Port, a small town on Cape Cod, Massachusetts, contracted strep throat. While her mother, Dorothy Sheridan, read *Science and Health* and prayed her Christian Science prayers for some three weeks, Lisa's illness turned into pneumonia, and she died in her bed on March 18, 1967. In a time and place in which few children caught pneumonia and fewer died of it, Dorothy Sheridan's failure to provide medical care for Lisa seemed cold, calculating, and ultimately criminal. A month after her daughter's death, she was indicted for manslaughter.

The death of Lisa Sheridan and its aftermath became the subject of the only full-length investigative report ever published on the human cost of Christian Science and the legal ramifications of the deaths of its children. *The "Crime" of Dorothy Sheridan,* by Leo Damore, a reporter who covered Sheridan's trial for the *Cape Cod News,* captured the bizarre clash of cultures that occurred when Christian Science theology entered the courtroom.

In Damore's portrayal, all the emotions engendered by the case— the puzzlement of the local police, the anger of the medical examiner, the district attorney's contempt, and the righteous outrage of the Church authorities who became involved in defending the actions of the Christian Science mother—seem to swirl around the benumbed figure of Dorothy Sheridan who, in the aftermath of the death, was stoic and unnaturally calm, as bereaved Christian Science parents often are, almost as if nothing had happened at all. That Damore's book opens with a description of Dorothy Sheridan's demeanor indicates how deeply troubling outsiders find Scientists' emotional response to death. Their blank faces and untroubled remarks approach what psychiatrists term "lack of affect"; their absence of expression is a subject that arises in virtually all the coverage of the deaths of these children. While it is not a crime to express no grief or sadness over such a death, the strange calm is taken by most observers as callousness, and as an indication that something has gone terribly awry.

When Sergeant David Monbleau, alerted by a funeral home director, arrived at the child's home at just past six in the morning on March 18, 1967, he found Sheridan urging her seven-year-old son, Stevie, to eat his breakfast cereal, despite his distress over his sister's demise. Monbleau, who felt great pity for Sheridan, was nonetheless surprised to learn that Lisa had been dead since one-thirty that morning and that her mother had not informed the funeral home until six o'clock because she "didn't want to disturb anyone in the middle of the night."[55] He was also astonished to hear Sheridan call her ex-husband and abruptly say, "Hello, Steve. This is Dorothy. Steve, Lisa died during the night."[56]

The medical examiner, Dr. Joseph Kelly, was less astonished than outraged by the mother's behavior. He told her that her daughter's death had been "unnecessary" and, over her objections, ordered an autopsy. After Lisa's body was removed from the house, Sheridan asked the police sergeant if he had any children. When he told her he had five, including a girl about Lisa's age, Sheridan offered him Lisa's Easy Bake oven, which had been a Christmas gift. " 'Would you please take it for your little girl?' " she said. " 'I don't care to have it in the house.' "[57]

The autopsy showed that Lisa had the worst case of empyema, or accumulation of pus in the lung cavity, that the pathologist had seen in twenty years of practice. Over a quart of pus had accumulated in Lisa's chest, displacing the diaphragm and the liver and collapsing her right lung. She had essentially "suffocated to death."[58] Both the pathologist and Kelly, the medical examiner, believed that the child could have recovered with early antibiotic treatment or, even a week before her death, with surgical drainage and chemotherapy.[59]

The impending trial garnered an unprecedented amount of attention. It was covered in the local and national press, becoming known throughout New England as "the Christian Science Manslaughter Case."[60] The Church employed some of the finest, most expensive lawyers in Boston to represent Sheridan and to claim that despite its long duration she could not have known how ill her daughter was. But her placidity and lack of remorse and sorrow disturbed the jury. While she was on the stand, Sheridan seemed not to realize the effect that her proud self-righteousness was having on those who observed her. The only emotion she displayed was a defensive anger when she insisted, oddly, "Our family is blessedly free from illness! There has never been a situation like this before!"[61]

The defense, too, erred in turning the most patronizing, pompous face of Christian Science toward the jury, parading before them a series of wealthy, prominent Christian Scientists—including Erwin Canham of the Monitor—to speak for the success of the religion. Damore reported that Canham made an effective witness, but not all the other Scientists did. A juror noticed that one of these witnesses, a municipal judge flown in from Indiana to attest to the fact that he had always provided only Christian Science treatment for his children, had "an impressive set of gold inlays" in his mouth; the juror found himself wondering "if the witness had procured such dental work through prayer" or if, like the juror himself, he had paid a princely sum for his orthodontia.[62]

In the end, Sheridan was found guilty and sentenced to five years' probation. The Church, which was paying the bills and making the legal decisions about the case, chose—against her wishes—not to appeal, fearing that a loss would establish a legal precedent damaging to the rights of Christian Scientists in the state.

David Sleeper, the manager of the Committees on Publication, who had testified in Sheridan's defense, expressed outrage at the legal system, attacking the prosecutor, the jurors, and the judge during a Church-sponsored lecture he delivered at the First Church of Christ, Scientist, Hyannis, Massachusetts, in December 1968. "Human law has nothing stronger to support it than human belief," Sleeper insisted. "God's law *rebukes* any claims of another law. There is *no* law that subverts God's law. Divinity will prove its evidence. Divine authority supports our rights. It is not for the courts or the legislature to provide us our freedom."[63] He urged Scientists to ignore "the enchantments of medicine, and its claims of power," and urged parents not to be afraid to radically rely on their religion, regardless of the law: "Do not let fear of consequences well up. . . . We must not yield to the mesmeric claims of medicine by calling a doctor and being forced to worship a false God."[64] On another occasion he said, "No jury is competent to judge the efficacy of Christian Science."[65]

Sleeper's bitter rhetoric reflected the Board's embattled attitude; indeed, the Board, which vets all Christian Science lectures before they are delivered, must have approved his language. In the aftermath of the Sheridan trial, the Church's policy regarding its children hardened. Since the law had failed Scientists, the law—and the fallible, uncomprehending officials, judges, and juries that enforced it—could not be trusted. Scientists must make it their responsibility to rewrite the laws and ensure that the laws were enforced to Scientists' advantage.

They began in Massachusetts. First, the Church sent the ever persuasive Dr. Stokes to the Massachusetts State House, an institution known less for moral probity than for old-fashioned political deal-making. Working with a sympathetic state senator, Stokes drafted and proposed to the appropriate committee a statute specifically exempting parents who were furnishing "nonmedical remedial treatment by a recognized religious method of healing under the permitted laws of the Commonwealth, such as Christian Science" from being considered neglectful of the "proper physical care" of a child, as Sheridan had. While the bill was working its way through the statehouse, the state's Supreme Judicial Court ruled in an unrelated case that limiting an exemption to those belonging to particular religions or churches was unconstitutional. Stokes revised his proposed statute but then managed to slip the unconstitutional language back into the bill before it passed, specifying no church by name but limiting the statute's applicability to a "recognized church" that just happened to offer the services of "duly-accredited practitioner[s]," language that could only refer to the Christian Science Church. The final bill read: "A child shall not be deemed to be neglected or lack proper physical care for the sole reason that he is being provided remedial treatment by spiritual means alone in accordance with the tenets and practices of a recognized church or religious denomination by a duly-accredited practitioner thereof."[66]

The problem with a bill that protected Christian Science parents from prosecution whether their children lived or died under prayer treatment was that American jurisprudence had long held it to be illegal for parents to martyr their children. Infuriated by the Sheridan trial and emboldened by their success in rewriting other state and federal laws to protect Scientists' rights, even against charges of neglecting their children, the Church was pressing against the limitations traditionally imposed on First Amendment freedoms by the Supreme Court. Reaching back to the beginning of the century, courts had ruled that, while the right to religious freedom of belief is absolute, the right to act on those beliefs may be limited by the interests of the state and society. The most famous formulation of that principle was written in the Supreme Court ruling of 1944 in the case of *Prince v. Massachusetts*, in which a Jehovah's Witness had been convicted of violating state child labor laws by having a child distribute Witness literature in the streets at night. Prince claimed that, because Witnesses are required by their beliefs to proselytize, her right to religious freedom was violated by the conviction. But the Supreme Court upheld it, writing:

> The right to practice religion freely does not include liberty to expose the community or child to communicable disease, or the latter to ill health or death. . . . Parents may be free to become martyrs themselves. But it does not follow they are free, in identical circumstances, to make martyrs of their children before they have reached the age of full and legal discretion when they can make that choice for themselves.[67]

As Damore wrote, with some prescience, at the end of his book, "The amended law did not diminish the risk to children. Its vulnerability remained—and still remains—ticking like a time bomb."[68] Vulnerable by virtue of its unconstitutional language, enacted by senators who were paying little attention to the consequences, the law actually worked to imperil

both children and parents by encouraging Massachusetts Scientists to radically rely on their beliefs, withholding medical care from their children,
and to believe themselves safe from prosecution in the event that their
beliefs radically failed.

It took Damore seven years to write his book and three years to find a
publisher for it. The "Crime" of Dorothy Sheridan was published by Arbor
House in 1978. In 1979, in response to letters he had received from a former Christian Scientist mother who had recently lost her baby to meningitis, Damore wrote,

> I'm afraid your "crusade" is up against a very skilled, well-financed lobby
> effort most effectively mounted by The Mother Church. Your only chance
> is Publicity and more publicity for your cause. The Church, as you know, is
> very secretive about such tragedies as yours and Dorothy Sheridan's and
> shuns any public discussion of them.[69]

The woman Damore was addressing, who had indeed launched a crusade
against the Church she had once loved and obeyed, took him at his word.
Her name was Rita Swan.

3. The Child Cases

The Sheridan case acted as a wake-up call to the Christian Science
Church authorities. They decided that they must spare no expense to
ensure that Scientists could not be tried for manslaughter in the future. In
1974, the Church successfully lobbied the U.S. Department of Health,
Education, and Welfare to enter this mandate in the Code of Federal
Regulations: "A parent or guardian legitimately practicing his religious
beliefs who thereby does not provide specified medical treatment for a
child, for that reason alone shall not be considered a negligent parent or
guardian; however, such an exception shall not preclude a court from
ordering that medical services be provided to the child, where his health
requires it."[70]

This mandate would require states to include religious exemptions in
their civil laws concerning negligence; those states that refused to comply
stood to lose substantial federal funding for child welfare programs. Eleven
states already had a religious exemption statute in 1974, but by 1984, all

states, and the District of Columbia, had passed such statutes, some specifically exempting Christian Scientists from both civil and criminal laws, others employing language supplied by the Church, allowing "duly accredited practitioners" of a "well-recognized religion" to provide "spiritual" treatment for children without their parents being considered negligent.[71] The Church, through its Committees on Publication, ensured the passage of these statutes by intensive lobbying at the state level. Although the Department of Health and Human Services, which succeeded HEW, eliminated the regulation in 1983, most states still retain the exemptions in their statutes.

The HEW requirement went into effect in 1974, the year that Rita and Douglas Swan moved to Grosse Pointe, Michigan, the well-to-do suburb of Detroit where they attended Sixth Church, one of Detroit's most prosperous and well-attended Christian Science branch churches. The Swans' story provides a rare and remarkably complete view of the theological and psychological pressures that can combine to bind Christian Science parents in a kind of paralysis, an inability to take action to save a child's life. It remains one of the most detailed pictures of the death of a child subjected to Christian Science treatment.

When they moved to Grosse Pointe, after Douglas Swan was offered a full-time teaching position at the Detroit Institute of Technology, the Swans were a young couple with one child, a daughter, Cathy, born in 1969. Douglas Swan held a doctorate in mathematics, and Rita was finishing a doctoral dissertation for Vanderbilt University on the poetry of Percy Bysshe Shelley. Over the next two years, Rita Swan would teach part-time at Wayne State University and at junior colleges in the Detroit area.

Douglas and Rita Swan were both devout Christian Scientists raised in the religion. As a teenager, Doug Swan tended to his Christian Scientist mother as she lay dying of colon cancer. Rita, who grew up in Pittsburg, Kansas, a small farming community in the southeast corner of the state, had known Christian Science since she was five, when her parents converted. She joined the branch church in Pittsburg in 1959, when she was sixteen.

Both of the Swans had had Christian Science class-instruction, and before moving to Grosse Pointe they had taught for a time at Principia, building a small house in Elsah, a town on the Mississippi River near the campus. Neither of them had much familiarity with modern medicine or medical doctors. After joining the Grosse Pointe branch church, they donated $100 a month to the church, although they were making less than $18,000 a year.

On March 3, 1976, Matthew, their second child, was born. The birth was uneventful, but the months leading up to it had not been. For several years, Rita Swan had experienced intermittent pain in her abdomen and irregular vaginal bleeding; when she became pregnant with Matthew, the pain became agonizing. Her obstetrician (again, Christian Scientists are encouraged to cooperate with a doctor before and during the birth of a child) felt a cyst on her left ovary. Swan reported the alarming news to her practitioner, Jeanne Steely Laitner, a prominent Christian Science teacher and member of Sixth Church, whose husband was chairman of the board of that branch. Laitner immediately began Christian Science treatment. After the obstetrician could find nothing resembling the cyst during an ultrasound exam, Swan was ecstatic, believing herself healed through Christian Science. She says, "I was absolutely convinced I'd had a Christian Science miracle. I was on cloud nine through the rest of the pregnancy."[72]

The "miracle" was merely a brief reprieve; the cyst had been hidden by the pregnancy. After Matthew was born, the pain returned; on Rita's follow-up visits, the obstetrician insisted that her condition—a cyst that was in danger of twisting and causing necrosis—was serious, probably fatal without surgery. During a bout of particularly unbearable pain and vomiting, unable to breast-feed her six-month-old son, Swan finally called the obstetrician's office and asked if she could merely have a "hypodermic," as Mary Baker Eddy allowed. The doctor told her it would be a violation of medical ethics to provide that kind of Band-Aid treatment and again urged her to go to the hospital.

The Swans agonized over their decision; Doug Swan was haunted by memories of his mother's illness and death. After Jeanne Laitner agreed to continue her metaphysical treatment (a violation of the code of behavior for Christian Science practitioners, who are not allowed to "mix" Christian Science and medicine), Rita Swan decided to have the surgery in October 1976. It saved her life; the cyst had already twisted twice, causing the bouts of pain. As Swan ruefully says now, "I had seen science do in twenty minutes what six years of Christian Science treatment couldn't do. . . . I still went crawling back to Christian Science."[73]

Because she had had surgery, Swan was placed on probation by Sixth Church and was not allowed to do committee work or teach her Sunday school class. A month after the surgery, Matthew Swan, eight months old, came down with a fever. The Swans called Jeanne Laitner for treatment, and Matthew recovered quickly, in about an hour. Again, Rita Swan says, "we gave Christian Science the credit."[74] In April 1977, Matthew came down with another high fever; again he recovered with Christian Science treatment. The Swans were so grateful for his recovery that they testified in church about this "healing."

Only a month later, Matthew developed yet another fever, and this time the Swans were so embarrassed by their perceived failure to maintain the previous healing that they called a different practitioner, whom they had known back in Elsah. Again, Matthew recovered, but more slowly this time, and on Saturday, June 18, 1977, the day before Father's Day, he began running the fever from which he would not recover.

Throughout that weekend, Matthew, now fifteen months old, lay unmoving, flat on his back in his crib, his clothes and bedding soaked with perspiration. "We were terrified," Rita Swan recalls. "My husband stayed up all night; we were terrified that he was going to die. We kept feeling guilty that our fear was causing the baby to be sick. Mary Baker Eddy says that fever is caused by fear, and we accepted at face value that we were the guilty party." By Monday, the Swans were so frightened that they asked Jeanne Laitner to make a house call. It is uncommon for practitioners to visit their patients at home; Christian Science treatment is presumed to be effective, perhaps more effective, when given absently, when the physical picture is not thrust before the practitioner. Jeanne Laitner visited twice on Monday and twice on Tuesday; this is an unusual number of visits for a practitioner to make, and it indicates both the Swans' terror and, perhaps, the practitioner's realization that this was a serious case. On one of these visits, according to Rita Swan's recollection, Mrs. Laitner gave a treatment to Matthew as he lay on his back on the Swans' couch, arguing with him in the way of practitioners, saying, "Matthew, God is your life. God didn't make disease, and disease is unreal. There is no false parental thought that could cause disease." Mrs. Laitner also instructed the Swans not to pray for Matthew themselves because the baby would get confused if more than one person addressed his thought.

But to Matthew's mother, Matthew seemed beyond thought, lost in a terrifying maelstrom of fever and pain. The Swans were struggling, every conscious moment, to control their fear and to "know the Truth" about Matthew, but it was becoming increasingly difficult. Tuesday evening, Rita

Swan broke down in tears, telling Mrs. Laitner that Matthew didn't seem to be making any progress and asking her to treat him alone, in his bedroom; she felt Matthew should be away from her fear. When Mrs. Laitner returned from his room, the practitioner told her that she was very encouraged and that Matthew seemed improved. Rita took the baby outside and thought that he did seem cooler; she sang hymns to him and began to hope that he was recovering.

But on Wednesday morning, she says, "he was horrible, probably in a coma again, really, although we didn't know those words at the time." She called Jeanne Laitner to tell her about this turn of events, only to discover that the practitioner had become irritable, asking if there wasn't something good Rita could report. According to Rita, she said, "It would have been nice if you'd put the good news first."

There wasn't, however, any good news. Matthew could not eat on his own. By Thursday of that week, the Swans had decided that they had to do something, either go to a doctor or employ a different Christian Science practitioner. They debated the options but were fearful of hospitals, Doug Swan saying that he was afraid of what medical science would do to Matthew. The whole medical system, says Rita, "was a mystery. We had no idea what it was, and we knew if we went to a doctor we couldn't get Christian Science treatment, that our thinking would be contaminated. We felt there was no way we could get back to Christian Science if we left. We didn't know if this disease was medically treatable or not. It honestly seemed safer to stick with Christian Science. We decided to try another practitioner for a day and a night."

The Swans called June Ahearn, another older woman and respected practitioner at Sixth Church. They told her that it was a "desperate emergency," and she told them she would take up the work immediately. Mrs. Ahearn also said that she was getting "a strong message" that the Swans were tempted to go to a doctor. They admitted that, if Matthew did not improve by Friday morning, they were planning to seek medical help, and she scolded them gently, telling them that Christian Science could not work under those circumstances, that their reliance on Christian Science had to be total. Their belief in medicine, she told them, rendered them like "a man hanging onto a branch over a cliff." Mrs. Ahearn spoke more truth than she knew when she urged the Swans to trust entirely in Christian Science, to let go of the branch. And they did.

Next, the new practitioner began exploring Rita's life, probing for past sins that might explain her young son's problems. Soon she discovered that Rita had recently had a fight with her father; she encouraged Rita to write him a letter seeking forgiveness. Healing the acrimony between daughter and father might clear the way for Matthew's healing to follow. On Friday, after having successfully, if painstakingly, fed Matthew milk with a baby spoon the day before, Rita felt that he might be getting better and called Jeanne Laitner, the first practitioner, to let her know the good news. Laitner was indignant, claiming that she herself, and not the second practitioner, June Ahearn, should get the credit for the healing. "In this case," she told Rita, "after all my hard work, it wouldn't be right for another practitioner to heal it." Rita says she was terrified by Mrs. Laitner's response, convinced that "this authority figure was putting a curse on my child." June Ahearn was continuing to do her metaphysical work on paralysis, because one of Matthew's symptoms was a stiff neck, but when Rita blurted out her fears over Mrs. Laitner's "curse," Mrs. Ahearn was aghast, convinced that the specter of malicious animal magnetism had entered the picture. She referred to her erstwhile competitor as a "kook."

The next day, Saturday—a week into Matthew's illness—Rita wrote the apologetic letter to her father; Sunday, Mrs. Ahearn dropped by the Swans' house after church. When Matthew grasped Mrs. Ahearn's thumbs, she believed the child had experienced an instantaneous healing; Rita Swan was not so sure. "Mrs. Ahearn said that he looked just like a little rose lying there with this terrible glassy look on his face. She had never had children of her own, and I think she thought he was like a newborn. Here was this fifteen-month-old child who could walk and do all kinds of things. . . . I was just crushed. He looked awful to me." In fact, he seemed to be in excruciating pain whenever his spine was moved. At midnight that Sunday, June 26, Matthew began screaming.

The Swans stayed up with him all night listening to him scream and decided in their despair that they must take him to a doctor. They called June Ahearn as early as they dared the next morning, following Christian Science protocol that practitioners must be taken off the case before the patient goes to a doctor, but Mrs. Ahearn was having none of it. She told the Swans she would not be able to pray for them if they crossed the line and told them they'd have "a long hard road" back to Christian Science if they once left it. Doug Swan suggested that Matthew's illness might be contagious—practitioners in many states are legally required to report contagious illnesses to health authorities—but Mrs. Ahearn was dismissive of that ploy, saying: "You're too concerned about what the community thinks." She counseled them instead to hire a Christian Science nurse who would not "interfere with the practitioner." The Swans called for a Christian Science nurse.

A nurse came out that evening to evaluate the situation. She told the Swans that Matthew was getting better and should be given more orange juice. A home aide who could relieve them so that they could sleep would not be available for several days. "They didn't regard this as an emergency," Rita says now. Indeed, Christian Science nurses and practitioners, following the precepts of the religion, regard nothing as an emergency; routinely, nurses and practitioners only call 911 after their patient is dead.

Immediately after the nurse left on Monday, the night of June 27, Rita saw that the pain seemed to have left Matthew's spine. "It was a dramatic change in symptoms," Rita says. "But he still couldn't blink, couldn't sit up, couldn't connect. He was just moaning incoherently. It tore my heart out to look at him." Rita called Mrs. Ahearn again, to report her continued fears; the practitioner responded by sharply rebuking her, telling her, "It's been one and a half hours since the healing of the spine! I've done my metaphysical work on this case for the evening." And she hung up. The next day, she told Rita not to call her so many times and that fever was simply the body's natural way of getting rid of heat.

By this time, Tuesday, June 28, Matthew was convulsing and gnashing his teeth. Mrs. Ahearn suggested that he was gritting his teeth because he was planning some "great achievement." Matthew was now completely unable to eat. Mrs. Ahearn came over to the Swans' home again Wednesday evening, sat in their rocking chair with Matthew, and pronounced him healed of his "paralysis," pointing out how he could move his arms and legs freely. "I was in total despair," Rita says, "because I knew it wasn't normal. She tried to make Matthew walk, holding him in an upright position. Matthew could no more have walked than June Ahearn could have flown to the moon."

The afternoon of Thursday, June 30, Cathy, the Swans' seven-year-old daughter, was scheduled to have a T-shirt-decorating party, invitations having gone out before Matthew fell ill. Cathy herself had wanted to cancel the party, telling her parents that morning, "My brother is going crazy." But Mrs. Ahearn insisted that the Swans go ahead with it—"Go on with your natural activity," Rita says she told them—and even suggested that they "include Matthew" on a blanket with the other children. During this surreal event, at which both Doug and Rita Swan were present, one of them would stay with the children in the basement while the other would run up to Matthew's room and, says Rita, "watch him convulsing." When the party was over, the Swans had reached the end of their passivity. They had previously managed to wring a concession out of June Ahearn: Matthew, she admitted, might have a broken bone, which, according to Mary Baker Eddy, could be set by a doctor. But Mrs. Ahearn counseled them not to go to a hospital but rather to an X-ray clinic, avoiding the prying eyes and questions of an emergency physician. They ignored her and drove, instead, to St. John Hospital in Detroit.

"When I walked into the emergency room with Matthew in my arms," Rita Swan says, "he was probably close to death. There was a doctor there who took one look at him and said, 'How long has he been like this, not responding?' I was shocked by the question. It was such a simple question." It was a question that would change Rita Swan's life.

"I stammered out my prepared statement and asked him to check for broken bones," Rita says. But the doctor rushed off with the child, soon joined by a number of nurses. "We'd been waiting for a Christian Science nurse or home aide since Monday. But these doctors, they took it seriously. They regarded the child as important." So, of course, did his parents, but it was a revelation to them to see the urgency of emergency medical treatment.

Matthew had bacterial meningitis, a virulent and life-threatening inflammation of the brain and spinal cord membranes that occurs most frequently in children under the age of five; it is treated with large doses of antibiotics and is frequently fatal without medical treatment and sometimes fatal with it. It is also contagious, and Mrs. Ahearn's dismissal of her responsibility to report it to health authorities could have endangered other children. Had Matthew been taken to a physician earlier in his illness, his stiff neck and high fever would immediately have suggested meningitis, a painful illness according to those who have survived it; the change in symptoms, when Matthew seemed to become free of the pain in his spine, indicated that the infection had moved to his brain, a development that is nearly always fatal.

The pediatrician who had been called in told the Swans that Matthew's case was grave and that he needed emergency neurosurgery, which was, however, a desperate measure; it might not improve his condition or save him from brain damage. The Swans had called June Ahearn to inform her of their change of heart; she was horrified at their "reliance on materia medica" and refused to pray for Matthew.

Having been told by the doctors that there was little time, the Swans reluctantly gave their permission for the neurosurgery. Matthew survived the surgery, but his condition continued to deteriorate. Soon he was unable to breathe on his own and was put on a respirator; he was being given several different kinds of medication.

The Swans continued to search for a Christian Scientist who would help them in their hour of need. Practitioners are subject to discipline from the Board of Directors if they pray for patients undergoing medical treatment, but Rita reasoned that, since the doctors had threatened to get a court order if the Swans refused to allow Matthew's surgery, perhaps a practitioner could pray for them since they hadn't actually wanted it. Rita called a man she knew, a Christian Science chaplain at Wayne State University, Robert Jeffery. The Swans say that Jeffery refused to pray for Matthew while he was on any medication or dependent on medical "machinery." He told the Swans that, if they wanted Christian Science treatment, they would have to take Matthew off the respirator and remove him from the hospital, with or without the permission of the doctors. According to the Swans, he told them, "You have to be willing to make fools of yourselves in the eyes of the world to get help from God." He also mentioned that he could not work with "all those minds" in the hospital. If Matthew was healed through Christian Science while still in the hospital, he asked, "Who would get the credit? The doctors would claim the credit for healing him."

As it turned out, no one would be able to claim any credit. On July 5, the hospital performed an EEG on Matthew; it indicated that he was nearly brain-dead. Matthew died in the early morning hours of July 7, 1977. "Until the moment Matthew died," Rita Swan says, "I retained the belief that Christian Science would heal him."

The Swans never returned to a Christian Science church. Although the doctors had been reluctant to tell them about their own role in Matthew's death, they had learned enough about meningitis during their time in the hospital to realize that he could probably have been successfully treated had they brought him in sooner. They both felt intense guilt and shame, as well as resentment of the two practitioners' continued rationalizations. When they informed June Ahearn of Matthew's death, she declared herself "shocked," saying, "I know medical science can scare you, but I know that Matthew felt more comfortable under my care." Jeanne Laitner claimed that Matthew had gotten better while she treated him. "It's incredible how these people wanted credit for this dead body," Rita Swan says.

Other Christian Scientists were no more empathetic. Doug Swan told Dean Joki, the Michigan state Committee on Publication, "I'm very repentant that I let that poor baby suffer like that." Joki, who had himself some years earlier lost an eleven-month-old son during Christian Science treatment (a fact that he did not reveal to the Swans at the time), replied, "That kind of resentment will never cure anything."[75]

Rumors began to fly throughout the Detroit Christian Science community about the fact that Rita Swan had had an operation only months before Matthew's illness and death; many Christian Scientists believe that once a person gives in to materia medica, illness inevitably follows. "That's what happens when you seek out medicine," Rita Swan says, explaining Christian Science logic. "All these diseases come crashing down on you."

When the Swans wrote to Sixth Church soon after Matthew's death to say that they wished to withdraw their membership, they say that friends predicted that "we'd be at the doctor's office every day if we left Christian Science." Members pleaded with them not to quit. One of them suggested that Matthew "had seen through this whole plane of existence." The Swans also say that Jeanne Laitner was dismissive about the importance of Matthew's death, saying, "Life on earth is such a pinprick, what does it matter?"

Rita Swan was particularly infuriated when she learned that Mrs. Laitner was letting it be known that she had healed another boy of meningitis; when Swan investigated, eventually talking to the boy's mother, she learned that Mrs. Laitner had treated a case of viral meningitis, not bacterial meningitis. The boy she had "healed" turned out to be a teenager, and his most severe symptoms were minor weight loss and an aversion to strong light. Viral meningitis is, in fact, a form of the illness so benign that it often does not require medical treatment. Swan discovered these medical facts while sitting on the floor in the library stacks of the Wayne State University School of Medicine. "I read and I read and I read," she says, "and finally I figured out that there are two different kinds of meningitis. That was really the liberating moment for me, when I could read that and figure out for myself that Christian Science was a fraud. Christian Science could not cure bacterial meningitis. The healing of that other boy was not a miracle. I didn't have to rely on magical thinking. I was very, very angry at Jeanne Laitner. If she could cure meningitis, she sure had an opportunity."

Rita Swan was also angry at herself. "It was terribly, morally wrong for us to let this happen," she says. It had taken her years of pain and the threat of death to push her into surgery for the cyst; afterward, she was shamed by her church for having done so. With Matthew, she and her husband had had thirteen days to make a decision and had, or so they now saw it, made a tragic mistake.

The Swans were not punished by the law. Ironically, Rita and Doug Swan were protected by one of the very laws that they would eventually devote their lives to overturning. As Matthew lay dying, Dean Joki had told them that they would most likely not be prosecuted for their son's death; the religious exemption statute protected Michigan parents providing spiritual treatment for their children from prosecution for neglect or abuse.

But if the law would not punish her, Rita Swan would punish herself; in essence, she would sentence herself to years of hard labor for the crime of failing her son. First, Rita and Doug Swan tried to reform the Christian Science Church from within. They wrote a letter to the Mother Church complaining about June Ahearn's self-justification and her refusal to acknowledge that her treatment had been ineffective; they suggested that her *Journal*-listing as a practitioner be dropped. The reply from the Mother Church informed them that they would "see Matthew again" in proportion to their understanding that he had never died. In the fall of 1977, when Rita wrote to the Church to withdraw her membership, she received a letter from the Clerk of the Mother Church, telling her that she needed a more spiritual understanding of the motherhood of God, which she could only obtain from the Bible and *Science and Health*.

The letters so angered the Swans that they began to think about suing the Church for negligence in having played a role in Matthew's death. They talked to several law firms but found little interest, nor were local newspapers that Rita Swan queried (the Grosse Pointe newspaper and the *Detroit Free Press*) interested in pursuing the story. While working as a technical editor at General Motors during the winter of 1977, Swan called dozens of people during her lunch hours: doctors, hospitals, child protection workers, to ask what could be done. "I'd grab somebody's ear and pour out this horrible story," she says, trying to make a connection, trying to make somebody care.[76] She learned from a neighbor that another child, a boy in a Christian Science family, had died only five blocks away from her home around the same time as Matthew had died; she subsequently learned that Matthew and this other boy were the only children aged between one and fourteen who had died in Grosse Pointe in 1977.

In 1978, the Swans had another child, a girl named Marsha, and moved to North Dakota, hoping to start a new life, but they did not forget their debt to Matthew's memory. In 1979, the International Year of the Child, they resolved to do something every day on what they called the Matthew Project, to get the word out that Christian Science can endanger children. Rita Swan wrote letters to magazines and newspapers but found no interest until she hit upon the idea of writing to 60 *Minutes* and the *Donahue* show. *Donahue* was immediately interested and, in December 1979, the Swans and their daughter Cathy were flown to Chicago to do the show, an entire hour devoted to the issue of Christian Science and children. The producers of *Donahue* had invited representatives of the Church to appear on the show as well. The Mother Church sent Allison Phinney, Jr., then the manager of the Committees on Publication, as well as several others— all of whom, however, refused to appear on camera. They simply spoke with the producers, who were mystified as to why they had bothered to come to Chicago at all.

The *Donahue* appearance heightened media interest in the Swans, and shortly after the show, they retained the Detroit firm of Charfoos & Christensen to represent them in their suit against the Church. They received angry mail from Christian Scientists; they also heard from angry ex–Christian Scientists, some of whom had tales of death and disability to tell that corresponded eerily with their own. A number of ex-Scientists wanted to donate money to a group or organization that would inform the public about Christian Science and its perils, but, as yet, there was no such group.

In the spring of 1983, Rita and Douglas Swan founded Children's Health-care Is a Legal Duty, Inc. (CHILD, Inc.), the only nonprofit group of its kind in the world, devoted to lobbying to change religious exemption laws and to educating the public as well as legal, medical, and media professionals not just about Christian Science but about all religious sects that encourage medical neglect of children.

The Swans' lawsuit against Jeanne Laitner, June Ahearn, and the First Church of Christ, Scientist, Boston, Massachusetts, took up much of their time in the years following their appearance on *Donahue*. Filed in 1980, it was the first civil suit for the wrongful death of a child ever filed against the Church; it was scheduled for trial in Wayne County Circuit Court in Detroit in September 1983. The complaint included counts that charged the two practitioners with not following the procedures of the Church; the Church publicly insists that all Christian Scientists have the right to make their own decisions regarding health care, but June Ahearn had repeatedly talked the Swans out of going to a doctor whenever they expressed an interest in that option. Another count concerned the Swans' assertion that both Jeanne Laitner and June Ahearn had offered inaccurate physical diagnoses of their son's condition; according to the Swans, Laitner had suggested that he was cutting a tooth, Ahearn that he might have roseola, a common virus in infants that causes fever and rash and is not life-threatening. Practitioners are forbidden both by the Church itself and by law from making diagnoses of physical illness.

The first day in court was a disaster for the Swans; the Church had filed a motion for summary judgment—or dismissal—of the case, and the judge, newly appointed after another judge had stepped aside, dismissed all but one of the counts in the complaint, the one regarding the diagnoses, on the basis that the counts regarding religious belief could not be adjudicated. "It was very humiliating and painful," Rita Swan says. The courtroom had been full of local and national media—the Grosse Pointe newspaper and the *Detroit Free Press*, which had spurned her years earlier, were now intensely interested in the story—and a trial that had taken years to prepare and was expected to take weeks to hear was suddenly reduced to a single issue. The second day, Rita says, the judge "gave a long speech about the power and dignity of the First Amendment" and dismissed the rest of the case. The Swans' appeals, which were not ruled on until December 1986, were also fruitless.

The legal case ended in failure, but it yielded some fascinating information, in the form of depositions taken from numerous Church officials: Ruth Jenks and DeWitt John, members of the Board of Directors (John was also the well-known author of a popular book, *The Christian Science Way of Life*); Allison Phinney, the manager of the Committees on Publication; the two practitioners, Laitner and Ahearn; Dean Joki, the Michigan C.O.P.; and Robert Jeffery, the practitioner who had refused to pray for Matthew unless the child was removed from life support, among others. For the first time, Church officials were forced to go on the record, describing the cursory qualification procedures by which practitioners and Christian Science nurses become *Journal*-listed and after which they are sent out to deal with life-threatening illnesses and injuries; the fact that no notice is taken by Church authorities of the number of Christian Science children who die; the fact that Christian Science practitioners cannot possibly diagnose and report—as they are legally required to do in many states—contagious diseases that could affect public health.

The defensiveness and anger of these officials on being questioned about the ability of Christian Science to heal potentially fatal illnesses revealed officials who were often startlingly smug in their self-assurance as healers, although they had no hard scientific or statistical evidence supporting them. They seemed confident of the power of their church and proud of their ignorance of the human body and of disease. In his deposition, Dean Joki said, "Our record of healing is at least as good as that of other forms of treatment. Might not be any better but it is just as good."[77] Shortly after these remarks, on being asked to return the next day to continue his deposition, he remarked that he had a dental appointment that he particularly didn't want to miss.

When pressed on how Church officials can determine whether the Christian Science treatment that children are being given is effective, Joki claimed that those officials learn this through "hearsay, fairly reliable hearsay."[78] Asked why it is permissible for a Christian Scientist to employ a physician for the birth of a child but not in order to diagnose and treat the illnesses of a child, Joki's reply defied even theological logic:

> The birth of a child is not a physical condition that has been brought about through vague thinking on the part of Christian Scientists who sometimes are caught up with disease. It is a determined procedure and, therefore, not something that they wish to terminate through spiritual treatment, that is, they do not wish to have the condition go away. They want to see it through. So that is a physical experience.[79]

June Ahearn explained that she did not "know a thing about disease" because she had been "exempt through the C.O.P. card that we filed with the office of the schools," when she attended high school, the extent of her education.[80] She claimed that she would "snap off" the radio or television whenever symptoms of illness were mentioned.[81] When asked, "Did your treatments as a Christian Science practitioner ever in your opinion fail?"

she replied, "I do not, you know, because God heals, I do not think it ever fails."[82]

Another Christian Science practitioner from the Detroit area, J. Thomas Black, who was not involved with the Swans' case directly, was called to give a deposition regarding the nature of the practitioner's work. He explained what the Swans had done wrong, and how, in his opinion, they themselves had caused their son's death. He was asked, "Assuming Matthew Swan is dead, do you have any opinions as to whether or not he was healed by Christian Science treatment?" Black replied, "Apparently he was not."[83] The Swans' attorney asked, "So that would be an instance when Christian Science treatment did not heal?" Black answered, "Incorrect. . . . Whenever Christian Science is properly applied it heals." He went on to say, "The patient, the parents, apparently from what I have thus far read, were much more intent on physical healing than on spiritual growth and moral regeneration. [Christian Science] was therefore misapplied." He was then asked, "And then it would have been the parents' misapplication because of their intent on physical healing?" He replied, "Yes, and their rejection of spiritual progress and moral regeneration."[84] J. Thomas Black was appointed president of the Christian Science Church in 1997 and First Reader at the Mother Church for a three-year term beginning in 1998.

The Swans' legal case was the beginning of an unprecedented era of disaster for the Christian Science Church, marked by seven criminal prosecutions of Christian Science parents, civil lawsuits for wrongful death, and the worst public relations that the Church had endured since the early years of the century. Throughout this ordeal, the Church responded with self-righteous indignation, claiming that its members were being unfairly singled out and persecuted for their religious beliefs, blandly insisting that the deaths of Christian Science children were infrequent events, even though nearly every newspaper story covering what would become known to Christian Scientists as "the child cases" proved them wrong.

In 1984, three Christian Science children in the state of California died of bacterial meningitis, the same illness that killed Matthew Swan. Shauntay Walker, a four-year-old living in Sacramento, California, died on March 9, 1984. Her mother, Laurie Walker, who had been a Christian Scientist for three years, had kept her child home from nursery school for seventeen days. The day before Shauntay's death, her aunt, Claudia Oswald, who had become concerned about the child's welfare, went to the Walker home and found Shauntay "comatose . . . just lying on the couch."[85] Oswald described her niece as nonresponsive and noticeably thin; in fact, Shauntay, who was nearly five years old, weighed only twenty-nine pounds at death. Oswald urged her sister to take Shauntay to a doctor; instead, Laurie Walker removed her to the home of another Christian Scientist, where she died within hours. The Christian Science practitioner who had been praying for Shauntay later claimed that the child had eaten lunch and taken a walk the day before she died, the same day that Oswald described her as "comatose."[86]

Two weeks later, the Sacramento district attorney's office filed charges of manslaughter and felony child endangerment against Laurie Walker, the first such charges against Christian Science parents in California since the case of Merrill Reed and his wife in 1902. One of the defense attorneys was Warren Christopher, a powerful figure in Democratic circles in California, who would eventually serve as Bill Clinton's secretary of state.

Walker's counsel argued in California Supreme Court that the state's religious exemption statute had led her to believe that she had the legal right to provide spiritual rather than medical care for her daughter and that, protected by the statute, she could not be tried for involuntary manslaughter. In 1988, in a unanimous ruling that has established precedent in California, the Supreme Court held that the statute did not exempt parents from providing "necessary" medical care, nor did it exempt them from prosecution for felony child endangerment or manslaughter. The ruling cited *Prince v. Massachusetts*, asserting that parents did not have the right to martyr their children.

The California Supreme Court also alluded to advances made in modern medicine and rejected the relevance of an 1874 case that Walker's defense team had suggested was applicable, a case in which manslaughter charges were dismissed against a parent who had chosen prayer rather than blisters and leeches: "Were blisters, leeches and calomel the medical alternatives to prayer today," the court wrote, that 1874 case might "more fully resonate." "Medical science has advanced dramatically," the court noted, "and we may fairly presume that the community standard for criminal negligence has changed accordingly."[87]

In 1990, Laurie Walker was convicted of manslaughter in a plea agreement that allowed her to retain her right to appeal. After the California Supreme Court declined to review her conviction, a federal court overturned it in 1996 on due process grounds, ruling that the wording of the California statute at the time of Shauntay's death did not provide Walker with fair notice of her criminal liability. The California Supreme Court ruling of 1988, however, still holds; Christian Science parents in California may not assume that they are free to withhold "necessary" medical care from a child without being subject to prosecution. The 1988 ruling also cleared the way for the trials of the other California Christian Scientists to proceed.

Seth Glaser, a seventeen-month-old infant, died of meningitis in Los Angeles on March 28, 1984, just weeks after Shauntay Walker. His parents, Eliot and Lise Glaser, were acquitted of manslaughter after a bench trial in 1989; their child's illness had been so short in duration—just over twenty-four hours—that the judge ruled that any parents might have responded to such an illness in the same way, with the same results.[88]

But Natalie Rippberger, eight months old, died on December 9, 1984, after an illness lasting two weeks; she, like Matthew Swan, suffered convulsions and high fevers. Natalie's parents, Mark Rippberger and Susan Middleton-Rippberger, were charged in Sacramento with felony child endangerment and involuntary manslaughter. In 1989, after a trial lasting seven weeks, they were acquitted of manslaughter but found guilty of endangerment. They were placed on probation and fined over $10,000; they were also ordered by the court to provide medical care for their five surviving children.

In 1986, Amy Hermanson, seven years old, died of untreated juvenile-onset diabetes in Sarasota, Florida, after a long, wasting illness that had left her noticeably weak and emaciated. Six days before her child's death, Christine Hermanson, a piano teacher, brought Amy with her to the home of one of her adult pupils, where she was to give a lesson. The pupil, Victoria Neuhaus, was appalled at Amy's condition and urged Hermanson to take her to a doctor immediately; she refused. Neuhaus later testified that, during the lesson, Amy crawled into the music room on her hands and knees, asking her mother to take her home. Hermanson told Neuhaus, "She'll be all right."[89] A few days before Amy died, her parents flew to Indianapolis to attend their Christian Science Class Association meeting.

Amy died on September 30, 1986, in her parents' bed, vomiting and urinating uncontrollably, attended by her parents, a Christian Science nurse, and the Christian Science Committee on Publication for Florida, who forbade the nurse to call 911 until he had called Boston, to inform authorities at the Mother Church of the situation. By the time the nurse made the call, Amy was dead. The Hermansons, charged with felony child abuse and third-degree murder, were convicted on both charges after a jury trial in 1989. At trial, it was reported by one of the Hermansons' neighbors, a non-Scientist, that she had asked Christine Hermanson how she could justify having withheld medical care from Amy when she had had two cesarean sections with anesthetics and William Hermanson had had painkillers while undergoing dental work. Christine Hermanson had replied, "Well, that was a different situation." The same neighbor testified that Hermanson remarked, after Amy's death, that "Amy had chosen to pass over."[90] The jury foreman later described the Hermansons' behavior as "a seeming lack of care, a coldness. It's hard for anybody to believe they could let it get that far."[91]

In 1992, in a unanimous decision, the Florida Supreme Court overturned the Hermansons' convictions on the grounds that Florida's religious exemption law was "ambiguous" and failed to give parents fair notice of their obligations under the law to provide medical care:

A person of ordinary intelligence cannot be expected to understand the extent to which reliance on spiritual healing is permitted and the point at which this reliance constitutes a criminal offense under the subject statutes. The statutes have created a trap that the legislature should address.[92]

The "trap" described by the judge had been set by the Christian Science Church itself, in its advocacy and lobbying for religious exemption laws. Believing that the laws would freely allow parents to provide Christian Science treatment instead of medical treatment no matter what the consequences, Church officials had urged Scientists to radically rely on their religion. But, in fact, the state statutes could not legally protect Christian Science parents from prosecution and, in some cases, conviction. The exemptions for which Scientists had fought so hard—the same exemptions that made them feel safe in staking their children's lives on their religion—would spare them little.

The public image of Christian Science was dealt another blow in 1985. Three people died during a severe measles outbreak at Principia College in Elsah. The majority of students had never had the disease and were not vaccinated. During the course of the outbreak, over 100 people, out of a total of 650 students and 175 staff, contracted the illness. Dr. Walter

Orenstein of the Centers for Disease Control in Atlanta told a reporter for the *St. Louis Post-Dispatch* that measles usually causes approximately three deaths for every thousand cases; that only three fatal cases had been reported in the United States over the past three years; and that the three deaths at Principia represented "the kind of mortality statistics we see" in the Third World.[93]

The outbreak began on January 11. On February 5, Charlotte Bertleson, twenty-three, a senior from Tucson, Arizona, studying interior design, died two days after being transferred from a "special care facility" at the school to Alton Memorial Hospital. The campus was not placed under voluntary quarantine until February 21, by which time nearly ninety cases had been reported; after that time no one was allowed to enter or leave the campus unless they could prove that they had either had the measles previously or had been vaccinated. On February 22, Scott Shadrick, a nineteen-year-old student from Massachusetts, died in a guest house on campus; on March 1, Jennifer Evans, the sixteen-year-old daughter of a campus counselor, died in her parents' on-campus apartment. Pathologists' reports officially confirmed that Shadrick's and Evans's deaths had been caused by the measles; no autopsy was performed on Bertleson, although her cause of death was reported as pneumonia, a common complication of the disease.

The reactions of both the parents and the Christian Science officials involved were typically defensive. Although Charlotte Bertleson was an adult, Bertleson's mother told the *Post-Dispatch* that she had sought medical care for her daughter against her own wishes because she was afraid she would be held legally liable in her death if she did not; she also suggested that her daughter might have gone into shock "from having medication because her system was not used to it."[94] Scott Shadrick's father said of his son, "Everything possible was done for him. I am very comfortable with that."[95] And John Boyman, the president of Principia, issued a statement saying that, while those on campus were "deeply concerned" about the deaths, he felt that "we are learning, as many medical people recognize, that contagion of fear is as much a factor as anything else."[96] There were measles outbreaks that winter at Boston University and Ohio State University, as well as in northern Florida and in Browning, Montana, a town on the Blackfeet Indian reservation. But none of these outbreaks involved as many cases as the one at Principia, and none involved deaths.

Boyman also claimed that the students who recovered demonstrated that Christian Science works, but a good proportion of his student body apparently had their doubts. Over four hundred Principia students chose to be vaccinated at clinics that had been set up on campus by state health authorities. Later that same year, yet another measles outbreak was traced to a Christian Science summer camp, Adventure Unlimited, in Colorado; it spread to twenty-five cases in nine states.[97]

The 1985 measles epidemics were not the first outbreaks of infectious disease involving Christian Scientists, nor would they be the last. In 1972, there was an outbreak of polio at Daycroft School, a Christian Science prep school in Greenwich, Connecticut. One hundred and twenty-eight students contracted polio; four were partially paralyzed.[98] In 1982, a nine-year-old girl, Debra Kupsch, came down with diphtheria at a Christian Science camp in Colorado. She died of the illness after having traveled to her home in Wisconsin by bus with a number of other unvaccinated children; it ultimately cost the state of Wisconsin some $20,000 to locate all those she had come in contact with to test them.

Measles returned to Principia in the spring of 1994, when a fourteen-year-old girl, a Christian Scientist from Elsah, Illinois, contracted measles while on a Colorado ski vacation. From this one case, measles spread to over 150 people in six states. Like the Elsah girl, most of the victims in Missouri were students at Principia's elementary and upper school, in St. Louis. The victims in Illinois lived in Elsah. Those in other states—New York, Maine, California, and Washington—had contracted the illness while visiting Principia; those in Colorado had contracted it from the Elsah girl.

This time, the Principia campus in St. Louis was placed under quarantine. Richard Nordahl, the Committee on Publication for Missouri, pointed out to Martha Shirk, a reporter for the *St. Louis Post-Dispatch*, that Christian Scientists consider rashes or other obvious physical symptoms of illness "an unreal picture" or "a dream."[99] By the time this particular "dream" was over, a total of 247 people had gotten the measles, including many non–Christian Science children who had not been vaccinated. The outbreak was the nation's largest since 1992 and cost St. Louis County over $100,000. All told, the Christian Science students in the St. Louis area have suffered four major outbreaks of measles between 1985 and 1994.[100]

The "time bomb," as Leo Damore described the Massachusetts religious exemption law lobbied for by the Church, exploded with the death of two-and-a-half-year-old Robyn Twitchell in a suburb of Boston, on April 8,

1986, of peritonitis caused by a bowel obstruction. His father, David Twitchell, was an administrator in a Christian Science retirement home; he and the boy's mother, Ginger Twitchell, were both graduates of Principia.

Robyn Twitchell was ill for five days. On the first day of his illness, his parents called Nancy Calkins, a practitioner. After the boy's symptoms grew progressively more serious over the next few days—he refused food, became weaker, and seemed to be in pain—the Twitchells called Nathan Talbot, the manager of the Committees on Publication, who told them that they could not be prosecuted for continuing with their course of spiritual treatment. David Twitchell later testified that, before he heard Talbot's reassurances and learned that he could arrange to have a Christian Science nurse pay a home visit, he had been considering taking Robyn to a doctor.

Linda Blaisdell, the Christian Science nurse, bathed Robyn and fed him two spoonfuls of applesauce during her visit. She also took some brief notes, describing him as "moaning in pain, vomiting, and listless . . . rejecting all food." She noted that he was not able to walk without assistance. She later testified, however, that, despite the alarming picture of Robyn's condition depicted in her own notes, he did not seem critically ill. On April 8, the last day of his life, Robyn vomited violently and repeatedly, dying on his father's lap as his mother and Nancy Calkins watched.

David Twitchell tried to perform CPR on his son; when this failed, he called Nathan Talbot, who told him to call a funeral home. The funeral home advised Twitchell to call the Boston police. Twitchell finally dialed 911 some two hours after his son had died.

After an autopsy and an inquest by the Suffolk County district attorney, Judge Lawrence Shubow of the West Roxbury District Court returned a thirty-five-page report in which he surmised that Nathan Talbot had "probably acted criminally" by discouraging David Twitchell from seeking medical care for Robyn; that Nancy Calkins had similarly discouraged emergency care and "recklessly and without legal excuse" contributed to Robyn's death; that the nurse had only made the child's illness worse by feeding him. His opinion held that the Twitchells should be prosecuted for manslaughter, and that the three Church officials should be indicted as their accomplices. Shubow also wrote that there was "an overwhelming case" for revising the 1971 religious exemption statute.[101]

The Twitchells were charged with manslaughter and, at their trial in 1990, were defended by a prominent Boston attorney, Rikki Klieman. According to prosecution witnesses, Robyn's twisted bowel had to have caused excruciating pain. Bowel obstruction and perforation had caused the child to vomit excrement and portions of the bowel before he died; his scrotum was black with necrotic tissue. Dr. Burton Harris, chief of surgery at Boston's Floating Hospital for Infants and Children testified, "It's beyond comprehension that the parents of a child who's vomiting stool wouldn't seek medical help."[102] There was also testimony indicating that Robyn Twitchell's condition could have been routinely diagnosed and surgically corrected had he been given medical care; and he could probably have been resuscitated had emergency medical aid been summoned after his final collapse. But the facts of the child's condition were sharply at odds with the testimony of his Christian Science caretakers. Nancy Calkins testified that Robyn had had a "super-good day" just before he died and had played with his "kitty."[103]

David Twitchell wept throughout his five days on the witness stand, and he went so far as to admit, "If medicine could have saved my son, I wish I had turned to it." But he also testified that he had had root canal surgery, with novocaine, in 1983, the year Robyn was born, and thus found it difficult to explain why he had felt justified in withholding medical care from his son. Members of the jury were just as emotional when they delivered their verdict finding the Twitchells guilty of manslaughter, and later told the press they would have acquitted the couple had they been allowed to hear the complete language of Massachusetts's religious exemption law, which the trial judge refused to read as part of their instructions. The Supreme Judicial Court of Massachusetts overturned the Twitchells' conviction in 1993, finding that they had not received a fair trial. The appeals court cited the fact that the trial judge had prevented the jury from viewing the Church-published guide on the rights and responsibilities of Scientists in Massachusetts, which had led the Twitchells to believe themselves safe from prosecution in refusing to seek medical care for Robyn. The decision was a victory for the Twitchells, but not, however, for the Church. The court also noted that the 1971 state law exempting Scientists from child neglect did not protect them from criminal prosecution and that parents had a legal duty to provide medical care for children in cases of serious illness. Later that same year, Massachusetts repealed its religious exemption law.[104]

Perhaps the most bizarre and horrifying of the documented "child cases" was that of Elizabeth Ashley King. The only child of John King, a real estate executive in Phoenix, Arizona, and his wife, Catherine, both

Christian Scientists, Ashley King was twelve years old when she contracted bone cancer. She was withdrawn from school in November 1987
because of "a problem with her leg."[105] Officials at Cocopah Middle
School, in Scottsdale, arranged for Ashley's teacher, Tammy Van Denberg,
to see her at home.

According to court records, in February 1988, Van Denberg went to the
Kings' home for a visit but was not allowed to see Ashley. She kept going,
hoping to see the child. Catherine King repeatedly reassured her until, in
April, she met Van Denberg at the door and said, "We finally have come
to the point where you place God before your own life."[106] School authorities called Child Protective Services.

She had alarmed the school officials with her absolutist rhetoric, but
Catherine King was simply echoing what she had been taught by her
church. She was, in fact, echoing the words of Mary Baker Eddy's faithful
servant and longtime chairman of the Board of Directors, Adam Dickey,
whose essay "God's Law of Adjustment," which first appeared in the
Christian Science Journal in 1916, is the only original theological writing,
aside from Eddy's own, that has been widely and continuously distributed
by the Church. "God's Law of Adjustment" may have provided the religious rationalization for the Kings' passivity in their behavior toward their
daughter:

> When we have reached the point where we are willing to do what seems to
> us the best and then leave the problem with God, knowing that He will
> adjust everything according to His unchanging law, we can then withdraw
> ourselves entirely from the proposition, drop all sense of responsibility, and
> feel secure in the knowledge that God corrects and governs all things right-
> eously. . . . If our good is evilly spoken of, this does not affect the situation
> in any degree, since God does not hold us accountable for the action of oth-
> ers. Our responsibility ceases when we have complied with the demands of
> good, and there we can afford to let any question rest. It makes no difference
> how much is at stake or what is involved.[107]

On May 5, Detective Edwin Boehm, of the Paradise Valley Police
Department, came to the house; he believes himself to have been the first
person other than her parents to see Ashley in months. Boehm later
recalled that it had taken some time before he "gained entry," because
Catherine King at first refused to answer the door. He said of Ashley, "I
knew first thing looking at her that she was dying."[108] He couldn't see her

leg, because "she had a pillow on it under the covers—she was hiding it." He would eventually tell a grand jury, "She was extremely white, ashen colored—to be specific, death color."[109] The next day Child Protective Services received a court order granting the agency temporary custody of Ashley for the purpose of medical examination.

Judging by photographs taken a year or so before her death, Ashley King was a beautiful girl, with long, straight, dark-brown hair and high cheekbones. When she was taken to Phoenix Children's Hospital, she had a tumor on her right leg that was forty-one inches in circumference.

Her hemoglobin count, according to Paul Baranko, the physician who examined her, was "almost incompatible with life."[110] Her heart was enlarged from the burden of pumping blood to the tumor, her pulse was twice normal, the cancer had spread to her lungs, and she was in immediate danger of dying from congestive heart failure. Immobilized by the tumor, she had been lying in the same position for months. Her buttocks and genitals were covered with bedsores.

Medical nurses who testified before the grand jury said that Ashley had told them, "I'm in so much pain" and "You don't know how I have suffered."[111] Baranko, who estimated that Ashley would have had a 55 to 60 percent chance of recovery if she had had timely medical treatment, recommended that her leg be amputated to reduce her pain in the time she had remaining; the Kings declined. He later said, "This has to be the most disturbing, depressing case I have ever seen in my twenty-five years as a physician. I have never seen a patient presented with this kind of situation . . . [which] could have been totally avoided."[112]

Ashley stayed in the hospital for only six days. Officials with Child Protective Services reached an agreement with her parents whereby Ashley would be transferred to Upward View, a nonlicensed Christian Science nursing home. At Upward View, under the care of Christian Science nurses who provided her with no medical care, Ashley lay in bed in conditions that must have been similar to those she had endured at home. When she cried out, a nurse reminded her to remember the other "visitors." She died on June 5, 1988.

Two months later, her parents were indicted on charges of child abuse and negligent homicide (the negligent homicide charges were dropped in a second grand jury hearing), and Nathan Talbot, the manager of the Committees on Publication, came to their defense. In front of the grand jury that indicted the Kings, one juror put a central question to Talbot:

It has been described, the little girl—her thigh had grown so large, it was larger than my waist, and the stench from the decaying flesh was so bad, it permeated the entire floor of the hospital.

It must have been obvious to the parents, their prayers had not been successful up to that point. Was it reasonable of them, as Christian Scientists, to continue the treatment only in the Christian Science faith as contrasted, perhaps, in seeking medical help?

I put great emphasis on that word "reasonable."[113]

Talbot's response was typical of the public response from the Church throughout this period; first, he defended the parents' actions by asserting, without offering any evidence, that Christian Scientists had been healed of other obviously terminal conditions: "Given the healings that have taken place, even [in] those difficult kinds of circumstances, I would have to honestly answer 'yes.' "[114]

Then Talbot turned his attention to the "agony" that children undergo at the hands of physicians in hospitals:

I don't know if any of you saw a couple of years ago a program on "60 Minutes" they did. The program was not trying to put anyone down. They were showing what doctors have to deal with sometimes. They showed some scenes in that program I don't know how any of us could get through without a tear or two—some of the agony and torture children have had to endure under some medical procedures—the best doctors could bring to it.

After seeing the program, I cannot imagine anything worse.[115]

Years later, the deputy county attorney who handled the prosecution of the Kings, K. C. Scull, is still infuriated by the behavior of the parents and their church. "It was a shocking case," he recalled. "The tumor—it was absolutely humongous, the size of a watermelon. You've just never seen anything like that on a human being. It was absolutely bizarre. I spent a fair amount of time with Nathan Talbot—I flew out to Boston and met with him for a full day, trying to figure out what to do with the case. And I came away from there stunned that Nathan Talbot believed that you can heal anything with this prayerlike procedure. He really takes it literally, and so did these people."[116]

Scull is particularly scathing about Talbot's motives for wanting to appear before the grand jury that indicted the Kings: "If there's a bad guy here, it's the Church. I really resented a guy like Nathan Talbot coming in. When I saw him, I thought, He doesn't care about these people; he cares about the Christian Science Church. It's obviously in serious decline, and he knows it. And he can't turn it around. He and the Church are doing dangerous things. I got a sense that the Kings were willing to make martyrs of themselves, and I think the Church pushed these people. Nathan Talbot was out here more than once."[117]

In 1989, a year after their indictment, John and Catherine King each pleaded no contest to one charge of reckless endangerment—a misdemeanor in this case. After their sentencing to three years' probation, the couple held a press conference at which Catherine King displayed a number of cardboard cutouts of her daughter, which she had made out of enlarged photographs. She told reporters that her daughter had been terrified not by her disease or her pain but by the doctors who examined her: "The only analogy I can use to describe the terror, resistance, and sense of injustice Ashley felt is to compare it to what it must have been like for Anne Frank to be taken to the prison camp in Nazi Germany." King also said, "I know I was a good mother, and no judge or jury in the country can convince me otherwise."[118]

4. Gaslight

Gaslight, the 1944 George Cukor film starring Charles Boyer and Ingrid Bergman, is the story of a vulnerable woman, Paula, whose devious husband tries to drive her into insanity. Unbeknownst to her, he has murdered her aunt and is frantically searching for a cache of jewels in the attic of their home. His searches make the gaslights throughout the house flicker, a phenomenon that his wife interprets as another symptom of her insanity. With his lies and schemes, he tricks Paula into believing that she is careless, delusional, irresponsible, hysterical. Confronted with one of her husband's accusations, she screams, "I couldn't have dreamed it, I couldn't have dreamed it, I couldn't have dreamed it, I couldn't have dreamed it!" In the climactic scene, with her husband tied in a chair in the attic, she takes a knife from a drawer. Pretending not to see the weapon, she advances on him, saying, "There is no knife, you must have dreamed you put it there. . . . Have you gone mad, or is it I who am mad?"

The heroine of *Gaslight* is torn between what she knows to be true and what she is told. Children of Christian Science are likewise faced with two irreconcilable and contradictory facts: their own bodies versus Eddy's statement that "Man . . . is not made up of brain, blood, bones, and other material elements."[119] The dilemma posed is not a minor one. Christian Science children faced with catastrophic illness or injury may have only Eddy's words to keep them alive, words that their own bodies tell them are lies. At the age of eleven, Ian Lundman came face to face with those two irreconcilable facts. He died not knowing who was mad.

On May 6, 1989, Ian complained to his mother, Kathleen McKown, that he had a stomachache. His mother, a Christian Scientist, lived with Ian in Independence, Minnesota, just outside Minneapolis, along with his older sister, Whitney, then thirteen years old, and Kathleen's second husband, William McKown. Ian and Whitney's biological father, Douglass Lundman, had been divorced from their mother since 1984 and was living five hundred miles away, in Manhattan, Kansas, where he was teaching architecture at Kansas State University. Douglass Lundman had been raised as a Christian Scientist, and he and his former wife had met as students at Principia. But over the years, Lundman had grown to question Christian Science. He left the Church in 1982. His abandonment of the faith led, in part, to the divorce.[120] The Lundmans had agreed that Kathleen would have custody, but Douglass Lundman saw his children often. He had once taken Ian to the doctor for an ear infection.

Ian had been losing weight and had been ill, on and off, for some time prior to his stomachache.[121] When his father last saw him, several weeks before Ian's final illness, he had noticed that his son seemed thin. But they played softball, and Douglass said later that the boy "was strong, hit well, and he seemed normal and happy."[122] Then on May 6, Ian complained throughout the day of his stomach hurting, and his mother could smell a fruity odor on his breath. She began to treat Ian through prayer.

The next day, Sunday, he complained again; Kathleen McKown called a practitioner in St. Paul, Mario Tosto, and asked him to pray for Ian. Despite his illness, Ian was taken to Sunday school, in keeping with the Christian Science belief that to acknowledge sickness (by, for instance, resting) is to give it power. His Sunday school teacher noticed that he seemed tired. By this time, Ian was being given mints to mask the odor of his breath. After Sunday school, Ian was taken to the home of his grandmother—Douglass Lundman's mother—who was also a *Journal-*

listed Christian Science practioner and teacher. While at his grandmother's house, Ian vomited and was too weak to do anything but lie on a
couch.

Throughout the night of May 7, Ian could not sleep and repeatedly complained of pain and discomfort, expressing fear and begging his mother not
to leave him alone. The following morning, he vomited again and was
unable to keep any food down. His mother would later acknowledge that
Ian's condition—his evident weight loss and his inability to eat—made her
afraid that he was going to die. At this point, she began to consider taking
him to a hospital.

But first, she called the Minnesota Committee on Publication, James
Van Horn; in turn, he called Nathan Talbot to tell him about the situa-
tion. Van Horn made sure, he said later, that McKown had contacted a
Journal-listed practitioner. Then she called Clifton House, a Christian
Science nursing home, and a Christian Science nurse there advised her to
give Ian fluids. William McKown, who is also a Christian Scientist, called
Van Horn again to get phone numbers of health authorities to call in case
Ian had a contagious disease (although how this was to have been determined is unclear). William McKown then called Clifton House again, to
report that Ian was unable to take any fluids.

By the afternoon of May 8, Ian could not eat, drink, or control his bladder. His mother asked him, "Are you part of the team?"—meaning the
Christian Science team—and later testified that he replied, "I am." But
that night he was beyond being part of anybody's team. He was carried
down to the dinner table in an apparently insensible condition. At one
point, he looked at his mother, did not recognize her, and said, "My name
is Ian, too." At eight o'clock that night, she called Clifton House again and
tried to have Ian admitted.

Christian Science nursing homes do not accept minor children as
patients, and Kathleen McKown had apparently determined, on learning
this, to take her son to North Memorial Hospital, in Minneapolis. But the
nurse on duty at Clifton House helpfully suggested that a Christian
Science nurse might be found who could come to the McKown home. The
on-duty nurse called Quinna Lamb, a *Journal*-listed Christian Science
nurse, who arrived at the McKowns' home at nine o'clock in the evening.
William McKown went to bed at eleven o'clock.

The notes that Lamb took that night while sitting beside Ian's bed,
watching him, were later entered into evidence in the lawsuit that followed. They encompass the rest of Ian Douglass Lundman's brief life:

9:00 p.m.	Arrived. Boy had urinated—prepared bed—dad carried—light e.c. [evening care] p.c. [patient care] given—P[atient] had juice earlier—eyes rolled back—P[atient] awakened when moved—seemed aware of people—breathing labored.
10:10	siphoned water.
10:50	turned P[atient] onto R[ight side]—siphoned water.
11:15	Pract[itioner Tosto] called—report given—onto back.
11:30	P[atient] vomiting brownish fluid—called Pract[itioner]—vomiting ceased.
12:30	labored breathing.
12:50	moistened lips [with] Vaseline—
1:00	P[atient] swallowing—facial spasms—called Pract[itioner]—report given.
1:05	immediate [change]—symptoms gone—labored breathing.
2:05	taking big breaths every other breath, gritting teeth.
2:10	called Pract[itioner]—report shallow, irregular breathing—eyes fixed.
2:20	called Pract[itioner]—P[atient] color white—passing possible.
2:36	P[atient] stopped breathing.
2:50	N[urse] called Pract[itioner].
3:02	husband called 911/M.E. [medical examiner] and C.O.P. [Van Horn][123]

Quinna Lamb's nursing care had consisted of dribbling water between her unconscious patient's lips, rubbing his lips with Vaseline, and, according to an addendum to her notes, wrapping a plastic bag and washcloth around his scrotum to catch his urine. She also read to him from the Christian Science Hymnal and from *Science and Health*.

Ian Lundman, as any medical physician in the country could have deduced from his visible symptoms—weight loss and the fruity odor on his breath—had juvenile-onset diabetes. Doctors later testified that, had he received an injection of insulin up to two hours before his death, he could have lived. The police officer who arrived at the McKown home shortly after his death later said that the boy looked "very fragile, like he had lost weight recently, very skinny, and just basically to tell you the truth, didn't even look human."[124] The practitioner, Mario Tosto, who never saw Ian, was eventually paid $446 for his services.

Shortly after two-thirty on the morning of May 9, 1989, Kathleen McKown called Douglass Lundman to tell him that his son was dead. The only information Lundman had been given about Ian's illness had come in two phone calls earlier that night. The first was from his own mother, Ian's grandmother, who had called to tell him that Ian was ill. Lundman had then called his former wife and asked about Ian's condition. McKown told him that Ian was ill but that it wasn't anything serious. He asked to speak to Ian, and she told him that he was sleeping. Ian was, in fact, in a diabetic coma, and Kathleen McKown had already, hours earlier, become alarmed for his life and had seen that Ian had lost bladder control and the ability to communicate. Douglass Lundman also asked his former wife if he should drive up to Minnesota. She told him that wouldn't be necessary.

Kathleen and William McKown were charged with second-degree criminal manslaughter in October 1989, but were ultimately protected by Minnesota's religious exemption law. The district court of Hennepin County, where the death took place, dismissed the indictments in 1990, and the dismissals were upheld by the Minnesota State Court of Appeals and by the state's Supreme Court. In 1991, Douglass Lundman was appointed trustee of Ian's estate and filed a wrongful death suit on behalf of himself and his daughter, Whitney, against Kathleen and William McKown, Quinna Lamb Giebelhaus (who had married), Mario Tosto, James Van Horn, Clifton House, and the First Church of Christ, Scientist, Boston, Massachusetts. It would be the most far-reaching and ultimately damaging lawsuit ever filed against Christian Scientists and their church.

The civil trial in Hennepin County District Court stretched out over seven weeks of July and August 1993. Kathleen McKown testified that Ian had previously been healed through Christian Science of warts and impetigo (a contagious skin infection) and that Whitney Lundman had been healed of a serious breathing problem when she was two. Quinna Lamb was questioned about her training as a Christian Science nurse. Asked how she had been trained to care for seriously ill children, she replied that she had been taught how to cut sandwiches into "interesting shapes." She also testified that Christian Science was a good and effective treatment for all diseases, including diabetes. Defense attorneys for the Christian Scientists argued that Douglass Lundman was himself negligent in not seeking medical care for Ian. James Kaster, one of Lundman's attorneys, told the jury that Ian's death was a team effort, led by the Church, which was acting through its representative, James Van Horn, the Minnesota C.O.P. He, the nursing home, the nurse, and the Church-listed practitioner had all colluded in convincing Ian's mother not to take her son to the hospital.[125]

On August 18, 1993, the jury of six women found all seven of those named in the suit negligent. They divided the liability for Ian's death among them: Kathleen McKown, 25 percent; William McKown, 10 percent; Mario Tosto, 10 percent; Quinna Lamb Giebelhaus, 5 percent; Clifton House, 20 percent; James Van Horn, 20 percent; and the First Church of Christ, Scientist, 10 percent. They awarded Douglass Lundman a total of $5.2 million in compensatory damages against all the defendants. Then, in a separate phase of the deliberations a week later, the jury awarded Lundman an additional $9 million in punitive damages against the Church alone. The jury had believed James Kaster when he said that Ian's death was a team effort orchestrated by the Church. It was the first time in the history of the Church that it had been held liable in the wrongful death of anyone. The Church vowed to appeal.

After the trial, Douglass Lundman said that the money meant little to him but for the fact that it "was the only thing the jury had for a tool" to force the Church to reevaluate its treatment of children.[126] Of the compensatory damages, Lundman said later, "No amount of money compensates me for the loss of Ian. No amount of money can compensate Ian for his loss. It means nothing." In 1994, the trial judge reduced the compensatory damages to $1.5 million, saying that the original $5.2 million was excessive compared to other damage awards in wrongful death cases, but let stand the $9 million assessed against the Church. The following year, in a two-to-one decision, the Minnesota State Court of Appeals overturned the award against the Church, asserting that such a judgment "imposing punitive damages on a church to force it to abandon teaching its central tenet" was unconstitutional. It was an intrusion "upon the forbidden field of religious freedom."[127] Lundman was deeply disappointed when the punitive damages were rescinded. "It meant," he said, "as either legal or political theory, that the death of a child is not a price too great to pay for anything labeled religious, especially if it also calls itself Christian." On the grounds that no "special relationship" incurring a duty to care for Ian existed for James Van Horn, the C.O.P., or for Clifton House, the decision also released them from responsibility.

But the appeals court upheld the $1.5 million judgment against the McKowns, Mario Tosto, and Quinna Lamb Giebelhaus, deciding that all four had had a "special relationship" to Ian:

> In the common law tradition, our holding today serves as notice to all professional Christian Science caregivers—be they practitioners, nurses, or others—that they cannot successfully disavow their professional duty to a child by deferring to the parent as the ultimate decision-making authority.[128]

These words seem like a powerful warning to Christian Science practitioners, at least in the state of Minnesota. But in some ways, they make little sense. Since practitioners and nurses not only cannot diagnose illness but are forbidden to by the Church and by law, what exactly is their "professional duty"? A practitioner, who is not responsible to any federal or state agency but only to the Church, would have to defy the rules and teachings established by the Church in order to summon medical aid. And yet the appeals court ruled that the Church—and the Committees on Publication—was free to promulgate its teachings rejecting medical care and encouraging radical reliance on Science without incurring punitive damages. According to the ruling, the Church can teach parents (and practitioners and nurses) to eschew medical care no matter what happens, but the Church's practitioners and nurses cannot act on those teachings. Although it held the four people most closely involved in Ian Lundman's "treatment" responsible, the decision was clearly based on ignorance of the Church's chain of command, its teachings, and its history of asserting to state and federal lawmakers that it constitutes a scientifically proven and effective alternative health care system.

In 1996, the U.S. Supreme Court, to which the Church had appealed on behalf of the McKowns, Tosto, and Giebelhaus (Douglass Lundman also filed a cross-petition asking the Court to review the exclusion of the Church from damages), refused to review the $1.5 million damage award or Lundman's petition. This refusal—which effectively rendered the appeals court's judgment final—stimulated a variety of high-profile responses from professional pundits in newspapers around the country. Cindy Adams, the New York socialite and gossip columnist for the tabloid *New York Post*, devoted her entire column to a lugubrious interview with Quinna Lamb Giebelhaus. In the interview, Giebelhaus accepted no responsibility and expressed no remorse for her role in Ian Lundman's death:

> "The jury had eight weeks to understand all this and couldn't. I felt like Joseph in the first chapter of the Bible. He was thrown in the pit and covered with dirt. But I knew it wasn't me personally. I'm only a cog. My church was on trial. Parents want the best care obtainable. Based on healings we experienced, knowing that millions choose this method because it works, the treatment selected was a reasonable choice."[129]

Adams, who described Ian's failed Christian Science treatment as "spiritual, prayerful care" and portrayed those responsible for his death as victims of the justice system, felt no responsibility to reveal her conflict of interest; she and her husband, the comic Joey Adams, have long espoused Christian Science. Nor did she challenge Giebelhaus's assertion that "millions choose this method," an astonishing inflation of the actual number of practicing Christian Scientists.

Stephen L. Carter's op-ed piece in the *New York Times*, "The Power of Prayer, Denied," also supported the Church's position. Carter's argument could have come straight out of the mouths of Christian Scientists: "Like parents everywhere," Carter asserted, the McKowns "made the best choices they could, relying on their religious faith to help guide them."[130] He compared Ian's mother's right to religious freedom to that granted by the famous Supreme Court case *Wisconsin v. Yoder*, which sanctioned the right of the Amish to educate their children in their own schools, and to that of the Seattle woman who sent her son to live with Tibetan Buddhist monks who believed he was a reincarnated lama. Treating children as the property of their parents, Carter failed to note the violation of Ian Lundman's right—that most inalienable of human rights, the right to live. Nowhere, for example, did he acknowledge that Ian's life could have been saved with insulin. The Christian Science Church was so pleased by Carter's editorial that they promptly invited him to give an interview touting his new book, *Integrity*, in the *Christian Science Sentinel*.[131] Subsequently, a full-page interview with him appeared in the *Monitor*.[132]

For Douglass Lundman, the case will never be over. In 1993, Lundman told the *Minneapolis Star-Tribune*, "Forgive myself? I don't think that's possible. . . . The fact is this: I was his father. Children have no one looking out for them but their parents. I was 500 miles away. If I'd been there, he would be here now. I have to live with that."[133] Douglass Lundman has to live with the fact that his son was killed not by an act of fate, an accident, or an incurable illness. His son was killed by Christian Science, whose dangers he knew all too well. In his forties, with gray-blond hair and wire-framed glasses, Lundman speaks thoughtfully and deliberately, with a slight speech impediment arising from hearing loss he suffered as a child, possibly because of untreated ear infections. He moved to Japan after the trial, in part to achieve some distance "psychologically and physically" from Ian's death and the ordeal that followed, in part to escape the incessant criticism and advice of strangers.[134]

The motive for his suit had been simple from the start. A few months after Ian's death, he told a television reporter, "I'm principally concerned about the strong possibility that other children will die in similar circumstances and I personally wish to do whatever I can to prevent that from happening."[135] But Lundman was never optimistic about the possibility of effecting a profound change in how Christian Science children are treated, and he seems uncertain about how much he has accomplished. Just after the astonishing initial judgments against the Church and the Scientists were announced, he had said, "Maybe because of this case some other child may not have to have the experience that Ian had. Maybe."[136] Now he speaks of the frustratingly slow progress of the justice system—"There's been almost nine years of litigation. . . . I don't know that I would litigate anything again"—and of the bewildering and ineffective bureaucracy of Child Protective Services, which denied him custody of his daughter after Ian's death.

Tragically, Douglass Lundman's fears about what might happen to other Christian Science children have been borne out. In 1992, James Andrew Wantland, a twelve-year-old boy who lived with his Christian Science father and sister in La Habra, a suburb in Orange County, California, began to lose weight. His friends noticed that he was drinking a lot of water and that he had developed a chronic cough. Andrew's parents had divorced in 1984. His father was a Scientist and his mother was not. On Sunday, December 20, 1992, Andrew Wantland's father called an ambulance, and his son was pronounced dead shortly after his arrival at St. Jude Medical Center in La Habra.[137]

Andrew weighed only 105 pounds at his death and was severely emaciated. The Orange County coroner's report listed three causes of death and their duration:

    A. Multiple system failure / days

    B. Diabetic ketoacidosis / months

    C. Diabetes mellitus / months[138]

Andrew Wantland, like Ian Lundman, died of juvenile-onset diabetes. On December 20, 1992, his mother, Gayle Quigley, who had remarried and was working as a schoolteacher in Philadelphia, Pennsylvania, arrived home after shopping at the mall to find a message on her answering machine from her daughter. When she returned the call, she learned that her son, of whose illness she had never been informed, was dead.

Nine days later, on December 29, 1992, Aaron Witte, who lived in St. Charles, Missouri, and attended the Principia prep school, died the day before his thirteenth birthday. The cause of death was diabetic ketoacidosis. His parents, Linda and Michael Witte, were both Christian Scientists. His death was ruled a homicide by the St. Charles County medical examiner, but prosecutors declined to file criminal charges.[139]

5. Fruitage

"Fruitage," the chapter that closes *Science and Health*, is an anthology of testimonies of healing. The term was inspired by Jesus' words: "Wherefore by their fruits ye shall know them."[140] To true believers, testimonials are the fruits—the demonstration—of the truth of Christian Science, and Scientists still use the word as a celebratory term to denote a collection of healings; at their annual meeting in 1993, the Church held a "Fruitage" gathering at which Scientists from all over the world gave testimonies.

What follows is fruitage of a different kind. In the Christian Science Church, there is no institutional acknowledgment of Christian Science failures, but failures, nonetheless, happen. When the subject has arisen in the press, Church spokesmen have always responded with the mournful plaint that the press pays attention only to Scientists' failures, not to their successes. But the Church's own bias in this regard has made it necessary for others to document the fruitage of failure.

One might expect those who have suffered permanent physical injuries or the losses of loved ones to bear resentment toward the Church that caused those losses, and, having interviewed many such people, I have often heard anger, frustration, and disappointment expressed about the faith. But another strain of feeling seems more prevalent and profound among former Scientists: despair over Scientists' inability to acknowledge and feel remorse for their failures, and over the public ignorance of what Christian Science is and what it does. This ignorance is expressed everywhere in society: by the court system, by child welfare bureaucracies, by adoption agencies, by the police, by the media, by the medical profession, and overwhelmingly by elected officials in state and federal legislatures.

A number of former Scientists who oppose the practices of the Church have joined the group founded by Rita and Douglas Swan, Children's Healthcare Is a Legal Duty. In years past, CHILD has sponsored a small, informal annual meeting that offers to its members some of the benefits of a support group and an educational conference. It provides a place for former Scientists to meet their peers and to exchange information and swap their often troubling tales. It can be an astonishing experience to attend these meetings. Rita Swan opened the 1998 meeting by singing, with another CHILD member, a song she had learned long ago at one of her Christian Science class-association meetings. Sung to the tune of "My Bonnie Lies Over the Ocean," the lyrics are, "My *body* lies over the ocean, My *body* lies over the sea, My *body* lies over the ocean, Don't bring back my *body* to me." The meetings combine a kind of giddy bonhomie—few people who have not experienced it can understand or even believe what goes on in Christian Science households—with accounts of deeply disturbing, even brutal neglect. Such accounts go a long way toward explaining the virulent emotions Christian Science can inspire.

Paul Michener, of Waynesville, Ohio, first saw Rita Swan when she appeared on *Donahue* in 1979, and immediately wrote to her:

> At age nine, my left leg was burned in a gasoline fire (1st to 3rd degree). Although the area burned was not too large, from the ankle to just above the knee, it became a lengthy trauma which at times I thought would be fatal. As I recall, I was fifteen years old before the injury had grown closed with scar tissue. In the meantime, the knee became stiff and the pain was beyond description. I was bedridden for about two years and walked on crutches for another two and a half years.
>
> Today I walk with a four inch limp, a curved spine and some recurring back and hip pain. Walking any distance would be impossible without a built-up shoe. I have undergone three surgical operations in the last four years trying to patch up the damage done by this insidious philosophy. I find it neither Christian nor a science.[141]

Michener subsequently became a member of CHILD.

Beth Young, a CHILD member who teaches writing and rhetoric as an assistant professor of English at the University of Central Florida in Orlando, was born in 1965 in California. She was adopted by a Christian Science couple from Chicago in a private adoption initiated by Harvey Wood, a popular Christian Science lecturer who later became the chairman of the Church's Board of Directors. She was born with hip dysplasia, or dislocated hips. Doctors routinely check for this congenital condition, and it is generally treatable and curable in infancy by dressing the infant in a special kind of diaper, called a Pavlik harness, that holds the legs in the correct position. But Beth had no neonatal exams and received no treatment. She didn't begin walking until she was over two years old, and one of her earliest memories is of a trip to the store after church one Sunday. Her parents, walking her through the door, jerked her upright by her arms and scolded her to "walk straight."[142] They adopted another girl when Beth was four.

Beth would never learn to "walk straight." As a child, she says, she "waddled like a duck," swaying back and forth. She was teased relentlessly in school, and whenever she cried in frustration at not being able to run or walk normally, her parents would ask her, "What's wrong?" They routinely denied the reality of her physical problems or those of her adopted sister. She remembers showing her mother the spots from a rash she had, only to be told, "I don't see them." She also remembers one occasion when she was violently sick to her stomach; her parents told her, "You don't have to throw up." She did not learn the name of her hip disorder—or the fact that it would have been easily treatable when she was a child—until she was in her twenties. Now her condition is no longer surgically correctable; it severely limits her activities and causes exhaustion and continuous pain. She worries that "every step I take might be one less step I have left." Members of her family who are still Christian Scientists tell her that they "forgive" her for going to the doctor, that she can't "blame" the religion for her disability, and that she could still be healed through Science, if she would only give it a chance.

Another CHILD member is Carolyn Joyce Hyatt, known as C.J. She was born in Los Angeles in 1952 and was also adopted as an infant. Her adoptive mother, forty-eight years old when C.J. was born, had been a Christian Scientist for many years, and her father eventually joined the Church as well. C. J. Hyatt became deaf in 1959, at the age of seven, after contracting several childhood diseases—measles, mumps, and chickenpox—in rapid succession; they were followed by a series of painful ear infections, all of which went untreated. She recalled the experience in a letter to me:

> It hurt so bad. I remember [my mother] holding my head on her lap while I cried. She told me that earaches were "not real, because God didn't make them," and I needed to "change" my thinking. Later, when I couldn't hear (except loud, low-pitched noises), she said, "If you would be more loving, you could hear." That made me feel like I was the worst, most evil person in

the world, because no matter how hard I tried to "be loving," good, and nice, I couldn't hear.[143]

Although she always found it difficult to understand her father, C.J. quickly learned to read her mother's lips. She had more trouble lip-reading in the public school she attended, because the teachers moved out of her line of sight so often. Astonishingly, however, her deafness seems to have gone largely unnoticed by school officials, because she spoke understandably, could lip-read, and, out of shame, did everything she could to hide her condition:

> I remember one day in 2nd grade, the teacher walked around the room with a stopwatch on the end of a yardstick. She was demonstrating how sound travels. I was so nervous, my hands sweated profusely and I wiped them on my dress. All the kids were smiling and nodding when the end of the yardstick touched their ears. I smiled and nodded, too. I didn't want anyone to know I couldn't hear, because then they'd know how bad I was, how evil. The only mention of my deafness was on a report card in 3rd grade, where the teacher wrote, "Carolyn does quite well in spite of her apparent handicap."[144]

She says she taught herself by "reading everything," and did well in all subjects except math. When her junior high school wanted her to transfer to a special program, she did obtain a hearing aid, but it was so uncomfortable she threw it out. The school did not pursue the matter.

In 1961, C.J.'s parents successfully adopted twin girls who had been under their foster care for several years, after winning an acrimonious and widely publicized court battle for custody, the state having argued that the couple was too old to adopt more children. The state did not, apparently, investigate the couple's Christian Science background or learn that C.J. had been medically neglected and had gone deaf while under their care.

Throughout her childhood, C.J.'s mother denied the reality of her daughter's deafness, insisting that she could hear if she really "wanted to." In this, she was obeying Eddy, who wrote in Science and Health, "Sound is a mental impression made on mortal belief. The ear does not really hear."[145] Of Christian Science, C.J. writes, "I could never really understand it. . . . I read Science and Health. I did the lessons every day. I prayed. The silence remained, like an oppressive cloud overshadowing my life." At the age of twelve, she began to refuse to attend Sunday school and was beaten for it by her father.

Although she did well in school, graduating from La Habra High School in 1970 and from California State University at Fullerton in 1978, she suffered through periods of severe suicidal depression, particularly when she found it difficult to find a job after college because her speech was noticeably affected by her deafness. As a young adult, she herself denied her deafness until confronted by friends and therapists. At the age of twenty-eight, she went to Gallaudet University, the college for the deaf in Washington, D.C., earning a master's degree in counseling. There, for the first time, she was able to learn sign language and to be in the company of other deaf people. Since 1981, she has been a career counselor at the California School for the Deaf in Fremont, California. Her mother continued to insist, until she died in 1991, that she had "a perfect family."

The refusal to acknowledge actual human need and suffering that is encouraged by Christian Science is perfectly captured by the account of Mark Woodall, now a patent lawyer in Washington, D.C., originally from Pittsburgh, Pennsylvania. Woodall comes from a family whose involvement in Christian Science stretches back four generations. At the age of four, he convinced his father to let him ride his Flexible Flyer on his own and promptly steered himself into a football goalpost, incurring a severe head injury. Unconscious, he was taken home and given Christian Science treatment. He did not wake up until two days later, when he found that his parents had taped cardboard over all the mirrors in the house so that his mind would not be affected by the evidence of the senses and interfere with his healing. They had drawn "smiley faces" on the cardboard with Magic Markers. Mark eventually found an uncovered mirror in his parents' room and discovered that both of his eyes were black and that his entire face was swollen dark purple. He believes that a still-visible deformity in his collarbone resulted from that injury.[146]

Like virtually all the former Scientists I have interviewed, Mark Woodall has had friends his own age who died, suddenly and needlessly, without medical treatment, an unusual phenomenon for young adults in this age of long life spans. His brother was attending Principia during the 1985 measles epidemic that killed three students. At Principia Upper School, Mark himself knew Jennifer Stitt, a fellow student who died in 1984 at the age of seventeen, during her senior year, of toxic shock due to septicemia, or blood poisoning. In a personal essay about his Christian Science experience that he read at a CHILD meeting, Mark wrote, "Jen's picture appears five times in our Senior Yearbook. Her name is mentioned eight times, but nowhere is she memorialized. Nowhere is her tragic death mentioned. Nowhere is her passing mourned."[147]

The denial of illness and the institutionalized fear-mongering that are a part of the religion have proved overwhelmingly traumatizing, as well as physically hazardous, to children. Bonnie Deckerhoff, of Jacksonville, Florida, has spoken vividly at CHILD meetings of her younger sister Jennifer's death, in 1967, at the age of seven, of what was probably untreated cystic fibrosis; Jennifer's condition was never diagnosed by a doctor. Deckerhoff recalls surreal scenes at the family dinner table toward the end of her sister's life, when Jennifer, barely conscious, her body grotesquely swollen, would be propped up in a chair at the table, as if nothing were wrong. Sleeping in the same room with her sister, Deckerhoff could hear her saying, the night before she died, "Call God, Call God." As a child, Deckerhoff herself had severe asthma attacks, during which her parents would prop her up in a recliner with a copy of *Science and Health* and she would try to pray about her "congested thoughts." "I can only imagine what Jennifer went through," she says now. "The fear, the guilt, the sense of responsibility." During her asthma attacks, she found herself obsessed with the notion that she might have the same illness that killed her sister, and that the illness was her fault. "What were the things I was thinking that kept me from breathing?" she wondered.[148]

Pam Mundell, of Piney Point, Maryland, attended several Christian Science private schools and camps while growing up. She remembers believing, along with her classmates, in the Christian Science concept of "malpractice," another of Eddy's words for malicious animal magnetism. The children, who called malpractice "malping" for short, were constantly afraid that this form of hex would be practiced on them; Mundell remembers the hair on the back of her neck standing up when she was afraid someone was "malping" on her. She also remembers one classmate who died in her dormitory room after a long illness and others who became seriously ill and simply disappeared from school, never to return.

The mental as well as physical pain that Christian Science can cause children is vividly described in several memoirs. *The Unseen Shore: Memories of a Christian Science Childhood* (1991), by Thomas Simmons, a poet and essayist, traces Simmons's Christian Science childhood through painful earaches, nagging doubts, a broken wrist, and periods of severe depression; it chronicles his mother's unrelieved pain and lingering death, of cancer, in a Christian Science nursing home. Simmons faces the cold realities of the religion, asserting that he does not recall "ever having been healed of a physical illness through Christian Science," and analyzes the tortured relationships that the religion forces on its devotees:

> Because my mother was an immensely kind woman, it seems grotesque to suggest that she was also cruel. . . . The cruelty my mother inflicted on me, and on my brother and sister, was scarcely intentional, and the power of her love should have reassured us that we were precious in her sight. From a very early age, however, we all knew that we were suffering unnecessarily, cruelly. "The opposite of cruelty is not kindness," says the philosopher Philip Hallie. "The opposite of cruelty is freedom. The victim does not need the ultimately destructive gift of kindness when offered within the cruel relationship. He needs freedom from that relationship."[149]

He finally concludes that "the perfection of the religion had produced, not more perfection, but misery."[150]

Blue Windows: A Christian Science Childhood (1997), by Barbara Wilson, author of several mystery novels and cofounder of two feminist publishing companies, offers a horrific account of her childhood in the Church. In 1960, when Wilson was ten years old, her mother, devoted to Christian Science and hoping to become a practitioner like her own mother, experienced a catastrophic psychotic break after finding and keeping secret for months a lump in her breast that continued to grow despite her desperate prayers. Hearing voices, tortured by delusions that her Christian Science teacher had been killed by malicious animal magnetism, Wilson's mother drank Drāno, disfiguring her face and burning her throat. After several more suicide attempts, she died of breast cancer in an institution in 1963; her children's loss was compounded by the family's inability to explain or acknowledge what had happened.

Spalding Gray, the actor, writer, and monologuist, has been compiling a kind of Christian Science fruitage of his own since the 1970s. Born in 1941 in Providence, Rhode Island, and raised in nearby Barrington, the middle of three sons of a "mixed" marriage between a nonbelieving father and a Christian Science mother who went mad and killed herself, Gray has been revisiting her death and other fragments of his Christian Science experience ever since, transforming them into an astonishing variation on the Christian Science testimony. His monologues—*Swimming to Cambodia, Sex and Death to the Age 14, Monster in a Box, Gray's Anatomy*—and his one novel, *Impossible Vacation*, are built around talismanic memories of

Christian Science. *Sex and Death to the Age 14* begins with a pivotal recollection of confronting his mother with an injury:

> So one day I was in the bathtub taking a very hot bath. It was a cold day and the radiator was going full blast. I got out of the tub. . . . I hit my head on the sink. . . . When I landed my arm fell against the radiator. I must have been out quite a long time because when I came to, I lifted my arm up and it was like this dripping-rare-red roast beef, third-degree burn. Actually it didn't hurt at all because I was in shock, a steam burn on my finger would have hurt more. I ran downstairs and showed it to my mother and she said, "Put some soap in it, dear, and wrap it in gauze." She was a Christian Scientist, so she had a distance on those things.
>
> The next day when I got to school, the burn began to drip through the gauze. I went down to the infirmary, and when the nurse saw it she screamed, "What, you haven't been to a doctor with this? That's a third-degree burn. You've got to get to a doctor right away." So I went back home and told my mother what the nurse had said, and my mother said, "Well, it's your choice, dear. It's your choice."[151]

His tone is at once flat and knowing, expressive of the blank confusion of a child faced with a burned arm and his mother's dismissive response.

Like V. S. Pritchett, Gray captures the hypochondria and narcissism that are characteristic of the Christian Science way of life: when you have no way of knowing what's wrong with you, particularly when you're a child, you fear the worst, becoming more obsessed with your body the more you try to repress any thoughts about it. Exaggerated fears can arise from the simplest symptoms, or even from no symptoms at all. Later in the monologue, Gray juxtaposes his recollection of being intensely afraid of catching polio while swimming, with a memory of a "little piece of flesh growing off my nose . . . like a little stalactite."[152] This embarrassing growth "looked like a piece of snot," and Spalding begs his mother to let him go to a doctor to have it removed; she asks him to continue praying. When it eventually falls off, the event is interpreted as a Christian Science healing.

This pair of reminiscences captures the anxieties and fantasies, the exaggerated fears and the magical thinking that are inevitably a part of the practice of Christian Science. Gray's work relentlessly emphasizes the physicality of life, a physicality that is denied to the Christian Scientist. The vivid elements of his titles encompass an uneasy *nostalgie de la boue*— sex, death, anatomy—and his language betrays a constant preoccupation with bodily functions and the curt Anglo-Saxon terms for them, once unmentionable in society and always unmentionable in the religion in which he was raised: farting, shitting, pissing, fucking.

Spalding Gray's older brother, too, was plagued by recurrent hypochondriacal fears. Rockwell Gray, a writer and teacher at Washington University in St. Louis, recalls that, at the age of eight or nine, he was sorting his elaborate collection of train timetables only to be struck by an intense fear that he was about to have a heart attack. The fear itself, he says, begat more fear. As a Scientist, he knew that if he feared a heart attack, he would get a heart attack. "There is a corollary in Christian Science," he says now. "If you can think something away, you can also bring it about. I remember distinctly sharing a bedroom with Spalding and praying in a compulsive, repetitive fashion."[153]

Children, of course, are not the only Christian Scientists who experience catastrophic failures to heal. On August 12, 1997, after an illness of nine days, Suzanne Quaife, twenty-nine years old, of Albuquerque, New Mexico, died of untreated Guillain-Barré syndrome, an inflamation of the nerves believed to be caused by an allergic reaction to an infection. The disease causes a creeping paralysis, moving from the extremities up to the chest, that, without treatment, can immobilize the muscles required for breathing. With hospitalization and intensive care, it has a high rate of recovery.

Quaife's husband, Evan Quaife, believes he might have succeeded in convincing her to go to the hospital but for the influence of her Christian Science practitioner, Carmen Templeton, and her parents, Richard and Patricia Brooks. The Brookses flew to Albuquerque and convinced their daughter that her husband's doubts about Christian Science were preventing her healing. Templeton, meanwhile, instructed Evan Quaife, while his wife was partially paralyzed, to get big sheets of paper and Magic Markers with which to write the seven characteristics of man that were discussed in that week's Christian Science lesson sermon.

Eventually Suzanne Quaife's parents removed their daughter to her brother's home, several blocks away. Quaife called police and paramedics the morning of his wife's death, and one patrolman interviewed the dying woman. In a whisper, she refused treatment. The paramedics were not admitted to the house where she died until forty-five minutes after her death, long after the possibility of reviving her had passed. One of his wife's Christian Science friends said to Quaife, "Perhaps Susie preferred to die. I'd rather die and work it out in the next life."[154]

It is well established in American law that adults of sound mind have a constitutional right to refuse medical treatment of any kind. But, particularly during a time when there is ongoing debate about the legality of assisted suicide and the right to die, deaths like Suzanne Quaife's raise compelling questions about Christian Science practices. From my interviews with former Christian Science practitioners and nurses, it became clear that, their denials to the contrary, Church functionaries often play a coercive and contributory role in the unnecessary pain and suffering, as well as in the fatalities, commonplace within the movement.

Suzanne Shepard is a graduate of Principia College and worked as a *Journal*-listed practitioner in St. Louis for thirteen years. Like many Christian Scientists who have trouble conceiving a child and refuse to seek medical treatment for infertility, Shepard and her husband adopted—in their case, four children. In 1987, she watched her six-year-old daughter, Marilyn, lapse into a coma on her sofa, and asked herself if she wanted "to be a good Christian Scientist and not have a daughter, or be a bad Christian Scientist and have a daughter."[155] Against the wishes of her practitioner, J. Thomas Black, and followed by two Christian Science friends who hoped to talk her out of her decision, Shepard drove her daughter to St. Louis Children's Hospital and saved her life; Marilyn had appendicitis and peritonitis. From the hospital, Shepard called Black and asked him to continue praying. She says he refused, telling her to "take Marilyn home, because it was better that she die." Shepard says, "He said that if she lived, her next healing would be more difficult, because she would not be able to understand Christian Science."[156] Black was not the only practitioner to suggest that death was preferable to medicine; Arthur Corey told of a prominent Christian Science teacher whose pupils described him as insisting it was "better to die for lack of an operation than to live in consequence of one, since the individual would progress spiritually in standing for Principle at any cost."[157]

Shepard came out of this experience convinced that prayer could be combined with medicine, and she began in a small way to try to reform the Church from within. In 1993, several months after Aaron Witte (with whom her own children had once played) died of diabetes, she took her story to the *St. Louis Post-Dispatch*.

The experiences with her family and as a practitioner that she described for that newspaper—and subsequently expanded on for me—verge on Grand Guignol. A fourth-generation Scientist, Shepard has seen many members of her family die prematurely and terribly. Her mother died at age fifty of untreated cervical cancer; her stepmother died of a melanoma that began on her chest and then metastasized; her grandfather developed a melanoma on his cheek that ate completely through the flesh. She told me, "You can't imagine the human torture and neglect of watching someone die without any painkiller. It's very abusive and very sad."[158]

Her father, an asthmatic, would spend days in bed during pollen season, wheezing and gasping until his family feared he would die. As a teenager, Shepard herself was paralyzed for several weeks after fracturing two vertebrae in her neck; her right side is still affected because she didn't go to a doctor until years after her injury. One of her sons was sent home from the Principia preschool at the age of four, a note pinned to his chest saying that he'd had a bad day and needed prayer. When she took his shirt off, she found that his collarbone was broken and pushing up against the skin.

About her work as a practitioner, Shepard says: "I know that no one actually died when I was praying for them. But I know that people suffered terribly and had malformations as a result of having no medical treatment, especially in the cases of cuts, deep wounds, and burns."[159] She remembers two children in particular. The parents of a six-year-old girl called to ask her to pray for the child because she had fallen and bruised her arm. The girl herself later called Shepard, crying uncontrollably. Shepard drove to her home and found her alone, lying on the floor with a protruding broken collarbone. Her parents had gone to work and left her on the floor with the telephone. On another occasion, a mother called and described her child as having a sore throat. Three days later Shepard visited the child and found that he had swallowed lye and had a hole in his throat.

After the newspaper article was published, she received numerous letters and phone calls from Christian Science parents, many anonymous, confessing to stories of suffering and death similar to those she had described, and she could not back away from what she now felt was the truth. Shepard refused to recant what she had told the *Post-Dispatch*, and in 1993 her branch church excommunicated her.[160]

6. Inside the Sanatoriums

Christian Science nursing homes, or sanatoriums, of which there are currently twenty-three in this country, are a law—a world—unto themselves. They are unlicensed by state or federal government. The Church has described them as "a religious activity," yet it has won them the right to act as Medicare and Medicaid providers. They are unlike any other nursing homes in this country; they receive federal money for religious services. They are intensely private; what goes on within their walls is strange beyond belief.

The Mother Church oversaw the administration of these institutions for many years, but in 1993, it severed its ties to them so as to protect their status as Medicare providers. Now independent entities without Church affiliation, they are accredited by the Commission for Accreditation of Christian Science Nursing Organizations/Facilities, a body staffed by Christian Scientists. Twenty-one of the sanatoriums are Medicare providers; six offer Medicaid.

Christian Science nurses are not registered nurses, and any registered nurse who converts to Christian Science and wishes to serve as a nurse in a Christian Science facility must renounce her credentials. No medical training or prior educational requirements are demanded of Christian Science nurses; anyone wishing to advertise as a nurse in the Christian Science periodicals need only have had Primary class-instruction in Christian Science, complete the Church's training course, and be able to fulfill Mrs. Eddy's specifications, spelled out in the *Manual*: "A Christian Science nurse shall be one who has a demonstrable knowledge of Christian Science practice, who thoroughly understands the practical wisdom necessary in a sick room, and who can take proper care of the sick."[161] The "practical wisdom" of the nineteenth century is far removed, however, from scientific knowledge of today. An informational booklet, "The Foundation for Christian Science Nursing," asserts that the nurse must "establish a defense against aggressive mental suggestion" and "make certain that the ethics of Christian Science will be respected—no mixing with, no intrusion, of materia medica . . . to assure radical reliance on Christian Science."[162]

There are four training centers for Christian Science nurses: the sanatoriums of the Christian Science Benevolent Association—or B.A.s, as they're called—at Chestnut Hill, in Massachusetts, and Arden Wood, in San Francisco; Tenacre, in Princeton, New Jersey, which is also one of two Christian Science institutions that provide care for cases "with mental disorders"; and one in London, England. The three-year "Nurses Training Course" offered at these institutions is unique. As Robert Peel described it, "The instruction is devoted as much to what the nurses are *not* to do as to what they *are* to do."[163] Entirely "nonmedical," the training, according to Peel, focuses on "basic nursing arts (for example, feeding, bathing, applying dressings, and bandaging), care of the elderly, cookery for invalids, nursing ethics, obstetric theory, and care of reportable diseases—but no medication or physical therapy of any kind."[164] All patients in these homes are required to be under the care of a practitioner, who provides the prayer treatment; the nurse, Peel notes, "must resist any temptation to diagnose a case, either medically or metaphysically," but is crucial in maintaining "a mental atmosphere that supports the patient's own spiritual endeavors."[165] Among the many things that nurses are *not* to do are: use any form of medical technology to assist patients who cannot breathe on their own or feed themselves; administer painkillers; react to medical emergencies as emergencies. Over the course of her career as a practitioner, Suzanne Shepard visited both patients and family members in nursing homes and had occasion to see many of the common practices. Once she was scolded by a Christian Science nurse for helping an elderly patient who was having difficulty breathing to sit up. For patients who cannot eat on their own, nurses are instructed to place a small amount of food on the mouth and leave it be. Christian Science nursing homes take the notion of not resuscitating to its ultimate conclusion. If you fall into a coma or experience a crisis while in one of these homes, you will not be helped.

The Church has argued in a recent court case that the kind of care Christian Science nurses provide—bandaging wounds, changing bedpans, moving patients, providing sponge baths, and the like—is essentially the same kind of care nurses provide in hospitals, and that, therefore, payment for the care they provide should be reimbursed through federal programs. Both the logic and the language of this explanation are twisted, however; the simple tasks performed by Christian Science nurses—the heavy lifting and bathing that are done by nurse's aides in hospitals—are not comparable to "skilled nursing care" as it is practiced in medical facilities, and for which Christian Science nursing homes are reimbursed under Medicare. And when the Church claims that its nurses are trained in bandaging wounds and burns, it is referring to something completely, bizarrely, different from the techniques practiced in hospitals and burn units.

Ruth Cook, born and raised in California and now in her fifties, went into training at Arden Wood immediately after graduating from high school. There, after learning basic housekeeping duties, the nurses-in-training took several classes, in dressings, Bible study, and poise. There was also an obstetrics class for learning how to help mothers with postpartum care. No anatomy or emergency medical procedures were taught. Cook served as a Christian Science nurse for over twenty years at numerous facilities and in private homes around the country. She described for me the unusual dressings and bandages used by Christian Science nurses. Of course, they do not utilize bandages and dressings to prevent infection or promote recovery—the nurses believe that only Christian Science itself can heal—but to cover up unsightly wounds, sores, and injuries, and to mask odors in order to prevent distraction from the ongoing mental "work." Christian Science nurses have, in the past, used plain gauze and Kotex pads for bandages.[166] Dressings that have been used in these facilities include Lux dishwashing liquid, as well as Bactine, an over-the-counter skin antiseptic, and something called ST 37, an antiseptic mouthwash. ST 37 was used, Cook says, for cleansing wounds that had no apparent odor; Bactine was used for "odorous dressings, cancerous stuff." When I asked her how the nurses determined which dressing to apply, she said, "Use your nose. If you've got a six-inch-wide hole with grayish matter in it, you sort of want to use the Bactine."[167] The nurses were then forced to abandon Bactine, because it was learned that lidocaine, a local anesthetic, was an ingredient in that preparation. In recent years, the nurses switched to saline solution for all dressings, because, Cook says, "they couldn't find anything that was not medicated." All of the nurses' unique procedures must be approved by the Mother Church.

In one instructional pamphlet for Christian Science nurses, there is a section entitled "After Care," which instructs nurses in the procedures to be followed after a patient's death. The first order of business after death is to "Read to the patient about 20 minutes," from, of course, the Bible and *Science and Health*. One of the next instructions is this: "*If the law permits,* close the patient's eyelids and straighten him. If he has experienced a breathing difficulty before passing, prop his head up on two pillows, or raise the head of the bed."[168]

In 1992, Cook married the pastor of an evangelical church and became a born-again Christian. She now believes that she was able to function in the rigidly controlled and often disturbing environment of the Christian Science nursing home by becoming dissociated from her emotions. "I was shut off," she says. "It was sort of a silent pain. If you talk to yourself enough, you can quiet yourself down, telling yourself that the disease is a lie. It was self-medicating. But there was a lot of pain." Cook routinely saw patients whose bodies had been eaten away by cancer. "I saw people who had half an eyeball, or their teeth were there but their tongue wasn't there." She regrets that, after years of service as a "nurse," she is not qualified to do any actual nursing. "With all these years of experience,

I can't go in and supervise a floor, I can't even take a pulse or a blood pressure."

Cook and others familiar with these facilities note that Christian Science nursing homes tend to be cleaner and better kept than many other similar homes, and that there are fewer patients per nurse. In 1993, the *American Journal of Forensic Medicine and Pathology* published a paper by several physicians and forensic scientists, "Pressure Sores in a Christian Science Sanatorium," that found that 11 percent of individuals who died in a Christian Science sanatorium in Texas and who were subsequently examined by the Dallas County medical examiner's office had pressure sores—bedsores—while among patients dying in nursing homes or hospitals the incidence could be as high as 54 to 57 percent. The study did not characterize the quality of the nonreligious nursing homes used for comparison.[169]

Exemplary institutions though they may be in some respects, Christian Science nursing homes have seen their share of controversy. In May 1965, during the same month when Dr. J. Buroughs Stokes visited the U.S. Congress to secure Medicare funding for Christian Science nursing, Isaac M. Lawrence, a sixty-five-year-old accountant and Scientist, checked into Chestnut Hill on crutches. He had been suffering severe pain in his left leg and was being treated by a practitioner; a Christian Science nurse had bandaged his foot. Over the course of the next several months, Lawrence was told that his condition was improving; in fact, several toes on his left foot were gangrenous, and his leg began to rot. Leo Damore, the author of the book about Dorothy Sheridan, gained access to the subsequent court filings and reported that Lawrence's treatment "consisted of washing the foot with a tincture of green soap and applications of Bactine to combat odor."[170] After five months, Lawrence's physical condition was so dire that a conservator had to be appointed. "Mummified and wizened, with profuse drainage of pus, all tissues and arteries, nerves and muscles had disappeared from Lawrence's ankle to an area aproximately one-third distant from the knee," Damore wrote. "The tibia was bare of flesh."[171] Lawrence was transferred to Norwood Hospital, where his leg was amputated. He died a year later. His heirs filed suit against the Christian Science Benevolent Association and the superintendent of nurses who had initially examined Lawrence's foot, charging them with "negligent, wanton and reckless misconduct"; the Church eventually settled out of court.

El Dorado Vista, located in Phoenix, Arizona, is a representative Christian Science nursing home. A nonprofit corporation, certified by

Medicare and accredited by the Commission for Accreditation of Christian Science Nursing Organizations/Facilities, it is a sparklingly clean facility consisting of several small buildings, fairly new, with pleasant rooms, sunny areas for sitting and reading or for Sunday church services, and French doors that open onto patios with attractive desert landscaping. It completely lacks the astringent odors of hospitals or medically oriented nursing homes, the chaotic air of frenzied activity so common in hospitals, or the depressing sight of the elderly and infirm abandoned in wheelchairs. Indeed, the only hints of its purpose are the hospital beds and the patients in them.[172]

In every way, El Dorado Vista seems, to the casual visitor, like an exceptional institution, dedicated to the health and well-being of its patients. Its history, however, tells a more ambiguous story. It has been located at its present site for a number of years, but its name was not always El Dorado Vista. Its name used to be Upward View, and it was the facility where Elizabeth Ashley King, the twelve-year-old girl with the forty-one-inch tumor on her leg, was sent to die in 1988. In 1989, it was renamed El Dorado Vista, and several years later, the building where she died was torn down and the new ones erected. It is entirely possible that the renaming of Upward View was an attempt to erase its most spectacular public failure from its institutional memory.

Patients applying for admission at El Dorado Vista are asked "Do you use any drugs/medication/tobacco/alcohol/medical treatments/home remedies?"[173] An article in its newsletter, written by Chris Mahlstedt, the superintendent of nursing, dismisses the importance of the physical side of patient care: "Have I left out anything? I didn't mention the beds, bedpans, bandages, food, wheelchairs, etc. That's because these things have been resolved into thoughts—spiritual ideas declaring man's dominion over the belief in the material laws of discomfort, hygiene, movement, nourishment, elimination, separation, etc."[174] Mahlstedt, who showed me around the facility, seemed warm, competent, and forceful, expressing her expectation that all patients entering El Dorado Vista would be healed. It is not, however, an expectation grounded in reality.

Applicants "must have been free from medical methods of treatment for a minimum of 30 days." They are asked to consent to the following "Agreement of Understanding for Admission":

I understand that the purpose of El Dorado Vista is to provide a place where an individual can come to commune with his Father-Mother God while radically relying on Christian Science treatment for healing in an atmosphere free from criticism, free from family cares, and free from medical involvement. The nursing care provided at El Dorado Vista is intended to be consistent with [the] theology of Christian Science, and therefore no mixing with or the intrusion of medical practice is permitted. This would include x-ray or dental services on the premises.[175]

Individuals who knowingly choose such care may feel well served by El Dorado Vista, but those, like Elizabeth Ashley King, who are suffering extreme pain, or who need oxygen, or who cannot feed themselves would not be. No matter how clean and quiet and attractive the facility it is, it is not equipped to respond to the human needs of those with real physical pain or real physical emergencies. El Dorado Vista is a perfect place to stay only for those who are already perfect.

In 1996, Rita Swan's organization, CHILD, Inc., and two of its Minnesota members filed a taxpayers' suit in federal court in Minnesota against the U.S. Department of Health and Human Services, alleging that the use of federal funds to pay for Christian Science nursing services was unconstitutional. In 1992, Swan pointed out, "more than $7,400,000 in Medicare funds was paid to Christian Science nursing homes."[176] The Christian Science Church entered the case as a "defendant-intervenor," and the U.S. Justice Department defended HHS. In August 1996, a judge in the federal District Court in Minneapolis ruled in favor of CHILD, striking down laws and regulations providing Medicare and Medicaid payments for Christian Science nursing as unconstitutional and unenforceable. The judge, however, issued a stay, pending appeals.

In a stunning reversal of its former position, in January 1997, the Justice Department realigned itself with CHILD's petition. Attorney General Janet Reno sent a letter to the House and Senate legal counsel advising them that the Justice Department would no longer continue to defend the Christian Science position, finding that Medicare/Medicaid coverage of nonmedical nursing violated the Establishment Clause of the Constitution. But Reno suggested a compromise, offering to assist Congress in drafting new legislation "that would address the needs of Christian Scientists and other faiths in a manner that comports with contemporary Establishment Clause jurisprudence."[177] The problem, she suggested, was that the 1965 legislation specifically mentioned Christian Science;

if new legislation could be drafted without mentioning any religion, it might be constitutional. She did not note that the Christian Science Church is the only church that could benefit from such legislation: it is the only religious institution in the country that maintains and accredits such facilities.

Congressmen, notably Senators Orrin Hatch, of Utah, and Edward Kennedy, of Massachusetts, hastened to respond to the Church's request for new legislation ensuring that their Medicare/Medicaid coverage would continue. Virginia Harris, chair of the Church's Board of Directors, personally wrote to Senator Hatch, a Mormon who believes that he was healed, through faith-healing prayer, of deafness in one ear.[178] Hatch replied, reassuring her, "I am very hopeful that legislation can be enacted in a timely manner."[179] It was. In August 1997, Bill Clinton signed a bill mandating Medicare/Medicaid payments for "religious nonmedical health care," and Christian Science nursing was once again assured of federal funding.

CHILD promptly filed a second suit, asking the federal court in Minnesota to rule the new statutes unconstitutional:

> The amended statutes effectively replicate the prior unconstitutional provisions, by adopting religious eligibility criteria applicable only to those persons and institutions holding religious beliefs about the effectiveness of religious methods of healing and abstinence from medicine, thereby effectively discriminating among religious sects.[180]

In January 1998, Senator Kennedy, who may believe that Scientists constitute a significant voting block in Massachusetts, home to the Mother Church, entered an amicus brief in the suit, defending the Church's right to federal money. The Department of Justice once again defended the statutes favoring the Church, and, in July 1998, a judge of the U.S. District Court in Minneapolis granted summary judgment for the defendants, throwing the suit out of court; CHILD is now appealing, but Kennedy and a variety of church groups, including the National Council of Churches of Christ and the National Association of Evangelicals, have filed amicus briefs in support of the Christian Science position. In an interview that ran in the *Christian Science Journal* in October 1998, Kennedy was lavishly supportive of the Church's position, saying, "I think it's basically an issue of fairness. . . . members of the Church have contributed to the Medicare and Medicaid programs over a long period—and continue to do so. I think the court was basically and fundamentally wrong. We have the authority and we have the power and we have the *responsibility* to make sure that the members of the faith are going to be able to participate in those programs. . . . I just regret that the courts were off on this judgment."[181] Kennedy failed to point out, however, that most Americans contribute, through their taxes, to many programs from which they may never personally benefit.

Swan has not committed herself exclusively to litigation in trying to correct the legal favoritism shown to the Church at the expense of children. She has recently written an article, "Children, Medicine, Religion, and the Law," which was published in the annual *Advances in Pediatrics*, summarizing the history of religious exemption laws and their human cost.[182] She has also co-authored, with Seth Asser, a pediatrician in San Antonio, Texas, the study "Child Fatalities from Religion-Motivated Medical Neglect."[183] Swan and Asser documented 170 children's fatalities due to religion-based medical neglect that occurred between 1975 and 1995; 28 were from Christian Science families.[184] The majority of the deaths, 140, resulted from illnesses in which survival rates, with medical care, would have been better than 90 percent.[185]

The studies highlight what Swan has known since she began researching the history of these deaths. The Christian Science Church, which is the largest church promoting faith-healing in the world, has created a legal environment in which members of other, smaller sects—many of them millennial sects or charismatic groups called Full Gospel or Word churches (including Faith Assembly, End Time Ministries, the Church of the First Born, Faith Tabernacle, and others)—feel free to medically neglect their children for religious reasons and then seek protection under the religious exemption laws lobbied for by Scientists.[186] After Swan and Asser's study was published, a particularly gruesome case came to light in a suburb of Portland, where a private cemetery belonging to the twelve-hundred-member faith-healing Followers of Christ church was found to contain the bodies of some seventy-eight children buried over the past thirty-five years. The state's medical examiner believes that, of those seventy-eight, twenty-one "probably would have lived with medical intervention, often as simple as antibiotics."[187] Many of the deaths, like those of Christian Science children, were caused by diabetes or easily treatable infections; according to the medical examiner, they were "painful, torturous deaths that sometimes lasted days, if not weeks."[188] But it is impossible to prosecute the parents who have caused these deaths in Oregon because of the state statute exempting faith-healers from manslaughter charges, a statute lobbied for by the Christian Science Church.

In a particularly bewildering response to a 1998 *Time* magazine article about these deaths, Gary Jones, manager of the Committees on Publication, said, "taking care of a child is a sacred responsibility. If one form of treatment is not working, parents have an obligation to investigate other alternatives," including medical care.[189] Christian Science parents have apparently never felt that particular obligation, and their children have died in virtually identical circumstances. Scientists, however, have always felt socially superior to other faith healers, whom they have referred to publicly as "fringe-group faith healers."[190] But the Church, blind to the harm it has caused, clearly feels no responsibility for the protection it has afforded these social outcasts. And that level of protection is still high. Only three states, Massachusetts, Hawaii, and Maryland, have removed their religious exemptions; all others still provide various degrees of legal immunity to religious parents who medically neglect their children.[191]

The numbers of dead children are not high, but the issue is not one of numbers. "Look at the number of children who have been killed by airbags, or hung by venetian blinds, or drowned in buckets," says Asser. "Look at the amount of attention those things have gotten, although from a purely statistical point of view, they don't add up to much. They're all preventable, but this [medical neglect] is clearly much more ongoing and more insidious."[192] Even in a world in which thousands of children die annually of malnutrition, Asser insists that Christian Science children's deaths are a moral issue: "The concept that this is a trivial issue is also bigoted. These people are viewed as fanatics—'They're not like us, so we don't have to pay attention to them.' If anything, the opposite is true. These kids are just abandoned. I don't care how many kids die—two hundred, fifteen hundred—it's equally tragic." As for the claims of Christian Scientists such as Virginia Harris and Nathan Talbot that Christian Science is at least as successful in treating children as medicine, Asser says, "I had an professor in college, and he always told us: 'If something is false, it doesn't matter how many times you say it. It's still false.' "

7. The Child Cases Come to Boston

Over the past several decades, the Christian Science Church has tried in several ways to repair and burnish its reputation. But every occasion that might have proved a boon to the Church's public relations has been ruined by the bad publicity attendant on the child cases. Dorothy Sheridan's conviction for manslaughter hung like a shroud over the construction of the elaborate new Church Center in the late 1960s and early 1970s. Most painful of all, the Robyn Twitchell case exploded just as the Church was launching the most expensive public project in its history.

The Twitchell case was clearly the most disturbing and damaging of the child cases for the Church, but not because the manner of Robyn Twitchell's death was so grotesque, not because his suffering was extreme, not because his fate personally affected the Board of Directors. Robyn Twitchell, two and a half years old, died in the very lap of the Mother Church, in Boston, Massachusetts. His was the most bitterly contested of the cases largely because it became national news, covered in national newspapers, on national television, on 60 *Minutes*, *20/20*, and *Nightline*.

The trial was a firestorm for the Church. The Board of Directors hired a political consultant and a public relations firm to help cope with the publicity surrounding the Twitchells. Full-page advertisements were placed in the *Boston Globe*, asking, "Why is prayer being prosecuted in Boston?"[193] There was much talk by Church spokesmen of religious persecution, and Nathan Talbot told the *New York Times*, "We're having dozens and dozens and dozens of examples of people coming to our churches and reading rooms who have heard about the Twitchell case and are asking if Christian Science can heal them. Something is happening here, and it's not what the prosecutors intended."[194]

Something else was happening, too. Simultaneously with the trial of the Twitchells and the other trials of Christian Scientists across the country, the Mother Church was embarking on an improbably grandiose scheme. Christian Science, a sect that had shrunk to an extent that most members of the press had not even begun to imagine, was entering the world of international media on a lavish scale, spending millions of dollars developing worldwide shortwave radio, a nightly news broadcast to rival those of the major networks, a twenty-four-hour cable television channel, and a new national news magazine.

But despite the trappings of media sophistication, Christian Science remained Christian Science: the Church spent as much energy pretending that all was right with its world as it did in fighting the Twitchells' legal battle. As one Christian Science scholar pointed out in dismay, the Church that fancied itself reincarnated as a media mogul had not yet mastered the art of appearances. During the same week that David Twitchell was on the stand testifying in his manslaughter trial, bright foreign flags were flying in front of the portico of the Mother Church in an inappropriate celebration of the Church's international media triumph, held during an unprecedented media disaster.[195] The Church was so desperate for a future, it was blind to the peril of the present.

Part V

"God's Requirement": Christian Science on the Air

God's Requirement. SECT. 5. God requires wisdom, economy, and brotherly love to characterize all the proceedings of the members of The Mother Church, The First Church of Christ, Scientist.[1]

—Mary Baker Eddy,
Manual of The Mother Church

1. Mrs. Eddy and Mr. Ed

God expects wisdom, economy, and brotherly love of all Church members, according to Mary Baker Eddy. But during the 1980s and 1990s, as Christian Scientists found themselves surrounded on all sides by prosecutors, press, and the prospect of the bankruptcy of their own church—which was emptying its coffers into the development of fantastically expensive media projects—wisdom, economy, and brotherly love were the first casualties.

The Church had dabbled in television and radio for many years. During the 1950s and 1960s, the Church produced two long-running series for radio and television, *How Christian Science Heals*, which featured testimonies of Christian Science healing, and *The Bible Speaks to You*, an educational program. As Robert Peel acknowledged in 1988, however, "Both series brought in thousands of appreciative letters from Christian Scientists and the general public, but neither filled the churches, as had been hoped."[2] In fact, nothing that the Church tried, including the hiring of management and public relations consultants, was filling the churches, or refilling them as they continued to empty year after year.[3]

In the late 1960s and early 1970s, the Church made a halfhearted attempt to transfer its lectures to television, approaching the former vaudevillian and situation comedy actor Alan Young, who wrote and directed the hugely popular television series Mr. Ed, about a talking horse, between 1961 and 1966. Young, who played Mr. Ed's beleaguered owner—the only person who could actually hear the horse's wisecracks—quit the show in 1966, in order to devote himself full-time to being a Christian Science practitioner.

In a memoir he wrote later about his attempts to bring the Church and modern television together, Mr. Young Goes to Boston, Young recalled that his first involvement with the Mother Church came when he was contacted by Cindy Adams, then a newscaster with ABC in New York. Adams, who was also a Scientist, was interested in putting together an hour-long special in which she would interview several prominent Christian Scientists; the show that was eventually taped included Young, Robert Peel, and Erwin Canham, the editor emeritus of the Christian Science Monitor, among others. But, although the interviews received a good review in Variety and prints were made by the Mother Church, nothing ever came of the project; the prints were never distributed, as originally planned, to branch churches. When Young called Cindy Adams to find out what had happened, she told him that the project had been "scrapped" because authorities at the Mother Church had decided that "somebody on the show," possibly Erwin Canham, "said something that wasn't absolutely metaphysical."[4]

In 1969, Young was hired by the Mother Church as its director of communications and assigned to develop promotional and educational material, but like Reginald Kerry, whose rebellion he would ultimately support, he was disturbed by what he saw as pervasive political infighting and lax morality at the Church Center. None of the projects he proposed was developed, not even when he put together a package in which a number of Christian Scientists with Hollywood connections volunteered free studio space and equipment for filming Christian Science lectures. In a move that he interpreted as an attempt to quash his initiatives, Young was eventually transferred to the Lecture Board, where his talks were enthusiastically received and well attended. When Young learned that the board was proceeding with its own plans to film a Scientist delivering a lecture in a church, in talking-head format, he was greatly disillusioned with the Church's commitment to modern media. "There is nothing in this world duller than photographing a man giving a speech for an hour," he wrote.[5] He continued to feel that, presented in a fresh and more spontaneous way, Christian Science lecturers could take their place among television's most popular religious personalities, offering a more tasteful and appealing product than most televangelists. He considered television the crucial means by which to reach the most people: "In one televised Crusade in the Los Angeles Coliseum," he wrote, "Billy Graham reached more than ten times the number of people the Christian Science Lecture Board reaches in a year. . . . more people than the Lecture Board has reached since Mrs. Eddy started it!"[6]

Discouraged by what he saw as the Church's tortoiselike refusal to stick its head out into the twentieth century and see the peril that faced it, Alan Young quit lecturing and resigned his membership in the Mother Church in 1977. He remains, however, a believer, lending his name, his voice, and some of his writings on Christian Science to dissident groups.

2. "To Live for All Mankind"

In 1977, the same year that Alan Young resigned his Church membership, a man who would have sympathized with and supported his ambitions for a televised Church was elected to the Christian Science Board of Directors. Harvey Wood, the driving force behind the Church's precipitous entry into the media age, was himself a driven man, propelled by a messianic fervor to lead his church out of the wilderness and into the world. That the world might not be particularly interested in Christian Science was something that he simply could not accept.

During the 1960s, when gentle folk-guitar renditions of Mrs. Eddy's hymns were au courant, Harvey Wood was the first and perhaps the last of the Church's hippie teachers, appearing in parks with long hair, a beard, bell-bottoms, and beads, hoping to attract youthful converts to the religion in a moment when anything seemed possible.

Born in Waco, Texas, in the mid-1920s, Wood had been raised as a Christian Scientist, lost interest in it growing up, and saw the light again as an enlisted man in the Navy during World War II. His recollection of his rediscovery of the religion speaks to the impulsive, fervent side of his nature and echoes Eddy's prophecies about Christian Science saving the world: "I got really philosophical about it," he told a reporter for *Boston Magazine* in 1992. "I thought if enough people could be influenced sufficiently, we could prevent World War III. And that became my self-appointed mission: I'm going to prevent World War III!"[7] Instead, at least among his brethren, he started it.

Wood became a full-time practitioner in 1950 and soon thereafter was appointed the Christian Science chaplain at the U.S. Naval Academy at Annapolis, Maryland. A few years later, he appeared as a moderator on *How Christian Science Heals*. By 1971, he was a Christian Science teacher and lecturer in Chicago who, according to several sources, became so popular that the Board of Directors eventually called him to Boston and asked him if he was trying to develop his own religious following, a practice forbidden by the *Manual*. Tearfully, Wood denied it, but a number of the dissident Christian Scientists who came to oppose Wood's plans for a global media empire believe that his 1977 appointment to the Board was the Board's means of keeping him under control. Whether or not Wood wanted a following, he was intensely dissatisfied with at least one aspect of the audiences and students he did attract; most of them were already acquainted with Christian Science. His watchword for the next decade—"We were talking to ourselves"—described everything that was wrong with the Christian Science movement; it had no dialogue with the wider world.[8] By the time of his Board appointment, Wood was tired of talking to other Christian Scientists; he wanted to reach the multitudes.

And so he did. In 1984, Wood presided over the biggest media extravaganza the Church had ever seen, a live, two-hour video teleconference linking Christian Scientists in 147 sites in twenty-five countries around the world via six satellites. The brainchild of Wood's weekly luncheon with several of his cronies, Hal Friesen, another Board member; Donald Bowersock, the Church's new treasurer; and Jack Hoagland, the manager of the Publishing Society, the conference was rapidly thrown together over ten weeks in the fall of 1984; it took place on Saturday, December 8, which Wood would later refer to as "an historic day for The Mother Church."[9] Although eager for publicity about the event, the Church did not reveal its cost, said to be in the millions of dollars.

The idea of such a conference was not unique to the Christian Scientists. Wood's 1984 conference may well have been inspired by the spectacular 150th anniversary celebration held in Salt Lake City by the Church of Jesus Christ of Latter-Day Saints. On Easter Sunday, April 6, 1980, an enormous television screen was hung from the rafters in front of the pulpit in the Mormon Tabernacle, with other television monitors placed throughout the room. Appearing on it live, via satellite uplink, was the Mormon Church's Prophet, Seer, and Revelator, Spencer Kimball, who had flown to Fayette, New York, to dedicate a restoration of the log cabin where the Mormon Church was founded on April 6, 1830. Signaling their regard for the future as well as the past, Mormon officialdom announced that an LDS satellite network was being installed around the world; "broadcast-quality television dishes at church properties [would] connect all the stakes of the tent called Zion to the mother church via uplinks."[10] The Mormon event was itself covered on national television and may have ignited in rival religionists a certain competitive spirit.

The purpose of the Christian Science conference—to encourage Scientists "to live for all mankind"—was grand but vague. The Lord's Prayer was prayed, but most of the two hours was filled by a staged "conversation" between Board members, including Wood and Friesen, and editors and writers of the Church's religious periodicals and the *Christian Science Monitor*. Responding to the *Boston Globe*'s religion reporter, a few days after the conference, Wood harked back to his ambitions to heal the world and prevent another world war: "What makes this message so important that it couldn't be communicated in some other way, with less cost, less work?" Wood asked himself. He answered his own question: "The urgency came from the state of the world. The message fit with Christmastime and the contest going on in the *Monitor*, in which we are inviting people to write us with their substantive ideas about how we can arrive at peace 25 years hence."[11]

Although the *Globe* reported that the conference "did not reach any specific conclusions," its effect on Harvey Wood was nonetheless electric. "The feedback has been thrilling," he said.[12] He was so pleased that two more conferences, each more elaborate than the last, were staged in 1985 and 1986, costing several more millions of dollars.

In 1984, Wood himself witnessed the miracle of the technology that made it all possible. Sitting with Jack Hoagland in an impromptu media center in the basement of the Mother Church, a satellite dish parked on the lawn outside, Wood saw the downlinks come online and the words "The Christian Science Network is fully operational" blink on a bank of screens. As John Strahinich put it in *Boston Magazine*, "the flashing phrase worked an almost hypnotic effect on him, like subliminal advertising."[13] It was an interesting choice of words. Hypnotism, like mesmerism and malicious animal magnetism, is one of the dark forms that the devil takes in Christian Science belief, and many Scientists, over the next decade, would come to believe that Harvey Wood, along with Hoagland, Friesen, and Bowersock—the group who would become known to their detractors as the Gang of Four—had indeed been mesmerized by forces bent on destroying the Church from within.

3. "Betting the Company"

During his days as a teacher and lecturer in Chicago, Harvey Wood hadn't been talking entirely to himself. One of those he helped to bring into Christian Science was a young divorcée with three children named Katherine Woodruff Field. She had been married to Marshall Field, Jr., the department-store heir, and publisher and editor of his father's newspaper, the *Chicago Sun-Times*. After her divorce in 1963, the former Mrs. Field went through a period of depression and confusion. In a memoir written later, she admitted to using tranquilizers and briefly considering suicide during this period.[14] But with her discovery of Christian Science, she threw away her pills, stopped drinking and smoking, and found the determination to move her family to Anchorage, Alaska, where she went to work as a librarian at the tiny *Anchorage Daily News*, then running a distant second to the *Anchorage Times*. Within months, she had become a reporter, and one of her early efforts won an Alaska Press Club award. In 1966, she married Lawrence Fanning, another Chicago newspaper editor, and in 1967, the Fannings bought the *Anchorage Daily News*.

Lawrence Fanning died in 1971, and Kay Fanning became editor of the paper, eventually leading it to a Pulitzer Prize Gold Medal for Public Service in 1976 for a series that explored the Teamsters' abuse of power in the building of the Trans-Alaska pipeline. She succeeded in a virtually all-male field, cementing her control of the paper by quietly refusing to acknowledge the disdain of her competitors and the doubts of some of her own staff. Repeatedly fighting off bankruptcy, Fanning eventually established the *Daily News* as Anchorage's—and Alaska's—premier newspaper. In May 1983, she was hired to be the editor of the *Christian Science Monitor*, by a Board of Directors now led by her Christian Science teacher, Harvey Wood. She joined Katharine Graham, of the *Washington Post*, as one of the few women in a position of power at a major American daily newspaper.

The *Monitor*, although still beloved and respected by a small but devoted readership, which included many non-Scientists, had become somewhat dated and stuffy; it was also bleeding cash at an ever more alarming rate, running deficits of $12 million to $15 million a year. Since the 1960s, the paper had been suffering from the malaise of all modern newspapers. Competition for advertising from metropolitan dailies, magazines, and television increased; the prices of paper and of mail delivery—crucial to the Monitor's national subscription base—rose relentlessly; and, although the Monitor's circulation reached a peak of 271,000 during the early 1970s, most of its revenues were coming from circulation rather than advertising. This was a recipe for disaster when the circulation dropped, as it inevitably did.[15] In 1982, the Board of Directors was warned by its consultants that the Monitor's growing deficit would eventually bankrupt the Church, probably before the end of the century; its subscribers, whose median age was over sixty and who numbered only around 130,000, might die with it.[16]

Kay Fanning, who had nothing but "reverence and admiration" for the newspaper of her chosen religion, nonetheless thought it could use "a little livening up."[17] She presided over a complete redesign and reorganization of the paper, adding staff; at the same time, Jack Hoagland, who had been appointed manager of the Publishing Society in 1983, the same year Fanning was hired as editor, devoted himself to rebuilding the Monitor's sales staff and its sagging circulation.

Fanning's and Hoagland's efforts showed slow but steady success; over the next several years, circulation increased, through direct mail, to 170,000, and the sales force was selling more ads. But the deficit also rose, to an astonishing $22 million in 1986.[18] By the following year, Kay Fanning's vision of the Monitor's future and Jack Hoagland's had sharply diverged.

Rumors flew throughout 1987. In September, an anonymous letter, thirteen pages, single-spaced, was sent to all Christian Science teachers, considered by the Field to be the spiritual leaders and protectors of the movement. It was signed "Workers at The Mother Church," and it raised the alarm about changes being made to the Church's lectures and reading rooms, which were also being smartened up electronically; about excessive spending; and about "the future of our newspaper."[19] As the letter pointed out, Christian Scientists were being told that the Monitor " 'is not a newspaper—it's a concept.' "[20] And it raised the central issue in many Scientists' minds: "What is nowhere near sufficiently known about these programs and plans is their staggering and unprecedented expense. They represent commitments and liabilities beyond anything the Church has ever conceived of having."[21]

A month later, one of the most alarming rumors was confirmed. During the second week of October, Hoagland brought Fanning four videotapes and a black binder along with a memo marked PERSONAL & CONFIDENTIAL.

She was instructed to submit the materials to "careful study" and to understand that the Board of Directors of the Church, including Harvey Wood, had seen the videos and the charts and tables in the binder and had indicated their "general acceptance of the overall course of action recommended during the presentation."[22] The videos, which she watched that weekend, were of a meeting, a presentation given by Jack Hoagland to the Publishing Society's Trustees two months previously, on August 17, 1987. That date, Fanning said later, was "indelibly impressed" on her mind; she had not been informed that any important meeting had taken place.[23] Watching the tapes, Fanning heard Jack Hoagland recommend that enormous resources be allocated to radio, television, and shortwave, as well as to something he called "an appropriate print product." Recommending that the Trustees adopt his proposal to move resources away from the newspaper and into television—and acknowledging its inherent risks, which were not justified by any sensible business plan—Jack Hoagland said, "We're betting the company on some of these programs in any normal commercial terms."[24] As she watched the videos and read the accompanying materials, Fanning realized that at this secret meeting, Hoagland had proposed folding the *Christian Science Monitor*, established by Mary Baker Eddy, the pride and joy of all Christian Scientists.

Fanning was aghast. She called Hoagland at home to confirm her impressions. Nowhere on the videotapes had he specifically said that the newspaper was to be abolished, but in one column in one of the tables, the projected future budget and revenues of the *Monitor* in 1989 were listed as zero. On the phone, however, Hoagland was more direct. Fanning asked him if he meant to shut down the *Monitor*; she says he replied by saying, "Let me be very clear. Yes." He told her that the *Monitor* would not be published after April 1989. He also told her that the Directors and the Trustees had approved the decision. Some days later, he would confirm this to two of Fanning's colleagues, telling them that the last issue of the paper would appear on May 1, 1989.[25]

What kind of manager would plan to shut down a venerable newspaper without discussing it with that newspaper's editor? While owners have been known to take such abrupt action, Jack Hoagland did not own the *Christian Science Monitor*. Indeed, before coming to work at the Church as a consultant and later as manager of the Publishing Society, Hoagland had had no experience in running a newspaper or in media of any kind. His act of concealment—hiding a pivotal meeting about the fate of the *Monitor* from its own editor—reflected the kind of background he did have. Jack

Hoagland started his professional career working for the Central Intelligence Agency.

4. "One Spooky Operation"

In a chapter of the Christian Science saga that is filled with fascinating characters—heroes and villains, fantasists and hard-nosed realists, yes-men and ladies-in-waiting—the most fascinating of all is John "Jack" Hoagland, Jr., a man at once seductive and sinister, a kind of sorcerer's apprentice who conjured up a maelstrom of frenzied spending, consulting, and developing that inevitably came crashing down, bringing the Church down with it.

Many of Jack Hoagland's colleagues, both Scientist and non-Scientist, describe him in extreme terms. "Jack is the most disarming and probably the most insincere man I've ever met," one top official who worked with Hoagland has said. "He's an elaborate bullshitter, very persuasive, a hell of a good salesman." A Christian Scientist who worked with him felt a similar ambivalence: "Jack Hoagland had a style of management designed to keep everyone in chaos. That was his approach, and it was conscious up to a point. He used the motto, 'Fire, ready, aim,' rather than 'Ready, aim, fire.' He believed in trying a lot of things; if something didn't work, pull it back and try something else."

Jack Hoagland grew up in Louisville, Kentucky, and, as a teenager, in Boston, where his father, Jack Hoagland, Sr., moved the family in 1944, and where he would serve the Church as manager of the Publishing Society.[26] Hoagland graduated from Yale in 1951, and it was at Yale that he was recruited into the intelligence community, serving first as a naval officer in the CIA where, according to one journalist, "he monitored Soviet aircraft advances and translated Russian scientific and technological journals. After the war, he stayed on with the agency, working as a local liaison with Cambridge scientists and the burgeoning Route 128 high-tech companies." In 1961, Hoagland left the CIA and spent the next twenty-odd years working as a consultant, eventually in his own firm, advising large corporations, such as Renault, on "strategic planning" and forecasting future technological applications. According to press materials released by the Church during the height of the television development, Hoagland had also "directed several major studies on arms control, international security, and UN peacekeeping," activities that led many of his detractors within the Christian Science movement to question whether his involvement with the CIA—institutionally or perhaps emotionally—had truly ended.[27]

Hoagland's commitment to Christian Science, however, seemed clear, as did a taste for the good life. He flew to Europe and back on the Concorde while simultaneously working with Renault and serving as a First Reader in his branch church in Wellesley, Massachusetts, during the 1970s.[28] Despite personal reservations stemming from his father's death in 1962— which he attributed to the exhausting job of managing the business side of the *Monitor*—Hoagland took on his father's old job as manager of the Church's Publishing Society in 1983.[29] After the excitement of the 1984 video teleconference subsided, Hoagland seems to have transferred his hopes from the newspaper—with all its deficits and slow growth—to electronic media. In his five-year plans and during his discussions with board members, Hoagland began emphasizing that the cost represented by every new *Monitor* subscriber who was attracted by direct mail and low subscription rates was prohibitive, whereas listeners and viewers attracted to new radio and television programs produced by the Church would be bargains by comparison. As evidence, he could point to the debut of Monitor Radio, a weekly show that first aired in 1984, which had gone well. It was picked up by over a hundred stations on the American Public Radio network that year. In 1985, at Hoagland's instigation, Monitor Radio—at a cost of $2 million a year—went to a daily format. The *Christian Science Monitor Reports*, a monthly and then weekly television show that examined news stories in depth, also appeared in 1985, eventually costing $6 million a year.[30] But although the show won Peabody and Emmy awards, it aired early on Sunday morning and never attracted much of an audience.

In 1986, the Church bought WQTV, a local Boston television channel (Channel 68) for $7.5 million. The Church's first big television purchase, WQTV would serve as a kind of proving ground for television experiments. In order to hold the operating licenses of both the shortwave and TV stations, the Christian Science Monitor Syndicate was formed; Jack Hoagland, Don Bowersock, and Hal Friesen, among others, sat on its board.

What Hoagland could never establish, at any point during the course of the lavish expenditures that he was to oversee, was that large numbers of television viewers were clamoring for lengthy daily doses of serious broadcast journalism beyond what PBS and CNN and shows like *Nightline* were already providing. Indeed, one of Hoagland's former television staffers later wrote, "There was a rumor that a study had concluded that there was no market interest in the kind of program that was being devised."[31]

Instead, Hoagland seemed to be operating under a religious imperative very similar to that issued by Mary Baker Eddy when she imperiously ordered her Publishing Society Trustees to start a daily newspaper: "Let there be no delay."[32] Jack Hoagland seemed to be counting on the same kind of alacrity that Eddy's followers had displayed in obeying her commands as he pulled ever more incredible plans out of his hat: a daily television newscast; a new monthly magazine, costing $7.5 million to start up; and, most astonishing of all: worldwide, twenty-four-hour-a-day religious and news programming on shortwave radio, at an initial cost of $38 million. Although Church members—lawyers, judges, accountants, financial advisers—soon began raising the alarm over these astounding costs, Hoagland seemed to view their objections as an irritating manifestation of malicious animal magnetism, while his budget predictions came to resemble religious visions. In one memo, dated December 8, 1987, Hoagland wrote that "the Monitor's mission to all mankind requires that the Monitor incorporate and be represented by a range of publishing media."[33] "The complete product line," he wrote, would include:

- the daily newspaper and its weekly edition;
- a new daily print edition delivered electronically to the user;
- continuous daily shortwave radio broadcasting to a global audience;
- daily radio broadcasting within the U.S. on public radio;
- a new daily television news program on U.S. commercial TV;
- a new monthly news magazine for global circulation[34]

The memo, however, gave no indication of how "the complete product line" would be supported financially in the years to come.

One impediment to the fulfillment of Hoagland's grand scheme was Kay Fanning. Jack Hoagland appears not to have factored into his charts and tables the human element and its power to overturn applecarts. Immediately after learning of the infamous August 17, 1987, meeting, Fanning went to work at convincing the Christian Science Board of Directors to grant her the time and money to assemble a task force that would determine how to cut the paper's deficit while maintaining its quality.[35] As she did so, virulent rumors about the possible demise of the Monitor began to waft out into the newsroom and, from there, to the Field. As the saying goes, there was hell to pay.

During a wildly acrimonious newsroom meeting between the *Monitor* staff and Jack Hoagland in December 1987, one staff member flatly told Hoagland that he wasn't trusted. On a cassette tape of the meeting, Hoagland can be heard responding to a question about the danger that the *Monitor* might be eliminated by suggesting that no such threat had ever existed:

> I think about all I can say in answer to any of these questions is these are challenges one approaches on one's knees. You don't debate them, you don't reason through them in any normal human way. And these are not problems or challenges that this management invented; it seems to me we have to address them together. . . . if you say you've been hearing from me some sort of guise to eliminate the daily, no, hang on a minute, that's very hard on me because every year we've been increasing the commitment to the daily newspaper, now that's a fact. It's very hard for anyone to predict the future, but that's the fact of what happened.[36]

In the face of vehement opposition not only from staff but also from the Field itself, Hoagland and Wood backed away from the plan of closing down the *Monitor* in order to transfer its budget to television and other projects. But they not only backed away from the plan, they began openly denying that they had ever considered it. Their denials, however, had a farcical element; Hoagland himself had had the August 17, 1987, meeting videotaped and had distributed those tapes, along with the damning tables showing the *Monitor* budget at zero and the Board's own memo approving his recommendations. While Wood and Hoagland issued their denials, others began circulating the documents that exposed their deception in a kind of parodic reenactment of CIA coverups and exposés. By the end of 1987, in the *Monitor* newsroom and even among those working on the burgeoning television operation, there was, as one journalist described it, "the growing feeling that Jack Hoagland was running one spooky operation."[37]

Kay Fanning was given her task force, but it was ultimately an empty gesture. Through most of 1988, a year in which she also served as the first woman president of the American Society of Newspaper Editors, Fanning worked on devising a plan to cut the deficit that involved laying off nearly forty staff members and redesigning the paper. By her estimates, the plan would have cut the *Monitor*'s then annual deficit of $19 million to a little over $8.6 million after three years. Hoagland, meanwhile, had given the nod to a second task force, one headed by his friend Richard Nenneman, the former managing editor of the *Monitor*. Nenneman's task force claimed that the deficit could be cut to a mere $2.5 million by reducing the number of editorial pages from over twenty to sixteen, cutting the staff from 170 to 88, closing several foreign bureaus, and eliminating all advertising, and thus all ad sales jobs.[38]

Kay Fanning's task force gave its presentation to the Publishing Society's Trustees and the Board members on Halloween, 1988; Nenneman's task force followed several days later. After her presentation, Fanning was deeply discouraged to hear Harvey Wood remark that her cuts were not deep enough and that the deficit had to be reduced to $5 million. Ten days later, Fanning learned that Nenneman's task force recommendations had been accepted by the Board; within another ten days, in November 1988, she was called to a meeting with Hoagland and Wood where they presented her with a revised organizational chart of the Publishing Society. The chart indicated that she, as editor of the *Monitor*, would no longer report to the Directors, but to a new editor-in-chief. The chart also introduced several other layers of management between herself and the Directors.

Three days later, on November 14, 1988, she resigned, along with her managing editor, David Anable, and assistant managing editor, David Winder. In her resignation letter to the Board, Fanning wrote, "The decisions that are being made now . . . will undo the efforts of the last five years. . . . I am convinced that the downsizing, downgrading of the Monitor will be seen in time as a tragic mistake, a serious blow to the church, and a step away from Mrs. Eddy's vision for her movement."[39]

Richard Nenneman was appointed editor-in-chief, and Richard Cattani, a longtime *Monitor* reporter, was named editor. Virtually every major newspaper and wire service in the country, including the *Boston Globe*, the *New York Times*, and the *Wall Street Journal*, covered the resignations and the controversies that lay behind them. The *Christian Science Monitor* did not.

5. "USA Yesterday"

What the *Monitor* did carry, the day the news broke, was a boxed notice on the editorial page announcing Fanning's resignation (although not Anable's or Winder's) and the appointments of Nenneman and Cattani. The new editors, after consulting with Harvey Wood, had rejected an article about the resignations and the issues involved that had been prepared by a staff writer; in this, they were effectively enforcing a policy of censoring news not considered beneficial to the Church and its fledgling media empire. That act initiated the deconstruction of what was once considered to be one of the world's finest newspapers.

The news of the resignations sent shock waves through the Christian Science Field as well as through the Church Center. Hoagland and Wood were caught off guard when Fanning and Anable released news of their resignations to the press, apparently having counted on the culture of compliant courtesy and obedience that had been built up at the Mother Church over many decades. Wood later declared himself in "great shock" at the fact that the editors had made their resignations public.[40]

For the first time, the divisions between *Monitor* staff and Church leadership over the vast sums being spent on television and other media opened up, like a visible crack in the foundation of the movement, before the astonished eyes of all Christian Scientists. Over the next several months, dozens of *Monitor* staffers would resign or be fired, and the Board of Directors and other Church authorities, including Jack Hoagland, would once again find themselves deeply at odds with the Church's own membership.

On November 15, the day after the resignations of Fanning, Anable, and Winder, Elizabeth Pond, the *Monitor*'s correspondent in Bonn, Germany, who had worked for the paper for thirty years, also resigned, citing the same concerns as Fanning and predicting that "trivializing the Monitor" would ultimately lead to the disappearance of Christian Science.[41] Jack Hoagland told the *New York Times*, "The daily newspaper is our flagship. It will always be our flagship," and "The paper will not be down-sized in any sense."[42] That same day, Church security guards were sent into the *Monitor* newsroom to police the photocopying machines and prevent the staff from making copies of resignation letters and other documents the Board deemed subversive. That afternoon, Board members Harvey Wood and Hal Friesen, along with Jack Hoagland, sensing that they had an insurrection on their hands, held an emergency meeting with the newsroom staff that was undoubtedly the most discordant in the Board's history. Over the vehement objections of the staff, Harvey Wood insisted that the Board could not let a story on the resignations run in the *Monitor* unless it was "very positive." And besides, Hoagland added, everything had been happening too fast.[43]

The following day, November 16, the same team, consisting of Wood, Hoagland, and Friesen, along with Nenneman and Cattani, traveled to

Washington, D.C., to meet with the Monitor's Washington bureau. There, Wood told the assembled reporters that in his twelve years on the Board, he had "never heard presented to the Board—or a vote taken—to discontinue the paper. Not ever."[44] It was a statement that most of those present, including, presumably, Wood—who was on the Board when its memo approving the decision to discontinue the Monitor was drafted—knew to be false. When the staffers asked about the drastically downsized prototype that Nenneman's task force had presented, they were given vague answers about the future of the paper and told that no final decisions had been made. They were also reassured that the Monitor's budget was not being diminished in order to feed the voracious budgets for television and radio programming.

On the first day of January 1989, when the redesigned Monitor appeared, it was clear that the Monitor as a full-fledged newspaper was gone and that the deficits would in no way be reduced by the new design. In fact, the expense of bringing out the new Monitor was exorbitant, by any standard. The paper was still a Monday through Friday daily, but it was reduced to twenty pages; the number of articles per issue dropped from thirty-nine to thirty; the staff had been reduced from 170 to 110; local and classified advertising had been dropped (the paper accepted only two full-page national ads); and three foreign and three domestic bureaus had been closed. What was added was four-color printing on heavier, forty-pound stock. (The heavier paper was required, as the trade publication Editor & Publisher reported, "to improve the color reproduction and the durability of articles readers clip from the paper.")[45] The last-minute decision—made in December 1988—to add color to the paper meant pushing the paper's deadlines back from four o'clock in the afternoon to the unheard-of hour of ten o'clock in the morning, making it virtually impossible for the Monitor to report breaking news. It also meant canceling contracts with five longtime Monitor printing plants on three days' notice, a decision that cost the Church $1.7 million in penalties. After the Church hired the plants that printed USA Today, disillusioned Monitor reporters began referring to their own paper as "Yesterday's News Tomorrow" and "USA Yesterday"; the Monitor had become a colorful little news magazine minus the news.

The costs of putting out the downsized Monitor—which included $1.8 million in new color-printing equipment and another $1.5 million in additional operating costs—pushed the annual deficit to roughly $12 million, far over the deficit of $5 million that Wood had demanded and several million in excess of what Kay Fanning's task force had foreseen for their version of the *Monitor*, which would have remained recognizably a newspaper.

Reaction to the new paper from both Christian Scientists and non-Scientists was overwhelmingly negative. Theo Sommer, the editor of the West German newspaper *Die Zeit*, sent his condolences to *Monitor* correspondents: "For whatever it's worth: the new lay-out of The Christian Science Monitor is an unmitigated disaster. The colors are awful, the type is hard to read, the print is abominable. I feel a physical aversion to read the hyped-up Monitor."[46] There were sorrowful editorials in the *Boston Globe* and other papers, and the 1990 edition of the *Repap Media Guide*, an industry watchdog, dropped the *Monitor* and its reporters from its annual evaluation, citing "the death knell of the newspaper."[47] It wrote, "The *Monitor* no longer breaks any new ground, reportorial or otherwise, looking more like the *Weekly Reader* than the prestigious daily newspaper it used to be."

Five days after the debut of the new *Monitor*, Charlotte Saikowski, the Washington bureau chief who had been with the paper for twenty-seven years, took early retirement. In her letter of resignation, she criticized the color as "glitzy" and deplored the poaching of young talent away from the newspaper to serve the Church's radio and television endeavors. She wrote:

> You should know that reactions in the Washington community to events at the Monitor . . . have been heart-rending. I have heard expressions of concern from members of Congress; White House, State Department and other government officials; foreign diplomats; academics; leading representatives of the print and television (yes, television) industry; and many other readers. "We treat you as a national treasure," a well-known scholar at the Council on Foreign Relations told me. "You have an obligation far beyond your church."[48]

Soon after the changes were made in the *Monitor*, subscriptions fell from 180,000 to around 120,000 and kept falling. By February, forty staff members had resigned or taken early retirement, another thirty-three were fired. The publishing director, David Els, resigned, and Joseph Harsch—after a column he wrote about freedom of the press was censored by the new editors—retired after sixty years with the paper, saying that the new *Monitor* "isn't a real newspaper" and that he considered it "journalistically unsound."[49] According to *Monitor* correspondent Elizabeth Pond's widely distributed analysis and chronology of events—as painstakingly reported as if it had been an article for the newspaper she no longer worked for— mail from subscribers themselves ran four to one in favor of the old design; mail to the Board of Directors ran nine to one against the new, emasculated paper.[50] In their rush to establish the electronic Church, Harvey Wood and Jack Hoagland had burned their bridges behind them; along the way, they'd destroyed the sterling reputation of the *Christian Science Monitor*.

6. The Big Room

The people Jack Hoagland had already hired to produce *Christian Science Monitor Reports* advised him not to try to put on an evening newscast. Among others, Richard O'Regan, the program's executive producer, explained that to cover breaking news required enormous resources in personnel, equipment, travel, and overhead and that the idea of going head-to-head with the major network newscasts was practically suicidal. The competition was too fierce, the expenses too high. O'Regan, along with some of his coworkers, agreed that if the Church wanted to put on a daily television show, a morning news show might be accomplished with a reasonable budget and would offer a unique service to viewers: serious analysis of the previous day's news and discussion of upcoming events in an environment in which it could compete with the softer morning shows of the networks.[51]

Hoagland was not pleased by this advice. In late 1988, he fired O'Regan for being "insubordinate" in refusing to support the idea of an evening newscast. Meanwhile, he had hired a number of people who would tell him what he did want to hear. Most were consultants who would profit enormously from Hoagland's determination to enter the television news market. One of them was Herbert Victor, a television consultant known for resurrecting a San Francisco station by introducing *Geraldo*-style talk shows. Victor explained to the bemused television staffers that a morning program simply wasn't satisfying to the egos of those involved: "When you're in Vegas," he said, "you don't want to play the small rooms. You want to play the big room. An evening program is the big room."[52] Jack Hoagland, member of a church that forbids gambling, took millions of dollars of the Church's money and bet it in the big room.

• • •

World Monitor: A Television Presentation of The Christian Science Monitor premiered on September 12, 1988, on the Discovery Channel, at seven P.M. Eastern time. The Discovery Channel represented a last-ditch effort to get the program on the air; it had failed to sell as a syndicated program. The Church's agreement with Discovery was highly advantageous to the cable channel: Discovery would pay $1 million for the program the first year and $2 million the second. Discovery had no obligation to pay anything after the second year unless *World Monitor* reached certain specified viewer ratings. For instance, in the sixth year, *World Monitor*, which by then, according to Hoagland's projections, was supposed to be profitable, was to have a rating of 3.5, up from its 1988 rating of .6 to .8, a viewership of roughly 350,000. As one skeptic noted, a rating of 3.5 was then four times the average viewership of other prime-time Discovery Channel programs, and Hoagland had not demonstrated how this astonishing jump in the ratings was to be achieved.[53] Because *World Monitor* would air on the cable channel, advertising revenues would go to Discovery, putting the Church in the position of paying some $20 million dollars annually to produce a nightly newscast while recouping only a small fraction of its costs.

One of the primary attractions of the show for the Discovery Channel, which did not then have its own nightly newscast, was its anchor, John Hart, a silver-haired, deep-voiced longtime correspondent with NBC who had anchored the Saturday edition of *NBC Nightly News* during the 1970s. Hart had covered everything from the presidential campaigns of Robert Kennedy and Richard Nixon to the Vietnam War and had served as national affairs correspondent and chief European correspondent for NBC News, winning the Edward Weintel Prize for Diplomatic Reporting for his coverage of relations between the Soviet Union and the United States. The Discovery Channel considered Hart such a crucial part of the package that they made his presence as anchor a condition of the show staying on the air; if Hart left, Discovery would drop the show. Hart himself was never apprised of this condition while he stayed with the show; indeed, hardly anyone at the Church was aware of the clause except for Jack Hoagland and his chief lieutenant, a young woman named Annetta Douglass, known as Netty.

Netty Douglass's meteoric rise through the ranks of Christian Science officialdom began with an entry-level job at the Publishing Society. Jack Hoagland took an interest in her career after she played a role in helping to plan the 1984 video teleconference, advising her to finish her college education. By 1990, she had a dizzying array of titles: manager and chief executive officer of the Christian Science Publishing Society; president and chief executive officer of the Christian Science Monitor Syndicate, the body that owned and operated the shortwave stations, among other properties; executive producer of radio and television broadcasting of the *Christian Science Monitor*; and executive producer of Monitor Broadcasting. Jack Hoagland had assumed the titles of chairman and chief executive officer of Monitor Television, Inc. Critics of the Church's expansion into television would later point to the close relationships of Board members Harvey Wood and Hal Friesen with Jack Hoagland and Netty Douglass as having created an unhealthy atmosphere which no dissenting or questioning voices penetrated. Like the hapless character played by Alan Young in *Mr. Ed*, only this small handful of people could hear the talking horse, the magical voice of television. It was telling them, as one Board memo entitled "A spiritual call-to-arms" put it, to "turn the face of this Church outward and keep it there."[54]

Just weeks before the debut of *World Monitor*, Jack Hoagland and Harvey Wood moved to consolidate their position within the Church and to quash the mounting opposition in the Field to the expansion of television and its related expenditures. In 1988, the venerable Robert Peel, who had spent most of his life in the service of the Church, had written *Health and Medicine in the Christian Science Tradition*, one of a series of books commissioned by an ecumenical publishing group to explore the beliefs concerning health and medicine in a variety of religious faiths. In July, Peel gave a copy of his soon-to-be-published manuscript to the Board of Directors as a courtesy. The Board responded by sending a long letter rebuking Peel to some fifteen hundred Church employees and teachers. With his usual circumspection, naming no names and proffering no figures, Robert Peel had, very mildly, suggested that the headlong rush into media development by the Church was, perhaps, a departure from its origins, concluding: "The question now is whether [the Church] can reach its destination more rapidly and more easily by turning onto the six-lane highway where the mainstream of twentieth-century traffic so confidently flows."[55] Perhaps the point Peel made that most offended Wood and Hoagland came when he quoted Mrs. Eddy's disapproving letter to her publisher, chastising him for his aggressive publicity: "The smartest business man is not scientifically a safe business man. He is not as smart as God, while he thinks himself smarter and is quite unconscious of this thought."[56]

It is a common ploy of the Church, and particularly of its Committee on Publication, to accuse critics of Christian Science of unspecified "inaccuracies"; the Board's letter now turned that tool against one of its own: "We felt the concluding chapter not only contained inaccuracies which would undermine the credibility of the rest of the book, but was also too strident in tone and too personal in opinion."[57] The Board saw fit, from its lofty position, to patronize Peel, suggesting that he should have taken "a more careful look" and that this elder statesman of Christian Science suffered from "cloistered nostalgia."[58] With their letter, the Board sent photocopies of the offending final chapter of Peel's book without obtaining his permission or his publisher's, a violation of copyright law.[59] In the Field, the letter inspired less sympathy for the Board's position than outrage. When Robert Peel died in January 1992, at the age of eighty-two—a man who had arguably done more than any other single individual in the Church's history to legitimize Christian Science in the mind of the public—the *Christian Science Monitor* took no notice and did not publish its customary appreciative article about the career of a man so important to the movement.

World Monitor was an excellent and in some ways unique program, offering in each half-hour show two or three in-depth reports from around the world as well as a summary of the day's news. Along with the *MacNeil-Lehrer NewsHour*, *World Monitor*—which offered the same high-quality coverage and analysis but focused on international rather than domestic news—was one of the most thoughtful and least sensational of all the newscasts then on the air. Virtually everyone who worked on the program, Scientist and non-Scientist alike, remains proud of his work. But the staff of *World Monitor* was itself divided, in a way that the staff of no Church project had ever been before. This was the first major endeavor in the Church's history to involve a majority of non-Scientists.

Traditionally, the *Christian Science Monitor* had always hired Scientists before non-Scientists, even if they were not as experienced, a practice that was legal because the *Monitor* was Church-owned and thus not required to follow equal-opportunity employment guidelines. Since Mrs. Eddy's day, the editor of the *Monitor* had always been a Scientist, as were most of the other top editors, correspondents, and columnists. But when it came to television, there were few Scientists qualified to fill the top jobs and not enough experienced in television journalism to staff the large operation. The Christian Science Monitor Syndicate, although Church-owned, would abide by equal-opportunity hiring practices in order to meet Federal Communications Commission regulations; the television operations would likewise comply.[60] Those regulations, however, contained no instructions on how to reconcile the unusual beliefs and practices of Christian Scientists with the outside world.

John Hart described the clash of cultures between believers and nonbelievers after leaving his position as anchor of World Monitor in 1991. "The News for God's Sake" appeared in the Columbia Journalism Review in 1992 and chronicled a series of run-ins Hart had with Jack Hoagland and others at World Monitor over conflicts caused by Christian Science beliefs seeping into the newscasts. The instances of such conflicts ranged from the absurd to the serious. When Hart wanted to report the death of an elderly elephant at the San Diego Zoo, David Cook, the managing editor and the highest-ranking Scientist on the staff, told him, "We don't normally do obits, unless the people are of overriding importance"; when Hart wrote that twenty million people are "afflicted" by leprosy, Cook wanted to change it to "affected"; when Hart wanted to use the phrase "poxes and fevers" in a piece about Native American health issues, Cook wanted to take it out.[61] The issue of censorship for theological reasons was central to Hart and to some other non-Scientists on the staff, and the conflicts assumed real importance when decisions on how World Monitor would cover the unfolding trial of David and Ginger Twitchell were imminent. The producer assigned to the piece, a non-Scientist, complained to Hart that David Cook was following her every move and examining all her work. Hart suggested to Cook that he recuse himself, but Cook did not.[62] As it turned out, World Monitor's coverage of the Twitchell trial was fair and balanced, but this exercise in journalistic integrity only outraged loyal Scientists, who seem to have felt that the Church's news broadcast should have favored the beleaguered couple.

Hart was also disturbed by other ways in which the Church culture penetrated the newsroom. "There was some kind of infantilization going on," he said later, speaking of Hoagland's patronizing behavior to his staff. One day, Hart said, "he marched us over to the Sunday school for a meeting." (The Sunday school building is across the Church Center plaza from the Colonnade building, which housed the broadcasting offices and studios.) "We all sat around in babies' chairs under sayings from the Bible. I don't know what message he was trying to send, but it didn't feel good."[63] Hart complained bitterly when Jack Hoagland announced to the staff in early 1990 that he would be going on a " 'fact-finding mission' " to Eastern

Europe for the State Department; he was unfazed when it was pointed out to him that the trip would represent a flagrant case of conflict of interest for the editor in chief of a news organization.[64]

In another, unrelated incident shortly thereafter, the Board of Directors wrote a letter to ABC News chastising its producers for having aired a piece about Monitor television that failed to take into account the Church's "unique worldwide mission."[65] Hart—who didn't care to be perceived as the figurehead for a church on a mission—threatened to resign. Not realizing the influence he wielded thanks to the Discovery Channel's cancellation clause, Hart was convinced to stay when Hoagland gave up the "editor in chief" title and invited Hart to help formulate written editorial guidelines for the news operation. Like a nonnative species brought into a delicate ecosystem to control a pest, the guidelines would inevitably threaten the whole environment.

The "Editorial Standards and Guidelines" were released in June 1990. Formulated by Hoagland, Douglass, Hart, and other newsroom editors, they contained some admirable (if obvious) points, as well as what Mark Twain would have called stretchers. Most of the guidelines concerned nuts-and-bolts television news ethics, forbidding such practices as presenting taped footage as live, staging or reenacting events, paying interviewees, and the like. But the crucial passages, those most intently negotiated by Hoagland and Hart, came under the heading of "Editorial Policies Related to Coverage of Topics Concerning the Christian Science Church." They were these:

> The Christian Science Monitor and its ancillary radio and television news broadcasts were established and are conducted with one purpose: public service. There is no second purpose or hidden agenda. . . . Monitor broadcasts are not a means to propagate Christian Science. They have no missionary or proselytizing role. Nor do they serve a public relations function for the Church.[66]

While the statements may have made Hart and the other non-Scientists on staff feel better about working as journalists for a church, they were demonstrably false. They directly contradicted Mrs. Eddy's own stated purpose for the Monitor and the Christian Science Publishing Society, which institution, Eddy wrote, was established for the purpose of "more effectually promoting and extending the religion of Christian Science as taught by me."[67] The statements also contradicted repeated explanations of the purpose of all *Monitor* journalism that were made by Wood, Hoagland, and the Church treasurer, Don Bowersock, to the membership of the Church over the preceding several years.

In fact, the *Christian Science Monitor* had been recognized both within and outside the movement as a newspaper inspired by a religious mission. Its longtime editor Erwin Canham wrote in *Commitment to Freedom: The Story of the Christian Science Monitor* that the *Monitor* was a "public service" that "does in fact serve to promote and extend the religion of Christian Science, which is the basic obligation of The Christian Science Publishing Society, set forth in its Deed of Trust." While characterizing the *Monitor* as a "real newspaper," he also acknowledged that it was a " 'religious newspaper' in the sense that its fundamental obligation is to a religious purpose . . . and many of its decisions and actions are motivated by profoundly religious criteria."[68]

In the first issue of the *Christian Science Monitor*, Mary Baker Eddy defined its purpose as follows: "to spread undivided the Science that operates unspent. The object of the *Monitor* is to injure no man, but to bless all mankind."[69] The architects of Monitor television consistently spoke out of both sides of their mouths, using parts of this crucial quotation to serve their own purposes. On the one hand, they repeatedly told Christian Scientists that the television programs they were funding through their donations would "spread undivided the Science that operates unspent." In 1989, for example, at the Church's annual meeting, Jack Hoagland got up before thousands of Christian Scientists and said:

> It's nice to think of the spiritual mission, the mandate, that Mrs. Eddy has given us for each of her periodicals . . . for the *Monitor* that wonderful mission that we just plumb time and again and find new meaning in: 'to spread undivided the Science that operates unspent.'. . . Every one of these activities is an extension, a further step of the periodicals that Mrs. Eddy has established.[70]

Eddy's crucial phrase was repeated several more times during his presentation for good measure. Two years later, the Christian Science Board of Directors published a statement in the *Christian Science Journal* that made a direct connection between "every activity" of the *Monitor* and the Church's religious mission: "All of the *Monitor*'s work in this way is unquestionably contemporary evidence of the spirit of Christ, Truth, moving among humanity according to God's saving purpose for the world.

Throughout the pages of the newspaper and the monthly magazine, through every broadcast over the airwaves, something tangible is going forward that embodies vital qualities. . . . The *Monitor's* mission in every format represents a deeply religious idea and a certainty that the world's ills can be healed."[71]

On the other hand, these same Church officials avoided using Eddy's first phrase about the *Monitor's* proselytizing mission when speaking to non-Scientists like Hart, emphasizing to them that Monitor journalism was simply intended "to injure no man, but to bless all mankind." Indeed, the first sentence of the "Editorial Standards and Guidelines" quoted only this second and more secular part of Eddy's formula for the *Monitor*. The editorial standards—with the misleading statement denying the "missionary or proselytizing role" of Monitor broadcasting—were finalized and reissued in March 1991.

Of course, John Hart and his fellow non-Scientists putting out *World Monitor* were not reading the Church's religious periodicals or its fundraising letters or attending its annual meetings. They had no way of knowing that they had been engaged, without their knowledge or consent, in a "deeply religious" mission; indeed, their employer, the Church, had assured them that they were not. But what they didn't know, the swelling ranks of Church dissidents were about to tell them.

7. The Dissidents and *The Destiny of The Mother Church*

The voices of those who objected to the Church's ever more expensive broadcasting endeavors had been raised loudly since the resignations of Kay Fanning and the other *Monitor* editors. But they reached a crescendo after May 15, 1991, the day the Monitor Channel was launched, raising the Church's deficit to $6.5 million a month. Jack Hoagland and his colleagues at the Publishing Society paid no attention, celebrating the launch with a peculiarly Scientific affair: an ice cream party.[72]

Many Church members had been distressed by the quality of programming on the Church's Boston television station, WQTV. The purchase of WQTV in 1986, apparently made on Hoagland's "Fire, ready, aim" principle, was one of many costly mistakes; the Church had originally contracted to run some $14 million worth of WQTV's regularly scheduled programming, which consisted of reruns of such shows as *Star Trek*, *Kojak*, *Charlie's*

Angels, and *The Addams Family*. The Church's decision to switch the channel to public service programming several years later—hardly surprising considering that Scientists all over the country were outraged by what they considered the vulgarity of WQTV's lineup and by the frequent pharmaceutical and other medically related advertising that accompanied it—lost approximately $7 million of that $14 million.

But the Monitor Channel, which aired on WQTV, was not, in the minds of many members, a significant improvement. It had little in the way of religious programming, and much of its serious-minded fare nonetheless managed to offend the faithful. Dr. Herbert Benson, the cardiologist noted for his theories on the placebo effect and "the relaxation response," was featured on one show, much to Scientists' horror; another roundtable show focused on the accomplishments of Harry Hay, a gay activist. Scientists would later point out, reasonably enough, that this was a strange programming choice for a church that, not that long ago, had fired two employees for being gay. Jack Hoagland and Netty Douglass signed a $10,000-a-month contract with the comedian Mort Sahl, a particular favorite of Hoagland's who entertained at a party celebrating the fortieth wedding anniversary of Hoagland and his wife.[73] Sahl was to appear on several Monitor shows, as well as something called *Weekend with Mort;* many Scientists could not understand what this aging satirist—who was not a Scientist—was doing on their channel.

But the biggest problem faced by the Monitor Channel was its general lack of purpose. The Church seemed to have trouble finding enough ways to fill the hours. One show, *50 Years Ago Today*, featured its host, Lincoln Bloomfield, an M.I.T. history professor who wore thick glasses, paging through old library volumes of the *Monitor*, from which he read. *Today's Monitor* focused, as one might guess, on that day's newspaper; it employed a host interviewing "the disembodied voice of a correspondent . . . as stills of the article were occasionally flashed on the screen."[74]

The fears of the membership were exacerbated by the increasing press attention focused on the Church's investment in its media projects, much of the coverage questioning how the Church could sustain such heavy expenditures. In September 1990, a year before the launching of the Monitor Channel, *Forbes* magazine had run an article, "Netty Douglass' Impossible Task," that skeptically examined the Church's revenues and losses. Over the previous year, *Forbes* pointed out, *World Monitor* production costs were $20 million while the program earned only $4 million; *World Monitor* magazine had lost $5.5 million; the Boston channel WQTV

$10 million; and the newspaper $11 million. Programming for what would become the Monitor Channel had cost $10 million, with another $14 million for purchase of a satellite transponder and construction of its earth station.[75] In all, *Forbes* noted, "programming operations will cost $30 million but will produce less than $10 million in revenues."[76] This did not include the $38 million that the Church was investing in its shortwave radio or the cost of its national radio broadcasting. To offset these costs, the Church then had roughly $70 million left in its unrestricted funds.

The numbers were incredible, but none of those at the Church who were interviewed seemed to realize the gravity of the situation. Harvey Wood told the reporter, "I'm not beleaguered. I'm so excited about where we are I can't stand it." Confronted with the numbers, Wood advised the reporter to "think through the Gideon story" in the Bible and said, "Dollars and numbers mean everything. But they don't to us. We sure don't measure our strength that way."[77] The piece ended with a projection of doom for the Church's investments:

> The day is fast approaching when Netty Douglass will find that she can no longer run over or around the central unanswered question: How long can a nonprofit institution with a public service philosophy afford to ignore the unforgiving laws of the marketplace?[78]

The piece was prophetic. Indeed, the Church had already been forced to borrow $15 million from its pension fund in April 1989—retirees were told that the account was "overfunded"—and another $25 million from the same pension fund in April 1991 in order to keep financing its operations. But Netty Douglass, although well aware of the borrowing, seemed as oblivious as Harvey Wood to what it portended. She responded with a letter to *Forbes*'s editor that betrayed the hubris behind the whole enterprise: "One of us is wrong, and we're pretty sure it's you!" she wrote. "Since you've granted us so little remaining time, we have a terrific idea. This is an invitation to your correspondent and editors to have lunch with us here in Boston this time next year and the following year. The only entertainment will be to re-read your article aloud; and the menu will be *corbeau* under glass."[79]

The Church members who were dubious about the Church's media investments might never have become as organized or as vocal in their opposition if Jack Hoagland had not unearthed that controversial old chestnut, Bliss Knapp's *The Destiny of The Mother Church.*

Knapp, a popular Christian Science lecturer and teacher in the early years of the movement, had deified Mrs. Eddy in his book, which was partly a memoir about his family's work for the early Church and partly theological instruction for Scientists regarding the "divinity" of their Leader. When he asked the Church to publish the book in 1948, he received a stinging letter of rejection instructing him not only to withdraw the copies he had placed with the Library of Congress but to destroy the plates that had been used to print them. Knapp had committed the ultimate Christian Science faux pas, asserting that Mrs. Eddy was personally on a par with Jesus, and he had failed to coat this observation in the vaguenesses and obfuscating rhetoric that made such conclusions acceptable to the Church. The Board's objections to Knapp's views seem like theological hairsplitting to an outsider, since the Board members, in their pamphlet "Mrs. Eddy's Place," came within a hairbreadth of claiming divinity for their Leader. Even their letter of rebuke to Knapp is full of grandiose statements about Eddy, whom they describe as a "feminine consciousness" who "by her works exemplif[ied] in human experience the Motherhood of God, as typified by the Woman of the Apocalypse."[80] They asserted the "divine right" of both Jesus and Eddy "to be acknowledged in their respective spheres as the highest human corporeal concepts of the divine idea."[81] Eddy and Jesus, they also noted, were "the two most transparent sources of spiritual light the world has ever known."[82] Knapp, however, stepped over some invisible line by suggesting that Eddy was known to God personally, along with Jesus, and that she was "ruler over the gates, by which we enter the Holy City," a view sharply at odds with the generally amorphous Christian Science conception of the afterlife.[83]

Knapp died in 1958, his sister-in-law, Bella Mabury, in 1964, and his wife, Eloise, in 1973. After their deaths, it was clear that the Board's letter had goaded Knapp for the rest of his life. It was also clear that he had learned a thing or two from Mrs. Eddy about leaving a legacy that would live on after him. His wife and her sister came from a wealthy California family, and in both women's wills—which he had helped to draft—Knapp dangled millions of dollars of temptation before the Church. As Mrs. Knapp wrote in letters to her attorney, "I want all possible pressure put on The Mother Church to publish Mr. Knapp's book."[84] She also commented, tersely, "Money talks."[85] According to the wills, if the Church published the book by 1993 and "prominently displayed" and sold it as "authorized literature" in "substantially all" of its reading rooms, the Church would inherit the Knapp-Mabury millions.[86] If it did not, everything would go to Stanford University and the Los Angeles County Museum of Art. By 1990, the combined legacies were worth more than $90 million. By the spring of 1991, the grand schemes by which the Church would turn its face to the world had nearly bankrupted it, and Jack Hoagland and Harvey Wood, as representatives of the Christian Science Board of Directors and Publishing Society, reached out and took the bait Bliss Knapp had left for them.

The Church had considered cashing in on the Knapp millions before. In 1973, suffering from the combined effects of a severe recession and the cost overruns of its elaborate Church Center, the Church found itself, in the words of Board member Otto Bertschi, "in a stringent situation" financially.[87] That year, the Board voted on whether to publish *Destiny* and obtain the money from Eloise Knapp's estate (then some $20 million dollars). And once again, the Board rejected the book, as their forebears had twenty-five years earlier, agreeing that it "contained points which were sharply contrary to Christian Science as taught by Mary Baker Eddy."[88]

In 1977, Peel published the last volume of his biography of Eddy, which sought to marshal all of Eddy's remarks about Revelation; his interpretation of these remarks was that Eddy had authoritatively denied that she was prophesied in the Bible, a key point with Knapp.[89] A year later, Lee Zeunert Johnson, the Church's archivist for nearly thirty years and a friend of Peel's, completed a new review of archival material on the subject, requested by the Board; he, too, concluded that Eddy had not identified herself personally with the prophecies of the Book of Revelation. On the basis of this review, the Board quietly withdrew the pamphlet "Mrs. Eddy's Place," the contents of which were quoted verbatim in Knapp's book, from circulation in Church reading rooms. Expressing a similar distaste for Knapp's views in 1987, the Board at first refused to consider the actor Robert Duvall as a potential narrator for a new Church-produced video documentary about Eddy's life, solely because his parents had studied Christian Science with Knapp. They relented only when no other suitable narrator could be found.[90]

But in 1991, with the Church facing imminent bankruptcy, *Destiny* suddenly didn't seem so abhorrent to the Christian Science Board of Directors. They met on April 22 with the Publishing Society Trustees to consider creating a series of biographies of Eddy, to be entitled the Twentieth-Century Biographers Series. Among the first books to be pub-

In 1899, Christian Science Reading Rooms began selling the "Mary Baker Eddy Souvenir Spoon," featuring Eddy's likeness, her signature, a picture of Pleasant View, and on the back of the handle, the words "Not Matter but Mind Satisfieth." Eddy asked that each Scientist purchase at least one. (Photograph by Aniko Horvath)

MONUMENT AT BIRTHPLACE OF MARY BAKER EDDY, BOW, N.H.

The granite pyramid marking the birthplace of Mary Baker Eddy, in Bow, New Hampshire, dedicated on the centennial of Eddy's birth in 1921 and subsequently donated to the Mother Church, was dynamited in 1962 on the order of the Board of Directors. (From Martin Gardner, *The Healing Revelations of Mary Baker Eddy*, Amherst, N.Y.: Prometheus Books, 1993. Reprinted by permission of the publisher.)

An aerial view and an interior of Arden Wood. This sanatorium of the Christian Science Benevolent Association on the Pacific Coast, in San Francisco, offered Scientists a luxurious and medicine-free setting for Christian Science study and treatment.

Lady Nancy Astor
during her illness
before she discovered
Christian Science

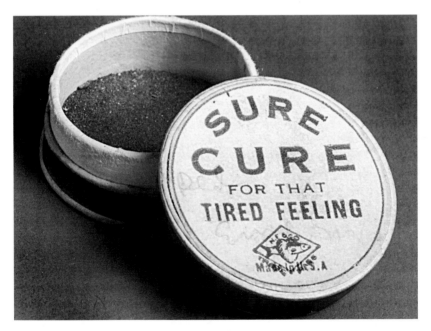

Pill box by Joseph Cornell, the eccentric and reclusive American artist, famous for his shadow boxes, who converted to Christian Science in his twenties (Collection the Joseph Cornell Study Center, National Museum of American Art, Smithsonian Institution. Gift of the Joseph and Robert Cornell Memorial Foundation.)

Bliss Knapp, the author of a controversial book deifying Eddy, which nearly brought down the Church (Harvard University Archives)

This book is not An Authorized Christian Science Publication

Christian Science Class Instruction

Arthur Corey

☆

THE FARALLON PRESS ☆ 58 SUTTER STREET
SAN FRANCISCO 4, CALIFORNIA, U. S. A.

EXPLAINING A CONTROVERSY
ABOUT THIS BOOK

The publisher states, "the only publication of Christian Science Class Instruction authorized by a duly accredited practitioner in good standing with the Church, this book is of value not alone to the follower of Mary Baker Eddy, but it is important to the historian, the philosopher, the critic."

In a letter dated November 13, 1945,, Mr. William D. Kilpatrick, manager of committees on Publication, the First Church of Christ Scientist in Boston, Massachusetts states that many of the authors' and publishers' claims are false. "For example the author speaks of "the bequest of full and accurate transcriptions of the private teachings of our most eminent Scientists" and then lists the names of certain teachers. Many of those listed have declared without qualification that Mr. Corey's statement is false; that full and accurate transcriptions of their private teachings have not been made available to anyone,- least of all Mr. Corey. Mrs. George Shaw Cook, and Mrs. Albert Gilmore have vigorously denied that accurate transcriptions of the teachings of their late husbands have ever been available. All these people have written to Mr. Corey and to the publishers protesting the deceptive and unauthorized use of their names in his book."

The book jacket containing the publishers claims and the correspondence referred to above are on file in the office of the librarian.
The Public Library of Des Moines, Iowa

The Church's press office, known as the Committee on Publication, encouraged public libraries to warn readers against such heretical books as Arthur Corey's *Christian Science Class Instruction*. (From Charles S. Braden, *Christian Science Today: Power, Policy, Practice*, Southern Methodist University Press, 1958)

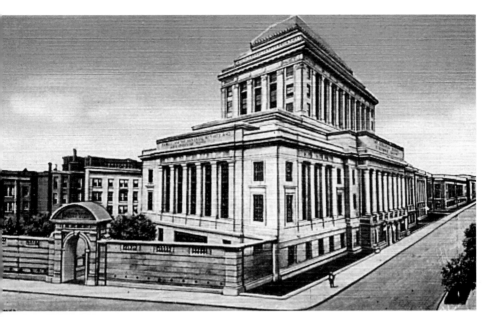

The Christian Science Publishing Society building, constructed between 1932 and 1935, where the *Christian Science Monitor* and the Church's religious periodicals and books originate

Housed in the Church's Publishing Society building and completed in 1935, the one-of-a-kind walk-through Mapparium, a stained-glass globe thirty feet in diameter spanned by a glass bridge, is meant to symbolize the worldwide reach of Christian Science. (Corbis)

Gilbert C. Carpenter, a Christian Science practitioner who had served as one of Eddy's secretaries, and his son, Gilbert C. Carpenter, Jr., a practitioner and teacher of the religion, were driven from the Church for circulating some of Eddy's more esoteric teachings.

Nathan Talbot, the Church's controversial manager of the Committees on Publication during most of what were called "the child cases" (Pat Greenhouse, *The Boston Globe*)

In 1969, the annual meeting at the Mother Church was disrupted by black protestors demanding "reparations for 520 years of slavery."

Rita Swan holding a picture of her son Matthew, who died in 1977 after Christian Science treatment failed (photograph from Chris Kleponis)

In 1989, after pleading no contest to reckless endangerment in the death of her twelve-year-old daughter, Ashley, Catherine King held a press conference at which she displayed cardboard cutouts of her daughter. (Michael Meister, *The Arizona Republic*)

Ginger and David Twitchell, right, consult with their defense attorneys, Rikki Klieman and Stephen Lyons, during their trial for manslaughter in 1990. (Janet Knott, *The Boston Globe*)

The Extension of the Mother Church dominates the fourteen-acre Christian Science Church Plaza in Boston's Back Bay, which was redesigned during the 1960s by the firm of I. M. Pei. On the left is the Publishing Society building. Behind the high dome of the Church rises the twenty-eight story Administration Building. (Rob Crandall, Stock Boston)

lished in the series was Bliss Knapp's. A few days before that meeting, the Church made the second of its transfers from its pension fund, shifting $25 million to its nearly exhausted "unrestricted fund," from which most bills for the television projects were being paid. On April 26, Jack Hoagland met in Los Angeles with the trustees for the estates of Bliss Knapp, Eloise Knapp, and Bella Mabury to discuss how the Church might satisfy the conditions for distribution of the trusts. Two days later, the Publishing Society voted to publish Destiny. Jack Hoagland was designated the sole representative of the Board of Directors and the Publishing Society in working out a legal agreement with the trustees of the Knapp and Mabury estates.

Unfortunately for the Board, the abrupt about-face concerning the Knapp book in the spring of 1991 could not have been worse timed. Only that January, the Board had sent a letter to all Christian Science teachers explicitly instructing them not to use "Mrs. Eddy's Place." Therefore, the attempt to pass off Destiny as a mere "biography" that contributed to a fuller understanding of Church history rang particularly hollow; only a few months before Destiny's publication, the Board had denounced a chief element of the book's conceptual foundation.

In June, at the Church's annual meeting, the Board announced the publication of the Twentieth-Century Biographers series, but neglected to mention that Destiny would be among the books published. At the end of July, an unsigned letter was sent to members of the Mother Church leaking the news; several days later, Netty Douglass sent a memo to managers at the Church Center and to Christian Science teachers announcing its publication and describing the series as offering "an expanded shelf of biographies" of Eddy.[91] The "expanded shelf" rationale would appear over and over again in the publicity materials and in explanations proceeding from the Church.

Early in 1991, not long before the Board had taken up the question of Destiny, Lee Johnson, who was known to disapprove of the Knapp book, was laid off from his job as Church archivist because of what he was told was a "reorganization" of the department. In August, having heard that the book was being rushed into print, he entered the fray, writing a seven-page letter to the Board asking them to reconsider its publication. Several weeks later, having received no reply to his letter other than a phone call acknowledging its receipt, Johnson sent copies of it, with a cover letter explaining the circumstances, to every Christian Science reading room librarian and branch church executive board, warning them that the blasphemous book was on its way. Johnson took particular note of Eddy's

372 | GOD'S PERFECT CHILD

bylaw in the *Manual* prohibiting Church members from buying, selling, or circulating "incorrect literature" on Christian Science. He referred to her prophetic warning: "A departure from the spirit or letter of this By-Law involves schisms in our Church and the possible loss, for a time, of Christian Science."[92]

This was no small matter to Christian Scientists. Over the years, many other Christian churches had come to accept Christian Science into the fellowship of Christianity. (It is still rejected by some fundamentalist groups.) Foremost in the minds of those who opposed publication of the Knapp book—including the Boards that had rejected it for over forty years—was the fear that they would find, in the Church's embrace of Knapp's open deification of Eddy, renewed reason to reject Christian Science as a cult.

It did not take long for wind of this massive doctrinal dispute to reach the offices of the *Boston Globe*. On September 18, 1991, Joan Vennochi opened her regular *Globe* column, "The Private Sector," with the following: "Judas sold out for just 30 pieces of silver. Today leaders of the cash-strapped Christian Science Church could be betraying their founder for a much bigger payoff . . . by publishing a book whose teachings the church has long considered unacceptable."[93]

Jack Hoagland was nearly apoplectic after the appearance of the "Judas" column, which featured his name and a photograph of him. He fired off a letter to the *Globe*'s editor that began with a classic passive-aggressive disclaimer—"My concern is just as much for the Globe as for ourselves"—and worked up to quoting Joseph N. Welch's famous denunciation of Senator Joseph McCarthy ("Have you no decency, sir, at long last?") and predicting that the *Globe* itself would soon face a "steep decline in revenues and the possibility of changes in ownership."[94] But none of Hoagland's rhetoric could turn back the wave of press coverage that was about to break over the Church.

The day the *Globe* column appeared, the wire services picked up the story. Throughout the rest of September and into October, the *New York Times*, the *Los Angeles Times*, the British *Independent*, *Time* magazine, and a host of others ran detailed accounts of the Knapp controversy and the financial peril faced by the Church, as did CNN. Clark Morphew, a minister and columnist for the *St. Paul Pioneer Press*, wrote a piece entitled "Church That Can Be Bought Is Poor Indeed," which was picked up in syndication and ran in Knight-Ridder papers all over the country. Most of these articles contained quotations from the Church's leading dissident, Stephen Gottschalk.

Gottschalk, a child of the Church, has dedicated his life to Christian Science. At Berkeley in the 1960s, he wrote a doctoral thesis that was eventually published (1973) by the University of California press. *The Emergence of Christian Science in American Religious Life* remains one of the few academic works about the historical context of the religion, which it follows up to the point of Eddy's death. After graduate school, Gottschalk taught at the U.S. Naval Postgraduate School in Monterey, California, but he soon found his way to the Christian Science Church Center. He spent nearly thirteen years working for the office of the Committee on Publication, first for Allison Phinney, Jr., and then, when Phinney left to become the editor of the Church's religious periodicals, for Nathan Talbot. With Talbot, Gottschalk had some differences.

To begin with, Gottschalk, a plump, deceptively cheerful man with a wicked tongue, was frustrated by the Church's approach to dealing with the "child cases." He felt that the response of the Church to bad publicity was clumsy and heavy-handed, and that it needed to do a better job of communicating with its own members. He felt strongly that healing in the movement had fallen off since Eddy's day and that Scientists needed to rededicate themselves to improving this crucial skill. He was also of the opinion that it was a grave mistake for the Church to portray itself as an alternative health-care system, instead of simply a religion, a policy which made the Church vulnerable to charges that its "system," such as it was, observed none of the state or federal regulations that governed the medical system. While Nathan Talbot was a follower of orders, invariably obedient to his directives from the Board, Gottschalk was essentially an academic, someone who wanted to discuss and debate. But discussion and debate are not hallmarks of the Christian Science way of life and have long been actively discouraged at the Church Center.

In 1989, Gottschalk told a reporter for *U.S. News & World Report* that "the church is becoming as worldly as the world it is trying to reach"; he was soon to feel its wrath.[95] Several months later, on March 1, 1990, during a departmental meeting at which a statement from the Board calling for "unity" and the calming of dissent was read, Gottschalk made his own statement. He read an open letter to his coworkers questioning the Church's "suppression of serious and responsible dissent."[96] He made no specific demands and expressed respect for both the *Manual* and the Board itself, but he also made the argument that Church members and workers had the right to express their views:

> The fact remains that nothing in the *Manual* or in Mrs. Eddy's continuing leadership requires, justifies, or permits repressing responsible expression of divergent viewpoints on church directions and policies. Far from being inherently divisive and detrimental to unity, allowance for such expression helps build unity. It gives members, including those of us at The Mother Church, needed assurance that their point of view is being taken account of, and that even if decisions go against them, they are not to be driven into silence or regarded as disloyal.[97]

It was a brave stand, considering that the Board had always displayed absolute intolerance for criticism of any kind, and it cost Gottschalk his job. The day after Nathan Talbot read Gottschalk's letter, he ordered him to go home and pray about his "attitude," and he was placed on indefinite leave. He stayed home for a month and then returned to tell Talbot that he could not agree to be silent. They failed to reach a compromise, and so a "parting of the ways," as Gottschalk calls it, occurred. By the end of 1990, five of Gottschalk's associates had also resigned or been fired. The Church-produced 1988 video documentary about Eddy's life, *Mary Baker Eddy: A Heart in Protest*—a lavishly sympathetic portrait prepared, in large part, by Gottschalk—was pulled from the shelves of reading rooms in 1991, despite having won several awards and critical acclaim. Many of those who had appeared in it—Kay Fanning, Lee Johnson, Gottschalk himself—had fallen afoul of the Church administration.[98]

An atmosphere of fear and repression had reigned at the Church Center for several years, particularly since the furor at the *Monitor* in 1988. Many of those who worked at the Center feared both for their jobs and, increasingly, for their religion, as rumors of bankruptcy and the publication of the Knapp book spread. Virginia Harris, the Clerk of the Church, whose job it is to serve the membership and respond to their questions and concerns, had personally contacted those suspected by the Board of subversive activities and officially rebuked them for not being supportive of it.

Ultimately, the Clerk seemed to be using the punitive powers of the Church to suggest the threat of both job termination and excommunication. Diane Manuel, a freelance writer for the *Monitor* who had once been an editor and staff writer there, was called by Harris at the beginning of 1989 and told that it had come to the attention of the Board of Directors that she had been "circulating literature."[99] Harris also read her the bylaw from the *Manual* concerning "Working Against the Cause," a crime punishable by excommunication, and told her that Mrs. Eddy had "pretty stiff things to say" concerning those who spread "incorrect literature."[100] The literature Manuel had been circulating, as she pointed out in a letter she sent to Harris after their phone conversation, consisted largely of documents and memos that had come from Church departments. "If these are 'not supportive of the church,' " she wrote, "I would suggest that I am not to blame. I did not originate them, nor have I tried to interpret them. I only xeroxed them."[101] She scolded Harris right back for defending the "closed climate" at the Church Center and for asserting that Board members have "an entirely different perspective that no one else has—an overall sense, a direction, a vision."[102] In response to the notion that Board members have a visionary role, a suggestion nowhere supported in Eddy's own writings (indeed, Eddy reserved that role for herself), Manuel wrote, "If the Board's 'viewpoint' is indeed founded on truth, then Board members shouldn't feel threatened or challenged in any way by the circulation of materials which merely confirm the facts surrounding their decisions."[103] Manuel also felt it necessary to assert that her opinions were hers alone, lest they endanger her husband's job at the *Monitor.*

In many ways, the disciplinary calls and letters going out to Church workers and members were in keeping with the Church's history of accepting rumors and anonymous accusations against Christian Science teachers and practitioners and acting on them. But when the dissidents themselves adopted anonymity and discovered in it a powerful tool of dissension and disruption, Church bureaucrats found themselves at a loss. Virginia Harris was rewarded for her loyalty to the Board: she was elected to it in December 1990.

Church authorities could not have picked a fight with a worse foe than their own members. Christian Scientists are generally well-educated, affluent, and influential. A number of those who were at first suspicious and ultimately incensed by the financial and moral direction of the Church as it entered the 1990s were judges, lawyers, accountants, businesspeople, and, of course—given the number of disaffected former *Monitor* staffers—reporters, writers, and editors with connections to the press. Some had a sophisticated understanding of the Church's financial history and present condition; some of them had worked at the Church Center in positions of authority, at the offices of the Committee on Publication and the

Committee on Finance, and as legal counsel; some had substantial clout with the Church itself, having donated to it thousands, if not millions of dollars.

In the summer of 1991, shortly after the editorial standards for *Monitor* journalism had been disseminated to the mostly non-Scientist television staff, an anonymous letter addressed to "All Non–Christian Scientists in Monitor TV and Radio Broadcasting" was placed in mailboxes. Signed "Christian Scientists for Honesty," it pointed out to the non-Scientists that, regardless of what they had been told by those in charge, their jobs were essentially religious, not secular. It directed them to look at the *Manual's* determination that the Publishing Society for which they worked was designed "for the promotion of the interests of Christian Science."[104] It advised them that there was "major opposition" to the downsizing of the print *Monitor;* that their salaries and the financial support for the programming they worked on were drawn from rapidly dwindling funds; and that "it would probably be very unwise to bank too much on the indefinite continuation of your present employment."[105] The Church responded with angry denials, but the damage was done, and seeds of doubt had been sown in a number of non-Scientist minds. In October 1991, disillusioned by the transfer of resources from *World Monitor* to the Monitor Channel and sensing that the entire television operation was beginning to crumble, John Hart left as anchor of *World Monitor,* and the Discovery Channel, itself disillusioned by the show's failure to attract an audience, promptly dropped it.

That same summer, another letter, signed only "Some of us in the newsroom," was sent by a group of *Monitor* reporters in Boston to their counterparts in the Washington, D.C., bureau. Bitterly acknowledging that "the Monitor is really gone" and that those of its reporters who were left were reduced to "playing journalistic 'doll house' with what used to be a great newspaper," it was alternately furious and hopeless as it noted the dishonesty of projections made and the dwindling resources available: "We sit here daily witnessing the fact that the present management team hasn't been honest with us and hasn't met a single management goal on time or in the way promised. They can't even make ends meet without draining the retirement fund two weeks before the end of the fiscal year (twice now)."[106] The letter ended with a long series of self-loathing questions— "Some of us . . . wonder why we aren't more honest and brave, why we don't have more self-knowledge, why we aren't less deluded"—that went to the core of the late-twentieth-century Christian Science crisis of faith and the still-unfolding, painfully apparent failures of the Church.[107] The

Church's two great, grandiloquent attempts to project itself into the future—the building of the Church Center and the foray into television—had nearly bankrupted it and had proved to be singularly ineffective ways to impress the faith's importance upon the world and attract people to its theology. The Church that does not believe in the material world was gradually learning that big is not necessarily better.

8. The Facts

Not every dissenter took refuge in anonymity. There was one dissident in particular whom the Church could neither silence nor intimidate, and whose voice was perhaps more damning than any other: United States District Court Judge Thomas P. Griesa. Griesa, as a federal judge in the Southern District of New York, was no stranger to conflict. In 1992, he sentenced real-estate tycoon Leona Helmsley to a prison term for tax evasion, and it was his ruling in 1982 that blocked construction of the Westway development, a vast highway and landfill project in New York City, for violating environmental regulations. Griesa had become concerned about the Church's financial picture starting in about 1986, as he listened closely to the Church's vague pronouncements about its media plans. Throughout the late 1980s, putting together the information given out at annual meetings, the stories beginning to appear in the press, and what he was able to learn from his own sources, he recognized that the numbers did not add up. In late 1988, after the story of the Monitor resignations and downsizing broke, he obtained some detailed figures from Church treasurer Don Bowersock, and wrote two pages of comments in which he concluded that "the Church's financial condition is extremely difficult. . . . This situation is caused by expanding much too fast into a number of very speculative endeavors."[108] He noted that the Monitor's deficit was not "the financial problem"; that the Church could, in fact, reasonably expect to handle that deficit as it had always handled it. "The problem," he pointed out, "is the *excessive number* of . . . activities which have been undertaken."[109]

Griesa was not alone in his concerns. Christian Science businessmen and businesswomen all over the country were aghast at the financial picture, which was becoming clearer as the Church informed retirees in 1989 and again in 1991 that it had borrowed from its own pension fund. After the story of the Knapp controversy broke in the press, Harvey Wood, Jack

Hoagland, and the other authorities at the Church defensively sent sixty thousand to ninety thousand copies of a letter to Church members, explaining the publication of the book and (as events would bear out) convincing only a fraction that their motivation was not venal. The letter, signed by Hal Friesen and Netty Douglass, put the blame for the press coverage and the Church's problems as a whole squarely on the "sad effort of a few individuals"—the dissidents—"to sustain . . . the impression of a deep split among our members."[110]

The Knapp book, it claimed, had been warmly received, which indeed it was: by Knapp's own followers, students, and descendants of his students, who had long felt aggrieved with the Church for rejecting it. But the press was not mistaken in estimating that the number of dissidents were far from few, as Church authorities who had seen the volume of angry mail knew all too well. Friesen and Douglass's letter went so far as to accuse the dissidents of supporting "censorship" for suggesting that the Church should not publish a book it had rejected years ago.[111] They also attempted to portray the Church as a body that "held firmly to the principle of preserving the greatest possible degree of intellectual freedom," an incredible position for an institution that has devoted itself throughout its history to suppressing the criticism of its own members as well as critical attention from outside its walls.[112]

With the book's October publication, Wood and Hoagland had clearly hoped to get the Knapp-Mabury bequests early in the following year, to stave off further borrowing and the ever nearer prospect of bankruptcy. They were disappointed. On February 7, 1992, the other potential beneficiaries of the Knapp-Mabury trusts, Stanford University and the Los Angeles County Museum of Art, announced that they would challenge the disbursement of the money. They argued that the Church had not completely met all the terms of the wills and their codicils, particularly in not having printed the phrase "Authorized Literature" anywhere in Knapp's book. Wood and Hoagland would not be laying their hands on the Knapp millions any time soon.

Two weeks later, on February 25, 1992, the Church nearly came to a halt again, as it had during the week that Kay Fanning and her colleagues resigned. All four senior editors of the Church's religious periodicals—the *Christian Science Journal, Sentinel,* and *Herald*—including Allison Phinney, Jr., resigned together, saying, in a letter issued jointly, "In good conscience, we are unable to continue serving as editors under present board policies."[113] One of the editors, Elaine Natale, had recently told the others of her conviction that the publication of the Knapp book was a tragedy for the Church and had refused to write an editorial justifying its publication; she had thereupon been barred from writing editorials for some weeks. On February 29, 1992, three days after headlines announced these resignations, the *Globe* broke perhaps the most stunning of its many stories on the financial collapse of the Church: "Church Digs Deep for Cash: Christian Science Crisis." An anonymous source within the Church had revealed that its officials had borrowed $45 million from reserve accounts, including an additional $20 million from the pension fund, $20 million from the restricted endowment fund of the *Christian Science Monitor*, and $5 million from the sacrosanct estate of Mary Baker Eddy herself.[114] Confronted with the details, Church officials admitted the truth. The "cash crisis," wrote James Franklin, religion reporter for the *Boston Globe*, "was precipitated by delay in payment of a $97 million bequest the church had expected to receive after publishing *The Destiny of the Mother Church*."[115]

On March 3, 1992, Netty Douglass and Jack Hoagland issued to their employees what would become perhaps their most infamous memo, "Staying the Course," in which they bemoaned the fact that "we are witnessing an all-out assault on the television activities of the Monitor, the purposes of which are not entirely clear."[116] They dismissed the news of their financial disaster: "Spurious reports questioning our financial stability and future prospects are being run as page-one stories."[117] And they insisted that the commitment of the Board and other Church authorities to Monitor television was "unanimous."[118] On March 4, Harvey Wood told the *Globe*, "Our resolve is unwavering."[119] Five days later, on March 9, he resigned from the Christian Science Board of Directors, and the Church announced that it was putting the Monitor Channel up for sale.

That was hardly the end of the story. In some ways, it was just a beginning. With Wood's resignation and the tacit admission that the Church could not continue to fund its cable channel came insistent demands by the membership on a scale that the Church had never before seen for further resignations of all of those involved in the failed enterprises—including the entire Board of Directors—and for full disclosure of information about the Church's spending and decision-making over the disastrous preceding years.

At the end of March, Judge Griesa faxed a letter to Virginia Harris, now chairman of the Board of Directors, asking for "a full and fair disclosure of the facts," along with a lengthy list of questions that Griesa hoped would be answered at that year's annual meeting in June.[120] He asked for specific information on the deficits of each of the Church's publishing and broadcasting activities; on the Church's internal indebtedness to its various funds, the balances left in those funds, and the interest, if any, that was being paid on those debts; and on the Discovery Channel's termination of *World Monitor* and the revenues earned by that program, among other things. Griesa's letter had been addressed to "Mrs. Harris"; the reply suggested that even in the throes of the most shameful and humiliating crisis of its existence, the Board was still taking a patronizing and unapologetic tone toward its subjects. Addressed to "Dear Tom," Harris's letter asserted that his questions were "inappropriate," and, once again, defensively laid the blame for the failure of the Church's enterprises at the feet of its critics:

> In service to the purpose of this Church, we launched a program of extension of *The Christian Science Monitor*. This plan had every reasonable opportunity for success, and had the capacity to fulfill one of Mrs. Eddy's requirements for the long-range financial health and continuity of her Church. However, the effort to interfere with and even induce the failure of this plan has been long and persistent and has actually brought about the very situation about which you quite reasonably have expressed deep concerns.[121]

Harris, who herself had little business and no judicial experience, saw fit to question Griesa himself: "In writing to you as a fellow member we have a very private concern that the form and even some of the substance of your request may carry with it a question of judicial impropriety. . . . Our affection for you is all that motivates our comment in this regard."[122]

Griesa's response pointed out the fallacy of Harris's logic:

> It has been a source of amazement to me that over recent years some Church officers have persistently sought to pin the Church's problems on certain persons said to be working in opposition to the new activities. . . . All this is sadly misguided. It is the *facts* that are the problem—facts about overspending, deficits, depletion of working funds, and lately the borrowings from the Monitor Endowment Fund, the Trustees under Mrs. Eddy's Will, and the Pension Fund. The reason for the recent front-page stories was the *facts*. If there had been no facts, there would have been no stories.[123]

In April 1992, three respected Christian Science teachers and former lecturers—Margaret Rennie, Nola Cook, and Roy Linnig—took the
extraordinary step of compiling those facts in a one-hundred-page report,
" 'Speaking the Truth in Love,' " that they sent to teachers, practitioners, and branch churches. Unlike the materials and letters circulated by
"Paul Revere" and Reginald Kerry, " 'Speaking the Truth in Love' " was
well-written and well-organized, extensively footnoted, and supported by
exhaustive documentation: over three hundred additional pages of evidence, including Church memos, transcripts of meetings, letters of resignation, press reports, and other materials. It was submitted, its authors
wrote, "in obedience to Art. I, Sect. 9, of the *Manual of The Mother
Church*." This was a reference to Eddy's bylaw stipulating that "it is the duty
of any member of this Church, and especially of one who has been or who
is the First Reader of a church" to inform the Board when any Church officer failed to perform his official duties. If the Board took no notice, the
Manual instructed, then the complaint was to be taken to the Church
Clerk, who was required to undertake an investigation.[124] Margaret Rennie,
whose late husband, David Rennie, had himself been a Board member,
attempted to carry out the conditions of these bylaws, which were based on
the Matthew Code.

Rennie and her two witnesses, Cook and Linnig, had brought their complaint to the Field only after they had sent their report and an accompanying letter of complaint to the Board and asked to meet with the Clerk.
They had encountered delays and refusals to meet. Indeed, there was good
reason to believe that the Clerk would not investigate the Board because
the Clerk, Olga Chaffee, was, in fact, a *member* of the Board.

The report and its accompanying materials were damning. They documented the deterioration of the Church's financial state and the extensive
pattern of dishonesty regarding projected figures on viewership, readership,
and revenues from television, the magazine, and shortwave. They documented the plan to eliminate the newspaper and the eventual cover-up of
that plan; they documented what the authors felt was the secular content
of *World Monitor* and the programming on the Monitor Channel and
WQTV that defied Eddy's stated purpose for the newspaper and the
Church's Publishing Society. The report expressed particular outrage over
the "damaging coverage" on *World Monitor* of the Twitchell trial: "the
result was almost as painful to watch as the trial itself."[125] If the circumstances documented by the Rennie report did not warrant the Clerk's
investigation—and the Board's resignation if "the complaint be found

valid"—it is hard to imagine what would.[126] But the Clerk did not investigate anything, and the Board did not resign.

9. "Schisms in Our Church"

Bliss Knapp's book was poison to the Church. It blackened the reputation of every Board member and every Publishing Society Trustee affiliated with its publication. It pitted branch church members against each other as they struggled to decide whether to display the book, as ordered, in reading rooms. It pitted state representatives of the Committees on Publication against their C.O.P. manager in Boston. It divided the Church against itself. If the Great Litigation was the Church's Civil War, leaving bitter divisions among Christian Scientists for decades, then its Vietnam was fought over *The Destiny of The Mother Church*. There have been no winners.

Jack Hoagland has defended his brief but expensive reign as the media mastermind of the Church, and Susan Bridge, who once worked with him at Monitor Television, has written an analysis highly favorable to him. Her *Monitoring the News: The Brilliant Launch and Sudden Collapse of the Monitor Channel* promotes an elaborate conspiracy theory by way of explaining what went wrong. According to this theory, the *Boston Globe* and its parent company, Affiliated Publications, waged "an undeclared war" on Monitor Television, "determined to retain primacy in New England."[127] Bridge alleges that there were ulterior motives behind the *Globe's* extensive and damaging coverage of the quick rise and disastrous fall of Monitor Television. She suggests that Kay Fanning—who joined the board of Affiliated Publications after leaving the *Monitor* and acquired shares of stock in that company, the value of which was enhanced when the *Globe* was acquired by the *New York Times* in June 1993, a year after the Monitor Channel shut down—was somehow involved in instigating this coverage; she points to the long friendship between Fanning and Tom Winship, a former editor of the *Globe*.[128] Her theory requires readers to believe that the *Globe* intentionally "played megaphone to the [Church] opposition's cheerleaders" and covered the Monitor Channel's failing financial health in order to queer possible deals for the Channel's sale to other regional media companies. With television projects of its own in the works, she surmises, the *Globe* feared local competition.

The glaring problem with this theory, besides the lack of factual evidence, lies in the paranoid interpretation of the *Globe*'s coverage; it is a classic case of blaming the messenger. In fact, the Monitor Channel hardly merits the suggestion that it was a fearsome competitor; its overreaching financial plans doomed it from the beginning. As for the *Globe*, the story of Monitor Television—the near bankrupting of a Church that is a historical institution in Boston, and the schism that broke out among its members over the publication of a blasphemous book—was perhaps the biggest breaking story on a religious issue to come along in that city for some time. As Robert Peel once said, "The hardest impositions to correct are the ones that are true."[129]

The Christian Science Board of Directors, including Harvey Wood and Virginia Harris, has always denied that it published Knapp's book for the money, but that conclusion is virtually inescapable. Judge Edward M. Ross, of the Los Angeles County Superior Court, denied the Church's motion for summary judgment in the Knapp-Mabury litigation on September 17, 1992; this was its last chance for immediate disbursement of the bequests. Judge Ross expressed his own suspicions about the Board's motives when he wrote that the "timing of the publication raises a question of fact in the mind of the Court. Although no new publication on the life of Mary Baker Eddy has come out for years, is it only coincidence that *Destiny* came out as a part of a proposed 15 volume work on the life and work of Mrs. Eddy? Are there really going to be 15 volumes or will the initial 3–4 volumes be all that are published and are these really publications or only a smoke-screen to hide and obfuscate the dissemination of *Destiny*?"[130] That question created "an inference of a triable fact in the mind of the Court," and the case to decide the disposition of the Knapp and Mabury millions was set to go to trial.*

Even after the Monitor Channel was put up for sale, rumors had continued to circulate to the effect that the Church was holding on to its television equipment in hopes of someday returning to broadcasting, but

---

* As of the spring of 1999, a total of eleven books and one videotape biography of Eddy had been published in the series, the majority of which were previously published by the Church or other publishers and had been widely available in libraries and bookstores for years. With the single exception of Knapp's book, much of which concerns itself with theological matters, all the books are biographical works about Eddy and her close associates. Other controversial books that were promised in the series—Adam Dickey's memoir and Hugh Studdert-Kennedy's biography of Eddy, which the Church rejected years before—have not been forthcoming.

two days after the judge's ruling, the Church announced that it would auction off some $8 million worth of equipment, a move interpreted by the
dissidents as the end of the television dream. It was also the end of the
dream of obtaining the whole of the Knapp-Mabury bequests. In March
1993, the Church announced that it was negotiating with Stanford and
the art museum in order to reach a settlement.

A settlement of any kind was not what the dissidents wanted. A group
of Christian Scientists, including Judge Griesa, calling themselves the
Objectors, attempted to oppose a settlement, but a judge ultimately ruled
that they lacked legal standing to prevent it. Steve Gottschalk had donated
his expertise free of charge as a consultant to the attorneys for Stanford and
the museum, hoping that they would prevail over the Church. The dissidents felt that the only solution to the theological dilemma posed by the
Knapp book was its complete withdrawal by the Church and the relin-
quishment of any affiliation with the money. The wills had stipulated that
the book remain for sale in all reading rooms until a full year passed without any requests for it, a condition that seemed to ensure its presence in
reading rooms in perpetuity. But the dissidents derived hope from the fact
that the Church seemed to be in violation of that condition; as of 1993,
nearly six hundred reading rooms around the country—approximately a
third of the total—were refusing to carry the book.

The Church began cracking down on the disobedient. In an unprece-
dented move, the Board refused to reappoint four Committee on
Publication officials—in Colorado, New Hampshire, Australia, and the
Netherlands—because they objected to the publication of the Knapp
book. Robert Shepherd, the C.O.P. who was relieved of his duties in New
Hampshire, Mrs. Eddy's home state, wrote to his fellow church members:

> On my way home from a final visit to the Committee Office in Concord I
> have stopped at Mrs. Eddy's birthplace in Bow. I'm sitting on a stone wall she
> may have played on as a child. . . . I wonder what she would think of the
> things that are going on in her Church today? . . . With only a few excep-
> tions, every faithful Christian Scientist I've known for twenty years who
> worked for The Mother Church has been forced out of service. So I am
> in good company with other CoPs, lecturers, and the dear editors of our
> periodicals.[131]

Since deciding to publish the Knapp book, the Board and other Church
officials had attempted to redefine some critical terms in Christian Science

discourse, notably "authorized literature" and "incorrect literature." In the book's third printing, after it became clear that the alternative beneficiaries to the wills would challenge the Church's right to the bequests on the grounds that they had not met all conditions, the Church inserted on the copyright page the phrase "Authorized literature of The First Church of Christ, Scientist." Heretofore, that phrase had been reserved solely for the works of Mary Baker Eddy. All other books, including biographies, the Christian Science Hymnal, and books on the history of the Mother Church, were "approved books," according to labels printed by the Church itself for use in libraries. But now the Church claimed that Mrs. Eddy's books were not "authorized literature"; they were "Christian Science literature." Anything the Church's Publishing Society published, they said, was "authorized literature," a definition that effectively rendered "authorized literature" meaningless.

Moreover, a number of those who had known Harvey Wood, now a vocal supporter of the Knapp book, declared in affidavits that in years past he had vociferously and repeatedly reviled it. Katherine Fanning, class-taught by Wood, declared she had discussed the Knapp book with him on several occasions:

> In one specific instance, I recall a lunch at the Colonnade Hotel, when Mr. Wood told me about the book Bliss Knapp had written and that, if the Directors would publish it, a great deal of money would come to the church. But, he said that even during the early seventies when the church was in dire financial straits, the Board refused to publish the Knapp book, and that no Board would ever publish it. He explained that the book contained seriously incorrect material at variance with Mrs. Eddy's own writing in her textbook, Science and Health.
>
> Harvey Wood has been my Christian Science Teacher and close friend for over twenty-five years. I have long had a deep affection for him and I find it difficult to understand his drastic change of position on the publication of The Destiny of The Mother Church.[132]

Rushworth Kidder, a former reporter, editor, and columnist for the Monitor, declared that Wood had told him that Knapp's ideas "were hopelessly and dangerously incorrect."[133] Elaine Natale, one of the editors of the Church's religious periodicals who resigned over the book, explained in her affidavit that, during a pivotal meeting with Wood in which she expressed her alarm about the Church's planned publication of it, "Mr. Wood stated his opinion, in no uncertain terms, that Mr. Knapp's teachings in Destiny were false and wrong. In fact, he went so far as to state that they were 'obviously ridiculous.' "[134] Natale went on to describe what was perhaps one of the first formulations of the new "Christian Science literature" rationale:

> As our conversation progressed, Mr. Wood espoused a theory for the publication of Destiny which I have never heard before—or since. Mr. Wood claimed that there are two distinct and separate categories of material published by The Christian Science Publishing Society—"books" and "literature"—and that only "literature" fell within the scope of Article VIII, Section 11, of the Manual. He then stated that Destiny is a "book" and therefore not "literature" subject to the requirements of this Manual provision.[135]

For his own part, Wood, in his long and defensive declaration, revisited and rationalized many of the decisions he had taken as a Director. He denied having said most of the things attributed to him by Fanning, Kidder, or Natale, and recollected that Fanning had frequently taken the initiative "of voicing strong personal opinions (frequently unfavorable) on management decisions by the Publishing Society that were clearly beyond the purview of her office."[136] As for Natale, she was guilty of "rank insubordination."[137]

In February 1994, the Church, the university, and the museum reached a settlement granting 53 percent of the money to the Church, with the remainder to be split between the two alternative beneficiaries. Such a settlement was barred by the conditions of the wills themselves, but after years of expensive litigation and frustrating maneuvering, the judge approved it anyway. The heirs of Bella Mabury, whose estate contained the bulk of the money, approximately $80 million, spent many months appealing the approval, but their effort was fruitless. The dissidents continued to feel that *"Every day this book is in print under the auspices of our Publishing Society is a day that the Manual is being violated by the officers of Mrs. Eddy's Church."*[138] They were pleased to have at least put on record much evidence suggesting that the Board had acted in violation of the Church's own governing documents, and they continued to hope that some future Board would withdraw the book and return the tainted bequests. But there was no getting around the fact that the Church got the money.

10. A Cancer

One of the most infamous phrases of the Watergate era was John Dean's warning "We have a cancer within, close to the Presidency, that is grow-ing." The bitterest denunciation of the Church's Board of Directors, and one of the most widely reported, echoed that famous quotation. In a May 1992 letter appearing in the *New York Times*, R. Crosby Kemper, the chair-man and chief executive officer of United Missouri Bank, one of the largest banks in the country, called for the Directors' resignations:

> To have naively and cavalierly wasted the good assets of the Church is incomprehensible. You have gambled away the wealth and reputation of the Church without having any good judgment or sense about what your com-mitment involved. Shooting dice with the assets of the Church and chang-ing the Church's mission from a religious one to a secular one is tragic. And then, in order to confuse the real condition of the Church, you have time and time again prevaricated and twisted the truth in your own self-interest. . . . You have failed massively in your mission and all of you respon-sible should excuse yourselves from further leadership. If the Church's principal mission is healing, then I must say you have created a cancer in splitting the church.[139]

Kemper, although not himself a member of the Church, was connected to it through his wife, and had given more than a million dollars to it over the past several years.

In their headlong rush to become media moguls, the Board and its fol-lowers had alienated many of the most renowned and accomplished mem-bers of the Church. Represented by its own attorney, a group of forty businessmen, lawyers, academics, and other Christian Scientists, includ-ing Brooks Wilder, the Church's former general counsel, joined Judge Griesa in his demands for a more detailed financial accounting. In April 1992, after Griesa's exchanges with Virginia Harris, the Church's legal counsel met with representatives from Griesa's group. Also that month, a letter signed by over twenty Christian Science teachers and practitioners, including all four of the former editors of the religious periodicals and one former Church president, was sent to the Board, asking them, "for the sake of our Church," to resign.[140]

That same month, the Church's assistant controller, June Thompson, resigned, citing the Church's failure to uphold Eddy's requirement to behave with "wisdom, economy, and brotherly love." She cited specifically the Church's continued efforts to mislead the press and Church members by concealing the fact that the Monitor Channel's expenses were already running several million dollars over budget so far that fiscal year. "What hides this fact," she wrote, "is that the overbudget portion of programming expense is kept on the Publishing Society's books rather than The Monitor Channel's."[141]

Charles Terrell, of the Church's three-member Committee on Finance, established by Eddy after a scandal in which an official absconded with Church funds, resigned in May 1992, also referring to violations of "God's requirement" for "wisdom, economy and brotherly love." Terrell noted that the Board, in 1980, had virtually crippled his office with a memo reducing its oversight function; the Committee on Finance had previously been required by the *Manual* to "visit" the Board "in case of any possible future deviation from duty" and demand compliance with the bylaws, but the memo reduced its role to approving the bills submitted to it.[142]

Finally, several prominent heads rolled. On April 17, 1992, Virginia Harris announced in a memo that Jack Hoagland was resigning as chairman and chief executive officer of Monitor Television, Netty Douglass as executive producer of radio and television, and Hal Friesen as chairman of the Publishing Society Trustees. The architects of the television fiasco had been sacrificed, but nearly all the Board members remained, to nearly universal dismay. As Steve Gottschalk told *Forbes* magazine in a follow-up to its 1990 article predicting disaster for the Church's television empire, "The people who made the mess shouldn't be in charge of cleaning up the mess."[143]

The annual meeting of 1992 was the most acrimonious of the Church's history. The most detailed, though still partial, financial accounting ever presented at an annual meeting was delivered, but there were no further resignations by Board members. No apology was forthcoming. Although Nathan Talbot, who as Church president was running the meeting, appealed to those present to behave as a unified Church family, there were several outbursts from the audience, which is traditionally never allowed a voice in the proceedings. "Why publish the book?" one woman yelled from the floor. Al Carnesciali, recently named manager of the Publishing Society, then tried to explain the difference between "authorized literature" and "Christian Science literature," as a justification for publishing the Knapp book.[144] His answer was followed by some thirty seconds of applause and booing, until Talbot threatened to adjourn the meeting. Some members were not satisfied by the partial financial accounting. Charles Terrell told Peter Steinfels, of the *New York Times*, that the qualified assurances of the accounting firm Ernst and Young, cited by the Church treasurer, "did not mean that the church is out of danger."[145] And Kay Fanning spoke for the growing ranks of Church dissidents in saying, "Frankly, until there is a complete change of direction, maybe involving a change of personnel, most Christian Scientists won't be convinced that a new day is dawning."[146]

The 1992 annual meeting was so disappointing to those who had hoped for remorse and resignations that it gave rise to the "Mailing Fund," a nebulous nonprofit group with a post office box in Astor Station in Boston. Steve Gottschalk, who had continued to speak out openly, frequently sharing with reporters his knowledge of and perspective on the inner workings of the Church, helped to organize it as a kind of clearing house of information for Church members. The Mailing Fund collated and disseminated information and commentary on the escalating crisis and would ultimately come to represent a movement within the movement. According to an unsigned statement that has appeared in the mailings, "The Mailing Fund has the sole purpose of making available to Christian Scientists accurate, responsible information about their Church." At various points, Steve Gottschalk and others have acknowledged that they are "officers" of the Mailing Fund, but it apparently holds no meetings, and a number of Christian Science teachers, practitioners, Church members, and former Mother Church workers have written pieces for its intermittent publications or signed letters included in them. One of the first mailings included an essay by Judge Griesa, "Democracy in the Mother Church," in which he argued that, although Christian Scientists have no voting rights within their Church, it is nonetheless essentially democratic. Although prohibited by the *Manual* from engaging in "unauthorized debating . . . on Christian Science in public debating assemblies," Christian Scientists have an absolute right to discuss and debate matters that are not religious in nature, Griesa wrote; he was referring specifically to the media activities and other "practical human steps" that the Church had taken.[147]

Like Rennie, Cook, and Linnig's " 'Speaking the Truth in Love,' " the Mailing Fund publications are well-written and well-edited; since the group's first mailing, "Waking Up and Coming Together," a response to what its writers felt were inaccuracies and omissions at the annual meeting, they have been a painful thorn in the side of the Church, providing news items, excerpts from court transcripts, and discussions of Church positions that the Church would rather not have its membership read. As of 1996, the Mailing Fund, which operates entirely on donations, claimed that its mailings reached about 25,000 Christian Scientists, "a substantial part of the working membership."[148]

As of mid-April 1992, the Monitor Channel began airing only reruns, and on June 28, after the Church could find no buyers for it, the channel went dark. It was estimated that any buyer would have had to make a considerable investment in order for the channel to become a viable concern. WQTV was sold to Boston University in 1993 for only $3.8 million, about half what the Church paid for it.[149] The entire television operation would ultimately cost the Church between a quarter of a billion and half a billion dollars, an amount that caused astonishment in the world of cable television. After the Board of Directors confirmed that at least $250 million had been spent on television, the trade publication *Cable World* ran an article entitled "$250M Question: How Did Monitor Spend All That Money?" It said that the "eye-popping figure has cable insiders scratching their heads in amazement" and pointed out that, by contrast, the cable channel Court TV, launched five months after the Monitor Channel, was projected to spend only an estimated $30 million over four years.[150] The president of the not-yet-launched Sci-Fi Channel, Mitch Rubinstein, responded to news of the losses by saying "How much? That sounds impossible. I think these [Monitor Channel] people were good people who deserve a lot of credit, but I don't think they were really that sophisticated about the economics of basic cable."[151]

The *Boston Globe*, in reports throughout 1992 and into 1993, revealed just how unsophisticated Jack Hoagland and Netty Douglass, as managers of television operations, had been. Christian Scientists were shocked to read about the extraordinary travel expenses incurred by television executives. John Palmer, who had replaced John Hart as *World Monitor* anchor, was put up at the Four Seasons Hotel in London at $400 a night; other Church officials flew first-class and stayed in some of the most expensive hotels in the world, including Brown's in London.[152] Over Christmas of 1991, as the Church ran out of working funds and borrowed from its restricted funds, Harvey Wood and his wife flew first-class to Australia and spent four weeks there at the Church's expense. The airfare alone cost $13,000.[153] Church members learned that television consultants had signed enormously lucrative contracts with the Church, one earning half a million dollars annually, plus expenses for dozens of first-class round-trip flights to Tokyo, London, and other cities; sometimes the Church paid airfare for a spouse as well. The Church bought out the contract of one consultant for WQTV operations, Alan Ginsberg, after the station moved to public service programming against his advice, for $900,000, and paid two consultants, Frank McGill and Malcolm Netburn, over a million dollars in the fiscal year ending April 30, 1991.[154] Members also learned that the shortwave station established in Scott's Corners, Maine, a station that could have been staffed by a handful of people working in a very basic facility, had been constructed with an expensive fieldstone fireplace and elaborately decorated with Thomas Moser furniture and oriental rugs.

That Maine station, which cost the Church $8.5 million to build, was sold in 1995 for $5 million to World Voice of Historic Adventism, Inc., an affiliate of Prophecy Countdown, Inc., a small evangelist group that had reportedly split from the Seventh-Day Adventists.[155] Church members were particularly scandalized to learn via the Mailing Fund that Prophecy Countdown was headed by a religious leader and conspiracy theorist known as Elder John Osborne, a supporter of the Branch Davidians (who had also broken away from the Adventists), David Koresh, and Randy Weaver. Osborne was given to denouncing all sects that worshipped on Sundays as "commandment-breaking apostate churches" representing "the habitation of devils, and the hold of every foul spirit, and a cage of every unclean and hateful bird."[156]

Many members were disturbed to hear that Elder Osborne had been given airtime—while the Church still owned the station—in order to conduct fund-raising that would enable him to buy it, and to air an eight-hour program entitled "The Military Takeover of America." As the Mailing Fund pointed out, during that program, Osborne seemed preoccupied with the self-sufficiency of the shortwave station, saying, "WCSN is so totally self-contained. It has a 10,000 gallon fuel tank of diesel fuel and a 750 kw generator. If the power's cut off, we go right up on our 750 kw generator with 10,000 gallons of fuel in the ground ready. . . . it's totally self-contained. . . . It's not God's will to get our station and be thrown off by somebody; it's God's will to own the station." The townspeople of Greenbush, Maine, near where the station is located, were understandably alarmed; the treasurer of the Mother Church comforted them in an ad in the local newspaper by asserting that those behind Prophecy Countdown were "deeply religious people."[157]

Month after month, the disclosures kept coming. *World Monitor* magazine, the monthly that rounded out Hoagland's "complete product line," printed its last issue in May 1993, having lost a total of $36.5 million, never having met its business plan, which called for it to become profitable after only three years and not to exceed a total deficit of $9.5 million.

Outraged Church members passed around copies of the menu of the 1991 Gridiron Club dinner held in honor of that year's Gridiron president, Godfrey "Budge" Sperling, Jr., the *Monitor*'s senior Washington columnist. The dinner was hosted by the Church at a time when its treasurer, who was also in attendance, was dunning members for millions of dollars. It was attended by all the Board members, Jack Hoagland, and Netty Douglass, as well as a host of Washington elite. The guests' lavish perks—each was given a box of chocolates decorated in white chocolate with the *Monitor*'s copyrighted wheat-sheaf design, and Sperling and his wife were presented with a crystal eagle and an all-expenses-paid vacation to the Virgin Islands—were particularly galling. It was also noted by Church members who lived in Boston and were privy to local gossip, that Jack Hoagland's wife was appointed to be a Christian Science teacher in December 1991, at the height of Hoagland's power and that his son-in-law, William Clark, a vice president at Fleet Financial, had been assigned to handle the stock sale of the Monitor Channel, which ultimately came to naught; and that Lincoln Bloomfield, host of the Monitor Channel's lugubrious *50 Years Ago Today*, was a longtime friend of Hoagland's.[158]

Observers within and outside the Church continued to respond to the growing suspicion that Wood, Hoagland, and those in charge had attempted to demonstrate, in the religious sense, that they could found a multimillion-dollar media operation entirely on prayer. A source "familiar with the church finances" told the *Boston Magazine*, "These guys are Christian Scientists. They believe in miracles and healing, which is dangerous in a business thing. They would have run down their pension fund and sold off their real estate. It scares the shit out of you. What they weren't ready to do is say, no magazine, no newspaper—and save $20 million."[159] The humiliation of Scientists was complete. As one highly placed Scientist said later, with some exasperation, "I'm a Christian Scientist, but I don't buy a Cadillac without the means to pay for it."

Finally, the disclosures of financial mismanagement and overspending were so offensive and the apparent position of the-Board-that-refused-to-resign so obdurate that a group of Christian Scientists calling themselves Members for the Manual turned to the law. On December 30, 1993, Elizabeth A. Weaver, a state appeals court judge in Michigan, and Roy D. Varner, a Church member in Houston, Texas, along with Members for the Manual, filed a lawsuit in Suffolk Superior Court in Massachusetts against fourteen present and former members of the Church administration, including Harvey Wood, Virginia Harris, Don Bowersock, Jack Hoagland, and Netty Douglass. The plaintiffs sought no damages, but rather "full financial disclosure and injunctions for Church officers to follow *Manual* By-Laws in future financial management." The "sole purpose" of the suit, they wrote, "is to align policies and procedures of Church officers with the *Manual* and Mrs. Eddy's Trusts."[160]

Over three and a half years of litigation, the suit survived the defendants' 1994 motion for summary judgment: essentially a motion by the Church administration defendants to throw the case out of court. In 1995, the defendants filed another motion for summary judgment on the ground that the court lacked "subject matter" jurisdiction over some of the counts in the complaint. In support of that motion, the Board of Directors submitted an affidavit asserting—in direct contradiction of the "Editorial Standards" issued by Hoagland and Douglass to their employees, claiming no missionary role for Monitor broadcasting—that "the Publishing Society's expenditures for expansion of the Christian Science periodicals into new print and broadcast forms were intended and designed to advance The Mother Church's religious interests and the Publishing Society's mission."[161] The Board's affidavit stated: "Christian Science Publishing activities are and always have been impelled by a religious purpose."[162]

Weaver and Varner did their best to expose all the contradictions in the Church's position, particularly the Board's insistence in its affidavit that it represented "the final ecclesiastical and administrative body of The Mother Church."[163] Like the Board's approving comments on the Knapp book, which so closely followed on their denunciation of it, their affidavit came back to haunt them. In years past, some of those named in the suit had published articles in the Church's religious periodicals that expressly contradicted their now expedient position. They had asserted that the

Christian Science Church had no ecclesiastical hierarchy, a type of structure that Eddy had herself denounced in *Science and Health*.

In addition to the self-contradictory arguments in their affidavit, the Board also issued a number of misleading statements in "legal updates" printed in the *Christian Science Sentinel* and, without qualification, clarification, or attribution, in stories on the case that appeared in the *Christian Science Monitor*. This suggested that the *Monitor* continued to be as journalistically compromised and biased when it came to the affairs of the Mother Church as it had been the day that Katherine Fanning resigned. In their "legal updates" and in the *Monitor*, the Board claimed that the plaintiffs were trying to overturn or alter church government; in fact, they were arguing that the Board itself had violated the bylaws of the *Manual* by interpreting the Committee on Finance as a rubber stamp designed to approve all Board expenditures and by destroying its power to serve as a check on spending.

Ultimately, however, although two state judges ordered the case to trial, none of these issues were heard. On June 19, 1997, in a unanimous decision, the Supreme Judicial Court of Massachusetts—the same court that had granted the Board of Directors its victory in the Great Litigation of 1921—threw out the lawsuit, reversing the decision of the lower state court, on the grounds that the Church is a "public charity" and that Weaver and Varner as individuals therefore had no legal standing to sue. "We consistently have held that only the attorney general can bring an action alleging the misuse of charitable assets," Justice Margaret Marshall wrote in the court's decision.

The Board declared a victory, but, as in 1921, it was a Pyrrhic one. They had convinced the court, once again, not to interfere in their internal affairs. But they had not convinced many of their own members of their moral authority or their honor.

11. "My Child Is Dead"

All in all, the Christian Science Church experienced, throughout the 1980s and into the 1990s, a massive institutional nervous breakdown. It is still, in many respects, in a state of schism. Although no large group within the Church has split off to form its own sect, there is a substantial minority of members who continue to support the Mailing Fund and other so-called dissident groups, who believe that the Board itself disobeyed the bylaws in the *Manual*, and who consider the present Board of Directors to be morally compromised and unfit to govern. Given such a state of affairs, it is impossible to see how this shrinking, shaken Church can pull its members together to perform the one act without which it must perish: attract new members.

Monitor Radio, one of the earliest incarnations of the media dream, survived the longest. Public Radio International had been distributing Monitor Radio to nearly two hundred public radio stations, but, in 1994, when the Church last released fiancial figures on its broadcasting projects, Monitor Radio's programming costs were $9.3 million, only a million of which was underwritten by outside grants and commercial sponsors. The show was often carried early in the morning, and it faced increasing competition not only from National Public Radio but from broadcasts from the BBC, now aired in this country, and from PRI's own programming, which focused, like Monitor Radio, on international news.

In April 1997, the Church announced that it was planning to lease or sell its two remaining shortwave stations and to put Monitor Radio up for sale. In June, no buyers for the radio service having been found, it too signed off. David Cook, who began as a *Monitor* reporter and also served as editor of Monitor Broadcasting, was appointed editor of the *Christian Science Monitor* in 1994. He told the *New York Times*:

I think that Monitor Radio was a worthwhile experiment on the part of the church, since we managed to reach over a million listeners a week domestically and uncounted millions over shortwave. On the basis of just public service alone, it was a good thing to expose our values and our Monitor name.[164]

What Cook left unmentioned was the indisputable fact that those "uncounted millions" had not translated into millions of Church members or even millions of people interested in learning more about Christian Science. Asked how he felt about the demise of Monitor Radio, David Cook said, not recognizing the irony of his statement: "How do I feel? My child is dead and how do I feel? I would say bittersweet."[165]

Part VI

"God Will Do the Rest": Resurrecting Christian Science

"Give your evidence," said the King.
"Sha'n't," said the cook.

—Lewis Carroll,
   Alice's Adventures in Wonderland

1. "God Will Do the Rest"

Mary Baker Eddy's child, her Church, is dying. But unlike the Church's own lost children, who have not been resurrected, Christian Science may well be. It may wear a different face or call itself by a different name, but in American life, extreme self-reliance is here to stay.

The Mother Church, however, finds itself in some peril. Spokesmen for the Church have downplayed the difficulties currently facing the institution, suggesting instead that it is on the brink of renewal. Indeed, the religion itself requires such a response: the metaphysical process of praying to *know* that the Mother Church reflects the perfection of an omniscient God entails a denial of the cold realities of its present situation. As a result, Scientists tend to look away from the numbers and to point instead to recent efforts to promote the sale of *Science and Health*, renovate the Mother Church and other Church buildings, restore the Church's pension plan to health after the disasters of the early 1990s, and redesign and update the *Monitor* and the religious periodicals. The symptoms of decline, however, remain visible and unmistakable.

Subscriptions to the *Monitor* have fallen to 77,000, a decline of some 100,000 since 1988, when Kay Fanning resigned.[1] Only 25 percent of the paper's subscribers—less than 20,000 people—are Christian Scientists.[2] Branch churches are closing at a steady rate of over 2 percent a year. Over

450 churches have been lost since 1987, 48 in 1997 alone. Only some 1,600 churches remain, and some estimates place the number of Scientists at 60,000 or less.[3]

The Church's religious periodicals, whose subscription base has been eroding in recent years, are being smartened up in an attempt to make them more appealing to modern readers; they offer Christian Science bromides on all manner of modern-day perils and problems: "Can God Be Found in Cyberspace?" "Rising Up Against Rage," "Tired of Diets?"[4] In 1998, the hundredth anniversary of the *Sentinel*, the Church substantially redesigned that weekly, expanding it from digest size to a standard magazine format; it may eventually be offered for sale at newsstands. The content has been radically revised to attract non-Scientists. Each issue now includes a spread called "Items of Interest" with ecumenical news about religion and spirituality drawn from other magazines and newspapers; references to Christian Science itself have been minimized throughout. The cover bears a new flag across the top—"Watching the world from a spiritual perspective"—and the words "Christian Science" in the title have been reduced in size, while "Sentinel" has been enlarged. Articles are packaged to touch on self-help themes. "You Can Quit Smoking," reads one headline; "Fearless about Food" is another.[5] Self-help gurus, long spurned by the Christian Science movement, are now front and center, with interviews and excerpts celebrating the work of Larry Dossey and Marianne Williamson.

Scientists are required by the *Manual* to subscribe to the *Monitor* and Church periodicals if they can afford it; the drop in subscriptions indicates both the declining membership and the disaffection of members during the controversies of the 1990s, a trend that may have been alleviated somewhat by the recent changes. In 1997, the *Sentinel* was at a low point, with a subscription base of 44,000; in 1998, after the redesign, it had climbed to nearly 51,000. The following year, a *Journal* editor announced that "for the first time in twenty-four years, the *Journal* has finished the past fiscal year with a higher average circulation than the previous year," but gave no specific numbers.[6]

In honor of the ninetieth anniversary of the *Monitor*, that ailing institution was redesigned yet again. In a 1997 speech before a gathering of Committees on Publication, its editor, David Cook, called for "a healing of the challenges we face at the *Monitor*." These he defined, accurately enough, as "uncompetitive news deadlines, a shortage of highly skilled Christian Science journalists who want to work for the paper, declining circulation, a low level of subscription support from church members, mea-ger advertising sales [the earlier no-ad policy having been abandoned], and decades of multi-million dollar operating deficits."[7] Cook's redesign, directed by the graphic arts team of Milton Glaser and Walter Bernard, ini-tially added special pull-out sections to each day's paper: "Work & Money," "Arts & Leisure," "Ideas," "Learning," and "The Homefront."

On November 25, 1988, just before the paper's ninetieth anniversary, a front-to-back redesign of the paper was unveiled. It introduced a bolder masthead logo and devoted more space to national and international news, although at the expense of placing the editorials, oddly, at the center of the paper and printing the special sections in such a way that they could no longer be pulled out. The Church then began an advertising campaign for the new paper; full-page ads ran in such outlets as the *New York Times Magazine* and the *New York Times Book Review*, positioning the *Monitor* as an antisensationalist organ that offered a "far more accurate . . . brand of journalism."[8]

But it is hard to see how cosmetic changes or the addition of special sec-tions can address the enormous problems now facing a newspaper that no longer even resembles a newspaper. At twenty-four tabloid-sized pages, shorter than any other national paper and most city papers, the *Monitor* reaches its subscribers by mail a day after its publication date and consis-tently reads more like a weekly reader or news magazine, with a focus on light fare. The Church has been proud of the *Monitor*'s popularity with teachers and in classrooms, but that popularity may derive from the fact that much of the paper now seems to be written for a high-school audience with a short attention span. With articles as simplified and abbreviated as they are upbeat, the *Monitor* cannot begin to compete in news coverage, breadth, sophistication, national distribution, or advertising with the *New York Times*, the *Wall Street Journal*, or *USA Today*. It has always been a "small" paper, with a highly selective audience, but it is now practically invisible in influence and readership. It continues to offer occasionally excellent in-depth reporting—as in a recent exposé on safety concerns at Boeing—and thoughtful features. But its approach to the news is scatter-shot, and it has acquired an amateurish and sometimes precious tone.

After the exodus of talent during the television years, the *Monitor* has had trouble finding and keeping experienced reporters. In the paper's finest achievement of recent years, David Rohde won a 1996 Pulitzer Prize for his reporting on Bosnia, breaking the news in 1995 of the discovery of mass graves of Muslims massacred by Bosnian Serbs. He subsequently left the

Monitor for the *New York Times*. As Cook himself described it, the *Monitor* is a "weak, tradition-bound, declining institution," reaching "few people," with the support of "only a fraction of all Christian Scientists."[9] Cook concluded his speech to the Committees by importuning the heavens, noting that "as with any Christian Science healing, there is no human pattern for what we are attempting" and quoting Eddy: "God will do the rest." As far as the future of the *Monitor* goes, it looks as if only God can.

Since 1956, the last year in which it made a profit, the *Monitor* has lost over $300 million, an average of some $7 million a year.[10] *Forbes* magazine, that doubting Thomas of the financial world, reported in 1997 that the *Monitor* has recently been losing $11.5 million dollars a year. "Church leaders," it wrote, "are said to have given the paper until the year 2000 to stop the bleeding."[11] If that cannot be done, the five-day-a-week paper may be cut back to a weekly. The Church is currently promoting the *Monitor*'s website and online subscriptions to the "Electronic Edition" available by e-mail; some Scientists have predicted that, in future, the *Monitor* will cease to exist on paper and appear only in cyberspace. The *Banner*, a dissident newsletter started in 1987, reports that the Church treasurer has projected bankruptcy for the Mother Church in ten years, should the paper keep losing money at its current rate.[12]

There are apparently so few Scientists qualified to fill jobs at the Church Center—many of which must be filled not just by Scientists but by *class-taught* Scientists—that it is now possible to call an 800-number to listen to a recording that lists the many jobs open there. The *Banner* has reported that "consideration has been given to selling the Administration Building," and the Church Center has recently been forced to rent out its buildings.[13] Thirty thousand square feet of the Publishing Society was recently rented out to an ice-making company; the Sunday school building and Colonnade building—which in years past were not available for rent—are now offered as meeting spaces during the week for both secular and religious groups.

But perhaps the most alarming sign of the approaching end concerns neither buildings nor jobs nor newspaper subscriptions, but the human heart of the Church, its healers, without which it cannot function. In 1941, there were over eleven thousand Christian Science practitioners in the United States alone. There are now fewer than two thousand in the world, and the number of practitioners and teachers continues to decline at a rate of approximately 5–6 percent a year. In 1997, the Normal class, offered only once every three years at the Mother Church to those who wish to become Christian Science teachers, had nine students; normally it would enroll thirty. Enrollment at Principia College, which traditionally provides the Mother Church and the *Monitor* with many of its workers, has also dropped, hovering at between five hundred and five hundred fifty students, down from around a thousand in the 1950s.[14]

But, while the numbers look unrelievedly grim, a whole new front in the battle to preserve Christian Science has opened up. Over the past several years the Church has been positioning itself to reap the whirlwind of interest in alternative spiritual healing. Looking beyond their own church walls, Scientists are now hoping to sell *Science and Health* as a form of alternative health care to the millions of enthusiasts in this country and abroad who are dissatisfied with increasingly expensive and technologically complex medical care and who yearn for a holistic and spiritual connection to their caregivers. And finally, after decades without a strong, competent leader, the Church has found a charismatic figure to promote their message. Following in the tradition of Mary Baker Eddy herself, a woman has emerged from the Field to lead the Church forward. Like Eddy, she is both authoritative and emotive, and she has a reputation as a potent healer. A survivor of the Church's media debacle, she has devoted her life to saving Christian Science by trying to bring it into the twenty-first century.

2. *Science and Health* for the New Age

Virginia Sydness Harris was born in Fargo, North Dakota, probably sometime during the 1940s (she declines to state her age, as do many Scientists). Her mother was a Scientist and her father was not; she describes being drawn to Christian Science after having seen "clear proofs as a young child." She attended Principia College for a year but eventually graduated, in 1967, with a degree in social studies and political science, from Moorhead State University in Moorhead, Minnesota, near Fargo. From 1967 to 1968, she worked as a personal assistant to one of President Lyndon Johnson's foreign-language interpreters. Her family has a history of seeking the public eye: her father, under the stage name Ken Kennedy, worked in radio and television for the NBC affiliate in Fargo; a brother has unsuccessfully run for a congressional seat in North Dakota.[15]

During the early 1970s, she became involved in the Junior League in

Birmingham, Michigan, where she and her husband, Reed Harris, who is also a Scientist, were then living, and where she spent time working for child advocacy groups on the issues of child abuse and neglect. In 1976, she was in a car accident and believes that she was healed through Christian Science of injuries she describes as grievous and potentially fatal. After her recovery, she went through a period of reevaluating her priorities and began to dedicate herself to her religion and to becoming a Christian Science practitioner. She subsequently served as a Christian Science lecturer and, in 1985, was invited to assume the roles of manager of Sunday school activities and superintendent of the Mother Church Sunday school in Boston. Within months, she was asked to become Clerk of the Church, in which crucial position she had extensive contact with those in the Christian Science Field.

Harris was elected to the Board of Directors in 1990, while the wave of turmoil generated by the media failures and the Knapp conflict was breaking over the Church. She emerged after that disaster as the only person at the helm of the sinking ship to have a plan; she was soon elevated to chairman of the Board. Turning her back on the Church's failures and its critics' clamoring for resignations from the Board (including hers), she began to take seriously her title as publisher of the Writings of Mary Baker Eddy and devoted herself to selling *Science and Health* to the New Age.

In 1994, under Harris's leadership, the Church published with great fanfare a trade edition of *Science and Health*, designed to be sold in bookstores to the hordes of buyers who, over the past decade, have been snatching up titles devoted to spirituality. Harris took the startling step of introducing new material into the book: a selective word index, referring readers to topics such as "Drink(s), intoxicating" and "Drug(s)," as well as a "Publisher's Note," describing the book as "one of the most effective and enduring books on spirituality and healing."[16] Harris touted the new edition in interviews with the *New York Times* and other major papers, and the Church designed ads that feature photographs of Scientists beside pull quotes, such as this one from "G. Plum": "I had tried everything to achieve satisfaction and fulfillment. I was a psychotherapist, but I still felt an inner hungering. So I took a vacation to try to sort things out. During my time off, I spent a lot of time thinking and reading *Science and Health*." "G. Plum," is, in fact, Giulia Plum, one of the most prized converts in the Church's recent history, a psychotherapist who left her profession to join the Church and become a practitioner; she has been invited to speak at the

Church's annual meeting and the story of her conversion has been featured in the *Journal*.

Over the last several years, the Church has invested heavily in the promotion of the trade edition, running these advertisements—which also feature the tag line "For People Who Aren't Afraid to Think"—in the *New York Times Book Review*, the *Los Angeles Times Book Review*, *Publishers Weekly*, and other publications reaching retailers and the book-buying public. The Church has also implemented a substantial support structure throughout the country of publisher's representatives: Church members who visit bookstores in their region and promote *Science and Health* to managers and retailers. Christian Science lecturers have been dispatched to give talks on *Science and Health* at bookstores.

Church periodicals have kept up a drumbeat of encouragement for "sharing" the book and proselytizing in a way that Christian Scientists never have before. Letters and reports from individuals and branch churches published in the periodicals frequently attest to success at giving away copies of *Science and Health* at book fairs, health fairs, and other outlets. Various promotional campaigns have encouraged Scientists to buy multiple copies of the book and give them away to neighbors, strangers, friends, local hospitals, and anywhere there might be interest. One recent campaign advertised in the *Christian Science Sentinel*—"Multiply the blessings!"— offered a free three-month gift subscription to the *Sentinel* for the recipient of one's choice to anyone who purchased six copies of the book.[17] Christian Science lectures sometimes feature tables stacked with copies of *Science and Health*, free for the taking.

It is difficult to gauge the success of Harris's campaign for "the book." She and the Church have been thrilled by several flattering public accolades recognizing *Science and Health* and its author as important milestones in American feminist and religious history. In 1992, the Women's National Book Association named *Science and Health* one of the "75 Books by Women Whose Words Have Changed the World." In 1995, Eddy was inducted into the National Women's Hall of Fame, along with such luminaries as Elizabeth Dole and Ella Fitzgerald; Virginia Harris appeared at the ceremony in Eddy's stead. And in 1998, a summer exhibit devoted to Eddy, "This Is Woman's Hour," was opened at the National Park Service's Women's Rights National Historical Park in Seneca Falls, New York, in celebration of Eddy's contributions to the women's rights movement.[18]

Not everyone, however, has shared Harris's enthusiasm. Although the

Church has presented a relentlessly rosy picture of the book's fortunes, less sanguine accounts have come from a number of directions. The Mailing Fund and other dissidents have objected to the trade edition on all fronts: to the Church's promotional campaign, run by "a well-known Boston-based publicist who is not a Christian Scientist," to the new "Publisher's Note" and index, and to promotional materials that claimed, startlingly, that *Science and Health*, Eddy's self-proclaimed pastor of her Church, is "non-denominational."[19] In 1995, the *Banner* reported that some branch churches refused to carry the trade edition because of the changes, and that state Committees on Publication had been instructed to obtain the names and addresses of all members in the offending branches.[20] In 1997, it reported that "a reading room in the Midwest received a telephone call from a local teaching hospital requesting that unsolicited copies of the trade edition of *Science and Health* be picked up because hospital staff members and interns had no interest. . . . the package was sent to various hospitals around the country from church headquarters."[21]

Sales figures for the trade edition are difficult to come by. The Church has variously claimed in the national press, as well as on the cover of the trade edition, that *Science and Health* had sold, over its lifetime, eight million copies by 1994 and over nine million copies by 1995. Virginia Harris has repeatedly claimed that *all* editions of *Science and Health* have sold over 100,000 copies per year since 1995. On requesting more specific information from Harris's office regarding the trade edition, I was told by her assistant, Alice Howell, that "we actually are not able to get real specific numbers from the bookstores." Howell repeated the same figure of 100,000 per year in the last several years and added that the book had sold "over fifty thousand copies each year for the last ninety years." When I pointed out that these figures seemed vague and also didn't necessarily add up to "over nine million," Howell said that the trade edition has been "blessing all flavors of *Science and Health*; it's not so much about a particular cover." She said that these were the numbers that the Church "has felt comfortable about sharing," because they "place [*Science and Health*] in the book industry as a best-seller."[22] *Science and Health* has not, however, appeared on the *Monitor*'s own quarterly list of religion best-sellers, drawn from *Publishers Weekly*.

Although no individual Christian Scientist would take credit for the project of revivifying *Science and Health*, Virginia Harris has been the most vocal and consistent promoter of the book. She has given interviews to the press and speeches around the country, at annual conferences of the National Order of Women Legislators and at the Religion Newswriters' annual meeting. She has spoken in places where no Christian Scientist has ventured before, boldly shaking hands with medical doctors and faith healers from other religious traditions who have in years past been belittled or dismissed in Church lectures or publications.[23] She has even been interviewed by Larry King for his book *Powerful Prayers*—which features celebrities talking about prayer—in which he states, "Quite frankly, I think people who won't avail themselves of modern medicine are a little wacko."[24]

In person, Harris is a charming woman, energetic and evidently sincere. When we met in Albuquerque in September 1997, she seemed eager to address my questions and to convey to me the great good that she feels Christian Science has brought to many lives. She willingly described her automobile accident, albeit in somewhat vague terms, struggling to put into words how she had been lifted away from the sensation of dying by her sense of God.

And yet, as we proceeded over the course of a two-hour interview, I was struck not just by a certain vagueness or sense of calculation in some of her answers but also by her lack of engagement with the issues troubling the Church, by a worldview that seemed almost impossibly insular. When I asked her what she thought Mrs. Eddy might have intended by including the various estoppel clauses in the *Manual*, one of the most crucial questions in the institutional history of the Church, she said briskly, "I don't have an interpretation of that. I wouldn't even begin to venture a guess." She would never, she said, "second-guess" Mrs. Eddy.[25]

She said that the Church had no official policy against printing testimonies that included Christian Science failures in its periodicals, although it had not done so for nearly a century. When I asked her why the Church had recently run a notice three times in its periodicals warning its members away from "incorrect literature," she insisted that Mrs. Eddy didn't want censorship in her Church; when I asked her if the Knapp book was "incorrect literature," she said, "No. It's one man's opinion." She referred to the failed media projects as "those dear endeavors."

At one point, the conversation took an uncomfortably fervent turn. I had asked her about the Christian Science view of nature, considering that Scientists believe in the unreality of the material world. She was explaining the "key, key point" that "nothing in Christian Science would do away with the human experience; it's not a rejection; it's seeing man as so much more than that." She suggested a little exercise, asking me to describe my best friend. I threw out some adjectives—warm, caring, smart—on which she seized triumphantly. "See," she said, "you described her qualities, not that she's five feet, six inches tall or weighs a hundred and thirty pounds." I said, "But I couldn't know her if she wasn't five feet, six inches tall." She said, "That's the package, not the person. Man is *more*." She leaned intently toward me, looking directly into my eyes. "Caroline," she said, "*you* are *more* than you appear."

The dissonance between the facts and her answers was most noticeable when I asked her about the child cases. I asked her why, given Eddy's various writings allowing "hypodermics" and other forms of medical care, insulin had not been made available to a Christian Science child like Ian Lundman, who had died without it. "It's not not available," she said. She seemed to have no recognition of the absurdity inherent in her answer. I expressed astonishment, and she went on to say, "Thousands of children are healed every day in Christian Science." I asked why society should trust children with diabetes to Christian Science, when insulin has been proved to control the disease in the vast majority of cases. "But why not?" she said. Of Christian Science treatment for diabetes, she said, "It's as effective, it's more effective. It gets down to a matter of choice: Where does one want to go for healing?" She spoke fervently for the parents' right to choose the kind of treatment a child should receive, emphasizing over and over that all she could do for a parent faced with a choice between Christian Science and medical care, as the head of the Church or as a practitioner, would be to "pray and support them," "to pray with all my heart," and "hope that they would do what is their highest sense of right for that child." As far as hospitals, she asserted that there are "children just begging to get out of [hospital] wards," and that there are "drugs that make those little bodies wrench." "I'm an advocate for children there too," she said.

Denying the realities of Christian Science treatment of children and bemoaning children's suffering in hospitals and under medical care is a standard method of defending Christian Science, pioneered by Nathan Talbot and many former Committees on Publication. But Harris's most original contribution as a would-be savior of her Church, a contribution designed not simply to defend but to revive interest in Christian Science, has been in her appearances before the Harvard Medical School's "Spirituality and Healing in Medicine" courses. Kissed with the cachet of Harvard, Harris's lectures have brought Christian Science before medical practitioners in an amicable, largely uncritical environment and exposed thousands of eager seekers after alternative medicine to Eddy's version of "the power of prayer." Reprinted often in the Christian Science religious periodicals, Harris's lectures have brilliantly married healing-through-prayer to the trendy diction of popular alternative therapies while suppressing the most radical element of Christian Science: its rejection of medicine.

Throughout the 1990s, books on the connection between health and spirituality have sold strongly, leading to intense media interest in religious and medical "experts" who claim to understand the so-called power of prayer. *Publishers Weekly* reported in 1995 that the consensus in the book industry put sales in the religion book market at $1.5 billion, while Christian bookstores reported $3 billion in sales, three times their business in 1980.[26] In 1995, Barnes & Noble increased its number of religious titles by 35 percent.[27] Books on angels have sold in the millions of copies. Devils are also popular, as are God, spiritual quests, and "spiritual laws," one of Eddy's favorite phrases.

In particular, the best-seller lists have teemed with books popularizing prayer and its practical as well as spiritual benefits. Many of these books are by medical doctors: *Healing Words: The Power of Prayer and the Practice of Medicine*, by Larry Dossey, M.D.; *Timeless Healing: The Power and Biology of Belief*, by Herbert Benson, M.D.; *Spontaneous Healing*, by Andrew Weil, M.D.; and *Timeless Body, Timeless Mind*, by Deepak Chopra, M.D. The relentless emphasis on positive terminology that can be seen in these repetitive titles—"healing," "power of prayer," and "timeless" come up again and again—is essentially a popular repackaging of old-fashioned Emersonian self-reliance; but this version of self-reliance is being sold as a nostrum. These books rely heavily on anecdotal testimonials, the stock-in-trade of Christian Science. Publishers have seemed less interested in the miraculous claims of these books than in the millions to be made off them. "As Seen on OPRAH and NOW with Tom Brokaw & Katie Couric!" reads a label on the cover of Dossey's *Healing Words*. Benson has been profiled in *USA Today*: "Medicine Catching Up with Pioneer Benson."[28] Weil has appeared on the television news magazine *20/20* and in numerous other media outlets; Weil's and Chopra's lectures to adoring audiences have been played and replayed on public television, which has hosted a multipart series on alternative medicine. In response to the enormous public interest in prayer, as well as "alternative" therapies ranging from homeopathy to acupuncture to "therapeutic touch"—a method of nursing care that essentially resurrects P. P. Quimby's old-fashioned laying on of hands—in 1992, the National Institutes of Health opened an Office of Alternative Medicine to investigate avant-garde healing therapies. Once again, as it was in the nineteenth-century, the union of prayer and science has proved profitable.

Herbert Benson, a cardiologist and associate professor at Harvard Medical School, acquired his notoriety in the 1970s after the publication of his book, *The Relaxation Response*, which promoted a secular version of Transcendental Meditation. The "relaxation response," as described by Benson, is brought about by the repetition of a word, phrase, sound, or prayer and by the "passive" return to that word or phrase when "intrusive" thoughts occur; it is much the same as the meditation technique taught in the TM movement, but lacks the secret mantra given during TM teaching. Benson's studies indicated that this kind of meditation results in decreased metabolism, heart rate, respiratory rate, a decrease in blood pressure, and measurably slower brain waves.[29] The relaxation response, he claims, has proved to be helpful in treating chronic pain, insomnia, anxiety, hypertension, and depression, as well as the side effects of various cancer and AIDS therapies.

Benson's interest had originally been inspired by studies he performed on Transcendental Meditators who had offered themselves to him as human subjects, hoping that a Harvard researcher's conclusions would help legitimize the TM movement's claims for their technique. That movement was not pleased when Benson went on to steal some of their thunder, essentially suggesting that secret mantras were not necessary to gain the physiological and psychological benefits of relaxing meditation.

The TM movement was not the only institution disturbed by Benson's work. So was Harvard Medical School. Benson says that, early on in his research, friends warned him against "throwing away a very promising career" by pursuing such flaky subjects.[30] After he received a large grant to pursue the mind-body connection, Harvard Medical School faculty members quarreled over whether he should be allowed to accept it. After threatening to resign, Benson prevailed.

Since 1995, Benson has directed a series of well-attended courses sponsored by Harvard Medical School's department of continuing education and by Benson's own Mind/Body Medical Institute, founded in 1992 and affiliated with Harvard and the Beth Israel Deaconess Medical Center in Boston. (Harvard, never an institution known to ignore the bottom line, has apparently recovered from its qualms over Benson's work.) These courses are underwritten, as are an enormous number of research projects examining the mind-body connection, by the John Templeton Foundation, the brainchild of retired mutual fund multimillionaire Sir John Marks Templeton, who, earlier in his life, considered becoming a missionary. The Templeton Prize for Progress in Religion, worth over a million dollars, is now the largest annual cash prize in the world and has been won by Mother Teresa and the Reverend Billy Graham, among others. According to Herbert Benson, the Templeton Foundation is devoted to "studying the scientific basis of God."[31]

Herbert Benson has had an interesting history with the Christian Science Church. He visited an official at the Mother Church sometime during the 1970s to inquire if the Church might be willing to participate in a study of its healing methods, and was turned down. He first met Virginia Harris in the early 1990s, when he appeared as a guest on *Monitor Forum*, one of the Church's short-lived television interview programs. Although one powerful group of Christian Science dissidents condemned Benson's *Monitor Forum* appearance as contributing to "spiritual illiteracy," being offended by his suggestion that prayer could be used as a relaxation technique in conjunction with medicine, Virginia Harris went on to discuss with Benson the possibility of participating in his "Spirituality and Healing" courses.[32] Harris eventually agreed to lecture at the courses on the subject of Christian Science healing practices and has been a fixture at them since their inception, in 1995. (The courses feature lectures on several religious traditions, including Pentecostalism, Judaism, and Islam, among others.) *Science and Health* is sold at the courses, along with copies of the *Christian Science Journal* and other Church publications.

Although the official Church has long refrained from appearing alongside other alternative or minority religious or healing groups, it now eagerly welcomes the opportunity presented by the courses to educate the medical profession and the ever-present media about Christian Science. A variety of articles, interviews, and dialogues promoting the lectures have appeared in the Church's periodicals and in the *Monitor*, and Harris and others have spoken to the press about the Church's participation and encouraged Christian Scientists to attend. The talk that Harris gives at these courses, held every December in Boston and during the spring at a Midwestern or Western venue, is dramatic. In it, she delivers her own Christian Science testimony, about her near-fatal car wreck.

"Twenty years ago, I was in a serious car accident," she says. "I was trapped alone in a mangled car." In the fear, pain, and chaos of the wreck, her thoughts turned instantly to God, to knowing that he "was right there with me," loving her and all the others involved in the accident. "Even in those first startling minutes," she says, "I felt actually cared for; I *felt* God's love." She also felt herself going in and out of consciousness; she says she was the last person extricated from the scene of the accident and taken to "a hospital emergency room," where she could hear doctors telling her husband that they feared her injuries could be fatal.

Within minutes, before being admitted to the hospital or being examined, X-rayed, or diagnosed, Harris, with her husband, decided to call a practitioner. Against the advice of hospital personnel who "didn't think I could survive the injuries," her husband signed release forms and took her home by ambulance to pray and recover. She describes the ensuing events very simply:

> Although I was in pain for about three days, I can honestly say it was a special time, a time filled with earnest prayer by me and my whole family, and with a dear sense of God's love for me. During the second day, however, there was a crisis—a time when I thought I was dying. The mental pull to let go of life was very strong. But I tangibly felt God's love and presence holding on to me, supporting me. I knew this Love was the greatest strength there was—it was the greater attraction—and, in fact, it was the only power that existed. . . . I knew God was my Life! And the pull to let go—to die—diminished. Then it ceased. For me, that was the turning point! I found myself on safe ground. I began to progress. I knew I could be healed.[33]

After this crisis had passed and the threat of death had been defeated by prayer, Harris claims, she recovered quickly and was "fully healed" within two weeks, able to go about her business and drive her three sons to school.

I attended one of the Harvard Medical School Spirituality and Healing courses, held in Los Angeles in March 1997. As scientists often point out, extraordinary claims must be supported by extraordinary evidence. If Harris's testimony were delivered in a Christian Science church, no one present would demand evidence. At the course I attended, whose audience was composed predominantly of doctors, nurses, and self-proclaimed "healers" of various stripes, Harris's talk was enthusiastically received, and no one thought to ask for any verification of her claims. At the course attended by the journalist Chip Brown (he does not give the year), someone did challenge her: "A man who identified himself as a retired anesthesiologist and a Christian said, 'A number of Christian Science patients have come to me with tumors the size of grapefruits, and it seems to me they're in denial about their condition. Their faith isn't working. When do you recommend that a Christian Scientist should see a doctor? Are there any conditions? Compound fractures? Balloon aneurysms?' "[34] According to Brown, Harris refused to specify any illnesses that Christian Science could not heal and insisted that it was effective.

At the time of her accident, which occurred in January 1976, Harris lived in Birmingham, Michigan, a well-to-do suburb of Detroit. Although she was a prominent figure in her community, the local newspaper carried no coverage of her accident, and, since she was never admitted to a hospital, there would be no medical records of her injuries. As with most Christian Science testimonies, Harris's offers no scientific verification that would prove or disprove her claim that her injuries were as severe as she believes or that her recovery was as extraordinary as she implies. This is not to cast doubt on her sincerity which, like most Scientists', is only too evident. It does cast doubt, however, on the scientific methodology behind Benson's courses.

The courses are not characterized by the traditional skepticism of scientific inquiry. Instead, the lectures have the air of an old-fashioned tent revival meeting, with participants whooping, hollering, and rising to proclaim their faith in God and his power to heal. At the course in March 1997, one doctor introduced himself by saying, "I've loved Jesus for thirty-five years," and was rewarded with thunderous applause.[35] An unseemly amount of adulation is expressed for Herbert Benson, with course attendees and lecturers heaping upon him praise and gratitude as if he were a religious figure, a guru of the power of prayer. Benson himself seems almost totally ignorant about Christian Science, its history and its claims. In a discussion I had with him following the course, he refused to comment on the controversy of Scientists' withholding medical care for their children. He seemed to believe that Christian Science does not teach a radical rejection of medicine, saying, "My understanding is that Christian Science practitioners do use medications occasionally."[36]

In addition to the lectures on various forms of faith healing in different religious traditions, the courses feature physicians and scientists who are exploring the now quite lucrative field of mind-body studies. Foremost among these are Dr. Dale Matthews, an associate professor at Georgetown University School of Medicine and a senior research fellow at the National Institute for Healthcare Research (funded by Templeton), and Larry Dossey, an M.D. who has written several books on the "power of prayer."

Both Matthews, a genial primary-care physician, and Dossey, an imposing figure with long gray locks and a rustic manner, are charismatic preachers presiding over the marriage of delicate Spirituality (generic religion) to manly Medicine.

Their presentations rely heavily on personal anecdotes, as well as on good-natured mockery of the God-hating triumvirate of Freud, Marx, and Albert Ellis (a founder of cognitive psychology who has criticized mind-body research). In his talks, Dossey has been dismissive of the need for randomized controlled trials or double-blind studies of the power of prayer. This is a controversial argument for a medical doctor. In 1996, he told *Healthcare Forum Journal:*

> While the double-blind method of evaluation may be applicable to certain alternative therapies, it is inappropriate for perhaps the majority of them. Many alternative interventions are unlike drugs and surgical procedures. Their action is affected by factors that cannot be specified, quantified, and controlled in double-blind designs. Everything that counts cannot be counted. To subject alternative therapies to sterile, impersonal, double-blind conditions strips them of intrinsic qualities that are part of their power. New forms of evaluation will have to be developed if alternative therapies are to be fairly assessed.[37]

Dossey also believes in something he calls "non-locality of consciousness": "the ability of my consciousness to affect your body at a distance, even when you are unaware this is going on, and the capacity of your consciousness to do the same."[38] Dossey believes in absent healing, essentially identical to what is practiced by Christian Science practitioners. He believes in concepts akin to mind-reading (which he calls "telesomatic events") and malicious animal magnetism.[39] Deeply impressed by Christian Science, Larry Dossey invited Virginia Harris to be his guest at a conference called "Spirituality and Health Care," held at the University of New Mexico in Albuquerque in February 1997. (This conference, like Benson's Harvard courses, was underwritten by the Templeton Foundation.) Dossey also included in *Healing Words* (1993) a serious consideration of the "Spindrift" studies, quasi-scientific experiments conducted by a small group of West Coast Christian Scientists and intended to demonstrate the efficacy of prayer. These studies were so controversial within the Christian Science Church—which has always opposed scientific experimentation involving its teachings—that the father-and-son team that headed the experiments, Bruce and John Klingbeil, were censured by the Church, and Bruce Klingbeil, a Christian Science practitioner, was dropped from the *Journal*. Eventually, he was excommunicated.

Conducted by the Klingbeils' Spindrift organization, located in Salem, Oregon, one of the experiments compared the progress of molds grown on the surface of rice agar plates. Some of the molds were subjected to what Dossey calls directed prayer (similar to the practice of "outlining," frowned on in Christian Science, in which a desired outcome is specified) and some to nondirected prayer (prayer specifying no desired outcome). The molds reportedly benefited the most from the nondirected prayer, forming "additional concentric growth rings."[40]

Although Dossey admitted to being "uncertain about generalizing these conclusions to human beings," he did speculate, "after becoming personally acquainted with some of the Spindrift experimenters," that, owing to the Klingbeils being "wonderfully introverted," the nondirected prayer method worked best for them, because it was the most "natural."[41]

Dossey's observation of the Klingbeils, at least, was not inaccurate. The Klingbeils, father and son, were so "wonderfully introverted" that, in 1993, they purchased shotguns and, in a remote area of Oregon, blew their brains out. According to the *Boston Globe*, they were "apparently despondent that their attempt to scientifically prove the value of prayer was not embraced by the First Church of Christ, Scientist."[42]

None of those attending Benson's courses betray the slightest awareness that they are reenacting American religious history and pouring new wine into the old bottles of Christian Science and the various New Thought groups. Only Harvey Cox, a Harvard historian of religion who has also lectured at the courses, seems to have noticed the irony. Cox commented dryly to the *Christian Science Monitor*, in one of its many articles covering the courses and Harris's lectures, that "this interest is a periodic event in American culture."[43]

Resurrecting Christian Science hinges on attracting new members. Harris's lectures at the Harvard courses are designed to do just that. She clearly hopes to position Christian Science as an alternative healing method, to bring *Science and Health* to those who've never heard of it, and to erase any negative images that course members may have absorbed through the press coverage of the child cases. For those proud, old Scientists accustomed to their Church's isolationist past, in which Scientists would never stoop to compare their faith with any other—much less appear at a *medical* course to do so—Harris's methods have come as a rude shock. As one lapsed Scientist suggests, "The Mother Church is living off of estates and property sales of closed churches. . . . The Mother Church has all but given up on the 'field' and will try to recruit new Christian Scientists through their own efforts." Although Nathan Talbot has traveled around the country delivering a Christian Science lecture called "Healing Church Wounds," it does seem that the Church's recent advertising campaigns have been geared toward gathering new Scientists into the fold rather than appeasing old ones; like the ads for the new edition of *Science and Health*, many of the pitches feature photographs of new converts next to quotations explaining how they turned to the faith.

In her appeals for respect from the medical practitioners and New Age aficionados at Benson's courses, Harris has claimed that there is "no shortage of statistical data" proving the efficacy of Christian Science.[44] Benson himself, in his book *Timeless Healing*, has limply raised the questions that inevitably follow from such claims, saying, "It would . . . be interesting to study Christian Scientists who eschew all medical care except dentistry and bone setting. Does faith alone make them well? Is there something to learn from a community that relies on faith, not pills and procedures?"[45]

There is indeed something to learn. Christian Science offers an excellent test case of the consequences of relying on faith, "not pills and procedures." The Church's claims have been accepted as scientific evidence by insurance companies and the U.S. Congress. But what exactly *is* that evidence? What lies behind the thousands of published Christian Science testimonies? Is Christian Science truly a science? Is it as good as or better than medicine? *Can it heal?*

3. Accentuating the Positive

Christian Science makes some of the most extraordinary claims of any Christian sect—indeed, of any religious movement in history. Christians believe that Jesus healed the lame, the halt, the blind. Christians believe that Jesus raised Lazarus from the dead and himself rose from the dead. Most Christians believe in miracles, in divine intervention, in the hope that God hears prayers and answers them. Many pray for healing, and some radical faith healers in the Christian tradition believe in refusing medical care and in throwing themselves on the mercy of the Lord. But only

Christian Scientists believe that they have literally rediscovered primitive Christianity by rediscovering the *exact method and means* by which Jesus healed. Only Christian Scientists believe they can duplicate those healings systematically and repeatedly, over a lifetime.

Christian Scientists deny that what they do is faith healing. In her autobiography, *Retrospection and Introspection*, Eddy called faith healing "blind belief" and implied that it was simplistic, where Christian Science was complex.[46] All but true believers, however, can recognize that Christian Science is a form of faith healing, differing from other Christian forms mainly in its rhetoric. Most Christian faith healers, who may engage in startlingly different methods of healing—everything from simple prayer to frenzied laying on of hands in crowded auditoriums to snake-handling— plead with God for divine intervention and accept the results as "God's will." Christian Scientists work not to accept but to "correct" their own perception of suffering or illness before them. They eschew completely the concept that God's will might include disease, accidents, or death, claiming instead that we can do nothing but reflect God's perfection. Therefore, when Scientists describe their testimonies of healing at meetings or in their periodicals, they sound different from other faith healers. They tend not to use the word "miracle" to describe a healing; healings are seen as the natural result of corrected thinking, a kind of realization of the truth, to which the body—or whatever is out of alignment—conforms. Where other kinds of faith healers praise God for his goodness, Christian Scientists express gratitude not only to God, but also to Mary Baker Eddy and Christian Science.

Scientists truly believe that their religion is a science; the "science" in Christian Science is taken literally, not metaphorically. They see their testimonies not as anecdotal expressions of faith but as actual proof, or demonstrations, as they call them, of the scientific method of Christian Science healing, amounting to statistical proof of its validity as a healing method. Scientists often speak of "God's laws," as taught by their religion, as if they can be mathematically proved. Over and over again in Christian Science teaching, an analogy is made between a mathematical equation and the Scientific truth about man. "It's like realizing that $2 + 2 = 4$, not 5," Sunday school teachers tell their pupils: "Finding the correct answer in math is the same as realizing the correct answer in metaphysics; everything else follows." The analogy originated with Eddy, who told some of her students at the Massachusetts Metaphysical College what was reprinted in the *Journal* in 1889: "How is a joint dislocated? Through mind. Then mind can put it back. We prove the rule of mind-healing mathematically. Four times five are twenty and five times four are twenty."[47]

Christian Scientists have also celebrated modern discoveries in physics and quantum mechanics, believing that scientific exploration into the nature of matter has proven that matter does not exist, a notion dear to the Scientific heart. The *Journal* in its early days eagerly reported on scientific developments suggesting the "Defeat of Scientific Materialism."[48] In an article entitled "Methods of Reasoning as Used in Christian Science," one *Journal* writer reasoned: "Like pure mathematics, Christian Science is a system of deductive reasoning, and when it solves a single problem correctly, such solution, like the solution of a mathematical problem, is a demonstration and not a mere experiment."[49] Apocryphal stories circulate throughout the Christian Science Field that Albert Einstein kept *Science and Health* on his bedside table, or attended Christian Science services in Princeton, New Jersey, or frequented reading rooms, remarking on *Science and Health*, "Do you people know what you have in these books?"[50] Robert Peel drew connections between Eddy's teachings and Einstein's theory on relativity, and asserted that "Einstein showed a slight but recurrent interest in Christian Science in his later years"; however, he provided no source for that information.[51]

Just as Christian Science makes more extraordinary claims than any other religious movement, so it goes to great lengths to validate those claims. There are many churches that also function as publishers, putting out religious tracts, books, periodicals, and so on, but the Christian Science Church has devoted itself to collecting and publishing testimonials of healing wrought through the practice of Christian Science. The *Christian Science Journal* and *Sentinel* have, almost from their inception, included testimonies of healing in every issue. In 1902, Eddy added the final chapter to *Science and Health*, "Fruitage," which consisted of eighty-five such testimonies attesting to healings of everything from deafness to "liver complaint."[52] Many of the Church-published biographies of Eddy, including the four volumes of her followers' reminiscences entitled *We Knew Mary Baker Eddy*, feature accounts of her healings or the healings wrought by her early followers.

In addition, the Church's Publishing Society has published two compilations of testimonies, *A Century of Christian Science Healing*, in 1966, and

Healing Spiritually, in 1996, each consisting of hundreds of pages of healings. Robert Peel's two books about Christian Science healing, published by mainstream publishers, *Spiritual Healing in a Scientific Age* and *Health and Medicine in the Christian Science Tradition*, include many Christian Science testimonies. Testimonies have also been featured extensively on Church radio and television programs and in public lectures.

By 1989, some 53,900 testimonies had been published in the Christian Science periodicals.[53] The publication of these testimonies has served several purposes. In the early days of Christian Science, they established a record that could be used both to attract new converts and to deflect the intense criticism of medical practitioners and other skeptics. An "Editor's Note" in the *Journal*'s "Healing and Reports of Cases" department in 1889 instructed the reader: "The publication of cases has two objects; the first, the help and encouragement of Scientists, and second, to lead those unacquainted with Science to look into its claims."[54]

The earliest testimonies have a flavor all their own. Few rules had been established, and Scientists felt free to go into detail, to excoriate the doctors who had frightened them with gloomy diagnoses and failed to heal them, and to laud Mrs. Eddy in the highest terms. Early on, Christian Science practitioners were allowed to write up their cases and publish them; eventually, only those healed were allowed to testify to their experience and were forbidden from naming the practitioner in the testimony, a practice intended to impersonalize the testimonies and to discourage the promotion of individual practitioners.

Several early testimonies, printed in the *Christian Science Journal* of September 1889, attest to the primitive nature of medical care at that time and to the powerful comfort that a belief in Christian Science brought to those suffering from a variety of physical and, perhaps, emotional ills:

I wish to give my testimony to the power and efficacy of CHRISTIAN SCIENCE. For three years I have been a helpless sufferer from complicated chronic diseases. I tried various physicians and remedies. I wore a German Electric Belt over one year. My Christian friends prayed for me two years ago, that I might be restored to health, but I could not see that I was bettered any. My doctor said I must leave here on account of the hard water. So my husband took me to Pratt Co., Kansas. I had to be taken on a bed. During my three years' sickness I had to be taken to Pratt Co. twice, each time on a bed, as I never was so I could sit up longer than an hour at a time.

Last fall when I came back to Eldorado I had about given up all hopes of ever getting well. So the Christian people of Eldorado took me up again as a subject of prayer, but there was no difference in my health, when, thanks be to God, I heard of a Christian Scientist, and we sent for her to come and see me. That was the 18th of February, and thank God, in less than three weeks I was up and doing my work. My cure has been truly a miracle of God.—R.A.S., ELDORADO, BUTLER CO., KANSAS

About three years ago I was taken with a belief of enlargement of the bowels. I knew nothing about Science then. Two physicians consulted on my case and decided that I had a tumor. The following year I had an opportunity to be treated by a Scientist, but was not cured. I grew better and then worse, until I felt as if I could not live and suffer so much. Then I made up my mind that I would go to K.C. and take treatment from Mrs. B. I was restored under her treatment. My gratitude knows no bounds. Thanks be to God for the Founder of Christian Science. Truly she is God-led. —E.P., SEDALIA, MO.

When I first came to you my eyes were swollen very much and out of place, now they are back in their proper place. When first treated, I had great pain in my eyes, which had continued for years. That has been relieved. I can now see the moon, see the lightning and the sunshine and the shadows when I sit by the Window, everything that is light. There has been improvement in all respects, so that I enjoy the best of health. Since I have been coming to you my hearing has improved also, so that I can hear the birds sing. I am very happy, for Science is curing me. It has done more than all the doctors have. It seems to me I could write volumes of wonderful things it has done for me.—F.S.[55]

With their talk of cures and miracles, these early testimonies focus on physical recoveries—albeit from complaints that may have been psychosomatic—and illustrate how the language of Christian Science had not yet become standardized. There is also a use of Christian Science jargon—"a *belief* of enlargement of the bowels"—that is rare in published testimonies today.

Modern testimonies lack the idiosyncrasy and immediacy of the earlier testimonies and adhere to a well-developed pattern. The testimony begins with a brief and nonspecific description of the problem that was healed and moves to a longer description of the Christian Science reading and logic that were used to correct the thought that seemingly caused the problem. Helpful prayers, hymns, or passages read in the Bible or *Science and Health* are cited, and a connection is usually made between the readings (which may have been discovered serendipitously by the sufferer or through the aid of a practitioner or the bible lesson) and the subsequent healing. A brief description of the resolution of the problem follows; the healing is always depicted as complete, total, and lasting. The testimony almost inevitably concludes with an expression of gratitude to Eddy or Christian Science or both. Some testimonies refer to diagnoses or opinions rendered by doctors consulted before the patient relied on Christian Science, or by emergency medical technicians who may have been present at the scene of an accident, but the names of doctors, EMTs, and hospitals are never given. The testimonies are generally nonspecific as to time, referring to conditions or accidents that happened "recently," "years ago," "about three years ago," and so on. Occasionally, an exact year is given. The length of testimonies can run anywhere from a half page to two pages.

In recent issues of the *Journal* and *Sentinel*, the testimonial section is prefaced by this claim:

> The statements made in testimonies and articles with regard to healing have been verified in writing by those who can vouch for the integrity of the testifier or know of the healing. Three such written verifications or vouchers are required before a testimony can be published.[56]

According to the guidelines printed in the periodicals and sent to those wishing to submit testimonies, the three verifiers must also be members of the Mother Church. Often the verifiers are practitioners or parents, spouses, siblings, or fellow Church members; occasionally, a verifying letter is printed following the testimony. The testimonies of young children are usually followed by a verifying letter from a parent.

Following the Church's annual meeting in 1993, held, as always, in the Mother Church, in Boston, there was a special "Fruitage" meeting featuring twenty testimonies of Christian Science healing from around the globe, delivered in person by the testifiers. A woman from Milan, Italy, told of being healed of a sprained ankle; a young man from Warsaw, Poland, described recovering from a variety of childhood ailments and "inharmonious conditions"; a mother from Helsinki, Finland, recounted her young son's recovery after being hit by a car while riding his bicycle; a woman from Athens, Greece, was healed of a long-standing corn on one of her toes.[57]

One of the most notable accounts was given by Linda Bumpus, a woman from Riverdale, New York. She was preceded onstage (the podium of the Mother Church) by her son, Aaron. He spoke of being healed of doubts about Christian Science, such as "What if this stuff I'm being told in Sunday School is just something somebody made up?"[58] But his mother stole the show when she told of "Aaron's first healing":

> When I was pregnant, a doctor said that the child had a severe birth defect. He was prepared to recommend an abortion, because he felt that even if the child survived the birth, which he said was unlikely, he would be severely retarded.
>
> Before another examination, we had time to pray about it. Without telling my husband or me, the doctor (who knew we were Christian Scientists) called the practitioner who was praying for me and described the condition in more detail. The practitioner continued praying.
>
> The second test showed a complete healing. I had a very smooth pregnancy and a very harmonious delivery. And the baby was perfectly healthy.
>
> It's hard to find words to say how grateful you are for a book and a religion that saved your child's life.[59]

The testimony was followed by loving, accepting, enthusiastic applause. It was clear to all present that young Aaron Bumpus was not "severely retarded" but was a normal child in every way. His mother's account of his gestational healing was acknowledged by the audience as profoundly moving.

This is typical of the reception Christian Scientists give Christian Science testimonies, whether published in the Church periodicals or delivered during a Wednesday evening testimony meeting at a branch church. It is impossible to exaggerate the effect such testimonies have on Christian Scientists. Testimonies validate not only their beliefs but their entire lifestyle, bolstering and supporting a profound reliance on Christian Science to the exclusion of other methods, including medical methods, even in the face of societal disapproval. It is testimonies like these that make Christian Science seem impregnable to its believers. All Christian Scientists have their own fund of such testimonies that they fall back on in moments of doubt or trouble or when they are questioned by curious or skeptical outsiders. These testimonies encourage and confirm Scientists in their faith, as Eddy knew they would. In the Preface to *Science and Health*, she wrote: "The question, What is Truth, is answered by demonstration,— by healing both disease and sin; and this demonstration shows that Christian healing confers the most health and makes the best men. On this basis Christian Science will have a fair fight. Sickness has been combated for centuries by doctors using material remedies; but the question arises, Is there less sickness because of these practitioners?"[60] The same question might now be asked of Christian Science.

4. Eliminating the Negative

In 1989, the Church's Committees on Publication published a small beige pamphlet entitled "An Empirical Analysis of Medical Evidence in Christian Science Testimonies of Healing, 1969–1988." It is the only systematic attempt that the Church has ever made to examine the nature and number of its published testimonies. It was clearly published in response to the ongoing and unprecedented number of prosecutions and convictions of Christian Science parents following the deaths of children under Christian Science treatment, and to the negative publicity these cases engendered.

It is an odd study. In certain respects, it apes scientific or sociological papers, opening with an abstract and containing a section on methodology and one on findings. But the resemblance ends there. No authors are listed, and the pamphlet, unlike scientific papers, was not published by a refereed professional journal that would have submitted it for evaluation to experts in its field. It was published by a church. And, like environmental studies bought and paid for by oil companies, it reaches predictable conclusions.

The study begins with a reference to a recent article in the *Southern Medical Journal*, "Positive Therapeutic Effects of Intercessory Prayer in a Coronary Care Unit."[61] This article, by Randolph C. Byrd, is now famous in the annals of alternative medicine, having inspired a rash of studies purporting to demonstrate the efficacy of prayer. Unsurprisingly, the Church held up the Byrd study as a model, after nearly a century of yearning for such a development to take place in the medical world. The authors of the "Empirical Analysis" hailed Byrd's work as an example of "a rigorous controlled study investigating the effects of prayer on the recovery of . . . heart patients."[62] Although that rigorousness has since come into some question, the point that the Christian Scientists wished to make was this: "There has been relatively little medical research on religious healing over the years, in spite of a growing body of evidence from its practice. The most substantial evidence is undoubtedly to be found in the experiences of Christian Scientists."[63]

The reason why little research has been conducted in this field, however, is rather obvious. Medical researchers generally believe that scientific studies on prayer cannot legitimately be performed under the conditions demanded by today's protocols. One of the criticisms of the Byrd study was that there had been no attempt (and possibly no way) to quantify or control the prayer that was performed for the patients: perhaps others, outside the study and unknown to the researchers, had prayed for the patients, skewing the results. The associations made in prayer studies other than Byrd's between prayer and higher rates of recovery or faster recovery are also suspect because there is no way to control for variables that may influence the results. Prayer is not quantifiable apart from the length of time it takes. Prayer is not visible. There is no way to interpret or evaluate the quality or effectiveness of types of prayer. By definition, it is spiritual. How can the spiritual be studied scientifically?

The Christian Scientists, in their "Empirical Analysis" prepared a database "recording and categorizing" what they termed the "medical information contained in testimonies published in the denomination's periodicals from 1969 to 1988."[64] The study paid particular attention to those testimonies that mentioned that a healed condition had originally been medically diagnosed. But it also acknowledged that even in diagnosed cases, "testifiers are often reporting in their own words what physicians have said to them."[65] It allowed that some of these testifiers might have misunderstood, misremembered, or inaccurately reported their diagnoses.

Doctors have been pointing out the perils of self-reported diagnoses since the earliest days of Christian Science. While running their long series of articles about Eddy in 1908, McClure's Magazine also published an article by Dr. Richard C. Cabot, a Boston physician and professor at Harvard Medical School, examining "One Hundred Christian Science Cures." Like most doctors today he expressed a certain skepticism about patients'—and Christian Scientists'—interpretations of doctors' diagnoses, remarking that he had rarely found such self-reported diagnoses to be "even approximately correct."[66]

In their findings, the author or authors of the "Empirical Analysis" reported "over 10,000" physical healings described in 7,154 published testimonies between 1969 and 1988.[67] Of those healings, 2,337 involved "healings of medically diagnosed conditions."[68] The study itemized the testimonies that mentioned "medically diagnosed conditions" in this fashion:

> The list of diagnosed conditions healed covers an extremely broad range of injuries, disorders, and diseases: at least 27 healings of malignancy or cancer (including bone cancer, lymph cancer, skin cancer, cancer of the liver, breast, intestine, and uterus), 42 of tumor, 16 of polio, 68 of tuberculosis, 38 of pneumonia (seven of double pneumonia, two with collapsed lung), at least 88 of heart disorders, 23 of kidney disorders (two of Bright's disease), 203 of broken bones . . . 71 of childbirth complications (such as uremic poisoning, four still births), nine of meningitis, 24 of appendicitis (eight acute), 16 of scarlet fever, 16 of rheumatic fever, 11 of cataract, 12 of diabetes (one as a complication of pregnancy, one juvenile case), 13 of pernicious anemia, 12 of rheumatoid or degenerative arthritis, two of gangrene, three of glaucoma, seven of hepatitis, three of leukemia, six of multiple sclerosis, seven of blindness (48 of other vision deficiencies such as astigmatism or nearsightedness), 13 of goiter, eight of curvature of the spine, 13 of epilepsy, three of crossed eyes, one of cleft palate.[69]

The questions raised by such a list are legion. Were these diagnoses preliminary or tentative; the result of first, second, or third opinions; were they made in doctors' offices or in hospitals after batteries of tests? What were the exact prognoses? What were the treatments, if any, and with what results? What kind of tumors were healed, malignant or benign? In what sense were the four stillbirths "healed"? Or were the mothers healed? Were those who received diagnoses and who subsequently chose Christian Science treatment particularly aggrieved over their medical treatment, a psychological state that may in itself have aggravated their reported symptoms? Again, since the diagnoses were reported by patients, not by the medical professionals involved, and were not accompanied by pertinent medical data—patients' charts, test results, and the like—virtually no credible scientific conclusions can be drawn from such a list. Moreover, the study failed to footnote any of the testimonies, so the reader cannot even read them for himself.

The most fascinating disclosure in the "Empirical Analysis" occupies a mere sentence. The study, its authors wrote, "does not provide comparative cure or mortality rates, *nor does it consider cases in which healing prayer has not been effective*" (my italics).[70] This remarkable qualification—one the

Church has rarely, if ever, acknowledged in print—captures the essential, central, inescapable problem in all the scientific claims of the Christian Science Church. In order to present Christian Science treatment as effective, the Church and its members have simply *eliminated the negative*. The Christian Science periodicals never publish testimonies about Christian Science failures. No Christian Scientist ever takes the floor during the Wednesday evening testimony meeting and talks about a failure. The Church never acknowledges failures in its editorials or articles.[71] By eliminating the negative, Christian Scientists have, at least in their own minds, willed it into oblivion.

The Church's claim in recent years that Christian Science works better for children than medical treatment is a case in point.[72] When the Church found itself confronted in court and in the media about its treatment of children during the early 1990s, it manufactured statistics regarding its "loss rate" of children in order to confute its critics. Nathan Talbot, then the manager of the Committees on Publication, told the *Washington Post* in 1990: "We've done a study looking at the loss rate of all children between age four days and age 14. For the general public, the loss rate is about 51 children per 100,000. For Christian Scientists, the comparable figure is 23 per 100,000."[73] Talbot also claimed that the seven criminal cases ongoing during 1989 represented "virtually all of the losses in our entire denomination in the United States since 1983."[74]

Both claims were utterly false. The Church had done no study. Talbot's claim regarding the loss rate among Christian Science children was based on a comparison of the seven children's deaths that had come to public attention with the total number of children's deaths in the United States published by the National Center for Health Statistics. The fatal flaw behind both Talbot's specious comparison and his tally of seven deaths lay in the fact that neither the Church nor its practitioners keep any record of the number of deaths, of children *or* adults.[75] It never has. In 1995, Victor Westberg, the manager of the C.O.P., admitted as much to me: "We never keep track of the records of how many [Christian Science] children pass on."[76] The Church therefore has no way of knowing what its "loss rate" is. It doesn't care to know.

Christian Scientists ignore all evidence of Christian Science failures in their periodicals, in their Church, and in their lives. But there is also evidence to suggest that some of their published testimonies are falsified or purged of information that would call into question the "healing" claimed.

One fascinating example concerns what may be one of the most famous Christian Science testimonies ever published, that of Lieutenant Charles Herbert Lightoller, the second officer of the *Titanic* and a devout Christian Scientist. Lightoller's testimony was originally published in the *Christian Science Journal* of October 1912, but an excerpt from it was recently reprinted in the December 8, 1997, issue of the *Sentinel,* just prior to the release of the film *Titanic.*[77]

The highest-ranking officer of the *Titanic* to survive the disaster, Lightoller faced intense questioning during the congressional hearings held in New York City only a week after the ship sank, concerning the safety procedures and the loading of the lifeboats during the early morning hours of April 15, 1912.[78] An employee of the White Star Line who stood to advance professionally if he protected the reputation of his employer, which owned the ill-fated vessel, Lightoller was evasive in his responses before the hearing. Both congressmen and historians have deduced that he lied when he claimed that he did not know that the ship was in the vicinity of icebergs and that he had not discussed the hazard with other officers.[79] (Indeed, he eventually recanted part of the latter claim when written evidence contradicting it came to light.) He is also believed to have lied about circumstances surrounding his survival; he and about thirty others clambered aboard an overturned lifeboat, where they spent most of that night. (Interestingly, twenty-seven of those who made it onto that particular lifeboat were crew; only three were passengers.)[80] Lightoller denied that others still in the water had struggled in vain to get aboard the boat, a claim that was later contradicted by eyewitnesses.[81]

Lightoller's published and much reprinted Christian Science testimony addresses and acknowledges none of these issues. It may, in fact, have been intended to even the score, for Lightoller had angrily denounced the congressional hearings that had exposed him to ridicule as "nothing but a complete farce."[82] An astonishingly smug document, the testimony makes several assertions that contradict the established facts regarding the sinking of the *Titanic.* It is well known that lifeboats were sent away from the sinking ship half-full, costing untold lives. Lightoller was responsible for the loading of passengers on the port side of the ship, and he writes, "It was hard work, and yet the very conditions which existed on the port side were in themselves a demonstration of the workings of Truth, for not the slightest hitch occurred, and all boats were got away."[83] Concerning the grim scene atop the overturned lifeboat, he observes: "I could not overcome the intense cold experienced, yet when a man handed me a bottle of something that smelt somewhat like essence of peppermint, the thought of material means was nothing short of repulsive, and needless to say, it was not taken."[84] He concludes that his experience proved that " 'with God all things are possible.' "[85] He makes no mention of the fact that, for more than fifteen hundred other people, all things were not possible. And he expresses no sense of responsibility, remorse, or sorrow for his role in what transpired that night.

Lightoller, who died in 1952 at the age of seventy-eight, is remarkable not as a physical coward (indeed, he distinguished himself at Dunkirk by rescuing over a hundred men in his own private yacht) but as a moral one. The fact that the editors of the Christian Science periodicals would see fit to reprint his self-serving and inaccurate testimony not once, but several times (it has recently been reprinted in the *Monitor*, as well as in the *Sentinel*) without explanation of the serious questions that surround it, says volumes about their dedication—or lack thereof—to the process they themselves have termed "verification."[86] In truth, the testimonies are not verified in any meaningful way, and if inconvenient historical fact seems to interfere with their claims, the writers and editors of such testimonies simply turn their heads and look away.

Those who are most misled by the continual overemphasis on successful healings in the Church periodicals are Scientists themselves, who sometimes believe themselves healed when their health is actually in grave danger. A practitioner who was interviewed at length for a 1992 *Yankee* magazine article about the Church, Dale Parker Edens, of Columbia, South Carolina, claimed in that article that he had recently been healed of self-diagnosed leukemia and of the effects of a severe fall off the roof of a building.[87] But Edens, who was then in his forties, was apparently not as healthy as he believed. He died less than a year after the article was published, of what a friend and fellow practitioner identified as a heart attack.

In 1984, Ruth Price Brewster, a *Journal*-listed practitioner in El Paso, Texas, published a testimony in the *Christian Science Journal* that contains a disturbing omission. "Rearing four children with total reliance on God for healing was a joy. I cannot remember an activity missed because of illness," Mrs. Brewster wrote.[88] In fact, Mrs. Brewster had *five* children. The unmentioned fifth child who has been revised out of this testimony—indeed, out of life itself—was Nancy Brewster. Rita Swan learned that Nancy died in 1963 at the age of seven, of what was probably malignant lymphoma.[89] Whatever disease Nancy Brewster had, it went entirely untreated, and she must have missed many activities. Ruth Price Brewster is still a *Journal*-listed practitioner.[90]

In the early days of the Christian Science movement, it was acceptable to the Church to publish queries about incomplete healings or failures. For a five-year period, 1889–1893, there was a "Questions and Discussions" department in the *Journal* in which its editors, who wrote that the *Journal* "ought to be the great market or exchange for Scientists," attempted to answer heartfelt queries about the practice of the religion.[91]

In November 1889, one woman wrote to the *Journal* begging for an explanation of why she had been unable to heal her failing eyesight, after having given up her eyeglasses for two years as part of her Christian Science treatment:

> I so wish that some one would suggest to us—if such explanation in Science is attainable,—why demonstration is not unexceptional; as it must be to be scientific. I see in your August issue, under heading, "Open Letters" signed "E.N.," a communication begins, "I have never studied, because my belief of deafness was increased under Christian Science and I have to be written to now almost entirely," etc. Why? Why?? If the reply be because of an increased understanding of the nothingness of material sense of hearing, my thought cries aloud, Why does not the spiritual power increase in proportion to diminution of material belief? . . .
>
> Now, what I do not understand is this,—that while my sight has slowly but steadily improved, in the face of what the world would call rashness and abuse; and while at times for intervals of several minutes I see with wonderful clearness and read the very finest diamond print as clearly and delightfully as a child; up to this time I cannot in any degree control or rely on these conditions. I write, read, and sew—but generally through a seeming cloud or mist. It is still struggle. I face dazzling sunlight from which others shrink, without flinching. Why, oh, why, in the name of Truth and Christ's promises, does "demonstration" seem to elude me? —F.A.G.[92]

It may have been questions such as this that inspired the editors to abruptly announce, in the February 1893 issue of the *Journal:* "We shall hereafter decline to answer questions relating to Christian Science, or the interpretation of SCIENCE AND HEALTH, and other writings of our Teacher, the Rev. Mary B. G. Eddy. Her works will answer all questions."[93]

It has been left to the world outside of Christian Science officialdom to investigate its failures. Earlier in the century, doctors, lawyers, and scientists eagerly took up the gauntlet thrown down by Eddy and closely examined her claims.[94] In *The Faith and Works of Christian Science* (1909), Stephen Paget, a British surgeon, analyzed some two hundred Christian Science testimonies and solicited doctors' recollections of their encounters with patients whom Christian Science had, sometimes catastrophically, failed to cure. Many of these accounts display a horror of and impatience with the Scientists' denial of physical symptoms and refusal to take swift medical action, as well as an occasionally patronizing amusement over the Scientists' ignorance of human biology; a few show an acceptance of Christian Science as an adequate treatment for psychosomatic illness.

After Paget's book was published, he engaged in a bitter exchange of letters in the London newspapers with Frederick Dixon, the Christian Science Committee on Publication for London, which continued for several months. In a note to the second edition of his book, Paget included an account of their debate and a number of additional cases sent to him by doctors, as well as a fascinating letter from a former Christian Science practitioner who had left the practice "because of the constantly increasing and at length overwhelming proof both in my own practice and in that of a large number of other so-called healers that there was *no science* in it and that cures were the *exception* and not the rule."[95]

Paget also, with some glee, presented the entire correspondence, which had appeared in the *Times* of London and other British newspapers, between the Honorable A. Holland-Hibbert and a Christian Science practitioner regarding the practitioner's absent treatment of a "favourite mare" belonging to Holland-Hibbert, which suffered from a condition its owner described as being "gone-in-the-wind." In *Science and Health*, Eddy had suggested that animals could be treated as readily as humans; even today, the Christian Science periodicals occasionally print a letter from a child or adult pet owner attesting to the healing of a beloved dog or cat.[96]

Holland-Hibbert's mare, however, was not so fortunate. Her owner and the practitioner eventually came to loggerheads after the practitioner criticized Holland-Hibbert's frame of mind, and he reminded her that "the mare has no mind, and you have been dealing with her."[97] Sometime later, Holland-Hibbert wrote to the *Times*, expressing, perhaps, the jaded sensibility that interfered with his animal's spiritual treatment:

My poor mare continued to blow like a grampus until her grievously afflicted career terminated in death. But I shall only be too glad to submit for treatment several more broken-winded animals, any age, any sex, and if a single one is cured I will gladly buy a hundred copies of 'Our American Mother's' book, and, further, I will promise to see to its distribution in railway and dentist waiting-rooms or in any other places where suffering is submissively borne.[98]*

More recently, the fate of another horse was entrusted to Christian Science. In September 1998, Smitty-Rose, a polo pony belonging to Florida millionaire and Scientist Ann Mallinckrodt, suffered a hairline fracture of its right rear leg in Saratoga, New York. Opposing veterinarians, who advised putting the horse down after the fracture shattered into bone fragments, which eventually worked their way through the skin, Mallinckrodt hired a practitioner to treat the horse mentally. Two months later, after the animal's condition had visibly deteriorated, the New York State attorney general's office sought a court order to euthanize it; a judge, however, ruled that the state could not proceed without the owner's permission. Smitty-Rose was found dead in December 1998.[99]

Whatever interest the contemporary scientific community might have had in investigating Christian Science has been discouraged by the Church's reluctance to participate and its failure to keep records. Nonetheless, although no double-blind studies on Christian Science have ever been done, there have been important statistical investigations.

In 1954, R. W. England, of the University of Pennsylvania, published a study in the *American Journal of Sociology*, "Some Aspects of Christian Science as Reflected in Letters of Testimony," which analyzed a sample of five hundred letters published in the *Christian Science Journal* during 1929, 1939, 1940, and 1946.[100] England was interested in determining what characterized people drawn to " 'fringe' religious groups" and "what factors

---

*Holland-Hibbert, it turned out, was an early-twentieth-century skeptic in the mold of James Randi—"the Amazing Randi"—the writer-magician who currently travels the globe investigating and, often as not, debunking psychics, spoon benders, dowsers, faith healers, and others whose claims strain credulity. Since 1968, he has offered a cash prize, now over a million dollars, to anyone who can demonstrate scientifically verifiable supernatural, occult, or psychic powers, including the power to heal. So far, no Christian Scientist has accepted the challenge.

stimulate and maintain adherents' interest"; he also, rather mysteriously, alluded to his own "one-time participation" in Christian Science, a reference that the Church, in its inevitable response, latched on to as an explanation for what it termed his "polemic tone."[101]

Whatever his tone, which seems to this author studiously academic, England's observations tend to support those of earlier critics and skeptics: the self-diagnoses of Scientists may be unreliable, and many healings concern minor, insignificant, or psychosomatic conditions:

> Most conspicuous was an apparent ignorance of or indifference to the natural healing powers of the human body. Thus, a vast number of minor ailments, ranging from athlete's foot to the common cold, were treated and cured by the application of Divine Truth. Furthermore, there is, among the 500 communicants, considerable attention given to types of disorders so insignificant as to be of practically no consequence so far as one's daily life is concerned. Chapped hands, lone warts, a burned fingernail, hangnails, vague fleeting pains, and momentary dizziness were not infrequently the "healings" for which testimony was given. Man, like most organisms, is subject to myriad minor and temporary ills which are of little importance to general health. The doctrines of Mary Baker Eddy, however, endow even these pathological minutiae with special meaning, for they become evidence of the workings of mortal mind. When they vanish, as they almost inevitably must, Christian Scientists give credit not to their resilient organisms but to their religion. Thus, by virtue of the peculiar emphases of their faith and the peculiar functioning of the human body, Scientists have a constant and automatic source of evidence confirming their beliefs.[102]

As Paget did before him, England casts doubt on the healings of more serious conditions:

> The number of cancers, tumors, broken bones, and cases of pneumonia and acute appendicitis which were self-diagnosed by the writers seemed large. . . . It seems likely that most of the more dramatic cures are due simply to mistaken diagnosis. In scores of letters the writers describe how they broke their skulls, dislocated organs, awoke in the night with pneumonia, decided that mysterious lumps were cancers, or found themselves in other ways serious victims of mortal mind. Their next move was to begin divine treatment, either with or without a practitioner's aid. Elated and gratified

when their skulls mended, their organs returned to place, their pneumonia and cancers vanished, they wrote letters of testimony to the *Journal*.[103]

But England also introduced a new element to the discussion when he observed that the Christian Science practitioner's role "seems not unlike that of the psychiatrist or psychiatric social worker," in supplying for patients "an object of affection, a rock of security, a confessor, and a source of hope, as well as a technical healer."[104] Christian Science, in redefining illness as a mental, not a physical, phenomenon recalled the origins of the movement in the nineteenth century's experimental fascination with mesmerism or hypnosis, the generative technique that inspired the early insights not only of Mary Baker Eddy, but also of Charcot and Freud.[105]

More recent statistical studies, though preliminary, have demonstrated the exact price that Christian Scientists pay for their beliefs. The first, conducted by Dr. Gale E. Wilson, a forensic pathologist, examined the records of the King County, Washington, coroner's office between 1949 and 1951 and found that the average age of death for those identified as Christian Scientists was slightly below the state average but not to an extent that was statistically significant.[106] Wilson also found, however, that 6 percent of the Christian Scientists' deaths would have been preventable with the medical care then obtainable, and that the death rate of Christian Scientists from cancer was double the national average.[107] As another writer has noted, Wilson's study "was confined to years when antibiotics were few and limited, and before the advent of polio, mumps, measles, and rubella vaccines."[108] This suggests that, if a similar study were undertaken today, it might show a statistically significant lower life expectancy for Scientists.

But a 1989 study published in the *Journal of the American Medical Association* indicated a more striking difference in life expectancy between Scientists and non-Scientists. "Comparative Longevity in a College Cohort of Christian Scientists" looked at the longevity of graduates of Principia College next to the longevity of a control group of graduates of the University of Kansas, in Lawrence, between the years 1934 and 1983.[109] The author of the study, William Franklin Simpson, a professor in the division of mathematics and physical science at Emporia State University in Kansas, was himself an alumnus of Principia, where students are likely to be practicing Scientists. He hypothesized "that Christian Scientists who graduate from Principia College survive graduation for a shorter period of time than persons of the same sex who graduate from the College of Liberal Arts and Sciences of the University of Kansas."[110] Simpson constructed two life tables, one for men and one for women.[111] Percentages of death were noticeably higher among Principia graduates in both tables and climbed particularly in the older graduates. Among the men graduated between 1939 and 1943, 24 percent of the Principia graduates were dead, compared with 19 percent of the University of Kansas graduates. Among the women graduated between 1949 and 1953, 8 percent of Principia graduates were dead, compared with 4 percent of the control group; among those graduated between 1939 and 1943, 15 percent of Principia women were dead, compared with 10 percent of the control group.

Simpson concluded:

> If Christian Science healing methods work as well as medical healing methods, one would expect to see Christian Scientists live as long as non–Christian Scientists. However, this study has shown that this is not the case. Christian Scientists (at least people who claimed to be Christian Scientists at the time they were students at Principia College) have a lower life expectancy than a control group of students from the University of Kansas.[112]

Simpson also noted that the results were "particularly interesting" considering that Christian Scientists neither smoke nor drink.[113] Mormons also eschew alcohol and tobacco, and studies have shown that they are "among the healthiest people on earth," with strikingly lower death rates from heart disease, liver disease, and stroke than the American population as a whole.[114] Mormons go to doctors, and Christian Scientists don't.

The JAMA study was picked up by the news wires and reported in newspapers across the country. The Christian Science Church lost no time in attacking it. They sent a letter to the editor of virtually every newspaper reporting the story, insisting that it was "a questionable study" that made "questionable assumptions."[115] They claimed that life insurance statistics showed a "somewhat longer life expectancy among Christian Scientists than others," although they cited no specific figures.[116] As Simpson pointed out in his response, life insurance figures include a cross section of society. Simpson's study, self-limited to college graduates, had the advantage of comparing Christian Scientists—overwhelmingly college-educated, middle- to upper-middle-class Caucasians—with their peers.

In 1991, Simpson repeated his study, comparing the Principia graduates with graduates from Loma Linda University, a Seventh-Day Adventist institution in Loma Linda, California, over a thirty-eight-year period, 1945–1983. Seventh-Day Adventists abstain from eating pork and shell-fish, usually follow a vegetarian diet, and eschew alcohol and tobacco, but, unlike Christian Scientists, they accept medical care. This time, the results were even more marked. "Total mortality," Simpson reported, was higher among Principia College graduates in twenty-two, or 85 percent, of the twenty-six age groups he examined.[117]

A rigorous analysis of the existing evidence, including the Church's own study, its testimonies, and the studies of sociologists and statisticians outside the Church, does not yield conclusions favorable to Christian Science. The Church's own "empirical" study is unreliable, because it takes no account of Christian Science failures. As for Christian Science testimonies themselves, they are essentially unverified and unverifiable. They can be and have been falsified. And the Church has refused to permit any scientific investigation of them, even punishing those in its movement who have sought to do so.[118] William Simpson's studies offer substantial evidence that Scientists' longevity is compromised by their refusal of medical care. The simplest and most logical explanation of Christian Science testimonies is that they are testimonies of religious belief, spiritual feeling, and faith. They do not present significant evidence of biological recovery from organic disease or serious injury. "Christian Science! as if there could be such a thing!" one of the characters in a John Updike novel exclaims. In fact, there is not. Christian Science is not a science.

5. Remarkable Providences

The history of the United States of America is a history of religious sects that have sanctified the power of self. It was once said that "it has been granted to the Americans less than any other nation on earth to realize the visible unity of the Church of God." True enough. The disunity of American religion is a direct result of visionary after visionary standing on his or her principles. Over a hundred years before the country was founded, the minister Roger Williams was driven into the wilds of Rhode Island for his separatist beliefs; Mistress Anne Hutchinson, who outrageously and blasphemously delivered her personal vision during weekly public lectures in her house, followed him into exile. Williams and Hutchinson were cultists breaking away from cultists who had themselves broken away from England. New England, as the Puritan scholar Perry Miller would say, was "the test tube."[119] We are the result of the experiment. We are a suggestible people, forever singing the song of ourselves.

Religious experimentation and excitation have always been the American norm. The jeremiad was the Puritan sermon of choice: the sermon as a violent and bilious attack upon and scourging of the sins of the congregation—indeed, an attack upon the congregation itself. These attacks were a welcome part of the fabric of life, a lifeline to a people convinced that every misfortune—destructive storms or drought, shipwrecks, earthquakes, smallpox—was the visitation of an angry God. "That God hath a Controversy with his New England people is undeniable," was the conclusion of the General Court in Boston in 1679, after a series of disasters punished the righteous.[120] Such ills could only be cured by the self-imposed humiliation, fasting, and humbling of God's people. Increase Mather, pastor of Boston's North Church for over sixty years and father of Cotton Mather, published a volume in 1684 entitled *An Essay for the Recording of Illustrious Providences*, also known as *Remarkable Providences*, in which he examined God's propensity to strike unworthy individuals with his extraordinary weapons: possession by demons, bolts of lightning, blizzards, comets, floods. Here was the kernel from which the stripling Christian Science grew. Sin in the people caused disease in the people. When sin was reformed, disease was cured.[121]

The Great Awakening (1734–1740) presaged the proliferation of sects to come. Led and defended by the minister of Northampton, Jonathan Edwards, whose violent sermon "Sinners in the Hands of an Angry God" is now the archetypal text of that event, the Awakening was characterized by "enthusiasm," a term that carried overtones of the contempt more restrained clergy felt for it and referred to untoward excitement and passion. Exhorted by Edwards, "the people yelled and shrieked, they rolled in the aisles, they crowded up to the pulpit and begged him to stop, they cried for mercy."[122] They were also healed in astounding numbers or, if not healed, saved.

The taste for enthusiasm worked like yeast in the air of freedom, and inevitably led to schism: the uncontrollable desire to break the molds of old religion and find purity in the new. The Second Great Awakening (1820–1860) bred new cults and sects like flies, bred whole new categories of cults. There were new "schools" that aimed at reform: the Congregational new school, the Presbyterian new school, the Lutheran General Synod. There were new schismatic sects that broke off from recalcitrant parent churches: the Missouri Synod, the Millerites, the Mennonites, the Shakers, the Unitarians, the Universalists, the Seventh-Day Adventists. There were brand-new cults, deviating from Christianity so widely that they seemed cut from whole new cloth: the Swedenborgians, the Spiritualists, the Mormons, the New Thought movement, the Christian Scientists. There were, as well, communal utopian movements espousing religious, political, and social beliefs—such as the Oneida Community, which famously practiced free love, and the Amana Society, which less famously went in for celibacy.[123] There were food fads founded by Graham and Kellogg that represented new beliefs about the body; there were astonishing new pseudoscientific, pseudoreligious beliefs growing up around homeopathy, mesmerism, phrenology, and astrology. There was spiritual freedom and spiritual chaos.

It is happening again. We may smile and shake our heads over the folly of the seventeenth, eighteenth, and nineteenth centuries, their healers, mesmerists, hypnotists, and layers on of hands, but there is very little difference between the credulity of those times and that of the present. We are an ahistorical people.

Remember Mesmer? And his magical, healing magnets? The magnets are back. And they're being used in ways that Mesmer never imagined. According to one science writer who examined the claims of current magnet vendors, "Magnets can be used to improve blood circulation, cure and prevent diseases, increase automobile mileage, improve plant growth, soften water, prevent tooth decay, and even increase the strength of concrete."[124] In the magnet market there are magnet wrist wraps, magnet back braces, magnet mattress pads, magnets to ease depression, and magnets endorsed by professional football players and golfers. In Europe, "human magnets," persons who claim that their very bodies have become magnetized, have recently become the rage, featured in magazine articles and television shows.[125] Many of these new magical claims concerning magnets have, of course, been proven false; initial experimentation suggests that magnetic therapy may produce some benefits in cases of depression or joint pain, although the results are still under investigation. But it hardly seems to matter what the experimental scientific evidence suggests; the *New York*

Times reports that "Americans spend large sums on magnets to seek pain relief."[126] Worldwide sales of one Japanese magnet firm totaled more than $1.5 billion in 1994.

Remember Lucius Burkmar, the mesmeric healer who claimed to be able to see inside people's bodies and diagnose their illnesses? He would feel right at home in today's spiritual marketplace. Caroline Myss, a Ph.D. and self-proclaimed "medical intuitive," now claims to be able to "see" specific illnesses in patients' bodies by intuitive means. Her videos, such as *The Energetics of Healing* and *Why People Don't Heal and How They Can*, have been called "the hottest new choices in the alternative health/spirituality scene" by *Publishers Weekly*. They have been sold through the PBS Home Video catalogue and featured on public television.

Remember Phineas Parkhurst Quimby's soothing hands? His work has been resurrected in "Therapeutic Touch," a strange theoretical combination of Quimby's metaphysics, the mystical Chinese notion of *qi* (a life energy that is supposed to flow through the body), and the Indian idea of *prana*, or life force. During the early 1970s, Dolores Krieger, a Ph.D. and registered nurse on the faculty of New York University's Division of Nursing, was heavily influenced by Martha Rogers, then the dean of nursing at NYU; Therapeutic Touch is their brainchild. Rogers saw the human body as an energy field, and labeled her theory, without much originality, the Science of Unitary Man (Eddy's early manuscript was entitled *The Science of Man*). Another figure behind Therapeutic Touch is Dora Kunz, who served as president of Madame Blavatsky's Theosophical Society of America from 1975 to 1987. Skeptics of the procedure have pointed out that the "human energy field" postulated by therapeutic touchers bears an uncanny resemblance to Mesmer's theories regarding "magnetic fluid" and "animal magnetism."[127]

Like Mesmer, practitioners of Therapeutic Touch make passes over patients' bodies with their hands and believe that they can manipulate the "human energy field" above the skin to the benefit of the patient.[128] Clothing or bedding that lies between skin and hands is not considered a "significant" barrier.[129]

The claims made by proponents of Therapeutic Touch are so preposterous and so easily refuted that, in 1996, a nine-year-old girl, Emily Rosa, of Chicago, the daughter of a registered nurse who is a longtime doubter of the practice, conducted a classically simple experiment on it for a school science fair. She set up a cardboard screen through which Therapeutic Touchers were instructed to put their hands (twenty-one were tested, multiple times); with their sight blocked, they were then asked to identify which of their hands was near one of hers. Designed to determine whether these practitioners could discern the "human energy field" so crucial to the practice of Therapeutic Touch, the experiment revealed a success rate of only 44 percent, less than the 50 percent that would be expected from random chance. Emily Rosa's research, which she wrote up with the help of her mother and two additional co-authors, was published by the *Journal of the American Medical Association* in April 1998. It concluded that the "failure to substantiate TT's most fundamental claim is unrefuted evidence that the claims of TT are groundless and that further professional use is unjustified."[130]

And yet, as the *JAMA* article points out, Therapeutic Touch has been granted extraordinary professional recognition, even though little well-designed research supports its efficacy. The practice is taught in over a hundred colleges and universities in seventy-five countries and used by nurses "in at least 80 hospitals in North America, often without the permission or even knowledge of attending physicians." *RN*, a professional journal for registered nurses, has published positive articles about it, and professional nursing organizations in the United States and Canada, including the American Nurses' Association and the National League for Nursing, the credentialing agency for nursing schools in the United States, have promoted it through books, videotapes, workshops, and journal articles.

Remember malicious animal magnetism? It, too, has seen a renaissance in the late twentieth century, celebrated by the medical doctor and friend of Virginia Harris, Larry Dossey. His most recent book, originally titled *Toxic Prayer*, was subsequently published under this title: *Be Careful What You Pray For . . . You Just Might Get It: What We Can Do About the Unintentional Effects of Our Thoughts, Prayers, and Wishes.*

In this volume, Dossey earnestly explores the deleterious effects of hexes, death wishes, and the evil eye; he sees these elements of folklore as not merely psychologically negative but physically destructive. He sets great store by quasi-scientific experiments in which bacteria and fungi exposed to positive prayer prosper, while their neglected fellows languish. He suggests that we might reconcile our moral concerns regarding experiments in which nonhuman organisms are subjected to harmful prayer by simply asking their permission: "Every research institution might need a Nonhuman Permissions Committee (NONPERC). The NONPERC would be made up of individuals who have special skills in sensing and listening to the responses of mice, rats, chimps, cats, dogs, rabbits, bacteria, fungi, yeasts, seeds, and plants."[131] (Of course, he nominates for these positions "Native Americans and other individuals who have not severed their communication skills with the nonhuman world.")[132]

Dossey, who was once chief of staff of Humana Medical City in Dallas, has garnered a wave of attention with such nonsense, appearing on national television on *Oprah*, *Dateline*, and *Larry King Live*. He apparently has no qualms about making statements such as this: "The evidence is abundant that our thoughts and intentions can inhibit or harm a variety of living, biological systems."[133] In fact, such "evidence" is *not* abundant. Thousands of years of recorded human history have shown that human beings are adept at causing harm to living things through all manner of physical means; it has also shown that thoughts alone cannot kill. Such a statement is as false as Virginia Harris's claim that "There is no shortage of statistical data" supporting Christian Science.[134]

Dossey is not the only doctor making simplistic connections between human health and emotions, thoughts, and feelings. Since the 1980s, Bernie Siegal, a medical doctor and author, has been telling cancer patients that their disease derives from their own anger and other negative emotions. Andrew Weil, author of *Spontaneous Healing* and other best-selling books, videotapes, and assorted health products, wants to have it both ways, suggesting that "cultivating anger or emotional isolation" can "obstruct . . . the healing system" but that "appropriate, focused expressions of anger can sometimes activate the healing system."[135] Dr. John E. Sarno, in *Healing Back Pain* and other best-sellers, has argued that most back pain, as well as the pain of carpal tunnel syndrome, fibromyalgia, migraine, hay fever, asthma, and other illnesses, is caused by "repressed rage," a syndrome he calls T.M.S., "tension myositis syndrome."[136] This diagnosis is not recognized by professional medical associations. Sarno has attracted crowds to his lectures and has a number of celebrity clients, including Howard Stern, Anne Bancroft, and even John Stossel, the correspondent for ABC's *20/20* who has made a career out of skeptical reporting on social trends, including medical fads and faith healing.

Likewise, Deepak Chopra, M.D., has been hugely successful, selling millions of books, CDs, seminars, lectures, herbal supplements, massage oils, and movie scripts that promote his prescription that an immersion in love can bring long life (120 years!) and a lot of money: "When your actions are motivated by love . . . the surplus energy you gather and enjoy can be channeled to create anything that you want, including unlimited wealth."[137] Chopra's message—he claims that merely reading his books has prompted cancer to go into remission—has certainly brought him great popularity, just as Eddy's similar message did for her, but whether his message derives from boundless love is questionable; like Eddy, Chopra is known for aggressively filing suit against critics.[138]

Also like Eddy, whose spiritual laws and seven synonyms for God were the backbone of her belief system, these new medical metaphysicians have cloaked their prescriptions in pseudoscience and disguised the fact that there is little scientific support for their theories by offering carefully chosen testimonials. Their therapies are simplistically systematized with numbers. Weil has "seven strategies of successful patients"; Sarno, "six basic needs"; and Chopra, "seven spiritual laws of success," as well as "seven spiritual laws for parents." Yet another pretender to the mind-healing throne, Rudolph Ballentine, M.D., offers "6 Integrative Medicine Practices for Mind, Body & Spirit" in his book *Radical Healing;* one of the six is "Flower Essences." All enjoy celebrity endorsements and connections, with Chopra in the lead, having served as pied piper to Donna Karan, Demi Moore, George Harrison, Mikhail Gorbachev, Benjamin Spock, Bonnie Raitt, Prince Charles, and—the crown jewel—Princess Diana.

But in the rush to revive magical thinking and to invoke the powers of magnets, malicious animal magnetism, mesmeric healing, spiritual laws, and the laying on of hands, Mary Baker Eddy herself looms large, although some of her heirs seem not to know it. The ideas and language of Christian Science have been enshrined in the popular religious culture of the twentieth century, often by those who have been Christian Scientists or been directly influenced by it.

Marianne Williamson, the popular, charismatic lecturer who travels the globe lecturing on *A Course in Miracles*—an inspirational text written during the late 1960s by two psychologists at Columbia University—has published a number of books that naively repeat concepts derivative of Christian Science, a fact of which she seems blissfully unaware.

A Course in Miracles itself is directly influenced by Christian Science. One of its two authors, William Thetford, was raised as a Christian Scientist. When he was seven, his nine-year-old sister died of a streptococcal infection after treatment administered both by medical doctors and by Christian Science practitioners failed. According to a biography of the co-authors, *Journey with Distance: The Story Behind A Course in Miracles,* Thetford's parents renounced Christian Science, "and neither of them stepped inside a Christian Science church again."[139] Thetford then fell ill, spending several years bedridden. In middle age, when he was a professor of medical psychology at Columbia and director of the psychology department at Presbyterian Hospital in New York City, Thetford met Helen Schucman, another psychologist in his department at Columbia, and the two gradually developed a folie-à-deux, a shared delusion. Schucman believed that a mysterious voice was speaking to her, compelling her to write down inspired wisdom; Thetford became her amanuensis, taking dictation from the voice. These "transcripts" eventually became A Course in Miracles, a three-volume set including a textbook, a workbook, and a "Manual for Teachers." Like Mary Baker Eddy, Thetford and Schucman believed that the voice dictating to them was divine. Thus, they have minimized their authorship; inside the three volumes of A Course, no authors are listed.

No one who has read A Course in Miracles can fail to notice its conceptual and rhetorical similarities to Science and Health. A Course in Miracles is more modern in style and contains much of the language of the miraculous that Eddy rejected. But essential elements are virtually identical. Man is not an individual but a reflection of God. "Healing . . . is a way of approaching knowledge by thinking in accordance with the laws of God."[140] God is love, love is God. As in Science and Health, man and God are "one indivisible divine mind," as Williamson writes.[141] As in Christian Science, "only love is real," and fear is the enemy: "God is not the author of fear."[142] Illness is seen as the physical manifestation of sin or error, as it is in Christian Science, and death is denied: "There is no death."[143]

But before Marianne Williamson delved into this rich vein of reconstituted Christian Science, Louise L. Hay had already made deep inroads. Born in 1928 and raised during the Depression by Christian Science parents, Hay ran away from home at fifteen, after a traumatic childhood in which she was raped by a neighbor. A number of abusive relationships followed until she discovered the Science of Mind, one of the New Thought faiths and an offshoot of Christian Science. She became a minister of the Science of Mind church in New York City, eventually writing a book entitled Heal Your Body, which consisted of simplistic correspondences between physical symptoms and their psychological counterparts.[144]

The parallels drawn by Hay and the brief prayers she outlines for them bear a remarkable similarity to the cryptic notes on metaphysical obstetrics and other bodily problems that Eddy's students preserved. Hay explains, for example, that "kidney problems" result from "criticism, disappointment, failure," and prescribes these positive thoughts to cure them: "Divine right action is always taking place in my life. Only good comes from each experience."[145] Problems with "bone marrow" represent "deepest beliefs about the self." She writes, "Divine Spirit is the structure of my life."[146] Hay believes that her positive philosophy healed her of cervical cancer without medical treatment. This kind of positive thinking may seem harmless, but its hidden message—that the sick have somehow generated their own illness and are to blame for it—is ugly. Still, many readers, if sales figures and best-sellers are any indication, are desperately eager to feel a sense of control over their lives and diseases, even if blaming themselves is the only key to that control. Hay's book *You Can Heal Your Life* became a best-seller in 1984, and her version of positive thinking became popular among AIDS sufferers in 1980s Los Angeles, where she regularly led a group prayer called the Hayride.

It is also clear that the eccentric leaders of what eventually became the Church Universal and Triumphant were strongly influenced by Eddy and *Science and Health*, as well as by Madame Blavatsky's Theosophy. The Church Universal and Triumphant, famous during the 1980s for its predictions of nuclear doom issued from its compound in southwestern Montana, where its members constructed a number of bomb shelters, was formed by Mark and Elizabeth Clare Prophet in the 1960s. In 1975, the Prophets published a document purportedly written by one of the Ascended Masters, a spirit named Master El Morya. El Morya had this to say about Eddy's role in religious history:

In 1876, Helena Petrovna Blavatsky was ordered by the Master Kuthumi and me, then known as the Masters K.H. and M., to write Isis Unveiled. . . . Commissioned by Jesus the Christ, the Ascended Master Hilarion, and Mother Mary, Mary Baker Eddy was given certain revelations that she set forth in Science and Health with Key to the Scriptures. Though at times beset with their own preconceptions and the burden of the mass consciousness, these witnesses codified the truth and the law of East and West as the culmination of thousands of years of their souls' distillations of the Spirit.[147]

Although the Prophets' Church displayed a millennial fervor that has no counterpart in Christian Science, other elements of their beliefs attest to the inspiration provided by the older church. As in Christian Science, God and man are part of the same creation, with man's relation to God being likened to the rays of light emanating from the sun, a notion similar to the Christian Science concept of man reflecting God. God is referred to as "Father-Mother." And Jesus is seen as the human man, Christ as the principle of divine consciousness, concepts nearly identical to those of Christian Science. Even the name of the Church may have been inspired by Eddy, who appropriated "the Church Universal and Triumphant" from the Catholic tradition to describe her own movement in her *Church Manual*.[148]

Elizabeth Clare Prophet did not learn from her millennial predecessors, however, specifically prophesying (as the Millerites had before her) that Armageddon would arrive in 1990. Up until then, her movement had been growing rapidly, both in this country and abroad, particularly in Ghana and in Sweden, but when the end of the world failed to arrive on time, numbers fell off and they have not risen.

Christian Science has also inspired the Pentecostal "Word of Faith" or "Faith" movement, which preaches faith healing; one of its most visible proponents is the televangelist Benny Hinn. According to those who knew him, E. W. Kenyon (1867–1948), one of the original preachers in the movement, was a great admirer of Eddy's.[149] Kenyon "acknowledged the similarity" between his teachings and Christian Science, claims one adherent. "I can remember him saying, 'All that Christian Science lacks is the blood of Jesus Christ.' He was very conversant not only with Christian Science concepts but also with a lot of details of how Christian Science originated. . . . He admitted that he freely drew the water of his thinking from this well."[150] Word of Faith preachers inspired by Kenyon, including Hinn, Kenneth Copeland, and Kenneth Hagin, preach a gospel promising the easy availability of health and wealth that parallels and encompasses Eddy's teachings on "supply."

Perhaps the most intriguing Christian Science progeny has been the Church of Scientology, one of the youngest and most controversial of the new sects. L. Ron Hubbard, the founder of Scientology, was born in 1911, only a few months after Eddy's death, and he, too, made a connection between science and health. In *Dianetics*, the foundational text of Scientology, Hubbard defined his scientific technique, called Dianetics, as a "spiritual healing technology."[151] Hubbard claimed to have discovered a new "science of mind": "It is an organized science of thought built on definite axioms (statements of natural laws on the order of those of the physical sciences) . . . with which can be treated all inorganic mental ills and all organic psychosomatic ills."[152] Although Scientology differs sharply from Christian Science in many ways—its teachings derive from not one but a number of texts, are largely secret and vigorously protected by the Church, and are based on a science-fiction premise about multiple worlds, galactic confederations, reincarnation, and other concepts foreign to the older sect—there are, nonetheless, fundamental similarities. Hubbard taught that the human body was essentially a phase; that each individual possesses an immortal soul; that illness, disease, and insanity are foreign "implants" or "engrams" that are artificially inflicted on people; and that, by using the techniques and technology he developed, Scientologists can free themselves of such "implants," much as Christian Scientists free themselves of infirmities through the techniques of thought developed by Eddy. Hubbard's *Dianetics* was, in essence, a new *Science and Health* based on a vision of the "natural laws" of the universe.[153] Like Christian Science, Scientology encourages a distrust of doctors, drugs, and especially psychiatry and psychology; it claims to cure addictions and psychosomatic and organic illnesses of all kinds. Hubbard claimed that he himself had been cured by his new technique of blindness and other serious injuries arising from his service in the navy. (His claim to have suffered serious injuries during his naval service was subsequently disputed by government authorities.) For a time, the Church of Scientology headquarters in Los Angeles was known as the Mother Church. Scientology periodicals regularly print testimonials from its members regarding successful healings of all kinds of problems.

Knowingly or not, Hubbard himself followed in Eddy's footsteps. Deeply intolerant of criticism, he isolated himself with certain handpicked followers and exhibited paranoid fears of unconscious mental attacks, believing that "unseen forces" were allied against him and accusing his followers of trying to poison his food.[154] Like Eddy, he had a tendency toward grandiosity, inflating his military exploits and record, boasting of honors and medals that were not his, much as Eddy embellished her genealogy. When Hubbard died in 1986, his followers celebrated, believing that he had made a passage to a new phase of existence where he would continue his work. Exceeding even that of the Christian Science Church, the now-infamous institutional paranoia of the Church of Scientology—its leaders, including Hubbard's wife, were convicted of conspiracy and burglary during the 1970s after engaging in elaborate attempts to intimidate and investigate the church's enemies—has most recently materialized in its many harassment suits against former members and critics and contributed to its long conflict with the Internal Revenue Service, resolved in 1993 in the church's favor. The Church of Scientology in Clearwater, Florida, was recently brought up on criminal charges relating to the death of a young woman who was removed by her Scientologist colleagues from a local hospital, a death that seems to have resulted from the Scientologists' fear of medical doctors and medical institutions.[155]

In the spring of 1721, a century before Eddy was born, an epidemic of smallpox broke out in Boston, and Cotton Mather, having read reports from Turkey asserting that a mild case of the disease could render a person immune, inoculated his own son, who nearly died. The community was frightened and outraged by Mather's insistence that inoculation was a safe and effective means of protecting the populace; a bomb was thrown into his house in November 1721, with a message attached: "Cotton Mather, You Dog, Dam you: I'l inoculate you with this, with a Pox to you."[156]

The Mathers were consistent Puritans: they believed in witches and in supernatural phenomena of all kinds. But they were also early naturalists, fascinated by crude scientific theories. Increase Mather's *Remarkable Providences* recounts tale after tale of wondrous attacks by God on the wicked through lightning, storm, and fire, as well as miraculous acts of salvation enjoyed by the devout; it also includes speculation about the mysteries of the physical world. To inoculate against smallpox was seemingly to deprive God of one of his dire powers, but the Mathers did not hesitate. Their critics denounced the preventative measure as another of the Mathers' follies, suggesting that the family had contributed to New England three periods of "infatuation": the persecution of the Quakers in 1659, the hanging of suspected witches thirty or so years later, and inoculation, or "Self-procuring the Small Pox," in 1721. "Infatuation," one writer noted, "seems to return to us after a Period of about Thirty Years."[157]

History, of course, has shown that inoculation was not an "infatuation." It was, in fact, arguably the greatest boon humanity has ever known, and through it smallpox—the killer of millions—became the first disease ever to be eradicated from the world. But the simultaneous condemnation of the Mathers for their experiments in inoculation and their role in hanging witches demonstrates how tragically difficult it can be to separate reason from faith, and science from religion. "Infatuation" still powerfully afflicts our spiritual lives, which are, just as they were for the Puritans, inextricably linked to how we perceive our bodies and our world. Hysterical fears of the sort that inspired a bomb to be thrown through Cotton Mather's window are still abroad in the land. In 1998, the critic Elaine Showalter was the target of death threats because she had suggested, in her book *Hystories*, that several currently fashionable medical conditions, such as chronic fatigue syndrome, are psychosomatic illnesses. Nation of Islam leader Louis Farrakhan has become allied with a dentist who advocates the theory that AIDS and the Ebola virus were created through the contamination of common vaccines by a shadowy conspiracy of government, military, and big business.[158] Extremists from both the political right and left have suggested that fluoridation of the water supply is deadly and that common vaccines are dangerous.

Mary Baker Eddy's fear of just such invisible foes was legendary, and her long, tortured life remains a tale that should caution us against the same excesses. So should the fate of her followers. The suggestibility, infatuation, and enthusiasm that sparked Christian Science and has also sparked many other religious cults and sects lies behind our current anxious fixations on imaginary perils and medical conspiracies. Florid though they may seem, such fears can have far from imaginary consequences. Should we continue to pursue them, our providences will surely grow ever more remarkable.

GLOSSARY

At the end of *Science and Health*, Eddy provides a glossary of her metaphysical and spiritual interpretations of God, biblical proper names, and such words as "devil," "sheep," and so on. Taking her cue, Christian Scientists have developed their own unofficial glossary of religious jargon, based both on her writings and on the day-to-day practice of their faith. An understanding of the ways in which Scientists use certain words is crucial to understanding both the religion and the folkways of its followers. The First Church of Christ, Scientist, for its part, has engendered an array of sometimes bewildering names, titles, and officialese, and it has often used the peculiar language of Christian Science to rationalize its policies to skeptical members of the press or to government officials. So, here, for the reader, is a glossary of the unique terminology of this religion, a window onto the world of Christian Science.

Aggressive mental suggestion

This term appears in the *Manual*, where Eddy writes that it is the "duty" of every Scientist "to defend himself daily against aggressive mental suggestion." The term refers to ideas or notions disturbing to the Scientific mind, often involving illness, disease, death, materialism, cynicism, or skepticism. Such suggestions would usually proceed from sources outside the Christian Science realm: from non-Scientists, from the media, from those who attack the religion. Aggressive mental suggestions may arise from the minds of Scientists themselves, in the form of unwelcome or discouraging thoughts; there is much discourse in the Church's religious periodicals about how to combat aggressive mental suggestions.

Authorized literature

This term appears nowhere in Eddy's writings but was adopted by the Church after her death in order to distinguish Church publications from mind-cure literature originating from outside individuals and institutions, and to control the reading of its members. Labels listing the "Authorized literature" issued by the Church's Publishing Society can still be found in library copies of such books; on many books, "Authorized Edition" is stamped on the spine.

The term has become fraught, particularly in recent years, as legal disputes have broken out between different Christian Science factions over its exact definition and over which books deserve to be labeled "Authorized."

Chemicalization

Chemicalization can occur in the body or mind of an individual, or in society as a whole. It is a process of disruption or upheaval—an obvious worsening of symptoms or situation—which Eddy described as taking place in response to *Christian Science treatment,* almost as if *error* or the devil were disturbed by the influx of good and were fighting back. Eddy wrote of it: "What I term *chemicalization* is the upheaval produced when immortal Truth is destroying erroneous mortal belief. Mental chemicalization brings sin and sickness to the surface, forcing impurities to pass away, as is the case with a fermenting fluid."[1]

Christian Science practitioners frequently use the term to rationalize a recurrence or explosion of symptoms in patients under Christian Science treatment; the *Committee on Publication* has used it to explain the Church's bad press or other societal outrages committed against Christian Science. This book may be seen as a form of chemicalization.

Christian Science branch churches and societies:

A Christian Science branch church is any Christian Science church under the control of *the Mother Church.* Such churches are officially titled by number according to their establishment in a city or community—First Church of Los Angeles, for example—but only "The" Mother Church (or "The" First Church of Christ, Scientist, Boston, Massachusetts) is prefaced by the article, always capped in Church literature. Members frequently refer to their churches simply by number (as in "I'm a member of Third Church"); this practice derives from the traditional numbering of Congregational and other churches.

The closing of many branch churches in cities has led to interruptions in the numbering. Los Angeles has a Forty-third Church, but only twenty branch churches remain in the city. A branch church is supposed to have at least sixteen members, four of whom are members of the Mother Church and one of whom is a *Journal*-listed practitioner. Some Christian Scientists have recently claimed that there are branch churches in existence that do not meet these guidelines.

Smaller groups of Scientists can meet as Christian Science societies, which hold the same services as churches but often in private homes or rented spaces.

Christian Science lectures and lecturers

Christian Science lecturers—some fifty to sixty Scientists who constitute the Church's Board of Lectureship—are approved annually by the Church's Board of Directors. Lecturers deliver one-hour free public talks on Christian Science; branch churches usually sponsor one or more such talks a year. The Church itself approves the written text of each lecture; some lectures have been recorded or videotaped for radio or television.

Lecturers are currently giving talks on *Science and Health* in bookstore chains, such as Borders Books and Barnes & Noble. Recent lectures have had such titles as "God Knows," "Prayer Is Power," and "God's Healing Law of Love." They are geared toward a general audience, but lecturers do not take questions from the floor (although they may address them individually after the presentation). The lectures, on Eddy's directive, are not to be considered social occasions; refreshments are not served.

Lectures are not regarded as Christian Science teaching; that can only be given by authorized *Christian Science teachers* during *class-instruction*.

Christian Science nurse

Christian Science nurses are not state licensed and generally have no medical or nursing training. If they have had such training before converting to Christian Science, they are required by the Church to drop any medical licensure they may have. They receive minimal instruction in rudimentary sanitary care, including how to bathe and turn bedridden patients; how to cover unsightly wounds with pads or bandages (but not how to treat them medically); how to prepare meals; and how to make beds. They read to patients from Church literature and sometimes sing hymns. For more on the training and unusual practices of Christian Science nurses, see "Inside the Sanatoriums" in Part IV.

Christian Science nursing home, sanatorium, or Benevolent Association

Christian Science nursing homes, or sanatoriums, offer only nonmedical, Christian Science care by Christian Science nurses and practitioners.

There are several Christian Science Benevolent Associations, including one in Chestnut Hill, Massachusetts, and one in San Francisco, California; these serve as training institutions for Christian Science nurses. Christian Science nursing homes are exempt from the licensing procedures and inspections required of other such institutions; they are inspected only by Christian Science officials.

Christian Science organization

Christian Science organizations can be formed, according to Eddy, by faculty and/or students at any college or university. They conduct meetings or services similar to those held at branch churches, which may include reading the Lesson, giving testimonies, or singing hymns, but may also include informal discussion.

These college groups used to be known in the vernacular as "Orgs," but the Church has recently put a stop to this practice, instructing Scientists to call them by their initials, "CSOs," perhaps because the Church of Scientology refers to one of its entities as the "Sea Org" (or Sea Organization).

Christian Science periodicals

The Church publishes the *Christian Science Journal*, a monthly religious periodical that lists all Christian Science branch churches, societies, and organizations, and the place and time of their services, as well as the names, addresses, and phone numbers of Church-approved practitioners, teachers, and nurses, and of the worldwide Committees on Publication.

The *Christian Science Sentinel*, a weekly, contains, as does the *Journal*, editorials and articles on Christian Science, church announcements, and testimonies of healing. The *Sentinel* also contains brief news notes of interest to Scientists.

The *Christian Science Herald* is an international version of the *Journal* published in twelve languages, monthly in some and quarterly in others.

The *Christian Science Quarterly—Bible Lessons* contains the weekly lesson-sermon read in all Christian Science branch churches and the Mother Church; it consists of selections from both the Bible and *Science and Health*.

The Church's Publishing Society also publishes the *Christian Science Monitor*, the international daily founded by Eddy in 1908. The *Monitor*, now published only on weekdays and available by mail or e-mail, contains a daily religious article, and its news standards are informed by Christian Science teachings; for example, it does not publish obituaries and avoids giving the ages of people mentioned in its news coverage. It also covers Church news.

Christian Science practitioner

A Christian Science practitioner is said to be in the public practice or healing ministry of Christian Science. Practitioners treat their patients through prayer and prayer alone, although they may advise a patient to read or study various passages in the Bible or *Science and Health*.

Practitioners take patients who are seeking healing of any of a multitude of problems: physical illnesses; mental illnesses; problems with relationships, marriages, or children; professional problems or problems relating to business; alcohol or drug abuse. Practitioners will not, however, accept a patient who wishes to continue seeing a medical doctor or who is taking medication; they also will not accept patients who are in hospitals receiving medical care or medication. Except in very severe cases or cases involving children, they generally discuss cases in their offices or over the phone; the latter is called absent treatment. They charge relatively modest fees for their services, from $5 to $50 for a treatment. Many insurance plans, including government insurance plans, cover these fees.

Practitioners who have demonstrated to the Church's satisfaction (by submitting testimonials) that they are successful in the healing practice are listed in the back of each month's *Journal*; this constitutes the Church's only form of licensing or certification of practitioners. Some practitioners who have not been able to achieve the prestigious *Journal* listing advertise in the yellow pages. Practitioners who are not also teachers of Christian Science may use the initials "C.S." after their names, particularly in their *Journal* listings, indicating that they have completed *class-instruction*.

Christian Science teachers, class-instruction, and Association

Christian Science teachers are generally practitioners who have taken the so-called Normal class offered once every three years by the Board of Education of the Mother Church. ("Normal school" was a term much in use in the nineteenth century for institutions that trained teachers; it is taken from the French *école normale*.) Some Christian Science teachers may have ceased to maintain an active practice, but they have been practitioners in the past. Teachers have no other institutional role in their branch churches or at the Mother Church (unless they happen to hold other positions), but their status is one of great prestige and respect within the Christian Science movement.

After completing the Normal class, teachers are then free to perform "class-instruction," also known as Primary class, a two-week course that Scientists may take once in their lives. Class-instruction is required for anyone who wishes to become a Christian Science practitioner or nurse; it is generally offered in the teacher's hometown. Class-instruction is often referred to simply as "class," and those who have taken it are said to be "class taught."

Eddy ruled that teachers could instruct only one class a year of not more than thirty pupils (apparently to prevent any teacher from obtaining too large a following). The curriculum is drawn largely from the question-and-answer chapter of *Science and Health*, "Recapitulation," but it is augmented by specific teachings on how to begin each day with various protective arguments and prayers designed specifically to vanquish *malicious animal magnetism*, hypnotism, spiritualism, and other Christian Science enemies.

Both class-instruction and Association meetings are surrounded with secrecy. Pupils are instructed not to take notes or, if notes are allowed, are forbidden to reproduce or share them and are requested to ensure that the notes are destroyed upon their deaths.

Those taught by teachers who fall afoul of the Church administration and are stripped of their status must be retaught by an approved or "loyal" teacher.[2]

Once a year, Christian Science teachers hold Association: a meeting of all former students, to whom they give a brief talk. Association typically takes place over a weekend.

Christian Science teachers use the initials "C.S.B." after their names, indicating that they have completed Normal class and received the degree of "Bachelor of Christian Science."

Christian Science treatment

Christian Science treatment consists entirely of prayer, whether administered by a *Christian Science practitioner*, by oneself, or by one's family or friends. Christian Science treatment is the only kind of treatment administered in Christian Science nursing homes.

Claim or belief

Christian Scientists routinely refer to any problem, but particularly to a physical illness, injury, or symptom as a claim or belief in matter or mortal mind, as in "I was healed of a *belief* of chronic liver complaint," or "She was struggling with the *claim* of weakness of the heart," or "She was dealing with a physical *claim*." Other common phrases indicating a belief or claim are "material sense testimony" or "mortal mind testimony." When discussing such physical problems, Scientists also tend to employ verbs implying that the problem has only a conditional or illusory reality, as in "I *seemed* to have a cold."

This language occurs frequently in the early years of the Christian Science periodicals but has been discouraged in recent years as confusing to non-Scientists.

Committee on Publication; Committees on Publication

For an extensive description of the history and function of the Committees on Publication, see "The C.O.P. and 'The Corrective Work,' " in part II of this book.

Demonstration

A demonstration is a healing of any inharmonious condition, including disease, illness, injury, unhappiness, joblessness, relationship difficulties, marital problems, etc. The term originated with Eddy, who frequently urged her followers to demonstrate the Scientific truths of Christian Science through healing.

Error

A central concept in Christian Science, error proceeds from mortal mind. It is a belief in mortality, materialism, and matter, as well as in all ideas and notions that proceed from the belief that the material world is a reality. Scientists devote themselves to recognizing, weeding out, and correcting the error in their thinking, any negative thoughts about others or about themselves that arise from lingering beliefs that the body or other physically imperfect forms of matter can wield power or feel pain.

Field

Eddy used this term in the *Manual* and elsewhere to refer to Christian Scientists around the world. The Field includes all Scientists who live and work outside

Christian Science officialdom, who do not work for the Mother Church. Christian Scientists also often refer to themselves as the movement, and sometimes as the Cause.

Handled

In Christian Science jargon, a person behaving in a way inappropriate for a Scientist (by, for example, seeking medical care or openly criticizing the religion) is said to be handled by malicious animal magnetism, handled by error, or handled by mortal mind. The term implies being in the grip of or being controlled by error or evil: being out of control. Being handled is a dangerous and undesirable state.

Knowing the Truth

This phrase, used so often by Scientists, refers to the mental act of holding fast to the belief that man is not material, that God is love and God is all, and that man is a reflection of God.

Malicious animal magnetism

Malicious animal magnetism (which Eddy also referred to as M.A.M.) is one of the most confusing concepts in Christian Science. It is the force of evil, which can affect just about everything on earth for ill, but it is also defined by Eddy as powerless. It is poorly defined in the chapter "Animal Magnetism Unmasked" in *Science and Health*, but Eddy referred to it copiously throughout her writings and private correspondence as a force that can poison, kill, and hypnotize people. She uses mesmerism, hypnotism, mortal mind, witchcraft, and priestcraft as synonyms for M.A.M.

Bryan Wilson, a sociologist, referred to it as "a type of institutionalised paranoia," and the externalization of Eddy's "own inner conflicts, elevated . . . to cosmic significance."[3]

Malpractice, malpractitioners, and "malping"

Malpractice, in Christian Science, is any intentional thought or effort to control the beliefs or condition of another person, either maliciously or without the express permission of that person. Eddy believed that malpractice by her enemies (nearly all of whom were either former students, critics, or Catholics) could and did sicken her; on two occasions, she instructed her followers to say that, if she should die, she had been killed by mental malpractice. Malpractitioners are those who engage in malpractice. Malpractice is sometimes called malping by Christian Science children.

Materia medica

This term, commonly used in previous centuries to denote the branch of medical science dealing with drugs, is still common parlance among Christian Scientists, who use it to refer to all aspects of medicine. Eddy denounced materia medica in the strongest possible terms, asserting that "the profession of medicine originated in idolatry" and proclaiming it "pitiful to lead men into temptation . . . to victimize the race with intoxicating prescriptions for the sick."[4]

Scientists also colloquially refer to anything having to do with medicine as "the medical," as if medical science were a political party or a religion in its own right. One writer notes: "Materia medica, as they call it, is believed to be a channel for mental malpractice, and in the field the warning is often heard that 'the doctor will put a law on the patient.' "[5]

Mental surgery

Eddy encouraged her followers to believe in mental surgery, and there are many testimonies in the Christian Science periodicals of bones resetting themselves, of foreign objects being expelled from the skin, and of Scientists hearing or feeling strange movements or sounds in their bodies as they are restored to perfect health.

The Mother Church

The Mother Church, also formally referred to as The First Church of Christ, Scientist, was the first Christian Science church, built in Boston in 1894. (It now consists of two churches, built one on top of the other: the original Mother Church, and the vast Extension, completed in 1906.)

The name refers not only to the edifice but to the headquarters of the Church and to the Church bureaucracy, which occupies buildings at the Christian Science Church Center surrounding the Mother Church, at 1 Norway Street (between Massachusetts and Huntington Avenues). These buildings include the Publishing Society building, built alongside the Mother Church during the 1930s, which houses the offices of the *Christian Science Monitor* and other Publishing Society business; the Mother Church Sunday school; the Colonnade building, which once housed the Church's radio and television enterprises; and the twenty-eight-story administration building, where the Committee on Publication, the Church archives, and the offices of the Board of Directors and other Church officials are located.

Outlining

"Outlining" was a term once commonly used by Christian Scientists, and appears frequently in early numbers of the Church periodicals, although it is less common today. It refers to a practice discouraged, if not forbidden, among Scientists: the practice of praying for a specific outcome or a desired result. Scientists are taught to pray to understand the perfection of all of God's creation, including man as God's reflection; to outline a specific need or desire—such as a physical healing, a particular amount of money or particular material goods—is thought to interfere with healing. Instead, Scientists are encouraged to pray about a specific issue by studying, often with a concordance to the Bible and Eddy's writings, the meanings of and allusions to words or concepts that are affiliated with the condition requiring the healing. For example, if a Scientist were dealing with a *claim* or *belief* of deafness, he might look up the word "Ears" in the glossary in *Science and Health*, as well as references to hearing or deafness in the Bible; he would not, however, pray asking God to heal his deafness, because the deafness originates in his own thought, which must be corrected. It cannot be corrected by outlining or begging God for some specific help.

Supply

This is a term used by Eddy, and her followers to this day, to refer to the infinite supply of all resources available to anyone who understands the true nature of God. It can be used to refer to a supply of anything—money, material goods, buildings, etc.—that may be needed; although Scientists do not outline their needs in their prayers, they may, should they find themselves in need, pray to understand that the infinite source of supply, God, provides for all. For further discussion of supply, see "Nothing Succeeds Like Supply" in part III.

NOTES

Works Frequently Cited

Bates and Dittemore
Bates, Ernest Sutherland and John V. Dittemore. *Mary Baker Eddy: The Truth and the Tradition*. New York: Knopf, 1932.

Cather and Milmine
Cather, Willa, and Georgine Milmine. *The Life of Mary Baker G. Eddy and the History of Christian Science*. Lincoln: University of Nebraska Press, 1993.

Dakin, Mrs. Eddy
Dakin, Edwin Franden. *Mrs. Eddy: The Biography of a Virginal Mind*. Blue Ribbon Books, 1930.

First Church of Christ, Scientist and Miscellany
Eddy, Mary Baker. *The First Church of Christ, Scientist and Miscellany*. In *Prose Works*. Boston: First Church of Christ, Scientist, 1941. [Paginated separately.]

Manual
Eddy, Mary Baker. *Manual of The Mother Church, The First Church of Christ, Scientist in Boston, Massachusetts*. Eighty-ninth edition. Boston: First Church of Christ, Scientist, 1936.

"Message to the First Church of Christ, Scientist"
"Message to The First Church of Christ, Scientist or The Mother Church, Boston." In *Prose Works*. Boston: First Church of Christ, Scientist, 1941. [Paginated separately.]

Miscellaneous Writings
  Miscellaneous Writings: 1883–1896. Boston: First Church of Christ, 1924. Also included in Prose Works. Boston: First Church of Christ, Scientist, 1941. [Paginated separately.]

Retrospection and Introspection
  Retrospection and Introspection. In Prose Works. Boston: First Church of Christ, Scientist, 1941. [Paginated separately.]

Science and Health
  Science and Health with Key to the Scriptures. Boston: First Church of Christ, Scientist, 1934.

Gottschalk, Emergence
  Gottschalk, Stephen. The Emergence of Christian Science in American Religious Life. Berkeley, Calif.: University of California Press, 1973.

Peel, Years of Discovery
  Peel, Robert.
  Mary Baker Eddy: The Years of Discovery. 1966.

Peel, Years of Trial
  Mary Baker Eddy: The Years of Trial. 1971.

Peel, Years of Authority
  Mary Baker Eddy: The Years of Authority. 1977.
  All originally published by Holt, Rinehart and Winston; now published by Boston: Christian Science Publishing Society.

Shannon, "Golden Memories."
  Shannon, Clara. "Golden Memories." Santa Clarita, Calif.: The Bookmark, photocopy.

Silberger, Mary Baker Eddy
  Silberger, Julius Jr. Mary Baker Eddy: An Interpretive Biography of the Founder of Christian Science. Boston: Little, Brown, 1980.

Smaus, The Golden Days
  Smaus, Jewel Spangler. Mary Baker Eddy: The Golden Days. Boston: Christian Science Publishing Society, 1966.

Thomas, "Footsteps"
  Thomas, Robert David. "With Bleeding Footsteps": Mary Baker Eddy's Path to Religious Leadership. New York: Knopf, 1994.

Wilson, Sects and Society
  Wilson, Bryan R. Sects and Society: A Sociological Study of the Elim Tabernacle, Christian Science, and the Christadelphians. Berkeley, Calif.: University of California Press, 1961.

Preface: God's Perfect Child

1. Christian Science children are still being taught that "there is no spot where God is not." See the testimony of a child named Wayne Ingram, of Ontario, California, in *Christian Science Sentinel* 99, no. 43 (27 October 1997), p. 38.

2. Details about the death of Michael Schram come from Richard Buck, "Christian Scientists to Probe Mercer Island Boy's Death," *Seattle Times*, 23 September 1979; Kathy Gay, "Memories of Michael Schram Surrounded with Controversy," *Mercer Island Reporter*, 26 September 1979; "Michael Edward Schram, 12" (obituary), *Mercer Island Reporter*, 26 September 1979; John McCoy, "12-year-old Mercer Island Boy Dies of Untreated Appendicitis," *Seattle Post-Intelligencer*, 13 October 1979; Kathy Gay, "The Schram Case: Recent Change in Washington's Negligence Statute Leads Prosecutor Not to File Charges," *Mercer Island Reporter*, 17 October 1979.

3. Jack Schram, telephone interview with author, 11 February 1996. Unless otherwise indicated, all quotations of Jack Schram are from this interview.

4. Jonathan Edwards, *Images or Shadows of Divine Things*, Perry Miller, ed. (New Haven: Yale University Press, 1948).

5. F. O. Matthiessen, *American Renaissance* (New York: Oxford University Press, 1941), p. 368.

6. Ralph Waldo Emerson, "Historic Notes of Life and Letters in New England," *The Transcendentalists*, Perry Miller, ed. (Cambridge, Mass.: Harvard University Press, 1950), pp. 494–95, 496.

7. For the number of churches, see Wilson, *Sects and Society*, p. 149. For membership figures for these years, see Rodney Stark, "The Rise and Fall of Christian Science," *Journal of Contemporary Religion* 13, no. 2 (1998), p. 191, table 1.

8. Wilson, *Sects and Society*, p. 149. Wilson cites figures compiled for the Institute of Social and Religious Research, New York, and published in Luther C. Fry, *The U.S. Looks at Its Churches* (New York: Institute of Social and Religious Research, 1930).

9. "Message to the Mother Church," in *Miscellaneous Writings*, p. 322. On Eddy's instruction, there are no communion services in the Mother Church. There are two communion services in Christian Science branch churches, one in January and one in July, but the form of the service is largely the same as on other Sundays. Members of the congregation are, however, invited to kneel on Communion Sundays at one point during the service.

10. Eddy herself encouraged this practice. In 1903, she wrote to the Christian Science Board of Directors: "It would be a good thing to have one of my hymns read and sung about every Sunday. It would spiritualize the thought of your audience, and this is more needed in the church than aught else can be." See Mary Baker Eddy, *Seven Hymns* (Boston: First Church of Christ, Scientist, 1992), not paginated.

11. See Peter Steinfels, "Beliefs," *The New York Times*, 1 November 1997.

12. Rodney Stark, "The Rise and Fall of Christian Science," *Journal of Contemporary Religion* 13, no. 2 (1998), p. 203.

13. Ibid.

14. Arthur O. Lovejoy, *The Great Chain of Being: A Study of the History of an Idea* (Cambridge, Mass.: Harvard University Press, 1964), pp. 25–31.

15. The Christian Science Publishing Society, *Mary Baker Eddy: Twentieth-Century Biographers Series, An Introduction* (Boston: Christian Science Publishing Society, 1991), p. 41, n. 6. The author of this pamphlet, introducing a series of biographies and memoirs about Mary Baker Eddy that the Church reissued beginning in 1991, is not identified. That shadowy figure has, of course, misused the idiomatic "tip his hat"; he really means "tip his *hand*."

16. See Marion Cates, "Never Born, Never Dying," *Christian Science Sentinel* 98, no. 40 (30 September 1996), p. 13.

17. Thomas P. Griesa, letter to Virginia S. Harris, 31 March 1992. The quotation from this letter also appears in James L. Franklin, "Prominent Member Issues Call for Account of Media Spending," *Boston Globe*, 6 April 1992.

18. Nathaniel Hawthorne, "The Minister's Black Veil," in *Twice-Told Tales* (1837).

Part I. Mary Baker Eddy: "Mere Historic Incidents"

1. Nathaniel Hawthorne, "Young Goodman Brown," *Mosses from an Old Manse* (1846).

2. The bibliographical history of Eddy's works is complex. After its first publication in 1875, *Science and Health* went through seven major revisions: the second edition in 1878, the third edition in 1881, the sixth edition in 1883, the sixteenth edition in 1886, the fiftieth edition in 1891, the 226th edition in 1902, and the final major revision in 1906, at which time Eddy discontinued the practice of numbering the editions. The final edition was the 432nd, according to *A Christian Science Library: A Descriptive and Extended Bibliography*, Ernest J. Brosang (privately printed, 1990), p. 6. Several authors have noted, however, that it was Eddy's practice to make numerous smaller corrections in other printings, in addition to the changes made in the major revisions. Brosang reports that "4000 changes were made [in *Science and Health*] from 1907 to 1910." William Dana Orcutt, a printer who worked with Eddy, reports in *Mary Baker Eddy and Her Books* (Boston: Christian Science Publishing Society, 1950), p. 31: "During 1886–1890 editions numbering through forty-eight of Science and Health were issued from the 1886 plates, each new printing containing textual corrections in cases where the author felt she could convey her message in clearer form or simpler language." Stephen Gottschalk, in *The Emergence of Christian Science in American Religious Life* (Berkeley: University of California Press, 1973), p. 39, also confirms that Eddy was an inveterate reviser: "Mrs. Eddy made numerous smaller changes from edition to edition. . . . These small changes she considered exceedingly important."

3. *Retrospection and Introspection*, in *Prose Works Other Than Science and Health with Key to the Scriptures*, pp. 21–22 [paginated separately]. According to Brosang's *A Christian Science Library*, pp. 11–12, the first version of this work appeared in

1885 and was entitled *Historical Sketch of Metaphysical Healing*; it was reissued and revised several times before appearing under its present title in 1891.

4. Cather and Milmine, p. 7.

5. Lyman P. Powell, *Mary Baker Eddy: A Life Size Portrait* (New York: Macmillan, 1930), p. 284.

6. Peel, *Years of Discovery*, p. 5.

7. Cather and Milmine, p. 8.

8. See Peel, *Years of Discovery*, p. 5; Thomas, "With Footsteps," p. 4.

9. *Retrospection and Introspection*, p. 5.

10. Rev. Irving C. Tomlinson, *Twelve Years with Mary Baker Eddy: Recollections and Experiences* (Boston: Christian Science Publishing Society, 1945), p. 17.

11. The photograph is reproduced in Cather and Milmine, facing page 10.

12. *Retrospection and Introspection*, p. 10.

13. This anecdote appears in Clara Shannon, "Golden Memories" (Santa Clarita, Calif.: The Bookmark, transcript) pp. 2–3; it also appears in Smaus, *The Golden Days*, p. 34.

14. *Retrospection and Introspection*, p. 11.

15. Smaus, *Golden Days*, p. 37.

16. Peel, *Years of Discovery*, p. 76.

17. Smaus, *Golden Days*, pp. 39–40.

18. Shannon, "Golden Memories," p. 2.

19. Adam H. Dickey, *Memoirs of Mary Baker Eddy* (1927; Santa Clarita, Calif.: The Bookmark, transcript, 1992), p. 50.

20. *Retrospection and Introspection*, p. 8.

21. Ibid., p. 9; 1 Sam. 3:9.

22. Dickey, *Memoirs of Mary Baker Eddy*, p. 53.

23. Thomas, "Footsteps," p. 196.

24. *Retrospection and Introspection*, p. 13.

25. Ibid., pp. 13–14.

26. Cather and Milmine, p. 20.

27. Luke 2:49.

28. Cather and Milmine, p. 19.

29. Eddy, "Reply to McClure's Magazine," *The First Church of Christ, Scientist and Miscellany*, in *Prose Works Other Than Science and Health* (Boston: First Church of Christ, Scientist, 1953), p. 311 (paginated separately).

30. Smaus, *Golden Days*, p. 62; Peel, *Years of Discovery*, p. 48.

31. Paul E. Johnson, *A Shopkeeper's Millennium: Society and Revivals in Rochester, New York, 1815–1837* (New York: Hill and Wang, 1978), pp. 3–4.

32. Ibid., p. 4.

33. Harold Bloom, *The American Religion: The Emergence of the Post-Christian Nation* (New York: Simon & Schuster, 1992), p. 87.

34. Fawn M. Brodie, *No Man Knows My History: The Life of Joseph Smith*, 2nd ed. (New York: Vintage Books, 1995), p. 259.

35. Ibid., p. 257.

36. Ibid., pp. 12, 14.

37. *Retrospection and Introspection*, p. 10.
38. Cather and Milmine, pp. 21–22.
39. Edward Shorter, *From Paralysis to Fatigue: A History of Psychosomatic Illness in the Modern Era* (New York: Free Press, 1992), pp. 5–10.
40. Bloom, *American Religion*, p. 133.
41. Peel, *Years of Discovery*, p. 13.
42. Ibid., p. 22.
43. Ibid., p. 44.
44. Ibid.
45. Ibid., pp. 44–45.
46. See Margery Fox, "Protest in Piety: Christian Science Revisited," *International Journal of Women's Studies* 1, no. 4 (July/August 1978), p. 409. Fox writes, "Curiously, but significantly, biographical references to Mary's physical disabilities, which seemed so severe a few years earlier, cease altogether at this time. . . . Catching sight of a larger goal and channeling her talents and energy into achieving it seem to have improved Mary's health."
47. Mary had some influential close neighbors near Sanbornton Bridge, later called Tilton; she was only five miles from a Shaker settlement at East Canterbury. Members of that group were, one of Eddy's biographers notes, "frequently tried in the courts for various supposed offences" and were the subject of much local news and gossip. See Ernest Sutherland Bates and John V. Dittemore, *Mary Baker Eddy: The Truth and the Tradition* (New York: Knopf, 1932), p. 155.

   The similarities between certain aspects of Shaker belief and practice and those of the Christian Scientists are striking. Ann Lee, the founder and leader of the Shakers, lived in Concord, New Hampshire, for a time, after arriving in this country from England in 1775. Ann Lee's followers called her "Mother" and regarded her as the woman of the Apocalypse clothed with the sun, as Eddy's followers would her. The Shakers' version of the Lord's Prayer began "Our Father *and Mother* which art in Heaven," and they called their founding body the Mother Church. Like Ann Lee, Eddy instructed her followers to prefer silent prayer over audible prayer and, while not advocating total celibacy as the Shakers did, implied that it was a higher spiritual state. Many early Eddy acolytes, particularly women, practiced it.

   How deeply it would impress the young Mary Baker Glover—who experimented unhappily with teaching youngsters and who dreamed of learning to play the piano so that she might support herself—that a *woman* had achieved such power, independence, and respect, at least among her own followers. Cather and Milmine, in an appendix to their biography, listed the "significant resemblances" between Shaker belief and Christian Science, supporting the idea that Eddy admired and coveted Mother Ann Lee's position. They particularly noted the fact that Ann Lee "declared that she had the gift of healing" and practiced a form of what would become, in Eddy's parlance, malicious animal magnetism: "The Shakers believed that Mother Ann had spiritual illumination. . . . her followers believed that, with her mental powers, she could inflict torment upon them in this world" (p. 495).

48. Peel, *Years of Discovery*, p. 320, n. 97.

49. See ibid., p. 62.

50. The most detailed account of the Glovers' married life is to be found in ibid., pp. 67–72.

51. Eddy's claims concerning writing about slavery and freeing her husband's slaves can be found in Shannon, "Golden Memories," p. 6; Sibyl Wilbur, *The Life of Mary Baker Eddy* (1908; reprint, Boston: Christian Science Publishing Society, 1994), pp. 37–40; Lyman P. Powell, *Mary Baker Eddy: A Life Size Portrait* (1930; reprint, Boston: Christian Science Publishing Society, 1991), pp. 81–83. These claims were first debunked in Bates and Dittemore, *Mary Baker Eddy*, pp. 35–36. Peel, too, puts them to rest in *Years of Discovery*, p. 71 and p. 322 n. 135. But the Church has recently reprinted both the Wilbur and the Powell biographies, with the controversial claims intact. It has also recently added material, including one of the "Bill" stories, to Irving C. Tomlinson, *Twelve Years with Mary Baker Eddy: Recollections and Experiences* (Boston: Christian Science Publishing Society, 1996), pp. 30–31. Compare this edition with the Church's edition of 1945.

52. Mary Baker Eddy, "Message to The First Church of Christ, Scientist or The Mother Church, Boston, June 15, 1902," in *Prose Works Other Than Science and Health*, p. 15 (paginated separately).

53. Peel, *Years of Discovery*, p. 72.

54. Ibid., p. 78.

55. See Shannon, "Golden Memories," pp. 6–7.

56. The "infant school" is described in Peel, *Years of Discovery*, p. 81.

57. Ibid., p. 98.

58. The furniture and procedures involved in "swinging Mrs. Glover" are described in Cather and Milmine, pp. 27–28, and in Peel, *Years of Discovery*, pp. 99, 328 n. 85. Peel, however, is offended by Cather and Milmine's use of the term "cradle."

59. Peel, *Years of Discovery*, p. 96.

60. Ibid., p. 97.

61. Ibid., p. 80.

62. See Cather and Milmine, p. 33.

63. *Retrospection and Introspection*, pp. 20–21.

64. Julius Silberger, Jr., *Mary Baker Eddy: An Interpretive Biography of the Founder of Christian Science* (Boston: Little, Brown, 1980), p. 47.

65. Ibid., pp. 48–49.

66. See Jewel Spangler Smaus, "An Important Historical Discovery," *Christian Science Journal* 101, no. 5 (May 1983), pp. 284–288; Jewel Spangler Smaus, "Family: From New England to the Black Hills, Part IV," *Quarterly News, Mary Baker Eddy Museum and Historic Sites* 20, no. 3 (autumn 1983), pp. 314–15.

67. Aside from Eddy's claim in her autobiography that George had been told she was dead, the only "evidence" lies in the Jewel Spangler Smaus interview conducted years after George Glover II's death with *his* son, George Glover III, when he was in his eighties. Smaus acknowledges that there is no explanation of how Eddy's son learned that she was still alive; he wrote to her in 1861. See Smaus, "Family:

From New England to the Black Hills, Part III," *Quarterly News, Mary Baker Eddy Museum and Historic Sites* 20, no. 1 (spring 1983), p. 306.

68. Peel, *Years of Discovery*, p. 98.

69. Ibid.

70. *Retrospection and Introspection*, p. 90.

71. See Peel, *Years of Discovery*, p. 126.

72. For Daniel Patterson's midnight ride to his wife's side, see Cather and Milmine, pp. 34–35; Peel, *Years of Discovery*, pp. 121–22. For Mary Patterson's contraption, see also Peel, p. 122. A primitive hospital bed perhaps similar in construction to Mrs. Patterson's, with an adjustable headboard, can be seen at Hancock Shaker Village, near Pittsfield, Massachusetts.

73. See Cather and Milmine, pp. 38–41; Peel, *Years of Discovery*, pp. 140–42.

74. Robert Darnton, quoted in Stephen Jay Gould, "The Chain of Reason versus the Chain of Thumbs," in *Bully for Brontosaurus: Reflections in Natural History* (New York: Norton, 1991), p. 184.

75. Gould, op. cit., pp. 184–85.

76. Ibid., p. 185.

77. Charles Mackay, *Extraordinary Popular Delusions and the Madness of Crowds* (1841; reprint, New York: Harmony Books, 1980), p. 305.

78. Ibid., p. 307.

79. Ibid., p. 317.

80. Ibid.

81. See Gould, op. cit., p. 184 n.

82. Ibid., pp. 186–87.

83. The lavender robe and magnetized wand are described in George Frederick Drinka, M.D., *The Birth of Neurosis: Myth, Malady, and the Victorians* (New York: Simon & Schuster, 1984), p. 130.

84. Gould, op. cit., 189.

85. Benjamin Franklin, Antoine Lavoisier, et al., "Report of the Commissioners Charged by the King to Examine Animal Magnetism," Charles and Danielle Salas, trans., *Skeptic* 4, no. 3 (1996), p. 83.

86. Horatio W. Dresser, ed., *The Quimby Manuscripts*, (New York: Julian Press, 1961), p. 34.

87. Ibid.

88. Ibid., p. 35.

89. See Paul Johnson, *The Birth of the Modern: World Society, 1815–1830* (New York: HarperCollins, 1991), p. 746.

90. Ibid., p. 747.

91. See Dresser, ed., *The Quimby Manuscripts*, p. 388. Nor was the term unique to Quimby. A completely unrelated volume on Christian ethics by William Adams, *The Elements of Christian Science, A Treatise upon Moral Philosophy and Practice*, had been published in 1850. See Peel, *Years of Discovery*, p. 139.

92. Dresser, op. cit., pp. 180–81.

93. Cather and Milmine, p. 43.

94. Ibid., pp. 58–59.

95. Ibid., p. 60.
96. Ibid.
97. Edwin Franden Dakin makes much the same point with regard to this passage—
"Here is 'truth' as opposed to 'error.' Here is a 'science capable of demonstration'"—in his *Mrs. Eddy: The Biography of a Virginal Mind* (New York: Blue Ribbon Books, 1930), p. 47.
98. Peel, for example, bent on establishing the absolute originality of Eddy's thinking, criticized the scholarly tendency to identify the "evolution" of religious ideas; he denies that Christian Science evolved from Quimbyism. "The germ of a new idea, alien to everything in Quimby," Peel writes, "is already present [in Eddy's writings] . . . the concept of man as a perfect spiritual idea, made in the image and likeness of a God who is wholly good and wholly Spirit" (Peel, *Years of Discovery*, p. 206). The concept that God is all good, however, also appears in Quimby's writings, albeit in a slightly different construction: "My object is to correct the false ideas and strengthen the truth. I make war with what comes in contact with health and happiness, believing that God made everything good, and if there is anything wrong it is the effect of ourselves, and that man is responsible for his acts and even his thoughts." (Charles Braden quotes this passage from "an introduction [Quimby] wrote for one of his collections of writings which he evidently thought he might some day publish," the original of which is in the Library of Congress [Braden, *Spirits in Rebellion: The Rise and Development of New Thought* (Dallas: Southern Methodist University Press, 1987), p. 68].) Peel's denial is an essential part of the official history of Christian Science, and it seems to arise in part out of Scientists' need to "own" the concepts of the religion and to elevate Eddy to the status of a visionary, a unique seer visited by God and chosen to receive His word. Quimby, with his grubby beard and his head-rubbing, could only detract from Eddy's image as the Discoverer of Christian Science.

As Charles Braden observed, Quimby's own manuscripts, published in 1921, "revealed beyond question to any but the most convinced Eddy disciples that Quimby had held the basic ideas of mental healing before Mrs. Eddy sought healing at his hands in 1862." See Braden, *Spirits in Rebellion*, p.57.

Questions have long been raised by Eddy's apologists, including, most recently, the biographer Gillian Gill, about the provenance of Quimby's manuscripts, since the majority of them were preserved by copyists and not in Quimby's own hand. Gill goes so far as to suggest that Quimby was illiterate and that his manuscripts may have been in whole or in part the original work of his son, George Quimby, or of his amanuenses, the Misses Sarah and Emma Ware, patients and devotees of Quimby, although she has little evidence on which to base this speculation. See Gillian Gill, *Mary Baker Eddy* (Reading, Mass.: Perseus Books, 1998), pp. 144–46. However well or poorly he himself wrote, letters by Quimby's patients preserved in *The Quimby Manuscripts* describe and confirm his practices—the absent treatment, the use of the capitalized word "Science," the notion that "mind is matter"—that later appear in Eddy's teachings. There is no doubt that Eddy was inspired in these matters by Quimby.

Eddy's harshest critics accused her of plagiarizing from Quimby's manuscripts, a charge that was never proved, but most commentators, including myself, are far more interested in the question of Quimby's undeniable influence than in the literal extent of Eddy's debt to him. The fact remains that Eddy's essay in the Portland (Maine) *Evening Courier*, written and published shortly after her life-altering initial meeting with and treatment by Quimby, contains language and concepts that simply do not appear in her letters or writings before she encountered him. Even Gill, after all her speculation about the Misses Ware and the true origin of Quimby's writings, must acknowledge that "this does not mean that Quimby did not have a profound influence on her" (p. 146).

99. Much of the argument about Eddy's debt to Quimby centers on a brief manuscript entitled "Questions and Answers," copies of which were, according to Horatio W. Dresser, who edited and published Quimby's manuscripts after his death, "kept on hand to loan to new patients," some of whom "made their own copies." (See Dresser, ed., *The Quimby Manuscripts*, p. 165.) The date and authorship of Quimby's "Questions and Answers" has been a matter of controversy ever since it was suggested that Eddy had plagiarized it in producing one of her first teaching manuscripts, "The Science of Man," which also consisted of questions and answers, although different from Quimby's. "The Science of Man," which went through a number of different versions and also exists in various handwritten copies by Eddy's students, eventually became the seminal chapter, "Recapitulation," of *Science and Health*; it is the text from which students of Christian Science are class-taught. For a detailed account of the history of these manuscripts, see Peel, *Years of Discovery*, pp. 230–36. Several versions of "The Science of Man" are reprinted in the privately printed volume entitled *Essays and Bible Lessons Ascribed to Mary Baker Eddy with Repaid Pages; Footprints Fadeless by Mary Baker Eddy with The Science of Man or Questions and Answers in Moral Science, Early Papers, Visions, Mind-Healing: Historical Sketch*, available from the Rare Book Company of Freehold, New Jersey.

100. Gillian Gill has argued that Quimby could not be the author of his own writings because his "personal letters or drafts . . . eloquently testify to his incapacity to spell simple words or write a simple, declarative sentence." The problem with this argument is that the same could be said of Eddy herself. One has only to read her letters or the first edition of *Science and Health* to find that, although her spelling may have been better than Quimby's, her grammar, word usage, and sentence construction were every bit as idiosyncratic as his. See Gill, *Mary Baker Eddy*, p. 144.

101. See Peel, *Years of Discovery*, pp. 162–63. Christian Scientists would later sneer at Quimby, suggesting that he was a mesmerist, not a Christian philosopher, but the Christian elements that would become so important to Eddy are present in his writings. Catherine L. Albanese has written convincingly of Quimby's "theology of healing" in *Nature Religion in America: From the Algonkian Indians to the New Age* (Chicago: University of Chicago Press, 1990), p. 108. She writes, "As Quimby's identification of Wisdom with Christ or Science . . . suggests, explicitly Christian teaching figured prominently in his thought. In fact, it is impossible to

read more than a few pages of his writing without confronting biblical rhetoric" (p. 113).

102. Dresser, ed., *The Quimby Manuscripts*, p. 267.

103. Ibid.

104. For Schelling and Swedenborg, see Braden, *Spirits in Rebellion*, pp. 99–100.

105. *Science and Health* (Boston: The First Church of Christ, Scientist, 1934), p. 266.

106. For a discussion of Quimby's interest in Swedenborg and Andrew Jackson Davis, see Peel, *Years of Discovery*, pp. 160–63.

107. *First Church of Christ, Scientist and Miscellany*, p. 307.

108. Peel, *Years of Discovery*, p. 195.

109. Ibid.

110. *Retrospection and Introspection*, pp. 24–25.

111. Cather and Milmine, p. 85.

112. Silberger, *Mary Baker Eddy*, p. 98.

113. Peel, *Years of Discovery*, p. 198.

114. Ibid., pp. 201, 347 n. 33. In the note, Peel seems to acknowledge, if unconsciously, the dubiousness of this anecdote of healing. The written account of a woman named Elizabeth Harding, telling of George's healing, exists in the archives of the Mother Church; Harding's mother was told "years later" of the healing by a Mrs. Norton, George's mother. To bolster support for this account, Peel refers the reader, without explanation, to a completely separate published account of a healing of malformed feet.

115. Silberger, *Mary Baker Eddy*, p. 102.

116. Cather and Milmine, p. 112.

117. Ibid., pp. 113–14.

118. Ibid., p. 118.

119. See ibid., pp. 121–27. Peel alludes to "a growing coolness" on the part of the Wentworths toward their houseguest, but suggests that the "frank scorn" of Horace Wentworth for Eddy was not shared by the rest of his family. See *Years of Discovery*, pp. 237, 229.

120. Peel, *Years of Discovery*, p. 252.

121. Mary Baker Eddy, *Essays and Bible Lessons*, p. 182. This book contains several versions of "The Science of Man," including the 1870 version published by Eddy in 1883 and other versions transcribed by her students.

122. "The Science of Man," much revised, turns up in later editions of *Science and Health* as the crucial chapter entitled "Recapitulation," but it is not present in the first edition. The Genesis manuscript eventually became the chapter "Genesis" in the "Key to the Scriptures" that was added to *Science and Health* in 1883.

123. Samuel Putnam Bancroft, *Mrs. Eddy as I Knew Her in 1870* (1923; transcript, Freehold, New Jersey: Rare Book Company, n.d.), p. 35.

124. John C. Lathrop, "Recollections of Mary Baker Eddy," *We Knew Mary Baker Eddy*, first series (Boston: Christian Science Publishing Society, 1971), p. 16.

125. Silberger, *Mary Baker Eddy*, p. 113.

126. Peel, *Years of Discovery*, pp. 262–63.

127. Ibid., p. 263. Eddy's reply (*Lynn* [Mass.] *Transcript*, February 3, 1872) is also

reprinted in full as Appendix 2 in Norman Beasley, *The Cross and The Crown: The History of Christian Science* (New York: Duell, Sloan and Pearce, 1952), pp. 569–72.

128. See Cather and Milmine, p. 147, for descriptions of the employment of many of Eddy's early students.

129. Ibid., p. 278.

130. Ibid., p. 282.

131. *The First Church of Christ, Scientist and Miscellany*, p. 114.

132. Mary Baker Glover, *Science and Health*, first edition (Boston: Christian Scientist Publishing Company, 1875), p. 15.

133. Ibid., p. 455.

134. Ibid., pp. 217, 219.

135. Ibid., pp. 374–76.

136. See Peel, *Years of Discovery*, p. 287; Bates and Dittemore, p. 165.

137. Peel, *Years of Trial*, p. 9.

138. Odell Shepard, ed., *The Journals of Bronson Alcott* (Boston: Little, Brown and Company, 1938), p. 464.

139. Ibid., p. 465.

140. Ibid., pp. 489–90.

141. A. Bronson Alcott to Mary Baker Eddy, 7 March 1877, quoted in Bates and Dittemore, p. 170.

142. Ralph Waldo Emerson, "The Divinity School Address," *Selections from Ralph Waldo Emerson*, Stephen E. Whicher, ed. (Boston: Houghton Mifflin Company, 1957), pp. 106, 105, 103.

143. Ibid., "Self-Reliance," p. 151.

144. Ibid., p. 150.

145. Bates and Dittemore, p. 171. Bates and Dittemore describe the source of this "undated letter to a Miss Lane of Chicago," as *Autograph*, no. 7 (September–October 1912).

146. Emerson, "Nature," p. 24.

147. Cather and Milmine, p. 172.

148. Ibid., p. 169.

149. Ibid., pp. 170–71.

150. Peel, *Years of Trial*, p. 16.

151. Ibid., p. 17.

152. Ibid.

153. This extraordinary letter has been popular with Eddy biographers both friendly and hostile. See Cather and Milmine, pp. 173–74; Peel, *Years of Trial*, p. 18; and Silberger, *Mary Baker Eddy*, pp. 127–28.

154. Eddy, *Science and Health*, first edition, p. 193.

155. See Bates and Dittemore, p. 177; Silberger, *Mary Baker Eddy*, p. 129.

156. Peel, *Years of Trial*, p. 21.

157. Ibid., p. 38.

158. Ibid., p. 43.

159. Silberger, *Mary Baker Eddy*, p. 133.

160. See Peel, *Years of Trial*, pp. 50–53.

161. Ibid., p. 51.

162. Ibid., p. 63.

163. Ibid., p. 48.

164. Ibid., p. 49.

165. Gottschalk, *The Emergence of Christian Science*, p. 145.

166. Silberger, *Mary Baker Eddy*, pp. 135–36.

167. Ibid., p. 139.

168. Peel, *Years of Trial*, pp. 97–98.

169. Julia S. Bartlett, "Reminiscences of Mary Baker Eddy and Personal Recollections in Connection with the Establishment of the Christian Science Movement," in *Miscellaneous Documents Relating to Christian Science and Its Discoverer and Founder, Mary Baker Eddy* (reprint, Freehold, New Jersey: Rare Book Company, n.d.), p. 177.

170. Ibid.

171. Beasley, *The Cross and The Crown*, p. 60.

172. Ibid., p. 78.

173. Mary Baker Eddy, *Science and Health*, 3rd ed., vol. 1 (Lynn, Mass.: Dr. Asa G. Eddy, 1881), p. xi.

174. Ibid., vol. 2, p. 20.

175. Ibid., p. 35.

176. William Dana Orcutt, *Mary Baker Eddy and Her Books* (Boston: Christian Science Publishing Society, 1950), p. 25. Orcutt reports: "During 1881 and 1882 three editions of one thousand copies each came off the press." See also Beasley, *The Cross and The Crown*, p. 77.

177. Peel, *Years of Trial*, p. 109.

178. Eddy, *Science and Health*, p. 63.

179. Ibid., p. 59.

180. In *Priestess, Mother, Sacred Sister*, a study of religions dominated by women, Susan Starr Sered concludes that "Christian Science differs from almost all other women's religions in several ways: Its belief system is complex and unconditionally obligatory, it is based on a large written literature, and the church organization is highly centralized." Susan Starr Sered, *Priestess, Mother, Sacred Sister: Religions Dominated by Women* (New York: Oxford University Press, 1994), p. 24.

181. "Miracles?" *Boston Sunday Globe*, 26 March 1882.

182. Ibid.

183. Ibid.

184. "What They Think of It," *Boston Sunday Globe*, 2 April 1882.

185. Ibid.

186. Ibid.

187. Ibid.

188. Beasley, *The Cross and The Crown*, 83.

189. Bates and Dittemore, p. 220.

190. Cather and Milmine, pp. 286–88; Peel, *Years of Trial*, p. 116.

Part II. "You Will Have to Learn to Love Me More": Mrs. Eddy Builds Her Empire

1. See Silberger, *Mary Baker Eddy*, p. 147. Silberger's discussion of Eddy's eulogy for her husband is particularly interesting: "It is hard to know whether she had much personal regard for Eddy. It had always been her way to replace one person with another, and now, when she set about to compose a poetic eulogy for Eddy, she simply took up a poem that she had first published thirty-odd years earlier for another man [an earlier suitor], and revised it to make it do for Gilbert. . . . [In the poem] Abigail Baker offers Gilbert Eddy, newly arrived in Heaven, the opportunity to speak some compassionate lines about the widow he has left behind but, naturally, very little about himself."

2. Margery Fox, "Protest in Piety: Christian Science Revisited," *International Journal of Women's Studies* 1, no. 4 (July/August 1978), p. 408.

3. See Peel, *Years of Trial*, p. 136; Silberger, *Mary Baker Eddy*, pp. 148–49.

4. Photocopies of the typewritten transcription that John V. Dittemore had made of the pages of the Calvin Frye diary that were in his possession are available from The Bookmark, Santa Clarita, California. At the back of this transcript there is a fascinating "Note" describing how Dittemore came by the pages and his disposition of them thereafter: "Although the originals were finally burnt Dittemore had taken care to have photostatic copies made for his own use while they remained in his possession. This he did before getting them photostated together. The copies in the foregoing pages are from copies of the Dittemore copies, thus accounting for the poor clarity, through much reproduction of some of Frye's original sheets." The Note concludes: "In 1930 or so Dittemore exhibited copies of the Diary in two bookstores (Los Angeles and New York) and invited Christian Scientists to go and read. Some went, and made copies which still circulate to some extent."

   Much other material purportedly written by Eddy or dictated by her to Frye or other students is available in the books privately printed by Richard Oakes and the Gilbert Carpenters, father and son (see the account of their careers in part III, "Paul Revere Rides Again"), also available from The Bookmark or from the Rare Book Company. See, for example, the volume entitled *Essays and Bible Lessons Ascribed to Mary Baker Eddy with Repaid Pages; Footprints Fadeless by Mary Baker Eddy with The Science of Man or Questions and Answers in Moral Science, Early Papers; Visions; Mind-Healing: Historical Sketch*, compiled by Richard Oakes from materials collected by the Carpenters; it is popularly known among Scientists who study it as the "Red Book," for the color of its cover; another popular Oakes volume of Eddy's works, *Divinity Course and General Collectanea*, is known as the "Blue Book." The "Visions" (chapter 8 in *Essays*) "were related by her [Eddy] to Calvin Frye and other students"; these may be contained in the original Frye notebooks to which outside researchers have been denied access by the Church (*Essays*, p. 241).

   Lyman Powell, a clergyman and Eddy apologist who wrote a reverent biography of her for the Church, first published in 1930, may have been an exception, a non-Scientist who was allowed to see these rare documents, but he did not quote from or describe them at length. To my knowledge, no other scholars who are non-Scientists have seen or described the original Frye diaries or notebooks. The scholar Robert David Thomas, whose *"With Bleeding Footsteps": Mary Baker Eddy's Path to Religious Leadership* was published in 1994, admitted in a letter to the *New York Review of Books* that, during his research at the Church archives, "some documents, most notably the diaries of Calvin Frye, were withheld." (See *NYRB*, 14 November 1996, p. 64.) Gillian Gill, in the "Research Note" of her 1998 biography, *Mary Baker Eddy*, (Reading, Mass.: Perseus Books), writes: "An even greater problem I encountered was with the so-called Eddy-Frye notebooks, written by Mrs. Eddy herself or dictated to Frye, which Robert Peel, Lyman Powell, and John Dittemore cite briefly and tantalizingly. I requested on at least two occasions to see these. . . . Unfortunately, here again I drew a blank. I was told that no effort had been made to transcribe these books, and since there were so many of them—a new fact in itself—and they were in such a difficult format, there was no way to photocopy them in sextuplicate for board approval" (Gill, p. 561).

5. Henry James, *The Bostonians* (1886; New York: Penguin Books, 1966), pp. 73, 277.
6. William Dana Orcutt, *Mary Baker Eddy and Her Books* (Boston: Christian Science Publishing Society, 1950), p. 25. Orcutt reports that the article was dropped from the subtitle after the fifteenth edition.
7. "Christian Science in Tremont Temple," in *Miscellaneous Writings*, p. 96.
8. Ibid., p. 97.
9. Peel, *Years of Trial*, p. 158.
10. Ibid.
11. "News from Abroad," *Christian Science Journal* 7, no. 5 (August 1889), p. 266.
12. "News from Abroad," *Christian Science Journal* 7, no. 7 (October 1889), pp. 364–65.
13. Ibid., pp. 365–66.
14. Rodney Stark, "The Rise and Fall of Christian Science," *Journal of Contemporary Religion* 13, no. 2 (1998), pp. 189, 191, Table 1.
15. See "The Following Official Announcement," *Christian Science Journal* 3, no. 3 (June 1885), p. 56.
16. "A New Home," *Christian Science Journal* 6, no. 6 (September 1888), p. 317.
17. Ibid.
18. Norman Beasley, *The Cross and The Crown: The History of Christian Science* (New York: Duell, Sloan and Pearce, 1952), p. 202.
19. Ibid., p. 160.
20. Ibid., p. 166.
21. Warren Felt Evans was another early patient of Quimby's (they met in 1863). The author of numerous texts on mental healing that would eventually form the literary foundation for New Thought, Evans may also have been a source for Eddy, as Quimby was. Two of his books on mental medicine, based on Quimby's teachings, were published years before *Science and Health*. Braden notes: "[Evans's] great distinction lies in the fact that he was the first to write of the new

healing and its basis as taught and practiced by Quimby. His first book, *The Mental Cure, Illustrating the Influence of the Mind on the Body, Both in Health and Disease, and the Psychological Method of Treatment*, was published in 1869, only three years after Quimby's death and six years before the appearance of *Science and Health* by Mrs. Eddy. . . . Although the books were never mentioned by Mrs. Eddy in any of her writings, she might well have read not only *The Mental Cure* . . . but also *Mental Medicine*, published in 1872, three years before *Science and Health*." Charles S. Braden, *Spirits in Rebellion: The Rise and Development of New Thought* (Dallas: Southern Methodist University Press, 1963), p. 92.

22. *Science and Health*, p. 464.
23. Rev. Mary B. G. Eddy, "Questions Answered," *Christian Science Journal* 4, no. 8 (November 1886), p. 192.
24. Ibid.
25. See Bates and Dittemore, p. 272; Braden, *Spirits in Rebellion*, p. 142.
26. The question of whether Eddy's borrowings prove her a plagiarist has plagued her Church for decades and distracted from a complete consideration of the origins of Christian Science. Earlier in this century, it was a something of a parlor game among intellectuals and hostile clergy to catch Eddy plagiarizing. Newspapers covered the various revelations on the subject, and whole books and pamphlets were devoted to it, such as *How Reverend Wiggin Re-wrote Mrs. Eddy's Book*, purporting to reveal that James Henry Wiggin was the true author of *Science and Health*. In 1904, the *New York Times* published an article comparing passages from Quimby and Eddy, in parallel columns, in an effort to show their suspicious similarities.

The irony of the plagiarism controversy, however, particularly as it involved Quimby, was that Eddy's defensive reaction to accusations that she had "stolen" Quimby's work fanned the flames of the "mind-cure" movement. Had she welcomed the other Quimbyites into her fold, instead of insulting them, Christian Science might ultimately have had a broader appeal. As it is, the plagiarism issue—while a hot topic in its day—is now, as Braden observed, "largely an academic question." While Eddy was in deep denial, if not dishonest, in her rejection of Quimby as her spiritual father and mentor, her appropriations were strangely creative. Quimby himself was a literary magpie, helping himself without reference or acknowledgment to morsels from Swedenborg and tidbits from the Transcendentalists and other philosophers that were then floating through the zeitgeist.

It was eventually shown that Eddy herself, apart from her wholesale adoption of Quimby's ideas and diction, had plagiarized from several sources. She plagiarized several passages of Carlyle and Ruskin from the anthology *Philosophic Nuggets*, during the years when she was editing the *Christian Science Journal* and *Sentinel* (indeed, Peel suggested that it was the haste engendered by deadlines that caused these mix-ups). Had Eddy acknowledged and apologized for these mistakes, the matter might have ended. But Eddy included in her *Miscellaneous Writings*, published in 1897, two full articles that were entirely plagiarized, one from Lindley Murray's *English Reader* about "the man of integrity," which she had sent as a letter to her Church members in 1895, and the other, "Taking Offence," from a newspaper article that she had pasted in one of her scrapbooks. Robert Peel piously notes that "since the discovery that these paragraphs were not in fact written by Mrs. Eddy, writers for the Christian Science periodicals have not been permitted to quote from them, cite them, or attribute them to her in their articles." But he has no explanation for the fact that Eddy continued to publish them as her own through a number of editions of *Miscellaneous Writings*. So has her Church. The offending articles remain in the book today, with not so much as a footnote to remark on their theft. In one of his most dubious rationalizations, Peel devotes more than two pages to an endnote asserting that Eddy's "shorter borrowings represent the fairly normal and probably unconscious process of assimilation and adaptation to be traced in many reputable writers," and goes on to suggest that everyone from Edgar Allan Poe to W. H. Auden engaged in a little harmless "unconscious borrowing" from time and time. Plagiarism, particularly to the extent that Eddy engaged in it, is never considered "normal" in the publishing world, nor is it excused or explained away as "unconscious." There is a vast difference between plagiarism and the kinds of literary influence Peel was describing. Notably, Peel also seemed to have forgotten that Scientists, who express contempt for all things relating to the field of psychology, do not believe in the unconscious mind. See Peel, *Years of Authority*, pp. 407–10 n. 56.

But not all the accusations of plagiarism were true. In 1936, Reverend Walter M. Haushalter, the rector of an Episcopal church in Philadelphia, published the sensational *Mrs. Eddy Purloins from Hegel: Newly Discovered Source Reveals Amazing Plagiarisms in Science and Health*, which spun an improbable tale of dark doings with manuscripts. Haushalter accused Eddy of having plagiarized parts of *Science and Health*, including the crucial "scientific statement of being," from an essay on Hegel written by a professor at New York's Columbia College (now University) that had fallen into the hands of Hiram Crafts, Eddy's first student, with whom she had boarded for a time.

Despite the Church's rejoinder in 1937 that Haushalter had tried to sell the offending document to them before publishing his book, the reverend's argument was widely disseminated over the years not only by his book, but by *The Kingdom of the Cults*, a polemical attack by the evangelical writer Walter R. Martin on groups ranging from the Jehovah's Witnesses to Christian Science. Martin claimed that the document in question "is above challenge by any Christian Scientist," and cited a source testifying to its " 'unimpeachably authentic' " origins. Unfortunately for Martin, however, in 1955 a Baptist seminary professor published a study demonstrating that the document was a forgery, a conclusion confirmed in the *New England Quarterly* in 1980 by Thomas C. Johnsen, a Christian Scientist and scholar who went on to work for the Committee on Publication. See Thomas C. Johnsen, "Historical Consensus and Christian Science: The Career of a Manuscript Controversy," *New England Quarterly* 53, no. 1 (March 1980), pp. 20–22.

The plagiarism scandals and forgeries demonstrated something that their promoters might perhaps have been chagrined to acknowledge. Christian Science was intensely threatening to mainstream clergy. Christian Scientists claimed to *heal*, the ultimate democratic claim, a claim that rang through the halls of the authoritarian, patrician, patriarchal Protestant churches of America and struck fear into the hearts of pastors. Characters like Haushalter and Martin took refuge in ad hominem attacks on the character of Mary Baker Eddy, leaving its ministry of healing to be examined by medical doctors.

27. See Peel, *Years of Trial*, p. 82; Silberger, *Mary Baker Eddy*, p. 138; Charles S. Braden, *Christian Science Today: Power, Policy, Practice* (Dallas: Southern Methodist University Press, 1958), p. 101. Peel claims that Chapter 375 of the Massachusetts Acts of 1874 "did not expressly grant the right to confer degrees," but Braden asserts that it did and that the Massachusetts Metaphysical College was the only institution of its kind chartered under the Act to do so. Eddy did grant degrees, often urging her followers in the Field to check the credentials of those purporting to teach or practice Christian Science. The act was repealed, according to Braden, in 1882.

28. Rev. Mary B. G. Eddy, "Questions Answered," *Christian Science Journal* 4, no. 8 (November 1886), p. 192.

29. "Invalidism in the College Classes," *Christian Science Journal* 5, no. 3 (June 1887), p. 159.

30. Ibid.

31. See Sarah Gardner Cunningham, "A New Order: Augusta Emma Simmons Stetson and the Origins of Christian Science in New York City, 1886–1910" (Ph.D. diss., Union Theological Seminary, 1994), pp. 32, 51. Eddy sometimes reduced or waived the tuition for students, such as Augusta Stetson, who were unwilling or unable to pay the tuition and whom she particularly wanted to take her classes.

32. C. Lulu Blackman, "The Star in My Crown of Rejoicing—The Class of 1885," in *We Knew Mary Baker Eddy*, second series (Boston: Christian Science Publishing Society, 1950), p. 1.

33. Ibid., pp. 4–5.

34. Ibid., p. 8.

35. Ibid., p. 9.

36. Ibid., p. 17.

37. Calvin Frye's diary contains an interesting entry that is suggestive of Eddy's fear of Roman Catholicism. The entry for Monday, August 10, 1908, reads: "Mrs. M. A. Scott's niece was playing with some catholic children when one of them said to her where do you go to church? She replied to the C.S. Church. The Cath. child said one of the sisters told me that when I go by a C.S. House or Ch to spit on the ground & cross myself & she has been seen doing it with *a venom*. Another R.C. child said you've got to die & old Mrs. Eddy has got to die and there are 60 R.C. Bishops praying for it." From *Photostats of a Portion of the Diary Kept by Calvin A. Frye*, privately printed (Santa Clarita, Calif.: The Bookmark, n.d.), p. 17.

In interviews with former Scientists who have taken class-instruction, several report that their Christian Science teachers have said that Jesuits pray for the destruction of Christian Science. See also Richard J. Brenneman, *Deadly Blessings: Faith Healing on Trial* (Buffalo, N.Y.: Prometheus Books, 1990), pp. 116–17 n. 27. Brenneman, a former Scientist, says that during class-instruction, he was taught "that the Roman Catholic Church is the Antichrist, the Beast of the Revelation of St. John; but, we were told, 'don't make a big deal of it.' "

38. "Notes from Primary Class as Taught by Laura Sargent," privately printed (Santa Clarita, Calif.: The Bookmark, n.d.), p. 54.

39. Ibid.

40. Ibid., p. 55.

41. *Manual*, p. 87; Braden, *Christian Science Today*, p. 108.

42. Richard Louis LePoidevin, "Recurring Back Pain Permanently Healed," *Christian Science Sentinel* 100, no. 11 (16 March 1998), p. 22.

43. *Science and Health*, p. 376.

44. See Eddy, *Science and Health*, p. 292; John 8:44.

45. *Science and Health*, p. 391.

46. See "Extreme Fear Overcome," in "Testimonies of Healing," *Christian Science Sentinel* 100, no. 13 (30 March 1998), p. 23; Isaiah 35:8.

47. See "Reports of Healing," *Christian Science Journal* 116, no. 3 (March 1998), p. 50; *Science and Health*, p. 393.

48. Testimony of Jean I. Tennant, *Christian Science Journal* 116, no. 7 (July 1998) pp. 43–44.

49. For discussions of Christian Science and its placebo effect during childbirth, see Silberger, *Mary Baker Eddy*, p. 171; Stark, p. 198.

50. "Notes from the Field," *Christian Science Journal* 17, no. 12 (March 1900), p. 840.

51. Cather and Milmine, p. 355.

52. Alfred E. Baker, "Notes on Metaphysical Obstetrics, Used to teach The Obstetric Class of June, 1900 of the Board of Education of the Massachusetts Metaphysical College, As prepared by Dr. Alfred E. Baker, Teacher of Obstetrics, Under the Direction and Approval of Mary Baker Eddy," pamphlet (n.p., n.d.), p. 8.

53. Ibid., pp. 9–10.

54. Ibid., p. 14.

55. Ibid., p. 18.

56. Silberger, *Mary Baker Eddy*, pp. 172–73.

57. Eddy, "Card," *Christian Science Journal* 6, no. 6 (September 1888), p. 322.

58. *Christian Science Journal* 20, no. 1 (April 1902), p. 38. There remains a single passage in *Science and Health* about "the obstetrics taught by this Science"; see *Science and Health*, p. 463.

59. Peel, *Years of Trial*, p. 243.

60. Ibid., p. 217.

61. Ibid.

62. Ibid., p. 218.

63. Peel is undoubtedly correct in noting that Mrs. Eddy arranged a place for her son and his family to stay and that she demonstrated fondness for her grandchildren by introducing them to her congregation at one Sunday service; nonetheless, her

letters to her son and her treatment of him indicate that her relationship with him continued to be a troubled one. See Peel, *Years of Trial*, p. 217.

64. Cather and Milmine, pp. 382–83.
65. Ibid., p. 383.
66. Ibid., p. 382.
67. Rev. Mary B. G. Eddy, "Fallibility of Human Concepts," *Christian Science Journal* 7, no. 4 (July 1889), p. 161.
68. Peel, *Years of Trial*, p. 252.
69. Ibid.
70. Dakin, *Mrs. Eddy*, p. 254.
71. See Silberger, *Mary Baker Eddy*, 192.
72. Bates and Dittemore, pp. 301–02.
73. Silberger, *Mary Baker Eddy*, p. 196.
74. Mark Twain, *Christian Science* (New York: Harper & Brothers, 1907), p. 199.
75. Silberger, p. 198.
76. Mary Baker G. Eddy, "Hints for History," *Christian Science Journal* 10, no. 4 (July 1892), pp. 133–34.
77. See Peel, *Years of Authority*, pp. 12, 179.
78. James F. Gilman, *Recollections of Mary Baker Eddy* (privately printed), pp. 4–5.
79. Peel, *Years of Authority*, p. 178.
80. Gilbert C. Carpenter and Gilbert C. Carpenter, Jr., *Mary Baker Eddy: Her Spiritual Footsteps* (privately printed), p. 55.
81. Matt. 26:40.
82. Carpenter and Carpenter, *Spiritual Footsteps*, p. 55.
83. Dakin, *Mrs. Eddy*, p. 527. Dakin obtained a copy of parts of the Frye diaries from John V. Dittemore, at one time a member of Eddy's Board of Directors. Dakin reprinted excerpts from the diaries in Appendix A of the 1930 edition of *Mrs. Eddy*, pp. 525–30. The amusing fallout of the hair-pulling incident between Eddy and Frye is reported in Cather and Milmine, p. 357. One of Eddy's students complained about seeing her pull Frye's hair, to which Eddy replied, " 'There is Calvin Frye. He has a good head of hair; let him speak for himself.' " Five weeks later, Frye replied with a letter, explaining that Eddy's action had been in his best interest because he was, at the time when his hair was pulled, contending with an attack of "malicious mesmerism."
84. Shannon, "Golden Memories," p. 56.
85. Dickey, *Memoirs*, p. 18.
86. Ibid., p. 19.
87. Shannon, "Golden Memories," p. 24.
88. Carpenter and Carpenter, *Spiritual Footsteps*, p. 5.
89. See Peel, *Years of Authority*, pp. 68–69.
90. Ibid., p. 68.
91. Ibid.
92. Ibid., p. 69.
93. Joseph Armstrong and Margaret Williamson, *Building of The Mother Church: The*

First Church of Christ, Scientist, in Boston, Massachusetts (Boston: Christian Science Publishing Society, 1980), p. 82.

94. For the Christian Science interpretation of Eddy's absence from the Mother Church dedication, see Peel, *Years of Authority*, p. 73.

95. Shannon, "Golden Memories," p. 39.

96. Ibid., p. 40.

97. Ibid.

98. Ibid., p. 41.

99. Paul R. Smillie, *Loving Our Leader* (St. Maries, Idaho: The Gethsemane Foundation, n.d.), frontispiece.

100. A number of Scientists report that this speech was delivered by Eddy from the balcony at Pleasant View on June 25, 1901; see Carpenter and Carpenter, *Spiritual Footsteps*, p. iv; and Andrew W. Hartsook, *Christian Science After 1910* (Santa Clarita, Calif.: The Bookmark, 1993), frontispiece. Peel says that the speech was given in 1895 before a meeting of the alumni of the Massachusetts Metaphysical College at Pleasant View; see *Years of Authority*, p. 83. These versions of the quotation are virtually identical, except for the last line, which Peel omits.

101. "Christmas Gifts to Mary Baker G. Eddy," *Christian Science Journal* 6, no. 10 (January 1889), pp. 534–35.

102. "The Mary Baker Eddy Souvenir Spoon," *Christian Science Journal* 16, no. 10 (January 1899), p. 739.

103. "Christian Science Souvenir Spoons," *Christian Science Journal* 16, no. 11 (February 1899), p. 742.

104. Cather and Milmine, p. 451.

105. Ibid., p. 451.

106. Peel, *Years of Authority*, p. 47. Peel offers an extensive discussion of the 1893 World Parliament of Religions and of Eddy's motives in viewing the event with some suspicion.

107. Ibid., p. 53.

108. Ibid., p. 58.

109. See Gilman, *Recollections*, pp. 8, 12.

110. For the tadpoles, see ibid., p. 37.

111. Ibid., p. 27. The entry in question, with reference to Eddy's foot, is that of May 15, 1893.

    The Christian Science Publishing Society has recently published as "Authorized Literature" of the Church an edited edition of Gilman's diary entitled *Painting a Poem: Mary Baker Eddy and James F. Gilman Illustrate Christ and Christmas* (Boston: Christian Science Publishing Society, 1998). The Church's version of the Gilman diary, an entry in their "Twentieth-Century Biographers Series," appears to be heavily edited and truncated, without the usual scholarly apparatus to indicate where material has been elided. The passage referring to Eddy's foot, for example, does not appear. The editors are not identified by name, and the note acknowledging the editing—"some of James Gilman's personal musings did not speak to the topic of this book and so have been omitted"—raises questions about this edition's reliability (*Painting a Poem*, p. viii). Much of what has been omitted from the Church's version can hardly be characterized as Gilman's "personal musings" but instead seems to consist of his description of Eddy's behavior and remarks that the Church has interpreted as likely to detract from the carefully constructed image of their Leader.

Also in the Church's introduction, its editor or editors write, "In the years after James Gilman's passing in 1929 several versions of his reminiscence were published. They were based on typed and revised copies of his writings, and as a result contained numerous errors. James Gilman's words in this volume are from his original handwritten letters, notes, and reminiscences—not fully available elsewhere" (pp. vii–viii). However, no bibliographical information about these different editions is provided. Gillian Gill, who was granted limited access to the Church's archives, was unable, due to time constraints, "to request to see the original and make a careful comparison." She notes, however, that the typed transcript of Gilman's diary that she read at the Longyear Museum and Historical Society contains passages omitted from the diary as published by Gilbert Carpenter, the version I have used. See Gillian Gill, *Mary Baker Eddy* (Reading, Mass.: Perseus Books, 1998), p. 670 n. 40. Robert David Thomas, however, *did* read Gilman's diary at the Church archives, and he reports that Eddy did pose for the artist, just as Gilman had reported. Thomas encountered copyright difficulties with the Church and was unable to quote from their materials at length. See Thomas, *"Footsteps,"* p. 189.

112. Mary Baker Eddy, *Christ and Christmas: A Poem* (Boston: The First Church of Christ, Scientist, 1925), final page. (The book is largely unpaginated.)

113. For accounts of the controversy that attended publication of *Christ and Christmas*, see Beasley, *The Cross and The Crown*, pp. 310–13; "Christ and Christmas: 'Song and Object Lesson,' " *Longyear Museum and Historical Society Quarterly News* 30, nos. 3 & 4 (1993), pp. 467–76; Peel, *Years of Authority*, pp. 59–64. None of these sources identifies by name the clergymen who objected to *Christ and Christmas*, but *Quarterly News* refers the reader to Raymond J. Cunningham, "The Impact of Christian Science on the American Churches, 1880–1910," *The American Historical Review* 62, no. 3 (April 1967), pp. 885–905.

114. The title of this illustration is "Christian Unity."

115. Eddy, "Queries," *Christian Science Journal* 11, no. 11 (February 1894), p. 474.

116. Peel, *Years of Authority*, p. 63. Eddy's professed horror over the fact that Christian Scientists were using her illustrated poem to heal themselves and others must be taken with a grain of salt. The *Christian Science Journal* hailed it, the month that it appeared, as "Christian Science in art" and asserted that "a study of the illustrations is enough to inspire and give a healing influence" ("Editor's Table," *Christian Science Journal* 11, no. 9 [December 1893], p. 426). The *Quarterly News* notes that "even after its withdrawal, three of the illustrations from the book were used as the basis for design of the stained glass windows in the room set aside for Mrs. Eddy in the original edifice of The Mother Church" (*Quarterly News 30*, 470). And, although Eddy claimed that she withdrew the book because students were using it to heal when they should have been using *Science and Health*, she apparently countenanced the publication of a testimony

in the *Journal* in 1898 that describes in glowing terms that onerous practice. Mrs. C. T. Letchfield, of Colorado Springs, Colorado, wrote to testify that her daughter was healed of "a very severe attack of malignant diphtheria" after reading "that wonderful book, 'Christ and Christmas.'" See "Notes from the Field," *Christian Science Journal* 16, no. 6 (September 1898), p. 437.

117. *Christ and Christmas* reappeared in a third edition in December 1897. Oddly, the illustration that caused the most offense, "Christian Unity," was left alone; the illustrations "Christian Science Healing," "Truth *Versus* Error," "Seeking and Finding," and "The Way" were altered, apparently because Eddy was dissatisfied with them. The text was also revised. See *Quarterly News* 30, 471.

118. See Orcutt, *Mary Baker Eddy and Her Books*, pp. 60–68.

119. Ibid., pp. 61–62.

120. *Miscellaneous Writings*, p. 148; also reprinted in *Manual*, p. 3.

121. Armstrong and Williamson, *Building of The Mother Church*, p. 69.

122. See Peel, *Years of Authority*, pp. 76–77.

123. Shannon, "Golden Memories," p. 58.

124. See Peel, *Years of Authority*, pp. 72–73. Peel reports that services conforming to Eddy's notion of the "impersonal pastor" took hold in Christian Science branch churches soon after they were instituted in the Mother Church. In 1891, Eddy had taken the first step in the direction of services that permitted only readings from the Bible and *Science and Health* by establishing a new "Order of Church Services" that relegated the sermon to a secondary position, after readings. See Mary B. G. Eddy, "Notice," *Christian Science Journal* 9, no. 9 (December 1891), p. 365.

125. *Manual*, p. 58.

126. *Miscellaneous Writings*, p. 322.

127. *Science and Health*, p. vii.

128. *Manual*, p. 44.

129. Ibid., p. 48.

130. Ibid., p. 43.

131. James Coates, *In Mormon Circles: Gentiles, Jack Mormons, and Latter-Day Saints* (Reading, Mass.: Addison-Wesley, 1991), p. 108.

132. See *Science and Health*, pp. 556–57; the detailed description of Woodbury's baptismal procedure and choice of reading matter can be found in Thomas, "Footsteps," p. 253.

133. Thomas, "Footsteps," p. 253.

134. Peel, *Years of Authority*, p. 80.

135. For the complete text of Eddy's Communion message of June 4, 1899, see *The First Church of Christ, Scientist and Miscellany*, pp. 124–131.

136. Dakin, *Mrs. Eddy*, Appendix A, p. 528.

137. *Manual*, pp. 97–98. An earlier version of the Committee on Publication was a three-man "Publication Committee"; see Peel, *Years of Authority*, p. 157.

138. Ibid., pp. 99–100.

139. Committee on Publication, *Setting the Course: Alfred Farlow and the Mission of the*

Committee on Publication (Boston: Committee on Publication, The First Church of Christ, Scientist, 1993), p. 20.

140. Ibid., p. 2.
141. Ibid., p. 14.
142. Mary B. G. Eddy, "Note," *Christian Science Journal* 9, no. 1 (April 1891), p. 16.
143. Braden, *Christian Science Today*, p. 126.
144. *First Church of Christ Scientist and Miscellany*, pp. 266–267.
145. Mark Twain, *Christian Science* (New York: Harper & Brothers, 1907), pp. 138, 82.
146. Stark, 191.
147. See Hamlin Hill, *Mark Twain: God's Fool* (New York: Harper & Row, 1973), p. 53.
148. Paul Baender, ed., *The Works of Mark Twain: What Is Man? And Other Philosophical Writings* (Berkeley, Calif.: Published for the Iowa Center for Textual Studies by the University of California Press, 1973), p. 23.
149. Wilson, *Sects and Society*, p. 359, Appendix D.
150. According to Peel, Mark Twain used this phrase in a letter to Frederick W. Peabody dated 5 December 1902; Peabody subsequently reprinted the letter in his book, *The Religio-Medical Masquerade* (Boston: Hancock Press, 1910). See Peel, *Years of Authority*, p. 446 n. 84.
151. Ibid., p. 204.
152. Peel, *Years of Authority*, pp. 202, 448 n. 97. Peel identifies the source of his information about Twain's Christian Science treatments as an account by Laura Lathrop, the New York City practitioner who reportedly treated him, in *Christian Science Sentinel* 10 (21 March 1908), p. 563f., but he adds that Lathrop does not identify Twain by name. He does not explain how he surmised that Twain was Lathrop's patient.
153. See Hamlin Hill, *Mark Twain: God's Fool* (New York: Harper & Row, 1973), p. 54: "His fear of the power [of Christian Science] was merely the surface expression of Mark Twain's real concern. . . . At a level too deep for comedy, he indisputably saw the relationship of Mrs. Eddy's new science of healing to the illnesses of his own family, a topic he could no longer mock."
154. Twain, *Christian Science*, p. 53.
155. Albert Bigelow Paine, *Mark Twain*, vol. 3 (New York: Harper, 1912), p. 1271.
156. Twain, *Christian Science*, p. 147.
157. Eddy, "Reply to Mark Twain," *First Church of Christ, Scientist and Miscellany*, 302; Eddy's claim that "it is a fact well understood that I begged the students who first gave me the endearing appellative 'Mother,' not to name me thus" and that her students used the term "without my consent" is dubious; she signed many of her own letters "Mother" and tolerated being so called by her household staff. See, for instance, *Letters of Mary Baker Eddy to Augusta E. Stetson, C.S.D., 1889–1909* (Cuyahoga Falls, Ohio: Emma Publishing Society, 1990), pp. 11, 22, 27.
158. "Reply to Mark Twain," in *First Church of Christ, Scientist and Miscellany*, p. 303.
159. Twain, *Christian Science*, p. 349.
160. Ibid., p. 130.
161. Ibid., p. 132.

162. See particularly, Twain, *Christian Science*, pp. 73–83. Twain also called Eddy "grasping, sordid, penurious, famishing for everything she sees," p. 285.

163. With regard to Eddy's donation to the local Concord hospital, see Robert Peel, *Health and Medicine in the Christian Science Tradition* (New York: Crossroad Publishing Company, 1988), p. 96; for a comprehensive list of Eddy's other charitable donations, see *Years of Authority*, pp. 255, 468 n. 2.

164. In the future, however, goaded by Twain's sneer, Eddy's Board of Directors would occasionally urge the membership to perform astonishing charitable feats, particularly during World War II, when they went to some lengths to publicize their efforts.

    In modern times, although the Church occasionally uses its periodicals to alert members to the fact that it is accepting donations following natural disasters such as Hurricane Andrew in 1992, or the 1995 earthquake in Kobe, Japan, it still maintains that charity begins in Christianly Scientific prayer. (See, for instance, the notice "Japan Earthquake Relief," in *Christian Science Sentinel* 97, no. 9 [27 February 1995], p. 45.) In a recent question-and-answer column in the *Sentinel*, in response to the question "What does your Church do for the local community?" the editors wrote, "It makes its biggest contribution through healing. This includes praying to heal community ills such as crime, drug addiction, and sexual and child abuse." *Christian Science Sentinel* 101, no. 1 (4 January 1999), p. 26.

165. *Science and Health*, p. 345.

166. Ibid., p. 167.

167. Bates and Dittemore, *Mary Baker Eddy*, p. 373.

168. See *Christian Science Sentinel*, 6 December 1900; "Christian Science and the Episcopal Congress," *Christian Science Journal* 18, no. 10 (January 1901), pp. 591–97.

169. *Science and Health*, p. 247.

170. In 1990, on cross-examination during his trial in Boston for the manslaughter and child endangerment of his two-year-old son, Robyn, David Twitchell was questioned about having had root canal surgery several years before refusing to seek medical care for his son, who died of complications caused by a twisted bowel. His inability to explain adequately the Christian Science rationale behind accepting dental surgery, while refusing medical surgery, may have contributed to the jury's guilty verdict (later overturned on appeal).

171. *Science and Health*, p. 254.

172. Ibid., p. 56.

173. Politically, the Church's accommodation to the expectations of society in this area has been a brilliant move. If Christian Scientists entirely refused prenatal care and medical assistance during delivery their mortality rate would skyrocket, which would lead to intense negative scrutiny. Scientists' positions on such matters seem to have evolved as a form of self-protection.

174. *Science and Health*, pp. 401–02.

175. Ibid., p. 444.

176. Ibid., p. 464.

177. See Peel, *Years of Authority*, pp. 238–42.

178. See, for example, the antiquated use of the word "surgeon" in the question-and-answer section of a recent *Sentinel*: "There are many documented accounts of the setting and mending of broken bones solely through prayer in Christian Science. Some choose to use the services of a *surgeon* to set the bone and then rely on Christian Science treatment for the healing." *Christian Science Sentinel* 100, no. 4 (26 January 1998), p. 26 (my italics).

179. Peel, *Years of Authority*, p. 238.

180. *Science and Health*, p. 396.

181. One example of a Christian Science teacher stripped of his position was Carl J. Welz of Santa Rosa, California, who was disciplined in 1982 for accepting dialysis when he experienced kidney failure. See Richard J. Brenneman, *Deadly Blessings: Faith Healing on Trial* (Buffalo, New York: Prometheus Books, 1990), p. 45.

182. Peel writes that Eddy's son George "suspected—probably with some justification"—that Calvin Frye had kept some of his letters from his mother; see Peel, *Years of Authority*, p. 276.

183. Bates and Dittemore, p. 391. See also Silberger, *Mary Baker Eddy*, p. 217.

184. *Manual*, p. 103.

185. Bates and Dittemore, p. 391.

186. Peel, *Years of Authority*, p. 223.

187. For "the largest church in the city of Boston," see Armstrong and Williamson, *Building of The Mother Church*, p. 92; for "a foot higher than the Bunker Hill monument," see Bates and Dittemore, p. 391.

188. Armstrong and Williamson, *Building of The Mother Church*, p. 124.

189. See Peel, *Years of Authority*, pp. 224, 321. This is one of the areas of Eddy's life where Peel is particularly misleading.

190. Bates and Dittemore, p. 391.

191. *The First Church of Christ, Scientist and Miscellany*, p. 6.

192. Armstrong and Williamson, *Building of The Mother Church*, p. 142.

193. Ibid., pp. 148–49; Dakin, *Mrs. Eddy*, p. 382.

194. Peel, *Years of Authority*, pp. 263–64.

195. Lyman P. Powell, *Mary Baker Eddy: A Life Size Portrait* (Boston: Christian Science Publishing Society, 1978), p. 224. This quotation is taken from the edition published in 1991 as part of the Church's "Twentieth-Century Biographers Series"; its pagination differs from earlier editions'.

196. Silberger, *Mary Baker Eddy*, p. 223.

197. Dakin, *Mrs. Eddy*, p. 451.

198. Silberger reports that this was Frederick Peabody's interpretation of the whole sad affair. See Silberger, *Mary Baker Eddy*, p. 229.

199. In fairness to Tomlinson, it should be pointed out that his decision not to mention the suicide of his sister may have had its basis in the social reticence of the day. In his autobiography, *The Education of Henry Adams*, Adams addresses only in the most elliptical way his wife's suicide. And yet, Tomlinson is so clearly devoted to Eddy and her beliefs that it seems reasonable to surmise that he found

it impossible to admit, much less discuss, an event so confounding to the teachings and teachers of Christian Science.

200. Silberger, *Mary Baker Eddy*, p. 230.

201. Peel, *Years of Authority*, p. 300.

202. A friend of Cather's, Elizabeth Shepley Sergeant, wrote in *Willa Cather: A Memoir* (Lincoln: University of Nebraska Press, 1963), p. 55: "The job seemed to her a little *infra dig*, not on the level where she cared to move."

203. See David Stouck, introduction to Cather and Milmine, pp. xvi–xvii.

204. For "yellow journalism," see M. Victor Westberg, "Report of the Manager, Committees on Publication," *Christian Science Journal* 111, no. 8 (August 1993), p. 17. *McClure's* was, in fact, one of the greatest periodicals of the "Golden Age of the American magazine," according to Peter Lyon's *Success Story: The Life and Times of S. S. McClure* (New York: Charles Scribner's Sons, 1963), p. 113. It was "the most exciting, the liveliest, the best illustrated, the most handsomely dressed, the most interesting, and the most profitable of an abundance of superior magazines." It ran the work of Rudyard Kipling, Hamlin Garland, Lincoln Steffens, and Ida Tarbell, whose series on Standard Oil, published in *McClure's* from 1902 to 1904, established a new standard of excellence in investigative journalism.

205. Lyon, *Success Story*, p. 300.

206. Ibid.

207. Ibid., p. 301.

208. David Stouck, afterword to Cather and Milmine, pp. 497–98.

209. Georgine Milmine, *The Life of Mary Baker G. Eddy and the History of Christian Science* (Grand Rapids, Mich.: Baker Book House, 1971), back cover flap.

210. Sergeant, *Willa Cather: A Memoir*, p. 56.

211. Stouck, afterword to Cather and Milmine, p. 497.

212. Victor Westberg's remarks were described to me by an editor at the University of Nebraska Press. The undated press release is quoted in its entirety.

213. Gillian Gill in her *Mary Baker Eddy* is highly critical of Cather and Milmine's book; see her appendix, "The Essential Published Source Books," pp. 563–568. Her observation that the Cather and Milmine book "is as much a work of polemic as a piece of reporting," is just as true of her own work. Nor is her point a new one; it is, in fact, the Church's old argument, that Milmine was biased and used biased sources. Gill is forced to conclude, however, as I do, that "there is no doubt that the Milmine biography is one of the most important sources of information on Mrs. Eddy" (p. 568).

214. Westberg, "Report of the Manager," p. 17.

215. Bates and Dittemore, p. 402.

216. Christian Science Publishing Society, *Mary Baker Eddy: Twentieth-Century Biographers Series, An Introduction* (Boston: Christian Science Publishing Society, 1991), p. 8.

217. Ibid., p. 9.

218. Powell, *A Life Size Portrait*, pp. 226, 225.

219. The Edwin Anderson letter is described in David Stouck's afterword to Cather

and Milmine, p. 500, n. 2: "The [New York Public] Library made a number of photographic facsimiles of the first edition for patrons, but the book was still protected by copyright so that when Trustees of Mrs. Eddy's estate learned about the library's practice they called on the library to destroy the negatives from which copies had been made and forced the library to recall those that had been sold."

The fear of the first edition of *Science and Health* displayed by those who work in the Church archives was described by Linda Fasig, a *Journal*-listed practitioner from 1979 to 1986, telephone interview by author, 11 November 1995.

220. "The New Book. Fiat Lux," *Christian Science Journal* 8, no. 12 (March 1891), p. 515. This was the lead article in that issue of the *Journal*; it was reprinted as the lead article of the April 1891 issue, "by request of the readers." Italics appear in the original. The piece was unsigned and speaks of Eddy in the third person, but, whether she wrote it or not, she was certainly aware of it and approved of it. This is particularly clear given that the article was reprinted.

221. The interview with Clara Barton, "Christian Science Most Potent Factor in Religious Life, Says Clara Barton," ran in the *New York American* on 6 January 1908; it was reprinted in the *Christian Science Journal* 25, no. 11 (February 1908), pp. 696–99.

222. Peel, *Years of Authority*, p. 308.

223. *First Church of Christ, Scientist and Miscellany*, p. 129.

224. *Science and Health*, p. 118.

225. Peel, *Years of Authority*, p. 310.

226. Erwin D. Canham, *Commitment to Freedom: The Story of The Christian Science Monitor* (Cambridge, Mass.: Houghton Mifflin Company, 1958), p. 7.

227. Ibid., p. 39; see also Archibald McLellan, "The Christian Science Monitor," *Christian Science Sentinel* 11, no. 7 (17 October 1908), p. 130.

228. For an extensive description of the first issue of the *Monitor*, see Canham, *Commitment*, pp. 58–62.

229. Eddy, "Something in a Name," in *The First Church of Christ, Scientist and Miscellany*, p. 353.

230. Ibid., p. xvi.

231. As Canham points out, the *Monitor* does occasionally cover Christian Science news, such as the Church's annual meeting, that is not covered, or not covered so extensively, by other newspapers. It formerly printed the texts of Christian Science lectures several times a year but ceased to do so in recent years. See Canham, *Commitment*, pp. 64–65.

232. Ibid., p. 65.

233. Ibid., pp. 121–22. Canham points out one interesting exception to the no-tobacco rule: Winston Churchill's famous cigar was left untouched.

234. Ibid., p. 119.

235. Ibid., p. 121.

236. According to Volney D. Hurd, who progressed from copyboy to Paris correspondent at the *Monitor*, the "passed on mules" story originated with a dispatch, perhaps written by a correspondent whose native language was not English, received in the *Monitor* offices during World War I; the original phrase was "passed-on

horses." Never published, what began as an office joke was eventually transformed by other newspapers and magazines into a telling example of *Monitor* taboos; Erwin Canham notes, however, that while the *Monitor* preferred to say that a person had "passed on," the word "died" was not taboo. See Canham, *Commitment*, pp. 119–21.

237. Ibid., p. xix.
238. I am indebted here and throughout this section on Augusta Stetson to the Ph.D. dissertation of Sarah Gardner Cunningham, "A New Order: Augusta Emma Simmons Stetson and the Origins of Christian Science in New York City, 1886–1910," Union Theological Seminary, 1994. Cunningham does not cite the source of this particular passage; see "A New Order," pp. 26–27.
239. Ibid., p. 42.
240. Mary Baker Eddy to Augusta Stetson, 21 March 1889, in *Letters of Mary Baker Eddy to Augusta E. Stetson, C.S.D.* (Cuyahoga Falls, Ohio: Emma Publishing Society, 1990), p. 11.
241. Ibid., p. 72.
242. Ibid., pp. 93, 100.
243. Peel, *Years of Authority*, p. 335.
244. Dickey, *Memoirs*, p. ix.
245. Ibid., p. 33.
246. Ibid.
247. Ibid., p. 40.
248. Ibid., p. 41.
249. Ibid., p. 42.
250. *Manual*, pp. 53–54.
251. Braden, *Christian Science Today*, pp. 164–65.
252. Dakin, *Mrs. Eddy*, p. 530.
253. Peel, *Years of Authority*, p. 359.
254. Ibid.
255. Ibid., p. 361.
256. Ibid.
257. Concord (N.H.) *Evening Monitor*, 15 October 1911; cited in Andrew W. Hartsook, *Christian Science After 1910* (Santa Clarita, Calif.: The Bookmark, 1993), p. 8. See also Dakin, *Mrs. Eddy*, p. 512; Dakin suggests that the amount was "approximately $3,000,000."
258. Harold Bloom, *The American Religion: The Emergence of the Post-Christian Nation* (New York: Simon & Schuster, 1992), p. 131.
259. Bates and Dittemore, pp. 153–54.
260. *Science and Health*, p. vii.
261. Ibid., pp. 678, 649, 690.
262. Ibid., p. 1.
263. V. S. Pritchett, "The Saint," *Collected Stories* (New York: Random House, 1982), p. 30.
264. Wilson, *Sects and Society*, pp. 125–26.

265. Audrey L. Miller, "Woman Conquers Pain," *Christian Science Sentinel* 100, no. 27 (6 July 1998), p. 20.

266. For Eddy's interpretation of the first two chapters of Genesis, see her chapter "Genesis" in the "Key to the Scriptures" section of *Science and Health*, pp. 501–57; for "Father-Mother God," see *Science and Health*, p. 16; for "radical reliance," see *Science and Health*, p. 167; for Eddy's strictures regarding alcohol, tobacco, drugs, and caffeinated beverages, see *Science and Health*, p. 406; for "animal magnetism," see the chapter "Animal Magnetism Unmasked," *Science and Health*, pp. 100–06; for "primitive Christianity," see *Manual*, p. 17.

267. *Science and Health*, p. 406.

268. *Miscellaneous Writings*, p. 21.

269. *Science and Health*, p. 468.

270. Ibid., p. 475.

271. Ibid., p. 465.

272. Ibid., p. 469.

273. Ibid., pp. 310, 469, 311, 335, 339, 312.

274. Ibid., pp. 207, 211, 472.

275. Gen. 1:26, 31.

276. *Science and Health*, p. 522.

277. Ibid., pp. 16–17.

278. Bloom, *American Religion*, p. 134.

279. Wilson, *Sects and Society*, p. 129.

280. *Science and Health*, p. 413.

281. Ibid., p. 557.

282. Ibid., p. 175.

283. Ibid., p. 389.

284. Wilson, *Sects and Society*, p. 123.

285. Arthur O. Lovejoy, *The Great Chain of Being: A Study of the History of an Idea* (Cambridge, Mass.: Harvard University Press, 1964), pp. 30–31.

286. *Science and Health*, p. 583.

287. Ibid., p. 313.

288. Ibid.

289. Ibid., p. 53.

290. Ibid., p. 55.

291. See Richard J. Brenneman, *Deadly Blessings: Faith Healing on Trial* (Buffalo, N.Y.: Prometheus Books, 1990), p. 116, n. 27.

292. Wilson, *Sects and Society*, p. 125.

293. Eddy refers to Jesus dozens of times throughout *Science and Health* as "Master." See, e.g., pp. 3, 4, 9, 16, 19, 24.

294. See ibid., pp. 430–32.

295. Ibid., pp. 431–33.

296. Ibid., p. 434.

297. Ibid., p. 438.

298. Ibid., p. 442.

299. Eddy, "Communion Hymn," *Seven Hymns* (Boston: First Church of Christ, Scientist, 1992), not paginated.

300. The Christian Science Board of Directors, "Mrs. Eddy's Place," *Christian Science Sentinel* (5 June 1943). See also the pamphlet "Mrs. Eddy's Place," reprint, Claremont, Calif.: Aequus Institute Publications, 1993.

301. Scientists' conflicted feelings over the woman they must not worship but *did* worship made any contemplation of Eddy by outsiders intolerable and any discussion by insiders problematic. Hollywood biopics about Eddy's life could not be countenanced, critical biographies had to be quashed, and the Church's own biographies had to be whitewashed. The Church flooded the Eddy market with flattering portraits, hagiographies, and memoirs after her death. It published a 1911 compilation of *Editorial Comments on the Life and Work of Mary Baker Eddy*, consisting largely of adulatory obituaries; *Christian Science and Its Discoverer*, by Mary Ramsay, in 1935; *Historical Sketches*, a compilation of *Journal* articles about Eddy by Clifford Smith, in 1941; *Twelve Years with Mary Baker Eddy*, by Irving Tomlinson, one of Eddy's secretaries, in 1945; *Mary Baker Eddy: Her Mission and Triumph*, by Julia Michael Johnston, the daughter of a woman taught by Eddy, in 1946; and, between 1943 and 1972, four anthologies of memoirs entitled *We Knew Mary Baker Eddy*. Church authorities also cooperated with Lyman Powell, an Episcopalian minister who first criticized and then came to revere Eddy; his *Mary Baker Eddy: A Life Size Portrait* was published by Macmillan in 1930 and later reissued by the Church. The Church established a pattern of acquiring the copyrights of books about Eddy, favorable or not; it therefore controlled the Eddy market.

Eventually the Scientists also published their own scholarly biography by their very own scholar, Robert Peel, who was such a booster for the religion that, during his lifetime (1909–1992), he was known as "Mr. Christian Science." A devout Scientist, Peel served the Church for most of his adult life. His early education and experience gave him the academic skills he needed to write his massive three-volume scholarly biography of Eddy: he completed a master's degree in English at Harvard in 1931, where he studied with the famous Americanist Perry Miller. He then entered the U.S. Army Counterintelligence Service, working for General Douglas MacArthur during and after World War II. He taught at Principia, the Christian Science college; he wrote editorials for the *Monitor* for nine years; he worked as an editorial consultant for the Committees on Publication from 1955 to 1989; and, most important, he wrote books, including *Christian Science: Its Encounter with American Culture* (1958), *Spiritual Healing in a Scientific Age* (1987), and *Health and Medicine in the Christian Science Tradition* (1989). All were intended to explain Christian Science to the layman and assert its healing prowess in a way accessible to a modern audience. His greatest work, however, was his three-volume biography of Eddy, the first and, as yet, the only biography by a Christian Science scholar with access to the archives of the Church. The Christian Science Church has not had a tradition of scholarship; indeed, the religion discourages wide reading and study. Most Scientists interested in literature or writing have traditionally gone to work for the *Monitor*. Peel was one of the finest—and one of the few—scholars that the Church ever produced.

Peel set out to counter all the aspersions cast on Eddy by Twain, Milmine, and Edwin Franden Dakin, whose *Mrs. Eddy: The Biography of a Virginal Mind*, one of the most famous critical biographies of Eddy, was published in 1929. Peel's exhaustive three-volume *Mary Baker Eddy: The Years of Discovery*, *The Years of Trial*, and *The Years of Authority*, was essentially the work of an apologist and contains startlingly inventive rationalizations for Eddy's strange pronouncements and paranoid behavior, suggesting that her much-loathed enemy, Richard Kennedy, was, in fact, a real devil and arguing that several passages she plagiarized from published sources reflected mere "unconscious borrowing" on her part. It was praised by reviewers, but the final volume in particular caused tremendous anxiety and concern among Christian Scientists.

From the point of view of many Scientists, that offending volume confirmed the damning anecdotes that Milmine and other biographers had told and that the Church had denounced. They confirmed that Eddy had taken morphine during illnesses, that she was tormented by fears, that her household was beset by petty rivalries among her followers and disrupted by her outbursts of rage and frustration. For everything, Peel had an explanation; every odd remark or outrageous tantrum was yet more proof of Eddy's brilliant leadership and her unique connection to God. But among some Scientists, Peel became a figure of suspicion. He had betrayed Eddy and her divinity. Because of his work, the Church could no longer assert that the facts of Eddy's life were simply the scurrilous and imaginative products of "yellow journalism." The facts are so disturbing to Scientists that one recent Christian Science dissident newsletter published an article, "Wonderful News Exonerating Robert Peel," claiming that Peel did not write the third volume of his trilogy: "A mental impairment precluded him from finishing his final volume. That job was left to a 'ghost writer,' another individual . . . [who] embodied nothing less than the Pharasaical thought bent on crucifying the Christ anew, if it could." (See "Wonderful News Exonerating Robert Peel," *Mary Baker Eddy Letter*, no. 9 [21 May 1998], p. 11.) The newsletter did not identify any source for the claim that Peel suffered a "mental impairment" that prevented him from writing his third volume, nor is the putative "ghost writer" named; indeed, the following issue of the *Mary Baker Eddy Letter*, no. 10 (16 July 1998), withdrew the claim, which was indubitably false. The volume in question, *Mary Baker Eddy: The Years of Authority*, was published in 1977, and Peel went on to write two more books. He appeared in a Church video about Eddy, *A Heart in Protest*, in 1988 and, although elderly, seemed physically and mentally fit. He lived at his own home until his death in 1992. Eddy has been dead for close to a century, but Scientists are still struggling to save her from herself.

302. Eddy, "Mrs. Eddy Shocked," *New York Herald*, 6 February 1895, reprinted in *Pulpit and Press* (Boston: First Church of Christ, Scientist, 1923), pp. 74–75.

Part III. "Nothing Has Gone Right Since 1910": Christian Science after Death

1. According to the curator of historical collections at Mount Auburn Cemetery, the body of Mary Baker Eddy is buried beneath the center of the monument. Meg Winslow, telephone conversation with author, 22 January 1998.
2. Dakin, *Mrs. Eddy*, p. 520. See also Bates and Dittemore, pp. 451–52, for a similar description of the guarding of Eddy's coffin.
3. Bates and Dittemore, p. 451.
4. Ibid. See also Peel, *Years of Authority*, p. 514 n. 116.
5. Peel, op. cit. As for Farlow's earlier belief that Eddy would demonstrate eternal life, see Sarah Gardner Cunningham, "A New Order: Augusta Emma Simmons Stetson and the Origins of Christian Science in New York City, 1886–1910" (Ph.D. diss., Union Theological Seminary, 1994), p. 107.
6. Peel, *Years of Authority*, p. 514 n. 116.
7. Ibid., p. 513 n. 116.
8. Ibid., pp. 360, 513 n. 114.
9. Ibid., p. 513, n. 114.
10. The minutes of this meeting and the press release can be found in *Proceedings in Equity 1919–1921 Concerning Deed of Trust of January 25, 1898 Constituting the Christian Science Publishing Society* (Boston: Christian Science Publishing Society, 1922), p. 374. This book was printed in a limited subscription edition; it can be found in the collection of the New York Public Library and several other large research institutions.
11. Ibid.
12. *Manual*, pp. 67–68, 48, 43.
13. Ibid., pp. 70, 71.
14. *Retrospection and Introspection*, p. 45.
15. Dr. Alfred E. Baker, "Notes on Metaphysical Work Done by Dr. Alfred E. Baker, M.D., C.S.D., While Associated with Mary Baker Eddy" (privately printed, n.d.), p. 14.
16. Dickey, *Memoirs*, p. 44.
17. *The First Church of Christ, Scientist and Miscellany*, p. 230.
18. See *Manual*, pp. 104–105.
19. Rodney Stark, "The Rise and Fall of Christian Science," *Journal of Contemporary Religion* 13, no. 2 (1998), p. 190.
20. Charles Braden, *Christian Science Today: Power, Policy, Practice* (Dallas: Southern Methodist University Press, 1958), p. 271.
21. For comparative purposes, see *Manual*, 88th ed., p. 120; *Manual*, 89th ed., p. 120. Christian Science dissident booksellers, such as the Rare Book Company (Freehold, New Jersey) and The Bookmark (Santa Clarita, California) sell reproductions of the 88th edition of the *Manual*.
22. *Manual*, p. 80.
23. Mary Baker Eddy, "Mrs. Eddy Talks," *New York Herald*, 1 May 1901, in *The First Church of Christ, Scientist and Miscellany*, p. 343.

24. This speech, with its martial imagery, is quoted in Braden, *Christian Science Today*, p. 75.

25. Herbert W. Eustace, *Christian Science: Its "Clear, Correct Teaching" and Complete Writings* (Berkeley, Calif.: Lederer, Street & Zeus, 1934), p. xxvi.

26. Ibid., pp. xxiii–xxiv.

27. *Proceedings in Equity*, p. 1141.

28. Braden, *Christian Science Today*, p. 87. The Board had already been held in contempt once, for violating the original injunction.

29. See "Paul Revere," "The Mother Church: Its Permanency" (privately printed pamphlet), no. 23, p. 7.

30. Braden, *Christian Science Today*, p. 89.

31. Ibid., pp. 91–92.

32. Ibid., p. 94.

33. Ibid.

34. Ibid., p. 95.

35. Eustace, p. xli.

36. Andrew W. Hartsook's *Christian Science After 1910* (Santa Clarita, Calif.: The Bookmark, 1993) is a virtual compendium of the Board's intrusions into the lives of Scientists; it summarizes Board statements in the *Journal* (the preferred medium for these communications) into the early 1990s.

37. Bicknell Young to Dr. Hendrik J. de Lange, 4 May 1937, in *The Continuity of the Cause of Christian Science* (Cambridge, England: Christian Science Foundation, 1995), frontispiece.

38. Norman Beasley, *The Continuing Spirit* (New York: Duell, Sloan & Pearce, 1956), p. 212.

39. Stark, "Rise and Fall," p. 191, table 1.

40. Beasley, *Continuing Spirit*, p. 229.

41. Ibid.

42. Ibid., p. 205. Beasley provides no source for this claim.

43. Christopher Sykes, *Nancy: The Life of Lady Astor* (New York: Harper & Row, 1972), p. 15.

44. David Sinclair, *Dynasty: The Astors and Their Times* (New York: Beaufort Books, 1984), p. 300.

45. Sykes, *Nancy*, p. 296.

46. Beate Ruhm von Oppen, introduction to *Helmuth James von Moltke: Letters to Freya, 1939–1945* (New York: Knopf, 1990), p. 5.

47. The historian Carroll Quigley has described how Christian Science became a part of the atmosphere of Cliveden. See Carroll Quigley, *Tragedy and Hope: A History of the World in Our Time* (New York: MacMillan, 1974); and *The Anglo-American Establishment: from Rhodes to Cliveden* (New York: Books in Focus, 1981).

48. Philip Kerr, Lord Lothian, as quoted in Hartsook, *Christian Science After 1910*, p. 61.

49. Mary Baker Eddy, "Christian Science and the Times," in *First Church of Christ,*

Scientist and Miscellany (Boston: First Church of Christ, Scientist, 1941), pp. 266–67.

50. Eddy, "Message to The First Church of Christ, Scientist, or The Mother Church, Boston, June 15, 1902," in *Prose Works Other Than Science and Health*, pp. 3, 4 (paginated separately).

51. One of the most prominent conservative Scientists who has advanced his objections to what he interprets as Canham's communistic leanings and deplored what he sees as the leftist leanings of the *Monitor* under Canham is Andrew W. Hartsook, who has published *The Banner*, a Christian Science dissident newsletter, since 1987, as well as a book, *Christian Science After 1910*, chronicling "the decline of this great movement." For Hartsook's interpretation of Lord Lothian's and Erwin Canham's roles in the movement, see his chapter 18, "The Foe in Ambush," pp. 101–105. Hartsook and other conservative Scientists are fond of quoting Eddy's endorsement of the Monroe doctrine and the U.S. Constitution; see *First Church of Christ, Scientist and Miscellany*, p. 282.

52. *Science and Health*, p. 494.

53. Ibid., p. 206.

54. *Miscellaneous Writings*, p. 45.

55. *First Church of Christ, Scientist and Miscellany*, p. 186.

56. "Report of Cleveland Association," *Christian Science Journal* 7, no. 5 (August 1889), p. 228; Alfred Farlow, "The Brotherhood of Man," *Christian Science Journal* 11, no. 9 (December 1893), p. 404.

57. "Business Men," *Christian Science Journal* 15, no. 4 (July 1897), pp. 203, 204.

58. See Altman K. Swihart, *Since Mrs. Eddy* (New York, Henry Holt and Co., 1931), p. 20; quoted in Wilson, *Sects and Society*, p. 140 n. 2.

59. See Stella Hadden Alexander, "Illuming Light: Glimpses of Home and Records, 1923–1939," vol. 3 (typescript, Burke Library, Union Theological Seminary, New York, 1939), p. 101; quoted in Cunningham, "A New Order," p. 110.

60. See Swihart, *Since Mrs. Eddy*, p. 43 f., as quoted in Peel, *Years of Authority*, p. 330.

61. Blanche Hersey Hogue, "Effectual Prayer," *Christian Science Journal* 28, no. 5 (August 1910), p. 295.

62. Stephen Gottschalk, *The Emergence of Christian Science in American Religious Life* (Berkeley: University of California Press, 1973), p. 252.

63. Ibid., p. 253.

64. "An Interview: She Built an International Corporation on a Spiritual Basis," *Christian Science Journal* 96, no. 10 (October 1978), p. 612.

65. For the Church's attempt to portray itself as a religion for Every Man, see DeWitt John, *The Christian Science Way of Life* (Englewood Cliffs, New Jersey: Prentice Hall, 1962), pp. 1–2: "Christian Science comes to all sorts of people. It comes to the rich and poor, the talented and the simple, the old and the young. . . . It comes to people of many races and many backgrounds and at varying stages of progress. It is hard to generalize about what kind of people Christian Scientists are."

66. Wilson, *Sects and Society*, p. 349.

67. Ibid., pp. 319, 317.

68. Eddy herself may well have been disgusted by this literary development; she had no use for imaginative literature, condemning novels as sinks of corruption: "It is the tangled barbarisms of learning which we deplore,—the mere dogma, the speculative theory, the nauseous fiction. Novels, remarkable only for their exaggerated pictures, impossible ideals, and specimens of depravity, fill our young readers with wrong tastes and sentiments." See *Science and Health*, p. 195.

69. Ada Carter, *The Seamless Robe* (New York: A. Wessels, 1909), p. 363.

70. Charles Francis Stocking, *The Diary of Jean Everts* (The Maestro Company, c. 1912), p. 339.

71. V. S. Pritchett, *A Cab at the Door* (New York: Modern Library, 1994), pp. 143, 151.

72. Ibid., p. 146.

73. Ibid., p. 147–48.

74. V. S. Pritchett, *Mr. Beluncle* (New York: Oxford University Press, 1986), p. 162.

75. Pritchett, *Cab at the Door*, p. 143.

76. V. S. Pritchett, "The Saint," *Collected Stories* (New York: Random House, 1982), p. 25.

77. Ibid., p. 30.

78. Ibid., p. 33.

79. Ibid., p. 34.

80. *First Church of Christ, Scientist and Miscellany*, p. 277.

81. Ibid., p. 278.

82. Mary Baker Eddy, "War," *Christian Science Journal* 26, no. 2 (May, 1908): 65; reprinted in *First Church of Christ, Scientist and Miscellany*, p. 286.

83. See Eddy, "The Prayer for Peace," in *First Church of Christ, Scientist and Miscellany*, p. 279.

84. Editorial, *The Christian Science Monitor*, 6 April 1917, as quoted in Joseph C. Harsch, "The Shifting Cast of Nations," *Understanding Our Century: Commemorating the 75th Anniversary of* The Christian Science Monitor (Boston: First Church of Christ, Scientist, 1984), p. 28.

85. For a full discussion of the Church's attitude toward conscientious objection, see Braden, "Christian Science in Wartime," *Christian Science Today*, pp. 288–90.

86. See "From the Directors: The Selective Draft," *Christian Science Sentinel* 43, no. 18 (January 4, 1941), p. 351; reprinted in *Christian Science Journal* 58, no. 11 (February, 1941), pp. 624–25; "Editorial Letter," *Christian Science Monitor*, 16 May 1940.

87. Of course, it could also be argued that the Tenets made no specific references to "radical reliance" or many of the other beliefs held dear by the Church and its members.

88. "Adolf Hitler, in an Exclusive Interview, Condemns Berlin Government's 'Liquidation' of Conflict, and Throws Down Gauntlet to Dr. von Kahr," *Christian Science Monitor*, 3 October 1923.

89. Ibid.

90. Erwin D. Canham, *Commitment to Freedom: The Story of The Christian Science Monitor* (Boston: Houghton Mifflin Co., 1958), p. 286.

91. Ibid., p. 290.
92. Beasley, *The Continuing Spirit*, p. 225. Beasley gives numbers similar to Canham's.
93. See Canham, pp. 287, 291. See also Beasley, *The Continuing Spirit*, p. 238. Beasley gives numbers similar to Canham's.
94. The full text of the letter banning Christian Science in Germany can be found in English and German in *The Story of Christian Science Wartime Activities: 1939–1946* (Boston: The Christian Science Publishing Society, 1947), pp. 254–55. It is also reprinted in English in Beasley, *The Continuing Spirit*, p. 242.
95. Information about the fates of Albert Telschow, Friedrich Preller, and the unnamed Scientist who was sent to Ravensbruck can be found in *Christian Science Wartime Activities*, pp. 252–56.
96. "Item of Interest Concerning Drugs or Medicine," *Christian Science Sentinel* 44, no. 19 (9 May 1942), pp. 812–813; *Christian Science Journal* 63, no. 9 (September 1945), p. 469.
97. Christian Science Board of Directors, "The Christian Science Standard of Healing," *Christian Science Journal* 75, no. 11 (November 1957), p. 598.
98. *Christian Science Wartime Activities*, pp. 48, 423.
99. Braden, *Christian Science Today*, p. 272; for "millions" see Eddy, "Reply to McClure's Magazine," in *First Church of Christ, Scientist and Miscellany*, p. 315; "The Blight that Failed" (New York: Blue Ribbon Books, 1930), p. 4.
100. For the period 1931–1941, see Braden, *Christian Science Today*, pp. 269–71.
101. Hearst's description appeared in the *Los Angeles Examiner* on 17 July 1941, and also in a pamphlet entitled "Faith" (San Simeon, Calif.: privately printed, 1941). The Hearst anecdote is also recounted in Peel, *The Years of Authority*, p. 495, and in *Christian Science: A Sourcebook of Contemporary Materials* (Boston: Christian Science Publishing Society, 1990), pp. 170, 173.
102. David Stenn, *Bombshell: The Life and Death of Jean Harlow* (New York: Doubleday, 1993), p. 230.
103. Ibid., p. 238.
104. Ibid., p. 236.
105. Irving Shulman, *Harlow: An Intimate Biography* (New York: Bernard Geis Associates, 1964), p. 397.
106. Ibid.
107. Stenn, *Bombshell*, p. 238.
108. Ibid.
109. Ibid., p. 247.
110. Ibid., p. 64.
111. Ibid., p. 228.
112. Ibid., p. 232.
113. Ginger Rogers, *Ginger: My Story* (New York: HarperCollins, 1991), pp. 4–7.
114. Ibid., pp. 380–81.
115. Arthur Corey, *Behind the Scenes with the Metaphysicians* (Los Angeles: DeVorss & Co., 1968), p. 209.
116. Ibid., p. 210.
117. Ibid.

118. Ibid., p. 211.

119. Hart Crane mentions Christian Science in several letters to and about his mother; see, for example, Hart Crane to William Wright, 2 May 1919, in *Letters of Hart Crane and His Family*, Thomas S. W. Lewis, ed. (New York: Columbia University Press, 1974), p. 109. For Mina Loy's church attendance with the Steins, see Carolyn Burke, *Becoming Modern: The Life of Mina Loy* (Berkeley, Calif.: University of California Press, 1996), p. 131. Henry Miller's remarks about Eddy can be found in Miller, *Big Sur and the Oranges of Hieronymus Bosch* (New York: New Directions, 1957), p. 360.

120. Mary Ann Caws, ed. *Joseph Cornell's Theater of the Mind: Selected Diaries, Letters, and Files*, (New York: Thames and Hudson, 1993), p. 304.

121. Deborah Solomon, *Utopia Parkway: The Life and Work of Joseph Cornell* (New York: Farrar, Straus and Giroux, 1997), p. 208.

122. Cornell, *Theater of the Mind*, p. 120.

123. Burke, *Becoming Modern*, p. 405.

124. Ibid., p. 404.

125. Solomon, *Utopia Parkway*, p. 61.

126. Ibid., p. 60.

127. Burke, *Becoming Modern*, p. 407.

128. Fred Lawrence Guiles, *Joan Crawford: The Last Word* (New York: Carol Publishing Group), pp. 154–55.

129. Louella O. Parsons, as quoted in "Doris Day," *Current Biography* (1954), p. 227.

130. Crosby Day, " 'Midnight' a Terror for a Day," *Orlando* (Fla.) *Sentinel*, 2 June 1996.

131. On *Larry King Weekend*, Tony Randall recently spoke of how Day had been "very, very serious about her religion," and said, "I don't know how a person can be so much in life, and then pull out of life." Tony Randall, *Larry King Weekend*, CNN, 19 April 1997.

132. Carol Burnett, *One More Time: A Memoir* (New York: Random House, 1986), p. 54.

133. Ibid., p. 10.

134. Enid Nemy, "Hello? Yes. Goodbye? Never," *New York Times*, 29 November 1995.

135. Bob Morris, "Glowing, Growing and Going Strong," *New York Times*, 22 October 1995.

136. David Richards, "Carol Channing: Still Lookin' Swell," *Washington Post*, 10 September 1995.

137. Ibid.

138. Leslie Bennetts, "All Lips and Lashes," *Vanity Fair*, October 1995, p. 265.

139. Richards, "Carol Channing: Still Lookin' Swell."

140. Bennetts, "All Lips and Lashes." p. 293. Bennetts describes Channing's planned eye surgery as well as cortisone cream she used on her lashes, a treatment most Scientists would not have contemplated.

141. Richards, "Carol Channing: Still Lookin' Swell."

142. Bennetts, "All Lips and Lashes," p. 265.

143. Richards, "Carol Channing: Still Lookin' Swell."

144. Lyrics of "Dyers Eve" as quoted in Michael Corcoran, "Speed Thrills: Metallica,"

Creem, May 1991, p. 62; for another description of "Dyers Eve" and "The God That Failed" as songs inspired by Christian Science, see David Fricke, "Metallica," *Rolling Stone*, 14 November 1991, p. 54.

145. Mike Gitter, "Somber No More," *Pulse!*, September 1991, p. 103.

146. Jill Smolowe, "Gymnastics: Don't Call Them Pixies!," *Time*, 27 July 1992, p. 56.

147. Len Pasquarelli, "Christian Science Beliefs Won't Be Problem, Vardell Tells Clubs," *Atlanta Journal and Constitution*, 26 April 1992.

148. Tommy Vardell, "Football, Mental Toughness, and Going Beyond Limits," *Principia Alumni Purpose*, summer 1992, p. 22.

149. For details on the relationship between Duvall and Foote, see Lynde McCormick, "Robert Duvall: Almost a Star, Definitely an Actor," *Christian Science Monitor*, 8 January 1981. The *Monitor* has covered Duvall's career almost religiously; see also David Sterritt, "Rediscovering the Drama in Decency and Compassion," *Christian Science Monitor*, 10 March 1983; David Sterritt, "Robert Duvall's Un-Hollywood Take on Movies, *Christian Science Monitor*, 23 January 1998; Robert Marquand, " 'The Apostle' Rewrites How Religion Is Depicted on Big Screen," *Christian Science Monitor*, 5 February 1998.

150. See Kathleen Tynan, "A Suffering Survivor Who Began on Velvet," *Independent*, 26 October 1990.

151. See Michael Blowen, "He's Off to Be the 'Wizard': Mickey Rooney's Happy Life in Front of the Curtain," *Boston Globe*, 24 January 1999; Carol Wallace, "From Liz to Imelda, Women Go Wild Over George Hamilton, Hollywood's Perennial Knight of 100 Stars," *People*, 21 April 1986.

152. Frank Rizzo, "Robin Williams' Prescription: A Laugh Is Almost as Good as a Pill," *Fort Worth Star-Telegram*, 25 December 1998.

153. For Val Kilmer's history as a Scientist, see Luaine Lee, "Val's Values," *St. Louis Post-Dispatch*, 4 April 1997; for Kilmer's interview, see Channing Walker, "Speaking for Moses: An Interview with Val Kilmer," *Christian Science Sentinel* 101, no. 2 (11 January 1999), p. 14.

154. Dakin subsequently edited and wrote the introduction and commentary for *Today and Destiny: Vital Excerpts from The Decline of the West of Oswald Spengler* (New York: Knopf, 1940).

155. Edwin Franden Dakin, *Mrs. Eddy: The Biography of a Virginal Mind* (1930; reprint with a new introduction by the author, New York: Charles Scribner's Sons, 1970), p. xiii.

156. Ibid., p. xiv.

157. Ibid.

158. Ibid.

159. Ibid., p. xv.

160. Ibid., p. xvi.

161. "The Blight That Failed" (New York: Blue Ribbon Books, 1930), p. 3.

162. Ibid.

163. Ibid., p. 4.

164. Ibid.; Dakin, *Mrs. Eddy*, 521.

165. "The Blight That Failed," p. 4.

166. Ibid., p. 5.

167. Ibid., p. 6.

168. Lewis Mumford, review of *Mrs. Eddy: The Biography of a Virginal Mind* by Edwin Franden Dakin, *New Republic* 61 (27 November 1929), p. 21.

169. Dakin, *Mrs. Eddy*, p. 362.

170. Ibid., pp. 523, 522.

171. In 1958, Charles Braden described Dakin's biography as "unusually comprehensive," and, although somewhat biased, still "the best and most thoroughly documented biography that has yet appeared." See *Christian Science Today*, p. 13.

172. "The Blight That Failed," p. 7.

173. Ibid., pp. 11, 7.

174. Ibid., pp. 8–9.

175. Ibid., p. 8.

176. Ibid., p. 9.

177. Charles Scribner's Sons, "Publisher's Note" in Dakin, *Mrs. Eddy* (1930), p. vi.

178. "The Blight That Failed," p. 12.

179. Committee on Publication, "Setting the Course: Alfred Farlow and the Mission of the Committee on Publication" (Boston: Committee on Publication, The First Church of Christ, Scientist, 1993), p. 31.

180. "The Blight That Failed," p. 9.

181. Ibid., p. 10.

182. Ibid.

183. Ibid., p. 14.

184. Ibid., p. 15.

185. Ibid.

186. Ibid.

187. M. Victor Westberg, letter to the editor, *New Republic* 216, no. 10 (10 March 1997), p. 7.

188. Braden, *Christian Science Today*, pp. 96–97. Since Braden wrote this, the Church has changed its position and is now actively encouraging professors to use *Science and Health* in their classrooms and to invite Christian Science lecturers to answer students' questions regarding, for instance, "how can you gain control of your health through what you think." This change of heart suggests how eager the Church is now to reach young people in their formative years. (See Marian Cates, "*Science and Health with Key to the Scriptures* at Colleges and Universities," *Christian Science Journal* 117, no 2 [February 1999], pp. 53–54).

189. Braden, op. cit., p. 204.

190. Ibid., p. 205.

191. Ibid., p. 206.

192. Robert David Thomas, letter to the editor, *New York Review of Books* 33, no. 18 (14 November 1996), p. 64. Thomas's account of his arrangement with the Church regarding copyright, and of his subsequent copyright travails was not, oddly, included in his book.

193. "Editor's Notebook: 'Denial' and 'Realization'; In What Do They Consist?" *Christian Science Journal* 8, no. 8 (November 1890), p. 359. The command to

burn was later rescinded, but many Scientists may not have seen the obscure correction. See "Notice," *Christian Science Journal* 8, no. 9 (December 1890) p. 412.

194. "Paul Revere," "Christian Science or Ecclesiasticism—Which?" pamphlet 24, p. 5; "Mene, Mene, Tekel, Upharsin," pamphlet 25, p. 14.

195. "Paul Revere," "Paul Revere Author Excommunicated," pamphlet no. 32, p. 1.

196. *Retrospection and Introspection*, p. 76.

197. The two most well-known dissident mail-order firms are the Rare Book Company, in Freehold, New Jersey, and The Bookmark, in Santa Clarita, California.

198. John Doorly, "To Those Interested, a Statement by John Doorly" (privately printed, 1945), p. 35.

199. Ibid., p. 38.

200. See Braden, *Christian Science Today*, p. 269.

201. Ibid., p. 168; Corey, *Behind the Scenes*, back cover.

202. Arthur Corey, *Christian Science Class Instruction* (Santa Clarita, Calif.: The Bookmark, 1993), p. 1.

203. For a complete account of Hugh Studdert-Kennedy's struggles with the Church, see Braden, *Christian Science Today*, pp. 128–63. Studdert-Kennedy was also the author of *Mrs. Eddy: Her Life, Her Work, and Her Place in History*, a biography that tried to replace the rose-colored view of Eddy then favored by the Church with a more realistic, if still sympathetic, portrait. Studdert-Kennedy and his wife had formed the Farallon Press specifically to publish his earlier book, *Christian Science and Organized Religion*. The Board of Directors of the Church then spent nearly a decade trying to persuade him to renounce that book by holding forth the promise of publishing his Eddy biography; the whole arrangement seems to have been an elaborate attempt to bribe Studdert-Kennedy to abandon his earlier, apostate views. Studdert-Kennedy died in 1943, his biography still unpublished, but his widow, the former Clarissa Hale (daughter of a department-store magnate), continued his fight with the Church, attempting to regain control of her late husband's manuscript, which had been heavily edited and rewritten by the Church.

    Eventually Arthur Corey and Studdert-Kennedy's widow would marry and run the Farallon Press and Foundation together, becoming a consistently irritating thorn in the Church's side.

204. Braden, *Christian Science Today*, p. 174.

205. Braden, *Christian Science Today*, plate III, facing p. 208.

206. Ibid.; see also pp. 182–83.

207. Ibid., p. 182.

208. Ibid., p. 187.

209. Ibid., p. 186.

210. Ibid., p. 194.

211. Ibid., pp. 193–94.

212. Corey, *Class Instruction*, p. 97.

213. Ibid., pp. 103–104.

214. Ibid., p. 161.

215. Corey, *Behind the Scenes*, p. 213.

216. Ibid., pp. 148–49.

217. Ibid., p. 224.

218. Ibid., p. 155.

219. Ibid., p. 228.

220. Robert E. Merritt and Arthur Corey, *Christian Science and Liberty* (Los Angeles: DeVorss & Co., 1970), pp. 39, 45.

221. *Christian Science Journal* 89, no. 8 (August 1971), p. 397.

222. Robin Wright, "Opposition Dies; Webster Gains Acceptance as Head of CIA," *Los Angeles Times*, 7 December 1988.

223. Turner was CIA director from 1977 to 1980, during the Carter administration, and William Webster served during the Reagan and Bush years (1987–1991).

224. Wright, "Opposition Dies."

225. He also criticized *Monitor* reporters for their critical coverage of the White House and the Vietnam War. See John Ehrlichman, *Witness to Power: The Nixon Years* (New York: Simon & Schuster, 1982), pp. 84, 284–85. On February 14, 1999, Ehrlichman died at the age of 73 at his home in Atlanta; he had been suffering from diabetes for two years. His son Tom requested that donations in his father's memory be made to Adventure Unlimited, a Christian Science children's camp located in Colorado. See Steve Terrell, "Watergate Co-Conspirator Ehrlichman Dies at 73," *Santa Fe New Mexican*, 16 February 1999.

226. Mark Twain, *Christian Science* (New York: Harper & Bros, 1907), p. 222.

227. Percy's campaign for Congress in 1966 was interrupted when one of his twin daughters, Valerie Jeanne, twenty-one, was murdered in his Chicago home by an intruder. The surviving twin, Sharon Lee, eventually married John D. Rockefeller IV, who has run for president and is currently a U.S. senator from West Virginia.

228. Leo Damore, *The "Crime" of Dorothy Sheridan* (New York: Arbor House, 1978), p. 315.

229. Hartsook, *Christian Science After 1910*, p. 127.

230. U.S. Constitution, Amdmt. 1.

231. See Hartsook, *Christian Science After 1910*, p. 127; Damore, *Dorothy Sheridan*, p. 316.

232. Dr. J. Buroughs Stokes, "Report of the Manager of Committees on Publication," *Christian Science Journal* 90, no. 8 (August 1972), pp. 435–436.

233. Peter Haldeman, "Growing Up Haldeman," *New York Times Magazine*, 3 April 1994, pp. 30–32.

234. Ibid., p. 31.

235. Ibid., p. 32.

236. "Christian Science Assumes New Posture," *National Observer*, 2 August 1965.

237. Ibid.

238. Merritt and Corey, *Christian Science and Liberty*, pp. 43–44.

239. John Dart, "Healing Church Shows Signs It May Be Ailing," *Los Angeles Times*, 20 December 1986.

240. See Stark, "Rise and Fall," p. 204. Stark also determined that the percentage of

Christian Scientists who are married is significantly below that of the United States population in general: two separate surveys, the General Social Surveys and the American National Survey of Religious Identification, indicated that 48 percent or 54 percent of Scientists were married versus 62 percent in the population at large. The percentage of Scientists over the age of forty who had never married was also higher than in other religious groups: 12.2 percent compared to 6.7 percent in Jehovah's Witnesses. Stark's conclusion—that Scientists' "inadequate fertility" and ineffective "socialization" of their children have contributed greatly to their population's decline—is inescapable. See Stark, p. 189.

241. In the Craig Rodwell Papers in the Rare Books and Manuscripts Division of the New York Public Library, there is a letter dated 23 November 1979, signed only "A Journal-Listed Practitioner (no longer 'colored')," attesting to the author's struggles against prejudice in the Christian Science Church. Craig Rodwell, a prominent gay-rights activist, was the founder, in 1967, of the Oscar Wilde Memorial Bookshop, advertised as "America's First Gay-and-Proud Bookshop," located in Greenwich Village in New York City. Rodwell, who died in 1993, headed a group called "Gay People in Christian Science," which lobbied the Church to end discriminatory practices and policies against gays and lesbians.

242. Stark, "Rise and Fall," p. 204.

243. See Ann Beals, *Crisis in the Christian Science Church* (privately printed, 1978), p. 32.

244. Ibid., p. 17.

245. Ibid., p. 2.

246. Reginald Kerry, Letter no. 1, pp. 10–11.

247. Beals, *Crisis*, p. 21.

248. Ibid., p. 22.

249. Ibid.

250. Ibid., p. 21.

251. Ibid., p. 31.

252. Ibid., p. 42.

253. Ibid.

254. Reginald Kerry, Letter no. 2, p. 1.

255. Ibid., p. 3.

256. Ibid., p. 1.

257. Reginald Kerry, Letter no. 4, p. 8.

258. Beals, *Crisis*, p. 33.

259. Ibid., p. 123.

260. Ibid., p. 143.

261. Ibid., p. 113.

262. Reginald Kerry, Letter no. 4, pp. 1–2.

263. Reginald Kerry, Letter no. 5, p. 11.

264. Reginald Kerry, Letter no. 6, p. 4.

265. Beals, *Crisis*, p. 130.

266. Kenneth L. Woodward, "Nursing the Faith," *Newsweek*, 21 June 1976.

267. James Franklin, "A Rift Among Christian Scientists," *Boston Globe*, 12 March 1978.

268. Ibid., 113.

269. See, for example, Carl J. Welz, "Homosexuality can be healed," *Christian Science Sentinel* 69, no. 16 (22 April 1967), pp. 681–83; Naomi Price, "The Bible and Homosexuality," *Christian Science Sentinel* 74, no. 47 (18 November 1972), pp. 2051–53. The Church recently weighed in again on this topic; see "A Perspective on Homosexuality," *Christian Science Sentinel* 101, no. 10 (8 March 1999), pp. 14–15.

270. See, for example, the editorial "Homosexual Rights," *Christian Science Monitor*, 8 November 1977.

271. See "My Freedom from Homosexuality," *Christian Science Journal* 96, no. 10 (October 1978), p. 609–10.

272. Rhea Becker, "Gay Writer Told: 'Heal Thyself,' " *The Tab* May 1982.

273. For these and other details relating to Ogan's firing, see Jil Clark, "Man Charges Homophobia in Firing from Church Job," *Gay Community News* (Boston), 3 April 1982; "Woman Sues Newspaper Over Firing," Associated Press, 2 December 1982.

274. Beals, *Crisis*, p. 113.

Part IV. "God's Law": Christian Science Goes to Court

1. For details regarding the case of *People of the State of New York v. Willis Vernon Cole*, I have relied upon Norman Beasley, *The Continuing Spirit* (New York: Duell, Sloan & Pearce, 1956).

2. Norman Beasley, *The Cross and The Crown: The History of Christian Science* (New York: Duell, Sloan & Pearce, 1952), p. 496.

3. Ibid., p. 498.

4. *Journal of the American Medical Association*, 10 December 1898, as quoted in Beasley, *The Cross and The Crown*, p. 497; *Continuing Spirit*, p. 87.

5. *Journal of the American Medical Association*, 12 August 1899, 29 July 1899, as cited in Beasley, *The Cross and The Crown*, p. 498.

6. *Journal of the American Medical Association*, 18 November 1899, as cited in Beasley, *The Cross and the Crown*, pp. 498–99.

7. See, respectively: "Dr. Rauch's Prescription," *Christian Science Journal* 5, no. 4 (July 1887), p. 215; "News from Abroad: Christian Science and Legislation," *Christian Science Journal* 7, no. 3 (June 1889), p. 153.

8. "Dr. Rauch's Prescription," *Christian Science Journal* 5, no. 4 (July 1887), p. 215.

9. "The Medical Bill at Albany," *Christian Science Journal* 16, no. 2 (May 1898), p. 100.

10. Ibid., p. 98.

11. For these quotations and details, I am indebted to Thomas C. Johnsen, "Christian Scientists and the Medical Profession: A Historical Perspective," *Medical Heritage* 2, no. 1 (January–February 1986), pp. 73, 75.

12. "Editor's Table," *Christian Science Journal* 16, no. 1 (April 1898), pp. 68–69.

13. William James to James J. Putnam, 2 March 1898, *The Letters of William James*, vol. 2, Henry James, ed. (Boston: Atlantic Monthly Press, 1920), pp. 66–67.

14. Ibid., p. 67.

15. *The New York Times*, 13 November 1898, as cited in "Editor's Table," *Christian Science Journal* 16, no. 9 (December 1898), p. 658.

16. Mark Twain, *Christian Science, with Notes Containing Corrections to Date* (New York: Harper & Brothers, 1907), 80.

17. Beasley, *Continuing Spirit*, Appendix 1, pp. 333–34.

18. Ibid., p. 334.

19. See Beasley, *Continuing Spirit,* p. 69.

20. Ibid., p. 333.

21. Ibid., p. 345.

22. Ibid., p. 347.

23. Ibid., p. 346; *People v. Vogelgesang*, 221 N.Y. Reports 290 (1917), Court of Appeals of New York.

24. William Carlos Williams, *The Autobiography of William Carlos Williams* (New York: New Directions, 1951), p. 167.

25. Ibid., p. 160.

26. "Practitioner Shot by Dad of Girl Who Died," *Chicago Tribune*, 31 January 1959.

27. For Whitney's acquittal, see Arthur Corey, *Behind the Scenes with the Metaphysicians* (Los Angeles: DeVorss & Co., 1968), pp. 152–53.

28. For an extensive discussion of the damage that religious exemption laws have done to the legal rights of children, see James G. Dwyer, "The Children We Abandon: Religious Exemptions to Child Welfare and Education Laws as Denials of Equal Protection to Children of Religious Objectors," *North Carolina Law Review* 74, no. 5 (June 1996), pp. 1321–1478. For other references to legal and scholarly articles on the subject, see Rita Swan, Ph.D., "Children, Medicine, Religion, and the Law," *Advances in Pediatrics* 44 (1997), p. 539 n. 142.

29. See Charles S. Braden, *Christian Science Today: Power, Policy, Practice* (Dallas: Southern Methodist University Press, 1958), p. 261.

30. Andrew W. Hartsook, *Christian Science After 1910* (Santa Clarita, Calif.: The Bookmark, 1993), p. 97.

31. For the complete list, see Beasley, *Continuing Spirit*, pp. 320–21.

32. Arizona Ann. Sec. 8-546 (8) (B), in the definition of a dependent child; see also Arizona Revised Statutes, Section 8-531.01.

33. Braden, *Christian Science Today*, p. 262.

34. Rita Swan, Ph.D., "Children, Medicine, Religion, and the Law," *Advances in Pediatrics* 44 (1997), p. 498.

35. See, for example, "Legal Rights and Obligations of Christian Scientists in Minnesota" (Saint Paul: Christian Science Committee on Publication for Minnesota, 1976), pp. 41–43.

36. Braden, *Christian Science Today*, p. 259.

37. See Swan, "Children, Medicine, Religion, and the Law," p. 499; "Legal Rights and Obligations of Christian Scientists in Minnesota," pp. 37–38.

38. See "Legal Rights and Obligations of Christian Scientists in Minnesota," pp.

7–8. This booklet advises practitioners to provide their own certificates, specifying that their judgment has been made "from my lay observations," or to cross out language that implies that a medical diagnosis has been made. While these qualifications may honestly allude to practitioners' limitations, they do not explain how practitioners can come to any rational or realistic judgments about their patients' true physical condition.

39. "Legal Rights and Obligations of Christian Scientists in Minnesota," p. 31.
40. Robert Peel, *Health and Medicine in the Christian Science Tradition* (New York: Crossroad, 1988), p. 109.
41. M. Victor Westberg, telephone interview with the author, 3 February 1995.
42. Leo Damore, *The "Crime" of Dorothy Sheridan* (New York: Arbor House, 1978), p. 305.
43. "TB Scare," *Time*, 24 May 1954, p. 55.
44. Ibid.
45. Damore, *Dorothy Sheridan*, pp. 148–49.
46. Braden, *Christian Science Today*, 257.
47. Arthur Corey, *Behind the Scenes with the Metaphysicians* (Los Angeles: DeVorss & Co., 1968), p. 153.
48. See Swan, "Children, Medicine, Religion, and the Law," p. 499.
49. U.S. Senate Committee on Finance, *Social Security: Hearings Before the Committee on Finance, United States Senate, First Session on H.R. 6675*, 89th Cong., 1st sess., May 10–14, 17–19, 1965, p. 697.
50. Ibid., p. 698.
51. Ibid., p. 700.
52. Ibid.
53. Ibid., p. 697, 699.
54. Ibid., p. 699.
55. These, like virtually all details of Lisa Sheridan's death and her mother's trial, are taken from Damore, *Dorothy Sheridan*; see pp. 12–13.
56. Ibid., p. 14.
57. Ibid., pp. 21–22.
58. Ibid., p. 26.
59. Ibid., pp. 26, 28.
60. Ibid., p. 110.
61. Ibid., p. 242.
62. Ibid., p. 233.
63. Ibid., pp. 296–97.
64. Ibid., p. 297.
65. Ibid., p. 161.
66. Ibid., pp. 312–13.
67. *Prince v. Massachusetts*, 321 U.S. 158 (1944).
68. Damore, *Dorothy Sheridan*, p. 314.
69. Leo Damore to Rita Swan, 23 March 1979. Collection of Rita Swan.
70. See Swan, "Children, Medicine, Religion, and the Law," pp. 510, 537 n. 118; see

also Laura Sessions Stepp, "More Children's Deaths Laid to Parents' Faith; Panel Faults Limited Child-Abuse Laws," *Washington Post,* 9 January 1988.

71. For a more complete breakdown of religious exemption laws by state and a discussion of their implications, see Swan, "Children, Medicine, Religion, and the Law," pp. 510–13.

72. Rita Swan, interview with the author, Sioux City, Iowa, 10 May 1997.

73. Ibid.

74. Rita Swan, telephone interview with the author, 5 July 1993. The following details regarding the illness and death of Matthew Swan come from this interview unless otherwise noted.

75. *May v. Laitner,* Michigan circuit court, county of Wayne, no. 80 004 605 N1 deposition of Douglas Swan, 4 September 1980, p. 283.

76. Rita Swan, interview with the author, Sioux City, Iowa, 10 May 1997. The following details regarding the founding of CHILD, Inc., are taken from this interview.

77. *May v. Laitner,* deposition of Dean Joki, 24 June 1980, p. 71.

78. Ibid., p. 76

79. Ibid., pp. 77–78.

80. *May v. Laitner,* deposition of June M. Ahearn, 26 June 1980, pp. 14–15.

81. Ibid.

82. Ibid., p. 27.

83. *May v. Laitner,* deposition of J. Thomas Black, p. 30.

84. Ibid., p. 33.

85. See "Conviction of California Christian Scientist Upheld," *Children's Healthcare Is a Legal Duty, Inc., Newsletter,* no. 3 (1992), pp. 1–3.

86. Ibid.

87. David Margolick, "In Child Deaths, a Test for Christian Science," *New York Times,* 6 August 1990.

88. The case of Seth Glaser is discussed at length in Richard Brenneman, "Nestling's Faltering Flight: The Short Life and Death of Seth Ian Glaser," *Deadly Blessings: Faith Healing on Trial* (Buffalo, New York: Prometheus Books, 1990), pp. 21–119.

89. Jeffrey Good, "Dead Girl's Parents Had Medical Care, Neighbor Testifies," *St. Petersburg* (Fla.) *Times,* 14 April 1989.

90. Ibid.

91. Jeffrey Good, "Christian Scientists Guilty in Girl's Death: Parents Relied on Prayer, Not Medicine," *St. Petersburg* (Fla.) *Times,* 19 April 1989.

92. "Florida Conviction of Christian Scientists Overturned," *Children's Healthcare Is a Legal Duty, Inc., Newsletter,* no. 3 (1992), pp. 1, 3.

93. Robert Goodrich, "Test Results Awaited in Causes of Deaths in Measles Outbreak," *St. Louis Post-Dispatch,* 4 March 1985.

94. Safir Ahmed, "Measles Suspected in Two Deaths," *St. Louis Post-Dispatch,* 27 February 1985.

95. Ibid.

96. Safir Ahmed, "Coroner: Measles Caused Student's Death," *St. Louis Post-Dispatch,* 5 March 1985.

97. Safir Ahmed, "Crucible: Faith Put to Test at Principia," *St. Louis Post-Dispatch*, 2 June 1985; UPI, "Measles Outbreak Traced to Christian Science Camp," *Los Angeles Times*, 9 August 1985.

98. See S. Barrett, *The Health Robbers* (Philadelphia: George Stickley, 1976), p. 268, cited in Swan, "Children, Medicine, Religion, and the Law," pp. 500, 534 n. 57.

99. Martha Shirk, "Measles Trail; Unvaccinated Students Turn 1 Case into 176," *St. Louis Post-Dispatch*, 8 May 1994.

100. See Swan, "Children, Medicine, Religion, and the Law," p. 500.

101. See Damore, *Dorothy Sheridan* (1978; Dell paperback reprint with new appendix, 1992), pp. 336–37. Both Rita Swan and Leo Damore played a role in bringing about the prosecution of the Twitchells; Damore had supplied Swan with a copy of a letter that J. Buroughs Stokes had written to the Massachusetts legislature while lobbying for the passage of the bill he had helped to draft. The letter read, in part: "I think it is important to emphasize and to understand that this amendment would not prevent a juvenile court judge from ordering medical or surgical care in an emergency to save a child's life if the judge felt it was necessary. This provision would protect a parent only from being prosecuted under Sec. 1 of Chapter 273 solely because he was providing his child with 'non-medical remedial treatment which is recognized under the laws of the Commonwealth.'" In turn, Swan sent a copy of Stokes's letter to the Suffolk County District Attorney, Newman Flanagan, who was considering filing charges against the Twitchells. Stokes's letter, as Damore points out in his appendix to the 1992 edition of his book, indicates that "seeking passage of the exemption to a misdemeanor charge of child abuse and neglect had never been intended by the church at the time of its petition to the legislature to protect Christian Scientists from other types of criminal action, including manslaughter." The Church, however, had attempted to portray the legislature that passed the law as appalled by the Sheridan verdict and determined to exempt Scientists from charges of manslaughter. Stokes's letter apparently convinced the D.A. to proceed.

102. Ibid., p. 334.

103. Christopher B. Daly, "Faith-Healing on Trial in Boston," *Washington Post*, 22 May 1990.

104. For coverage of the overturning of the Twitchell verdict, see Tom Coakley, "Christian Science Couple Reprieved in Death of Son," *Boston Globe*, 12 August 1993.

105. J. W. Brown, "Girl Died in Agony, Transcripts Show," *Phoenix Gazette*, 21 October 1988.

106. Ibid.

107. Adam H. Dickey, "God's Law of Adjustment," *Christian Science Journal* 33, no. 10 (January 1916), pp. 559–564.

108. Edwin Boehm, telephone interview with author, 13 October 1994.

109. J. W. Brown, "Girl Died in Agony, Transcripts Show," *Phoenix Gazette*, 21 October 1988.

110. Ibid.

111. Ibid.

112. Ibid.
113. Proceedings Before the 102nd Maricopa County Grand Jury, in re: John Harold King, Catherine Justin King, no. CR-88-07284, 15 November 1988, vol. II, p. 26.
114. Ibid., p. 27. ·
115. Ibid.
116. K. C. Scull, telephone interview with the author, 1 June 1993.
117. Ibid.
118. Brent Whiting, "Parents Draw Probation in Girl's Death, Christian Scientists Pawns in Church-State Struggle, Lawyer Says," *Arizona Republic*, 27 September 1989.
119. *Science and Health*, p. 475.
120. Douglass Lundman, telephone interview with the author, 19 August 1997.
121. Much of the description of Ian Lundman's last days is drawn from the opinion written by Judge Jack Davies in *Lundman v. McKown, et al.*, State of Minnesota Court of Appeals, Hennepin County, District Court File 918197. See particularly pp. 6–11.
122. "Dimension," WCCO News, Channel 4, Minneapolis, Minnesota, July 1989.
123. *Lundman v. McKown et al.*, p. 27.
124. Aaron Epstein, "High Court Permits Verdict in Christian Science Case," *Times-Union* (Albany, N.Y.), 23 January 1996.
125. Margaret Zack, "Mother Didn't Realize Spiritual Healing Was Failing, Lawyer Says," *Minneapolis Star-Tribune*, 18 August 1993.
126. Doug Grow, "Victory Over Christian Science Church Gives No Solace to Father," *Minneapolis Star-Tribune*, 3 September 1993.
127. See *Lundman v. McKown, et al.*, pp. 13–14. The Court of Appeals had essentially agreed with the arguments offered in an amicus curiae brief submitted by a coalition of religious groups. The coalition brought together a bizarre set of bedfellows: the Roman Catholic Archdiocese of St. Paul and Minneapolis, the Baptist Joint Committee on Public Affairs, the Church of Jesus Christ of Latter-Day Saints, the National Association of Evangelicals, the Worldwide Church of God, and others. That these churches supported the Christian Science Church on such an issue suggests that their ecumenicism disguised a certain element of self-interest. The Catholic Church, caustically critical of Christian Science during the early years of the movement (although many Catholics engage in faith healing), was supporting the right of Scientists to medically neglect their children to the point of death; ironically, this was the same Catholic Church that so vehemently supports right-to-life positions and opposes abortion. The evangelical movement—many sects of which practice faith healing, some refusing medicine—derides Christian Science as a satanic cult, but it, too, was on the side of Christian Science in this case. But the overwhelming motivation for this strange coalition of churches to unite in support of the Christian Science Church was simple enough: they all wanted to protect themselves against potential lawsuits. The Catholic Church was particularly sensitive to the legal vulnerability the Lundman suit might bring, having been the target of a number of lawsuits brought by those who claimed to have been sexually abused by priests.

128. Ibid., p. 29.

129. Cindy Adams, "Christian Science Nurse Reflects on a Losing Case," *New York Post*, 29 January 1996. The actor Alan Young reported, in a memoir first published in Reginald Kerry, Letter no. 7, pp. 8–9, that Cindy Adams "told me she was a student of Christian Science." Joey Adams's entry in *Who's Who in America*, 1997, ends with a quotation from Mary Baker Eddy, "a dose of joy is a spiritual cure," which may be apocryphal, as it does not appear in her published writings.

130. Stephen L. Carter, "The Power of Prayer, Denied," *New York Times*, 31 January 1996.

131. Kim Shippey, "The Hunger for Integrity," *Christian Science Sentinel* 98, no. 21 (20 May 1996), pp. 3–6; the *Sentinel* also reprinted Carter's op-ed piece in its issue of 4 March 1996.

132. Jane Lampman, "Fostering Trust and Civility Is a Moral Issue," *Christian Science Monitor*, 28 May 1998.

133. Doug Grow, "Victory over Christian Science Church Gives No Solace to Father," *Minneapolis Star-Tribune*, 3 September 1993.

134. Douglass Lundman, telephone interview with the author, 19 August 1997.

135. "Dimension," WCCO News, Channel 4, Minneapolis, Minnesota, July 1989.

136. Grow, "Victory over Christian Science Church."

137. See Associated Press, "Christian Scientists Face Another Death Suit," Associated Press, 16 December 1993.

138. Re: James Andrew Wantland, Certificate of Death, Orange County, California, 26 January 1993.

139. Martha Shirk, "Death of St. Charles Boy Renews Ethics Debate," *St. Louis Post-Dispatch*, 14 March 1993.

140. Matt. 7:20.

141. Paul Michener to Rita Swan, 26 November 1979.

142. Beth Young, telephone interview with the author, 10 February 1996. Subsequent quotations from Young come from this interview.

143. Carolyn Joyce Hyatt, letter to author, 16 August 1996.

144. Ibid.

145. *Science and Health*, 213.

146. Mark Woodall, interview with the author, Alexandria, Virginia, 24 November 1995.

147. Mark Woodall, "A Personal Statement and Essay for CHILD, Inc.," 18 July 1996.

148. Bonnie Deckerhoff, interviewed on videotape on 19 July 1996 by Rita Swan, Grafton, Illinois, at the 1996 CHILD meeting. Author was present during the interview.

149. Thomas Simmons, *The Unseen Shore: Memories of a Christian Science Childhood* (Boston: Beacon Press, 1991), pp. 63, 3.

150. Ibid., p. 144. The Church's reaction to Simmons's book was predictable. In 1991, the year it was published, the Church published a special issue of the *Christian Science Journal* devoted to the "practice of spiritual healing," particularly as it involved children. It included an editorial by Elaine Natale entitled "Memories of Medicine and Childhood," that described Simmons's book—without referring

to its title or the author's name—as "portraying Christian Science as a cold, intellectual system of words and a strange, ritualistic denial of normal human needs." Natale then related her own childhood experiences, in which a doctor mistakenly punctured her eardrum and, by administering "an experimental vaccine," caused her to develop temporarily "the symptoms" of polio. Somewhat disingenuously, she added: "Blame isn't the purpose here." This kind of tit-for-tat logic—doctors hurt children's ears, too!—is a graphic example of the kind of fear and loathing Scientists truly feel, and deny they feel, about medicine. See Elaine Natale, "Memories of Medicine and Childhood," *Christian Science Journal*, special issue on "Christian Scientists and the Practice of Spiritual Healing" (1991), pp. 57–58.

In a letter to the *Atlantic Monthly* after my article about the Church appeared in 1995, Simmons disclosed that Natale's editorial was not the only step the Church took to counter the perceived effect of his book:

> In 1992, I was interviewed by a reporter for a major television news network about my book.... This reporter had interviewed then–church spokesman Nathan Talbot just before coming to see me. A few minutes into our interview, she paused to tell me that Mr. Talbot had warned her that I was an unreliable source on Christian Science because (in Talbot's words) "He's either divorced or separated" and "his life is falling apart." ... According to the reporter, Mr. Talbot made these statements while referring to a medium-sized manila folder with my name on it.

151. Spalding Gray, *Sex and Death to the Age Fourteen* (New York: Vintage Books, 1986), p. 4.
152. Ibid., p. 13.
153. Rockwell Gray, interview with the author, St. Louis, Missouri, 7 May 1997.
154. Evan Quaife, interview with the author, Santa Fe, New Mexico, 21 November 1997.
155. Martha Shirk, "Mother Defied Doctrine to Save Dying Daughter," *St. Louis Post-Dispatch*, 14 March 1993.
156. Ibid.
157. Corey, *Behind the Scenes*, p. 155. The teacher was George Shaw Cook. Corey also mentions that a lecturer, John M. Tutt, of Kansas City, told his 1956 class that "*materia medica* is the anti-Christ, its hospitals an invention of the Devil."
158. Suzanne Shepard, telephone interview with the author, 27 May 1993; Suzanne Shepard, interview with the author, St. Louis, Missouri, 6 May 1997.
159. Ibid.
160. In 1994 she wrote an article for *Redbook* in which she described her Christian Science experience in graphic detail: Suzanne Shepard, as told to Marti Attoun, "Suffer the Little Children," *Redbook*, October 1994, pp. 66–72. Since her break with the Church, she has completed a doctorate in social work at Washington University, where she is now a professor.
161. *Manual*, p. 49.

162. The First Church of Christ, Scientist, Boston, Massachusetts, "The Foundation for Christian Science Nursing" (n.p., n.d.), p. 8.

163. Peel, *Health and Medicine*, p. 141 n. 13.

164. Ibid., p. 95.

165. Ibid., pp. 141 n. 13, 94.

166. Ruth Cook, telephone interview with the author, 16 April 1997. All following quotations from Cook are taken from this interview. Cook's observations about Christian Science nursing home practices are similar to those of Suzanne Shepard and Linda Fasig, both longtime *Journal*-listed practitioners. I interviewed Fasig on 17 November 1995; Shepard on 27 May 1993 and 6 May 1997.

167. Ibid.

168. The First Church of Christ, Scientist, Boston, Massachusetts, "After Care," in an instructional pamphlet for Christian Science nurses.

169. See James H. Holmes IV, et al., "Pressure Sores in a Christian Science Sanatorium," *American Journal of Forensic Medicine and Pathology* 14, no. 1 (1993), pp. 10–11. It is also interesting to note that, of the 116 dead from the Christian Science sanatorium who were examined, eight were relatively young, between the ages of thirty-one and sixty.

170. Damore, *Dorothy Sheridan*, p. 331.

171. Ibid.

172. I visited El Dorado Vista in April 1998, posing as the daughter of a woman interested in checking into the facility. I was given a brief tour of the buildings and grounds. I saw more staff than patients, glimpsing only a single elderly woman patient, in bed in her room.

173. "Application for Admission," El Dorado Vista: A Care Facility for Christian Scientists, Phoenix, Arizona.

174. Chris Mahlstedt, "Be a Christian Science Nurse!," *El Dorado Vista Messenger*, fall 1997, p. 1.

175. "Application for Admission," El Dorado Vista: A Care Facility for Christian Scientists, Phoenix, Arizona.

176. Swan, "Children, Medicine, Religion, and the Law," p. 498.

177. Janet Reno to The Honorable Thomas B. Griffith, 23 January 1997, reprinted in *Children's Healthcare Is a Legal Duty, Inc., Newsletter*, no. 1 (1997), p. 10.

178. See Jane Lampman, "Talk-Show Host Listens to Why People Pray," *The Christian Science Monitor*, 12 November 1998.

179. Orrin G. Hatch to Virginia Harris, 25 April 1997.

180. Rita Swan, "CHILD Files Second Suit Against Payments for Christian Science Nursing," *Children's Healthcare Is a Legal Duty, Inc., Newsletter*, no. 3 (1997), p. 1.

181. "Viewing Legal Challenges from a Spiritual Perspective," *Christian Science Journal* 116, no. 10 (October 1998), p. 51.

182. Rita Swan, "Children, Medicine, Religion, and the Law," *Advances in Pediatrics* 44 (1997), pp. 491–543.

183. Seth M. Asser, M.D., and Rita Swan, Ph.D., "Child Fatalities From Religion-Motivated Medical Neglect," *Pediatrics* 101, no. 4 (April 1998), pp. 625–29.

184. Ibid., p. 628, table 4.
185. Ibid., p. 626, table 1.
186. See Swan, "Children, Medicine, Religion, and the Law," p. 491.
187. David Van Biema, "Faith or Healing?," *Time*, 31 August 1998, p. 68.
188. Ibid., p. 69.
189. Ibid.
190. Allison W. Phinney, Jr., "The Spirituality of Mankind," *Christian Science Sentinel* vol. 86, no. 36 (3 September 1984), pp. 1529–33.
191. See Swan, "Children, Medicine, Religion, and the Law," p. 519.
192. Seth Asser, telephone interview with the author, 10 December 1997.
193. Daly, "Faith-Healing on Trial."
194. Margolick, "In Child Deaths."
195. The flags are described in a draft of an essay by Stephen Gottschalk, which he showed to me in October 1993.

Part V. "God's Requirement": Christian Science on the Air

1. *Manual*, 77.
2. Robert Peel, *Health and Medicine in the Christian Science Tradition* (New York: Crossroad Publishing Company, 1988), 122.
3. For a description of the Church's experiment with public relations and management consultants, see ibid., p. 123.
4. Alan Young, *Mr. Young Goes to Boston* (Seattle, Wash.: H. M. Wright Publishing, Inc., 1998), p. 10. This memoir, under the title, "My Boston Experience," was first excerpted in Reginald Kerry, Letter no. 7, pp. 8–9.
5. Young, *Mr. Young Goes to Boston*, p. 48.
6. Ibid., p. 55.
7. John Strahinich, "Not Ready for Prime Time," *Boston Magazine*, July 1992, p. 49.
8. Ibid., p. 50.
9. Superior Court of the State of California, County of Los Angeles, Estate of Eloise M. Knapp, P 488 062, Reply Declaration of Harvey W. Wood in Support of Petitions for Confirmation of Settlement Agreement, Etc., 14 December 1993, p. 2; reprinted in *Staying Loyal to Our Leader's Vision of Church, Supplement*, privately printed by the Mailing Fund, 5 February 1994.
10. James Coates, *In Mormon Circles: Gentiles, Jack Mormons, and Latter-Day Saints* (New York: Addison-Wesley Publishing Co., 1991), p. 110.
11. James L. Franklin, "100,000 Christian Scientists Talk World Peace via Satellite," *Boston Globe*, 27 December 1984.
12. Ibid.
13. Strahinich, "Not Ready," p. 69.
14. See the chapter written by Katherine Woodruff Fanning in *New Guardians of the Press: Selected Profiles of America's Women Newspaper Editors*, Judith G. Clabes, ed. (Indianapolis: R. J. Berg & Co., 1983), pp. 61–62.
15. Strahinich, "Not Ready," p. 49.
16. For these figures, see ibid., pp. 50–51.

17. Katherine Fanning, interview with the author, Boston, Massachusetts, 9 June 1993.

18. See Strahinich, "Not Ready," pp. 68–69.

19. "Workers at The Mother Church" to "Beloved Teachers," 26 September 1987.

20. Ibid., p. 9.

21. Ibid., pp. 12–13.

22. Jack Hoagland to Kay Fanning, memorandum re: Review of Presentation to Trustees, 13 October 1987.

23. Kay Fanning, interview with the author, 9 June 1993.

24. "Presentation to the Board of Trustees by the Manager and Senior Managers," 17 August 1987. Transcribed from videotape.

25. See Strahinich, "Not Ready," p. 70.

26. See Susan Bridge, *Monitoring the News: The Brilliant Launch and Sudden Collapse of The Monitor Channel* (Armonk, N.Y.: M. E. Sharpe, 1998), p. 32.

27. For Hoagland's background, see Strahinich, "Not Ready," pp. 50, 72; press kit for *World Monitor: A Television Presentation of the Christian Science Monitor* (n.d., n.p.).

28. See Daniel Golden, "Can Mary Baker Eddy's Church Heal Itself?" *Boston Globe Sunday Magazine*, 17 May 1992.

29. See Strahinich, "Not Ready," pp. 48–49. Strahinich gives 1961 as the year of Jack Hoagland, Sr.,'s death; Susan Bridge reports, based on personal interviews with Jack Hoagland, Jr., that it was 1962. See Bridge, *Monitoring the News*, p. 32.

30. For the $6 million figure, see Golden, "Can Mary Baker Eddy's Church . . . ?"

31. Richard O'Regan to Kay Fanning, 15 January 1989.

32. Peel, *Years of Authority*, 310.

33. John H. Hoagland to B. Helmick, A. Robertson, L. Wright, R. MacLachlan, J. Parrott, K. Fanning, D. Anable, J. Hughes, D. Willis, J. Yemma, E. Foell, R. Nenneman, D. Morse, D. Els, memorandum re: Approved Courses of Action Related to the Monitor, 8 December 1987.

34. Ibid.

35. Jack Hoagland would vehemently claim, in a letter to the editor of the *Columbia Journalism Review*, which had published an article describing the infighting between Fanning and Hoagland, that Fanning's task force was his idea: "The task force headed by the editor was in fact established *entirely and solely at the initiative and urging of the manager of the publishing society*" (italics in original). This claim seems to be contradicted by Hoagland's own memo to Kay Fanning regarding the establishment of the task force: "This memorandum constitutes approval of your proposal to convene a Daily Newspaper Task Force, starting December 1, 1987, under your chairmanship." Jack Hoagland to Kay Fanning, memorandum re: Establishment of a Daily Newspaper Task Force, 17 November 1987. For the original *Review* article, see Stephen J. Simurda, "Can the Stripped-Down *Monitor* Stay Afloat?" *Columbia Journalism Review*, March 1989, pp. 42–45. For Hoagland's letter and Simurda's reply to it, see "Letters," *Columbia Journalism Review*, July–August 1989, pp. 59–60.

36. Jack Hoagland, *Monitor* newsroom meeting, December 1987, cassette recording.

37. Strahinich, "Not Ready," p. 72.

38. For an excellent description of the dueling task forces, see Simurda, "Stripped-Down Monitor," pp. 42–44.

39. Kay Fanning to The Christian Science Board of Directors, 14 November 1988.

40. Harvey Wood, Meeting of Monitor Washington, D.C., bureau staff and Church and Christian Science Publishing Society officials, 16 November 1988, transcript, p. 9.

41. Several months later, Elizabeth Pond sent an extraordinarily detailed, meticulously reported, thirty-two-page, single-spaced chronology of the recent history of the Monitor to the Church's Board of Directors. This chronology was later circulated widely throughout the Field. Elizabeth Pond to the Christian Science Board of Directors, 15 February 1989; Elizabeth Pond, "Chronology of The Christian Science Monitor, 1988 Task Force, and 1989 new Monitor." Pond quotes from her own letter of resignation on page 15 of the Chronology.

42. Allan R. Gold, "Editors of Monitor Resign Over Cuts," New York Times, 15 November 1988.

43. Meeting of Monitor newsroom staff and representatives from management, Board of Directors, and Trustees, 15 November 1988, transcript of question-and-answer period, p. 13.

44. Meeting between Monitor Washington, D.C., bureau staff and Church and Christian Science Publishing Society officials, 16 November 1988, transcript, p. 4.

45. Jim Rosenberg, "More Color for the Monitor," Editor & Publisher, 4 February 1989.

46. See Pond, "Chronology," p. 26.

47. "The Monitor's Reasoned Voice," editorial, Boston Globe, 19 November 1988; entry on The Christian Science Monitor, 1990 Repap MediaGuide, Jude Wanniski, ed. (Morristown, New Jersey: Polyconomics, Inc., 1990), pp. 87–88.

48. Charlotte Saikowski to Richard Cattani, 5 January 1989.

49. See Simurda, "Stripped-Down Monitor," p. 45. Joseph C. Harsch died on June 3, 1998. The Monitor, which does not run obituaries, did publish an appreciation of his career as well as a column by John Hughes on his life, neither of which addressed the circumstances under which he left the newspaper. See Peter Grier, "Joseph C. Harsch: A Journalist with the 'Vision of an Age,' " Christian Science Monitor, 5 June 1998, and John Hughes, "On This Century's Stage of Titans, Harsch Fit In Well," Christian Science Monitor, 17 June 1998.

50. Pond, "Chronology," p. 28.

51. Richard O'Regan to Kay Fanning, 15 January 1989.

52. Ibid.

53. Thomas P. Griesa, "Figures Obtained by T. Griesa from D. Bowersock 12/2/88," memorandum, 5 December 1988; see also Griesa's comments in Simurda, "Stripped-Down Monitor," p. 45.

54. John J. Selover, Chairman of the Christian Science Board of Directors to Senior Managers and Officers, memorandum re: A spiritual call-to-arms, 21 February 1990.

55. Peel, *Health and Medicine*, p. 133.

56. Ibid., p. 124.

57. The Christian Science Board of Directors to All Employees, memorandum, 26 July 1988.

58. Ibid.

59. See Martin E. Marty, "Church Dispute Reveals 'The Dynamite in Tradition,' " *Bulletin of the Park Ridge Center* 3, no. 4 (July/August 1988), p. 1.

60. See "What Ever Happened to the Syndicate?" *Church Center News* 5, no. 3 (fall 1989), pp. 1–2.

61. John Hart, "The News for God's Sake: An Account of the Conflict Between a Church's Mission and a Journalist's Job," *Columbia Journalism Review* (September–October 1992), pp. 46, 45.

62. Ibid., p. 47.

63. John Hart, telephone interview with the author, 20 May 1993.

64. Hart, "The News for God's Sake," p. 46.

65. Ibid., p. 48.

66. Jack Hoagland to All Monitor Television and Radio Staff, memorandum re: Editorial Standards and Guidelines, 21 June 1990.

67. See Mary Baker Eddy, Deed of Trust for the Christian Science Publishing Society, 1898, reprinted in Norman Beasley, *The Continuing Spirit* (New York: Duell, Sloan & Pearce, 1956), pp. 348–52.

68. Erwin D. Canham, *Commitment to Freedom: The Story of The Christian Science Monitor* (Boston: Houghton Mifflin Co., 1958), pp. xvii, xvi, 6.

69. *First Church of Christ, Scientist and Miscellany*, p. 353.

70. "Report of the Christian Science Publishing Society, read by John H. Hoagland, Jr., Manager," *Christian Science Journal* 107, no. 9 (September 1989), pp. 18–19.

71. The Christian Science Board of Directors, "Christian Scientists, Their Lives, Their Church, and the World They Serve," *Christian Science Journal* 109, no. 1 (January 1991), p. 3. In fund-raising letters sent to the Church membership in the late 1980s and early 1990s, Church treasurer Don Bowersock repeatedly asked for members to contribute to the millions needed to fund the shortwave program. In a 1990 letter, he wrote, "One responsibility today is to place before the public ideas and models that elevate thought." See "Speaking the Truth in Love" (privately printed), p. 49. In 1990, Netty Douglass replied to a church member troubled by perceived irreligious elements in *World Monitor* by describing it as "an opportunity to extend the message of Christian Science to a greater community." "Speaking the Truth in Love," p. 43.

72. Some accounts say the Monitor Channel was launched May 1, 1991. The channel was previewed on that date; the official launch date was May 15. For the ice cream party, see Bridge, *Monitoring the News*, p. 118.

73. See Bridge, *Monitoring the News*, pp. 126–27.

74. Paul Hemp, "The Christian Science Monitor's Big Cable Gamble: Church Enters Tough Industry with Missionary Zeal," *Boston Globe*, 24 March 1991.

75. Norm Alster, "Netty Douglass' Impossible Task," *Forbes*, 17 September 1990, pp. 186–90.

76. Ibid., p. 188.

77. Ibid., p. 190.

78. Ibid.

79. Netty Douglass to James W. Michaels, 7 September 1990.

80. The Christian Science Board of Directors to Bliss Knapp, 20 February 1948.

81. Ibid.

82. Ibid.

83. Bliss Knapp, *The Destiny of The Mother Church* (Boston: Christian Science Publishing Society, 1991), p. 258.

84. Eloise M. Knapp to Ralph Kohlmeier, 20 March 1954, as quoted in "Accompanying Material" to "Supplemental Complaint, submitted to the Clerk of The Mother Church, April 21, 1993" (privately printed), pp. 4, 7.

85. Eloise M. Knapp to Ralph Kohlmeier, 9 September 1951, as quoted in "Accompanying Material" to "Supplemental Complaint, submitted to the Clerk of The Mother Church, April 21, 1993" (privately printed), pp. 4, 7.

86. Alex S. Jones, "A Book Proves Divisive for Christian Scientists," *New York Times*, 30 September 1991.

87. Superior Court of the State of California, for the County of Los Angeles, In the Matter of the Estate of Eloise M. Knapp, no. P 593 650, Declaration of Otto Bertschi, 14 December 1993. Reprinted in "Excerpts from the Objectors' Submission to the Los Angeles Superior Court," 16 November 1993 (privately printed by the Mailing Fund), p. 39.

88. Ibid.

89. For his views on Eddy's interpretation of Revelation, see Peel, *Years of Authority*, pp. 164–66, 169, 347–48, 431–32, nn. 83–93. Peel was deaf to Eddy's self-serving ambiguities, citing such passages of hers as this to demonstrate that she repudiated personal deification: "What God has spoken to this age through me is the *way* and *sure foundation*, and no man entereth by any other way into Christian Science." *Years of Authority*, p. 432, n. 88. To my mind, this passage seems to prove that Eddy believed herself to be special, gifted, divine—the opposite of what Peel suggests.

90. Golden, "Can Mary Baker Eddy's Church . . . ?" p. 16.

91. Netty Douglass to Senior, Group, Department, and Division Managers, memorandum re: Twentieth-Century Biographers Series, 1 August 1991.

92. *Manual*, pp. 43–44; see also Lee Z. Johnson to Librarian, Christian Science Reading Room, Chairman, Executive Board, 6 September 1991, and Lee Z. Johnson to The Christian Science Board of Directors, 19 August 1991.

93. Joan Vennochi, "The Private Sector: Money Changes Everything," *Boston Globe*, 18 September 1991.

94. John H. Hoagland, Jr., to John S. Driscoll, 23 September 1991.

95. Jeffrey L. Sheler, "Healing an Ailing Church: Christian Science Is Struggling to Reverse Its Steady Decline," *U.S. News & World Report*, 6 November 1989, p. 76.

96. Stephen Gottschalk to Co-workers, 1 March 1990.

97. Ibid.

98. I caused a stir in the main reading room of the Mother Church in 1993, when I asked to buy a copy. Distraught clerks, wringing their hands, sent me from office to office in the Publishing Society, explaining that they knew the video existed but didn't know why it wasn't available.
99. Diane Manuel to Virginia S. Harris, 4 January 1989.
100. Ibid.; see also *Manual*, pp. 52–53.
101. Ibid.
102. Ibid.
103. Ibid.
104. Christian Scientists for Honesty to All Non–Christian Scientists in Monitor TV and Radio Broadcasting, memorandum re: Your role in the purpose of Monitor broadcasting, 12 July 1991; see also *Manual*, pp. 79–80.
105. Ibid.
106. "Some of Us in the Newsroom" to Washington Bureau, memorandum, 26 June 1991.
107. Ibid.
108. Griesa, "Figures Obtained by T. Griesa from D. Bowersock 12/2/88."
109. Ibid.
110. Hal M. Friesen and Netty Douglass to "Friends," 3 October 1991.
111. Ibid.
112. Ibid.
113. James L. Franklin, "A Christian Science Dispute: Four Editors Quit Following Publication of Book on Church's Founder," *Boston Globe*, 26 February 1992.
114. James L. Franklin, "Church Digs Deep for Cash, Christian Science Crisis," *Boston Globe*, 29 February 1992.
115. Ibid.
116. Netty Douglass and Jack Hoagland to All Employees in the Christian Science Publishing Society and Monitor Television, Inc., memorandum re: Staying the Course, 3 March 1992.
117. Ibid.
118. Ibid.
119. James L. Franklin, "Church Officials Defend Loan from Pension Fund," *Boston Globe*, 4 March 1992.
120. Hon. Thomas P. Griesa to Mrs. Virginia S. Harris, 24 March 1992.
121. Virginia S. Harris to Thomas P. Griesa, 27 March 1992.
122. Ibid.
123. Hon. Thomas P. Griesa to Mrs. Virginia S. Harris, 31 March 1992.
124. See *Manual*, pp. 28–29.
125. " 'Speaking the Truth in Love' " (privately printed), p. 45.
126. See *Manual*, p. 29.
127. See the book jacket copy on Bridge, *Monitoring the News*.
128. Ibid., pp. 149, 187–88.
129. Stephen Gottschalk, interview with author, Wellesley, Mass., 8 June 1993; see also Caroline Fraser, "Suffering Children and the Christian Science Church,"

Atlantic Monthly 275, no. 4 (April 1995), p. 120. Gottschalk told me that Robert Peel said this in connection with the Knapp affair.

130. Superior Court of California, County of Los Angeles, Estate of Eloise M. Knapp, P 593 650, Order on Motion for Summary Judgment by Judge Edward M. Ross, 17 September 1992, p. 7.

131. Robert Shepherd to Christian Scientists in New Hampshire, 1 October 1992, reprinted in "For the Dignity and Defense of Our Cause: Preserving the Integrity of the Committee on Publication" (privately printed by the Mailing Fund), pp. 11–12.

132. Superior Court of the State of California, for the County of Los Angeles, In the Matter of the Estate of Eloise M. Knapp, no. P 593–650 [hereinafter "Matter of Knapp"] Declaration of Katherine Fanning, 28 October 1993. Reprinted in "Staying Loyal to Our Leader's Vision of Church: Supplement," 5 February 1994 (privately printed by the Mailing Fund).

133. Matter of Knapp, Declaration of Rushworth M. Kidder, 1 November 1993.

134. Matter of Knapp, Declaration of Elaine H. Natale, 10 November 1993.

135. Ibid.

136. Matter of Knapp, Declaration of Harvey W. Wood, 29 November 1993.

137. Ibid. In addition to these affidavits, "Staying Loyal to Our Leader's Vision of Church: Supplement" also included Elaine Natale's letters to the Board and her boss, Allison Phinney, Jr., containing extensive notes on her meetings with them, notes that tended to corroborate Natale's version of events.

138. "Moving Forward with Mrs. Eddy's Leadership," January 1995 (privately printed by the Mailing Fund), p. 4. Italics in original.

139. R. Crosby Kemper to the Christian Science Board of Directors, 5 May 1992; see also Peter Steinfels, "Christian Science Leaders, Accused of Improprieties, Face Members Today," *New York Times*, 8 June 1992.

140. Earle Armstrong, C.S.B., et al. to the Christian Science Board of Directors, 16 April 1992.

141. June Thompson, letter of resignation, 3 April 1992.

142. Charles Terrell, letter of resignation, 12 May 1992, printed as appendix C in "God's Requirement," 26 February 1993 (privately printed by the Mailing Fund), n.p.; *Manual*, pp. 77–78.

143. "Christian Science Meltdown," *Forbes*, 8 June 1992, p. 14.

144. See James L. Franklin, "Church Gives Grim Fiscal News, After Unity Plea, Christian Scientists Hear of TV," *Boston Globe*, 9 June 1992.

145. Peter Steinfels, "Troubled Church Discloses Its Financial Records," *New York Times*, 9 June 1992.

146. Ibid.

147. Thomas P. Griesa, "Democracy in The Mother Church," in "Loyalty and Democracy in The Mother Church," 30 January 1993 (privately printed by the Mailing Fund).

148. In fact, the Mailing Fund may reach as many as a third of all Scientists, but there are dissidents who dissent even from its views. In many ways, the so-called Christian Science dissidents seem to be the most vigorous, energetic, and

involved Scientists. Besides the aforementioned Rare Book Company, The Bookmark, and Andrew Hartsook's *Banner*, there are many other dissident publishers, including the Gethsemane Foundation, in St. Maries, Idaho, which publishes books and articles intended to restore Mary Baker Eddy to her rightful place of importance in Scientists' minds; the Emma Publishing Society, in Cuyahoga Falls, Ohio, publishing and promoting the works of Augusta Stetson; Helen M. Wright Publishing, Inc., in Seattle, which puts out the quarterly *Mary Baker Eddy Letter* and publishes books by Alan Young and Wright herself, who supports obedience to the *Manual*'s estoppel clauses; the Aequus Institute, in Claremont, California, which, like the Gideon organization, distributes copies of *Science and Health* to motels and hotels across the country and publishes a quarterly newsletter, as well as a CD-ROM with the complete texts of all of Eddy's published writings; and the Christian Science Endtime Center in Denver, Colorado, which offers seminars and publications on Mrs. Eddy's millennial waftings. The dissident Christian Science church in Plainfield, New Jersey, also publishes and distributes Christian Science literature.

149. See James L. Franklin, "BU to Buy Christian Science Church's TV Station for $3.8 Million," *Boston Globe*, 24 June 1993.

150. Al Stewart, "$250M Question: How Did Monitor Spend All That Money?" *Cable World* 4, no. 12 (23 March 1992).

151. Ibid.

152. See James L. Franklin, "Ex-Officials Troubled by Church's Big Spending," *Boston Globe*, 7 June 1992.

153. Ibid.

154. Ibid.

155. Andrew W. Hartsook, "More Shortwave Station Fallout," *Banner* 8, no. 4 (summer 1995), p. 3; "Sale of Shortwave Station Completed," *Christian Science Sentinel* 97, no. 14 (3 April 1995), p. 45. Hartsook takes his information regarding the sale of the station from the *New Hampshire Sunday News*, 30 April 1995.

156. See "The Sale of the Maine Shortwave Station: Facts Members Must Know," in "Mailing Fund Update," 24 June 1994 (privately printed by the Mailing Fund), p. 3.

157. "Mailing Fund Update," 20 January 1995, pp. 2–3.

158. The fact that Mrs. Sara Hoagland, Jack Hoagland's wife, became a Christian Science teacher after December 1991 is apparent from a comparison of her listing in the *Christian Science Journal* before and after that date; for William Clark's relationship to Hoagland and his role in the stock sale of the Monitor Channel, see Bridge, *Monitoring the News*, p. xix; for Bloomfield, see Bridge, p. 88.

159. Strahinich, "Not Ready," pp. 72–73.

160. Members for the Manual to Friends, 30 December 1996, reprinted in the Mailing Fund, letter of 1 January 1997.

161. Affidavit of the Christian Science Board of Directors, Commonwealth of Massachusetts, Superior Court Department, Civil Action # 93-7320H, *Weaver and other v. Wood et al.*, p. 31.

162. Ibid., p. 32.

163. Ibid., p. 14.
164. Iver Peterson, "Christian Science Radio Service Is Signing Off," *New York Times*, 28 June 1997.
165. Ibid.

Part VI. "God Will Do the Rest": Resurrecting Christian Science

1. Mark Jurkowitz, "Making the Monitor Matter," *Boston Globe*, 6 August 1997.
2. Ibid.
3. Because the *Christian Science Journal* lists the name and address of every Christian Science branch church in the world in every issue, it has been possible for journalists, sociologists, and concerned Scientists to keep tabs on the number of churches that have closed. Andrew W. Hartsook has published a running total of church closures in his newsletter for Scientists, *The Banner*, since 1987. See also Rodney Stark, "The Rise and Fall of Christian Science," *Journal of Contemporary Religion* 13, no. 2 (1998), pp. 193–94. Over the course of my research, I have learned that actual Church-compiled membership figures for the state of California fell from 14,208 in 1992 to 13,351 in 1993; membership in individual states is tallied confidentially by the Church in order to compute each branch's financial responsibility for maintaining the state Committee on Publication. Florida's membership, over the same two year period, fell from 4,900 to 4,697. One CHILD member, working with these figures, has calculated that, for 1998, if one assumes 55 members in each church and 10 members in each society, the total number of Christian Scientists is 94,035; if one assumes 27 members for every practitioner/teacher, the total number of Christian Scientists is 54,864.
4. See the *Christian Science Sentinel* for 13 January, 28 April, and 8 September 1997.
5. See Erik Tomas Carlson, "You Can Quit Smoking," *Christian Science Sentinel* 100, no. 36 (7 September 1998), front cover and p. 15; Michelle Boccanfuso, "Cover Story: Food Fights?" *Christian Science Sentinel* 100, no. 44 (2 November 1998), cover and p. 6. ("Fearless about Food" appears on the cover as the headline of the latter article.)
6. The U.S. Postal Service requires periodicals delivered by second-class mail to print in an October issue a "Statement of Ownership, Management, and Circulation" that includes current figures for "Total Paid and/or Requested Circulation." For the *Sentinel* circulation figures cited here for 1997 and 1998, see *Christian Science Sentinel* 99, no. 40 (6 October 1997), p. 46; *Christian Science Sentinel* 100, no. 42 (19 October 1998), p. 27. For the *Journal* announcement, see "The Christian Science Journal, Designed to Heal," *Christian Science Journal* 116, no. 8 (August 1998), p. 45.
7. David Cook, "Speech to the Committee on Publication Conference," dated 9 October 1997.
8. See, for example, *The New York Times Book Review*, 29 November 1998, back page.
9. Cook, "Speech to the Committee," 9 October 1997.
10. Paul D. Colford, "Articles of Faith," *Brandweek* 38, no. 29 (21 July 1997), p. 22.
11. Maura Smith, "Science Friction," *Forbes*, 15 December 1997, p. 14.

12. Andrew Hartsook, "More News from Boston," *Banner* 11, no. 2 (winter 1998), p. 2.
13. Ibid.
14. For the decline of practitioners, see Stark, "Rise and Fall," 192, table 2; and Andrew W. Hartsook, "Warning to Practitioners," *Banner* 12, no. 2 (Winter 1999), p. 1. Hartsook calculates that the total number of teachers and practitioners "dropped from 2,045 in 1997 to 1,953 one year later." For recent Principia enrollment, see Otto Johnson, ed., *1997 Information Please Almanac* (Boston: Houghton Mifflin, 1997), p. 884; this reference gives Principia's enrollment as 543. For past enrollment, see, for example, Peter Wyden, "The Principia," *St. Louis Post-Dispatch*, 9 September 1951; this article reports that 1951 enrollment was "nearly 1,000 students from 45 states and 14 foreign countries."
15. Information about Virginia Harris is drawn from a biographical statement sent me by her office and from Glen Elsasser, "Going Public; Christian Scientists Drop Their Research in a Spat over Where the Church Is Headed," *Chicago Tribune*, 12 December 1994.
16. See the paperback trade edition of *Science and Health*. The Publisher's Note and the Word Index are not paginated; the Note precedes the title page, and the index follows p. 700, the last page of "Fruitage."
17. See tip-in card stapled in *Christian Science Sentinel* 99, no. 39 (29 September 1997).
18. Eddy's role in the women's rights movement was negligible. She favored equal rights under the law for women but never took a political stand for women's voting rights. Her view of the role of the sexes was startlingly conventional, given the extraordinary power and wealth she would accrue during her lifetime; she wrote in *Science and Health*, "Man should not be required to participate in all the annoyances and cares of domestic economy, nor should woman be expected to understand political economy." *Science and Health*, p. 59.
19. "Preserving the Integrity of the Christian Science Textbook," 10 September 1994 (privately printed by the Mailing Fund), pp. 2, 4, 16.
20. Andrew Hartsook, *Banner* 8, no. 4 (summer 1995), p. 2.
21. Andrew Hartsook, *Banner* 10, no. 4 (summer 1997), p. 2. The copies were sent, Hartsook reports, "as an adjunct of the Spirituality & Healing in Medicine seminars held at Harvard University."
22. Virginia Harris originally gave me the figure of 100,000 copies since 1995 in our interview on 13 September 1997. This number was repeated (along with the figure of "over 50,000" copies each year for the last 90 years) in a letter to me from Alice Howell, Harris's senior executive assistant, on 8 October 1997. Howell and I also discussed the figures over the telephone on 18 November 1997. In *Years of Authority*, p. 382, Peel claims that "By 1906 . . . 418,000 copies of the book had been sold."

    Adding up 50,000 × 90 years = 4.5 million. 4.5 million + the 300,000 sold since 1995 + Peel's 418,000 = 5.2 million. Assuming that "over 50,000" actually means 60,000, the total number is closer to 6.5 million. Even assuming that "over 50,000" actually means that *Science and Health* sold some 75,000 copies every year for ninety years, the total equals less than 7.5 million. Therefore, the Church's own figures do not add up to "over nine million sold."

When I questioned the Church's math, Alice Howell patiently explained: "A best-seller is over 50,000 copies and then a religion bestseller is over 100,000 copies, so we felt it was important in showing the evergreen status of this book, that there is an ever-growing demand." I asked if "over 50,000" meant between 50,000 and 60,000. She said, "Now that I think about it, there was a year when we sold over 75,000 units, so it means between 50,000 and 100,000." When I requested specific figures by year, still questioning how the Church had derived its 9 million figure, she said, "You're comparing apples and oranges. You would just have to take our word for it. I don't think that's an important thing for people to know." She also remembered that there had been several years with sales over 75,000.

23. I refer here to Harris's willingness to appear with medical professionals, such as Dr. Herbert Benson, and Pentecostal healers, such as Samuel Solivan, who has lectured at Benson's courses; both doctors and faith healers from other traditions have been dismissed by the Church in the past. David Sleeper, then manager of the Committees on Publication, expressed the Christian Science contempt for medicine in his lecture "Christian Science and the Law," delivered at the First Church of Christ, Scientist, in Hyannis, Massachusetts, soon after the manslaughter conviction of Dorothy Sheridan in 1967. Sleeper said: "We must not yield to the mesmeric claims of medicine by calling a doctor and being forced to worship a false God." See Damore, p. 297. In a representative editorial, "The Spirituality of Mankind," in the *Christian Science Sentinel* in 1984, Allison W. Phinney, Jr., editor of the Church's religious periodicals, wrote dismissively of "fringe-group faith healers." See Phinney, *Christian Science Sentinel* 86, no. 36 (3 September 1984), p. 1530.

24. Larry King with Rabbi Irwin Katsof, *Powerful Prayers* (Los Angeles: Renaissance Books, 1998), p. 115.

25. Virginia Harris, interview with the author, Albuquerque, New Mexico, 13 September 1997. All of the following quotations of Harris in this section are taken from this interview.

26. Jim Milliot, "Do Religion Sales Add Up?" *Publishers Weekly*, 10 April 1995, 25, 27; Mary B. W. Tabor, "Of Grace, Damnation and Best Sellers," *New York Times*, 31 July 1995.

27. See Tabor, "Of Grace, Damnation and Best Sellers."

28. Marilyn Elias, "Clearer Link Between the Head and Healing: Medicine Catching Up with Pioneer Benson," *USA Today*, 31 March 1997.

29. Herbert Benson, M.D., *The Relaxation Response* (New York: Times Books, 1984).

30. Elias, "Clearer Link."

31. Herbert Benson, M.D., with Marg Stark, *Timeless Healing: The Power and Biology of Belief* (New York: Scribner, 1996), p. 201.

32. " 'Speaking the Truth in Love' " (privately printed), p. 51.

33. I attended the "Spirituality & Healing in Medicine" course held in Los Angeles in March 1997. Virginia Harris's presentation has also been published several times: see "Christian Science Spiritual Healing Practices," *Christian Science*

Journal 114, no. 2 (February 1996), pp. 33–38; "Christian Science Spiritual Healing Practices," *Christian Science Journal* 115, no. 3 (March 1997), pp. 20–26; "Christian Science Healing Practices," *Christian Science Journal* 116, no. 3 (March 1998), pp. 39–41; "Christian Science Healing Methods Explained," *Christian Science Journal* 117, no. 3 (March 1999), pp. 30–37.

34. Chip Brown, *Afterwards, You're a Genius: Faith, Medicine, and the Metaphysics of Healing* (New York: Riverhead Books, 1998), p. 341.

35. Author's notes, 15 March 1997.

36. Herbert Benson, telephone interview with the author, 17 November 1997.

37. David O. Weber, "The Mainstreaming of Alternative Medicine," *Healthcare Forum Journal* 39, no. 6 (November–December 1996), pp. 16–27.

38. Ibid.

39. For "telesomatic events," see Larry Dossey, M.D., *Healing Words: The Power of Prayer and the Practice of Medicine* (San Francisco: HarperSanFrancisco, 1993), pp. 85–86.

40. Ibid., p. 98.

41. Ibid., pp. 99–100.

42. Thomas C. Palmer, Jr., "Deaths Tied to Religious Dispute: Father, Son Apparently Kill Selves When Research Fails to Gain Acceptance," *Boston Globe*, 16 May 1993.

43. Robert Marquand, "Healing Role of Spirituality Gains Ground," *Christian Science Monitor*, 6 December 1995.

44. Virginia Harris, "Christian Science Spiritual Healing Practices," *Christian Science Journal* 115, no. 3 (March 1997), p. 23.

45. Benson and Stark, *Timeless Healing*, p. 293.

46. Eddy's justification for this position is practically incomprehensible: "[Faith-cure] demands less cross-bearing, self-renunciation, and divine Science to admit the claims of the corporeal senses and appeal to God for relief through a humanized conception of His power, than to deny these claims and learn the divine way,— drinking Jesus' cup, being baptized with his baptism, gaining the end through persecution and purity." *Retrospection and Introspection*, p. 54.

47. Eddy, as quoted in "Healing and Reports of Cases," *Christian Science Journal* 7, no. 1 (April 1889), p. 38.

48. See Louise Schmidt, "Scientific Materialism," *Christian Science Journal* 14, no. 3 (June 1896), p. 115; see also Peel, *Years of Authority*, p. 303.

49. Clarence A. Buskirk, "Methods of Reasoning as Used in Christian Science," *Christian Science Journal* 22, no. 7 (October 1904), p. 405.

50. For a typical example of such an apocryphal story, see "Children's Corner: Einstein's Advice to Parents," *Mary Baker Eddy Institute Letter*, no. 3 (1 May 1997), p. 9.

51. See Peel, *Years of Authority*, pp. 302–303, 492 n. 27. In fact, the major biographies of Einstein contain no references to Christian Science, Eddy, or *Science and Health*. See Ronald W. Clark, *The Life and Times of Einstein* (New York: World Publishing Co., 1971), and Denis Brian, *Einstein: A Life* (New York: John Wiley & Sons, Inc., 1996).

52. For Eddy's inclusion of the "Fruitage" chapter in *Science and Health*, see Peel, *Years of Authority*, p. 190.
53. Committee on Publication, *An Empirical Analysis of Medical Evidence in Christian Science Testimonies of Healing, 1969–1988* (Boston: Committee on Publication, 1989), 2.
54. Editor, *Christian Science Journal*, "Healing and Reports of Cases," *Christian Science Journal* 7, no. 6 (September 1889), p. 303.
55. Ibid., pp. 304–305.
56. See, for example, "Reports of Healing," *Christian Science Journal* 115, no. 12 (December 1997), p. 42.
57. I attended the 1993 annual meeting and heard these testimonies, which were later published in written form in the *Christian Science Journal* in a series that ran from September 1993 to May 1994. The testimonies from Riverdale, New York, Finland, and Greece can be found in "A Journey of Healing with *Science and Health*," *Christian Science Journal* 112, no. 2 (February 1994), pp. 52–53; the testimonies from Italy and Poland appeared in "A Journey of Healing with *Science and Health*," *Christian Science Journal* 112, no. 5 (May 1994), pp. 54–56.
58. "A Journey of Healing with *Science and Health*," *Christian Science Journal* 112, no. 2 (February 1994), p. 52.
59. Ibid.
60. *Science and Health*, p. viii.
61. Randolph C. Byrd, M.D., "Positive Therapeutic Effects of Intercessory Prayer in a Coronary Care Unit," *Southern Medical Journal* 81, no. 7 (July 1988), pp. 826–29. This and other studies purporting to demonstrate that prayer has a positive effect on physical health were recently criticized in *The Lancet* for failure to control for intervening variables and other flaws. See Richard Sloan, E. Bagiella, and T. Powell, *The Lancet* 353 (20 February 1999), pp. 664–67.
62. "Empirical Analysis," p. 1.
63. Ibid.
64. Ibid., p. 5.
65. Ibid., p. 4.
66. Dr. Richard C. Cabot, "One Hundred Christian Science Cures," *McClure's Magazine* (August 1908), cited in Stephen Paget, *The Faith and Works of Christian Science* (London: Macmillan, 1909), p. 150.

Paget, a British surgeon and author, was even more blunt than Cabot about the reliability of patients and scientific laymen:

> Many of these witnesses are not telling the truth. They are so excitable, so ill-educated, that they fail to distinguish truth from falsehood. They have given false evidence, have perjured themselves, not wilfully, but from sheer inability to be accurate.
>
> Again, we all know that no statement is more inaccurate than the average statement of "what the doctor said." We listen with politeness to it, but without acceptance: we think to ourselves, *I wish I knew what he really did say* [Paget, p. 152].

Yet there was still room for ambivalence, even for medical doctors so sure of their position, simply because medicine was so inexact a science and the psychosomatic contribution even to diseases deemed organic was so poorly understood. Cabot, some years after his uncompromising conclusions in *McClure's*, softened his position in a speech delivered at Harvard University:

> I see no reason why we should admit only one of the different ways through which healing comes to our bodies. I want to take them all, and in that I disagree with Christian Science, the good effects of which I see on all sides. I have not the slightest doubt that it does good, that it cures disease, organic as well as functional, only I do not want anybody to say, "And nothing else cures."

See Richard C. Cabot, *Harvard Alumni Bulletin*, 31 December 1925, as quoted in Robert Peel, *Christian Science: Its Encounter with American Culture* (New York: Holt, Rinehart, and Winston, 1958), p. 145.

67. "Empirical Analysis," p. 6.
68. Ibid.
69. Ibid., p. 7.
70. "Empirical Analysis," p. 11. My italics.
71. The *Journal* recently opened up enough to publish an article responding to a letter from a physician who asked, "What happens if a person doesn't get the healing for which he or she is praying?" The *Journal's* response, not surprisingly, put the onus on the patient, not on Christian Science itself: "When healing hasn't come, and we're relying on God's power, we may need to consider how we can yield more fully to the divine will. . . . What's being asked of us, perhaps, is more humility and increased devotion to God, the great healer. . . . When healing hasn't come, it's not a failure of divine Love, or of Love's reflection." See Barbara M. Vining, "When Healing Hasn't Come—What Now?" *Christian Science Journal* 116, no. 5 (May 1998), pp. 40–41; see also a letter written in response by Jacqueline MacDermott, about a "respiratory problem" that lasted thirty-five years, *Christian Science Journal* 116, no. 11 (November 1998), p. 43. In the eyes of the Church, the religion itself never fails; only its followers do.
72. For the Church's claim that Christian Science works better for children than medical care, see Richard J. Brenneman, "Appendix: The Committee on Publication Answers," *Deadly Blessings: Faith Healing on Trial* (Buffalo, New York: Prometheus Books, 1990), pp. 337–38. The Appendix features an interview with Nathan Talbot, then the manager of the Committees on Publication, who claims here, and in other interviews in newspapers, that there is a lower "loss rate" for children in Christian Science households than in the general public. See also Edward Dolnick, "When Faith and Medicine Collide: A Child's Death Brings Christian Science Parents into Court," *Washington Post*, 25 September 1990.
73. Dolnick, "Faith and Medicine."
74. Brenneman, *Deadly Blessings*, p. 337.
75. Another problem with Talbot's assumptions was pointed out in 1990 by Norman Fost, a medical doctor and then chairman of the American Academy of

Pediatrics Committee on Bioethics: "Christian Scientists tend to be well-to-do people. Their death rates should be lower than for the general population. The question is, what are their mortality rates for the diseases in which they're accused of being negligent, like diabetes and meningitis?" Dolnick, *Washington Post*, 25 September 1990.

76. M. Victor Westberg, telephone interview with the author, 3 February 1995.

77. Lieut. C. H. Lightoller, R.N.R., "The Night the Titanic Sank," *Christian Science Sentinel* 99, no. 49 (8 December 1997), pp. 7–9. See also the accompanying article, Channing Walker, "Safe Travel: A Titanic or an Ark Experience?," pp. 4–6. For the original, unedited testimony, see *Christian Science Journal* 30, no. 7 (October 1912), pp. 414–15.

78. An exhaustive account of the congressional hearings and of Lightoller's role in them can be found in Wyn Craig Wade, *The Titanic: End of a Dream* (New York: Viking Penguin, 1986).

79. Wade, *Titanic*, pp. 125–31.

80. Ibid., pp. 147–48.

81. Ibid.

82. Ibid., p. 313.

83. Lightoller, "Titanic," (1997) p. 7.

84. Ibid., p. 9.

85. Ibid.

86. See "The Night the Titanic Sank," *Christian Science Monitor*, 3 April 1998.

87. See Edie Clark, "The Price of Faith: A Special Report on the Trials of Christian Science," *Yankee* 56, no. 7 (July 1992), pp. 117–21.

88. Ruth Price Brewster, "Testimonies of Healing," *Christian Science Journal* (January 1984), p. 49.

89. A neighbor of the Brewsters wrote to the Swans after their appearance on *Donahue*, describing Nancy's death; Rita Swan subsequently obtained a copy of the child's death certificate.

90. For Ruth Price Brewster's listing, see, for example, *Christian Science Journal* 115, no. 12 (December 1997), pp. 119, 129.

91. "Editor's Notebook: Questions and Discussions," *Christian Science Journal* 7, no. 6 (September 1889), p. 312.

92. "Editor's Notebook: Questions and Discussions," *Christian Science Journal* 7, no. 8 (November 1889), pp. 401–402.

93. "Editor's Table," *Christian Science Journal* 10, no. 11 (February 1893), p. 528.

94. See, for example, *Christian Science, Medicine, and Occultism*, by Dr. Albert Moll, M.D. (1902); *The Religio-Medical Masquerade*, by Frederick W. Peabody (Boston: Hancock Press, 1910); and *The Faith, the Falsity, and the Failure of Christian Science*, by Woodbridge Riley, Frederick W. Peabody, and Charles E. Humiston (1925).

95. Stephen Paget, *The Faith and Works of Christian Science* (London: Macmillan and Co., 1909), p. 249.

96. For more on Christian Science treatment of animals, see the new publication from the Christian Science Publishing Society: *Pets, People, and Prayer: For Pet*

Lovers of All Ages. An advertisement for this new book that recently ran in the *Christian Science Sentinel* 100, no. 5 (2 February 1998), p. 18, says, "Dogs, cats, horses, and a hamster were healed through prayer."

97. Paget, *Faith and Works*, p. 265.

98. Ibid., pp. 258–59.

99. See Mike Fricano, "Video Shown in Trial Over Horse's Fate," *Times Union* (Albany), 22 December 1998; Michael P. Bruno, "Polo Pony in Lawsuit Found Dead," *Times Union* (Albany), 30 December 1998.

100. R. W. England, "Some Aspects of Christian Science as Reflected in Letters of Testimony," *American Journal of Sociology* 59 (1954), pp. 448–53.

101. Ibid., p. 448; Will B. Davis, The First Church of Christ, Scientist, "Letter to the editor, May 26, 1954," *American Journal of Sociology* 60 (1954), pp. 184–85.

102. England, "Some Aspects," p. 451.

103. Ibid., p. 542.

104. Ibid., pp. 452–53.

105. In addition to the statistical studies, there has also been valuable work on the sociology of Christian Science. Margery Fox, in her 1973 doctoral dissertation for the department of anthropology at New York University, "Power and Piety: Women in Christian Science," and in a subsequent paper, expanded on Wilson's foundation by examining the implications of the role that Eddy, and subsequently the women practitioners in her movement, assumed at a time when women were largely excluded from the healing professions and were denied roles in religious institutions. Fox conducted ten months of fieldwork for her dissertation, observing and interviewing at Christian Science branch churches in two separate communities, "one in a Western resort city of over 320,000, the other in a suburban town of 28,000 in the metropolitan area of a large Eastern city in the United States" (Fox, "Power and Piety," p. v). She interviewed a number of practitioners, enrolled her two sons in Sunday school, and participated "in rituals and social events," even engaging a practitioner to treat one of her sons for "a minor complaint" (p. viii). Fox's dissertation, which has unfortunately never been published, is thus the only study of its kind, one in which a researcher and outsider penetrated the lives of Christian Scientists and their church and observed them at work: as they worshipped, prayed, and practiced their healing rituals.

Fox noticed that, although there are worldly aspects to Christian Science theology and the ways in which it has historically been applied, particularly by businessmen and others seeking material success, there are also profound ways in which Scientists isolate themselves from the world, through "the secrecy surrounding the educational system [class-instruction], the special vocabulary Christian Scientists use, the exclusiveness of their social relations" (p. 226). She also examined the interface between the "absolute level" of Christian Science beliefs—that matter does not exist and that mankind is perfect—and the "relative level" of Christian Science behavior, whereby Scientists reach some accommodation with society (p. 225). Christian Scientists, for example, frequently shun funerals or hold funeral ceremonies without the ritual observances or expressions of sorrow and loss, a behavior which "supports the doctrinal denial of

biological processes" (p. 229). But Scientists feel free to attend such social functions and rituals as weddings without the tension caused by conflicting beliefs.
Scientists also feel free to express their essentially religious bias against traditional observances of age and aging, since that bias is also held by modern
American society, which worships youth and values attitudes expressed in such
saws as "You're only as old as you feel."

106. G. E. Wilson, "Christian Science and Longevity," *Journal of Forensic Science* 1
(1965), pp. 43–60.

107. Ibid.

108. Brenneman, *Deadly Blessings*, p. 88.

109. William Franklin Simpson, Ph.D., "Comparative Longevity in a College Cohort
of Christian Scientists," *Journal of the American Medical Association* 262, no. 12
(22–29 September 1989), pp. 1657–58.

110. Ibid., p. 1658. Simpson compared 5,558 Principia graduates to the control group
of 29,858 University of Kansas graduates and noted that 3 percent of the
Principia graduates had no current address, compared with 13 percent of the control group; to account for this discrepancy, he assumed all missing Principia
graduates to be alive and all missing control group members to have the same
mortality rate as their classmates of the same sex.

111. Simpson divided the numbers of graduates into five-year blocks and enumerated
the exact numbers graduated during those five years from Principia and the
University of Kansas; the number (and percentage) from each institution who
were dead; and the number (and percentage) who were alive.

112. Ibid., p. 1658.

113. Ibid.

114. James Coates, *In Mormon Circles: Gentiles, Jack Mormons, and Latter-Day Saints*
(New York: Addison-Wesley Publishing Co., 1991), p. 102.

115. Nathan A. Talbot, Manager, Committees on Publication, "Letter to the Editor
[of newspapers]," reprinted in "The Committee on Publication Replies to the
JAMA Allegations," *Principia Purpose*, winter 1990, p. 18.

116. Ibid.

117. William Franklin Simpson, "Comparative Mortality of Two College Groups,
1945–1983," *Morbidity and Mortality Weekly Report* 40, no. 33 (23 August 1991),
p. 580. Simpson's conclusion was that "Total mortality was higher among PC
[Principia College] graduates in 22 (85%) of the 26 cohorts."

118. Herbert Benson has hinted during his courses that additional experimentation
on prayer is under way but will not answer questions about whether his experiments involve Christian Science.

119. For the quotations and information cited in this paragraph, see Dietrich
Bonhoeffer, as quoted in Sydney Ahlstrom, *A Religious History of the American
People* (New Haven: Yale University Press, 1972), p. 5; John Winthrop, "The
Antinomian Crisis," in Perry Miller, ed., *The American Puritans: Their Prose and
Poetry* (New York: Anchor Books, 1956), p. 56; Perry Miller, *Errand into the
Wilderness* (New York: Harper & Row, 1956), p. 185.

120. The General Court as quoted in Ahlstrom, *Religious History*, p. 160.

121. For my understanding of the Puritan jeremiad and the Puritan logic regarding disease and other misfortunes, I am indebted to Perry Miller, *The New England Mind: From Colony to Province* (Cambridge, Mass.: Harvard University Press, 1953).

122. Miller, *Errand*, p. 155.

123. I am indebted for this categorization of cults to Margaret Thaler Singer, "A Brief History of Cults," in *Cults in Our Midst: The Hidden Menace in our Everyday Lives* (San Francisco: Jossey-Bass, 1995), pp. 29–37.

124. Mike R. Powell, "Magnetic Water and Fuel Treatment: Myth, Magic, or Mainstream Science?" *Skeptical Inquirer* 22, no. 1 (January–February 1998), p. 27.

125. Massimo Polidoro, "The Human Magnets," *Swift: Newsletter of the James Randi Educational Foundation* 1, no. 1 (1997), pp. 10–11; included in *Skeptic* 5, no. 1 (1997), paginated separately.

126. Lawrence K. Altman, M.D., "Study on Using Magnets to Treat Pain Surprises Skeptics," *New York Times*, 10 December 1997.

127. Information about the history and practice of Therapeutic Touch has been drawn from Linda Rosa, B.S.N., R.N.; Emily Rosa; Larry Sarner; Stephen Barrett, M.D., "A Close Look at Therapeutic Touch," *Journal of the American Medical Association* 279 (1 April 1998), pp. 1005–1010.

128. Ibid.

129. Ibid.

130. Ibid., p. 1005.

131. Larry Dossey, M.D., *Be Careful What You Pray For . . . You Just Might Get It: What We Can Do About the Unintentional Effects of Our Thoughts, Prayers, and Wishes* (San Francisco: HarperSanFrancisco, 1997), p. 167.

132. Ibid.

133. Ibid., p. 188.

134. Virginia Harris, "Christian Science Spiritual Healing Practices," *Christian Science Journal* 115, no. 3 (March 1997), p. 23.

135. Andrew Weil, *Spontaneous Healing* (New York: Knopf, 1995), pp. 82, 100.

136. John E. Sarno, M.D., *The Mindbody Prescription: Healing the Body, Healing the Pain* (New York: Warner Books, 1998), p. 145.

137. Deepak Chopra, *The Seven Spiritual Laws of Success* (San Rafael, Calif.: Amber-Allen Publishing, 1993), p. 55.

138. For Chopra's claim about cancer remission, see John Leland and Carla Power, "Deepak's Instant Karma," *Newsweek*, 20 October 1997, p. 57; for Chopra's lawsuits, see Larry Reibstein with Theodore Gideonse, "Don't Mess with Deepak," *Newsweek*, 20 October 1997, pp. 56–57.

139. Robert Skutch, *Journey Without Distance: The Story Behind A Course in Miracles* (Berkeley, Calif.: Celestial Arts, 1984), p. 2.

140. See Marianne Williamson, *A Return to Love: Reflections on the Principles of A Course in Miracles* (New York: HarperPaperbacks, 1993), p. 230. This book quotes extensively from *A Course in Miracles*, offering commentary on various passages; endnotes cite the correlative passages in *A Course*.

141. Ibid., p. 31.

142. Ibid., p. 22.

143. Ibid., p. 261.

144. Details about Louise Hay's life come from Michael D'Antonio, *Heaven on Earth: Dispatches from America's Spiritual Frontier* (New York: Crown Publishers, 1992), p. 94.

145. Louise L. Hay, *Heal Your Body: The Mental Causes of Physical Illness and the Metaphysical Way to Overcome Them* (Santa Monica, Calif.: Hay House, 1988), p. 46.

146. Ibid., p. 20.

147. El Morya, *The Chela and the Path* (Colorado Springs, Colo.: The Summit Lighthouse, 1975), pp. 121–22, as quoted in George A. Mather and Larry A. Nichols, *Dictionary of Cults, Sects, Religions and the Occult* (Grand Rapids, Mich.: Zondervan Publishing House, 1993), p. 125.

148. *Manual*, 19.

149. See Hank Hanegraaff, *Christianity in Crisis* (Eugene, Ore.: Harvest House Publishers, 1997), p. 32.

150. D. R. McConnell, *A Different Gospel*, updated edition (Peabody, Mass.: Hendrickson Publishers, 1995), p. 25.

151. L. Ron Hubbard, *Dianetics* (Los Angeles: Bridge Publications, 1991), p. vi.

152. Ibid., p. 11.

153. Ibid.

154. For these and the following details of Hubbard's life, see Joel Sappell and Robert W. Welkos, "The Making of L. Ron Hubbard," part one of a six-part series, "The Scientology Story," *Los Angeles Times*, 24–29 June 1990.

155. See Douglas Frantz, "Scientology Faces Glare of Scrutiny After Florida Parishioner's Death," *New York Times*, 1 December 1997.

156. Miller, *The New England Mind*, p. 355.

157. Ibid., p. 357.

158. See Arthur Allen, "Injection Rejection," *New Republic*, 23 March 1998, pp. 20–23.

Glossary

1. *Science and Health*, p. 401.

2. See *Manual*, p. 85.

3. Wilson, *Sects and Society*, p. 349.

4. *Science and Health*, p. 158.

5. Charles S. Braden, *Christian Science Today: Power, Policy, Practice* (Dallas: Southern Methodist University Press, 1958), p. 251.

SELECTED AND ANNOTATED
BIBLIOGRAPHY

Works by Mary Baker Eddy

Glover, Mary Baker. *Science and Health*. First ed. Boston: W. F. Brown & Co., Printers, 1875. Reproductions of the first edition are now published and distributed by the Rare Book Company, Freehold, New Jersey.

Eddy, Mary Baker. *Christ and Christmas: A Poem*. Boston: The First Church of Christ, Scientist, 1925. Originally published in 1893.

———. *Science and Health with Key to the Scriptures*. Boston: The First Church of Christ, Scientist, 1934.

———. *Manual of The Mother Church, The First Church of Christ, Scientist in Boston, Massachusetts*. Boston: The First Church of Christ, Scientist, 1936. Originally published in 1895, Eddy's *Manual*, the governing document of her church, was finalized in the eighty-ninth edition.

———. *Miscellaneous Writings: 1883–1896*. Boston: The First Church of Christ, Scientist, 1924. Originally published in 1896, this volume contains sermons, letters, lectures, and articles, including the famous address delivered in Tremont Temple in 1885 and the address delivered in Chicago in 1888.

———. *Prose Works other than Science and Health with Key to the Scriptures*. Boston: The First Church of Christ, Scientist, 1953. This volume, originally published in 1925—the only volume of Eddy's work to be published posthumously—collects thirteen of Eddy's volumes and pamphlets: *Miscellaneous Writings; Retrospection and Introspection; Unity of Good; Pulpit and Press; Rudimental Divine Science; No and Yes; Christian Science versus Pantheism; Message to The Mother Church, 1900; Message to*

The Mother Church, 1901; *Message to The Mother Church*, 1902; *Christian Healing*; *The People's Idea of God; The First Church of Christ, Scientist and Miscellany.*

Biographies and Memoirs of Mary Baker Eddy

Bancroft, Samuel Putnam. *Mrs. Eddy As I Knew Her in 1870*. Boston: Geo. H. Ellis Press, 1923; Freehold, New Jersey: Rare Book Company, n.c.

Bates, Ernest Sutherland and John V. Dittemore. *Mary Baker Eddy: The Truth and the Tradition*. New York: Alfred A. Knopf, 1932. Dittemore, who was ousted from the Church's Board of Directors, later recanted his heretical biography.

Cather, Willa, and Georgine Milmine. *The Life of Mary Baker G. Eddy & The History of Christian Science*. Lincoln, Neb.: University of Nebraska Press, 1993. Reprinted from the original 1909 edition published by Doubleday, Page & Company, 1909.

Dakin, Edwin Franden. *Mrs. Eddy: The Biography of a Virginal Mind*. New York: Charles Scribner's Sons, 1929.

Dickey, Adam H. *Memoirs of Mary Baker Eddy*. Boston: Merrymount Press, 1927. Copies of this rare volume can be found at the Library of Congress, the Boston Public Library, the New York Public Library, and Harvard University's Houghton Library. Transcripts of it are also available from The Bookmark, Santa Clarita, California.

Gill, Gillian. *Mary Baker Eddy*. Reading, Mass.: Perseus Books, 1998.

Gilman, James F. *Recollections of Mary Baker Eddy, Discoverer and Founder of Christian Science, as Preserved in the Diary Records of James F. Gilman Written During the Making of the Illustrations for Mrs. Eddy's Poem*, Christ and Christmas, in 1893.

Miscellaneous Documents Relating to Christian Science and its Discoverer and Founder, Mary Baker Eddy, Author of the Textbook Science and Health with Key to the Scriptures. Privately printed. Distributed by the Rare Book Company, Freehold, New Jersey. Includes memoirs written by Eddy's students, including Clara E. Choate, M. Adelaide Still, Janet T. Coleman, Julia S. Bartlett, etc.

Peel, Robert. *Mary Baker Eddy: The Years of Discovery*. New York: Holt, Rinehart and Winston, 1966. Published since 1972 by the Christian Science Publishing Society.

———. *Mary Baker Eddy: The Years of Trial*. New York: Holt, Rinehart and Winston, 1971. Published since 1977 by the Christian Science Publishing Society.

———. *Mary Baker Eddy: The Years of Authority*. New York: Holt, Rinehart and Winston, 1977. Published since 1982 by the Christian Science Publishing Society.

Powell, Lyman P. *Mary Baker Eddy: A Life Size Portrait*. New York: MacMillan Company, 1930.

Silberger, Julius, Jr. *Mary Baker Eddy: An Interpretive Biography of the Founder of Christian Science*. Boston: Little, Brown, 1980.

Smaus, Jewel Spangler. *Mary Baker Eddy: The Golden Days*. Boston: Christian Science Publishing Society, 1966.

Smith, Louise A. *Mary Baker Eddy: Discoverer and Founder of Christian Science*. Boston: Christian Science Publishing Society, 1991.

Studdert-Kennedy, Hugh A. *Mrs. Eddy: Her Life, Her Work, and Her Place in History*. San Francisco: The Farallon Press, 1947.

Thomas, Robert David. *"With Bleeding Footsteps": Mary Baker Eddy's Path to Religious Leadership*. New York: Alfred A. Knopf, 1994.

Tomlinson, Irving C. *Twelve Years with Mary Baker Eddy: Recollections and Experiences*. Boston: Christian Science Publishing Society, 1945.

Von Fettweis, Yvonne Caché, and Robert Townsend Warneck. *Mary Baker Eddy: Christian Healer*. Boston: Christian Science Publishing Society, 1998.

We Knew Mary Baker Eddy. First Series. Boston: Christian Science Publishing Society, 1943.

We Knew Mary Baker Eddy. Second Series. Boston: Christian Science Publishing Society, 1950.

We Knew Mary Baker Eddy. Third Series. Boston: Christian Science Publishing Society, 1953.

We Knew Mary Baker Eddy. Fourth Series. Boston: Christian Science Publishing Society, 1972.

Wilbur, Sibyl. *The Life of Mary Baker Eddy*. New York: Concord Publishing Co., 1908.

Works of History and Analysis Concerning the Christian Science Church and Movement and the Practice of Christian Science, by Both Scientists and Non-Scientists

Armstrong, Joseph, and Margaret Williamson. *Building of The Mother Church: The First Church of Christ, Scientist, in Boston*, Massachusetts. Boston: Christian Science Publishing Society, 1980.

Beasley, Norman. *The Cross and The Crown: The History of Christian Science*. New York: Duell, Sloan and Pearce, 1952. Beasley was a non-Scientist who, nonetheless, wrote about Eddy and her movement with lavish admiration, verging on hagiography.

———. *The Continuing Spirit*. New York: Duell, Sloan and Pearce, 1956. This admiring survey of the post-Eddy Church contains useful summaries of the Church's early legislative battles to protect the rights of its practitioners and members, the development of its system of sanatoria, and its role in World War II.

"Blight That Failed, The." New York: Blue Ribbon Books, 1930. This pamphlet describing the Church's organized boycott of Edwin Franden Dakin's controversial biography of Mary Baker Eddy, *Mrs. Eddy: The Biography of a Virginal Mind*, was distributed with copies of the Blue Ribbon Books edition of Dakin's book.

Braden, Charles S. *Christian Science Today: Power, Policy, Practice*. Dallas: Southern Methodist University Press, 1958. Second printing with a new foreword by the author, 1969. One of the few histories of the post-Eddy Church by a historian of American religion.

Bridge, Susan. *Monitoring the News: The Brilliant Launch and Sudden Collapse of the Monitor Channel*. Armonk, New York: M. E. Sharpe, 1998. An account of the Church's adventures in media by a former vice-president at Monitor Television.

Canham, Erwin D. *Commitment to Freedom: The Story of* The Christian Science Monitor. Boston: Houghton Mifflin Company, 1958. The definitive history of the *Monitor* by its most influential editor.

Century of Christian Science Healing, A. Boston: Christian Science Publishing Society, 1966.

Christian Science: A Sourcebook of Contemporary Materials. Boston: Christian Science Publishing Society, 1990. A collection of excerpts of sympathetic writings on Christian Science and brief explanations of the religion, published by the Church during the period when a number of its members were embroiled in criminal or civil trials following the deaths of their children due to medical neglect.

Christian Science War Time Activities: A Report to the Board of Directors of The Mother Church by The Christian Science War Relief Committee. Boston: Christian Science Publishing Society, 1922.

Damore, Leo. *The "Crime" of Dorothy Sheridan*. New York: Arbor House, 1978; paperback with new appendix released by Dell, 1992.

Freedom and Responsibility: Christian Science Healing for Children. Boston: First Church of Christ, Scientist, 1989. A defense of Christian Science treatment of children distributed free-of-charge by the Church in its reading rooms, including, as an appendix, "An Empirical Analysis of Medical Evidence in Christian Science Testimonies of Healing, 1969–1988."

Gardner, Martin. *The Healing Revelations of Mary Baker Eddy: The Rise and Fall of Christian Science*. Buffalo, New York: Prometheus Books, 1993. A survey of Eddy's life and the fate of her church by a noted skeptic.

Gottschalk, Stephen. *The Emergence of Christian Science in American Religious Life*. Berkeley: University of California Press, 1973.

Healing Spiritually: Renewing Your Life Through the Power of God's Law. Boston: Christian Science Publishing Society, 1996.

John, DeWitt, and Erwin D. Canham. *The Christian Science Way of Life* with *A Christian Scientist's Life*. Englewood Cliffs, New Jersey: Prentice-Hall, 1962.

Leonard, Edwin S., Jr. *As the Sowing: The First Fifty Years of The Principia*. St. Louis: The Principia, 1980. A history of the only Christian Science college.

Morgan, Mary Kimball. *Education at The Principia: Selections from Letters, Messages, and Statements by Mary Kimball Morgan*. St. Louis: The Principia, 1965. A collection of writings by the founder of Principia.

Orcutt, William Dana. *Mary Baker Eddy and Her Books*. Boston: Christian Science Publishing Society, 1950.

Paget, Stephen. *The Faith & Works of Christian Science*. London: Macmillan and Co., 1909.

Peel, Robert. *Christian Science: Its Encounter with American Culture*. New York: Holt, Rinehart and Winston, 1958.

———. *Spiritual Healing in a Scientific Age*. San Francisco: Harper & Row, 1987.

———. *Health and Medicine in the Christian Science Tradition*. New York: Crossroad, 1988.

Report to the Members of The Mother Church of the Committee on General Welfare, Appointed Pursuant to Resolution of The Christian Science Board of Directors of The First Church of Christ, Scientist, in Boston, Massachusetts, Completed March 3rd, 1920. New York: Printed for the Committee on General Welfare, 1920.

Snowden, James H. *The Truth about Christian Science: The Founder and the Faith*. Philadelphia: Westminster Press, 1920.

The Story of Christian Science Wartime Activities: 1939–1946. Boston: Christian Science Publishing Society, 1947.

Twain, Mark. *Christian Science, with Notes Containing Corrections to Date*. New York: Harper & Brothers, 1907.

Understanding Our Century: Commemorating the 75th Anniversary of The Christian Science Monitor. Boston: Christian Science Publishing Society, 1984.

Wilson, Bryan R. *Sects and Society: A Sociological Study of the Elim Tabernacle, Christian Science, and Christadelphians*. Berkeley: University of California Press, 1961.

Works about the History of Positive Thinking, Mesmerism, the New Thought Movement, the New Age Movement, and Indigenous American Religious Sects

Bloom, Harold. *The American Religion: The Emergence of the Post-Christian Nation*. New York: Simon & Schuster, 1992.

Braden, Charles S. *Spirits in Rebellion: The Rise and Development of New Thought*. Dallas: Southern Methodist University Press, 1963.

James, William. *The Varieties of Religious Experience: A Study in Human Nature*. New York: Viking Penguin, 1982.

Meyer, Donald. *The Positive Thinkers: Popular Religious Psychology from Mary Baker Eddy to Norman Vincent Peale and Ronald Reagan*. Rev. ed., Middletown, Conn.: Wesleyan University Press, 1988.

Podmore, Frank. *From Mesmer to Christian Science: A Short History of Mental Healing*. New Hyde Park, New York: University Books, 1963.

Wills, Garry. *Certain Trumpets: The Call of Leaders*. New York: Simon & Schuster, 1994. This volume contains a chapter about Mary Baker Eddy and her influence on American culture as a religious leader.

Zweig, Stefan. *Mental Healers*. New York: Viking Press, 1932.

Works of Protest against Christian Science Church Authorities and Theological Teachings by Dissident Christian Scientists

Baker, Alfred E., M.D., C.S.D. *Notes on Metaphysical Work Done by Dr. Alfred E. Baker, M.D., C.S.D., While Associated with Mary Baker Eddy*. Privately printed. Distributed by The Bookmark, Santa Clarita, California.

Beals, Ann. *Crisis in the Christian Science Church*. Santa Clarita, Cal.: The Bookmark, 1978.

Carpenter, Gilbert C., Sr., and Gilbert C. Carpenter, Jr. *Mary Baker Eddy: Her Spiritual Footsteps*. N.p., n.d.

The Continuity of the Cause of Christian Science. 2nd ed., 1995. Cambridge, England: Christian Science Foundation. Also known as "The Compendium," this is a collection of photocopied primary and secondary source materials distributed by the Christian Science Foundation, a dissident group devoted to educating Christian Scientists about the *Manual's* estoppel clauses, which this group feels should have been interpreted and obeyed literally.

Corey, Arthur. *Christian Science Class Instruction*. San Francisco: Farallon Press, 1945;

now pub. in transcript by Freehold, New Jersey: Rare Book Company and Ann Beals, 1993.

———. *Behind the Scenes with the Metaphysicians*. Los Angeles: DeVorss & Co., 1968.

Essays and Bible Lessons Ascribed to Mary Baker Eddy with Repaid Pages; Footprints Fadeless by Mary Baker Eddy with The Science of Man or Questions and Answers in Moral Science; Early Papers; Visions; Mind-Healing: Historical Sketch. Freehold, New Jersey: Rare Book Company, n.d.

Eustace, Herbert W. *Christian Science: Its "Clear, Correct Teaching" and Complete Writings*. Berkeley: Lederer, Street & Zeus, c. 1934.

Hartsook, Andrew W. *Christian Science After 1910*. Santa Clarita, Calif.: The Bookmark, 1993.

Kerry, Reginald. The Kerry Letters, #1-11. Privately published. Distributed by The Bookmark, Santa Clarita, California.

Knapp, Bliss. *The Destiny of The Mother Church*. Boston: Christian Science Publishing Society, 1991.

Merritt, Robert E., and Arthur Corey. *Christian Science & Liberty*. Los Angeles: DeVorss & Co., 1970.

Notes on Mary Baker Eddy's Course in Divinity, Recorded by Lida Fitzpatrick, C.S.D., and Others; Watches, Prayers, Arguments Given to Students by Mary Baker Eddy; Items from Gilbert Carpenter's Collectanea Not Already Included in the Above; Instructions in Metaphysics From Mary Baker Eddy, Recorded by Dr. Alfred E. Baker, M.D., C.S.D., Together with Some Notes on Metaphysical Work. Freehold, New Jersey: Rare Book Company, n.d.

Paul Revere Pamphlets. Issues #1–32. Privately printed. Distributed by The Bookmark, Santa Clarita, California.

Stewart, Myrtle. *The 1910 Coup*. Privately printed, 1979.

Studdert-Kennedy, Hugh A. *Christian Science and Organized Religion*. San Francisco: The Farallon Press, 1930.

Young, Alan. *Mr. Young Goes to Boston*. Alan Young, 1998.

Memoirs or Autobiographical Writings about Christian Science

Cornell, Joseph. *Theater of the Mind: Selected Diaries, Letters, and Files*. Ed. Mary Ann Caws. New York: Thames and Hudson, 1993.

Gray, Spalding. *Sex and Death to the Age Fourteen*. New York: Vintage Books, 1986.

———. *Monster in a Box*. New York: Vintage Books, 1992.

———. *Gray's Anatomy*. New York: Vintage Books, 1993.

Haldeman, Peter. "Growing Up Haldeman." *New York Times Magazine* (3 April 1994): 30–35, 48, 58, 64–65.

Pritchett, V. S. *A Cab at the Door and Midnight Oil*. New York: Modern Library, 1994.

Simmons, Thomas. *The Unseen Shore: Memories of a Christian Science Childhood*. Boston: Beacon Press, 1991.

Wilson, Barbara. *Blue Windows: A Christian Science Childhood*. New York: Picador, 1997.

Articles about Christian Science and Mary Baker Eddy

Asser, Seth M., M.D., and Rita Swan, Ph.D. "Child Fatalities from Religion-motivated Medical Neglect." *Pediatrics* 101, no. 4 (April 1998): 625–29.

Clark, Edie. "The Price of Faith: A Special Report on the Trials of Christian Science." *Yankee* 56, no. 7 (July 1992): 76–92, 112–124. An excellent article about the Church and its members during the period of the "child cases," this piece is also noteworthy for being published in a magazine that was founded by a family of Christian Scientists (Robb and Trix T. Sagendorph).

Dwyer, James G. "The Children We Abandon: Religious Exemptions to Child Welfare and Education Laws as Denials of Equal Protection to Children of Religious Objectors." *North Carolina Law Review* 74, no. 5 (June 1996): 1321–1478.

England, R. W. "Some Aspects of Christian Science as Reflected in Letters of Testimony." *American Journal of Sociology* 59 (1954): 448–53.

Fox, Margery. "Protest in Piety: Christian Science Revisited." *International Journal of Women's Studies* 1, no. 4 (July/August 1978): 401–416.

Fraser, Caroline. "Suffering Children and the Christian Science Church." *Atlantic Monthly* 275, no. 4 (April 1995): 105–20.

———. "Mrs. Eddy Builds Her Empire." *New York Review of Books* 33, no. 12 (July 11, 1996): 53–59.

Kohn, Alfie. "Mind Over Matter." *New England Monthly* (March 1988): 58–63.

McDonald, Jean A. "Mary Baker Eddy and the Nineteenth-Century 'Public' Woman: A Feminist Reappraisal." *Journal of Feminist Studies in Religion* 2, no. 1 (Spring 1986): 89–111.

Simpson, William Franklin, Ph.D. "Comparative Longevity in a College Cohort of Christian Scientists." *Journal of the American Medical Association* 262, no. 12 (September 22–29, 1989): 1657–58.

———. "Comparative Mortality of Two College Groups, 1945–1983." *Morbidity and Mortality Weekly Report* 40, no. 33 (August 23, 1991): 579–82.

Stark, Rodney. "The Rise and Fall of Christian Science." *Journal of Contemporary Religion* 13, no. 2 (1998): 189–214.

Swan, Rita, Ph.D. "Children, Medicine, Religion, and the Law." *Advances in Pediatrics* 44 (1997): 491–543.

INDEX